List of Patterns

Adapter Microservice (135) How can the application take advantage of existing functionality without abandoning the microservices approach?

Aggregate (211) How do you tie together the groups of tightly related concepts and the values that belong within them in a subdomain?

Anti-Corruption Layer (229) How can we design the system so that the Bounded Contexts (BCs) can interact without being tightly coupled together?

Application Database (329) How should a cloud-native application store the data it uses so that it can run as a stateless application?

Application Package (62) What features of a computer language ecosystem are required to implement a Cloud Application?

Backend Service (106) How can multiple applications share the same reusable functionality?

Big Ball of Mud (22) What is the simplest possible architecture for an application that helps get something working quickly to get needed feedback?

Bounded Context (201) How do you clearly define the logical boundaries (edges) of a

domain and subdomain(s) where particular terms and rules apply?

Browser Application (410) What is the easiest, most universal Client Application for any user that does not assume a specific hardware or software configuration?

Client Application (406) How can an end user take advantage of the services provided by an application running in the cloud?

Cloud Application (6) How can I build applications to take the maximum advantage of all the features of the cloud for the best future proofing and agility?

Cloud Database (311) How should a cloud-native application store data persistently in a cloud environment?

Cloud-Native Architecture (58) How can I architect an application to take maximum advantage of the cloud platform it will run on?

Columnar Database (357) How can an application most efficiently store data for performing analytics, such as in a data warehouse?

Command-Line Interface (437) How can an end user automate activities like bulk loads, bulk changes, or scheduled execution of activities using the services provided by an application running in the cloud?

Command Query Responsibility Segregation (CQRS) (383) How do you optimize throughput for query and updates by multiple clients that have numerous cross-cutting views of the data?

Configuration Database (324) How can a cloud service store its service state such that all of the nodes in the service can share and access the state?

Containerize the Application (478) How can an application be packaged to facilitate greater deployment density and platform portability?

Data Module (367) How can I align my data model with my application model so that both are easier to maintain and can evolve quickly?

Database-as-a-Service (379) How does an application have access to an Application Database?

Dispatcher (140) How can a client access a microservices application through a channel-specific service interface when the business functionality is spread across an evolving set of domain-specific APIs?

Distributed Architecture (38) How can I architect my application so that parts of it can be developed, deployed, and run independently?

Document Database (339) How can an application most efficiently store and retrieve data when the future structure of the data is not well known?

Domain Event (193) How do you model those aspects of a design that correspond to things that happen during the various scenarios encountered by the system?

Domain Microservice (130) How should a set of microservices in an architecture provide the business functionality for an application?

Domain Service (222) How do you model those operations within a subdomain that do not belong to a specific Entity or Aggregate?

Event (255) How do you represent a change in one component to be communicated to other components?

Event API (274) How can the reactive components in an event-driven architecture know what events to expect?

Event Backbone (279) How can reactive components receive the events they are interested in without being coupled directly to the event notifiers that generate the events?

Event Choreography (246) When a change occurs in one component, how can a variable number of other components react accordingly?

Event Notifier (269) How and when should a component announce changes to other components?

Event Sourcing (289) As an application's state changes constantly and unpredictably due to evolving conditions, how can you audit the history that created the current state?

Event Storming (189) How do you get the stakeholders to understand and describe the elements and events around the domain and subdomain?

External Configuration (97) How can I build my application once and yet be able to deploy it to multiple environments that are configured differently?

Extract Component (535) How do you separate loosely related parts of the code in our monolith into distinct deployable units?

Graph Database (352) How can an application most efficiently store and retrieve interrelated data entities by navigating their relationships?

Hairline Cracks (530) How do you identify the areas within a monolith application that are candidate boundaries for microservices?

Interaction Model (448) How do you avoid mixing business and presentation logic inside your **Client Application?**

Key-Value Database (345) How can an application most efficiently store and retrieve independent data entities that are always looked up by the same key?

Lift and Shift (470) What is the simplest possible way to move an existing application to the cloud?

Micro Frontend (426) How do you avoid creating a monolithic Single-Page Application by placing too much functionality in a common front-end?

Microservices (119) How do you architect an application as a set of interconnected modules that can be developed independently?

Mobile Application (430) How do you provide the most optimized user experience on a mobile device and take advantage of the features that make mobile computing unique?

Model Around the Domain (183) How can you encourage stakeholders to explain enough of the domain requirements in a way that reveals the relevant capabilities for the application you are building?

Modular Monolith (29) How can I architect my application to make it easier to maintain and evolve quickly?

Monolith to Microservice Proxy (552) How can developers change the code in the monolith to access and use the functionality that was replaced with microservices?

New Features as Microservices (521) While strangling a monolith, how do you avoid adding new functionality to the monolith

that will later have to be modernized into microservices?

Pave the Road (496) How can we encourage teams to move to the cloud and adopt these new technologies without letting each team go in their own direction and work at cross purposes?

Playback Testing (556) How do you ensure that the new microservices architecture maintains the same functionality as the old monolithic system, especially when the amount of detailed end-to-end application knowledge of the existing application may be limited?

Polyglot Persistence (375) How can an application store its Data Modules in the type of database that works best for the application's data structure and how it accesses the data?

Polyglot Development (146) What computer language(s) should be used for implementing microservices?

Public API (443) How do you best enable third-party applications to interact programmatically with a Cloud Application?

Reactive Component (260) How can you construct an application that can react to events?

Refactor the Monolith (484) How can I make an existing application easier for multiple teams to maintain and able to run effectively in a multi-computer environment?

Refactor then Extract (542) How do we address coupling within the monolith to facilitate extraction into microservices?

Relational Database (334) How can an application store well-structured data that it needs to query dynamically?

Replace as Microservice (546) How can we move complex and important pieces of functionality that are tightly coupled in the monolith to microservices with minimal impact?

Replicable Application (88) How can an application run reliably on an unreliable platform and scale to handle greater client load the way the platform scales?

Replicated Database (316) How can a Cloud Database provide the same quality of service as a cloud-native application, with the same availability, scalability, and performance as the application?

Repositories (215) How do we address coupling within the monolith to facilitate extraction into microservices?

Self-Managed Data Store (154) How does a microservice store its state?

Service API (70) How should an application expose its functionality to clients that want to use the application?

Service Orchestrator (160) How does a microservice perform a complex task, one that is performed in multiple steps?

Single-Page Application (421) How do you design the front end of your application to provide the best mix of client responsiveness and server optimization?

Start Small (492) How can we start adopting cloud services and moving existing applications to the cloud or writing new applications for the cloud, possibly using microservices?

Stateless Application (80) How can an application support concurrent requests efficiently and recover from failures without losing data?

Strangle the Monolith (514) How can we replace a monolithic architecture with a microservices architecture while reducing overall risk?

Transform Monolith into Microservices (526) How do you keep the original monolithic system working while you substitute pieces of functionality with microservices over time?

Virtualize the Application (475) What is the simplest possible way to package an application so that it can easily be deployed to traditional IT or to the cloud?

Web Form Application (414) How do you build a user interface to provide basic functionality to the largest possible set of users using the largest possible set of devices and hardware?

List of Supporting Patterns

Application Services (205) How can you protect the internals of a bounded context?

Context Map (206) How do you understand the relationships and boundaries between different domains within a complex system?

Macro Service (538) How can we extract larger internally entangled components from the monolith to implement with microservices?

Repositories (215) How do you mediate between an Aggregate's entities and the persistent storage for their values?

Ubiquitous Language (186) How can adopting shared vocabulary minimize communication gaps between stakeholders for various domains and subdomains?

Wrap the Monolith (518) How do we decouple the monolith and new microservices from one another during the migration process?

Praise for *Cloud Application Architecture Patterns*

I've witnessed the authors' deep understanding of software architecture for decades. *Cloud Application Architecture Patterns* distills that hard-won wisdom into a blueprint, a practical guide for building and modernizing applications in the cloud. From cloud-first thinking to microservices and event architecture design, this book is an essential resource for developers and architects navigating the complexities of modern software development.

—Kerrie Holley, author of LLMs and Generative AI for Healthcare: The Next Frontier

Years of knowledge on migrating and evolutioning complex, high-volume systems, distilled into an easy-to-digest format. If I had access to this material at the start of my career, many projects would have been far easier!

—Diego Oliveira, software developer manager, Amazon

This book has been an absolute pleasure to read. *Cloud Application Architecture Patterns* is exactly what I've been looking for to help level up my teams and tech leads. I'll be recommending it for our tech book club later this year.

—Michael Keeling, senior staff software engineer at Kiavi and author of Design It!: From Programmer to Software Architect

These patterns give you a simple path to building cloud applications the right way. A valuable read for developers at any skill level.

—Steve Berczuk, principal software engineer, Cambridge Mobile Telematics

As someone who's wrestled with the complexities of cloud application architecture, I can confidently say this book is a game-changer. Brown, Woolf, and Yoder have delivered a truly practical and insightful guide. It's not just theory; it's a roadmap. They expertly break down proven architectural practices, clearly explaining why certain choices are superior in the cloud. I particularly appreciated how they connected the dots between different technical decisions and adoption patterns, showing how they all fit into a cohesive strategy. Finally, a resource that empowers you to not just follow a template, but to intelligently chart your own course. If you're serious about building efficient, robust cloud applications, this book is an absolute must-read.

—William A Brown, CEO, CIO, architect, cloud
application engineering, distinguished engineer emeritus, and coauthor of
SOA Governance: Achieving and Sustaining Business and IT Agility

This book will help architects to apply the right pattern in cloud architecture development, as well as application modernization and migration.

—Elizabeth Koumpan, distinguished engineer, BPO CTO

This is probably the most comprehensive book covering end-to-end cloud architecture that I have read. The chapters are easy to read and have a great flow. This will be my go-to playbook for years to come.

—Jim Episale, IBM CIO chief integration
and data architect, STSM

This book belongs on the bookshelf of every software engineer and architect! It was written by three seasoned software experts, each with decades of practical, real-world experience. Unlike many vendor platform-centric publications, the authors are delightfully technology-neutral. The book covers everything one needs to architect and design modern cloud applications. The authors explain the principles and practices of cloud architecture using well-established architecture patterns. I strongly recommend this book for those developing new applications or migrating a legacy monolith to the cloud.

—Dave Thomas, CEO, Bedarra Corporation

This book is all about getting applications to work *with* the cloud, rather than *in spite of* the cloud.

—Sam Newman, technologist, author of
Building Microservices *and* Monolith To Microservices

Cloud Application Architecture Patterns

Designing, Building, and Modernizing for the Cloud

Kyle Brown, Bobby Woolf, and Joseph Yoder
Foreword by Sam Newman

Cloud Application Architecture Patterns

by Kyle Brown, Bobby Woolf, and Joseph Yoder

Published by O'Reilly Media, Inc., 1005 Gravenstein Highway North, Sebastopol, CA 95472.

O'Reilly books may be purchased for educational, business, or sales promotional use. Online editions are also available for most titles (*http://oreilly.com*). For more information, contact our corporate/institutional sales department: 800-998-9938 or *corporate@oreilly.com*.

Acquisitions Editor: Megan Laddusaw	**Indexer:** Ellen Troutman-Zaig
Development Editor: Melissa Potter	**Interior Designer:** David Futato
Production Editor: Ashley Stussy	**Cover Designer:** Karen Montgomery
Copyeditor: Piper Editorial Consulting, LLC	**Illustrator:** Kate Dullea
Proofreader: Helena Stirling	

April 2025:   First Edition

Revision History for the First Edition
2025-04-15:   First Release

See *http://oreilly.com/catalog/errata.csp?isbn=9781098116903* for release details.

978-1-098-11690-3

[LSI]

Table of Contents

Foreword

Make it work. Make it right. Make it fast.

   —Kent Beck

Cloud computing isn't a new thing. Long gone are the days of hype, and what we are left with is reality. Many organizations have already taken the leap, and with the emergence of cloud infrastructure in the mid to late 2000s more and more of the software we write runs on the cloud. Against this backdrop, it might seem odd therefore for me to talk about a book on cloud application architecture being important, but it is.

Fundamentally, the easy stuff has already gone to the cloud. Those applications that haven't made the move haven't done so because it is hard for them to make that jump. The low hanging fruit has been picked—we're now reaching into the high branches, and we need help and support to get there. And this is where this book comes in.

Given how long we've had access to cloud infrastructure, it's important to understand why many applications still haven't made the switch. Legal and regulatory restrictions have long since ceased to be a roadblock in most situations. But fundamentally, a lot of applications are not built with the cloud in mind, so a planned transition is difficult.

Even for the applications that have made the move over, there is work to be done. As Kyle, Bobby, and Joe put it, "There are more applications running in the cloud than there are ones that run well in the cloud". I don't have a problem with a lift-and-shift approach to get applications into the cloud—what I have always objected to is seeing that as the entirety of the process, rather than an initial step. This book is packed with concrete patterns and practice to help take an application that runs uneasily on the cloud, to one that is cloud native—built with the ethos and understanding of its environment, rather than some awkward, ungainly alien transplant. This book is all about getting applications to work *with* the cloud, rather than *in spite* of the cloud.

This is also not a book with purist intentions, looking at beautiful and elegant architectural patterns without any care to wider context. The appropriate systems architecture is always a function of tradeoffs. The authors acknowledge this well, while at the same time giving you a pathway of where to go when the expedient choices made to quickly get a new product off the ground need to give way to something more appropriate for a longer-lived, cloud-based application.

In a book about tradeoffs, it can be easy for the reader to become overwhelmed with choice. But the authors clearly lay out their thinking, the variety of choices that exist, but then articulately distill this down with concrete advice. Those looking for useful guidelines will find them aplenty in these pages, but they will also find the well reasoned rationale behind them.

If you're a developer or architect struggling to understand how your existing application can make the switch to the cloud, then this book is packed with useful advice. If you're already dealing with a cloud-based application where you feel that you aren't getting full use of the cloud, then again this is for you. At its core, though, the authors of this book recognize that the route to the cloud isn't necessarily linear. And whatever path you might take, this book will be a very useful guide.

— Sam Newman
Technologist, author of Building Microservices *and*
Monolith to Microservices

Preface

This is a book about how to architect applications so that they will run well in the cloud. It is not based on any particular technology or product. Rather, it is designed for application architects using a variety of cloud platforms and technologies. Because the concepts in this book are product-neutral and vendor-neutral, the concepts will remain relevant even as technologies evolve and as old products fall out of favor and are replaced by newer, better products. A book focused on a single product will become obsolete when the product does, but one focused on architectural concepts remains relevant as long as the architecture does, potentially even outlasting the usefulness of the platforms that host the architecture.

Because this book focuses on designing applications to be deployed on the cloud, we do assume a fundamental set of technologies that have become a de facto standard stack that applications make use of to take advantage of cloud computing. These technologies include Linux, containers, and container orchestrators. These technologies and ones like them are referenced in this book.

To get the discussion rolling, we'll explain why we wrote this book and who we intend to read it. Adopting cloud is a very broad topic, more than can fit in one book, so we'll discuss what you can expect to learn, what topics are covered, and what is outside the scope of this book. Lastly, we'll give a quick overview of how this book structures the material.

Why We Wrote This Book

Through our experience with hundreds of applications, we have discovered that there are more applications running in the cloud than there are ones that run well in the cloud. This may be because architects do not realize that applications should be designed differently for the cloud than for traditional IT, or because they realize the need but don't know how to do it. By traditional IT, we mean applications that have been written to run on premises using technologies and methods that were optimized for the reality of computing prior to the introduction of the cloud. We (the authors) have hard-earned experience in making applications work well in the cloud, usually through making mistakes and thereby realizing what does and does not work. We have also successfully taught others these lessons and have captured that experience in this book. We hope that we can convince you that the cloud is different from traditional approaches, and teach you how to architect your applications differently, thereby making cloud adoption much easier for you than it has been for us.

Who Should Read This Book

This book is for application architects and developers who want to learn proven practices about how to design applications for the cloud. Architects who want their applications to run well in the cloud need to know these proven practices and employ them. These practices apply to any application that will run in the cloud. We assume most developers are writing business applications for commercial enterprises—let's face it, that's where the money is—but these techniques apply equally well to other fields such as research and science, government, nonprofits—any field where users have requirements for what an application should do and the organization wants to deploy their applications on the cloud.

What You Will Learn

This book briefly explains what the cloud is, and it does not justify the business case for using the cloud. We assume the reader already wants to use the cloud, so we focus on how to develop applications that run well in the cloud. You will learn how to architect applications for the cloud by understanding the following:

- The advantages and limitations of cloud computing architecture compared to traditional IT architecture and the consequences for application architecture

- How to make an application cloud native so that it will run well in the cloud

- How an application can encompass collaborating microservices and how to design a set of microservices for a particular domain of functionality

- How to make multiple microservices and other software components collaborate, both through orchestration as well as via choreography

- How to apply agile development techniques to designing a cloud application

- Strategies to rehost and replatform an existing IT application to run in the cloud, and to refactor an existing application while it is running in production

This understanding will enable you to create better cloud applications.

What This Book Covers

This book organizes its approximately 70 practices into these 10 topics:

Cloud Applications (Chapter 1)
> Architect a cloud application to take advantage of the strengths of cloud computing while avoiding and compensating for its limitations.

Application Architecture (Chapter 2)
> As traditional IT infrastructure has evolved, so has its application architectures.

Cloud-Native Application (Chapter 3)
> As traditional IT evolved to become the cloud, application architecture evolved to work well on the cloud.

Microservices Architecture (Chapter 4)
> Decompose a large application into many small applications so that each performs a separate responsibility.

Microservice Design (Chapter 5)
> Analyze interactions within the application to discover where one well-encapsulated responsibility ends and another begins.

Event-Driven Architecture (Chapter 6)
> Enable components to interact indirectly through dynamically discovered relationships modeled as choreography.

Cloud-Native Storage (Chapter 7)
> Incorporate newer databases that model data more flexibly, simplify how applications access the data, and run better on the cloud.

Cloud Application Clients (Chapter 8)
> Enable users to access the cloud application from a variety of device types via user interfaces that are simple to install and update.

Application Migration and Modernization (Chapter 9)
> Develop a cloud application by moving an existing application from traditional IT to the cloud and updating it to work well on the cloud.

Strangling Monoliths (Chapter 10)
> Incrementally convert an application from traditional IT to the cloud while keeping it running in production.

With these practices, you are prepared to stop designing applications for traditional IT and instead design them for the cloud.

What This Book Does Not Cover

This is a book on application architecture, specifically for cloud applications. One might be tempted to think that once you've designed the architecture for an application, you're finished. Instead, architecture is only the beginning. Architecture is the foundation for developing applications for the cloud, but there is a lot more to do that is beyond the scope of this book.

Once the architecture and design for an application is established, additional work is necessary to make the application usable and useful. It must be developed to create the application from its design and then deployed to become a running application. The application needs a custom environment defined in the cloud platform for the application to be deployed into, an environment that may be distributed geographically to enable the application to be more scalable and reliable. That application running in production must be monitored and managed to keep it running and ensure it is running correctly. The production application needs updates to fix bugs and add features. All of this is beyond the architecture and design of the application and is beyond the scope of this book.

This book does not focus on particular cloud platform hyperscalers; it is vendor-, product-, and language-neutral. For specific technologies, it focuses on widely used open source standards that most vendors incorporate into their platforms and tooling. Some of the examples do cite specific languages and products, but only to illustrate how the pattern can be used and is used, not how it must be implemented. As such, this book is not a tutorial on specific products, platforms, or even open source technologies. This book focuses on the design decisions that apply to using any of those, both ones that currently exist as well as many that may be invented in the future.

How This Book Is Structured

As the title says, most of the content in this book is structured in the form of *patterns*. Patterns are a proven and efficient technique for experts to capture knowledge and convey it to novices, enabling them to gain expertise quickly. Patterns encapsulate knowledge as reusable solutions to common problems, and they are given memorable names so those solutions can be used to clearly and concisely discuss design alternatives. Because reusable knowledge is rarely one-size-fits-all, patterns capture not just what to do but when and why it should be done—enabling the reader to customize their application of the pattern each time they use it. Patterns are harvested from experience and proven success, based not just on one person's opinion but on consensus among industry experts. Readers with expertise in this field have already internalized these practices and so should find the patterns very familiar. Novices are not familiar with these patterns, but learning them will help novices rapidly advance their knowledge. An expert may point a novice to this book as an efficient way to learn the basics without needing an expert's years of experience.

This book organizes its patterns into a pattern language—which interconnects the patterns to form pathways for combining multiple related patterns to solve more complex problems. More than just a catalog of solutions within the same problem space, the patterns in a pattern language build upon one another into a blend the reader customizes for a particular design.

Sets of patterns address a common topic, and we've organized each of those sets of closely related patterns into a chapter. A pattern in the pattern language may well refer to other patterns in other chapters but will refer primarily to other patterns in the same chapter because they all address problems for the same topic.

O'Reilly Online Learning

 For more than 40 years, *O'Reilly Media* has provided technology and business training, knowledge, and insight to help companies succeed.

Our unique network of experts and innovators share their knowledge and expertise through books, articles, and our online learning platform. O'Reilly's online learning platform gives you on-demand access to live training courses, in-depth learning paths, interactive coding environments, and a vast collection of text and video from O'Reilly and 200+ other publishers. For more information, visit *https://oreilly.com*.

How to Contact Us

Please address comments and questions concerning this book to the publisher:

O'Reilly Media, Inc.
1005 Gravenstein Highway North
Sebastopol, CA 95472
800-889-8969 (in the United States or Canada)
707-827-7019 (international or local)
707-829-0104 (fax)
support@oreilly.com
https://oreilly.com/about/contact.html

We have a web page for this book, where we list errata, examples, and any additional information. You can access this page at *https://oreil.ly/cloud-application-architecture-patterns-1e*.

For news and information about our books and courses, visit *https://oreilly.com*.

Find us on LinkedIn: *https://linkedin.com/company/oreilly-media*.

Watch us on YouTube: *https://youtube.com/oreillymedia*.

Acknowledgments

This book has been a group effort since day one, and we want to make sure that we try to recognize the contributions of everyone who has been a part of this project who is not listed on the cover. We want to begin by thanking the Hillside Group and the patterns community that this project emerged from. This effort never would have taken place without the PLoP conferences and the community that they established.

This project began as a series of (loosely) related papers submitted to the PLoP conference in 2016—by Kyle Brown and Bobby Woolf, and another by Cees De Groot. At the conference, we decided to explore the idea of joining the two papers into a common pattern language. While we ended up not using any of Cees's patterns in this volume, we very much consider him to be part of our author community and look forward to another opportunity for collaboration. Chris Hay was another paper coauthor who became part of our community and whose patterns again have been left for a later volume, but whose contributions are much appreciated.

Joseph (Joe) Yoder published early versions of some of the patterns in this book at previous PLoP conferences and would like to acknowledge several collaborators and coauthors. Brian Foote and Joseph Yoder wrote the original Big Ball of Mud pattern for an early PLoP conference; it was published in 1998. Joseph Yoder and Paulo Merson wrote some of the Strangler patterns for PLoP 2020—Paulo was instrumental in the creation in 2019 of the IDEALS design principles for microservices. A couple of the modernization and migration patterns evolved from a submission for PLoP 2023 by Martin Neubert and Joseph Yoder.

Every pattern language involves a constellation of collaborations. In this vein, Joe thanks Ademar Aguiar, Eduardo Guerra, and Rebecca Wirfs-Brock for their collaborations in writing related architecture and design patterns. Likewise, Kyle, Bobby, and Joe wish to thank all the shepherds and members of the Writers' Workshops where our papers were workshopped.

When we decided to take our patterns and bring them together to publish them to the world at large, we first did so through a website, *https://cloudadoptionpatterns.org*. Ian Mitchell gave us critical pattern feedback and helped in solving the mysteries of GitHub pages in setting this site up. As the project transitioned into a book, we then received valuable feedback from the members of a PLoP 2022 "Cloud Architecture Patterns Exploration Workshop" group. The members of that group included Matthias Kittner, Thalia Hooker, Kirk Davis, Filipe Correia, Mark Weitzel,

Cees De Groot, Antanas Kaziliunas, Joe Rice, Leandro Rodriques, Neil Harrison, and others whose names we have lost.

After we submitted our book to O'Reilly, we began work with the wonderful O'Reilly staff and would like to make sure that we've thanked them adequately as well. When Kyle promoted the website, Mary Treseler, director of content strategy at O'Reilly, contacted him and suggested that he publish the content as a book, and their conversation got this book rolling. Our acquisitions editor, Megan Laddusaw, and our development editor, Melissa Potter, gave us very patient and ongoing guidance as we transformed a heap of random advice into a coherent story. Our production editor, Ashley Stussy, her copyediting team, and the proofreader, Helena Stirling, have taken our mess and rendered it consistent and grammatically correct, for which we are very grateful. Kate Dullea, our illustrator, makes us look much better at drawing diagrams than we really are. We also thank cover designer Karen Montgomery, interior designer David Futato, and indexer Ellen Troutman-Zaig for all of their work to make our book look much more professional than what we initially gave them.

Our technical reviewers went above and beyond the call of duty in providing detailed feedback on a monster of a manuscript. They include Lee Atchison, Elizabeth Koumpan, Mark Weitzel, Jim Episale, Thalia Hooker, Steve Berczuk, Diego de Oliveira, and Eduardo Crivelli. Richard Gabriel helped us edit and improve the manuscript. He not only gave us technical and pattern advice, but he also provided feedback on writing style and readability. Finally, we also want to acknowledge the very helpful feedback received toward the end of the editing process from Chris Richardson and Vaughn Vernon. And we want to thank Sam Newman for contributing such an excellent Foreword, as well as all of those who contributed praise quotes.

We have probably forgotten to name some people deserving of credit; to them, we apologize. To everyone who helped us improve this book—both those we have listed and those we should have listed—thank you for all of your help. We are proud of this book and hope that you are too.

Introduction

Almost everything runs in the cloud now. Music and television stream from the cloud, documents are stored and edited in the cloud, and cars' navigation systems use the cloud to calculate the route to a destination. Today, we can't imagine using a personal computer that isn't connected to the internet. Put a smartphone in airplane mode and it suddenly does much less because it doesn't have cloud access.

Most applications either run in the cloud or on a device that connects to applications running in the cloud, but many of the applications running in the cloud don't run as well as they could because they were never designed for the cloud. We begin with Cloud Applications (Chapter 1), which will explore why we architect applications differently to deploy them to the cloud.

Before we get to that, let's consider the phases of adopting the cloud, some newer application development techniques, and how the cloud can help, as well as the many aspects of managing a cloud application through its full lifecycle—bearing in mind that many of these phases, techniques, and aspects, while important, go beyond how to architect the application and therefore are beyond the scope of this book. We will begin by reviewing how computer hardware architecture has evolved and how application architecture has changed along with it, leading us to today's cloud platform hardware and cloud-native applications. Then, we will review the pattern format used to structure most of the content in this book and how it documents best practices to make them reusable. Next, we will review how this book is organized, containing chapters that explore different aspects of how to architect an application for the cloud, with each chapter anchored by a root pattern—an overall best practice that leads to the other more detailed best practices in the chapter. Last, we'll present some strategies for how to get started reading this book. With that, you'll have a pretty good idea of what these best practices are going to teach you.

Phases of Cloud Adoption

Fundamentally, cloud applications run in Linux, containers, and container orchestrators—all in a cloud-native architecture. In putting these fundamental technologies to work, IT professionals can adopt cloud computing in three main phases:

Application Architecture and Design
> Structure an application such that it will work well when deployed to the cloud

Application Development and Deployment
> Create an application iteratively, configure an application environment in the cloud to host the application, and deploy the application in the environment frequently to make the improvements available to users

Cloud Operations and Nonfunctional Requirements
> Monitor and manage a deployed application to keep it running reliably, distribute it geographically to avoid single points of failure, and build in compliance and security

Cloud applications are designed for and deployed using the fundamental cloud technologies and are operated using them to keep the applications running.

This book focuses on the first phase of adopting the cloud: how to architect and design applications to work well in the cloud. The explanation for how to do that will start with the root pattern for this entire book, Cloud Application (6).

Modern Application Development

Let's consider how applications are developed. Modern application development incorporates several desirable software development techniques:

Modular code
> Code should be developed in modules, each built by a separate team working independently. Each team for developing a module should have about 5–10 people, often described as a two-pizza team because the team is small enough that two pizzas are enough to feed everyone. Modules lend themselves to the integration of external services (that are also modular), which rather than duplicating/re-creating code that already exists, encourages not only the reuse of existing code but also the integration of existing services.

Polyglot development
> All of an application's modules shouldn't need to be developed in a single computer language or technology. Some developers prefer one language over another, and some problems are more easily solved by some languages instead of others. Each module can be written in any preferred language regardless of what languages are used to implement the other modules.

Iterative development

One of the main tenets of agile development is that code should be written in small batches that can be developed in short iterations. Large code changes should be deconstructed into these smaller batches and performed iteratively.

Continuous delivery

Continuous delivery is the practice of automating the process of building, testing, and releasing software. User functionality, bug fixes, and other improvements should be delivered frequently. When users report a bug or request a new feature, once it is fixed or developed, that code change should be quickly deployed into production so that the users can benefit from it immediately. When code in production hasn't been updated in weeks or months, it apparently must have no bugs and the users don't want any improvements—which probably means no one is using this functionality.

Automated builds

When a team produces a new or revised set of code, an automated system should build it into deployment artifacts, run automated tests on it, and ultimately deploy it into production. Frequent builds are known as *continuous integration* (CI), and frequent deployment is known as *continuous deployment* (CD). Together they're known as a *CI/CD pipeline*. An important part of achieving continuous delivery—making code improvements frequently and available to users as soon as possible—is running code changes through the pipeline as soon as they're available. In addition, CI/CD pipelines should be instrumented with automated evidence collection to provide auditors and security teams with significant pipeline events and results that might be needed for enterprise or regulatory compliance.

These techniques can be accomplished without cloud computing, but the cloud greatly facilitates this style of development. The first two techniques impact an application's architecture, so this book incorporates them.

Aspects of Software Development

So far, we've talked about modern application development techniques that can be performed better using the cloud. Yet creating the application is just the beginning. The full software development lifecycle (SDLC) for a cloud application includes many stages, from architecture, development, and testing the application to deploying and operating it. The lifecycle incorporates several aspects of software development, including the following:

Application architecture

Architect and design a new application to fulfill users' functional requirements and run well in the cloud. Delegate common tasks to a set of backend services such as databases and messaging systems.

Application migration and modernization

Migrate an existing application to rehost it in the cloud, and modernize it to make it run better in the cloud. This can be accomplished through various methods—such as adopting a cloud-native architecture and refactoring to microservices.

Application development

Continuously deliver the application with small development teams developing independent modules in short, agile iterations.

Build pipeline

Automate building source code into deployment artifacts, including enforcing quality controls and building images for virtual servers and containers.

Application deployment

Design deployment strategies such as virtual server management and container orchestration, service mesh, external access, and the means to automate the strategies such as GitOps.

Environment creation

Utilize infrastructure as code (IaC) to build the application environment (aka landing zone) that the application will be deployed into.

Application operations

Augment the environment with tooling for site reliability engineering (SRE): observability capabilities such as monitoring, log aggregation, and activity tracking; and autonomic capabilities such as failover, restart, and elastic autoscaling.

Cloud topology

Architect a strategy for deploying an application across more than one data center, including public cloud zones and regions, private cloud, hybrid cloud, and multicloud.

Security

Protect data and functionality in a multitenant, public environment, as well as enforce and audit compliance.

All of these aspects are too broad and too numerous to cover adequately in a single book. This book will cover the first two aspects, with an eye toward enabling these other aspects that will come later in the lifecycle.

Evolution of Application Architecture

Some people describe the cloud as if it were a completely new technology, totally different from anything IT has done before. Others derisively dismiss the cloud as nothing new, just someone else's computer but with better marketing. The truth lies somewhere in between, that the cloud is an evolution from earlier computing technologies that has culminated in bringing those technologies together and making them more widely accessible. We can see how the industry has gotten to cloud computing by looking at how application architectures have evolved.

The architectural structure of a computer application has evolved over time into what, today, we call a cloud application. Here's a whirlwind overview of some key milestones in the evolution of computer hardware architecture and how application architectures evolved along with it, which shows how the IT industry has ended up with today's cloud-native architecture. This won't teach you how to architect applications, but it is an interesting history of how we got to where we are today.

Mainframe Application

Starting in the 1950s, the first computers were mainframe computers. The 1960s witnessed the invention of minicomputers—so named because whereas a mainframe took up all the space in a raised-floor computer room, a miniature computer took up only half of a room. Users in their offices accessed the mainframe using dumb terminals, so called because the terminal was just a display and keyboard without processing capabilities—only a dedicated connection to the mainframe that served as a hardline network.

As shown in Figure I-1, a mainframe application was a monolith that ran entirely on the mainframe in the computer room. All of the CPU, memory, and storage was on the mainframe. Therefore, the entire computer program and all of its program logic ran on the mainframe. The terminal just provided input and output for people but no computation. It could be housed in the office where the people were located, but it still needed to be near the computer room because the terminal required a connection to the mainframe via a dedicated network cable that was short and slow with very low bandwidth.

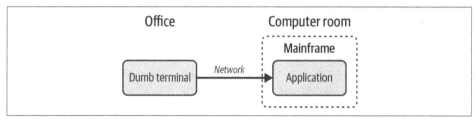

Figure I-1. Mainframe application structure

Desktop Application

The 1970s and '80s saw the advent of the personal computer. Like a dumb terminal, a personal computer sat on the desktop and provided input and output via a display, keyboard, and eventually a mouse. What made the personal computer unique is that it contained a CPU, memory, and storage. This gave the computer the ability to run its own programs; while it looked like a terminal, it worked like a very small mainframe.

Personal computers originally didn't have network connections, although some personal computers had modems that dialed up over a telephone line to act as terminals to remote servers. In the late '80s, companies adopted LANs (local area networks) to connect to nearby computers within a building. Offices with LAN networks added file servers enabling users to share files easily.

A personal computer application was a monolith that ran entirely on the user's desktop computer (Figure I-2). Structurally, its architecture was very much like a mainframe application but simpler. Whereas a mainframe application might support multiple users, a personal computer application was highly interactive but supported just one user. Multiple users in the same office each had their own computer. If they were all using the same application, each user had their own copy of the application installed on their computer, where it ran separately from all of the others, with each copy using its own data stored locally on the computer. With a LAN and file server, the application could use centrally stored files as well, but each desktop computer still ran its own copy of the application.

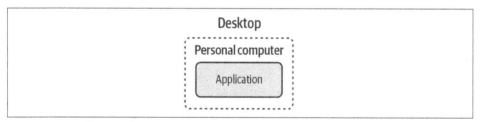

Figure I-2. Desktop application structure

Client/Server Application

In the 1990s, computing capacity became centralized once more. LANs added server computers with compute and storage that could be shared by all of the users on the LAN. Unlike the mainframe, the office workers didn't use dumb terminals; they used the personal computers they already had on their desktops. So each worker had their own compute and storage capacity on their desktop, as well as access to shared compute and storage capacity on the server computers.

Companies first used server computers to host database servers. The application still ran on the desktop computer, but it could access not just centralized files but also managed data. This enabled multiple workers to use data at the same time, even editing data at the same time without overwriting one another and always having access to the data with the latest changes.

Databases on centralized servers were a big improvement over sharing files on file servers, but what office workers really needed was applications that ran on the server computers. The application server emerged to centrally host applications so that running applications could be shared much the way files and data were, as shown in Figure I-3. Application servers are software platforms that run and manage business applications. Meanwhile, offices and homes became connected to the internet. Application servers were hosted in centralized data centers that workers' personal computers connected to through their LAN and the internet.

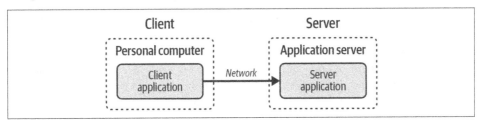

Figure I-3. Client/Server application structure

With application servers, many of the applications that office workers relied on became centralized and shared once more, much like the mainframe applications before them. While simple applications for tasks like word processing still ran entirely on the desktop, many applications became hosted in a centralized application server. Multiple workers using the same application could all share a single application running in the application server. But these workers weren't using dumb terminals; they had compute capacity on their desktops in their personal computers.

This led to the advent of client/server computing, where shared program logic and data ran on the server and were accessed by personalized program logic running on the client. As logic was spread across computers throughout the network, a slogan emerged: the network is the computer. In other words, the computer isn't one machine; it's all of the computers connected by the network. The desktop computers hosted thick client applications, full mini-applications that used the shared applications in the application server to perform the complex work that needed to be shared with other users. Server computers were much more powerful and expensive, so they performed complex work. But networks had limited bandwidth, so the thick client application performed as much of its individual user's work as possible to avoid the network.

The application server didn't eliminate the need for a centralized database server; it changed the purpose of a database. The application server and the database server ran side by side on one or more server computers. An application running in an application server didn't need to manage its data; it could delegate that responsibility to the database server. Multiple applications and multiple users in an application could all share the same data in the database.

Service-oriented architecture (SOA) applied the client/server architecture to the server application, dividing it into components that perform work for other components. Service components within the application that model business domain entities are able to vary independently and be maintained by separate development teams.

Cloud-Native Application

In the 2000s, application servers evolved into cloud computing. Whereas application servers were typically specialized to run a particular programming language or technology, cloud computers were generalized to run any program in a virtual machine. The virtual machine acted logically like a server computer—a virtual server instance —with not just virtualized compute capacity but also virtual storage and virtual networking. The cloud also hosted databases; whereas data center operations personnel who installed application servers also installed the database servers, the cloud could host databases as a service so that application developers could easily create their own databases without needing help from operations or a database administrator (DBA).

The cloud extended this database-as-a-service model to make everything a service, which became known as software-as-a-service (SaaS). Workflow engines, messaging systems, authentication directories, and anything else an application needed became hosted as a service, as shown in Figure I-4.

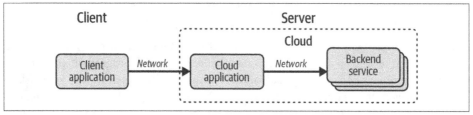

Figure I-4. Cloud-native application structure

With the cloud, the application running on the server could focus entirely on domain logic. It accessed any of the capabilities common to multiple applications—database, workflow, messaging, authentication, etc.—as shared backend services. The application server simplified into a virtual machine with the technology to run the code the application was implemented in—a runtime for a language like Java, Node.js, Python, and so on. While the server was no longer necessarily an application server, the client was no longer necessarily a desktop computer or even a laptop computer. With the popularity of the World Wide Web (WWW), web browsers became universal, and application developers learned to create user interfaces for their server applications that could run in any web browser. A user could access an application without having to install a thick client; they could just use a single web browser to access any server application. Furthermore, the client didn't even have to run on a desktop. With the advent of the smartphone and tablet, mobile devices became practical. They could also run web browsers, then quickly evolved to also run small thick client apps for accessing the server applications, often via a wireless network connection.

The cloud is mainframe-like compute capacity distributed across multiple server computers running generalized application servers with built-in SaaS services for common capabilities. Therefore the structure of a cloud application is a client/server application. The server application only runs the logic for user requirements and delegates all shared functionality to backend services. The client application can be a web browser, mobile app, or even a kiosk or a chatbot.

A cloud-native application is one written or modernized specifically for the cloud, to take full advantage of the cloud computing model. The application is designed to run well in the cloud—to take advantage of the strengths of cloud computing while avoiding and compensating for its limitations. Cloud native has become the de facto best practice for designing many applications, even those to be deployed on traditional IT, and so somewhat ironically refers less to where an application resides and more to how it is built and deployed.

The cloud facilitates a new world of massive computing power available on demand cheaply. Cloud-native applications are designed to take advantage of this on-demand computing power, resulting in applications that are highly scalable, always available, and that any user can access with a device and an internet connection.

Patterns and Pattern Format

This book documents best practices as patterns. We use the pattern format because we don't want to simply enumerate *what* tasks an application architect should perform; we want to teach *why* these practices work well and *how* to apply them. While explaining how to solve a problem, a pattern teaches a reader about the problem, why it is difficult to solve, and why this solution solves it well. Each pattern is a decision that can be made. A set of patterns is a very efficient way for an expert to document their expertise and for a novice to not only learn that expertise but also how to apply that expertise.

Simply put, a *pattern* is a reusable solution to a problem in a context. More specifically, it's a structured way of representing design information in prose and diagrams that facilitate communicating time-tested solutions to common problems.

Developing complex solutions requires applying multiple related concepts, which is where a pattern language becomes important. A *pattern language* is a set of related patterns that shows how the patterns are interconnected, how they fit together to form a whole greater than the sum of the parts, and how each pattern leads to others. A pattern language is generative, showing when and how to apply patterns to build solutions.

Learning a new domain of knowledge is difficult, especially in domains that are just inside the bleeding edge of a field of study. One of the issues with traditional academic approaches is that they aren't up to the problem of conveying "common" knowledge. There can be limited enthusiasm for documenting know-how if "everyone knows it." Yet not documenting what experts know makes it difficult for a novice to gain all of the information they need to be able to start working on something that uses ideas from the bleeding edge. When something is just relatively new, it's often hard to distinguish good ideas from bad ones, especially when you don't have the experience in a field to make that distinction.

As we use these patterns to describe how to design cloud applications, we avoid saying to always do one thing or never do another. Rather, designing an application involves a series of choices, and these patterns highlight many of the most important decisions to be made. They don't say what developers must do, they explain the pros and cons of making the decisions one way or another. It is up to each reader to judge their own organization's context, determine which pros and cons are most important for meeting their requirements, and decide accordingly. That will lead to a design that is best for their circumstances and preferences.

The pattern idea came to computer science not from software architecture but instead from the brick-and-mortar architecture world. The architect Christopher Alexander published two important books, *A Pattern Language* (1977) and *A Timeless Way of Building* (1979). In the brick-and-mortar world, Alexander uses patterns to express the interaction of forces in a problem and shows how you can resolve those forces to arrive at an elegant solution. He is also concerned with demonstrating how each pattern fits in with other patterns to convey to a novice architect the broader scope of how all the different issues come together. Several computer scientists in the late 1980s and early 1990s picked up these techniques from Alexander and found that they can also be applied successfully for developing computer software.

This book uses a modified Alexander style for the patterns. Each pattern consists of these sections:

Name
> An identifier for the pattern that describes the solution in a short phrase, usually a noun, that can easily be used in a sentence to describe applying the pattern as part of a design.

Context

A description of the sort of work you might have been performing that caused you to encounter this problem. The context often refers to other patterns that you may already have applied.

Problem

Formatted in bold, this describes the difficulty you are facing, expressed as a question. The problem statement should quickly tell you whether this pattern is currently relevant to where you are in your design.

Forces

This elaborates on the problem and the opposing constraints that make it difficult to solve, exploring possible solutions and showing their shortcomings. This is where an expert can teach a novice about the problem and why it is difficult to solve and help them appreciate that a solution isn't necessarily easy.

Solution

Specific guidance that you can apply to solve the problem, not just in your current situation but in the range of situations where the problem can occur. The solution answers the question posed by the Problem. The Name, Problem, and Solution are the core of the pattern.

Sketch

An illustration of the solution and how it's typically applied. As this is a book on architecture, the sketch is often a part of an architectural diagram.

Results

How the design changes because of applying the solution and how the solution resolves the forces and balances them, improving the design better than the other possible solutions.

Consequences

After a divider, a consideration of the strengths of the solution and its challenges.

Related Patterns

Guidance on other patterns to consider after this one, especially because solving one problem can lead to new ones. The links to patterns in the Context and Related Patterns sections are what make the patterns into a pattern language.

Examples

Optional sections showing the pattern in use, often citing well-known solutions and explaining how they embody the pattern.

The patterns in a pattern language form a methodology for designing complex solutions in a domain and a vocabulary for discussing those designs. Once a team has internalized the patterns, design discussions become much more efficient. The team no longer needs to explain what they mean by an **Adapter**, **Intention Revealing Interface**, **Data Transfer Object**, or **Message Channel**—those concepts are well-known patterns, so the team's discussion can focus on how the concept contributes to the design. In the seemingly endless quest to make components reusable, capturing knowledge as patterns in pattern languages has proven to be more reusable than any executable code.

We use the following convention for pattern names in this book. All pattern names are capitalized throughout the book. Any patterns that we cover in this book are *italicized*. We will also include a link to the pattern in the book the first time we mention it in a chapter or section. Any patterns that we mention but do not cover within the book are formatted by using a **bold** font with external references to the patterns the first time they are mentioned. Pattern problem statements and solution statements are shown in **bold**.

Organization of This Book

The pattern language in this book forms a web of patterns referencing one another. At the same time, some patterns are more fundamental than others, forming a hierarchy of patterns introducing big concepts that lead to more finely detailed patterns. The big-concept patterns form the load-bearing members of the pattern language. They are the main ones, the *root patterns* that provide the foundation of the language and support the other patterns.

Table I-1 lists the root patterns in this book.

Table I-1. Root patterns

Chapter	Root pattern
Chapter 1: Cloud Applications	Cloud Application
Chapter 2: Application Architecture	(none)
Chapter 3: Cloud-Native Application	Cloud-Native Architecture
Chapter 4: Microservices Architecture	Microservice
Chapter 5: Microservice Design	Model Around Domain
Chapter 6: Event-Driven Architecture	Event Choreography
Chapter 7: Cloud-Native Storage	Cloud Database
Chapter 8: Cloud Application Clients	Client Application
Chapter 9: Application Migration and Modernization	(none)
Chapter 10: Strangling Monoliths	Strangle the Monolith

This book groups patterns into chapters by level of abstraction and by topic area. Figure I-5 shows the primary relationships between the chapters in this book.

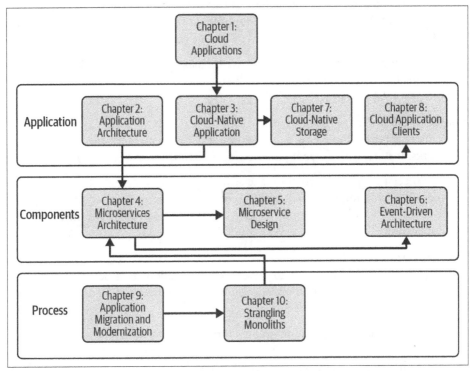

Figure I-5. Book organization

Now we've seen the chapters in this book, how they relate to one another, and their root patterns. Next, let's look at what the chapters are about.

Relationship of Root Patterns and Chapters

The pattern language is divided into 10 chapters, which follow the relationships shown in the diagram. The relationships are among these chapters:

Chapter 1: Cloud Applications
The pattern language begins with this chapter. It introduces the root pattern for the entire book, Cloud Application (6).

The way to adopt the cloud is to host applications on the cloud. The architecture and design of an application that works well in the cloud is significantly different from one that works well in traditional IT. The cloud also facilitates adding many great capabilities to applications.

Chapter 2: Application Architecture

This chapter is a tangential discussion that applies to traditional IT as much as the cloud. It explores three of the main approaches to architect an application: Big Ball of Mud (22), Modular Monolith (29), and Distributed Architecture (38).

Application architectures have evolved to make applications easier to develop and to run more efficiently. We will discuss common architectures and how they have evolved over time.

Chapter 3: Cloud-Native Application

This chapter explores how to design an application to work the way the cloud works. It starts with the root pattern Cloud-Native Architecture (58).

Architect a cloud application to take advantage of the strengths of cloud computing while avoiding and compensating for its limitations. This requires designing a cloud application differently to give it advantages beyond any traditional IT application.

Chapter 4: Microservices Architecture

This chapter explores how to model an application as a set of individually deployable units that can be developed by separate teams. It starts with the root pattern Microservice (119).

The traditional IT application architecture is one big monolith, which makes it difficult for a large team to develop and cumbersome to deploy. To avoid the same challenges in one big cloud application, break it into many small applications that each performs a separate responsibility.

Chapter 5: Microservice Design

This chapter shows a strategy for discovering and scoping individual microservices in an architecture. It starts with the root pattern Model Around the Domain (183).

How can developers design one big application as many small applications that each perform a separate responsibility? Analyze interactions with the application to discover where one well-encapsulated responsibility ends and another begins.

Chapter 6: Event-Driven Architecture

This chapter explains how to choreograph microservices that react dynamically to one another and to external events. It starts with the root pattern Event Choreography (246).

Complex functionality is often decomposed into a predefined set of orchestrated steps. However, some components interact indirectly through dynamically discovered relationships that are more easily modeled as choreography.

Chapter 7: Cloud-Native Storage

This chapter explains how to model data the way the application works and manage it the way the cloud works. It starts with the root pattern Cloud Database (311).

Enterprise IT has embraced the relational database as the best and only way to store and access the data the enterprise depends on. Newer databases have emerged that model data more flexibly and simplify the applications using the data. These databases not only run better on the cloud but often are also included as part of the cloud platform.

Chapter 8: Cloud Application Clients

This chapter explores how users outside the cloud interact with applications in the cloud. It starts with the root pattern Client Application (406).

Cloud applications run in the cloud, but their users do not. Users need to be able to access the cloud application from the device they're using, via user interfaces that are simple to install and update and that support an increasingly wide variety of device types.

Chapter 9: Application Migration and Modernization

This chapter explores how to transform and modernize existing applications into cloud applications. Strategies include Lift and Shift (470), Virtualize the Application (475), Containerize the Application (478), and Refactor the Monolith (484). It is best to Start Small (492) and Pave the Road (496) when you are migrating and modernizing existing applications to run in the cloud.

Cloud applications can be developed from scratch, but they often start as traditional IT applications that the enterprise later decides to host on the cloud. Simply moving a traditional IT application onto the cloud as is has limited success. The enterprise can achieve greater success by updating the application to make it work well on the cloud.

Chapter 10: Strangling Monoliths

This chapter describes how to iteratively transform an application from a monolith into microservices. It describes the process used while migrating and modernizing a monolith application to a microservices application.

A traditional IT application can be updated for the cloud in one big bang, but a complex application that is already running in production can be converted more easily by doing so iteratively. The trick is to keep the application running when it is half traditional IT and half cloud.

Getting Started

The standard way to read most books is straight through following the page numbers and chapter numbers. That will certainly work with this book as well and will help you gain familiarity with the patterns. While that can be the most effective way to read a book, it is not necessarily the most efficient way to use a pattern language.

In a pattern language, rather than only following a fixed chapter order, you can jump in where you need to and follow a path through the patterns that are helpful to you. No two readers may read the same pattern language exactly the same way, and a single reader may not read the same pattern language exactly the same way twice.

The best place to start reading a new pattern language is with the first pattern. That's true for this book's pattern language, so a good place to start is with Cloud Applications (Chapter 1) and the root pattern for the entire book, Cloud Application (6). From there, the *Related Patterns* section at the end of the pattern lists other patterns you might want to read next. And those patterns also have *Related Patterns* sections. Following these pattern links will eventually lead to most of the book, though often not in page or chapter order.

This pattern language is designed to facilitate learning at a high level before diving into all of the details. To get a good feel for the pattern language overall, read only the root patterns. They are listed in Figure I-5 and are the first pattern in each of the chapters. Some chapters don't have root patterns, and it's OK to skip those chapters for this overview; they're not as key to the pattern language as the chapters with root patterns. The root patterns don't have to be read in chapter order, but that's a pretty good way to understand them. In fact, the book presents the chapters in this order because it is a logical progression through the main topics of the book and likewise for the topics' root patterns. As with any pattern language, this ordering isn't the only path through and may not always be the best for all audiences, but it is a good way to get started.

Keep in mind that the chapter relationships shown in Figure I-5 also demonstrate a good order for following the root patterns. The order of the chapters in this book is one suggested ordering but only one of many useful approaches, and some readers will find other orderings more helpful for focusing on the material most relevant to them.

Once you're familiar with a pattern language, the best way to apply it is to think about the specific design problem you're facing currently. Read through the patterns that seem like they may help you solve that problem, pick one that seems promising, apply it, and then see if and how it helps. The *Related Patterns* section will lead to other patterns you should consider. Once you've applied all of the patterns that seem relevant, step back and repeat the process to consider what is now the next problem you're facing in your design and look for patterns that may apply. In this way, you'll use the pattern language to create a custom design by applying the patterns in a specific order to create that design.

The act of reading a pattern language customizes it for each reader and each particular application. As you get used to navigating the patterns in this way, you'll find the chapter order is irrelevant, and you may find that some of the patterns are never relevant to your design and so may never read those pages of the book. That is OK; each reader will use the patterns differently, and how you use the patterns is the right way for your design.

CHAPTER 1

Cloud Applications

Cloud computing is revolutionizing information technology. As the IT environment evolves, application architectures need to evolve to take advantage of the new technology, and IT professionals need to evolve their skills to succeed with the new technology. These cloud application techniques apply to developing a new application so that it will run well on the cloud, as well as migrating an existing application from traditional IT to cloud computing.

Introduction to Cloud Applications

Some readers may wonder why applications need to be structured differently for the cloud. To explain why, let's cover a couple of background topics:

- In Cloud Computing Defined, beginning on this page, we'll discuss how IT infrastructure in the cloud works.
- In Cloud Computing Practices, we'll discuss IT practices for making applications work with cloud computing.

Then, once we're all on the same page, we'll go to the first pattern, which is the root pattern for this entire book, Cloud Application (6).

Cloud Computing Defined

Let's begin with what we mean by "the cloud."

As the saying goes, the cloud is just someone else's computer (*https://oreil.ly/VLXn0*). However, the cloud is way more than just a computer—and far more useful as well. What makes a cloud valuable is the large number of computers available for you to use, your ability to manage your own usage, and the ability for your team members to readily access the computers.

The National Institute of Standards and Technology (NIST) provides this definition of cloud computing (*https://oreil.ly/Dlk9t*):

> Cloud computing is a model for enabling ubiquitous, convenient, on-demand network access to a shared pool of configurable computing resources (e.g., networks, servers, storage, applications, and services) that can be rapidly provisioned and released with minimal management effort or service provider interaction.

Cloud computing has several qualities that make a pool of configurable computing resources easy to share:

Universal access
A cloud can be accessed from any network connection, typically the internet, but an enterprise may host its own private cloud internally, and public clouds can support private network connections.

Shared resources
A cloud enables multiple applications to run on the same hardware. Capacity that is not being used by one application is available to be used by others.

Distributed computing
A cloud isn't just one computer; it's lots of computers, plus storage and networking, which function like one huge computer. An application doesn't run on just one computer; it runs on several, and the parts need to work together over the network.

Virtualized computing
The cloud's compute, storage, and networking hardware is managed by a layer of virtualization that can divvy up one computer to act like many smaller ones. This virtualized layer can also combine many computers to behave like one large computer—the cloud—with a giant pool of capacity.

Elastic computing
An application is not limited to a fixed amount of capacity. The capacity can grow and shrink dynamically as the client load on the application changes.

Multitenant
Multiple users and organizations share a cloud. The cloud controls who has access to which applications and resources and enforces isolation between them.

Self-service
When an organization wants to provision some capacity or deploy a workload, they don't need to send a request to the cloud's central administration staff. Users are able to perform these tasks themselves.

API-driven
> The resources and services that comprise the cloud are used and managed via APIs. Some APIs are only available internally, enabling the cloud provider to monitor and manage the cloud. Other APIs are available externally, enabling self-service by the customers.

Multicloud
> As much as it's convenient to think of "the cloud," there isn't just one cloud; there are lots of them: ones for different stages of the software development lifecycle (SDLC), for different geographies, and for different lines of business. Multiple vendors host different public clouds, and enterprises host their own private clouds.

These qualities are what make a cloud more than just someone else's computer.

Now we have a basic idea of what the cloud is. Next, to understand why cloud applications are different and need to be developed differently, let's review how cloud computing compares with traditional IT.

Cloud Computing Practices

As developers create applications to be deployed on traditional IT, they bake into the application a number of assumptions about how the hardware works, and therefore how the application can and should work. When an application is going to be deployed on cloud computing, many of these assumptions are significantly different.

Cloud computing has certain characteristics that differ from traditional IT and affect how cloud applications need to work:

Reliability through redundancy
> A traditional IT application is only as reliable as its hardware, so developers tasked with making their applications reliable expect either 100% reliable hardware or accept downtime as unavoidable. Cloud computing embraced inexpensive commodity machines, any one of which is less than 100% reliable, and also expects that planned outages are necessary for maintenance and that unplanned outages can't be avoided completely. To run reliably on unreliable infrastructure, a cloud application must be more reliable than its infrastructure, which it achieves by using redundancy.

Eventual consistency
> A traditional IT application uses atomic, consistent, isolated, and durable (ACID) transactions to enforce immediate consistency, even distributed across multiple resources. This requires the complexity and overhead of a transaction manager, concurrency locking, rollback, recovery, and retry. Cloud computing services often employ eventual consistency. Cloud application developers should design

for eventual consistency, which counterintuitively actually makes the applications more reliable.

Generic hardware

A traditional IT application typically requires specific hardware, whereas cloud computing provides generic hardware that will evolve in the future. A cloud application must be infrastructure neutral so that it can run anywhere.

Application mobility

Traditional IT developers assume that once an application is deployed on a computer, it will always run on that computer. Cloud computing moves a running application from one computer to another to balance load and avoid outages. A cloud application must be transportable so that that cloud platform can easily relocate it and it will keep working after relocation.

Multitenant

Developers design a traditional IT application to be the only one running on a computer and to use all of its resources. Cloud computing often runs multiple applications on the same computer and isolates each one to limit the resources it can use. A cloud application must be designed to share its hardware.

Horizontal scaling

A traditional IT application runs on a single computer and scales by growing on that computer, whereas cloud computing scales a cloud's capacity by adding more computers, and scales a workload by running it on multiple computers. To support scaling across multiple computers, a cloud application must be able to run as multiple copies that act like a single bigger application running on one big computer. Multiple copies also make the application more reliable by avoiding a single point of failure. Horizontal scaling can be applied manually or automatically.

Stateless

A traditional IT application stores user data for long-term use by multiple units of work. A cloud application loads data to perform a unit of work but must not store data between units of work.

Immutable

When bugs are found in a traditional IT application, fixes are applied by patching the running application. A cloud application is deployed as a release that does not change while running.

Componentized

A traditional IT application is often a single complex set of code with little separation of concerns, all deployed in a large process that requires a large computer. Cloud computing hosts workloads on parts of multiple smaller computers. A cloud application runs better when designed as multiple components with limited interdependencies that can each run on a different computer.

Service catalog

Many traditional IT applications either implement their own low-level services—such as data persistence and multithreading—or must be deployed into an application server that includes middleware services the applications require. Many cloud computing platforms provide a catalog of reusable middleware services. As much as practical, a cloud application should delegate middleware functionality to shared services.

Cloud database

A traditional IT application stores all of its data in a single relational database that the application must force-fit its data into, whereas cloud computing platforms often provide a variety of database types that are easy to provision and can fit different types of data more naturally. A cloud application should provision databases from the cloud platform's service catalog and should use the best database for each set of data.

Self-provisioning

When a development team needs a traditional IT environment provisioned for their application, they submit requests, and the IT's central operations team performs the provisioning. For a cloud environment, that same development team can perform the provisioning themselves. A cloud application should be designed to deploy into a cloud environment that is self-provisioned.

These differences explain how an application developed for the cloud needs to work differently than one developed for traditional IT. They also show how a traditional IT application moved as is to the cloud doesn't work as well in the cloud as an application designed specifically for the cloud. The more an application's design takes advantage of these cloud capabilities, the better it will run in the cloud. As you can see, adopting the cloud means that application developers need to adopt a new mindset embodying a new set of practices.

We've now seen what the cloud is and how cloud computing differs from traditional IT. With all of that under our belts, it's time to begin discussing how to architect applications for the cloud. We'll start with the root pattern for this entire book, Cloud Application (6).

Cloud Application

You are developing a new application or modernizing an existing application. You want your application to take advantage of cloud technology, both so that it will run better and so that your team will be able to follow better development practices.

How can I build applications to take the maximum advantage of all the features of the cloud for the best future proofing and agility?

Experienced application developers who are new to the cloud are used to developing traditional IT applications and tend to fall back on those practices out of habit. Those practices tend to develop an application that doesn't work well on the cloud, so even a newly developed application doesn't work much better on the cloud than a traditional IT application migrated onto the cloud with minimal changes. The developers either ignore these limitations or get into a game of Whack-a-Mole trying to fix problems in code that wasn't designed well for the cloud.

The cloud offers highly desirable capabilities that traditional IT applications cannot take advantage of:

Low cost, commodity hardware
> Traditional IT applications expect hardware to be specialized and highly reliable, but the most cost-effective cloud infrastructure is generic.

Equivalent computing
> Traditional IT applications hardcode assumptions about the hardware they will be deployed on, whereas the cloud is a loosely defined pool of hardware, and the application could be deployed anywhere.

Unlimited scalability
> Traditional IT applications are not designed to take advantage of the seemingly infinite compute capacity of the cloud.

Traditional IT applications are unable to take advantage of these cloud capabilities. These characteristics that work fine for traditional IT applications work poorly in the cloud:

Monolithic
> A traditional IT application is typically architected as one big program that runs on a single computer.

Complex transactions
> A traditional IT application typically performs several steps that must all complete successfully or none of them should, requiring that all of the steps are performed in a transaction and each step can roll back.

Infrastructure dependent

A traditional IT application is typically designed for a particular operating system with device drivers for specific hardware.

Stationary

A traditional IT application is typically deployed once to run forever on a computer that is expected to run forever.

Vertical scaling

A traditional IT application can scale only as much as its computer is able, becoming constrained by its computer's limits on CPU, memory, storage and network bandwidth.

Stateful

A traditional IT application will often store information in memory, making it so that copies of the application are not fully equivalent from a client perspective.

Patchable

To fix bugs and add features in a traditional IT application, patching is often preferred because a new version of the application that includes the fixes would be too difficult to redeploy.

Exclusive resources

A traditional IT application is typically designed to be the only application running on a computer, such that two applications may conflict.

Homogeneous data

A traditional IT application typically stores all of its data in a single enterprise database of record with a strictly defined one-size-fits-all schema.

Not all traditional IT applications have all of these characteristics; some newer applications may avoid some of these characteristics. While an application with some or all of these characteristics may run well on traditional IT, the more of these characteristics that are embedded in an application, the more difficult it will be to migrate the application to the cloud and have it run well on the cloud. Developers who have designed applications with these characteristics for traditional IT need to learn newer approaches for designing applications that work better in the cloud.

Therefore,

Architect an application as a *Cloud Application*, designing it to take maximum advantage of the capabilities of the cloud while avoiding its shortcomings.

Structure a cloud application as a set of services, preferably microservices, that takes advantage of backend services provided by the cloud platform, accessed by client applications that run outside the cloud (see Figure 1-1).

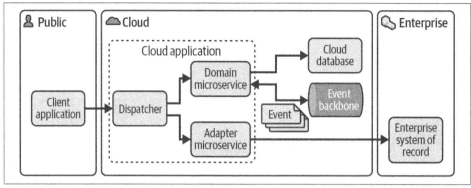

Figure 1-1. Cloud Application

Developers adopting the cloud need to make a conscious effort to develop applications with these qualities, to design the application to take advantage of the strengths of the cloud (such as shared resources and elastic computing) while working around its weaknesses (such as unreliable infrastructure and eventual consistency).

Cloud application design avoids the characteristics that make traditional IT applications run on the cloud less effectively and instead embodies these corresponding characteristics:

Modular and distributed
   A cloud application is composed of multiple components that can run on multiple computers.

Simple transactions
   A cloud application performs tasks as units that can succeed or fail independently.

Infrastructure independent
   A cloud application can run unchanged on a range of commodity hardware that evolves over time.

Movable
   The cloud can relocate a cloud application from one computer to another to balance load and avoid outages.

Horizontal scaling
   A cloud application can run across multiple computers, each with its own resources and bandwidth, avoiding bottlenecks.

Stateless
   A cloud application works best when the latest data is always persistent in the databases.

Immutable
> A cloud application does not change after it is deployed and can always easily be redeployed.

Shared resources
> Multiple cloud applications often run on a single computer.

Data persistence flexibility
> A cloud application often uses multiple databases designed for different tasks with varying approaches to storing data.

These characteristics of a more flexible application are beneficial to traditional IT but practically required to run well on the cloud. The more of these characteristics that are embedded in an application, the better it will work in the cloud.

Some of the main benefits of building *Cloud Applications* are availability, scalability, and flexibility. An application developed for the cloud tends to more modular. The application's modules that can be deployed and scaled independently of other parts of the application.

As explained in Cloud Computing Practices (3), designing applications for cloud is fairly different from the way traditional IT applications are designed. Organizations accustomed to developing applications for traditional IT may find the cloud difficult to adopt until they adopt these new architectural approaches for cloud applications.

Follow these best practices and related patterns to architect an application that works well in the cloud:

Cloud native
> The application is a Cloud-Native Application (Chapter 3), embodying a Cloud-Native Architecture (58) that takes advantage of cloud capabilities.

Microservices
> The application is not just cloud native but can be implemented as a Distributed Architecture (38), usually incorporating a Microservices Architecture (Chapter 4) composed of Microservices (119) that modularize the application into decoupled components that limit the boundaries of code changes and can run distributed across multiple computers. This supports Polyglot Development (146) so that each module can be implemented in a different language. The microservices incorporate a Microservice Design (Chapter 5) that models the enterprise's business domain and the user requirements.

Event driven

> While it is typical for a business process or microservice to orchestrate preplanned work of other microservices, it can also be helpful to use an Event-Driven Architecture (Chapter 6) of Reactive Components (260) to choreograph ad hoc interactions between microservices.

Cloud storage

> The application takes advantage of Cloud-Native Storage (Chapter 7) that is scalable and reliable in the cloud. A cloud platform typically includes a variety of Cloud Databases (311), each of which is optimized for a particular data structure and usage, so an application can take advantage of Polyglot Persistence (375) to segment data into encapsulated sets and store each set of data in the storage technology that works best for that data.

Client applications

> The application running on the servers in the cloud supports a variety of Cloud Application Clients (Chapter 8), with different Client Applications (406) for different platforms such as computers, mobile devices, and even other applications.

Cloud applications facilitate an application development process that makes agile development easier to achieve. A cloud application can be the goal of developing a new application from scratch, or it can be the result of Application Migration and Modernization (Chapter 9) that transforms an existing traditional IT application into a cloud application.

One of the most difficult aspects of modernization can be transforming an application while it is already being used in production. One way to address this is to Strangle the Monolith (Chapter 10), which transforms an application incrementally while keeping the existing application running.

Examples

Following are some examples of applications hosted on the cloud that use a cloud application architecture:

Ecommerce

> A retailer's website that enables consumers to purchase products for mail-order delivery.

Banking

> A customer self-service website that enables customers to view their accounts, deposit checks, and transfer money.

High performance computing (HPC)

> An enterprise uploads data to the cloud for analysis and processing by artificial intelligence.

Ecommerce: Three-tier architecture

An ecommerce application enables its users to order products, often by placing them in a shopping cart and checking out to make payment and place the order for delivery. Modern remote shopping began with ordering by telephone. The telephone customer service representative used an application hosted on traditional IT, often hosted in the computer on their desk. The first websites, though accessible over the web, were hosted in traditional IT on servers that were little more than fancy desktop computers. As the cloud became commonplace, these applications became hosted on the cloud.

Whether the user is the customer buying products or a representative facilitating the purchase, the architecture for the cloud application is the same. The application has functionality and databases for customers purchasing products. Both the customer and representative access the cloud application via client applications that run in web browsers and on mobile devices and even as thick clients deployed on desktop computers.

As Figure 1-2 shows, the business logic for purchasing products runs as a program hosted in the cloud. In this example, the business logic and its corresponding data consists of product catalogs, warehouse inventories, customers, and orders. The enterprise has an existing payment processing system still hosted on traditional IT that is payment card industry (PCI) compliant, so the cloud application uses it to manage payments. The warehouse has an existing inventory management system hosted on-site on traditional IT, which the cloud application uses to query product availability. Customers can make self-service purchases by accessing the website in a web browser or using a mobile application. If the customer calls to place their order, the customer service representative uses the same cloud application but accesses it via their own client, perhaps a thick client application running on their desktop terminal.

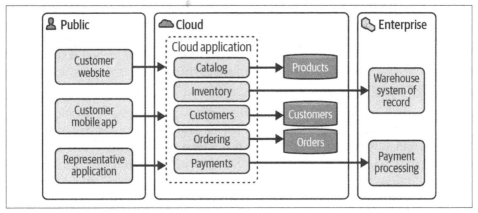

Figure 1-2. Ecommerce Cloud Application

Banking: System of engagement

Many enterprises have existing systems of record (SoRs) that cannot be moved to the cloud (or at least haven't been moved so far). Yet the cloud can still be helpful for making those systems accessible to large numbers of users across a variety of user interfaces. To do so, the enterprise implements a *system of engagement* (SoE) deployed in the cloud that provides controlled access to functionality in the SoRs. The SoE provides a new customer experience through a single modern user interface—such as a web browser—that facilitates access to existing SoR functionality. In both a three-tier cloud application and an SoE cloud application, the middle tier runs in the cloud. In a three-tier application, the middle tier contains the majority of the domain logic, relying on existing SoRs relatively little. In an SoE, the middle tier is mainly a facade that delegates to the SoRs for all domain logic and computation. Whereas the SoRs are difficult to use because of their legacy technology (such as COBOL copybooks, a limited number of concurrent network connections, and batch processing), SoEs use modern technology—such as JSON and XML, web services, and scalability for a huge numbers of concurrent users. The SoE adapts the SoRs so users can access them as a unified, modern application.

Consider a bank that wants to enable its customers and partners to interact directly with its financial services. Those services are often provided by systems of record that almost certainly do not run in the cloud and will not be migrated anytime soon. Rather than rewrite these business-critical systems, and rather than giving public internet users direct access to these business-critical systems, an SoE running in the cloud can scale to support numerous concurrent users on a variety of devices with security to control access to the SoRs via a limited number of shared connections. The SoE provides the external functionality while reusing the existing systems to implement much of that functionality.

The bank may rely on existing systems to manage different types of accounts—such as checking, savings, mortgages, and credit cards. These systems may not even know that multiple accounts are owned by the same customer, or that two customers with separate accounts also own a joint account. Part of the goal for an SoE is to enable a customer to see all of their accounts and manage them together, such as transferring funds between accounts.

Another driver for an SoE is supporting new types of client applications made possible by the internet. Whereas bank tellers used to access the bank's SoRs via dumb terminals, customers today want self-service access to their accounts using websites and mobile apps. Meanwhile, other devices like automatic teller machines (ATMs) need access. Telephone customer service representatives, bank tellers, and even telephone voice prompt systems and internet chatbots need access to these systems and need to be able to see all of the accounts for a customer. This system of engagement is a new application and should be developed to run in the cloud.

Notice that this banking architecture diagram (Figure 1-3) looks a lot like the e-commerce architecture diagram (Figure 1-2). This is the basic architecture of a cloud application. The business domains—ecommerce and banking—are very different, but the cloud architectures are very similar.

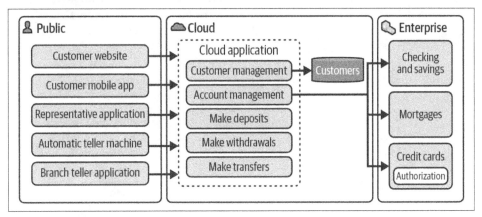

Figure 1-3. Banking Cloud Application

Figure 1-3 shows a bank with the following:

Systems of record (SoRs)
Existing applications in the enterprise, such as ones for different types of accounts like checking, savings, mortgages, and credit cards

Client applications
New client types such as web browsers and mobile apps, and support for new and existing roles like tellers, ATMs, and customer service agents

System of engagement (SoE)
A program in the middle, hosted in the cloud, that integrates with the SoRs to reuse their functionality and that is able to support the range of client applications and large numbers of concurrent users

An SoE can be thought of as a facade for the SoRs, but it's a very powerful facade. It implements security to protect the SoRs and control which users can access what. Most SoRs were never designed to handle very many concurrent users, but SoEs scale to handle large numbers of users connecting at the same time over the internet and internal networks, managing a small number of connections to the SoRs and sharing them among a large number of users.

The cloud makes it possible for many old-school businesses—such as banks, insurance companies, airlines, hotels, phone companies, utility companies, hospitals, ticket sellers—to make their old technology new again without changing it by adding an SoE that reuses what they already have and exposes it in new ways.

Data analytics: Cloud-scale job management

High-performance computing (HPC) hardware—such as high-performance graphics processing units (GPUs)—can greatly accelerate performing analytics and artificial intelligence (AI) on data. An enterprise can avoid the expense of installing HPC hardware in their own data center by instead using the compute capacity in a cloud. The cloud vendor incurs the expense of continuously installing the latest-model GPUs as well as provides large capacities that enable more data to be analyzed concurrently. If the enterprise needs the capacity only at specific times, rather than own capacity that often sits idle, it can pay-as-you-go: rent cloud capacity only when needed, and pay for only what they use.

To facilitate this model, the enterprise doesn't have to store its data in the cloud. Instead, it can break its data into sets and send them to the cloud to process in batches. Figure 1-4 shows the architecture.

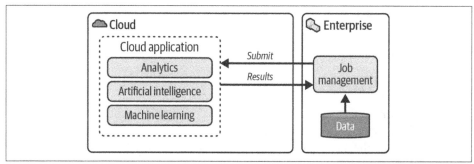

Figure 1-4. HPC Cloud Application

The client application runs where the data is stored, often in its own data center. That application breaks the data into jobs, then uploads each job for the cloud to perform and receives the results. Each job is managed in the cloud serverlessly. The cloud may have the capacity to manage large numbers of jobs concurrently, perhaps in multiple data centers in multiple locations. Multiple enterprises can submit jobs to be managed, all sharing the cloud's capacity and each paying only for the capacity they use. The data is not stored in the cloud long-term, so access to it in the cloud is limited.

Some public clouds make uploading data expensive. If multiple jobs will upload the same data, it can be stored on the cloud instead so that it has to be uploaded only once. If all of the on-prem data will eventually be processed as jobs, the cloud database can be a replica of the on-prem database, such that synchronizing the replica keeps the data current.

A domain-specific example of cloud-scale job performance: a user's survey equipment could take numerous photographs of a large terrain over time and upload them to the cloud for visual analysis using AI. The AI could identify the photos that show interesting anomalies and send their IDs back to the user, filtering for the interesting photos far faster than people could. When the equipment takes lots of photos, the cloud can scale to process them all at the same time, and the user pays only for the capacity they use. This approach also applies to other problem domains, such as enabling next-generation machine learning tools, performing simulations, and supporting research.

Conclusion: Wrapping Up Cloud Applications

In this chapter, we've examined the fundamental pattern for this whole book, Cloud Application (6). For an application to work well in the cloud, it needs to be designed for the cloud.

As we have seen in this chapter, there are important considerations that should be addressed when developing a new application or modernizing an existing application for the cloud. The Introduction showed how cloud computing has evolved from previous computing architectures. Then this chapter addressed the latest iteration of computing architecture—the cloud—as well as what the cloud is and how cloud computing differs from traditional IT.

Cloud applications are different from traditional IT applications. The cloud has newer, better qualities that traditional IT does not, qualities that make a set of computers easy to share. While traditional IT incorporates several practices that don't work well on shared computing, the cloud incorporates rather opposite practices that make shared computing useful. Meanwhile, the industry is adopting several newer application development practices, and the cloud helps facilitate applying those practices. The cloud application topic space is vast, with a lifecycle including numerous aspects that range from application architecture to deployment to complex topologies—more subject matter than can fit in one book, so this book focuses on the first part, the application's architecture.

We've seen that while cloud applications may seem completely new and unknown, their structure has evolved from earlier technologies—from mainframe computers to desktop computers to client/server computing to what is now known as cloud-native computing.

We've reviewed the basic structure of a cloud application, how it solves the challenge of designing an application to work well on the cloud. We reviewed examples for ecommerce, banking, HPC, showing that this cloud application solution can be applied across a range of industries using several architectural variations.

The next chapter will explore the fact that although traditional IT and cloud applications are different, they both run on computers and therefore both embody the same fundamental Application Architectures (Chapter 2). Then, we'll discuss the basic capabilities an application should include to make it run well on the cloud, best practices for designing a Cloud-Native Application (Chapter 3).

CHAPTER 2

Application Architecture

Cloud applications can seem exotic, but their fundamentals evolved from traditional IT. The architectures for applications are largely the same for the traditional IT and cloud. Some of what can make cloud applications seem advanced is that they incorporate advanced architectures that are used less commonly in traditional IT.

The three patterns in this chapter embody three broad approaches for how to architect an entire application. These architectures are not specific to the cloud; they apply equally well to both traditional IT and to the cloud. Developers experienced with developing architectures for traditional IT applications may well already be familiar with these patterns.

Introduction to Application Architecture

Before we dive into the architectures, we'll review some background information that is helpful for understanding them. An application architecture is a kind of software architecture, so first we will define software architecture itself. Architectures are all about trade-offs, so we will discuss the design constraints these architectures resolve and the trade-offs they balance. Architectures arrange functionality into components, so we'll introduce some terminology for describing the components in an architecture.

Once we have that background, we will then present the three application architecture patterns in this chapter—Big Ball of Mud (22), Modular Monolith (29), and Distributed Architecture (38)—and discuss the evolution they embody.

Software Architecture

In the software industry, there are various opinions on what "software architecture" means. For example, one definition (*https://oreil.ly/yWnGy*) states that architecture is the system's structure that comprises software elements with their visible properties and the relationships between them. IEEE defines (*https://oreil.ly/iVhZZ*) software architecture as "fundamental concepts or properties of a system in its environment embodied in its elements, relationships, and in the principles of its design and evolution." In general, many of these definitions view software architecture as the "big picture" of a system that shows the fundamental structures and the organization of a software system. Less formally, the architecture of a system is, as Ralph Johnson (*https://oreil.ly/kvqK6*) puts it, "those parts which are harder to change" or "the decisions you wish you could get right early in a project."

One of the most important yet difficult decisions that teams make early on in a project is deciding which application architecture they will use. An application's architecture does not change its functionality; rather it changes how that functionality is developed and how it runs. An architecture organizes the code that implements an application into a set of components, a collection of parts that form a whole. Components can operate with relative independence from one another, interact with one another, be reused, and be implemented and maintained by developers and small squads working relatively independently from one another.

Architectural Trade-Offs

There are always trade-offs when making decisions about architecture. When developing an application, you must resolve competing business and technical drivers such as performance, availability, security, maintainability, modifiability, time to market, developer skill-set, and more. Each architecture embodies decisions that address these drivers by balancing these trade-offs.

A common trade-off that needs to be made early on for any application is development time. Teams and organizations need to decide whether they need to develop something quickly and refactor it later—or whether they should think hard and try to do it right the first time. Building something quickly does allow teams to release sooner, thus providing user value earlier with the opportunity for needed feedback. Doing "exploratory programming" to experiment in order to find a good solution is sometimes the right choice. However, this comes at a cost in areas such as maintainability, performance, reliability, or developer experience, to name a few.

Another common architectural trade-off is technical debt. *Technical debt* is the implied cost of future effort required to keep a solution's existing functionality working and extend it with new functionality. Architectural decisions can avoid technical debt or incur it intentionally. The development effort to maintain conformance with an architecture can choose to completely eliminate existing technical debt, make a minimal effort to keep it under control, or ignore it entirely.

Figuring out how to budget your development effort over time is another important trade-off we will examine. Functionality developed quickly may require less effort but incur greater technical debt. Repairing the debt or at least keeping it contained will require greater development effort down the line.

If an important consideration for an application is to minimize risks and make the system easier to change, a team will need to think about an application architecture with these advantages. Doing something quick and dirty will not work well for minimizing risks and maintainability. For example, if there are many teams that need to work independently on different parts of the application without affecting other teams or parts of the system, having an architecture where you have pieces (modules) that can be developed independently is a good decision. Ultimately, this could lead to a requirement that the architecture enable different parts of the application to be bundled and deployed in separate processes or computers and be able to scale independently and run concurrently.

This chapter will examine some of these trade-offs and characteristics for deciding on an application architecture and when to choose one architectural style over another.

Component Terminology

This book uses the following terms for different types of components in an architecture:

Module
　　A cohesive set of code that implements a unit of functionality.

Service
　　A module designed to run in a different process than the clients that use it.

Program
　　A set of modules and services that implement a complete set of useful functionality to accomplish a particular domain purpose.

Workload
　　A deployable component, deployed on a physical or virtual server. A monolithic application is a single workload, whereas a distributed application is composed of multiple workloads.

Application
　　A program and the resources it needs to run, such as a web server and a database.

Architecture

A strategy for decomposing functionality into modules comprising services that collaborate. A single application can have different parts with different architectures, such as a single application with a combination of cloud-native architecture, microservices architecture, and event-driven architecture.

An application's architecture is an architecture that applies to the entire application. It defines what its components represent and how they are organized into these component types.

Components structure solutions

The component types in an application architecture define how the architecture structures solutions.

In an object-oriented architecture, each component is an object, and functionality is divided into classes that can each be implemented by different developers. In a service-oriented architecture, each component is a service, functionality is divided into services, and separate teams can work independently to develop each service provider and each service consumer.

Functional programming architects an application as a set of functions. Languages that incorporate functional programming aspects (often together with object-oriented aspects) such as JavaScript and Scala often explicitly declare modules as part of the language definition or through language or platform extensions. For example, Node.js adds modules for organizing JavaScript programs in Node.js, and Require.js is a commonly used module loader for use in both Node and browser-based programs.

Similarly, a layered architecture organizes components into layers, where the dependencies between one layer and the next are all unidirectional, such that the upper layer is optional and the lower layer can operate without it. Like a module, each layer has a purpose, the components in that layer all fit that purpose, and each layer can be developed by a different team with well-defined dependencies on the lower layers. For example, a three-layer architecture encompasses a user interface layer that depends on a domain layer that depends on a data persistence layer.

Application architectures are independent of programming language. An application can be implemented in assembler, FORTRAN, C, Java, Lisp, Clojure, or Go and still have the same architecture. Some architectures can be implemented more easily with some languages than others. For example, an application with an object-oriented architecture can be implemented more easily with a language that includes built-in features for method invocation, inheritance, and polymorphism.

Architectural Patterns

Although there are many architectural styles and patterns, an application is commonly structured with one of three fundamental architectures:

Big Ball of Mud (22)
> An application with no discernable modularity or structure, where any component has access to all other components and where any code can access all variables

Modular Monolith (29)
> A monolithic application composed of modules whose code is cohesive, well-encapsulated, and loosely coupled

Distributed Architecture (38)
> An application composed of code modules built as separately deployable workloads

The first two architectures are monoliths where the application is a single workload that runs in a single executable process—we have seen distributed balls of mud. Often a monolithic application is packaged as a single deployment artifact that runs in an application server. The monolith consists of many components that may contain domain logic for various functionality, which have dependencies among themselves, and code maintenance over the years often increases these dependencies. In an application with a *Distributed Architecture*, each module is a service that runs in a separate process, possibly on a separate computer.

Architectural evolution

These application architectures are milestones in application evolution, increasing the application's sophistication. We see this in Figure 2-1.

Over two centuries, bicycles have evolved to become more sophisticated, to work better, and to be easier to ride. Likewise, over time, application architectures usually evolve from *Big Ball of Mud* to *Modular Monolith* to *Distributed Architecture*. Developers may evolve an individual application through these stages over its lifetime. As developers maintain and extend an application, they must reinvest into the architecture of the application throughout its life, otherwise even a *Modular Monolith* and a *Distributed Architecture* can devolve into a *Big Ball of Mud*.

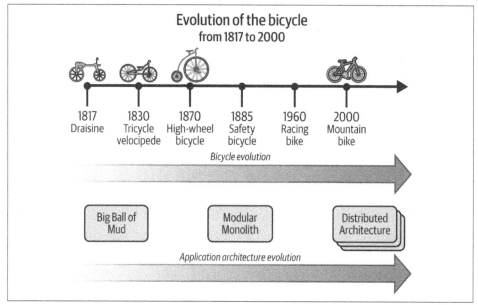

Figure 2-1. Application Architecture evolution

Design is always about tradeoffs. Building a *Distributed Architecture* is challenging; a *Distributed Architecture* is not always an improvement over a *Modular Monolith*. Sometimes building a *Modular Monolith* is the right solution for your problem. The key is knowing how far to take the evolution of the architecture of an application based on the requirements of the particular application, which we will discuss later in Application Migration and Modernization (Chapter 9).

This introduction has covered several topics that are helpful to be familiar with to understand the patterns in this chapter. We've talked about the industry perspective on what software architecture is, enumerated architectural trade-offs that these architectures balance, defined terminology for the components in an architecture, and introduced the patterns and how they evolve an application's architecture.

With this background in mind, let's explore patterns for how to architect an application. Those three application architecture patterns are Big Ball of Mud (22), Modular Monolith (29), and Distributed Architecture (38).

Big Ball of Mud

You are developing an application to be deployed on traditional IT or on the cloud. Perhaps you are in the early stages of development and therefore some or all of the requirements are provisional or evolving quickly. For business reasons, the team needs to get the software working and out the door quickly. You might need to engage in exploratory programming to learn about the requirements, get needed feedback, and understand the best ways to approach the problem.

What is the simplest possible architecture for an application that helps a function work quickly—allowing you to get needed feedback as early as possible

Often an application needs to be developed quickly and at limited cost in order to explore novel functionality. It can be a bare-bones implementation described as a demonstration, prototype, or proof-of-concept. Agile development techniques encourage starting a new project by first developing a minimum viable product (MVP). Lean startup methodologies for software show an application's viability by rapidly developing a simple version and using it to gather customer feedback.

Many application architectural practices make maintenance easier but can slow down coding speed. Function headers and method signatures create barriers between units of code that need to work together. Scoping variables makes them inaccessible to other code that needs them. A reusable component takes time to design and requires coordination between the developers that will reuse it. These are all positive factors but are often overlooked when time and resources are limited.

Many developers aspire to create a well-designed system with clean code, applying proven design patterns. Clean code and a well-designed architecture take significant effort and time. However, teams in the early stages of development often need to experiment with concepts to validate them and strive to find simple ways to develop applications without a lot of overhead.

Too much focus on rapid prototype development and quick delivery, rather than on sustainable architecture, often leads to a (correct) focus on business priorities but can also lead teams to overlook architectural concerns, resulting in technical debt.

Developers differ in their levels of skill, as well as in their expertise and experience. Such variation of experience covers domains, languages, and tools. These different levels of skills lead to a large variation in implementation especially in larger systems with many teams.

Therefore,

Focus on features and functionality before focusing on architecture and performance. Develop an application as a *Big Ball of Mud*—building the system by any means available: produce simple, expedient, disposable code that adequately addresses just the problem at hand.

Long before cloud computing, "Big Ball of Mud" (*https://oreil.ly/glMzX*) was already recognized as the most common, de facto standard software architecture. A *Big Ball of Mud* (*BBoM*) can be considered a lack-of-architecture architecture, the architectural equivalent of the number zero or the empty set. The telltale sign of a BBoM is that everything talks to everything else with circular dependencies, as shown in

Figure 2-2. Every shred of important state data might be global. Variable and function names might be terse, uninformative, or even misleading. Some BBoM architectures are the result of well-intentioned design ideas gone wrong or evolve from an accretion of expedient implementation hacks.

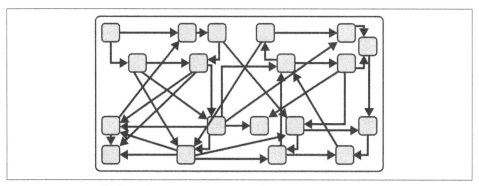

Figure 2-2. Big Ball of Mud

A BBoM architecture defies structured code practices. Function signatures might include long lists of poorly defined parameters, while their function bodies make extensive use of global variables. Variables seemingly intended as constants have changing values; variables seemingly intended as variables remain constant. Many functions are lengthy and convoluted, each performing several unrelated tasks instead of a single, well-defined task. The code is duplicated, and each copy is slightly different. The flow of control is difficult to follow. The programmer's intent is next to impossible to discern. The code is simply unreadable and borders on indecipherable. The code exhibits the unmistakable signs of patch after patch at the hands of multiple maintainers, each of whom seems to have barely understood the consequences of what they were doing. Did we mention documentation? What documentation? Any code comments might be as indecipherable as the code, and the code and its comments might not match.

Although a BBoM is a mess, sometimes intentionally developing an application as a BBoM is exactly the *right thing* to do. The simplest application architecture is no architecture. Rather than wasting time designing for encapsulation, reuse, brevity, and efficiency, simply implement each new feature with the simplest brand-new code that might work. This is the easiest way for a developer to make progress quickly and enables a group of developers working concurrently to all work independently. When a new feature has functionality in common with an existing feature, copy and paste code from the old feature into the new one and make changes. Make variables global so they can be accessed by any code that needs them. Don't worry about which values are constant; just store them all as variables. It can always be refactored later.

A common misconception about BBoM is that it is always an anti-pattern (*AntiPatterns*, 1998). However, a good pattern in one context can be an anti-pattern in another. A BBoM can be an *anti-pattern* in an application that needs to be maintained long-term, but it can be advantageous in the short term.

The BBoM pattern can help make sense of complex systems, whether your ultimate goal is to clean up or contain the mud or not. Many good reasons can lead to overly complex architectures. In fact, architects and development teams doing exactly the right thing can end up with some mud and unnecessary complexity in their systems.

Consider the often-used approach of a minimal viable product (MVP): teams work toward building the smallest possible product—with the fewest extraneous features—that can meet their business needs. Given the narrow focus on only the current product release, teams building with an MVP approach usually end up either unintentionally or quite possibly intentionally building a BBoM. Only if the MVP is successful will a team be able to move on to later releases, in which considerations of extension or expansion become more important than immediate practical value. However, teams following this approach easily get locked into a cycle of repeatedly doing "just enough," and as a result, technical debt (and mud) accumulates. What was a good decision at the beginning ends up becoming less so over time.

You may not always end up with just a single *Big Ball of Mud*. Instead, another possibility is building several mini "mud pies" that could then form a later focus for refactoring. This assumes that you put some effort into modularity even at this early stage. We will address this possibility in the next pattern.

"Big Ball of Mud" (*https://oreil.ly/pVSro*) presents patterns that start to clean up a *BBoM* when it starts to get out of control—such as **Shearing Layers, Sweep It Under the Rug**, and **Reconstruction. Shearing Layers** says to factor your system to group together artifacts that change at similar rates. **Sweep It Under the Rug** says that if you can't easily make a mess go away, at least cordon it off. This restricts the disorder to a fixed area, keeps it out of sight, and perhaps sets the stage for additional refactoring. You are at least not adding to the mess.

"Patterns for Sustaining Architectures" (*http://www.wirfs-brock.com/PDFs/Patterns ForSustainingArchitectures.pdf*) outlines some patterns for sustaining an architecture: **Paving the Wagon Trail** and **Wiping Your Feet at the Door**. These patterns can help prevent your system from getting out of control and keep existing components in your system clean. They help prevent mud from creeping into your design and help you deal with improving evolving systems that might already have muddy parts. They capture proven practices for sustaining complex and typically muddy systems. They do so by shoring up architectural boundaries, identifying and preserving core functionality, and providing easier ways to accomplish repetitive programming tasks.

The main advantage of a *BBoM* is that you are able to quickly develop something that works and thus are able to promptly show progress and get feedback. In many cases, getting a system up and working can be achieved without expending (wasted) time and effort designing what might turn out to be the wrong architecture, undermining the system's grander architectural potential. A casual approach to architecture is emblematic of the early phases of a system's evolution when programmers, architects, and users are learning their way around the domain.

Perfection can be the enemy of "good enough," and it is often the case that something not as good wins. Richard Gabriel's "Worse Is Better" (*https://oreil.ly/0upgk*) argues that in making software (and perhaps in other arenas as well), it is better to start with a minimal working program or system and grow it as needed. In other words, do what is expedient and build what you need; do not worry about the architecture or clean code until later, but use the running system to learn what is needed next. Also, in spite of the best intentions, good decisions can lead to muddy architecture. Only in hindsight can you see what a better, less muddy solution might be.

Kent Beck is known for this mantra: "Make it work. Make it right. Make it fast." "Make it work" means that we should focus on functionality up front and get something running; "Make it right" means that we should concern ourselves with how to structure the system only after we've figured out the pieces we need to solve the problem in the first place; "Make it fast" means that we should be concerned about optimizing performance only after we've learned how to solve the problem and after we've worked out an architecture to elegantly encompass this functionality. Problems arise when there is not enough attention given to the "Make it right" phase, thus leading to substantial technical debt that if not addressed might lead to a bad *BBoM*.

The main disadvantage of a *BBoM* is that they can be very difficult to maintain primarily because there is a lot of coupling between various parts of the system. Changes in one part can break other parts, requiring them to be changed accordingly, and so on, causing a cascade of changes throughout various seemingly unrelated sections of code. Multiple developers working on the same *BBoM* might need to coordinate their changes to prevent code collisions. Michael Feathers outlines some useful techniques that are helpful for dealing with *BBoMs* in *Working Effectively with Legacy Code* (2004).

A *BBoM* application is deceptively easy to build but can be riddled with technical debt. To manage this technical debt, code can be better organized by Refactoring the Monolith (484) into components to become a Modular Monolith (29) that is easier to maintain.

A *BBoM* executable that runs in traditional IT will also run in the cloud. If it ain't broke, don't use the cloud as an unnecessary excuse to fix it. Just Lift and Shift (470) it onto the cloud as is. Developers can Virtualize the Application (475) or Containerize the Application (478) as a *BBoM*, packaging it more like a cloud application. Once it's replatformed onto the cloud, demo the success and deploy it into production. If needed, refactor it later after moving it to the cloud. Alternatively, Refactor the Monolith (484) before moving it to the cloud. A good way to modernize a *BBoM* incrementally while moving it to the cloud is to Strangle the Monolith (Chapter 10), which is an evolutionary approach to moving functionality out of the monolith and replacing it with Microservices (116) and deploying it on the cloud.

A Cloud Application (6) can be developed incredibly quickly by developing each additional feature with yet more code, resulting in a *BBoM* application.

Examples

A general example of an application with a *BBoM* architecture looks like spaghetti code, with many parts connected to many others.

PayPal has publicly documented their application's *BBoM* architecture and how they refactored it to make it modular, to make those distributed, and to make them into microservices.

Ecommerce application

Consider an ecommerce system developed quickly as a *BBoM* monolith—as outlined in Figure 2-3. Ecommerce systems have functionality for *buying products*, which includes functionality for putting items into a Shopping Cart and ways to Checkout and pay for those items. A *BBoM* monolith might have many dependencies, shared global information, and coupling between different functions. Notice that in this example, the Buying Functionality, which includes the Shopping Cart and Check out to pay for items, are overlapped and tightly coupled with many parts of the monolith.

Functionality such as Shopping Cart and Checkout should each be encapsulated within a single part of the application, but this diagram shows how the functionality is spread across multiple parts and how some overlapping parts provide multiple units of functionality. It also shows how each part depends on many others and that the dependencies can become circular. No wonder a change in one part may have unintended consequences in other, seemingly unrelated parts.

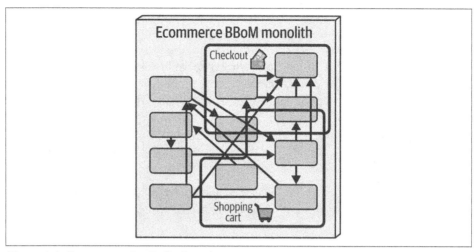

Figure 2-3. Ecommerce Big Ball of Mud

PayPal

One of the most intriguing published stories of refactoring a *BBoM* is David Mosyan's "PayPal's Microservices Architecture Journey" post (*https://oreil.ly/O1iHA*) about how PayPal was refactored from a complex set of monolithic applications, each of them a *Big Ball of Mud*, into a more modern Microservice (119) over a period of several years.

PayPal launched the initial web version of its electronic payments system (what we now know and recognize as PayPal) in 1999. This version was written as a CGI application, which grew substantially over time as more features were added. By 2007, it consisted of over 70 linked monolithic applications, providing significant business value to PayPal at the time. Big-bang releases were scheduled once a month, and the release process often took an entire night or weekend, with accompanying problems in supporting and maintaining the code.

The PayPal team began changing this code into something much more like a Modular Monolith (29) around 2007 with their "isolated releases" idea. This concept essentially made each monolith a module and provided mechanisms to release only those parts of the monolith affected by the changes in the release.

Around that time, they also abandoned a language-specific remote communication technology and moved to a more generic XML-based communication mechanism. There was a single C++ class that embodied most of the domain logic of the system, and they even referred to it as a "big ball of mud"! That one class had well over 5,000 methods and over 500,000 lines of code, and each application that used it had to pull in that enormous class and all of its dependencies—making it difficult to change or maintain. This class included much of PayPal's core functionality, and it became critical to refactor this class to make it easier to change.

The team spent parts of 2007 and 2008 breaking up that class and reorganizing things in a more modular way. That set the stage for a later reorganization to a fully Distributed Architecture (38) that was essentially a Microservices (119) Architecture. They used REST for everything, adopted a more Polyglot Development (146) approach (for example, using Node.js for some modules), and finally refactored the system as a set of Microservices (119). They now have over 2,500 microservices and 750 externally published APIs.

Modular Monolith

You are developing an application for either traditional IT or the cloud. Maybe you've performed some exploratory programming that developed a Big Ball of Mud (22) that has been successful and you now need to maintain it. Or perhaps you want to develop an application from scratch that should be more maintainable than a BBoM. The system is important for your organization and therefore requires you to be able to maintain and add features reliably and cleanly.

How can I architect my application to make it easier to maintain and evolve quickly?

While many projects fail before the application ever gets deployed into production, the applications that do get deployed tend to get used for the long run. Many that are developed quickly to meet an immediate need end up still in use years later. Having developed a prototype, the enterprise may decide to ship the prototype and deploy it into production. Describing an application as a legacy is conceding that the application is still useful. Because useful applications get used for a long time, most of the development effort goes not into initially developing an application but into maintaining it.

The easier an application is to maintain and evolve, the more valuable it is to an enterprise. Not only does it provide useful functionality, but developers can efficiently fix and expand that functionality to keep making the application even more valuable, even as requirements and circumstances change. An application that doesn't need bug fixes and doesn't need new features is one that no one's using. Applications need to be designed not only to provide the desired user functionality but also to be maintainable.

When an application starts as a Big Ball of Mud (22), once it proves viable, maintaining and evolving it becomes a problem. Convoluted code with complex interdependencies causes a fix for one thing to break several other things, and causes code changes that work for each individual developer to fail when integrated into the same build. Crosscutting concerns such as security are difficult to implement because the hidden dependencies complicate both code reviews and security scans. To make the application useful in the long run, developers must spend additional effort making it maintainable. It contains a lot of technical debt that needs to be paid down: making code reusable, removing duplicate code, encapsulating code within functions and classes, limiting variables' scope, etc.

When a project starts with a clear understanding of the requirements, exploratory programming may not be necessary. In this case, starting it as a Big Ball of Mud (22) may ultimately slow down the project. Developers should strive to create maintainable code from the beginning rather than have to dedicate time later to make it maintainable.

The question then is—What sort of application architecture should you morph a BBoM into to make it maintainable? How can you structure an application from the beginning so that it is always maintainable? Developers need a way to structure an application into parts that can be maintained, built, tested, and validated more independently.

Therefore,

Architect an application as a *Modular Monolith*—a single executable composed of separate encapsulated modules designed with limited dependencies between them.

In an application with a *Modular Monolith* architecture, the code has been structured by dividing it into modules. Each unit of functionality is implemented in a single module or small set of modules. Each module implements just one unit of functionality or a set of closely related units. The architecture creates limited dependencies between one module and other modules and avoids circular dependencies (as shown in Figure 2-4).

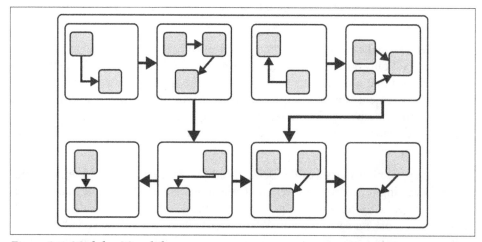

Figure 2-4. Modular Monolith

Earlier, we defined a module. Modules generally do "one thing," that is, they are unified by a single concept. In *Structured Design* (1975), Larry Constantine introduced two important concepts about modules: modules should have high cohesion and low adhesion. That is, one module should contain all of the code to implement one unified thing, and only that code and multiple modules should be loosely coupled so that one doesn't overly rely on others. This led to object-oriented programming, which groups multiple related routines together into classes that hide implementation to enforce loose coupling. That information hiding evolved into APIs that define the boundaries of modules.

This book uses this definition:

> A *module* is a cohesive set of code that implements a unit of functionality.

Each module can be designed to work fairly independently, with an explicit interface that defines the module's boundaries and encapsulates its responsibilities—as shown in Figure 2-4 by the larger blocks with the heavier lines between the blocks. The interfaces declare and limit dependencies between modules and therefore limit the impact of changes in one on the others. Each module can be developed by a separate team of developers working independently of the other teams, needing to coordinate primarily to design the interfaces.

This difference in organizing the code within a monolith makes a world of difference for a team of developers trying to work together to develop an application. Individual developers and small teams can work on different modules at the same time and avoid interfering with one another. This enables the codebase for an application to grow in scale and capability beyond what a single developer can produce.

Because the modules are parts of a single monolithic unit, the application as a whole can be built as a single executable that is easy to run. It is also easy to deploy to the cloud and run in the cloud. Because all of the modules run in a single process, their interfaces can share data using pass-by-reference (e.g., pointers), so the parameters don't have to be serialized. All of the modules are implemented in the same language, with built-in capabilities for function lookup and method invocation. A single executable process is easy to monitor and restart.

There are many *Design Patterns* (1994) that can help with creating *Modular Monoliths*. Patterns such as **Adapter**, **Bridge**, **Decorator**, **Facade**, **Proxy**, and **Strategy** are useful for making reusable components that help create separate modules within your monolith. Additionally, there are many *Pattern-Oriented Software Architecture, Volume 1* (1996) patterns that assist with evolving your monolith to a more modular system such as: **Layers, Master-Slave,**[1] **Pipes and Filters, Broker, Model-View-Controller, Blackboard,** and **Interpreter.**

There are definite advantages when building a *Modular Monolith*. The main advantage is that individual modules within a monolith are easier to develop and maintain. A large development team can work in small squads assigned to individual modules. The modules are still a single code base built into a single deployment artifact and run as a single executable. They can make the application easier to deploy, test, debug, and deal with crosscutting concerns such as security. It is also easier to change individual modules without affecting other parts of the monolith.

There are several other aspects that adding modularity within a monolith will improve. These include better maintainability since it will be easier to locate code within the monolith. Likewise, if each module only does one thing, it is easier to reason about the code. Finally, testing is simpler because you can more easily isolate changes within modules, each of which has fewer tests.

However, there are many challenges to building a *Modular Monolith*. It can take quite a bit of experience and effort to properly design modules around the domain. There is a need for extra time and budget to properly develop and maintain modules in modular programming. It is a challenging task to get the design right and to be able to combine all the modules. It also requires good documentation so that developers can properly use and extend modules without affecting other modules. Getting reusable modules without partly repeating the tasks performed by other modules can also be challenging. However, with well-designed modules, it can be easier to build, test, and deploy into production. Well-designed systems also become easier to maintain.

A *Modular Monolith* that runs in traditional IT will also run in the cloud, just Lift and Shift (470) it onto the cloud as is. Developers can Virtualize the Application (475) or Containerize the Application (478) of a *Modular Monolith*, packaging it more like a cloud application.

A Cloud Application (6) can be developed more methodically by organizing its functionality as a set of modules and assigning each module to a different team to develop it. The teams' work will be better organized, the outcome more predictable, and the result more maintainable.

---

1 **Master-Slave** is the name of the pattern as described in *Pattern-Oriented Software Architecture* (POSA). There has been multiple concerns with the evocations that the name brings. It has been suggested that it is time to change the name (*https://oreil.ly/LsJ6S*). Note: This language is also used in Figure 7-10.

To enable the modules in an application to scale and fail independently, develop it with a Distributed Architecture (38), which is a step toward building a Microservices (119) Architecture. A good design principle to practice for modular programming is to design your modules by Model Around the Domain (183).

Examples

Here are several typical examples of a *Modular Monolith*:

Transformation from Big Ball of Mud to Modular Monolith
   The general approach for refactoring a *BBoM* into a *Modular Monolith*

Ecommerce application
   The ecommerce example from the *BBoM* pattern, refactored into modules

Java
   Built-in support for modules implemented as JAR, WAR, and EAR files

Eclipse
   An open source IDE with a pluggable architecture

Firefox
   An open source web browser with a pluggable architecture

The first two are general techniques, the third is a language feature, and the last two are public applications with documented modular architectures.

Transformation from Big Ball of Mud to Modular Monolith

A common way to create a *Modular Monolith* is to refactor (484) an application with a Big Ball of Mud (22) (BBoM) architecture. Figure 2-5 shows the contrast between a BBoM and modules with well-defined interfaces.

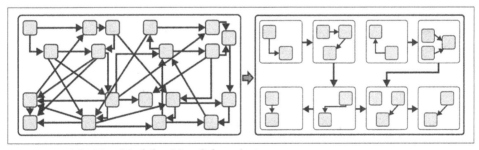

Figure 2-5. BBoM to Modular Monolith evolution

In both architectures, the number of components is the same, but the modules reduce the number of dependencies and make them more orderly with no circular dependencies. The modules help limit technical debt, or at least scope it into smaller parts that can be cleaned up more easily.

To transform a BBoM into a *Modular Monolith*, extract functionality into modules that model the domain. Each module can then evolve independently without affecting other parts of the system.

Ecommerce application

In the ecommerce example, the Buy functionality is separated into two smaller separate functions, such as Shopping Cart and Checkout (see Figure 2-6).

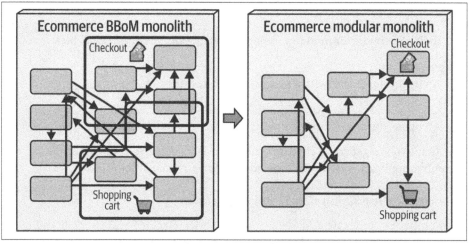

Figure 2-6. Ecommerce BBoM to Modular Monolith evolution

Once these functions have been extracted into separate modules, different teams can now work on them and deploy them with a much lower risk of breaking other parts of the system.

Java

In Java, each module can be compiled as a separate JAR file, and then the collection of JAR files can be built into a single executable JAR. Running the application is one simple action that runs the JAR file in an application server.

In Jakarta EE, several WARs can be packaged together into an EAR along with other JAR files. In this way, the specification encourages one form of a *Modular Monolith* by making it possible to package together multiple WAR and JAR files. While the basic specification encourages these WAR and EAR files to be loosely coupled, in practice, this often devolved into a *Big Ball of Mud* through tight coupling between classes packaged in different JAR files. This was exacerbated by the fact that the standard specification does not declare versions of classes or packages that are exported, often leading to issues when multiple modules are integrated.

Eclipse

One of the best, and most well-studied, examples of a *Modular Monolith* is the venerable Eclipse open source Integrated Development Environment (IDE). Eclipse was released to open source in 2001, having been originally internally developed by IBM, and control was turned over to the new Eclipse Foundation in 2004.

The key design principle that has defined Eclipse from its inception is that everything in Eclipse is defined as a plug-in. In the original version of Eclipse, a plug-in was a JAR file together with a manifest file (plug-in.xml) that described the dependencies of that plug-in and what APIs were available for extension or consumption. A plug-in is essentially, as we have described—a module. Eclipse runs inside a Java Virtual Machine (JVM)—when Eclipse starts, it scans a set of directories for the manifest descriptors and then builds an in-memory plug-in registry of the available plug-ins. Plug-ins can then be built on top of the existing extension points of other plug-ins. We show this in Figure 2-7:

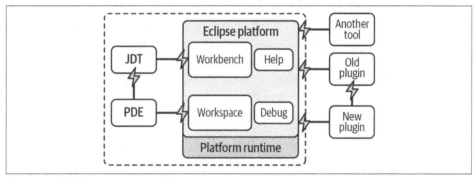

Figure 2-7. Eclipse plug-in architecture

This very flexible modular architecture has allowed Eclipse to be extended well beyond its original heritage as a Java IDE to provide support for languages and environments from Ada to Xtest, covering nearly every letter of the alphabet in between. One of the key things the Eclipse architecture has addressed that has often plagued other *Modular Monolith* systems is that it fixed the issue of isolation between modules when modules share common code elements (such as nested JAR files). This was addressed in the Eclipse 3.0 release, which adopted the OSGi framework, turning plug-ins into OSGi bundles.

OSGi is a set of specifications, implementations, and test compatibility kits that constitute a dynamic module system for Java that goes well beyond the standard Java

JAR specification. In OSGi, the unit of deployment (the module) is called a *bundle*. A bundle addresses the shortcoming of the Java class loader by providing visibility only to Java packages that are explicitly exported from a bundle and by declaring its package dependencies explicitly. What's more, it also provides a versioning mechanism for exporting and importing packages at only a specific version level or range of levels.

Firefox

This concept of a plug-in architecture—that is, an architecture of a platform that is specifically designed for extension—is one of the most common ways that a *Modular Monolith* can survive over the long term without becoming too unwieldy. However, even when an extension architecture becomes unmanageable due to accumulated technical debt, you can refactor it to bring the architecture back to a more manageable state. An excellent example of this is the evolution of the Mozilla (Firefox) extension architecture, which underwent a similar transformation.

Firefox is another venerable open source project—it was originally released in 2004, and the project was originally named "Firebird" to signify it was rising from the ashes of the older Netscape browser. One of the design decisions made in the original Firefox project was to build it using a component architecture—in particular, the architects of Firefox designed one specifically for this project. That was XPCOM (The Cross-Platform Component Object Model).

XPCOM was a cross-language component model developed by Mozilla that was similar to both Microsoft COM and Open Group's CORBA. Nearly all of the internal capabilities of Firefox were developed as XPCOM components. That was important to the original extension architecture of Firefox, in which third-party extensions to the platform were called "add-ons." Figure 2-8 shows the main components of this architecture.

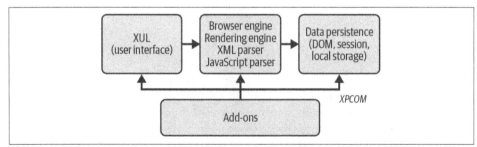

Figure 2-8. Original Firefox architecture

The key here is that the developer of an add-on could use nearly all of the internal XPCOM components within the platform from their extensions. The extensions themselves were also built using XPCOM components. However, over time this turned out to create some issues. One was that the performance of the

communication between the core platform modules was hampered by the requirements (such as parameter marshaling) of the XPCOM standard. Another was that
the broad set of capabilities made available to add-on developers resulted in them
using services that probably should have remained private to the platform—making
it hard for platform developers to make changes without breaking the extensions. In
other words, tight coupling between the code within the platform and the code in the
extensions made changes difficult.

Those factors, among others, led to a major change in the architecture in 2016. Motivated by the newer extension architecture of Chromium-based browsers (Chromium
was released as open source in 2008), Firefox released a new extension architecture in
2016. This led to the deprecation of XPCOM in 2017.

This new architecture consists of a simpler approach where extensions are written
using the exact same technologies as are used in building web pages—HTML, CSS,
and JavaScript. For the most part, a browser extension is simply a collection of HTML
and CSS pages and JavaScript code. An extension is defined as a directory containing
a JSON manifest, pages (in HTML and CSS), actions (button icons with optional
HTML and JavaScript), scripts (in JavaScript), and web-accessible resources. The final
piece of this architecture is that scripts and actions can call the WebExtensions API,
which defines a much more narrow, tightly controlled public API that limits the
access that extensions have to the browser internet. This is shown in Figure 2-9:

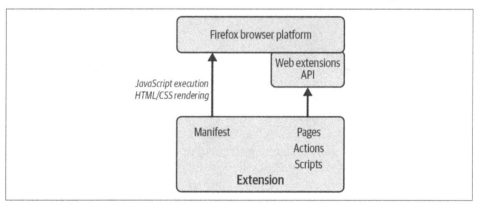

Figure 2-9. Post-2016 Firefox architecture

Web Extensions are standard APIs that cover browser functions like manipulating cookies, setting bookmarks, adding to menus, reading the DOM or taking
actions based on the content of a page, setting notifications, manipulating tabs, and
much more. This API is broadly compatible with the extension API supported by
Chromium-based brokers, which makes it easier to write extensions for both sets of
browsers. This new architecture is loosely coupled, based on languages and tools that
are already in use by web developers and aligned with the rest of the industry for

greater portability. We will see all of these requirements and features again when we start to examine how to evolve component models into a Distributed Architecture (38). The fact that they are still required even when building a *Modular Monolith* is very telling.

Distributed Architecture

You are developing an application for either traditional IT or the cloud. If any development has occurred so far, the application has been architected either as a Big Ball of Mud (22) or a Modular Monolith (29). Parts of the system need to evolve independently and possibly by different teams. Various parts of the system have different resource requirements, and some parts of the system can possibly run concurrently with other parts.

How can I architect my application so that parts of it can be developed, deployed, and run independently?

A monolithic application is built, deployed, and run as one big application. A single executable can be easier to test and debug because there are fewer moving pieces to keep track of. However, over time as a monolith increases in size, testing becomes cumbersome, because a change in one part requires retesting all of it. As a monolith gets bigger, running it requires computers with greater capacity. An application running as a single monolith runs on a single computer and is a single point of failure.

Deploying a new version of a monolith, even a Modular Monolith (29), is a big bang. Parts cannot be deployed independently; to deploy one part, developers must redeploy the entire application. To change one part of the application, all of it needs to be rebuilt, retested, and redeployed. Developers and teams may be able to independently improve different modules, but rebuilding and redeploying cannot be done independently. This means that development teams working on the various modules must coordinate to reach a stopping point and all be ready at the same time to build the application. Deploying a monolith requires testing all the modules together and ensuring that the modules are integrated properly. Therefore, everyone (all the teams) must be ready for a new build, and improvements in one module won't be deployed until all of the modules are rebuilt and redeployed. The bigger a monolith gets, the more complex and burdensome it may be to redeploy, often requiring an outage while the old version is shut down and uninstalled. Then the new version is installed and started. If the redeploy fails, the entire application is down until recovery is successful.

Even if you have spent the time to refactor a monolith into modules, it is still a single unit. Development teams would prefer an architecture that not only allows them to develop the modules independently but also to deploy them independently and have them run independently.

Therefore,

Architect an application with a *Distributed Architecture*, which creates a composite application that is a collection of modules, each designed to run separately in its own process.

A *Distributed Architecture* structures the modules in a Modular Monolith (29) to each run as a workload in a separate process and to be able to invoke one another remotely over the network. The architecture enables modules in a single application to run distributed across multiple computers and still connect to operate as a unified application, as shown in Figure 2-10.

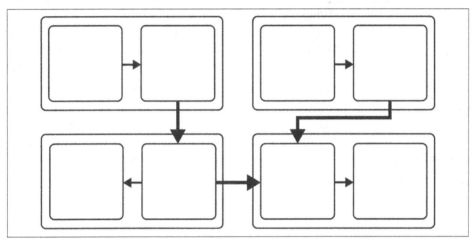

Figure 2-10. Distributed Architecture

A *Distributed Architecture* enables the modules in a single application not only to be developed independently but also to be built and deployed as separate workloads that run in their own processes. A distributed architecture application runs as a composite application, a collection of workloads—each a module running in a process—often called services. One service invokes another remotely via its interface. Multiple services can run on the same computer, and they can each run on different computers.

A *service* is a coherent, ready-to-use software component that is designed to provide a unit of domain functionality. Services are modules that clients access through APIs that encapsulate and hide the underlying implementation and technology. A service is implemented by a service provider that performs automated tasks, responds to events, or listens for data requests from other software. A service consumer invokes a service to request information or perform a task. The consumer passes parameter values in the request, and the provider passes a result value or error in the response.

A service consumer and provider communicate over a network connection via either a remote call or message distribution technology. Most commonly today, that will mean an RPC technology like gRPC or a more general remote technology like REST. Message passing with a queuing system like RabbitMQ or an Event Backbone (279) like Kafka is also common. All of these remote technologies transmit parameters and result values across the network by marshaling or serializing each value's data. Remote invocation and value marshaling can create performance overhead, which an API should limit by defining course-grained tasks that reduce the round-trip interactions between the consumer and provider. (See **Session Facade** (*Core J2EE Patterns*, 2003) and **Remote Facade** (*Patterns of Enterprise Application Architecture*, 2002).)

The services in a *Distributed Architecture* are deployed independently and can scale and fail independently. When one service becomes a bottleneck, it can be scaled without the others needing to scale. If one service's process crashes, the others running in their own processes keep running. When an infrastructure component fails, only the services running on that component fail with it; the services on other components keep running.

A distributed application may run more efficiently not only on multiple computers but even on a single CPU. Today, the CPUs in most devices are multicore CPUs. When combined with modern operating systems, any such device can multitask concurrently both by multithreading within a process and by running multiple processes simultaneously in multiple CPU cores.

Making an application distributed does increase design complexity by introducing challenges such as concurrency, failure handling, and crosscutting concerns such as performance, logging, security, debugging, and testing. To distribute components effectively, the data the components use must be stored in a data store that is also distributed; otherwise the data store will become a bottleneck and single point of failure.

A *Distributed Architecture* is often built by extending a Modular Monolith (29), where the services are modules that can be deployed independently, so the design patterns for developing modules also apply to developing services. Many distributed computing patterns are also helpful for designing services, including **Publisher-Subscriber** and **Presentation-Abstraction-Control** (*Pattern-Oriented Software Architecture, Volume 1*, 1996); **Message Channel**, **Message Endpoint**, **Message Translator**, and **Message Router** (*Enterprise Integration Patterns*, 2003); and **Client Request Handler**.

There are many advantages to building a Distributed Architecture. An obvious advantage, as previously discussed, is scalability across multiple computers. Another advantage is that the services can be developed and deployed independently. Resilience and redundancy are also key advantages. Each module in a Distributed

Architecture scales and fails independently. When one module becomes a bottleneck, it can be scaled without the others needing to scale. If one module's process crashes, the others running in their own processes keep running.

There is another advantage in modern systems that may not be as obvious. With almost no exceptions, all CPUs in desktops, mobile devices, and even embedded devices are multicore. That means that, when combined with modern operating systems, nearly any device can not only handle multithreading within a process but will easily handle multiple processes running simultaneously. Using all of those cores effectively almost always requires running multiple processes. Thus, even in a single CPU, building a Distributed Architecture of multiple cooperating processes may be advantageous. Likewise, even on a single CPU, there are advantages in that each process has its own memory space. Splitting across multiple processes that communicate therefore limits the "blast radius" of some types of memory issues.

There are also challenges to building a distributed architecture, such as concurrency, failure handling, and crosscutting concerns like performance and logging. One particularly serious challenge is related to data. A monolithic application typically uses a centralized database, whereas distributed architecture can follow the Self-Managed Data Store (154) pattern. The simplest alternative to splitting data across multiple databases is for an extracted service to directly access the monolith database, but that alternative creates undesirable coupling and, if applied, should be temporary. A common approach requires replicating the data across dedicated service data stores and any monolith data store. This option increases the design complexity, requires the implementation and constant overseeing of a data synchronization mechanism, and may cause the services to access stale data due to the eventual consistency setup.

Additionally, there is the challenge of dealing with crosscutting concerns such as security. It is much harder to ensure security when you have multiple services running in different memory spaces. Providing adequate security in distributed systems is challenging because the services and their connections need to be secured as well. This can also make debugging and testing more difficult.

An application with a *Distributed Architecture* that runs in traditional IT will also run in the cloud. To move these to the cloud, simply Lift and Shift (470) each of its services to the cloud as is. Developers can apply the Virtualize the Application (475) or Containerize the Application (478) patterns for each of the services in a distributed architecture, packaging them into components in a cloud application.

A Cloud Application (6) can be developed for more flexible deployment by organizing its functionality as a set of services that run independently. The application can more easily take advantage of cloud capacity if it can distribute its components. An important design principle for services is to Model Around the Domain (183).

A Microservices Architecture (Chapter 4) is a *Distributed Architecture* where each service is a Microservice (119).

Services are often developed as an Event-Driven Architecture (Chapter 6) where the services can be a Reactive Component (260).

Examples

Here are several typical examples of a *Distributed Architecture*:

Transformation from Modular Monolith to Distributed Architecture
The general approach for repackaging modules for distributed deployment

Ecommerce application
The ecommerce example from the BBoM and *Modular Monolith* patterns, repackaged into workloads

Airline reservation system
Three applications in one with differing requirements

AJAX Frameworks and Node.js
Distributed architecture for user interfaces hosted in web browsers

VS Code
Distributed architecture that deploys support for each computer language as a "Language Server"

Eclipse Theia
Distributed architecture with separate IDE frontends and backends

The first two are general techniques, the third is domain-specific, the fourth is a language feature, and the last two are public applications with documented distributed architectures.

Transformation from Modular Monolith to Distributed Architecture

A common way to create a *Distributed Architecture* is to transform each module in a Modular Monolith (29) by augmenting it with a remote API and packaging it to run in its own separate runtime. Figure 2-11 shows the contrast between an application composed of modules and the same one composed of processes.

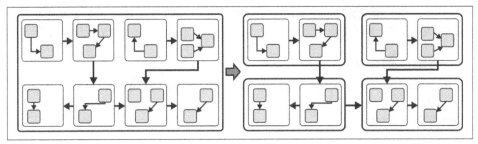

Figure 2-11. Modular Monolith to Distributed Architecture evolution

In both architectures, the number of components is the same, but the modules packaged in one process can be deployed separately from the modules in another process. Whereas the monolith can be deployed only on one computer, the processes in the distributed application can be deployed on the same computer or on different computers.

Ecommerce application

Expanding on our example from the BBoM evolution to the *Modular Monolith*, we can take a step toward a distributed architecture by extracting (*refactoring*) the "Buy Service," which includes both the Shopping Cart and Checkout modules into a separate service (see Figure 2-12).

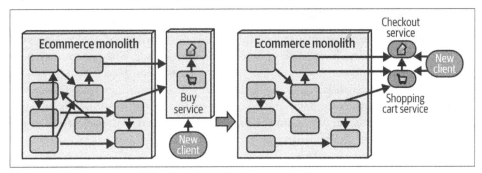

Figure 2-12. Ecommerce Distributed Architecture evolution

This new service can then be deployed independently of the monolith, either on the same virtual computer or on a completely separate computer running in its own process. Ultimately, this buy service can be *refactored* further into two separate services for the Shopping Cart and Checkout functionality, each running independently of the other and the monolith.

Rather than deploy a new version of a monolith as one "big bang," each new version of a module can be deployed as its own "little bang." An outage still occurs, but it affects only one part of the application rather than the entire application. Compared to redeploying an entire application, a smaller deployment goes faster and can be performed more reliably.

Airline reservation system

As an example of this separation of services, let's consider an airline frontend reservation system. Airlines in general are interesting in that they are the intersection of two different businesses:

Product sales
> The process of selling seats, which is much more like an ecommerce problem than anything else

Transportation management
> Moving passengers (who hold tickets for specific seats) from point A to point B safely, efficiently, and on time, which is a classic logistics problem

The result of this is that different parts of the backend of the same mobile app or website have different scalability needs. Most customers, especially during busy times of the year like holidays, are just browsing for flight prices—they may specify a pair of dates and an origin and destination, and then "abandon the cart" if nothing looks attractive from a price or time perspective. A much smaller number of customers will actually complete the transaction and purchase tickets on a particular flight. An even smaller number of customers are the elite fliers who want to check their account status or redeem points or miles for a ticket.

This means that the different parts of this application (browsing, purchasing, and tracking frequent fliers) have vastly different scalability needs. The system may need 10x the computing power to handle the browsing transaction load than it needs for the purchase load, which is again 10x larger than the frequent flier load. Developers deploying a monolith only have one option: deploy the entire monolith as many times as needed to cover the compute load of the most loaded part of the entire application. But that also means tying together the deployment processes of all of these different pieces.

If the system had a shopping service, a reservation service, and a frequent flier service that are each implemented by distributing the relevant modules behind a remote interface or messaging system, then it becomes easy to see how the shopping service could scale independently of the reservation service, if each is deployed as its own workload. The downside is that the system will still need to coordinate between these services. For example, the shopping service may need to pass the selected flight off to the reservation service to enable the customer to complete the reservation and purchase the ticket. This may amount to only a few pieces of information in our example (perhaps a few K of XML or JSON text), but this would expand in a more complex area of the domain, for example, in managing the complexity of the inventory of spare parts that would be involved in servicing an airplane. That is why it is critical to carefully craft interfaces and limit the amount of information transmitted between parts of a distributed architecture.

AJAX frameworks and Node.js

A hallmark of a true pattern is that when it becomes so common and so ingrained into the way that people think about a problem, no one talks about the particular solution as a pattern anymore.

When developing a new application with JavaScript, nearly 100% of developers will assume the solution will be developed with Node.JS and a frontend JavaScript AJAX framework like Angular or Axios. These are, of course, based on AJAX (Asynchronous JavaScript and XML), a feature that is such a common part of modern web development that an entire generation of developers has grown up through the industry assuming that user interfaces always worked this way. AJAX was added to JavaScript as the XMLHttpRequest class, which wasn't even supported in all browsers until as late as 2007 and wasn't made an official W3C standard (*https://oreil.ly/qnB3m*) until 2008. XMLHttpRequest was a revolution in how developers wrote JavaScript code in the browser, introducing the idea of fine-grained server calls within the JavaScript running on a web page, enabling one part of a page to be updated while another part is rendered, and enabling for controls that changed the content of the page based on a server-side query when the control was activated. The basic flow of this process is shown in Figure 2-13.

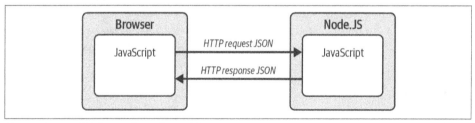

Figure 2-13. AJAX as a Distributed System

That revolution led to the introduction of all of the client-side AJAX frameworks we now have today, beginning with now-venerable libraries like jQuery and Backbone and leading up to more modern frameworks like Angular and Axios. This idea of now having JavaScript in both places—in the client code running in the browser and also in the Node.js server code, usually seamlessly communicating via JSON (which is nothing more or less than a method for marshaling JavaScript objects)—is so much a part of web development that few developers stop to think that they are actually building their web browser user interface as a *Distributed Architecture*.

Visual Studio Code

One of the interesting evolutions of this idea is that the newest generation of development tools has evolved from traditional desktop IDEs like Eclipse to systems rooted in the *Distributed Architecture* paradigm promoted through JavaScript in the Browser and JavaScript in Node.JS described previously. The first of this generation, and still by far the most popular, is Microsoft Visual Studio Code (VS Code).

At this point, if you've ever installed VS Code, you may be saying, "Wait a minute! VS Code is a desktop application, not a browser application—how is it a distributed system based on JavaScript and Node.JS?" That is one of the interesting and unique design features of VS Code—how it is based on the Electron framework (see "Why did we build Visual Studio Code?" (*https://oreil.ly/a-pKM*)) and the way it is architected to be in some ways the best of both worlds (e.g., see the VS Code extensions built in this project (*https://oreil.ly/AfB5L*) at Delft University of Technology). Electron (*https://oreil.ly/zDrUX*) is a framework for building desktop applications that embeds both Chromium and Node.JS as part of its Application Package (62). Thus it allows you to build desktop applications that use all the same technologies—and patterns —as *Distributed Architectures*. There are several communicating processes in VS Code, which often confuses people when they first look at VS Code in tools like the Windows Task Manager or Mac Activity Manager and see it represented as several processes.

One simple and straightforward example of this is how VS Code handles support for different languages. The way in which they have implemented multilanguage support is to separate the Developer Tool (which hosts the Code Editor) from the Language Server for each computer language that can be edited in VS Code (see "A Common Protocol for Languages" (*https://oreil.ly/QigpO*)). This is shown in Figure 2-14.

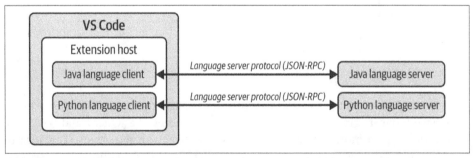

Figure 2-14. VS Code Language Server

The two processes communicate via a specialization of JSON-RPC that they call the Language Server Protocol (LSP). This allows the Language Server (which actually understands the abstract syntax tree (AST) of the program in the target language) to respond to changes in the document being edited and send back diagnostic information in the form of errors and warnings that are displayed in the code editor as the document is being edited.

Eclipse Theia

Not to be outdone, the Eclipse Foundation responded to the advances in VS Code by starting new projects that ended up adopting many of the patterns and design principles, and even protocols, that were introduced in VS Code. For instance, the Eclipse Theia project parallels VS Code in that it also encompasses several cooperating processes in a *Distributed Architecture* that each handles different aspects of the development process. Eclipse Theia adopted the Language Server Protocol from VS Code and has the same separation of code editing from language-specific syntax understanding. Where Eclipse Theia (*https://oreil.ly/myKBo*) goes even further than VS Code is that it allows for several different styles of packaging, starting with the same local packaging of frontend and backend using Electron that VS Code follows, but also including a Web Client frontend and remote backend (a cloud IDE) and a local Electron-based frontend that is combined with a remote backend.

These options are shown in Figure 2-15:

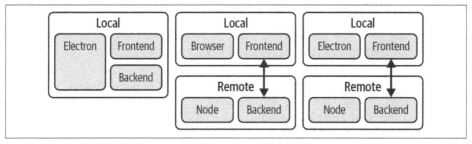

Figure 2-15. Eclipse Theia deployment options

A simplified component diagram of Eclipse Theia is shown in Figure 2-16. It demonstrates how you can combine modularity in several ways—both in the idea of packaging things as a *Modular Monolith* (which we can see in the packaging of the frontend) and as a *Distributed Architecture*, especially in considering the backend packaging.

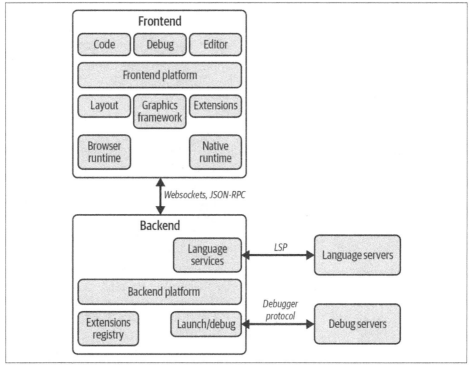

Figure 2-16. Eclipse Theia Architecture

Eclipse Theia has been used as the basis of several products from a number of companies, including Red Hat CodeReady Workspaces.

Conclusion: Wrapping Up Application Architecture

In this chapter, we've examined a set of patterns related to application architecture. Although there are many architectural styles and patterns, applications are generally structured with one of three fundamental architectures:

Big Ball of Mud (22)
> An application with no discernible modularity or structure, where any code has access to all other code and variables

Modular Monolith (29)
> A monolithic application composed of loosely coupled, well-encapsulated code modules

Distributed Architecture (38)
> An application composed of code modules that can run on separate computers

The first two architectures are monoliths where the application is a single workload that runs in a single executable process, whereas a Distributed Architecture has many pieces that can run independently in their own processes. It should be noted that we have seen distributed balls of mud which is far worse than a monolithic *BBoM*.

The three architectures all balance the same set of trade-offs, but each one balances them differently. Which architecture is better for a particular application at a particular point in its lifetime depends on how the development team wants to balance those trade-offs. There is no one right answer for how to solve these trade-offs, which is why there are multiple solutions embodied in multiple architectures. The generic answer is that *it depends*. It depends on context, and selecting the important criteria and qualities for your solution allows you to capture and describe them. Architecture and design is always about making trade-offs. When you are designing, you are making a design decision. For every architecture or design decision, you are compromising on some factors. When you choose one thing, you are going to sacrifice something else.

Sometimes a monolithic architecture is the right approach. If an existing monolithic solution works fine, is understandable, and helps the organization to promptly address new requirements, there's no pressing reason to change it. *BBoM* architectures are still seen today. BBoMs can be a mix of doing what it takes to meet business requirements and being obliviousness to technical debt when business drivers do not allow time to address such debt. Sometimes it is difficult to know the best design or even how to approach a problem. In these situations, doing some exploratory programming to experiment to find a good solution is exactly the right approach.

Over time, technical debt can accumulate in parts of the system that are integral to the business—especially parts of the system that require regular maintenance. When this happens, refactoring these parts of the monolith to make it easier to change is a good decision. This can lead to a better design that is easier to change: a *Modular Monolith*. Modular systems make changes less risky, facilitate reuse, and, most importantly, enable teams of developers to work independently with each team focusing on separate modules.

Distributed Architecture is the next step of this evolution. It extends the idea of modules as well-encapsulated units of independent development to execution bundles deployable in separate processes or computers and able to be run concurrently. Not all *Modular Monoliths* need to evolve to a *Distributed Architecture*. Building a *Distributed Architecture* is very challenging. Sometimes avoiding distributed complexity is the right approach.

Even though an architecture can evolve from a *BBoM* to a *Modular Monolith* to a *Distributed Architecture*, in practice it can be much more complicated. When building complex systems, it can be all too easy to primarily focus on features and overlook software qualities, specifically those related to the architecture and dealing with technical debt. Some believe that a clean architecture will magically emerge by simply following agile practices—starting as fast as possible, keeping code clean, and having lots of tests. Indeed, an architecture will emerge, but if not enough attention is paid to the architecture and the code, technical debt and design problems will creep in until the overall system becomes muddy, making it hard to deliver new features quickly and reliably. Often a *Modular Monolith* devolves into a *BBoM*, making it difficult to add new features or maintain the system. This even becomes worse and scarier when you have a distributed *BBoM*.

Of these three main strategies to architect a complete application, *Distributed Architecture* is the most fundamental one for Cloud Applications (6). While a *Cloud Application* can be a monolith, most are distributed because cloud computing is distributed.

Next, we will discuss best practices for designing a Cloud-Native Application (Chapter 3). Then we'll explore two specializations of *Distributed Architecture*, Microservices Architecture (Chapter 4) and Event-Driven Architecture (Chapter 6). Like *Distributed Architecture*, neither of these requires cloud computing but both are important building blocks for an application that runs well on the cloud.

CHAPTER 3

Cloud-Native Application

While the fundamental architecture for an application is the same for both traditional IT and the cloud, the architecture selected must then be refined further to optimize the application for the cloud. We've discussed how cloud computing enables you to run your applications on someone else's computer, how it incorporates practices that are different from traditional IT, and how those practices impact the way that applications work. With that in mind, let's look at how to architect an application to incorporate these cloud computing practices. To make an application run well on the cloud, architect and design it as a Cloud-Native Application.

Introduction to Cloud-Native Application

We need to distinguish between these two separate but closely related topics:

cloud computing
    How the cloud makes its IT infrastructure available

cloud native
    How to architect and design an application to work well with the cloud

These two topics are two different sides of the same coin: the compute infrastructure that the cloud provides and the application that works well within that infrastructure. These topics are counterparts because to understand why cloud native works the way it does, it is helpful to first understand how cloud computing works.

While cloud computing is well defined, the characteristics that make an application cloud-native have not been articulated as clearly. This chapter will introduce seven patterns that provide guidance on how to architect and design Cloud-Native Applications. Those patterns assume some background on how the cloud works, so let's review that first. Let's take a look at how the industry defines cloud computing and Cloud-Native Applications, along with a widely accepted methodology of 12 practices for building modern applications. Then we'll introduce the patterns and briefly review how they fit together.

With this background, we'll then start with the root pattern for this chapter, Cloud-Native Architecture (58).

Cloud Computing

"The cloud" is shorthand; it is how we refer to the infrastructure provided by cloud computing. Beyond the definition of what cloud computing is, there are multiple dimensions to how cloud infrastructure embodies itself as "the cloud."

As we've already seen in Cloud Applications (Chapter 1), the National Institute of Standards and Technology (NIST) provides a definition of cloud computing (*https://oreil.ly/A2oDo*) that says it's a shared pool of computing resources, widely available with self-service provisioning. The NIST definition elaborates further to say that the cloud model is composed of five essential characteristics, three service models, and four deployment models.

The NIST's five essential characteristics of cloud computing are as follows:

On-demand self-service
    A consumer can provision computing capabilities as needed without requiring human interaction with the service providers.

Broad network access
    Capabilities are available over the network.

Resource pooling
    The provider's computing resources are pooled to serve multiple consumers using a multitenant model.

Rapid elasticity
    Capabilities can be elastically provisioned and released to scale rapidly outward and inward commensurate with demand.

Measured service
    Cloud systems automatically control and optimize resource use by leveraging a metering capability.

The NIST's three service models of cloud computing are as follows:

Software as a Service (SaaS)
    The capability provided to the consumer is to use the provider's applications running on a cloud infrastructure.

Platform as a Service (PaaS)
>The capability provided to the consumer is to deploy onto the cloud infrastructure consumer-created or acquired applications created using programming languages, libraries, services, and tools supported by the provider.

Infrastructure as a Service (IaaS)
>The capability provided to the consumer is to provision processing, storage, networks, and other fundamental computing resources where the consumer is able to deploy and run arbitrary software, which can include operating systems and applications.

The NIST's four deployment models of cloud computing are as follows as follows:

Private cloud
>The cloud infrastructure is provisioned for exclusive use by a single organization comprising multiple consumers (e.g., business units).

Community cloud
>The cloud infrastructure is provisioned for exclusive use by a specific community of consumers from organizations that have shared concerns (e.g., mission, security requirements, policy, and compliance considerations).

Public cloud
>The cloud infrastructure is provisioned for open use by the general public.

Hybrid cloud
>The cloud infrastructure is a composition of two or more distinct cloud infrastructures (private, community, or public) that remain unique entities but are bound together by standardized or proprietary technology that enables data and application portability (e.g., cloud bursting for load balancing between clouds).

This NIST perspective has been widely adopted by the industry.

These definitions from NIST help us understand what the cloud is, and they introduce a lot of terminology used to describe aspects of the cloud. Clearly, the cloud is rather different from traditional IT. The IT industry has perfected techniques for producing applications that run well on traditional IT. However, because the cloud works so differently, many of those techniques don't work as well for producing applications that run well on the cloud. Instead, we need to learn new techniques to develop applications for the cloud, techniques that are generally known as "cloud native."

Cloud Native

The IT industry commonly uses the term *cloud native*, yet while the industry has generally accepted the NIST definition of cloud computing, there is no one highly agreed upon definition of what it specifically means for an application to be cloud native. The industry refers to a "cloud-native application" to describe one that works better in the cloud than one that is not so cloud native, but that's a self-referential definition at best, and those using the term otherwise tend to assume its meaning. Let's look at some authoritative sources that offer their own definitions.

Ironically, a so-called Cloud-Native Application doesn't necessarily have to run in the cloud. But if it were deployed to the cloud, it would run well. "Cloud Native Applications" by IBM (*https://oreil.ly/XDKWB*) points out:

> Cloud native refers less to where an application resides and more to how it is built and deployed.

Cloud native does not mean an application runs on the cloud but that it is built to be deployed on the cloud and to run well, which also makes it run better on traditional IT. Explaining cloud native further, Microsoft's "Architecting Cloud Native .NET Applications for Azure" (*https://oreil.ly/q_ClB*) elaborates:

> Cloud-native architecture and technologies are an approach to designing, constructing, and operating workloads that are built in the cloud and take full advantage of the cloud computing model.

For this book, we'll introduce our own working definition, one consistent with a range of industry perspectives:

***Cloud native* is an approach that designs an application to run well in the cloud, to take advantage of the strengths of cloud computing while avoiding and compensating for its limitations.**

Applications that are cloud native are often built using technologies like microservices and container orchestration and take advantage of services like autoscaling. The patterns in this chapter will articulate practices that make an application cloud native, that is, that make it run well in the cloud.

Cloud-Native Maturity

It's tempting to think that cloud native is just about developing an application with a cloud-centric architecture and design. However, making the application work well in the cloud is just one aspect of adopting the cloud into an organization.

Developing Cloud-Native Applications involves more than just modernizing technology, it permeates how the IT department works and how it supports the business. The Cloud Native Computing Foundation (CNCF), part of the Linux Foundation, developed the Cloud Native Maturity Model 2.0 (*https://oreil.ly/P-Pil*) that elaborates on these five aspects of maturity:

People

> How do we work, what skills do we require, what does our organization look like as we move through this process, and how do we weave security into how people work?

Process

> What processes do we need, what technology is required, how do we map workflows and CI/CD using infrastructure as code (IaC), and how do we shift security as "far left" as possible?

Policy

> What internal and external policies are required to achieve security and compliance mandates? Do these policies reflect your business's operating environment?

Technology

> What technology is required for you to deliver on the benefits of cloud native and support people, processes, and policy as well as the technology for CI/CD, adoption of GitOps, observability, security, storage, networking, etc.?

Business outcomes

> What can the business expect to achieve from cloud native? How are you going to communicate the benefits to the CXO and/or business leadership?

Cloud native embraces the cloud, and that affects all IT practices.

While these definitions and goals are aspirational, they don't provide actionable steps that guide a development team on what to do. Teams want to follow a specific set of technology practices, ones that remove obstacles to gaining benefits from the cloud, ones that they can focus on to achieve these goals more easily. Next, let's look at a well-known methodology that you can apply to make your application more cloud native.

The Twelve-Factor App

Ask a developer how to make an application cloud native and often they will point to the Twelve-Factor App practices. Heroku (*https://oreil.ly/FCdfU*) developed these practices to explain how to develop applications that work better on Heroku's PaaS cloud platform. Although the practices were discovered while developing *Cloud Applications*, a Twelve-Factor App does not have to be deployed on a cloud, and the approach has become recognized as advantageous for developing applications for traditional IT as well as the cloud. Nevertheless, because these 12 factors help make applications work better in the cloud, they are often used to explain cloud-native architecture.

The Twelve-Factor App (*https://oreil.ly/l91R4*) is a definitive guide to developing modern applications. Twelve Factor is a methodology for building SaaS applications that are very scalable and can deploy easily on modern cloud platforms: they are declarative, offer maximum portability between operating systems, enable continuous delivery, and minimize the differences between development and production environments. Twelve-Factor Apps help developers collaborate more effectively, evolve well over time, and avoid technical debt.

As the name implies, the methodology consists of 12 practices (*https://oreil.ly/ uZQuQ*):

1. *Codebase*
   One codebase tracked in revision control, many deploys

2. *Dependencies*
   Explicitly declare and isolate dependencies

3. *Config*
   Store config in the environment

4. *Backing services*
   Treat backing services as attached resources

5. *Build, release, run*
   Strictly separate build and run stages

6. *Processes*
   Execute the app as one or more stateless processes

7. *Port binding*
   Export services via port binding

8. *Concurrency*
   Scale out via the process model

9. *Disposability*
   Maximize robustness with fast startup and graceful shutdown

10. *Dev/prod parity*
    Keep development, staging, and production as similar as possible

11. *Logs*
    Treat logs as event streams

12. *Admin processes*
    Run admin/management tasks as one-off processes

To make an application cloud native, these 12 practices are a good start. Next, let's see an overview of this chapter's patterns for how to develop Cloud-Native Applications.

Designing Applications for the Cloud

This chapter defines a collection of seven patterns that together explain how to design Cloud-Native Applications. Figure 3-1 shows the patterns and their relationships.

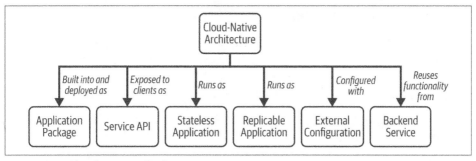

Figure 3-1. Cloud-Native Application patterns

A Cloud-Native Architecture (58) is the foundation of a Cloud-Native Application. The architecture structures the application in two parts that lead to several other practices:

Application
> This is the program part of the application that a development team implements using a programming language. It is built into and deployed as an Application Package (62), exposes its functionality to clients via a Service API (70), runs as a Stateless Application (80) that is also a Replicable Application (88), and is configured with an External Configuration (97).

Services
> These programs reuse functionality from Backend Services (106), specialized SaaS services that are reusable across applications, typically stateful, and often part of the cloud platform or otherwise developed by third-party vendors. A common example is a database service hosted on the cloud platform and managed by either the cloud vendor or the database vendor.

Follow these best practices to produce an application that runs well in the cloud, taking advantage of the strengths of cloud computing while avoiding and compensating for its limitations.

This introduction has covered several topics that are helpful to be familiar with to understand the patterns in this chapter. We've talked about the industry perspective on what cloud computing is, presented an explicit definition of what the industry generally means when it describes an application as cloud native, and summarized the Twelve-Factor App methodology for creating applications that work well on the cloud.

With this background in mind, let's discuss patterns for how to architect and design Cloud-Native Applications. We'll start with the root pattern for this chapter, Cloud-Native Architecture (58).

Cloud-Native Architecture

You are developing a Cloud Application (6) or perhaps refactoring a piece of a larger application to run on the cloud. You may be tempted to architect this application the same way you've always architected traditional IT applications. Yet the cloud offers new capabilities and imposes new challenges.

How can I architect an application to take maximum advantage of the cloud platform it will run on?

Developing an application to run in the cloud has some significant differences from developing one for traditional IT. You might think, "How different can the cloud be? Isn't an application designed for the cloud pretty much the same as ones I've designed for traditional IT?" A *Cloud Application* works differently in some respects.

One difference is application mobility. A traditional IT application is installed on a computer and runs there for the rest of its lifetime. Often a traditional IT application is designed for a specific hardware architecture and operating system version, so if it can be redeployed to a different computer, the new one must be exactly like the old one.

A traditional IT application that expects to always run on the same computer in the cloud is in for a shock. The cloud moves an application around from one computer to another to balance load and avoid outages. An application must be packaged as a simple unit which can be moved easily, that means it must have limited dependencies.

Another difference is middleware functionality. A traditional IT application that needs a business process engine or a rules engine is deployed in a middleware server that provides that functionality. The functionality is built in, easy to access, and reliable. The application becomes very dependent on that functionality and can move to another server only with that same middleware.

Cloud Applications don't assume all services are packaged inside the application. Instead, the cloud includes a catalog of external services that provide "middleware" functionality. An application that relies on that functionality must delegate to these services. The services are remote, which makes accessing them more complicated than if they were incorporated into the application itself. This means a *Cloud Application* must be built on an architecture that facilitates mobility and delegation to services.

Therefore,

Structure the application with a *Cloud-Native Architecture* by implementing the custom domain logic in an application separate from the reusable services.

The basic architecture of a Cloud-Native Application looks like Figure 3-2. This representation is intentionally very high-level, a starting point for understanding the overall structure of an application that is cloud native. The rest of this book will go into much greater detail.

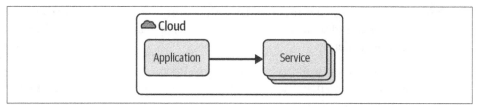

Figure 3-2. Cloud-Native Architecture

As the diagram shows, an application with a cloud-native architecture fundamentally consists of two main parts:

Application
> This is the part created by the application development team. It implements the user requirements, or at least all of those that the application has been unable to delegate to the services. It is typically implemented in a computer language, which can be almost any language. Popular ones include Java, Node.js, and Python.

Services
> These are solutions from the platform's service catalog—or other third-party services—which are specialized SaaS services that are reusable across applications. They are already written, so the application development team can buy rather than build. They are managed by the cloud platform, so the application's operations team can outsource managing the services and focus on managing the application.

A Cloud-Native Application also has one or more clients running outside of the cloud that use the application. See Figure 3-3.

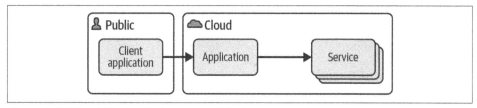

Figure 3-3. Cloud-Native Architecture with client

The client is typically a user interface, such as a web browser or mobile application. The client can also be another application, where someone else's application is invoking this one.

The application runs separately from the services and the clients. The application can run on any computer as long as it can access the services and the clients can access it.

Separating the application from its middleware facilitates mobility within the cloud. The application is smaller and easier to deploy. It can run on a simple server without having to first install middleware on that server. The application and its services can move around independently.

Separating the application from its middleware facilitates reusing services from the service catalog. When an application requires middleware functionality, it can't delegate to functionality built into its server; it must delegate to functionality built into services from the catalog. This separates the part the custom application developers create from the reusable parts created by third-party vendors.

An application with a cloud-native architecture splits the application from the services that it uses, separating the part that implements unique user requirements from the parts that provide reusable functionality. This enables the application to incorporate several features that make it run better on the cloud—particularly packaging, statelessness, and replicability.

However, there are some potential downsides to a cloud-native architecture that a team must plan for:

New skills
> Developers who are used to implementing traditional IT applications can find cloud-native development practices difficult to adopt. Traditional IT developers must learn new skills to develop Cloud-Native Applications.

Deployment simplicity
> In traditional on-premises development with an application server, the application is easy to deploy; just add it to the server. There is no need to bind to or authenticate against remote services. An application that runs in a middleware server accesses simple built-in middleware functionality via local function calls.

Cost
> Each element of a cloud-native architecture, from the VMs or containers that run the application to the *Backend Services* that the application relies upon, are individually priced and metered. When a team is not careful with their application,

the use of cloud services can expand quickly, leading to very high costs—often more than is planned for.

Fine-grained control
When you build an application in a cloud-native way, you give up some of the control that you otherwise exercise in an on-premises application. For instance, you may not have the ability to tune or control the hypervisor your application VM runs within. You may also lose control over the fine details of tuning your database servers and the operating systems that the application and database server runs on.

A Cloud-Native Application incorporates many best practices to help it work well with cloud computing:

Virtualized, multitenant computing with shared infrastructure
The application is deployed as an Application Package (62) so that it can be deployed anywhere, and it keeps itself isolated from anything else running there.

Distributed computing with universal access
The application exposes its functionality as a Service API (70) that makes it remotely accessible for client/server computing across the network.

Elastic scaling
The application runs as a Stateless Application (80) that is also a Replicable Application (88), which makes the application able to replicate across multiple computers, making the application more reliable than any one of the computers.

Deployment to multiple environments
The application has an External Configuration (97), enabling it to be deployed unchanged in different environments for multiple lifecycle stages, geographical regions, and cloud platforms.

Service catalog
The application uses multiple Backend Services (106) to implement stateful functionality that can be built into the cloud platform and reused across applications.

By following these practices, a Cloud-Native Application architecture takes advantage of the strengths of cloud computing while avoiding and compensating for its limitations.

A cloud-native architecture serves as the foundation for the rest of a *Cloud Application*. That creates the opportunity for additional decisions:

Microservices Architecture (Chapter 4)
A Microservices Architecture is a special kind of a Distributed Architecture (38) that breaks up a monolithic application into multiple components, to improve reliability of each component and to simplify the development and testing of

each component. Each component is a microservice—a small, specialized cloud-native application.

Event-Driven Architecture (Chapter 6)
Another kind of Distributed Architecture (38), often composed of microservices, where the services are coordinated through event choreography rather than service invocation.

Cloud-Native Storage (Chapter 7)
Cloud-Native Applications are stateless, but applications use data. The data tier of an application needs to be as scalable and reliable as the application tier.

Cloud Application Clients (Chapter 8)
Users need to be able to access the application, which they do using applications that run on client computers that access the *Cloud Application* remotely over the network.

All of these choices add additional flexibility and capability to the application, at the cost of increased complexity. However complex a *Cloud Application* becomes, it all begins with being cloud native.

Application Package

You are implementing an application with a Cloud-Native Architecture (58). You have a choice of computer languages to use to implement the application and want to choose one that will work well in the cloud.

What features of a computer language ecosystem are required to implement a *Cloud Application*?

The cloud is very flexible and able to run pretty much any program implemented in any language that can run in a standard operating system, such as Linux or Windows. Yet for a program to run well in the cloud, some conventions must be followed to remove dependencies the cloud may not be able to provide.

Traditional IT applications tend to be highly dependent on their hardware and operating system. A program written in a language like Assembler or C would run correctly only on a certain hardware model running a specific operating system version, and even then it would often require installing optional features and otherwise configuring the OS in a very specific way. Before the application could be installed, the operating system had to be customized for the application. The program might even be dependent on a specific version of the operating system. When a new version of the OS was released, some programs that worked in the old version wouldn't work in the new one. Programs needed complicated installers to verify all of these dependencies and perform the necessary configuration.

Programs can not only be dependent on a specific operating system with optional features and a specific configuration; they can often have other dependencies as well. Programs often require additional libraries, and each program requires different libraries. At best, these libraries have to be installed on the OS as part of installing the program. A way to avoid this complexity is to have the program dynamically load the required libraries from elsewhere. At startup, the program downloads the libraries from a central catalog. This creates a major dependency on the catalog that can cause problems for starting the program. If the program cannot access the catalog, it cannot run. If the catalog doesn't contain the right libraries or contains the wrong versions of the libraries, the program cannot run.

Traditional IT applications often customize their platform so much that two applications cannot be installed on the same platform. One application requires an extensive set of configuration settings, and another requires its own incompatible settings. Two applications delegate to the same library, but require two different versions of the library, yet only one can be installed on the platform. Each application must be run on a separate computer so that it can uniquely customize its computer.

For a program to run in the cloud, it needs to be portable. It needs to be isolated from the OS and able to run on a range of compatible versions. It needs to include everything needed to run, with no dependencies on outside catalogs or other resources. It needs to be able to install on the same computer as other program—none of them can customize it.

Therefore,

Implement an application's program in a language and toolset that encapsulates the application as an *Application Package*. Package the application with all dependencies that the program requires to run.

An *Application Package* contains a program and everything else needed to run the program. Figure 3-4 shows an *Application Package* that contains a program and two libraries.

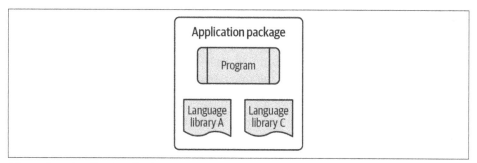

Figure 3-4. Application Package

An *Application Package* is specific to a particular language. It contains a program implemented in that language, includes code libraries implemented in that same language, and includes configuration settings meaningful to that language.

An *Application Package* is not a running application, but the cloud platform can deploy it as an application.

As Figure 3-5 shows, the cloud platform's management functionality includes an application deployer, which performs the function of creating a new workload instance of an application from its *Application Package*.

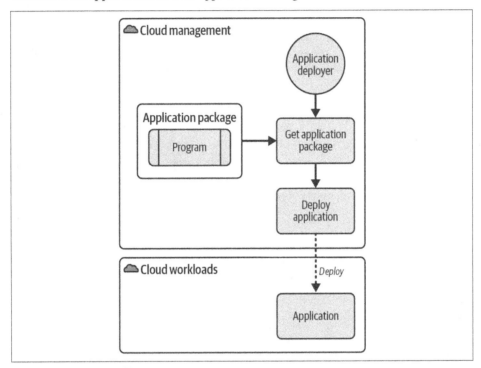

Figure 3-5. Service API

Modern programming languages such as Java, Node.js, and Go are cloud-friendly because they encapsulate a program in an *Application Package*. To build and run a program as an *Application Package*, the language uses two features:

Runtime environment
> A separately installable, language-specific runtime that executes the program. Any program written in this language can reuse the runtime environment. The runtime isolates the program from the OS, so that the program has no direct dependencies on the OS and the same program can run unchanged on multiple

OSs. The runtime environment may be a different executable for each OS and hardware architecture.

Package manager
  An application that packages the program with all of the libraries, dependencies, and configuration that the program specifies. This packaged program will run in the runtime environment on any operating system. The package manager needs access to a registry of libraries to build the package, but the runtime environment does not need access to the library registry because the package contains the libraries. The package manager may be part of the runtime environment or may be separate.

An *Application Package* runs in its runtime environment, which runs in the operating system. Figure 3-6 shows that stack for running the program.

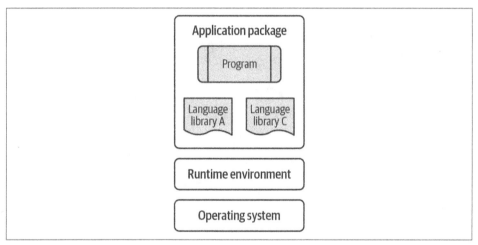

Figure 3-6. Running program

Programs that run in a runtime environment are more portable because they can run anywhere the runtime environment is installed. Java was one of the first programming languages to introduce a runtime environment. The Java Runtime Environment (JRE) that incorporates the Java Virtual Machine (JVM) provides a standard set of functionality for running a program. Different implementations of the JVM run on different operating systems, such as Windows, macOS, and Linux. The Java slogan was "Write once, run anywhere," meaning that the same Java program can run on any platform that has the JRE installed. Other languages such as Node.js and Python adopted this convention of running programs in a runtime environment.

While a runtime environment enables the same program to run on different platforms, an *Application Package* makes deploying the program in a runtime environment simple and reliable. The runtime environment is standard, and every

Application Package runs in equivalent runtime environments. The package is immutable; once it is built, it can be deployed repeatedly without changes.

The program is implemented in a language that can build it as an *Application Package*. A package manager builds the *Application Package* for a program, as shown in Figure 3-7.

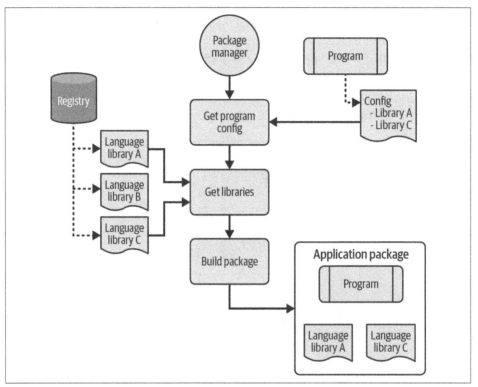

Figure 3-7. Package manager

The package manager has access to a registry of code libraries for the language it packages. The program includes a configuration that lists the program's dependencies, including the code libraries the program requires. The package manager packages the program with its libraries and other dependencies.

As explained in The Twelve-Factor App: II. Dependencies (*https://oreil.ly/ayVX7*):

> **A twelve-factor app never relies on implicit existence of system-wide packages.** It declares all dependencies, completely and exactly, via a dependency declaration manifest. Furthermore, it uses a dependency isolation tool during execution to ensure that no implicit dependencies "leak in" from the surrounding system. The full and explicit dependency specification is applied uniformly to both production and development.

To deploy an application to run in the cloud, install the runtime environment for the application's programming language onto the cloud platform's OS (usually Linux but possibly Windows), then deploy the *Application Package* into the runtime environment. Once deployed, the cloud can start and stop the application as needed.

An *Application Package* makes a program simple and reliable to deploy anywhere a runtime environment is installed. The package has no external dependencies other than the runtime environment. Anywhere the cloud can run the runtime environment, it can run the program in its *Application Package*.

However, not all programming languages support packaging applications and running them in runtime environments. Programs written in those languages will be more difficult if not impossible to run on the cloud.

Each *Application Package* is deployed to its own copy of the runtime environment, so each application can be implemented in a different language using Polyglot Development (146).

Cloud management's application deployer typically does not actually deploy copies of the *Application Package* but rather deploys copies of a virtual machine image (475) or container image (478) that includes the *Application Package*. One advantage of packaging an application as an *Application Package* is that the package makes it easier for the cloud platform's application deployer to deploy the application simply and reliably. By packaging the *Application Package* as a virtual machine or container, it is even easier for the application deployer to deploy.

The program in an *Application Package* to be deployed on the cloud should be a Cloud-Native Application, which means it exposes its functionality via a Service API (70), is implemented as a Stateless Application (80) that is also a Replicable Application (88), and has an External Configuration (97). The program uses Backend Services (106), specialized SaaS services that are reusable across applications, typically stateful, and often part of the cloud platform or otherwise developed by third-party vendors. A typical example is a database service hosted in the cloud.

Examples

Some examples of popular languages with runtime environments and package managers include the following:

Java
> The runtime environment is the JRE, which includes the JVM. Server environments such as Spring Boot, Open Liberty, and Quarkus, incorporate the JRE plus additional code libraries. A Java program is packaged as a web application

archive (WAR or .war) file or an enterprise application archive (EAR or .ear) file. The Java JDK (Java Development Kit), which includes the JRE, doesn't include a built-in package manager, but Maven and Gradle are optional third-party package managers for Java.

JavaScript

The server runtime environment is Node.js. TypeScript extends Node.js with additional code libraries to support type-safe JavaScript. The Node Package Manager (NPM) packages the program with the libraries specified in the program's configuration and can then run the package.

Go

The runtime environment can run a Go source code file on any system architecture. It can also build a compiled Go package that runs natively in the system architecture used to build it.

Python, PHP, Ruby, and even COBOL have runtime environments. On the other hand, C, C++, Assembler, and shell scripts don't have separate runtimes; those programs are highly dependent on the underlying OS.

Java

Java is a particularly interesting example for a package manager because the JDK doesn't include a built-in package manager, but there are two commonly used third-party package managers available for Java: Maven and Gradle. This separation clearly shows where the language ends and the package manager begins; it also shows alternative approaches for achieving the same application packaging goal.

A Java program runs in the JRE, which is part of the JDK for developing Java applications, and it is run using the java command. The command java <program> runs a program contained in a class file in the JRE, and java -jar <program>.jar runs a program contained in a Java Archive (JAR) file. The runtime environment contains a catalog of code libraries. When running a program, more code libraries can be added to those in the JRE by specifying them on the class path. The JRE includes the Java Virtual Machine (JVM). There are JVM implementations for Linux, Windows, and macOS and even Unix distributions such as Solaris, any of which can run any Java program.

Maven specifies a project's configuration in the pom.xml file. The project specifies the libraries a program requires in the dependencies section. Run mvn clean compile to build the runtime artifacts. Run mvn package to create a JAR file containing the runtime artifacts, which can easily be deployed and run on any computer with the JRE installed.

Gradle specifies a project's build script in the build.gradle file. The project specifies the libraries a program requires in the dependencies section, which also specifies how to find those libraries in the catalogs specified in the `repositories` section. The items in the `plugins` section add tasks that assemble the package using the dependencies. Run `gradlew assemble` to run the set of tasks to build the runtime artifacts in a JAR file that can run anywhere the JRE is installed.

Open Liberty

Open Liberty is an application server that implements Java Platform, Enterprise Edition (Java EE), and Jakarta EE. A program that runs in Open Liberty uses the `server.xml` file to configure its environment. It includes a section to configure the feature manager to load the features (which are Java libraries) that the program requires. The configured program runs in Java's JRE.

For example, the `server.xml` in Example 3-1 configures the server with the library for REST web services (see Service API (70)).

Example 3-1. Open Liberty server.xml

```
<server description="Sample Liberty server">
  <featureManager>
    <feature>restfulWS-3.0</feature>
    ...
  </featureManager>
  ...
</server>
```

Then build a server starting with the `openliberty-kernel` package—which is the Liberty server with the minimum set of features possible. The build will load only the features specified in the server configuration, ensuring that the application has access to the features it needs and that the server is as small as possible—only containing features that the application requires.

Node.js

A Node.js program specifies the libraries it requires as dependencies in the `package.json` file. For example, to specify that the program requires the `upper-case` module, include the configuration in Example 3-2.

Example 3-2. Node.js package.json

```
{
  "dependencies": {
    "upper-case": "^2.0.0",
    ...
  },
  ...
}
```

Use NPM to package and run the program. Node is just a runtime environment, but NPM is both a package manager and a runtime environment that uses Node to run the packages it creates.

Service API

You are developing an application with a Cloud-Native Architecture (58) that runs in an Application Package (62). You want clients to be able to connect to your application in a way that makes both of them easier to write and maintain, that supports connecting remotely over a network, that performs well over the network, and that supports the internet—the universal network.

How should an application expose its functionality to clients that want to use the application?

An application on a client device invoking behavior in a *Cloud Application* is fundamentally a client/server relationship: the client application is invoking behavior on the server. Making client/server interactions work well for the cloud entails four levels of difficulty:

Clean separation of client functionality from server functionality
> To separate the client from the server, both must be well encapsulated. The code in traditional IT applications is often difficult to separate into components. Spaghetti code, which is code that depends on any and all other code in the application, is difficult to separate into parts. (See Big Ball of Mud (22).) What is needed is a wall between the client code and the server code that separates the two sets of code, encapsulates the server, prevents the server from depending on the client, and restricts and controls the dependencies the client has on the server. Yet this wall must enable the server to expose its functionality to the client so that they can still work together. This wall will enable the client and server to evolve independently. It will also enable the two development teams working on the client and server to work independently, only needing to coordinate on designing the wall between the client and server.

Remote access to the server from the client
> The code in a single application runs in a single process, but a client and a server are more useful when they can run in different processes—perhaps on different computers—connected by a network. However, interprocess communication (IPC) is a lot more complicated than one function calling another within the same process. *The fallacies of distributed computing* (*https://oreil.ly/XDQY4*) by L. Peter Deutsch explain how remote invocation is more complex than it appears. Martin Fowler summarized them as his First Law of Distributed Object Design (*https://oreil.ly/VoBuv*): "Don't distribute your objects!" What is so complicated about **Remote Procedure Invocation** (*Enterprise Integration Patterns*, 2003) (aka

remote procedure calls (RPCs) and remote method invocation (RMI))? First, invocations between processes need a synchronous network protocol. To use the protocol, applications need a method to serialize complex objects so they can be sent across the wire, such as Java or .NET serialization. While there are many implementations to choose from, for example, XML-RPC, REST, and gRPC, all have disadvantages. This is why there are so many to choose from and why new remote protocols are added every few years. To communicate, the client and server have to agree on the option they're going to use.

Efficient communication between the client and server

Practices that work well for function calls in the same process can become incredibly inefficient when used between processes. Communication between functions can be very chatty, implementing behavior with lots of small, frequent calls between the participants. These participants also like to share data often pass by reference where all the participants share pointers to a single copy of the data, but they also pass by value where the caller receives its own copy of the data. Since pointers are difficult to use between processes, remote calls usually share data between processes using pass by value. But passing copies of large objects or data sets across the network harms performance as serialization takes time to perform and consumes memory and bandwidth. To make the communication efficient, the remote procedures need to be invoked less frequently and exchange less data.

Access over common networks

For cloud computing to be truly ubiquitous, the client and server need to support connecting over the public internet, since that is the network that connects everything. At the same time, when components in a *Cloud Application* are distributed, they need to support connecting over internal networks as well as the internet. The internal networks and the internet need to work the same so that clients and servers can connect over either as needed. Hypertext Transfer Protocol (HTTP) is universally used by modern systems yet has limited capabilities for connecting applications. Protocols like Distributed Component Object Model (DCOM) and Common Object Request Broker Architecture (CORBA) work for application integration but don't work as well with worldwide networks optimized for HTTP.

An application integration approach must overcome these challenges in order to allow clients and servers to work well together over the internet.

Therefore,

An application should expose a *Service API* consisting of tasks the application can perform. Implement the API as a web service to make the application easy to use in a cloud-native architecture.

The *Service API* is a contract between a service provider (i.e., the service application) and a service consumer (i.e., the client). The provider implements the contract, and the consumers depend on it. The consumers can invoke any of the tasks in the *Service API* but do not know how the provider implements those tasks. The provider can change its implementation of the tasks without impacting the consumer as long as the provider does not change the API.

As Figure 3-8 shows, the *Service API* defines a set of tasks that are the use cases the service application can perform. The service application implements each of those tasks so that each one performs the behavior it's supposed to. The client can invoke any of the tasks, but it has access only to the definitions of the tasks, not to the service application's internal implementations of the tasks. The set of tasks in the *Service API* is a contract between the client and service application. It is implemented as a web service so that the client and application can connect across the internet or any network built on internet technology, such as a data center's internal network.

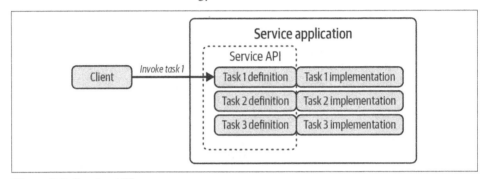

Figure 3-8. Service API

A *Service API* combines the application functionality of a service-oriented interface with the network protocol of a web service. It exposes a service-oriented interface as a web service that clients on the internet can invoke efficiently. This solution resolves all of the challenges of enabling a client and server to communicate effectively and efficiently over the internet, incorporating solutions that have already been developed for technologies other than cloud computing:

Clean separation of client functionality from server functionality
How can a client and server be separated into two separate sets of code?

As computer programs have grown in complexity, the need to encapsulate functionality and make it reusable has become well understood. Procedural programming evolved into object-oriented programming. In object-oriented programming, the only way to interact with an object is through its interface—which is the set of messages to which the object can respond (*Smalltalk-80*, 1983).

A **Facade** (*Design Patterns*, 1994) defines a unified, higher-level interface for a set of interfaces in a subsystem, making the subsystem easier to use.

An *application programming interface* (API) is an interface that is designed to be invoked by client code (rather than used by a human). An API makes an application easier to work with, enabling the application to expose a set of behaviors for clients to invoke while also enabling the application to hide its implementation. The API creates a clear separation between the client and application, acting as a contract between them. By using the API to hide its implementation, the application preserves its ability to change its implementation without impacting the clients, so long as it maintains its API. The client and server can evolve independently, and the client and server development teams can work independently, only needing to coordinate to develop the API itself. Often, the server team designs the API and the client team uses whatever the server team designed, so even that coordination can be pretty minimal.

Remote access to the server from the client
How can a client invoke a server remotely across a network?

A procedural programming language supports function calls within a process—an object-oriented language supports invoking methods on objects within a process, but something more is needed for a client to invoke a server remotely across a network between processes. A **Remote Procedure Invocation** (*Enterprise Integration Patterns*, 2004) enables one application to invoke behavior in another application across a network. The behavior could be procedural, invoked via a remote procedure call (RPC), or it could be object-oriented, invoked via remote method invocation (RMI).

Remote procedure invocation enables a client to invoke a server remotely. However, as the pattern explains, the fact that remote procedure invocation works so much like local procedure calls can actually become more of a disadvantage than an advantage. There are big differences in performance and reliability between local and remote procedure calls because the later occur over a network. Remote access enables a client and server to work remotely, but they will achieve rather poor performance.

Efficient communication between the client and server
How can a server expose its functionality so that a client can invoke it efficiently?

A **Session Facade** (*Core J2EE Patterns*, 2003) or **Remote Facade** (*Patterns of Enterprise Application Architecture*, 2002) improves efficiency over a network by providing a course-grained facade on fine-grained objects. A **Service Layer** (*Patterns of Enterprise Application Architecture*, 2002) gathers multiple remote facades as services in a layer that encapsulates a domain model as a set of available operations that can also be made remotely accessible. **Service Facade** (*SOA Design*

Patterns, 2008) generalizes services in a service-oriented architecture (SOA) that abstracts a part of the service architecture and increases its decoupling from the rest of the architecture.

An API implemented as a set of service tasks encapsulates a set of use cases for what the application can do as well as for how clients will use the application. With a service interface, the application exposes its behaviors as a set of tasks it can perform for clients, enabling the client to treat the application as a service. When a client invokes a service task in the application, it can pass any context necessary as parameters in the invocation. When the application produces a result or error while performing the task, the invocation can return that result or error back to the client. Because large objects are expensive to transfer (that is, copy) across the network, the parameters and return values for each service task should be primitives and simple objects that are easy to serialize. Often a primitive is a unique identifier—a **Claim Check** (*Enterprise Integration Patterns*, 2003)—for a complex object, so that when the receiver wants to use the object, it can use the primitive to find the object in a shared data store and load it for use.

Access over common networks

How can a server expose its efficient application interface for use over the internet and similar internal networks?

As the internet evolved into the World Wide Web (WWW), the *hypertext transfer protocol* (HTTP) became the common protocol of choice for web-based applications. HTTP enables a caller to specify not just the application listening on a port but also individual endpoints within that application. The firewalls, routers, browsers, and the rest of the backbone of the global internet support HTTP since it is already used to access web pages. This enables simpler connections between the user's desktop and servers running backend code—new ports do not need to be opened for each application. Applications thus evolved to expose their functionality via HTTP as web services.

While the concept of web services itself has become fairly stable, the protocol for performing web services has evolved over time. All of the protocols use HTTP as the universal transport, but they differ in the format of the data on that transport and in the schema to describe the protocol's API and its data formats. The first major web service protocol was Simple Object Access Protocol (SOAP), which used Extensible Markup Language (XML) to define application interfaces expressed as Web Services Description Language (WSDL) that work much like the objects in object-oriented programming. SOAP was eventually replaced by Representational State Transfer (REST) protocol, which makes parts of an application available as resources that the client specifies using HTTP Uniform Resource Identifiers (URIs) and operates on using HTTP methods (such as GET, PUT, POST, and DELETE to CRUD resources as units of data). REST APIs can be published as Swagger documents that define the API as a contract. The service application implements the Swagger API's contract and the client depends on the Swagger API's contract to invoke service behavior. Specifications such as OpenAPI and gRPC standardize web service protocols for universal integration by development teams who are then able to otherwise work independently.

Thus a *Service API* resolves the difficulties of making client/server interactions work well.

Service API incorporates and expands upon the practice explained in The Twelve-Factor App: VII. Port binding (*https://oreil.ly/wiK-X*):

> The web app exports HTTP as a service by binding to a port, and listening to requests coming in on that port....The port-binding approach means that one app can become the backing service for another app, by providing the URL to the backing app as a resource handle in the config for the consuming app.

A *Service API* defines a service-oriented API that clients must adhere to as they access the service. A *Service API* can be easily implemented as a border for remote access, making the application accessible across a network connection by any client running in a separate process.

A *Service API* creates a clean separation between an application and the clients that use it, reducing coupling between them, making both easier to implement, and enabling them to evolve independently as long as they preserve the API. It can support remote access, providing course-grained tasks that make remote invocation more efficient.

One of the biggest challenges to applying *Service API* is designing the API. It must make the producer's functionality available while hiding the implementation details. Once an API is put into use, it can be difficult to evolve, often requiring an API versioning strategy.

A service can be stateful or stateless. A Cloud-Native Application with a *Service API* is typically implemented to run as a Stateless Application (80).

These services are often part of a Microservices Architecture (Chapter 4). Services with broad responsibilities can be implemented by a Service Orchestrator (160) that orchestrates other services with more specialized responsibilities. Services can also be choreographed more loosely in an Event-Driven Architecture (Chapter 6).

Examples

An easy way to understand APIs is as the interface feature in languages such as Java. The interface's functionality should be abstracted as a service capability comprised of service tasks. An interface is a contract between the object and its client that separates what the object needs to be able to do from the class that implements how it's done.

OpenAPI (*https://oreil.ly/CYImY*) is the prevailing industry standard to publish a web *Service API* as a contract. It's typically implemented using Swagger to create a REST over HTTP web service. The service application implements the OpenAPI contract, and the client depends on the OpenAPI contract to invoke service behavior. gRPC is an alternative to REST that defines a web *Service API* as an RPC instead of resources.

Java interface

Here is a service that converts money from one currency to another. It has a very simple *Service API* that performs a single task, convert.

First, let's specify the money conversion *Service API* as a Java interface. Example 3-3 shows the code to create a Java interface named MoneyConverter that declares a single convert method.

Example 3-3. Java interface for MoneyConverter

```
import java.math.BigDecimal;
import java.util.Currency;

public interface MoneyConverter {
  public BigDecimal convert(BigDecimal amount, Currency from, Currency to);
}
```

The convert method accepts an amount of money in one currency (from) and returns the amount in another currency (to). It is an interface, so it does not implement the method, just declares its signature. Each method in a Java interface is essentially a **Template Method** (*Design Patterns*, 1994), except that rather than implement the skeleton of an algorithm, an interface method implements no algorithm at all. This sort of interface that defines methods for performing tasks is the essence of a *Service API*.

A class that actually performs the conversion implements the interface. Example 3-4 shows MyConverter, which implements the MoneyConverter shown in Example 3-3.

Example 3-4. Java class for MyConverter

```
import java.math.BigDecimal;
import java.util.Currency;
```

```java
public class MyConverter implements MoneyConverter {
  public BigDecimal convert(BigDecimal amount, Currency from, Currency to) {
    /* Code that converts the amount from one currency to another. */
  }
}
```

A client that needs the conversion performed delegates the work to an instance of MoneyConverter. Example 3-5 shows how the converter object, myConverter, is initialized as an instance of MyConverter, the concrete class with code that actually performs the conversion.

Example 3-5. Java client code using MyConverter as a MoneyConverter

```java
BigDecimal unconvertedMoney = 1000.0;
Currency originalCurrency = Currency.getInstance("INR");
Currency newCurrency = Currency.getInstance("USD");
BigDecimal convertedMoney = null;

MoneyConverter myConverter = new MyConverter();

convertedMoney = myConverter.convert(unconvertedMoney,
                              originalCurrency, newCurrency);

// For example, 1000.00 Indian Rupee equals 12.23 US Dollar
System.out.println(unconvertedMoney + " " + originalCurrency.getDisplayName()
        + " equals " + convertedMoney + " " + newCurrency.getDisplayName());
```

After myConverter is initialized, all subsequent code treats it as a MoneyConverter, not knowing whether the converter object is actually an instance of MyConverter or some other concrete class. This makes the code able to handle any concrete class that implements the MoneyConverter interface. The interface, MoneyConverter, is a contract between the client and the concrete class, MyConverter. The majority of the client code just knows the object implements the contract represented by the interface, so it can use an instance of any concrete class that implements the interface.

JAX-RS interface

The MoneyConverter service can only be used locally within a Java program. Let's use the Java API for RESTful Web Services (JAX-RS) to expose this local service as a web service.

Example 3-6 shows the web service declaration. Its root URI is /api.

Example 3-6. JAX-RS web service declaration

```java
import javax.ws.rs.*;
import javax.ws.rs.core.*;
```

```
@ApplicationPath("/api")
public class RestApplication extends Application {
}
```

Example 3-7 shows the resource `CurrencyResource`, which has a `convert` method. It's implemented using the `MyConverter` class from Example 3-4.

Example 3-7. JAX-RS web resource

```
import java.math.BigDecimal;
import java.util.Currency;
import javax.ws.rs.*;
import javax.ws.rs.core.*;

@Path("/currency")
public class CurrencyResource {
  @POST
  @Path("/convert/")
  @Consumes(MediaType.APPLICATION_FORM_URLENCODED)
  @Produces(MediaType.TEXT_PLAIN)
  public String convert(@FormParam("amount") String amount,
                        @FormParam("from") String from,
                        @FormParam("to") String to) {
    BigDecimal unconvertedMoney = new BigDecimal(amount);
    Currency originalCurrency = Currency.getInstance(from);
    Currency newCurrency = Currency.getInstance(to);
    BigDecimal convertedMoney = null;

    MoneyConverter myConverter = new MyConverter();

    convertedMoney = myConverter.convert(unconvertedMoney
                                   originalCurrency, newCurrency);

    return convertedMoney.toString();
  }
}
```

When a web service client invokes <domain>/api/currency/convert with an HTML form containing the three parameters, it gets a response containing the converted money.

Go interface

Like Java, the Go language also has an interface feature. The code in Example 3-8 declares a `MoneyConverter` interface using the types Float and Currency.

Example 3-8. Go interface for MoneyConverter

```go
type MoneyConverter interface{
  Convert(amount Float, from Currency, to Currency) Float
}
```

OpenAPI interface

A Swagger document for our API would include a /convert path. It requires the usual three input parameters: amount, from, and to. And it returns a number. (See Example 3-9.)

Example 3-9. OpenAPI document for Convert task

```yaml
openapi: 3.0.0
. . .
paths:
  /convert:
    post:
      description: Convert money from one currency to another
      requestBody:
        required: true
        content:
          application/json:
            schema:
              type: object
              required:
                - amount
                - from
                - to
              properties:
                amount:
                  type: number
                from:
                  type: string
                to:
                  type: string

      responses:
        '200':
          description: Successfully converted the money amount
          content:
            application/json:
              schema:
                type: number
```

Stateless Application

You are developing an application with a Cloud-Native Architecture (58) that has a Service API (70). You want it to scale easily, shut down cleanly, and recover from failures gracefully.

How can an application support concurrent requests efficiently and recover from failures without losing data?

Applications, whether hosted on the cloud or traditional IT, manage two types of state: *session state* is data used temporarily and limited to a single user; *domain state* is data used long term and is available to all users in all sessions, and it can even be shared between different applications.[1]

Developers creating applications for traditional IT have learned that they can improve application performance by loading domain data into the application and keeping it there. Applications store domain data—data that is available to all applications and services across all transactions—in databases to keep it safe and so they can share it. When database access is slow—due to overloaded data center networks, inefficient disk drives, and data locking and contention—an application can provide better throughput by prefetching any data that might be needed, caching it in memory, and never letting go because it might eventually be needed again.

Storing domain data read-only in an application causes a couple of problems:

Performance
> Holding data in memory helps improve performance by responding to client requests faster without having to retrieve data from a slow database, but hurts performance by making the application start slower and spend CPU managing the copies of the data. Prefetching data takes time, which makes the application's startup take longer. The application can avoid prefetching by only caching data the first time it's retrieved, but that hurts the throughput for users waiting for uncached data to be retrieved the first time.

Scalability
> Each object will hold its own copy of the same data. Storing so much data in memory causes the application to run out of memory sooner—limiting scalability. Multiple objects could try to share the same data, but then they have to implement a shared cache, which gets complicated. To avoid running out of memory, the objects could limit how much data they will cache, but then they

---

1 In *Patterns of Enterprise Application Architecture* (2003), Chapter 5: Concurrency and Chapter 6: Session State, Fowler has an extensive discussion of how applications use business and system transactions, session state and what he calls record data.

---

need to implement an eviction policy for removing cached data so that more data can be added.

An application that delays persisting the changes it makes to domain data can suffer even bigger issues:

Consistency

When multiple objects each hold their own copy of the same data and one of them changes that data, only one copy gets updated. The other objects continue to use old copies that haven't been updated. Stale copies of data mean that different users get different answers based on what is supposed to be the same data.

Graceful shutdown

To shut down a stateful application cleanly, before the application can shut down, any changes in its data must be persisted first by writing all of the data—or at least the data that has changed, if the application knows which data that is— to that slow database that the application has been avoiding. If the application crashes, all those data changes are lost.

Recoverability

A stateful application's tendency to lose data changes when it crashes wreaks havoc on disaster recovery (DR). A DR strategy tries to minimize the recovery point objective (RPO), which is the point before the application crashed that can be recovered. All changes in the application after the RPO are lost, which is why a DR strategy strives to keep the RPO short. A stateful application is an RPO tragedy waiting to happen. If an application enables users to make data changes but persists those changes only once an hour, the RPO effectively becomes an hour. When the application crashes, all of those changes the users thought they had made as long as an hour ago are lost. When DR restarts the application, it will not have those users' changes.

An application can avoid these issues by not caching domain data in memory.

An application that stores session data limits how many users it can support. When an application ran on a user's desktop computer, it needed to support only that one user. But when client/server computing technologies like Java 2, Enterprise Edition (J2EE) moved the application's business logic back onto the server, multiple users became able to access a single copy of the application.

How can an application on the server support multiple users? A client interacts with the application repeatedly via a session that associates the client's calls. The session includes session data—data gathered from the history of what the client has done.

Where should session data be stored? For web browser clients, that somewhere becomes an HTTP session object, server objects that servlets use to support web browsers running on the client. Each user's browser has its own HTTP session that keeps session data on the server, which greatly improves performance because it avoids sending data back to the browser using what is (or used to be) often a very slow internet connection.

HTTP sessions create their own scalability problems. Each user's browser has its own HTTP session object, so a server is limited in how many browsers it can support by how many HTTP sessions it can host. Furthermore, each browser has to send its series of requests to its own HTTP session, not any others. The browser stores its HTTP session's identifier in a cookie named JSESSIONID, which the server uses to implement sticky sessions where a browser's requests are always routed not just to any HTTP session but to the specific HTTP session with that session ID. While keeping session data on the server helps avoid performance problems caused by slow network bandwidth, the trade-off is scalability problems that limit how many concurrent users an application on the server can handle.

As long as session data is stored on the server, there will always be a limit how many concurrent users an application on the server can handle. As long as an application stores domain data in memory, the application will run into problems with performance, scalability, consistency, graceful shutdown, and recoverability.

Therefore,

Design the application as a *Stateless Application* that stores its domain state in databases and receives its session state as parameters passed from the client.

What makes an application stateless is not that it has no state but that it stores its state elsewhere, which makes it more scalable and resilient.

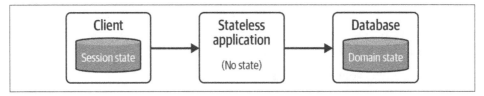

Figure 3-9. Stateless Application

As shown in Figure 3-9, a *Stateless Application* has three parts: the *Stateless Application*, its databases where it stores its domain state, and its clients, each of which separately holds its own session state. The application still operates on domain state, but it stores that state in databases, not in the application. The application uses session state to decide what to do, but it doesn't store session state; it gets the context for performing requests as parameters to the request. Each application client maintains its own session state and uses it to populate the parameters in each of its requests. For example, the client might pass in a bank account number or a product ID from its session state, then the *Stateless Application* uses that parameter to load the bank account or product details from it domain database.

Making an application stateless resolves the problems with a stateful application:

Performance
> The *Stateless Application* doesn't spend bandwidth populating the cache and CPU managing the cache.

Scalability
> The *Stateless Application* doesn't spend memory duplicating data that is already stored in databases.

Consistency
> The *Stateless Application* doesn't duplicate data from the database, and so it cannot get out of sync; it is always in sync with the database.

Graceful shutdown
> The *Stateless Application* is always ready to shut down cleanly between business transactions. The application can be quiesced to finish performing business transactions before shutting down.

Recoverability
> When a *Stateless Application* crashes, the only data that is lost is changes in any business transactions that did not complete successfully. The application can minimize these by keeping its business transactions brief. All other domain data is persisted to the databases and can be recovered easily.

A *Stateless Application* can perform requests concurrently for multiple clients because they each have the same state—which is no state. It performs each business transaction in its own thread with its own context from the request that loads the domain data it needs from the database. When the application finishes performing the business transaction, the thread ends and the data is discarded, making the application stateless once again.

The drive toward applications with no session state arose with web services—which work the way the WWW does and are accessed via faster internet connections. Each web service is stateless; the Client Application (406)—be it a web application, a mobile application, a CLI, or a chatbot—is responsible for maintaining session state and passing it to the web service as parameters. Each client typically runs on its own computer, so the solution scales quite well.

Most applications have domain state, so if the program is stateless, where does the state go? The application stores domain data in Backend Services (106), such as databases. Cloud platforms typically provide numerous different Cloud Database (311) services.

A *Stateless Application* loads its domain state from storage while it performs work for a client. Each call to the *Service API* defines a logical transaction. The application can cache data temporarily during the transaction but not between transactions. Concurrent transactions in the same *Stateless Application* each run in a separate thread that caches its own data. At the beginning of a transaction, a *Stateless Application* uses the context in the request parameters to find and load the relevant domain data from the database to perform business logic. At the end of a successful transaction, a *Stateless Application* stores any updates to the data back to the database before returning a result to the client. After a transaction, a *Stateless Application* effectively flushes all of its data before starting the next transaction.

As explained in The Twelve-Factor App: VI. Processes (*https://oreil.ly/WP8Rl*), applications should persist their data:

> Twelve-factor processes are stateless and share-nothing. Any data that needs to persist must be stored in a stateful backing service, typically a database. The memory space or filesystem of the process can be used as a brief, single-transaction cache.

The practice goes on to say that an application also should not store session data:

> Sticky sessions are a violation of twelve-factor and should never be used or relied upon. Session state data is a good candidate for a datastore that offers time-expiration, such as Memcached or Redis.

Stateless services are the building blocks for service-oriented architecture (SOA). "Service Statelessness," Chapter 11 in *SOA: Principles of Service Design* (2016), discusses at length how to design stateless services.

Statelessness enables an application to start quickly and shut down cleanly and simplifies crash recovery. To shut down a stateful workload cleanly, the platform must first persist the state. To restart a stateful workload, the platform must start the workload and then load its persisted state before making the workload available to handle client requests. When a stateful workload crashes rather than being shut down cleanly, the platform doesn't have the opportunity to persist its state first, and so that state is lost. These problems go away when the workload is stateless. A stateless workload is much easier to quiesce and shut down with no data loss because it doesn't have any state that needs to be persisted. It is easier to restart because it doesn't have any state that needs to be reloaded. When a stateless workload crashes, the only state that is lost is the intermediate state of logical transactions that haven't yet completed, so the lesson is to keep those transactions brief and that intermediate state small and persist it quickly.

A challenge for a *Stateless Application* is that retrieving the same domain data repeatedly may degrade network performance between the application and its database. This can be remedied with a caching service, which keeps the application stateless. Likewise, if a client's session state becomes extensive, it may degrade network performance between the application and its client. This encourages designing an API with parameters that are few and simple, limiting the session state that is necessary.

Statelessness makes scalability much easier. Making an application into a Replicable Application (88)—one that scales the way cloud scales—is much more complex when the replicas have state. When the replicas are stateful, the platform must use sticky sessions, a technique from traditional IT that should be avoided in the cloud. Furthermore, each replica's state has to be duplicated or persisted so that it's not lost if the replica crashes or needs to fail over. With a *Stateless Application*, all of the application's replicas are equivalent because they're all stateless. All replicas have the same data because it's all stored in a shared database. Routing is simpler—any replica can serve any client request because they're all equivalent. When scaling in, it does not matter which replicas the platform selects to shut down because they're all equivalent.

A *Stateless Application* is easier to implement when it has a Service API (70). The workload doesn't expose its state via the API—it doesn't have any state to expose. Rather than expose the domain state that it manages, the workload should use its API to provide tasks that keep the state encapsulated and hidden from the client and limit the scope of the session state.

A *Stateless Application* with a *Service API* is a stateless service, which is the preferred model to implement functionality in a cloud-native architecture. It is the basis for implementing a Microservice (119).

If an application still wants to cache domain data to improve performance, it should use a Backend Service (106), that is, an in-memory database, such as Redis or Memcached.

Examples

When a team that is new to cloud-native architecture is told that their application needs to be able to run statelessly, their first reaction typically is to say that their application won't work that way. "You don't understand," they explain, "our application has state." No kidding. Every application more complicated than a calculator has state. The trick is to figure out what in the application's implementation is storing data and move the data *outside* your program. In a sense, this is a form of functional programming, and if your language of choice supports functional programming constructs, it may be easier to implement these approaches in that way. Two common ways of storing data in your application can be addressed with these fixes:

- Make domain state external

- Make session state external

Make domain state external

With traditional IT, it is common to cache data from the database so that it only has to be fetched once. The most common way to do this is to define an instance variable to keep cached data. When retrieving a piece of data, retrieve it from the cache; if it's not already in the cache, first load it from the database into the cache, then retrieve it from the cache. A very simple version of the code (in Java) looks like Example 3-10.

Example 3-10. Stateful ProductManager stores products

```
public class ProductManager {

    private Map<Product> products;  // products is an instance variable

    private Database getDatabase() {
        Database database;
        database = /* Get the database connection */
        return database;
    }

    public getProductNamed(String name) {
        Product product = products.getOrDefault(name, null);
        if (product == null) {
            product = this.getDatabase().get(name);
            products.put(product.name(), product);
        }
        return product;
    }
}
```

If you want your application to be stateless, the object should be stateless. So, don't cache the data, retrieve it from the database every time. As shown in Example 3-11, the class no longer declares an instance variable, and the getProductNamed() method becomes much simpler.

Example 3-11. Stateless ProductManager does not store products

```
public class ProductManager {

    // Do NOT declare a products instance variable

    private Database getDatabase() {
        Database database;
        database = /* Get the database connection */
```

```
        return database;
    }

    public getProductNamed(String name) {
        Product product = null; // products is a temporary variable
        product = this.getDatabase().get(name);
        return product;
    }
}
```

But won't this stateless version be inefficient? In the cloud, databases have gotten faster, especially if they're NoSQL databases and have their own caches. Network connections have gotten faster. Run multiple replicas of the database so that each replica has less work to do and can do it faster; see Cloud Database (311). If data still needs to be cached in memory, use a *Backend Service* specialized for that purpose, such as Redis or Memcached. Making the database faster and the application stateless will ultimately be a much better solution.

Make session state external

Session state refers to an application's data that is unique to a particular user. When processing multiple requests that are related through a common interaction with a user, session state is that data that needs to be carried across all of those requests. For example, session state might include the identity of a user, so that the right records could be fetched back from the database using the approach previously described. The user identity can't only be in the database, because it's part of the key that's used to find the right data. Luckily, there are approaches to externalize session state as well.

The most common approaches involve storing a key (such as the user's identity) in something that is attached to every user request. In the example of a request carried over HTTP, this could be in the contents of an HTTP cookie or in the parameters of the request itself. Regardless of which protocol or framework you are using, that's the usual approach—make sure that a top-level key that is associated with the user gets passed in with each request.

However, even in this case, there is the temptation to store this information within the program, typically in a **Singleton** (*Design Patterns*, 1994) or in a class variable. Similar to the example above, classes should use temporary variables, not instance variables. Temporary variables passed as parameters are part of the thread running the method, so each thread gets its own copy, and the variables' lifetime ends when the thread does. That means that your class can be completely threadsafe, which makes debugging easier.

The side benefit of following these approaches is that the application is now a *Replicable Application*. Not only does it not matter if any particular copy of the application fails and is restarted (because no state is stored in the application), but it also does not matter how many copies of the application are running and receiving requests at any time, because all copies can handle any request equally well. Statelessness is difficult to achieve in that it takes more work to think about developing applications in this way, but the benefits are often well worth the trouble.

Replicable Application

(aka Horizontally Scalable Application)

replicable *adjective*

rep·li·ca·ble (ˈre-plə-kə-bəl)

- that which can be replicated
- that which can be produced again to be exactly the same as before

You are developing an application with a Cloud-Native Architecture (58) encapsulated in an Application Package (62). You want your application to always be available, even though the cloud can be unreliable and client load can grow greater than a single instance of the application infrastructure can handle.

How can an application run reliably on an unreliable platform and scale to handle greater client load the way the platform scales?

When developers of applications for traditional IT are asked how reliable their application is, they often reply, "My application is as reliable as the hardware it's running on." In this way, traditional IT applications punt responsibility for reliability and make it the responsibility of the hardware engineers and operations staff to make their IT environments reliable. This also avoids the uncomfortable truth that sometimes applications fail even when the hardware is functioning properly. These failures can have many causes, such as memory leaks, deadlocked threads, blocked I/O connections, or storage issues.

There are limits to how reliable hardware can be, not to mention the reliability of the OS and other system services the application depends on. As the reliability of hardware goes up, the price tag rises even faster—mainframes cost more than commodity computers, RAID arrays cost more than simple storage. Even if hardware can be made to fail infrequently, that only lowers the frequency of unplanned outages; it doesn't eliminate them completely. Furthermore, there are also planned outages—from OS patches to system upgrades—that cause the ubiquitous "system is currently unavailable because of maintenance" status that systems frequently display on weekends and holidays. (Not to mention that planning maintenance outages at times that avoid inconveniencing the users requires that the operations staff spend their weekends and holidays at work upgrading systems. And they do so with the ever-present threat that they'd better have their work completed and the system functioning again by Monday morning!)

Cloud computing embraces a new perspective: nothing is truly reliable, including computer systems. Rather than wasting money on trying to make your systems infinitely reliable, it's more practical and cost effective to design them to be redundant in the hope that even as some parts fail—or are intentionally shut down for maintenance—other parts will keep operating, thereby keeping the overall system reliable. This approach enabled one vendor who embraced cloud techniques to intentionally purchase RAM chips with a greater failure rate because they were cheaper. If the vendor found that a batch of RAM chips was too reliable, they assumed that they were being overcharged and that they should be able to get less-reliable chips instead at a significantly better price.

Accepting that hardware is unreliable recognizes the problem but doesn't solve it: How can a Cloud-Native Application run reliably even when a cloud platform is less reliable? The key is to not only structure the hardware as redundant parts but to structure the application as redundant parts as well.

Meanwhile, an application running in the cloud is shared by numerous users. When many of them start using the application at the same time, it can become overloaded with more client requests than it can handle. Some user requests may still get processed efficiently, and to them the application will still seem reliable. But for others, either their requests suffer very poor performance, or requests get lost and ignored completely, or the application becomes overloaded and crashes. Whatever the problems, the application becomes less reliable, even on reliable hardware, when too many users create too much load.

Ideally, the application should be reliable for all users at all times. With traditional IT, there are two main approaches for providing capacity for client requests:

Vertical scaling
Grow the application to use more of its computer's capacity.

Maximum sizing
Size the application to handle the maximum client load that can occur.

Vertical scaling requires that the application is able to access additional CPU and memory capacity in its computer. The application uses this additional capacity to serve more concurrent client requests. The application cannot grow once the computer runs out of CPU or memory and can also become constrained when it is using all of the computer's network bandwidth or storage. While an application can scale up vertically, it often cannot scale down again—memory and storage, once acquired, can be difficult to release, often at a minimum requiring the process to restart.

Maximum sizing ensures reliability at all times by determining the maximum client load that is likely to occur, then sizing the application for that. The problem is that most of the time the client load is much less and the application uses only a fraction of its capacity. An application that reserves a lot of capacity but uses much less of it is wasting money paying for capacity that it is not using. And however high the application's maximum client load may be, there's always the possibility it could receive even greater load and still become unreliable.

How can a *Cloud Application* reserve a lot of capacity when it has a lot of client load but less capacity when it has less load, so that its capacity is always proportional to the current level of client load? And how can the application always have the capability to grow more and more if it needs to? The key is to structure the application to scale bigger and smaller as client load increases and decreases.

The application should run as redundant parts for reliability and should be able to scale bigger and smaller as client load changes.

Therefore,

Design the application as a *Replicable Application* that is able to run as multiple redundant application replicas that all provide the same functionality without interfering with one another.

By designing a Cloud-Native Application to be replicable, the cloud platform will be able to deploy replicas of the application.

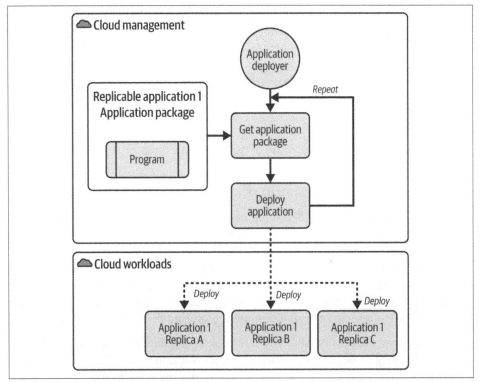

Figure 3-10. Replicable Application

As Figure 3-10 shows, the cloud platform's management functionality includes an application deployer, which performs the function of creating a new workload instance of an application from its *Application Package*. When cloud management runs the deployer repeatedly, it creates multiple replicas of the application.

Because a Cloud-Native Application is encapsulated as an *Application Package*, the cloud platform can easily create new replicas of the application by deploying the package repeatedly. Each replica is a deployment of the same *Application Package*, so all of the new replicas are equivalent. The replicas run independently of one another, do not even know about one another, and do not interfere with one another.

Application replication is a fundamental feature in most cloud platforms. Platforms that provide autoscaling use replication for that as well, but autoscaling isn't a requirement of replication. Some examples include the following:

Amazon EC2
   EC2 Auto Scaling adds EC2 instances when demand spikes

Kubernetes ReplicaSet
   Guarantees the availability of a specified number of identical Pods

Azure Function
   As requests increase, Azure automatically runs more functions

IBM Cloud "Auto Scale" for VPC
   Dynamically creates virtual server instances to improve performance based on metrics like CPU, memory, and network usage

With each of these examples, the platform is able to deploy new replica instances of the application that are equivalent to existing replica instances, such as to start an application by deploying redundant replicas or to replace a replica that has crashed or become unresponsive.

The cloud platform treats multiple replicas of an application as a group and makes the group behave like one big copy of the application. Running multiple replicas rather than one big replica solves both of the challenges of making an application more reliable than its hardware:

Scalability
   Each replica can run on a different computer, providing the capacity of multiple computers, which is greater than the capacity of any single one of those computers.

Reliability
   If one computer fails, only the replicas running on that computer fail; the rest of the replicas keep running.

The multiple replicas provide greater capacity for serving more concurrent client requests than a single replica could. While all of the replicas could run on a single computer, running on multiple computers enables them to use the capacity of multiple computers. When a computer fails, only the replicas running on that computer fail; the rest of the replicas keep running, making the application highly available and providing greater reliability for the clients.

The application can run as a single replica, but as explained in The Twelve-Factor App: VIII. Concurrency (*https://oreil.ly/WYQFC*), "The application must also be able to span multiple processes running on multiple physical machines." A significant advantage of this approach is that scalability becomes much simpler: "The process model truly shines when it comes time to scale out. The share-nothing, horizontally partitionable nature of twelve-factor app processes means that adding more concurrency is a simple and reliable operation." Each workload replica can still employ other techniques for scaling: "An individual process can handle its own internal multiplexing, via threads inside the runtime, can support the async/evented model, and vertical scaling is possible."

The application can not only scale out to add capacity, it can also scale in and reduce capacity simply by shutting down some of the replicas. As explained in The Twelve-Factor App: IX. Disposability (*https://oreil.ly/FV2bs*):

> The twelve-factor app's processes are disposable, meaning they can be started or stopped at a moment's notice. This facilitates fast elastic scaling, rapid deployment of code or config changes, and robustness of production deploys.

For an application to be replicable, avoid anything that fits the the **Singleton** pattern (*Design Patterns*, 1994) in which an object has only a single instance that cannot be replicated and must be shared globally. Avoid any design details that mean the application can run only as a single workload and therefore on a single computer, such as components with shared memory, concurrency semaphores, or a fixed IP address or domain name. Such designs were common with traditional IT, but they cannot support multiple copies in the cloud.

Fortunately, business applications and many multiuser environments typically replicate easily. When the user buys a book, views a bank account, or browses movies to stream, the business transaction is implemented by a logical thread performed in a slice of the application architecture from the graphical user interface (GUI) through the business logic to the database and back. A replica may have capacity to handle tens or hundreds of such transactions in isolated, concurrent threads. Multiple replicas can handle many more, each handling its share of the total concurrent transactions and none of them interacting with one another except for updating shared *Backend Services*.

A *Replicable Application* can run multiple redundant copies of itself without them interfering with one another. The cloud platform is what deploys the replicas. The cloud platform makes multiple replicas of the same application work like one big application, which improves the application's scalability and reliability. Replication works well for typical business applications.

However, developers who have never designed an application to be replicable often find doing so a challenge. Traditional IT developers are accustomed to designing an application with a single replica that scales vertically. The number one enemy of replication is the **Singleton** pattern and variations thereof—such as block storage and fixed IP addresses. These should be avoided.

The cloud platform will have an easier time distributing requests across replicas and scaling them in if the application is a Stateless Application (80). Stateful replicas require that the load balancer implement sticky sessions, a technique that the cloud avoids. When replicas are stateless, they are all equivalent, not only when new replicas are created from the same *Application Package* but throughout their lifetimes. To scale in, any stateless replica is an equally valid candidate to be shut down because they are all equivalent.

While replicas do not know about one another, they do coordinate via shared Backend Services (106). Because all of the replicas of an application share the same set of *Backend Service* instances, they all have access to the same external functionality and state—helping them all work the same way.

Replicas often share a common set of domain data in a shared Cloud Database (311). Many cloud databases are able to replicate across multiple computers and storage, thereby scaling the same way the application does. A distributed database has better high availability and throughput than a database running in a single server. The application should avoid managing its own storage directly by employing measures such as a file system or especially block storage—which typically cannot be shared, as that can break the equivalency of the replicas.

This ability to dynamically replicate on demand is a key advantage of a Microservice (119), which enables part of an application to scale rather than the entire monolith.

Application replicas typically are not simply copies of the *Application Package*, but rather are copies of a virtual machine image (see Virtualize the Application (475)) or container image (see Containerize the Application (478)) that includes the *Application Package*. One advantage of packaging an application as an *Application Package* is that the package makes it easier for the cloud platform's application deployer to deploy the application simply and reliably. By packaging the *Application Package* as a virtual machine or container, it is even easier for the application deployer to deploy repeatedly.

Examples

When a team that is new to cloud-native architecture is told that their application needs to be able to run multiple copies simultaneously, often their first reaction is to say that their application won't work that way. The trick is to figure out what in the application's implementation prevents multiple replicas running at the same time from working correctly. The following are some typical problem scenarios that would occur if multiple replicas of the application were running at the same time:

- The application depends on a **Singleton** (*Design Patterns*, 1994). Managing a **Singleton** within a replica may be straightforward, but managing it across replicas is complex.
- They will interfere with one another—such as overwriting one another's data—and keep any of them from working.
- They will each store their own data—such as in their own disk storage—and each will work but will not know about the data in the other replicas.
- The first replica will establish a lock on a resource, and the others will block while waiting to establish their own locks on the same resource.
- To establish a lock on a resource only once, all of the replicas will coordinate to elect one replica that will establish the lock that they will all then share. This might work until the replica that established the lock crashes without releasing the lock. Then, none of the replicas work, including the replacement for the replica that crashed.
- A scenario similar to a resource lock is an application that can run only on a particular IP address. The first replica reserves that IP address and assigns it to its network interface, then the other replicas cannot use it.

A theme here is that typically multiple replicas work OK internally; the problem is how they use external resources and that the program was designed with the assumption that it would be the only replica using the external resource. The trick is to discover where these problem scenarios occur in the program, discover the design assumptions that led to the problem, and redesign that part of the program with better assumptions that eliminate the problem and enable replication.

Here is some detail about a few specific examples:

- Avoid **Singletons**.
- Store data in a shared database service, not in disk storage.
- Manage a connection pool using an integration service.

Avoid Singletons

An application that uses the **Singleton** pattern will have difficulty running application replicas. When the application runs, it will create a single instance of an object that all of the application will share. If the application is run twice, each replica of the application will create its own **Singleton**. Two threads running in an application replica will share the same **Singleton**, but two threads running in two separate replicas will each access its replica's **Singleton**, which usually defeats the purpose of making the object a **Singleton**. If two threads can successfully use two different **Singleton** copies, the object doesn't need to be a **Singleton**.

Perhaps the application can be structured such that the first replica creates the **Singleton**, then subsequent replicas will all access the **Singleton** in the first replica. This creates a couple of problems. First, it is complex to implement, with each new replica needing to know that the original replica already exists and how to access it and its **Singleton**. Second, any network problems between the replicas will make accessing the **Singleton** slow and unreliable. Third, if the first replica—the one with the **Singleton**—crashes, none of the other replicas will work because they have lost access to the **Singleton**. The surviving replicas need to detect that the **Singleton** is lost and create a new one, working together to ensure that only one of the surviving replicas creates the replacement and they all know how to access it.

Rather than confront this coding complexity, a much simpler approach is to design an application to avoid any **Singletons**. Then, it is easy to run as a *Replicable Application*.

Store data in a shared database service, not in disk storage

An application that stores data directly in block or file storage will be difficult to replicate. It should instead use a database that the replicas can share.

An application has some data to persist, so it creates a block storage volume and stores blocks of data. The problem with running multiple replicas of the application is that each one creates its own storage volume and stores its own data, but each replica knows only the data it stores in its volume and has no access to the data the other replicas have stored in their volumes. This is an even bigger problem if any replicas shut down or crash—the data in those replicas' volumes becomes inaccessible, effectively lost.

Rather than each replica creating its own volume, they could create one volume and share it. The first replica does not find the volume creates it, then subsequent replicas find the existing volume and also attach to it. This will not work because block storage volumes typically cannot be shared by more than one workload process. Even if they could, how would each replica know about the blocks stored by the other replicas while avoiding overwriting one another's data? The application might be able to implement enough functionality to solve all of these constraints, but in doing so would end up implementing its own database.

While traditional IT applications used to implement their own data persistence, *Cloud Applications* don't have to. Instead, the solution for a *Cloud Applications* is to store its data in a database that has been created in a platform-managed database service and can be shared by multiple replicas of the application. This can even be a relational database or some other database running in a single server. The database coordinates requests from multiple threads—whether they are running in the same application replica or in different replicas—and coordinates writing data to blocks, remembering where the blocks are and avoiding overwriting blocks in use. As new application replicas are started and old ones are shut down, they all continue to share the same database. Such database services already exist, so no application should write its own. See Cloud-Native Storage (Chapter 7).

Manage a connection pool using an integration service

A *Replicable Application* can grow big enough to overwhelm a legacy system of record (SoR). Care must be taken in the application's design to avoid this problem.

When an application accesses an SoR, the SoR can typically handle only a limited number of concurrent connections. Too many concurrent connects will result in a crash. If the SoR can handle only 10 concurrent connections, the application creates a connection pool with 10 connections, perhaps using a programming language's connection pooling framework such as Java EE Connector Architecture (JCA). It channels all access through the pool so that it uses up to 10 connections at the same time. The problem with running multiple replicas of the application is that each one creates its own connection pool, each with 10 connections. Multiple application replicas using 10 connections each can create more than 10 concurrent connections to the SoR and crash it.

Again, coordination between application replicas may be the solution to the problem. Each replica adds only a few connections to its pool so that they all have only 10 connections total. This won't scale for more than 10 application replicas. Even with ten or fewer, how are they going to coordinate to know how many connections each one has and make sure each gets a fair proportion of the connections to use? When a replica shuts down, how do the others know so that they can start using its connections? Implementing a shared, distributed connection pool will not be easy.

The solution is for the application to not implement a shared connection pool at all, much less one distributed across multiple replicas of the application. Rather, the application should use an integration solution to connect to the SoR and let it manage the connection pool. An integration solution such as IBM App Connect Enterprise (*https://oreil.ly/hSZbo*) or MuleSoft AnyPoint (*https://oreil.ly/Hxt4p*) can manage connections to the SoR and be shared by multiple workload replicas.

Figure 3-11 shows a *Replicable Application* that accesses an SoR. Rather than connect to it directly, the replicas share a connection pool managed by an integration service.

The integration service enforces the constraints for connecting to the SoR, such as a limited pool of connections that it creates and shares. The workload replicas then share the integration service. Much like a database service coordinates multiple replicas accessing the same data, the integration service coordinates multiple replicas accessing the same SoR.

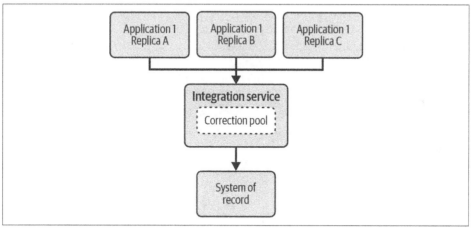

Figure 3-11. Replicable Application with a connection pool

External Configuration

You are developing an application with a Cloud-Native Architecture (58). You want to be able to deploy the same Application Package (62) to multiple environments without rebuilding it.

How can I build my application once and yet be able to deploy it to multiple environments that are configured differently?

An application is not deployed only once to a single environment; it is deployed multiple times to different environments. Each of these environments may be set up and operated differently, possibly requiring the application to work differently in each environment.

Cloud Applications (Chapter 1) are portable, designed to run on whatever hardware is available. Developers should be able to deploy a *Cloud Application* to different environments as long as they are equivalent. One common environment is the developer's local computer, where the developer may test out their latest changes. Other common environments are the stages in the software development lifecycle (SDLC) (such as dev, test, stage, and prod), which are separate but equivalent environments. An enterprise may also encompass multiple production environments, perhaps for different geographies (such as north america and europe) or different lines of business in the enterprise (such as marketing and accounts receivable). Equivalency of these separate environments is the principle behind The Twelve-Factor App: X. Dev/prod parity (*https://oreil.ly/JZwUd*). The application must be able to run equally well in any of these equivalent environments.

While various environments are equivalent in many ways, they are not the same. A developer's laptop is not running the same services as a cloud platform. The cloud environments for testing should include equivalent but separate service instances from those for production. For example, if the application requires a relational database with a particular schema, the database is provided as one installation on the developer's laptop, another service instance is provided for testing environments full of fake test data, and at least one more service instance full of proprietary enterprise data is provided for production. The equivalent databases are hosted on separate network endpoints (e.g., IP address, domain, or URL) and certainly have different authentication credentials. These databases are equivalent, but because they're separate servers, they're accessed differently.

An application has access only to the services in its environment. When the application is deployed to a development environment, it should have access only to the development database. Only when it is deployed to the production environment should it have access to the production database.

The application should be built to be immutable. This is one of the principles behind The Twelve-Factor App: V. Build, release, run (*https://oreil.ly/Vuh7Y*), as well as both a consequence and benefit of packaging an application as an application container image (*https://oreil.ly/nGh0l*)—such as a Docker image. An *immutable application* means that the exact same deployment artifacts are deployed into each environment. Deployment should not recompile or rebuild an application to deploy it into a new environment. When the application is immutable, the exact same artifacts that were used for testing are also deployed into production. Otherwise, if an application must be changed and rebuilt to deploy it into production, what's running in production is not what was tested and approved in the testing environment.

How can the same application use a different service instance (e.g., a different database) depending on the environment it's deployed into? One approach is to hardcode literals for the service instance's endpoint and credentials. But then every time the application is deployed into a new environment with a new service instance, the application's code needs to be modified to change those literals, be recompiled, then retested. An immutable application cannot be modified and recompiled between environments.

Another approach might be for the application to hardcode the endpoint and credential literals for all of the service instances in all of the environments. This assumes that the developers know all of the environments the application will ever be deployed into, that the service instances' connection properties can never change, and that the developers should have access to all of these settings. That would mean giving developers access to the authentication credentials for the production services, settings that the production operations team should treat as a closely guarded secret. Even if this would work, the unchanged application has no way to know which environment it has been deployed into and therefore which set of literals to use.

Another problem with hardcoding settings comes with committing code into the source code management (SCM) system. An SCM is widely shared with all developers who need access to the code. Environment settings should not be widely shared because anyone who knows the settings gains insight into how the enterprise's internal environments are set up. Secret credentials should be even more closely guarded, not stored someplace widely shared.

In traditional IT, a common approach to avoid hardcoding settings within an application is to store them in a properties file. That way, developers can change the settings by editing the file, and they do not have to recompile the rest of the application. However, this approach doesn't work well in the cloud. A Cloud-Native Application is stateless, and a properties file is state (unless you are storing it in an external service like a secrets store). Even if properties are an exception, a cloud environment may not even have a file system to store the properties file into. Also, the properties file is deployed with the rest of the application, so the application still cannot deploy to multiple environments unchanged.

Cloud Applications support Polyglot Development (146), where an application's modules don't all need to be developed in a single computer language. Settings need to be stored in a way that is language-independent, using an approach that will work for all languages and all environments, including cloud environments.

Therefore,

Store an application's settings in an *External Configuration* separate from the application's code so that the settings can be changed without changing the application artifacts.

Configuration is typically stored in environment variables.

An application accesses its configuration as an internal set of variables, populated from values that are stored externally. Because these configuration values are stored externally from the application, the values can be changed without having to change the application's code and recompile it. An application can be deployed to different environments with different configurations without having to change the code, just change its set of *External Configuration* values in each environment.

As shown in Figure 3-12, the application stores its configuration internally as variables and sets their values from a configuration that is stored externally.

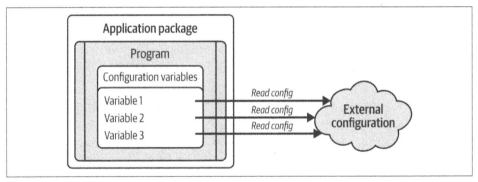

Figure 3-12. External Configuration

The *External Configuration* values are typically stored in the OS as environment variables, as shown in Figure 3-13. Most include environment variables as a feature. Most programming languages have features for reading environment variables, so the program just needs to use those features. For each configuration variable the program needs to read, the program just needs to know the name of the corresponding environment variable.

Operating system	
External configuration environment variables	
Key	**Value**
Variable 1	Value 1
Variable 2	Value 2
Variable 3	Value 3

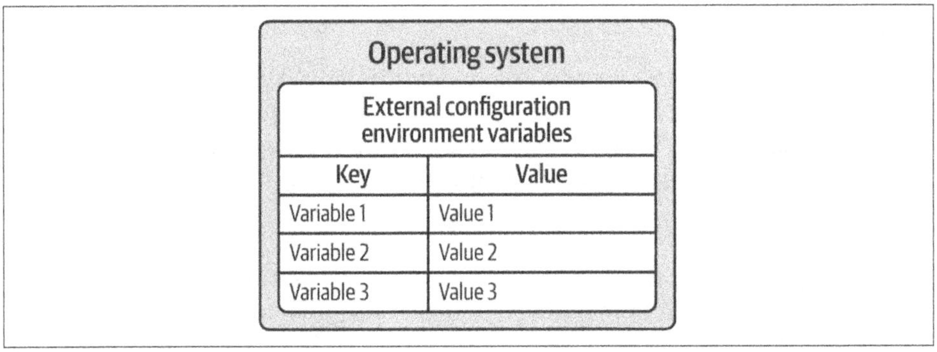

Figure 3-13. Environment variables

As Figure 3-14 shows, configuration for the application is stored in environment variables in the OS's environment. The deployment process, whether manual or automated, declares the environment variables and sets their values when it deploys the application into the OS. When the application runs in the OS, the program reads its configuration from the environment variables, optionally stores these values in its own internal variables, and uses the values as needed.

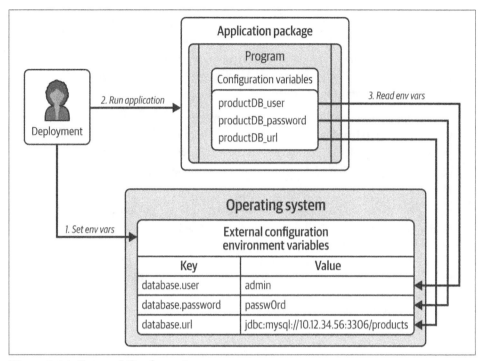

Figure 3-14. External Configuration usage

In this example, the configuration specifies the credentials to access and authenticate with an external MySQL database containing data for products. The deployer can set this configuration for one database in the development environment and a different database in production without having to change the program code, so the same *Application Package* can be deployed without modification in both environments.

As explained in The Twelve-Factor App: III. Config (*https://oreil.ly/htlXG*):

> **The twelve-factor app stores config in *environment variables*** (often shortened to *env vars* or *env*). Env vars are easy to change between deploys without changing any code; unlike config files, there is little chance of them being checked into the code repo accidentally; and unlike custom config files, or other config mechanisms such as Java System Properties, they are a language- and OS-agnostic standard.

Environment variables are a very good place to store the configuration settings for an application. They are not specific to any one language or OS. Unlike a properties file, environment variables do not require a local file system. If needed, each variable can be shared by multiple applications, as long as that doesn't create an unnatural coupling between the applications. If multiple applications always need the same setting, such as sharing the same database, they should share a single environment variable. If they may eventually need different settings, such as each using its own database, they should use separate environment variables that may or may not contain the same value.

Application settings may include private data such as credentials that should not be stored in a public SCM. Whereas properties files may accidentally get checked into an SCM, environment variables will not.

While storing an application's configuration in the OS's environment solves many issues, setting an environment's variables can be a chicken-and-egg problem. As part of the deployment process, something must set the environment's variables with the configuration settings, which must be set before the application is deployed into an environment.

An easy way to initialize the environment variables is to store the settings in a properties file that a deployment script can use to set the variables before deploying that app. The environment variables decouple the application from how the values are stored—only the deployment process needs access to the properties file and the file system. If the values are stored in a properties file, that file shouldn't be checked into SCM. Settings can also be stored in two files, sensitive and nonsensitive, where only the nonsensitive file is checked into SCM. The sensitive settings should be stored in a secrets vault.

Rather than storing the *External Configuration* in environment variables, it is sometimes stored in a database. While convenient, this approach requires that the application have access to a database, an extra middleware service that is not built into an OS like environment variables but one that most applications are likely to need anyway. This database approach also creates its own chicken-and-egg problem for initializing the application: the application needs settings for accessing the database that contains the settings.

Environment variables are often populated from a values management service provided by the platform—such as HashiCorp Vault, Parameter Store on Amazon Web Services (AWS), and Secrets Manager on IBM Cloud. An application can access such a service directly via an API, bypassing environment variables. However, that approach makes the application directly dependent on the service, with all of the problems of making the application directly dependent on a database of values. Furthermore, each service has its own API, locking in the application so that its code works only on the platform with that service. Environment variables avoid this lock-in by separating how the application accesses the values from how the values are populated, enabling the deployment process to easily switch between different storage methods without needing to modify the application, and without making the application dependent on the storage method.

Externalizing an application's configuration into environment variables makes the settings part of the environment the application is deployed into. Each environment independently sets the variables for its configuration. The application is able to run unchanged in multiple environments and use a different configuration in each environment. Cloud environments and their OSs support storing environment variables, and modern programming languages support reading environment variables. Unlike with a properties file, environment variables do not require a file system and cannot accidentally get checked into an SCM.

When an application externalizes its configuration as a set of environment variables, the cloud environment must provide a way to set environment variable values when running the application. Each platform handles that differently. Setting these environment variables' values can be a chicken-and-egg problem. The configuration for the code that initializes the variables should not be checked into SCM, and credentials should be stored in a secrets vault. Thus, many cloud platforms provide some sort of Configuration Database (324) to solve this problem for applications running on their platform.

When the application is a Replicable Application (88), the platform sets the environment once so that all of the replicas share the same configuration.

Externalizing your configuration enables other design principles. For example, a developer may choose to test locally with a local copy of a database like Postgres and then connect to an AWS or Azure database service when testing in the cloud. This toggling of features and environment-specific configuration choice is critical when testing applications built using a Microservices Architecture (Chapter 4). Each component can be tested individually and integrated within the system before testing, rather than always having to test a component with all of its dependencies—which can lead to having to test an entire system just to test one component in the system.

Examples

Application languages that support deployment techniques like application packaging also support accessing environment variables. Likewise, cloud technologies like containers and container orchestrators provide features for setting environment variables. Cloud platforms provide services for storing credentials securely and making them available to applications by setting them in environment variables.

Read environment variables in Java

As Oracle documents in Environment Variables (*https://oreil.ly/lsLY-*), a Java application can read environment variables using the System.getenv static methods.

An application can read all of its environment's variables into a Map, as shown in Example 3-12.

Example 3-12. Java code for reading all of an environment's variables

```java
Map<String, String> env = System.getenv();
for (String envName : env.keySet()) {
    System.out.format("%s=%s%n", envName, env.get(envName));
}
```

An application can also read an individual environment variable's value by specifying its name, as shown in Example 3-13.

Example 3-13. Java code for reading one of an environment's variables

```java
String name = "PORT";
String value = System.getenv(name);
if (value != null) {
    System.out.format("%s=%s%n", name, value);
} else {
    System.out.format("%s is" + " not assigned.%n", name);
}
```

A deployment tool that the Java application doesn't even know about can set the values of environment variables, and the application can read them simply by knowing the variables' names. This works on a range of platforms and helps keep the application platform-independent.

Read environment variables in Node.js

A Node.js process makes all environment variables accessible using a global env process object. Example 3-14 shows how an application can read all of its environment's variables from this object.

Example 3-14. Node.js code for reading all of an environment's variables

```javascript
const process = require('process');
var env = process.env;
for (var key in env) {
    console.log(key + ":\t\t\t" + env[key]);
}
```

An application can also read an individual environment variable's value by specifying its name, as shown in Example 3-15.

Example 3-15. Node.js code for reading one of an environment's variables

```javascript
const app = require('http').createServer((req, res) => res.send('Ahoy!'));
const PORT = process.env.PORT || 3000;

app.listen(PORT, () => {
```

```
console.log(`Server is listening on port ${PORT}`);
});
```

A deployment tool that sets the values of environment variables and the application that reads them do not need to know about each other. The setter doesn't need to know the language used to implement the application—Java, Node.js, or another—only that the application is able to read environment variables.

Docker container environment variables

Like application programs and packages, container images should also be built with an *External Configuration* so that their containers can be deployed to a number of environments. The running container will read the environment variables and make them available to its processes. For example, when running a container using Docker (*https://oreil.ly/FqPzr*), use -e flags in the docker run command to specify environment variable settings.

Kubernetes Configuration Map and Secret

Kubernetes, a popular container orchestrator, enables an application to access settings as environment variables using two features: ConfigMap (*https://oreil.ly/B216f*) and Secret (*https://oreil.ly/3l809*). Both a configuration map and a secret store a set of data as key-value pairs. The data in a configuration map is stored as plain text and so should not be confidential. The data stored in a secret is encoded and so can be as confidential as the encoding method.

For example, the YAML code in Example 3-16 creates a ConfigMap named game-demo that sets the values for two properties.

Example 3-16. Kubernetes configuration map

```
apiVersion: v1
kind: ConfigMap
metadata:
  name: game-demo
data:
  # property-like keys; each key maps to a simple value
  player_initial_lives: "3"
  ui_properties_file_name: "user-interface.properties"
```

An application in a pod that reads this configuration map has access to those two values named player_initial_lives and ui_properties_file_name.

The YAML code in Example 3-17 creates a Secret named mysecret that sets the values for two properties.

Example 3-17. Kubernetes Secret

```
apiVersion: v1
kind: Secret
metadata:
  name: mysecret
type: Opaque
data:
  USER_NAME: YWRtaW4=
  PASSWORD: MWYyZDFlMmU2N2Rm
```

An application in a pod that reads this secret has access to the plain text data for the values named USER_NAME and PASSWORD.

Secrets storage and encryption

An enterprise should store the sensitive settings in a secrets vault such as HashiCorp Vault (*https://oreil.ly/l4jIz*), or better yet a hardware security module (HSM) that only the enterprise can access. If sensitive settings must be stored in SCM, they should be encrypted using tools like git-crypt (*https://oreil.ly/NMopt*).

AWS Systems Manager Parameter Store and AppConfig

AWS Systems Manager Parameter Store (*https://oreil.ly/8Y9Va*) stores configuration data and secrets. This data can be accessed in compute services such as Amazon Elastic Compute Cloud (Amazon EC2), Amazon Elastic Container Service (Amazon ECS), and AWS Lambda. A feature within AWS System Manager, AWS AppConfig, allows users to store and manage custom application configuration from within application programs.

IBM Cloud Secrets Manager

IBM Cloud Secrets Manager (*https://oreil.ly/F8Bu_*)—built on HashiCorp Vault— stores configuration settings that should not be stored in source code management. It manages their lifecycle, controls access to them, records their usage history, and optionally encrypts them with user-provided keys. It can also be configured to create Kubernetes secrets, and those secrets can be encrypted with user-provided keys. Applications can use these secrets to authenticate to databases and storage, and continuous delivery services can use them to gain access to deployment environments.

Backend Service

You are developing an application with a Cloud-Native Architecture (58). The application implements custom business logic that deploys as an Application Package (62). The application needs some functionality that is common among many applications—such as data persistence or messaging.

How can multiple applications share the same reusable functionality?

A common approach in traditional IT to make functionality reusable has been to implement it as a reusable code library. Any application that needed the functionality would compile and link in the library as part of its executable process. For example, a Java program can include separate JAR files, Node.js programs can include modules, and a C# program can use the .NET libraries.

The library approach has several limitations:

Language
> An application implemented in a particular language can typically only use libraries written in the same language.

Distribution
> The libraries are part of the application process and therefore can only run on the same computer as the rest of the application.

Scalability
> The library scales with the application process. The library cannot scale independently of the rest of the application.

Failure
> If the library fails, it causes the rest of the application to fail, perhaps causing the entire application process to crash.

Composable
> To reuse multiple libraries, an application must be able to include them all in its process. This can be a problem for libraries unless they were designed to work together.

Duplication
> Multiple applications that embed the same library each load their own copy, causing bloat that limits scalability.

Traditional IT applications typically run in middleware servers that provide capabilities like automating business processes, running rules, and queuing messages. Middleware that also hosts the application is essentially a giant code library, with the same code library limitations.

The cloud needs to be able to vary the application independently of code libraries.

Therefore,

A Cloud-Native Application should connect to reusable functionality remotely as a *Backend Service*. The service can be stateful, reused by multiple applications, and managed by the cloud platform.

A single Cloud-Native Application can delegate to multiple *Backend Services*. A single *Backend Service* can be used by multiple applications.

As shown in Figure 3-15, a *Cloud Application* can delegate to several *Backend Services*, such as a database, a messaging system, and a process automation engine. Many cloud platforms include a catalog of services hosted as SaaS that applications can reuse as *Backend Services*. Many *Backend Services* perform the sort of functionality provided by middleware servers on traditional IT.

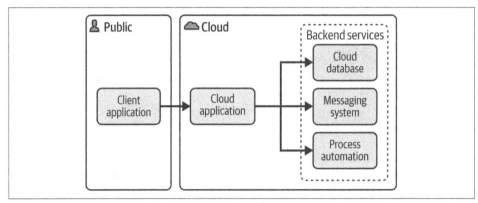

Figure 3-15. Backend Services

While *Cloud Applications* can embed reusable code libraries the way a traditional IT application can, they gain even greater flexibility by being able to connect to *Backend Services* remotely. A *Cloud Application* can even reuse other applications by treating them as *Backend Services*.

In cloud, reusing code libraries as a *Backend Service* overcomes the limitations of a library:

Language
> The application and the service can be implemented in different languages and technologies.

Distribution
> The application and the service run in different processes, so they can run on the same computer or on separate computers.

Scalability
> The application and the service run in different processes, so they can scale independently.

Failure
> The application and the service run in different processes, so a failure that crashes one does not crash the other.

Composable

An application can connect to multiple services and combine their functionality.

Duplication

Multiple applications that reuse the same service share a single copy, thereby consuming just one set of capacity.

The role of a *Backend Service* is distinct from that of the application program. *Backend Services* are specialized for reusable application functionality, whereas an application's program is specialized for the business logic that implements a particular set of user requirements. A *Backend Service* performs a single capability that many applications need, such as data persistence, messaging, rules processing, or event processing. Whereas business logic is often industry-specific and gives an enterprise competitive advantage, *Backend Services* are usually industry-neutral. The *Backend Service* does not give an enterprise competitive advantage as is; the advantage to the enterprise is in how they use the service and the fact that they could buy the service rather than build it themselves. An application program typically runs on behalf of a single enterprise, whereas a *Backend Service* is typically used by multiple enterprises while enabling an enterprise to isolate its usage by creating its own instance of the service.

As explained in The Twelve-Factor App: IV. Backing services (*https://oreil.ly/N17QY*):

> A *backing service* is any service the app consumes over the network as part of its normal operation….Backing services like the database are traditionally managed by the same systems administrators who deploy the app's runtime. In addition to these locally-managed services, the app may also have services provided and managed by third parties.

The *Backend Service* paradigm works so well that cloud platforms tend to make all functionality into services, yet some of the services in a service catalog are more backend than others. The services in a catalog come in two broad varieties:

Application service

The application connects directly to the service as a *Backend Service*. Its implementation includes client code that invokes the service's API, such that the service is required for the application to work. For example, for an application to work with a database or a messaging system, it must be written to do so.

Platform service

The cloud platform environment is configured to include the application and services that enhance how it runs. The application does not depend on these services directly—they are optional. For example, an application usually does not interact with a key vault directly; the database does. Observability services can be added to the environment and gather information about the application without changing the application.

The concept of *Backend Service* existed before the cloud. Even in traditional IT, most databases and messaging systems run in separate servers that applications connect to remotely. The cloud takes this to an extreme, whereby a program is only the code implemented by the development team and perhaps some embedded code libraries, and everything else in the application is *Backend Services* the program connects to remotely.

Backend Services can be developed by third-party vendors so that application developers can focus on the user functionality that makes their application unique. Many cloud platforms provide a catalog of *Backend Services*, available for applications deployed on that platform to use. Many software vendors make their products available as SaaS that applications can use as *Backend Services*. OperatorHub.io and Red Hat Marketplace make libraries of Kubernetes operators available, which can be installed in application environments so that applications can use them as *Backend Services*.

A single application can delegate to multiple *Backend Services*, and a *Backend Service* can be shared by multiple applications. Each *Backend Service* can be written in a different language and used by applications written in different languages. An application and its *Backend Service* can run on different computers, and they are able to scale independently. Each *Backend Service* focuses on a specific set of functionality that is highly reusable by multiple applications. Applications can connect to application services directly and indirectly make use of platform services embedded in the cloud platform. *Backend Services* can be developed by third-party vendors and made available built into a cloud platform in a service catalog.

However, *Backend Services* can complicate an application architecture. The application must be able to access the service remotely via a network connection, which can be slow and unreliable. It is not always clear where and how a *Backend Service* is hosted, which can be a challenge for applications with data sovereignty restrictions. It is not always clear whether a *Backend Service* is single-tenant or multitenant, and how multiple tenants are isolated. A *Backend Service's* reliability can be lower than an application requires, effectively lowering the application's reliability. Each *Backend Service* should include a user agreement that stipulates its service-level agreements (SLAs), which the application developer must confirm are compatible with their application's requirements.

If an application is designed as a Replicable Application (88), all of its replicas will share the same *Backend Services*. These shared services help the otherwise unrelated replicas coordinate to act like one big application.

Any Cloud Database (311) can be a *Backend Service*, as long as it runs in a separate process from the application. Some databases can be embedded within an application: Apache Derby in Java programs, SQLite as a C library, eXtremeDB for C and C++ programs. When embedded, a database is not a backend system. When the database server runs independently of the application and can be shared by multiple applications, *Cloud Applications* use it as a *Backend Service*.

A *Backend Service* is part of a Distributed Architecture (38) that can be implemented as a Microservices Architecture (Chapter 4).

An Event Backbone (279) is a *Backend Service*. It connects event consumers to event producers, all of which use it as a shared *Backend Service*.

Examples

A compelling advantage of many public cloud platforms is that the platform is chock full of *Backend Services*. These services are designed for applications to use as *Backend Services* or otherwise to add capabilities to an application that the development team doesn't have to implement itself. Infrastructure-as-a-Service (IaaS) and Platform-as-a-Service (PaaS) services such as virtual servers and container orchestrators host applications but are not *Backend Services* for applications. An application can connect directly to application services, which are SaaS services for adding functionality to the application, such as data persistence, caching, messaging, and process automation. An application's environment can be configured to include platform services that the application doesn't connect to directly, such as API gateways, authentication, key management, monitoring, and log aggregation.

Database services (application service)

A Cloud-Native Application runs as a Stateless Application (80). A problem with making an application stateless is that most applications have state, so where does the state go? It goes in databases and other data stores, which the application uses as *Backend Services*. The database server runs as a service, available for any client application that wants to use it to create a database and store data. Cloud platforms provide numerous different Cloud-Native Storage (Chapter 7) services.

Examples of database *Backend Services* include Amazon Relational Database Service (Amazon RDS) and Amazon DocumentDB, Azure Cosmos DB (document) and Azure Cache for Redis (key/value), and IBM Db2 on Cloud (relational) and IBM Cloudant (document). Object storage services—such as Amazon Simple Storage Service (Amazon S3), Azure Storage, and IBM Cloud Object Storage—are also *Backend Services*.

Integration services (application service)

Messaging services connect applications; each application connects to a messaging service as a *Backend Service*. Examples include Kafka, Amazon Managed Streaming for Apache Kafka (MSK), Azure Event Hubs, and IBM Event Streams; IBM MQ on Cloud, Azure Service Bus, Amazon MQ, RabbitMQ, and Apache ActiveMQ; and IBM App Connect on IBM Cloud.

An API gateway exposes internal application APIs as external endpoints and can authorize their use. An application doesn't try to manage this itself. The gateway runs as a service, but rather than connect to the gateway as a *Backend Service*, the deployment process publishes the application's APIs as endpoints in the gateway. Examples include Amazon API Gateway, Azure API Management, and IBM API Connect.

Security services (platform service)

A *key management service* (KMS) or a key vault that stores cryptographic keys securely is a *Backend Service*. Keys are stored in the KMS for safe keeping. When a database or storage service needs a key, it retrieves it from the KMS. Examples include Azure Key Vault Managed Hardware Security Module (HSM), AWS Key Management Service (AWS KMS), and IBM Cloud Hyper Protect Crypto Services.

External Configuration (97) talks about storing secrets in a secrets vault. Like a key vault, a secrets vault is typically hosted as a *Backend Service*. The application may interact with the secrets vault directly, making it an application service. Or the application may be able to interact with the secrets vault indirectly, such as by sharing Kubernetes secrets, making it a platform service.

A user authentication service enables the user to log in to the application. Rather than the application implementing this functionality itself, multiple applications can all share a service that sits in front of the applications and authenticates users on behalf of the applications. Examples include IBM Cloud App ID and Azure Front Door.

Observability services (platform service)

Monitoring services and log aggregators gather events from applications while they are running to display to the operations staff. Rather than each application performing this functions itself, separate services perform this work. The application may not even know these services are connected to it. Examples include Prometheus for monitoring and Fluentd for log aggregation.

Conclusion: Wrapping Up Cloud-Native Application

This chapter discussed how best to build applications that not only run in the cloud but work well in the cloud. A Cloud-Native Application is an application that is designed for the cloud. It incorporates a Cloud-Native Architecture (58) that takes advantage of the cloud computing model by dividing an application into an application program and services. A Cloud-Native Application is built and deployed as an Application Package (62). It exposes its functionality to clients via a Service API (70), runs as a Stateless Application (80) that is also a Replicable Application (88), and is configured with an External Configuration (97). It delegates to reusable functionality provided by Backend Services (106).

The program part of a Cloud-Native Application implements the custom domain logic for the application's desired user functionality. The program is built into an *Application Package* that can be deployed on any cloud platform. It runs as a stateless, replicable workload that clients access as a service via an API. This makes a single program able to support concurrent requests from multiple clients and run multiple replicas that share the same data. The interface hides the program's implementation, enabling the implementation to evolve without requiring code changes in the clients. Once built, the package is immutable with an externalized configuration, enabling it to be configured differently for deployment to multiple environments without requiring modification to the immutable package. The cloud platform can relocate the application to maintain availability even while outages occur in the platform.

Separating the program from the *Backend Services* achieves several advantages. It separates the stateless parts of the application from the stateful parts, which makes the program lighter weight, less error-prone and able to start quickly, shut down cleanly, and recover from crashes more easily. It separates the services that can be reused by multiple applications from the custom domain logic unique to a single application. It enables the application development team to implement the program in almost any computer language they choose, regardless of the technologies used to implement the *Backend Services*. It enables the program to scale independently of the *Backend Services* and enables the *Backend Services* to be topologically and geographically dispersed from the program and each other.

The patterns in this chapter for making an application cloud native can be applied to any of these architectures to make the applications embodying the architectures run well on the cloud. Nowadays, most *Cloud Applications* are built using the Microservices Architecture (Chapter 4) and Event-Driven Architecture (Chapter 6) styles, which we'll discuss in the next two chapters.

Later in Cloud-Native Storage (Chapter 7), we'll explore how a Cloud-Native Application can persist data that is distributed and replicated just like the application. We'll also discuss Cloud Application Clients (Chapter 8) that enable users and other applications to interact with the application hosted in the cloud.

CHAPTER 4

Microservices Architecture

While a *Cloud-Native Architecture* structures an application to incorporate cloud computing practices, a Microservices Architecture refines that further to modularize the application and distribute the cloud-native modules across the cloud infrastructure.

Back in the day, all applications were monolithic applications. Developers didn't need to specify that what they were producing were monoliths; they were just applications. Then with the advent of client/server computing, developers started designing applications with Distributed Architecture (38), structuring a single application as coordinated parts that could run on different computers. Service-oriented architecture (SOA) evolved to structure the distributed parts as services that could invoke one another to perform functionality. This is when monolithic architecture became one of multiple possibilities: an application could be a monolith or distributed.

With the advent of cloud computing, developers started creating Cloud-Native Applications (Chapter 3). Likewise, developers designed the services in service-oriented architecture to run on the cloud by incorporating Cloud-Native Architecture (58) into services, evolving services into miniature applications that became known as microservices.

Introduction to Microservices Architecture

This chapter explains how to build applications that work the way cloud does: composed of a constellation of small components that can be replicated easily and distributed across infrastructure. Microservices Architecture accomplishes this by combining *Distributed Architecture* with *Cloud-Native Architecture*. Each *Microservice* is a component in the *Distributed Architecture* that is not only a service but a cloud-native service, one designed to perform a capability in the application's business domain.

These patterns assume a basic understanding of microservices, so let's review that first. We'll take a look at how the industry defines a microservice, how a *Microservices Architecture* differs from a monolith, and how it relates to *Cloud-Native Architecture*. We'll then introduce the patterns and how they fit together to architect and design a microservices application.

With this background on what microservices are, we'll then present patterns for designing an application with a *Microservices Architecture*, starting with the root pattern for this chapter, Microservice (119).

Microservices

An application with a *Microservices Architecture* is one composed of *Microservices*.

In "What are Microservices?" (*https://oreil.ly/l8H0u*), Amazon AWS provides this definition:

> Microservices are an architectural and organizational approach to software development where software is composed of small independent services that communicate over well-defined APIs. These services are owned by small, self-contained teams.

In *Building Microservices* (2015), Sam Newman defines a microservice as follows:

> An independently deployable service that communicates with other microservices via one or more communication protocols.

What is a microservices architecture? In *Microservices Patterns* (2018), Chris Richardson defines microservices architecture this way:

> An architectural style that structures an application as a collection of microservices that are:

- Highly maintainable and testable
- Loosely coupled
- Independently deployable
- Organized around business capabilities
- Owned by a small team

From the outside, an application with a *Microservices Architecture* looks like any other server application, presumably one with a monolithic architecture. Application Clients (Chapter 8) running in web browsers and mobile devices interface with the application, typically over the internet via REST APIs that should define the services that the server can perform for the clients. The clients cannot tell whether the server application is a monolith or composed of microservices. The server application could even start out as a monolith and later be refactored into microservices (see Refactor the Monolith (484)) while preserving the services' interfaces and without ever changing the clients.

Microservices Architecture Versus Monolithic Architecture

The difference between the microservices and monolithic architectures is in how the server application works. A monolithic application is developed by a single large team, built and deployed as a unit, scales vertically in a single process or horizontally by duplicating the entire application, and fails as a unit. A *Microservices* application is composed of modules for individual business capabilities with their own *Service APIs*. It differs from traditional services approaches in that each module is developed by a separate small team working independently from the others, able to build, deploy, and scale those modules independently.

An application with a *Microservices Architecture* has significant advantages over one with a monolithic architecture. A *Microservices* application scales more efficiently and isolates failures better. *Microservices* help users avoid experiencing outages—both because microservices are deployed redundantly and because new versions can more easily replace old ones with zero downtime. A primary reason to adopt the Microservices Architecture is to accelerate the delivery of large, complex applications by many small, independent teams. Smaller development teams mean that each team member only has to coordinate with the other members of their team, not with everyone else in the department. This way, they can spend less time in meetings and more time writing code. The teams can iterate more rapidly, improving agile development and continuous delivery, because they can test and deploy their microservice when it is ready without having to wait for the rest of the department to be ready to build and deploy the entire monolith.

The *Microservices Architecture* also has disadvantages—they are typically outweighed by the advantages, but they cannot be ignored. These disadvantages are generally related to complexity: microservices applications, like distributed applications before them, are more complicated than monolithic ones. More microservices means more service interfaces, which require time to design and coordination between otherwise independent teams that implement and use a microservice. Each team needs to create and run its own build pipeline to deploy its microservice independently. Distributed transactions are more complex than simple ones. More components makes end-to-end testing more difficult. The operations team needs to monitor and manage lots of little microservices instead of one big monolith, aggregating their logs and measuring individual resource consumption. Traceability becomes more complex, as a request is passed from one microservice to another and performed in stages. On the other hand, each service interface is a convenient point for testing and monitoring that can actually help visualize what is working and pinpoint where problems are occurring.

Each microservice is essentially a small application. Lots of small applications are more complicated than one big application, but each small application is simpler and works better so that the whole works better as well.

Microservices and Cloud-Native Architecture

Microservices do not have to run on a cloud platform, but regardless of their deployment platform, Microservices Architecture is an extension of Cloud-Native Architecture (58). Just like a cloud-native application, microservices are Stateless (80) with Service APIs (70). Microservices need to be able to deploy easily in multiple environments with limited dependencies on the environment, so they encapsulate their program as an Application Package (62) with an External Configuration (97). Stateless packages are easier to make into Replicable Applications (88). And microservices access specialized, reusable functionality as separate Backend Services (106).

Although not required, a cloud environment makes lots of small microservices much easier to manage. Multiple microservices can more easily share a pool of capacity, and the environment can more easily provision capacity for each individual microservice as needed. Capacity can also be made available more easily for a new version of a microservice to replace an old one without causing an outage. The environment provides load balancers that enable clients to access a pool of microservice replicas as though they are a single instance that is both highly reliable and highly scalable. Microservices can get their *Backend Services* from the cloud platform's service catalog.

Architecting Microservices Applications

This chapter defines a collection of seven patterns that explain how to architect and design applications with a Microservices Architecture. Figure 4-1 shows the patterns and their relationships.

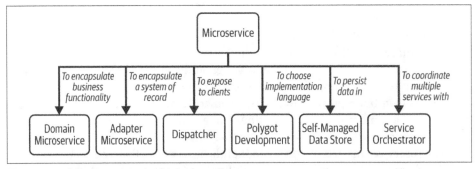

Figure 4-1. Microservices Architecture patterns

An application with a Microservices Architecture is composed of multiple Microservices (119) that each perform an independent business capability and make it available via a *Service API*. We classify microservices into four different types:

- Domain Microservices (130) that implement functionality from a business domain as a complete capability with a *Service API* and manage the data for that capability
- Adapter Microservices (135) that access existing external functionality and give it a *Service API*, thereby encapsulating the rest of the application's dependencies on the external functionality
- Service Orchestrators (160) that implement complex functionality by combining the functionality of multiple simpler microservices into one that's more complex, providing a means to perform transactions in a cloud environment
- Dispatchers (140) that provide clients with a single *Service API* to access the business functionality distributed across multiple microservices

Microservices are language-neutral and support Polyglot Development (146), enabling each one to potentially be implemented in a different computer language. To maintain their independence even at the data layer, each microservice manages its own persistent data in a Self-Managed Data Store (154).

This introduction has covered several topics that are helpful to be familiar with to understand the patterns in this chapter. We've talked about what a microservice is, how it brings together *Distributed Architecture* with *Cloud-Native Architecture* and forms the basis of implementing a Microservices Architecture. Microservices do not require a cloud platform, but microservices work the way the cloud does, and the cloud makes microservices easier to manage.

With this background in mind, let's discuss patterns for how to architect and design applications with a Microservices Architecture. We'll start with the root pattern for this chapter, Microservice (119).

Microservice

You are designing a server-side, multiuser application with a Cloud-Native Architecture (58). The application may be deployed to run in either the cloud or traditional IT. Typically, you would architect an application as a single monolithic program.

How do you architect an application as a set of interconnected modules that can be developed independently?

The code a developer writes has two audiences: the computer that will run it and the other developers who will maintain it. When computers were new, developers focused on making the program as efficient as possible so that it would run on a machine with limited memory and CPU. When networking was new, bandwidth was limited, so even powerful programs needed to limit the amount of data they sent across the network.

Over time, computers became available with greater capacity at much lower prices, a pattern known as Moore's Law (*https://oreil.ly/-vhzO*). The computer's and network's capacity were no longer the main limitation on computer software. Of the two audiences, the developers were the constraint limiting computer software.

As computers became more powerful, the priority became to make developers more productive. Higher-level computer languages evolved whose compiled code might be less efficient than hand-crafted assembler, but that enabled developers to program in abstractions with which they could describe functionality more easily. That helped developers write more functionality faster with less code that was easier to maintain. But applications are still a Big Ball of Mud (22) whose functionalities were difficult to maintain. Multiple developers working on the same application tended to break one another's changes unless they coordinated very carefully. Even with higher-level languages, the application's (lack of) architecture lowered the developers' productivity.

Developing ever more complex applications requires ever greater amounts of code written by larger numbers of developers. Even with higher-level computer languages, to make developers more productive, multiple developers need to be able to work independently on different parts of the application with minimal coordination, and their efforts to integrate together smoothly into a single merged application that works properly.

An evolutionary step to make developers more productive and enable more complex applications is to make an application a Modular Monolith (29) with a modular architecture. A modular architecture does little to benefit the computer it runs on because the application is still a monolith, but dividing code into modules should enable developers to maintain modules separately and therefore work independently. This works somewhat, but dependencies between modules still mean that changes by one developer will mess up another developer's work in another module, so the developers still have to coordinate. Distributed Architecture (38) enables running modules on separate computers, but now modules are even more complex because of remote interfaces, and distributed modules still cannot be developed independently. Dependencies between modules, even districted ones, still decrease developer productivity.

One popular modular architecture is the four-layer architecture that divides a traditional IT application into four stacked horizontal layers: view, application model, domain model, and persistence (see Figure 4-2).

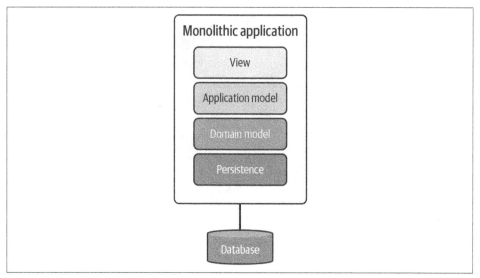

Figure 4-2. Four-layer application architecture

Although the four-layer architecture separates the concerns into layers, the layers are still developed and deployed as a monolith. The architecture can be distributed by making the layers into tiers deployed on separate computers—making the architecture somewhat client/server. Either way, the layers or tiers are still developed by a coordinated team and deployed as a set. Each layer or tier must be designed to depend on others, and if one layer stops working, the entire application stops working. The developers of each layer must coordinate with those developing others, limiting developer productivity.

Another popular modular architecture is the service-oriented architecture (SOA) that wrappers legacy systems as services with Service APIs (70) that can then be orchestrated to form higher-capability services (see Figure 4-3).

Each SOA service and orchestration is a module, and they can be distributed. The services are supposed to align with the business and abstract business functionality such that a business analyst would recognize the *Service APIs*, making services reusable and allowing for multiple implementations of the same *Service API* by different service providers. In reality, each service's API often does little to abstract the existing functionality of the existing system it wrappers. The orchestration and other service clients are written for services aligned with the business, so an increasingly complex enterprise service bus (ESB) is required between the services and their consumers to make them work together. This SOA approach increases developer productivity by making existing systems-of-record (SORs) easier to integrate into newer systems-of-engagement (SoEs), but it does little to enable developers to work independently because of the dependencies between the services and within the ESB.

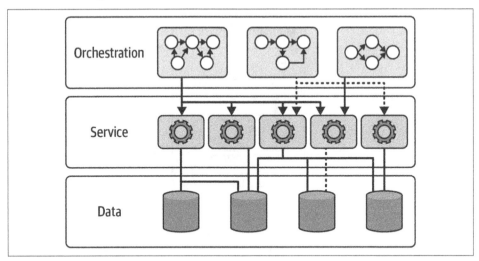

Figure 4-3. SOA stack architecture

Developers need an approach that treats modules as first-class objects, not just as sections in a code base or even as services that can be reused individually, but as units that can be developed, built, and executed fairly independently of one another. We need a way for development teams to create modules that can be developed independently.

Therefore,

Architect the application as a set of *Microservices*. Each *Microservice* is an independent business capability with its own data, developed by a separate team, and deployed in a separate process. The *Microservices* work together to provide the application's full set of business functionality.

A *Microservice* exposes its functionality as a *Service API*, implements its functionality statelessly, and persists its state in a data store, as shown in Figure 4-4.

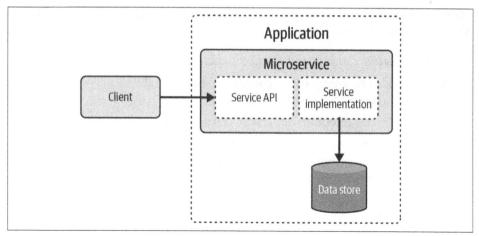

Figure 4-4. Microservice

Microservices implement the domain-specific logic of a complete application. There are multiple kinds of *Microservices*, such as *Dispatchers, Domain Microservices*, and *Adapter Microservices*. Figure 4-5 shows a complete application with these three types of *Microservices*.

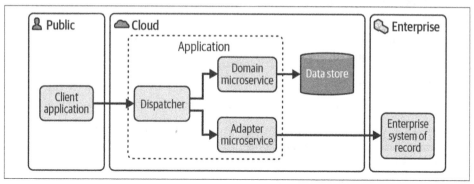

Figure 4-5. Microservices application

Each *Microservice* is implemented with a Cloud-Native Architecture (58), which makes it stateless and replicable with a *Service API* and an implementation that delegates to *Backend Services*.

Once James Lewis and Martin Fowler popularized the concept in "Microservices" (*https://oreil.ly/kliOG*) in 2014 and Sam Newman expanded upon it in *Building Microservices* (2015), the *Microservices* approach has become a de facto standard for developing large-scale business applications.

Microservices make modularity practical and solve the challenges of monolithic and distributed applications:

- Each *Microservice* implements a single domain capability.
- *Microservices* are composable, combining their capabilities to implement an application's complex domain functionality.
- *Microservices* communicate via *Service APIs* and events.
- Each *Microservice* has an interface that defines the domain tasks the *Microservice* performs, which clients use to interact with *Microservices* and which *Microservices* use to interact with one another.
- Each *Microservice* can be developed by a separate team, enabling teams to work independently.
- Each team develops a *Microservice* as a separate code base, ensuring modularity.
- Each code base can be built and deployed separately, enabling each team to work at its own pace.
- The *Microservices* in an application can all run on a single computer or distributed across multiple computers.
- Each *Microservice* runs in its own process that can scale and fail independently of other *Microservices.*
- Each *Microservice* can own and manage its own data, keeping it separate from the data used by other *Microservices.*

The Microservices Architecture has become so popular precisely because the combination of these points and the benefits obtained from following them is so powerful.

Figure 4-6 shows the structure of a more complete *Microservices* application. It shows four *Domain Microservices* that implement domain logic, each with its own data store, and *Dispatchers* for three different types of clients: a web application, a mobile app, and the API for a CLI or partner application developed independently.

At its simplest, a Microservices Architecture has four layers:

Clients
These enable users and other applications to interact with the *Microservices* application. They are applications separate from the *Microservices* application that typically run outside of the cloud. Typical client types include web clients that run in a web browser, mobile clients that run on mobile devices, and thick-client tools such as CLIs and other applications that interface with the *Microservices* application.

Dispatchers

These are *Microservices* that run on the server as part of the *Microservices* application and act as interfaces between the clients and the rest of the application. Each client type—such as web clients, mobile clients, and thick clients—has its own customized *Dispatcher* on the server.

Domain services

These are the heart of the *Microservices* application, implementing functional requirements as business entities with business logic. Although shown as a single layer for simplicity, the domain layer is often a hierarchy and web of interconnected services.

Domain state

These are databases, storage, automation engines, and legacy systems that persist the state for domain services and help perform their functionality.

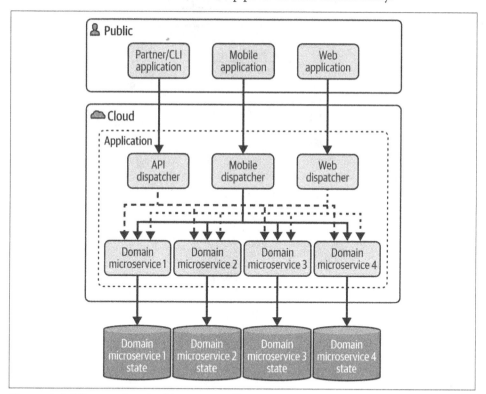

Figure 4-6. Microservices Architecture application

Figure 4-7 shows how the Microservices Architecture actually incorporates the layers from the four-layer architecture that was shown in Figure 4-2.

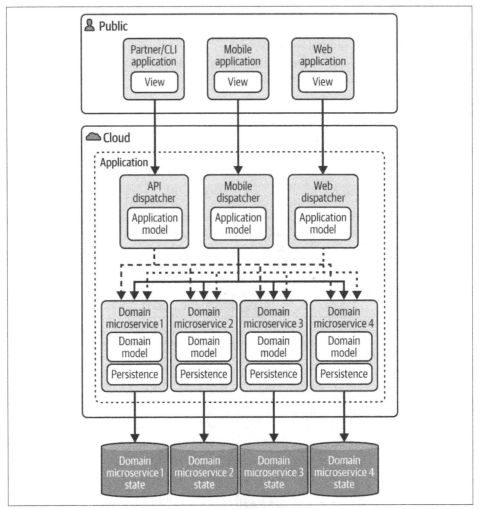

Figure 4-7. Four layers in Microservices Architecture

Rather than each layer being global to the entire application, each *Microservice* contains its own layers:

- Each client is an individual view.
- Each *Dispatcher* contains the application model for its individual client.
- Each *Domain Microservice* contains the domain model for its functional requirements, as well as the persistence logic for accessing its domain state.

The four-layer architecture is alive and well within the Microservices Architecture, but like *Microservices* themselves, the four layers are broken into smaller modules.

Microservices can be thought of as "service orientation done right" (*https://oreil.ly/ Wvx0s*). Whereas services in an SOA focus on wrapping existing systems, each *Microservice* focuses on modeling a complete domain capability. A Microservice and its clients are designed with a common *Service API* so that no ESB is needed to integrate them.

By incorporating a single, complete set of domain functionality within a *Service API*, packaged to be deployed separately, *Microservices* more than any previous architecture finally achieve the nirvana of distributed code modules that developers can create and maintain independently.

The quickest, easiest way to develop functionality is to write a whole bunch of code structured as a *Big Ball of Mud*. Developing and following the architecture for a *Modular Monolith* takes more effort, a *Distributed Architecture* takes even more effort, and a Microservices Architecture takes more effort still. The benefit of this effort is increased developer productivity and runtime efficiency, but it requires an initial and ongoing investment.

Develop a Microservices Architecture by following several best practices:

- Split an application's domain functions into individual Domain Microservices (130), each a domain capability. This designs *Microservices* that model a business domain and enables each to be developed by a separate, small team.

- Existing external or internal components may implement functionality needed in the application but may not implement a good *Microservice* interface. Use an Adapter Microservice (135) to incorporate an existing component into a Microservices Architecture.

- Application clients need the functionality in a network of *Microservices* but need a single connection point. Add a Dispatcher (140) that implements the API the client expects by delegating to the *Microservices* on the backend.

- Each development team will develop their *Microservice* as an Application Package (62). With many languages to choose from, separate teams may want to use different languages. Polyglot Development (146) enables each team to implement their *Microservice* using their language or technology of choice.

- Each stateless *Microservice* persists its state in its own Self-Managed Data Store (154).

- A Service Orchestrator (160) combines the functionality in multiple *Microservices* into a unified higher-level *Microservice*.

It is often difficult to determine how to model a complex domain of functionality as a collaborating set of *Microservices*. Microservice Design (Chapter 5) explains a process for discovering and scoping individual *Microservices* within a domain.

Microservices can be called explicitly via their *Service APIs*, and they can also interact in an Event-Driven Architecture (Chapter 6) that choreographs the interactions between *Microservices* rather than explicitly orchestrating the interactions.

Example

As an example of a Microservices Architecture, let's consider how an airline would architect their application. Then let's review Netflix's transition to the cloud and *Microservices*.

Airline application

An airline's application built with a Microservices Architecture has components specific to its functionality, as shown in Figure 4-8.

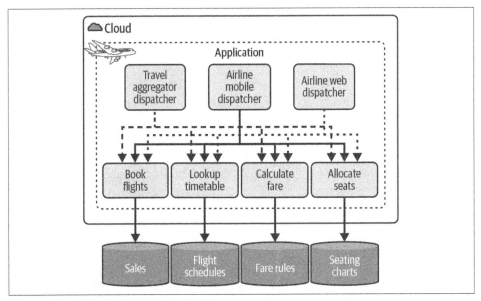

Figure 4-8. Airline Microservices Architecture

This application architecture is the standard Microservices Architecture, customized for the airline. The application includes the following:

Dispatchers
   The application supports three client types: the airline's website, its mobile app, and an API for other travel websites and apps.

Domain services

It models its business functionality as four domain services: booking flights, performing lookups in timetables, calculating fares, and allocating seats.

Domain state

Each service has its own persistence, and calculating fares uses a rules engine rather than a database.

In a similar fashion, any domain functionality can be modeled as a Microservices Architecture.

Netflix

One of the earliest and most vocal success stories of applying a Microservices Architecture has been Netflix, the video DVD and streaming company. The story of Netflix's transformation to the cloud is detailed in the following interviews and presentations:

- "Adrian Cockcroft on Architecture for the Cloud" (*https://oreil.ly/aYEbe*) and "Migrating to Cloud Native with Microservices" (*https://oreil.ly/D2Q7g*) by Adrian Cockcroft, Director of Architecture for the Cloud Systems team at Netflix

- "How Netflix Leverages Multiple Regions to Increase Availability: An Active-Active Case Study" (*https://oreil.ly/9v_Gr*) and "Microservices at Netflix Scale: Principles, Tradeoffs & Lessons Learned" (*https://oreil.ly/ozXnR*) by Ruslan Meshenberg, Director of Platform Engineering at Netflix

- "Completing the Netflix Cloud Migration" (*https://oreil.ly/IX4cF*)

When Netflix started moving to the cloud—specifically Amazon Web Services (AWS)—in 2009, they first moved non-customer-facing tasks like batch jobs for encoding movies and storing logging data because it gave them much greater data center capacity than they had on-premises. By early 2010, Netflix foresaw that they needed to move all of their IT operations to the cloud, including the customer-facing functions, because the business was growing so fast that Netflix would run out of on premises capacity by the end of 2010. Even with this move, many existing SoRs would remain on premises for the time being because they weren't growing as rapidly and would be difficult to move.

When Netflix moved their software from traditional IT to the cloud, they couldn't just lift and shift the existing systems as is; they had to rearchitect the software. A major portion of that effort was transforming a single giant monolithic Java WAR application into *Microservices*. The transition took seven years from 2009 to 2016, and as a result Netflix runs on *Microservices*. Netflix's development methodology evolved from a single release plan were all developers created a single monolithic application to multiple release plans for parts of the application so that they could be developed and deployed independently. This required structuring functionality as fine-grained services with REST interfaces, where each small group of developers worked on only one service. These services always ran as at least three replicas in three different availability zones so that the application kept running even when a zone went down. Each service had its own database, which meant that the database couldn't manage transactions across multiple sets of data because the data wasn't in the same database, which forces the application-level code to handle transactions, joins, and consistency. The billing service was the last one transitioned to the cloud and *Microservices* because it is stateful, transactional, and has to work properly.

To manage all of this, Netflix developed a suite of utilities to augment the AWS platform's capabilities, especially its EC2 virtual machine service, and manage these running application services. Netflix started releasing these utilities in 2012 as the Netflix Open Source Software Center (Netflix OSS) (*https://oreil.ly/MOPuM*). The software center included utilities like Eureka for service discovery, the Zuul gateway service, and Ribbon for client-side load balancing. When Kubernetes was released for container orchestration, it incorporated many Netflix OSS capabilities, such as service discovery, managed ingress, and server-side load balancing. The Netflix OSS utilities eventually became known as a service mesh and lead to infrastructure layer libraries like Istio, Consul, Kuma, Open Service Mesh (OSM), and AWS App Mesh.

Domain Microservice

(aka Decompose by Business Capability (*Microservices Patterns*, 2018))

You are architecting a new application using Microservices (119) or refactoring an existing application into *Microservices*. Users have functional requirements for an application, expecting it to provide certain business functionality. Despite the hype associated with the Microservices Architecture, it's not entirely clear from the basic *Microservices* principles exactly what the *Microservices* should do.

How should a set of *Microservices* in an architecture provide the business functionality for an application?

SOA makes traditional IT applications more modular by dividing an application into services, each of which defines a Service API (70) between the service provider and service consumer. SOA often derived services by wrapping existing systems to give them service interfaces. This resulted in services that were often just a thin veneer over the existing system, with a service interface that did little to abstract the existing system's implementation. The service was not designed to implement particular business capabilities or user requirements but rather to expose whatever capability the existing system already provided. This process created SOA services that varied greatly in level of abstraction, granularity, and often didn't even agree on the data formats being exchanged. These mismatches often required an ESB to make service consumers and providers fit together. Even when multiple services provide the same functionality, their interfaces might differ enough that consumers require an ESB to use them interchangeably.

An application with a Microservices Architecture should be composed of *Microservices* that represent individual business capabilities that align with how the business actually works, regardless of the capabilities implemented by existing systems. They should be designed to work together with compatible APIs and data models so that they don't require an ESB for integration.

When designing services from scratch, it is not necessarily obvious what the individual business capabilities are. An application can be designed as a few course-grained *Microservices* or many fine-grained *Microservices*. This is easier to determine when wrapping existing systems: a good start is to design a *Microservice* for each existing system (even if that doesn't model the domain as an individual business capability). When designing *Microservices* from scratch, how big is too big or too small?

It's not enough to know what a *Microservice* is. A team also needs to figure out how to model an application and its business domain as a set of *Microservices*.

Therefore,

Develop each business capability as a *Domain Microservice* that implements a *Service API* for that capability and encapsulates all the business functionality that implements the capability.

A *Domain Microservice* encapsulates a single business capability. It implements the business functionality for that capability and, like any *Microservice*, exposes it as a *Service API*. If the business functionality has state, the *Microservice* persists it in one or more data stores. Figure 4-9 shows the structure.

Build an entire application by composing together all of its individual business capabilities, each implemented as a *Domain Microservice*. *Domain Microservices* form the business functionality layer in a Microservices Architecture.

Figure 4-10 shows a complete application with the *Domain Microservices* highlighted. All of the application's business functionality is divided into this set of *Domain Microservices*.

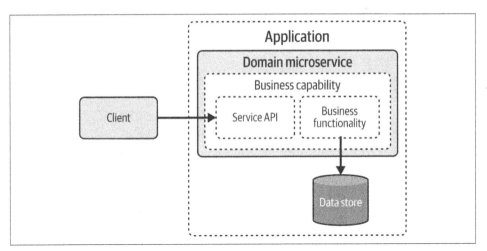

Figure 4-9. Domain Microservice

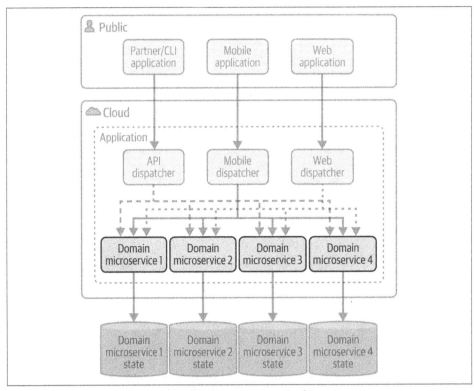

Figure 4-10. Domain Microservices in Microservices Architecture

The scope of a *Domain Microservice* is defined by the business transactions it performs and the data they use. Here are some guidelines for deciding how broad a *Domain Microservice* should be:

Manages a business transaction and its data
> Scope a *Microservice's* responsibilities broadly enough that it can perform entire business transactions and do so using only the data that it manages. When a business transaction is split across multiple *Microservices*, the design risks that one *Microservice* might succeed while another fails, resulting in a business transactions where the "transaction" is performed but only partially. If both *Microservices* manage their own data, one database might get updated while another does not, resulting in inconsistent data. Avoid dependency chaining—where one *Microservice* calls another that calls another—to perform a business transaction. If two parts of a business transaction are performed by two different *Microservices*, especially a transaction that updates data, consider merging the *Microservices* into a larger one. There are, however, situations where this is not possible. Eventual consistency, compensating transaction, or other techniques might need to be part of the solution in these cases.

Avoid tightly coupled microservices
> Scope a *Microservice's* responsibilities broadly enough that it can perform its functionality without having to be tightly coupled to other *Microservices*. For example, if one *Microservice* produces the data that another *Microservice* processes, a client will always have to use them together. Encapsulate both functions in a single *Microservice* that produces the data and also processes it, simplifying the *Service API* and the client.

Dividing business functionality into a set of individual business capabilities will make it easier to maintain and reuse.

Like building blocks, *Domain Microservices* that perform individual business capabilities can easily be composed into complex applications.

Designing *Domain Microservices* around business capabilities is rather difficult when the individual business capabilities are difficult to identify. Fundamentally, designing the functionality in *Domain Microservices* is much like designing the domain objects in a **Domain Model** (*Patterns of Enterprise Application Architecture*, 2002) in object-oriented programming.

Model Around the Domain (183) explains how to design *Domain Microservices* by applying domain-driven design (DDD) techniques and Event Storming (189). How a business operates can be assessed both statically and dynamically. The static view models the structure of a business domain as a set of Aggregates (211) augmented with Domain Services (222). The dynamic view models the interactions within a business domain, which can be discovered through *Event Storming* and captured as Domain Events (193).

While a Microservices Architecture is comprised primarily of *Domain Microservices* that are designed from scratch and implement their own behavior, the architecture can also use Adapter Microservices (135) to incorporate existing systems.

To compose a complex business capability from multiple *Domain Microservices*, implement it as a Service Orchestrator (160).

Since each *Domain Microservice* runs in its own process, Polyglot Development (146) enables developers to implement each *Domain Microservice* in a different language or technology.

Each *Domain Microservice* that has state should persist it in one or more Self-Managed Data Stores (154).

Building a single new *Domain Microservice* is a great way to introduce a team to how to Start Small (492) by starting with *Microservices*. It is often best to do this with a new business area rather than trying to start off the bat with refactoring a monolith. There is a lot of learning that a team needs to do to become productive with *Microservice* development, and starting with a simple, green-field *Domain Microservice* is often the best way to do that.

Example

As an example, let's return to the airline application from the *Microservice* (119) pattern, shown again in Figure 4-11.

This application architecture divides the airline's business functionality into four *Domain Microservices*:

Book flights
Overall functionality enabling the user to purchase an airline ticket.

Lookup timetable
Functionality to find the flights available between the desired cities on specified dates.

Calculate fare
Functionality to determine how much to charge for the selected flight. It doesn't persist state in a data store; it delegates to a rules engine.

Allocate seats
Functionality to either assign a seat to the passenger or enable the passenger to select a seat.

Domain Microservices like these can implement all of the business functionality for an airline.

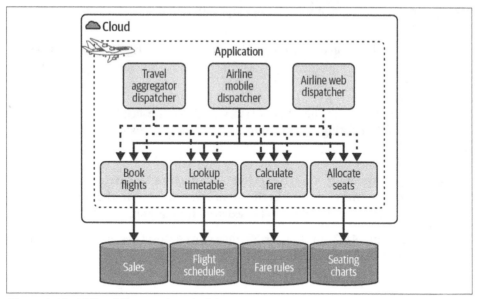

Figure 4-11. Airline Microservices Architecture

Adapter Microservice

You are architecting a new application using Microservices (119) or refactoring an existing application into *Microservices*. The application needs to incorporate existing sources of functionality.

How can the application take advantage of existing functionality without abandoning the *Microservices* approach?

The ideal way to incorporate existing functionality into a Microservices Architecture is to reimplement the existing code as *Microservices*, for example by Strangling the Monolith (514). Then the existing functionality will be reimplemented to be cloud native, to run well in the cloud, and will run better and be easier to maintain as *Microservices*. However, this approach assumes that the current development team controls the code for the existing functionality and has the time and expertise to modernize it.

There are several reasons why an existing system may need to be reused as is without modifying it:

- The existing functionality may be hosted by a third party that develops and maintains it, such as a software-as-a-service (SaaS) web service.

- The existing functionality is the only API that can access specific enterprise data sources.
- The existing functionality is a legacy application that is too difficult to modify or replace.
- The existing functionality is a legacy application that a future phase will eventually replace by reimplementing it as *Microservices*, but for now it needs to be reused as is.

The new application with the Microservices Architecture needs to incorporate the functionality of the existing system without modifying the existing code.

Therefore,

Add an existing system to a Microservices Architecture by developing an *Adapter Microservice* with a *Service API* like the other *Microservices* in the application and an implementation that delegates to the existing functionality.

As shown in Figure 4-12, an *Adapter Microservice* encapsulates an existing, external system of record (SoR) as a capability.

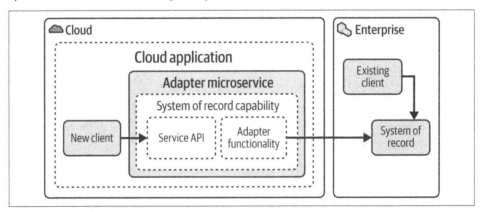

Figure 4-12. Adapter Microservice

The SoR capability in the *Microservice* is like a business capability that is limited to the behavior in the SoR. The *Microservice* implements adapter functionality for accessing the SoR remotely. Like any *Microservice*, an *Adapter Microservice* exposes its functionality as a Service API (70), yet this API is limited by the SoR's existing interface. New clients, such as other *Microservices* in the new application, use the *Adapter Microservice's Service API*, while existing clients can continue to use the SoR's interface directly as is.

An *Adapter Microservice* converts the interface of an existing SoR much like an adapter object. In object-oriented programming, sometimes an existing object has one interface but an existing client expects a different interface. Rather than modify either of the existing sets of code, a developer can employ the **Adapter** pattern (*Design Patterns*, 1994) converting the interface that an existing object has into the interface that a client expects. The *Microservice* also acts as a **Proxy** (*Design Patterns*, 1994), providing local access within the Microservices Architecture to the remote SoR outside of the architecture.

An *Adapter Microservice* works similarly to an endpoint in an ESB that converts one service's interface into another. The SOA approach for incorporating existing functionality is to implement an ESB that converts the APIs the service consumers wish the functionality had into the interfaces the functionality actually has. The ESB can also transform the existing functionality's data models into ones that work better for the consumer. ESBs are often implemented using products like IBM App Connect Enterprise (*https://oreil.ly/KQdUM*) (ACE), Mule ESB (*https://oreil.ly/fjd-r*) from MuleSoft, or open source solutions like Apache Camel (*https://oreil.ly/TSy1t*).

Whereas a Domain Microservice (130) is an evolution of an SOA service that models a complete business capability, the implementation of an *Adapter Microservice* is more like that of a traditional SOA service that attempts to wrap a service interface around an existing SoR:

- The service implements little to no domain logic; it reuses domain logic already implemented in the SoR. If additional domain logic is needed, it should be implemented in *Domain Microservices* that use an *Adapter Microservice* to access the external SoR through a well-designed service interface.

- The service's functionality is based on the SoR's functionality. The SoR's scope of functionality and how it enables functionality to be accessed dictates how the service and the service's API will work.

- The service predominately contains integration logic, implemented as adapter functionality focused on how to connect to the SoR over the network and how to work with the SoR's interface, functionality that SOAs often delegate to an ESB. The adapter functionality may include data validation logic.

Even if the existing SoR already has a perfectly good *Service API*, such as a well-designed SaaS web service, incorporating an *Adapter Microservice* improves the maintainability of the Microservices Architecture:

- The adapter isolates the application from the external SoR's existing API, protecting the application when the API provider changes the API or discontinues support for it.

- The adapter can transform the external SoR's data model into data formats that better fit the Microservices Architecture. For example, if the external SoR's data format is a COBOL copybook or binary, the adapter should transform the data into a more modern format like JSON or XML.

- One or more *Adapter Microservices* can perform significant API translation. The adapter can add the existing SoR's functionality into the Microservices Architecture by reusing only a subset of the existing functionality, or reusing that functionality by splitting it into multiple *Microservices* that each reuse a subset, or combining the functionality from multiple SoRs into a single *Microservice*.

- The existing system's quality of service (QoS) model may not meet the QoS needs of the *Microservices*. For example, the adapter can improve performance using caching or improve the reliability of unreliable functionality by adding retry behavior.

An *Adapter Microservice* can be a temporary step, reusing an existing SoR until it can be replaced. The existing SoR can be reimplemented as a *Domain Microservice* with the same *Service API* as the adapter so that it can replace the adapter. If the existing SoR is better modeled as multiple *Domain Microservices*, coordinate them with a *Service Orchestrator* that implements the same *Service API* as the adapter so that the orchestrator can replace the adapter.

If the existing SoR provides callbacks to its clients, the *Adapter Microservice* can handle those callbacks and even expose corresponding callbacks to its clients as part of its *Service API*.

Some ESB products have evolved to support *Microservices*, including IBM App Connect Enterprise (ACE) and Camel. This way, a Microservices Architecture can use an existing ESB. Furthermore, the architecture can replace the ESB by splitting apart the ESB into independent APIs and implementing each API as an *Adapter Microservice*.

Adapter Microservices enable a Microservices Architecture to incorporate existing SoRs as *Microservices* without changing the SoRs.

However, the *Adapter Microservice's* functionality is constrained by the existing SoR's functionality. While the adapter makes the SoR more reusable, the SoR is no more scalable than it ever was, and it continues to be a single point of failure in an otherwise highly available architecture. An SoR with an interface that exposes its implementation leads to a *Microservice* whose API may lack the abstraction of a service interface.

Having developed an *Adapter Microservice*, an application will also need *Domain Microservices* and Service Orchestrators (160) that reuse the adapter's functionality.

The SoR that an *Adapter Microservice* integrates is typically a monolith with a Modular Monolith (29) architecture or even a Big Ball of Mud (22) lack of architecture.

Since each *Adapter Microservice* runs in its own process, Polyglot Development (146) enables developers to implement each *Adapter Microservice* class in a different language or technology.

Whereas an *Adapter Microservice* adapts an existing external system, a Dispatcher (140) adapts multiple *Microservices* into a single Public API (38) expected by an external client.

Example

As an example, let's return to the ecommerce application from the Cloud Application (6) pattern, shown again in Figure 4-13.

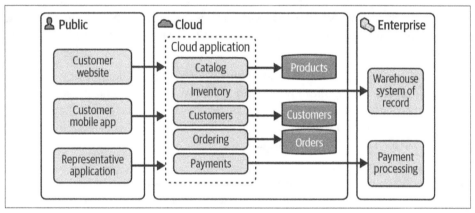

Figure 4-13. Ecommerce application with Adapter Microservices

This application is composed of five *Microservices*. Three of them are *Domain Microservices*: Catalog, Customers, and Ordering. They implement ecommerce business functionality and persist their data in data stores.

The other two, Inventory and Payments, are *Adapter Microservices*. They wrapper existing SoRs, Warehouse System of Record and Payment Processing, respectively. They don't implement business functionality like the *Domain Microservices* do; they delegate to the SoRs for the business functionality the SoRs already implement. The SoRs may have fairly ugly interfaces that are difficult to reuse—they may even require screen scraping!—and antiquated data formats, but the *Adapter Microservices* have clean *Service APIs* that fit easily into the rest of the Microservices Architecture. The adapters may improve on the SoR's nonfunctional quality of service, such as adding security features like enforcing authorization and encrypting data.

The architecture may eventually replace one of the SoRs by modernizing its functionality as *Microservices*, which would also replace the corresponding *Adapter Microservice*. The adapter can be replaced by a single *Domain Microservice* with the same API, or by a set of *Domain Microservices* coordinated by a *Service Orchestrator* with the same API.

Dispatcher

(aka Backend for Frontend (*Building Microservices*, 2015), API Gateway (*Microservices Patterns*, 2018), Aggregator)

You are architecting a new application using Microservices (119) or refactoring an existing application into *Microservices*. You notice a mismatch between the Domain Microservices (130) that implement the business functionality and client GUIs that enable people to use the functionality.

How can a client access a *Microservices* application through a channel-specific service interface when the business functionality is spread across an evolving set of domain-specific APIs?

When the server application is a monolith running in traditional IT, it's easy for a client to connect. The application is a single process running statically, so the client connects through a single endpoint or set of endpoints that never changes. The application has just one client for all of the users, or different clients work the same so that they can all use the same endpoint.

Cloud-native applications, especially *Microservices* applications, are more complex to connect to. Cloud applications (6) are much more dynamic, with components replicated horizontally, running in IP addresses assigned dynamically. In a Microservices Architecture, not only is each *Microservice* replicated independently (see Replicable Application (88)), but multiple *Microservices* break one set of business functionality into multiple Service APIs (70). Meanwhile, the easiest way for a client to interface with a server is still through a single API, not multiple *Microservices'* APIs.

An application's set of *Microservices* and their APIs change over time as the application evolves. A single *Microservice* might be refactored into two, and two *Microservices* that are highly dependent on each other might be merged into one. Once a *Microservice* has been implemented, although ideally its API shouldn't change because then its clients have to change as well, realistically an API may evolve over time as its responsibilities change.

All of this evolution in the *Microservices* on the server cause havoc for the clients. When the *Microservices* APIs change, the clients must be reimplemented to use the new APIs. Deploying new versions of *Microservices*, although complex, is relatively easy compared to updating all of the devices that have the clients installed. It would be much easier if the clients didn't have to change just because the set of *Microservices* and their APIs changed.

Different types of clients—web browsers, mobile apps, CLIs—may need different APIs even when they offer the same business functionality. Likewise, clients for use by an enterprise's employees may require different APIs from the clients for the enterprise's customers because the client applications for these different types of users offer access to different functionality. Yet all of these different clients with their differing API needs should not duplicate business functionality. These clients should still access the same set of *Microservices* so that they all consistently offer the same business functionality.

We need a way for various types of clients to have easy, stable access to a dynamic and evolving set of microservices on the server.

Therefore,

Build a *Dispatcher* (aka a Backend for Frontend, or BFF) that provides a unified API for clients to use the functionality in multiple *Microservices*. Implement different *Dispatchers* for different types of clients, each with an API customized to what that client type needs.

As shown in Figure 4-14, a *Dispatcher* exposes a single API for an external client and implements that API by delegating to *Microservices* in the architecture.

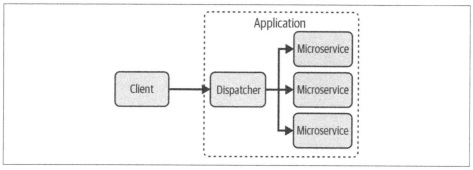

Figure 4-14. Dispatcher

The *Dispatcher* provides a single endpoint for the client to access the application, one with an API the provides the exact functionality the client requires. The client does not need to know how that functionality is distributed across the *Microservices*. Rather, the *Dispatcher* encapsulates the logic for how the functionality is distributed, delegates to those *Microservices* to invoke the functionality, and consolidates it into the API the *Dispatcher* provides for the client. Each type of client requiring a different API uses a different *Dispatcher*.

Building Microservices (2015) introduced this pattern as **Backends for Frontends**:

> Rather than have a general-purpose API backend, instead you have one backend per user experience—or a Backend For Frontend (BFF). Conceptually, you should think of

the user-facing application as being two components—a client-side application living outside your perimeter, and a server-side component (the BFF) inside your perimeter.

Dispatchers form the client-facing layer in a Microservices Architecture.

Figure 4-15 shows a complete application with the *Dispatchers* highlighted. The clients all access the same application but through different *Dispatchers*. The architecture includes a *Dispatcher* implementation for each client type, such as a web Dispatcher for web apps, a mobile *Dispatcher* for mobile apps, and an API *Dispatcher* for partner/CLI apps.

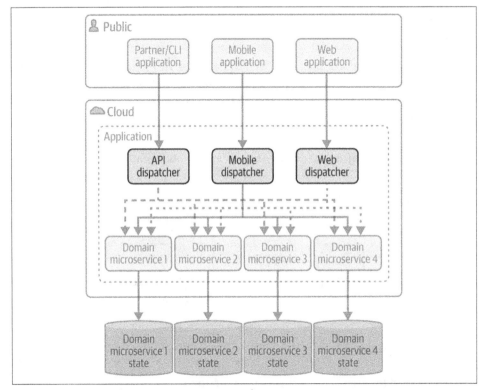

Figure 4-15. Dispatchers in Microservices Architecture

The *Dispatchers* define the external APIs that clients outside the cloud use to access the *Microservices* application hosted in the cloud. A *Dispatcher's* API is a Service API (70), typically implemented as a web service, that makes the entire *Microservice* application look like a single API. Each client type—web browser, mobile app, CLI, etc.—should have its own *Dispatcher*. Each *Dispatcher* should have an API that's customized for its client, so each client type gets exactly the API it needs to use the server application.

Dispatchers encapsulate a Microservices Architecture, which protects clients from changes in the architecture and protects the architecture from changes in the clients. As the architecture evolves—refactoring behavior, adding new *Microservice* classes, removing obsolete ones—and the *Microservices'* APIs change, the *Dispatchers'* implementations will evolve as well and absorb the changes, leaving the clients unaffected. Likewise, when a client needs new functionality or different data formats, its *Dispatcher's* API and its implementation evolve accordingly, yet as long as the *Microservices* still provide all of the functionality that the client needs, the Microservices Architecture is unaffected by changes in the client.

A *Dispatcher* should not contain any domain logic. Because each *Dispatcher* is specific to a single client type, any domain logic implemented in *Dispatchers* won't be shared across all client types. The *Dispatcher* delegates to *Microservices* in the architecture, based on which ones implement the functionality needed to implement the *Dispatcher's* API. Each *Microservice* can be any type, such as a *Domain Microservice*, *Adapter Microservice*, or *Service Orchestrator*.

A *Dispatcher's* internal implementation performs routing and conversion between the API the client wants to consume and the APIs the *Microservices* provide, such as the following:

Orchestration
   It can orchestrate several calls to *Microservices* to implement a single client action.

Translation
   It can translate the results of a *Microservice* into a channel-specific representation that more cleanly maps to needs of the user experience of that client type.

Filtering
   It can alter the results from the *Microservices* to remove items or details that are not needed by a particular client type.

The scope of a *Dispatcher* is usually straightforward: its API is customized for the client type it supports. Its implementation is usually pretty simple, implementing the API to route requests to *Microservices* as necessary.

This pattern is a key part of building the range of Client Applications (406) that can be used to access a cloud application with a Microservices Architecture. Client types such as Mobile Application (430) and Single Page Application (421) introduce unique translation or filtering requirements that often necessitate the use of a different *Dispatcher* for each client type. For example, in a mobile application, don't send a large set of data to the device that may have limited bandwidth; only send what it can display on its small screen. Likewise, a single page application may walk the user through a multi-screen wizard that requires orchestrating separate *Domain Microservices* on the server.

Because a *Dispatcher's* API is customized for its client type, the client and its *Dispatcher* tend to evolve together. Because of this coupling of their functionality, the same development team should implement both the client and its *Dispatcher* and modify them together, as shown in Figure 4-16.

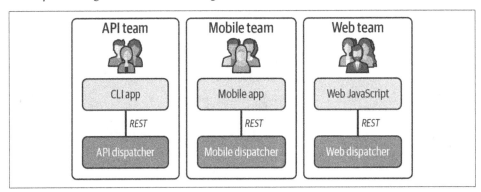

Figure 4-16. Dispatcher teams

Since both the client and *Dispatcher* are implemented by the same development team, the team often finds it convenient to implement them both in the same language. For example, the developers building a single page application using JavaScript will want to develop their *Dispatcher* services using Node.js on the server side. Likewise, Java developers building a native application for Android may want to develop their *Dispatcher* services with Java.

A *Dispatcher* is often a convenient place to cache data for the client. When *Domain Microservices* produce a large data set as a result, it may not make sense to return all of that data to the client at once, since bandwidth to the client may be limited, the client's storage may be limited, and its screen may be able to display only a small amount of data. Instead, the *Dispatcher* can make one call to the *Domain Microservices* to get the result, cache the data set, and enable the client to request it a page at a time.

A *Dispatcher* organizes all of the APIs in all of the *Microservices* in an architecture into a single API that does exactly what a client needs, encapsulating the application for the client and simplifying the client's interface with the application.

A *Dispatcher* can only provide functionality that the *Microservices* provide. When a client requires additional functionality, it will need to be implemented in the Microservices Architecture, and the changes will ripple through the *Microservices*, the *Dispatchers*, and the clients.

A *Dispatcher* is a type of *Microservice* but a specialized one that works differently. A *Dispatcher* is stateless and replicable, but its simple routing implementation rarely becomes a performance bottleneck that requires replication. Its *Service API* isn't based on a domain capability but more so on the requests that a client wants to make of the application. *Dispatchers* don't delegate to other *Dispatchers*, and microservices don't delegate to *Dispatchers*; *Dispatchers* are a single layer in the architecture, the architecture's client-facing layer.

A *Dispatcher* adapts multiple *Microservices* within an architecture, whereas an *Adapter Microservice* adapts a single system of record outside of the architecture.

A *Dispatcher's* API is often a Public API (443) expected by the client.

Since each *Dispatcher* runs in its own process, Polyglot Development (146) enables developers to implement each *Dispatcher* class in a different language.

Example

Let's examine how *Dispatchers* can help implement a banking application. Let's suppose we are part of a bank that has two disparate sets of customers (common with retail banks today). The first set of customers wants a simple web application to allow them to check their balances, do electronic transfers, and schedule payments. The second set wants all of those things but also wants to be able to trade equities, manage their investment portfolio, and explore new investment opportunities. What's more, the second set is more comfortable with technology and wants a richly featured mobile application they can use on their phones or tablets.

These two types of customers will need two different user interfaces, but those UIs can share the same *Microservices* functionality. Since the set of features that the second type of customer wants is a superset of the features needed by the first type of customer, one might assume that the two UXs can simply use the same *Microservices* directly. That may be true in some cases, but the odds are that the mobile app team wants to display the information on Accounts differently than the web app team does. They likely do not need to display all of the same information at the same time, nor do they necessarily need to show the same amount of information. Thus, the mobile team would need their own *Dispatcher* to filter information from the (shared) Accounts *Microservice*. This approach is shown in Figure 4-17.

The application needs two user interfaces, one for simple banking that runs in a web browser and another for stock trading that runs on a mobile device. These two UIs require two *Dispatchers*, each of which provides its UI with exactly the API and behavior it needs, and in doing so encapsulates the *Microservices* from the client. The *Dispatcher* for the banking UI encapsulates functionality in the bank account *Micro-services*. The *Dispatcher* for the stock trading UI encapsulates functionality in the equity *Microservices* and, because the stock trading UI enables banking functionality as well, also delegates to the bank account *Microservices*.

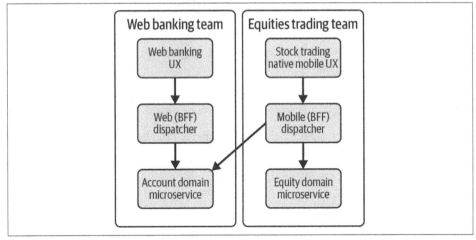

Figure 4-17. Banking UIs and Dispatchers

Polyglot Development

You are architecting a new application using Microservices (119) or refactoring an existing application into *Microservices*. The languages used to implement programs for traditional IT can also be used for cloud, but other languages should possibly be considered as well.

What computer language(s) should be used for implementing *Microservices*?

Computer science has created many different computer languages and keeps creating new ones. How should an IT department select the best language for implementing its *Microservices*?

For decades, an enterprise IT department would develop all of the programs in the same language. A science and engineering department would implement all of its programs in FORTRAN. The data processing department used COBOL. More recently, some huge companies wrote everything in Java, whereas others exclusively used PowerBuilder, Visual Basic, or C#. Most developers specialize in one particular language—typically the one that the department they work in uses the most.

This uniformity with computer languages was the result of several drivers:

Monolithic applications
> When the code for an entire application runs in a single process, all of it is usually written in the same language. Even in a Modular Monolith (29), all of the modules are usually implemented in the same language.

Interoperability

Applications are easier to connect together if they're written in the same language. If a COBOL program uses COBOL copybooks, other programs that work with it will need to be written in COBOL as well. Universal support for SQL databases gave some language flexibility, but then interconnectivity technologies like sockets and CORBA limited language choice once again.

Platforms and frameworks

The runtime environment supported by the enterprise's operations team could dictate language or technology. When the preferred deployment platform is Java EE application servers, all programs need to be written in Java. In a department that prefers the advantages of .NET, Java programs are useless; they need to be written in languages like C#. Android OS supports Java programs well, while iOS lends itself to Swift. Web browsers are optimized to run JavaScript, which also implements UX platforms like Angular and React.

IT department staffing

When all of the projects in a department write programs in the same language, staff can more easily move between projects. The department hires only new staff who have skills with that language.

Cloud computing and *Microservices* can run programs written in any language that runs on commodity hardware. An enterprise IT department or product development team accustomed to writing all of its programs in the same language may be tempted, by design or out of habit, to also develop all of the *Microservices* in an architecture in the same language.

With *Microservices*, language uniformity isn't required. The traits of a Microservices Architecture provide isolation between *Microservices*, and these same traits support developing *Microservices* in different languages, even in the same application. Cloud-Native Architecture (58) practices enable distributed modules to be written in different languages. Not only does each *Microservice* run in its own process, but it is bundled as an Application Package (62) with its own runtime, enabling each package to embed a different runtime. *Microservices* communicate through Service APIs (70), typically through a universal protocol like REST, enabling components written in different languages to interoperate nevertheless. Backend Services (106) separate the stateful shared resources from the stateless *Microservices*, so a *Microservice* and its *Backend Service* can be implemented in different languages. Cloud computing's dominant operating systems—Linux and Microsoft Windows—support hosting runtimes for a variety of languages.

Therefore,

Microservices Architecture supports *Polyglot Development*, where each *Microservice* can be implemented in a different computer language, allowing each team to select the language they use to develop their *Microservice.*

In a Microservices Architecture, each *Microservice* doesn't have to be implemented in a different language, but it can be. Figure 4-18 shows a standard example of an application with a Microservices Architecture, including an application client, a *Dispatcher*, and three *Microservices*. The *Microservices* are implemented in three different languages: Node.js, Java, and Go.

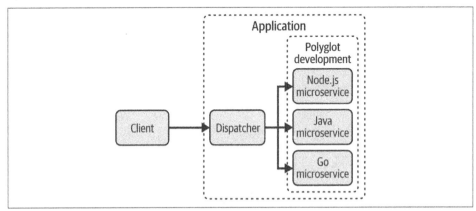

Figure 4-18. Polyglot Development

A monolithic application runs in a single process, and so it must be implemented in a single language. *Polyglot Development* takes advantage of the fact that each *Microservice* runs in its own process and so can be implemented in a different language. Multiple *Microservices* can still be implemented in the same language, and usually are. However, *Microservices* that work very differently may be easier to implement and may work better by using different languages and technologies.

Polyglot Development offers a key opportunity: for each *Microservice*, figure out how to implement it, and choose the best language for the task. Suit the solution to the problem. If a *Microservice* needs to model a business domain with procedural rules and complex interactions, a good approach is to Model Around the Domain (183) and implement the *Microservice* using an object-oriented programming language such as Java. Alternatively, if a *Microservice* needs to make classification decisions or determine best choices from incomplete data, implementing machine learning with Python may work well. If a *Microservice* needs to manipulate complex mathematical rules or construct models of physical activities, implementing functional programming with Scala or even JavaScript may be a good way to go. An additional feature of Polyglot Development with *Microservices* is that when implementing a service that needs the capability of specialized hardware (such as a GPU) you can implement that *Microservice* (and that *Microservice* only) in a language that supports that hardware. That means that you only deploy this *Microservice* onto hardware that has that specialization.

A single application with a Microservices Architecture could use some or all of these approaches, plus additional approaches such as scripting or Event-Driven Architecture (Chapter 6), as shown in Figure 4-19.

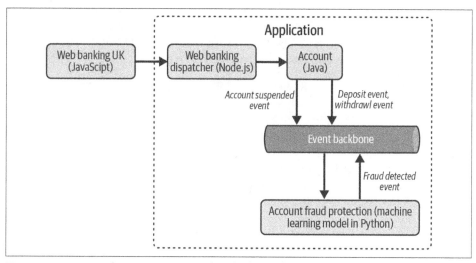

Figure 4-19. Event-driven program with polyglot components

Each component in this architecture is implemented in a different language. The web client is implemented in JavaScript, the *Dispatcher* is written in Node.js, the `Account` *Microservice* is written in Java, and the `Account Fraud Protection` *Microservice* is implemented using Python.

In a Microservices Architecture, individual *Microservices* must communicate using network transports (e.g., HTTP) and payload data formats (e.g., JSON, Google Protocol Buffers) that support cross-language operations. This means that it does not matter which language each *Microservice* is implemented in, since that detail is abstracted away by the protocol and encoding.

Polyglot Development can be used not only to implement each solution with the best language but also to enable each development team to program with the language they prefer. If some developers are more highly skilled with one language and some another, rather than putting them all together and making them fight it out, put them in separate teams and let those develop separate *Microservices*. Each should choose a *Microservice* they can implement well using the language they prefer. If a solution requires a language that the developers lack experience using, put those who want to learn that language on a team and provide them with education to learn the language.

Polyglot Development makes sharing libraries more difficult because two *Microservices* implemented in different languages cannot always share the same library. That is actually an advantage, however, because a library shared between two *Microservices* creates a dependency between the *Microservices* that can make them difficult to maintain and evolve independently. Imagine if the development team maintaining one *Microservice* wants to make changes to the library, and the other team doesn't want those changes. Each *Microservice* should develop its own libraries in its own preferred language. The *Microservice's* application package will bundle the *Microservice* program with its own copies of the libraries it requires.

An enterprise should provide guidance to its development teams on which languages are supported in order to prevent a development team from selecting a language that the enterprise cannot support. The enterprise must ensure it has a sufficient pool of developers to create not only *Microservices* in a supported language but also ones who will be able to maintain it over the long run and that have sufficient tooling, frameworks, and technical support to be successful with the enterprise's approved technologies. Without this governance, a team may select a niche or outlier language that may become difficult for the enterprise to support long term.

The Microservices Architecture enables *Polyglot Development*, which enables each team to implement its *Microservice* in the language that works best, regardless of the languages used to implement other *Microservices*.

An enterprise needs to govern the selection of languages to avoid developing a *Microservice* that lacks sufficient staff to maintain it.

Each kind of *Microservice* can be polyglot, whether it is a Domain Microservice (130), Adapter Microservice (135), Dispatcher (140), or Service Orchestrator (160). Some may even be implemented not with a programming language but with a technology such as a process engine, rules engine, machine learning engine, etc.

A *Microservice* can be implemented in almost any computer language, but to run well in a Microservices Architecture or hosted on the cloud, the language should be one that supports delivering a program in an Application Package (62). A language whose programs are difficult to package may be able to implement a *Microservice* adequately, but that *Microservice* will be difficult to deploy and manage.

Polyglot applies not only to language and technology but to persistence as well. Stateless *Microservices* with data store it in Self-Managed Data Stores (154). When the data stores are Cloud Databases (311), Polyglot Persistence (375) enables each development team to select the database type that works best for its *Microservice*.

Examples

In the following sections, we'll discuss a common multilanguage architecture, as well as the different language selections that are more common for each component.

Polyglot Node.js Dispatchers with Java Microservices

A common implementation strategy for a *Microservices* application is to implement the *Dispatchers* in Node.js and the *Microservices* (domain, adapter, and orchestrators) in Java, as shown in Figure 4-20.

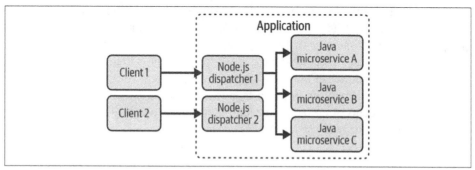

Figure 4-20. Polyglot Node.js Dispatchers with Java Microservices

A *Dispatcher* must support web clients, a task Node.js does well. A popular web application can have thousands of web clients, so the *Dispatcher* must scale well. A web client spends most of its time waiting on its user rather than performing work, so the *Dispatcher* shouldn't block waiting as well. A web client communicates via HTTP request and response. When a web client does submit a request, it will be input that is fairly simple to process even if it's for a task that's complex to perform.

Node.js is optimized for these web client requirements. It works well with HTTP. It runs single-threaded, dispatching each HTTP request quickly to a callback and moving on to the next. This way, it can scale well without managing multithreading or blocking threads. A complex request would bog down the Node.js process and block all of its web clients, but a Node.js *Dispatcher* can be designed to dispatch its request to another process to perform the task.

A *Domain Microservice* performs business functionality and attaches to external resources—capabilities that Java does well. Java is good at performing CPU-intensive computations and data processing. Its multithreaded process can scale efficiently to perform tasks for multiple concurrent clients. Its adapters make it easy to connect to Backend Services (106) such as databases (JDBC), messaging systems (JMS), and any other external resource that supports a connector (JCA). Its HTTP interface (JAX-RS and JAX-WS) maps requests to concurrent threads.

When in doubt about which language to use for which parts of a Microservices Architecture, Node.js *Dispatchers* with Java *Microservices* is a good approach to consider.

Dispatchers

There is usually a one-to-one correspondence between *Dispatchers* and clients: web clients connect through corresponding web *Dispatchers*, mobile clients via mobile *Dispatchers*, etc. Each dispatcher runs in a separate process, so they can employ *Polyglot Development* and each *Dispatcher* can be implemented in a different language.

Each *Dispatcher* should be implemented by a single team, and the same team should develop the client and its corresponding *Dispatcher* together. The team can choose to implement the *Dispatcher* in the language that makes the most sense, and each team can develop their *Dispatcher* in a different language. Often a team chooses to implement the *Dispatcher* in the same language as the client so that the team can use the same skills implementing both parts, and the two parts can interoperate more easily. Different clients often require or lend themselves to different languages, which helps guide the language to use for the *Dispatcher*:

Web browser
> As we discuss in Single-Page Application (421), SPAs are often implemented using JavaScript, so implement the *Dispatcher* using Node.js (since Node is the server-side version of JavaScript; the ".js" in the name Node.js stands for JavaScript).

Apple iOS
> The client is often implemented in Swift, so implement the *Dispatcher* using Swift as well.

Google Android
> The client is usually implemented in Java, so also use Java to implement the *Dispatcher*.

The *Dispatcher* can be implemented in a completely different language from the client, but that is often less convenient, especially since the *Dispatcher* and client should usually be written by the same team.

These examples notwithstanding, as noted in the previous example, Node.js is typically a good language to use for implementing *Dispatchers*. *Dispatchers* need to handle HTTP web service I/O efficiently to support large numbers of concurrent clients, and Node.js scales well for network I/O.

Domain microservices

Each *Domain Microservice* runs in a separate process, so they can employ *Polyglot Development*—with each *Microservice* implemented in a different language. *Domain Microservices* often use databases and other *Backend Services*. When they do, each can choose its own database service.

Each *Domain Microservice* should be implemented by a single team. The team should choose a language that works well for implementing the *Microservice's* solution, and a database service that works well for how the data will be stored and used, and the language should work well with the database. Each team makes these decisions for their *Microservice* independently of what other teams choose for their *Microservices*.

The team can use the best language for their domain and the problem they are solving. For example, when implementing *Domain Microservices*, if the business logic requires business calculations to be multithreaded and use CPU efficiently, Java is a good choice. Java is also good for *Microservices* that need to connect to external legacy systems, since Java includes adapter technologies to facilitate these connections. On the other hand, if it's a heavily network-based application, Go Lang could be a good option instead.

Adapter microservices

Adapter Microservices are much like *Domain Microservices*, in that each runs in a separate process and so can be implemented in a separate language and each is developed by a separate team that can use the language it chooses. Even more than *Domain Microservices*, *Adapter Microservices* focus exclusively on connecting to external legacy systems.

Java is typically a good language to use for implementing *Adapter Microservices* because of the multithreaded connectors it provides. Another choice for implementation of an *Adapter Microservice* is to use a commercial API Gateway (*https://oreil.ly/pYqus*) (such as WebMethods, Apigee, API Connect, or many others), which will often provide low-code or no-code options for common protocols and SaaS systems.

Again, since each *Adapter Microservice* is implemented independently, some can be implemented in Java while others are implemented using one gateway technology and others use another gateway technology. How one is implemented does not limit how the others can be implemented.

Self-Managed Data Stores

(aka Database per Service (*Microservices Patterns*, 2018))

You are architecting a new application using Microservices (119) or refactoring an existing application into *Microservices*. A *Microservice*, such as a Domain Microservice (130) or Service Orchestrator (160), implements its Service API (70) using domain data.

How does a microservice store its state?

Microservices are Stateless Applications (80), so they don't store state internally. Yet most applications have state, and *Domain Microservices* implement business functionality that has data. If the *Microservice* doesn't store its business data internally, it has to persist that data somewhere.

A traditional IT application persists its data in external storage, typically a database. The entire application is connected to the database and has access to its data. A Modular Monolith (29) is a single application and so typically has one database that all of the modules share. When multiple modules need to use the same data, it's simple for them to all access it in the shared storage. The application is developed by a single team, or multiple teams working together, so it is easy to coordinate as necessary to make the data persistence work for all of the code that needs to use it.

For developers of traditional IT applications, the modules in an application sharing data in a database is a natural extension of the way multiple applications in an enterprise share a database of record (DoR). A complex enterprise includes several mission-critical applications and at least one DoR, typically a relational database, that is shared by many of those applications. DoRs become huge, containing any data that any application needs. Any one application typically uses only a small subset of the data in the DoR. Yet all of the data in the DoR is used by some application, and typically a useful set of data is used by multiple applications. The applications share the data, often integrating the applications as a **Shared Database** (*Enterprise Integration Patterns*, 2003) that passes data when one application stores it and another application reads it.

Any shared database—especially one as widely shared as a DoR—creates couplings and dependencies between the applications. The database schema cannot evolve because changes often necessitate updating all of the applications that use the data. When one application messes up some shared data, that in turn messes up all of the other applications that use the data. Even worse, if one application deletes a record that other applications still need, those application's actions can become flawed because of the missing data. Enterprises sometimes develop policies that prohibit deleting data from DoRs. The reasoning behind these policies is that enterprises find it cost-prohibitive and difficult to be sure that none of their various applications is using the data—because data that has no use in their current applications might become useful again in the future. Databases become bloated with data that hasn't been used for years but looks as valid as any other data in the DoR.

Not only is the data difficult to maintain, but the applications become difficult to maintain as well. Each application must store its data in a certain format, not because that format is natural for the application but because the DoR uses that format. That format must have been useful to some application at one time but possibly has become a poor fit for all of the applications that still use it. Meanwhile, if an application has data to store that is not part of the DoR's schema, the application may be out of luck and must throw away the data.

DoRs also become performance bottlenecks. When too many applications access a shared resource, performance limitations in that shared resource slow down all of the applications using it. When one application locks a row or table, any other application that needs the data must block and wait. Many DoRs run in older database servers that can support only a very limited number of connections, limiting the applications that can use the data. Enterprises develop data access strategies with read-only copies of the DoR to enable greater access. As described in Command Query Responsibility Separation (383), applications must queue their data updates so that one processing application can perform the updates in batches that optimize limited connections and avoid locking conflicts. The enterprise effectively reinvents the capabilities a database is supposed to perform in the first place.

Compared to a DoR shared by many applications, storage shared by modules in a single application seems much simpler. Yet just as storage shared between applications creates a coupling between them that makes it more difficult for those applications to evolve independently—storage shared between modules in an application creates a similar dependency that limits evolving the modules.

Microservices should be independent, able to be developed by different teams, and able to be deployed separately. If they share the same data storage, that creates a dependency between them. Teams developing multiple *Microservices* must coordinate how their independent sets of code will store and share common data. To evolve the data format, all of the *Microservices* must be updated to use the new data format. To deploy the *Microservices*, whichever is deployed first must allocate the storage, then the others must be sure not to create duplicate storage but rather to share the storage that has already been created by whichever *Microservice* came first. The shared storage can become a performance bottleneck as differing *Microservices* compete to read and update its data, and likewise is a single point of failure.

Microservices need to remain independent even when they share the same data.

Therefore,

Each *Microservice* with state should include a *Self-Managed Data Store* to store that state, storage the *Microservice* manages that is accessed exclusively by the *Microservice*. Each different *Microservice* has its own data store, while replicas of the same *Microservice* share the same data store.

Two *Microservices* do not share the same *Self-Managed Data Store*; they each have their own, as shown in Figure 4-21.

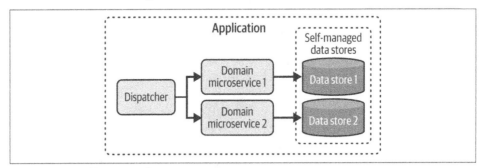

Figure 4-21. Self-Managed Data Stores

The two *Microservices* will be developed independently. Separate data storage enables each team to develop its *Microservice's* storage independently as well. If the *Microservices* shared the same storage, that would be a dependency that would require coordinating the development and maintenance of the *Microservices*.

When one *Microservice* needs to use another *Microservice's* data, it delegates the work to the other *Microservice* via its *Service API*, enabling the other *Microservice* to perform the work using the data in its own storage. This way, no matter how many different *Microservices* may use a set of data indirectly, the only *Microservice* with direct access to the data is the single *Microservice* that owns the data.

When a *Microservice* is a Replicable Application (88), its replicas all share the same *Self-Managed Data Store*.

As shown in Figure 4-22, multiple replicas of a *Microservice* share a single data store. Replicas are interchangeable, which is possible only if they share the same data. Each replica could try to store its data in its own data store, but then each replica would have different data. Replicas with different data behave differently from one another and therefore are not interchangeable.

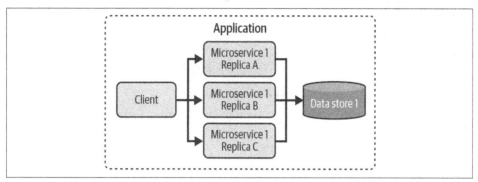

Figure 4-22. Microservice replicas share a data store

If multiple *Microservices* all depend on the same shared database, such as a DoR, they run into the same problem of shared dependencies that occurs with multiple traditional IT applications depending on the same DoR. Any *Microservice* that updates the data incorrectly will corrupt it for all other *Microservices*. If one *Microservice* creates a lock on the data, it blocks all of the other *Microservices*. If one *Microservice* wants to change the data format, all of the other *Microservices* also need to be updated to use the new format. The *Microservices* may seem to run independently, but by sharing the same storage, they all share a performance bottleneck and single point of failure.

Microservices avoid these dependencies by not sharing storage. One will not fail because another has corrupted its data, nor will it be blocked by another using its data. One *Microservice* can change the way it stores its data without impacting the other *Microservices*. One *Microservice* using its data heavily will not affect the performance of other *Microservices*, and storage becoming temporarily unavailable affects only one *Microservice's* replicas, not all other *Microservices* as well.

Each *Microservice* managing its own data store helps keep the *Microservices* independent. Each *Microservice* is the only code using its storage, so it controls its data and the data's lifecycle, and can evolve its format.

Data is no longer centralized in one massive DoR; it is dispersed among multiple specialized databases. Multiple data stores require additional management, such as to back up the data.

Each *Self-Managed Data Store* should be a Cloud Database (311), which works better than a *Microservice* using block or file storage to store data. The database should be a Replicated Database (316) so that it will scale the way the replicable *Microservice* scales, and an Application Database (329) whose functionality favors making the data simple to access rather than optimizing storage. A data store that supports the data formats that are incorporated into the *Microservice's* interface will make the *Microservice* simpler to implement with less conversion of the data. Likewise, a data store that enables the *Microservice* to access the data—find it, update it—the way the *Microservice's* interface works will also simplify the *Microservice's* implementation.

Not only can *Microservices* have separate storage, they can each have different kinds of storage. With Polyglot Persistence (375), each set of data is stored in the type of storage that is best suited to that data.

Example

To illustrate a Microservices Architecture with multiple *Microservices* that each has its own *Self-Managed Data Store*, let's consider an airline reservation system. An airline reservations application may have a *Microservice* that enables the passenger to select seats on their flights. The seat selection *Microservice* doesn't read the seating chart for each flight and try to interpret it. Instead, a flights *Microservice* manages each flight, including its seats, and the seat selector delegates to the flight manager. Some flights might be on different airlines. Each one encapsulates rules for when to show a seat as taken, not only because it's been assigned to another passenger but also perhaps because this passenger is told that that a premium seat is unavailable, or that a block of seats is unavailable because it's being held so that a family can sit together. The flight *Microservice* manages its seats, and the seat selection *Microservice* enables the passenger to choose one they're allowed to reserve and records that selection in its storage.

The Microservices Architecture for this airline reservations application might divide it into several *Microservices*, as shown in Figure 4-23.

To make a reservation, a user logs in as a particular customer, purchases a ticket, and selects a seat. The Microservices Architecture is composed of several *Microservices* to manage this functionality, such as `Customer Management`, `Ticketing`, `Flights`, and `Seat Selector`.

These multiple *Microservices* could all share one massive data store containing several sets of data. Instead, each *Microservice* includes its own *Self-Managed Data Store*, so the solution includes multiple data stores, each of which is specialized for the data that one *Microservice* needs and manages:

- `Customer Management` has its own `Customer Data`, a data store containing data about `Customers`. Only the `Customer Management` *Microservice* needs access to this `Customers` data.

- `Ticketing` has its own `Ticketing Data`, a data store containing `Tickets` data. `Ticketing` is the only *Microservice* with access to the `Tickets` data.

- The Flights *Microservice* has its own data store for Flight Data that contains two sets of data, Flights and Seating Charts, and only it can access that data. The Flights and Seating Charts data are encapsulated together in a single data store because part of Flights' responsibilities is to keep the Flights and Seating Charts data consistent with referential integrity so that every flight has exactly one seating chart and each seating chart is part of an existing flight's data.

- The Seat Selector *Microservice* is pure functionality, so it doesn't have any additional data and therefore doesn't have its own data store.

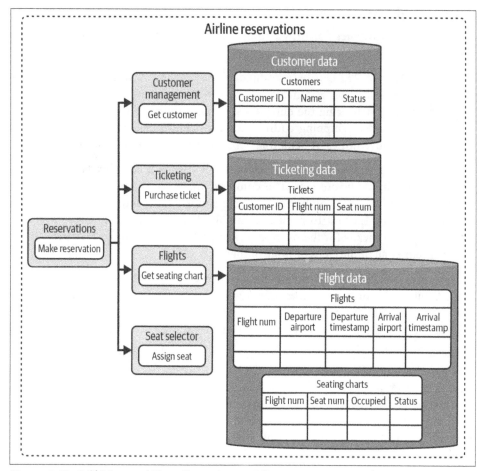

Figure 4-23. Self-Managed Data Stores in an airline reservations application

The Seat Selector *Microservice* enables the user to assign a seat by using Flights to find an available seat and using Ticketing to assign that seat to the customer. The Seat Selector *Microservice* never accesses any of that data directly; it does so indirectly by invoking behavior in the other `Flights` and `Ticketing` *Microservices* that do have direct access to the data. `Flights` and `Ticketing` are each responsible for keeping the data they manage consistent; there is no way for `Seat Selector` to make the data inconsistent.

Service Orchestrator

You are architecting a new application using Microservices (119) or refactoring an existing application into *Microservices*. Each *Microservice* has a Service API (70) and its own Self-Managed Data Store (154).

How does a *Microservice* perform a complex task, one that is performed in multiple steps?

A task in a *Service API* can be a complex task, one that a *Microservice* performs in multiple steps. Buying a concert ticket requires reserving the seat, processing the payment, and delivering the entry pass. Planning how to ship a product means finding the customer's shipping address, the product's dimensions and weight, and the warehouses' inventories. A bank transfer requires updating both accounts.

This seems like a simple problem to solve. Each step in a complex task should be a simpler task in a *Microservice*. The complex *Microservice* implements its task to invoke the simpler tasks, combining multiple simpler tasks into the single complex task. For the complex task to be successful, all of the simpler tasks must complete successfully. The trick is for the *Microservice* to perform the complex task such that it performs either all of the steps or none of them.

This problem might be simpler if all of the tasks were implemented in a single *Microservice*, but that's not the way *Microservices* work. Because each *Microservice* implements a single business capability, diverse subtasks may be distributed across multiple *Microservices*, so the complex *Microservice* invokes multiple simpler *Microservices*.

Likewise, it might be easier if the *Microservices* all shared a single database, but that's also not the way *Microservices* work. Each *Microservice* is stateless and persists its state in a *Self-Managed Data Store* such as a database. Each *Microservice* manages its own data and the persistence of that data. For one *Microservice* to access another's data, the one must delegate to the other and use its tasks that have access to the data. So a complex task incorporates not only multiple *Microservices* but also their multiple databases.

Applications in traditional IT solve this problem using transactions. Data is kept immediately consistent; updates to the data transition it from one consistent state to another by making a complete set of changes. A simple transaction runs in a single resource and ensures that a set of updates either all commit at once or none of them do. A distributed transaction runs across multiple resources and ensures that the updates in all of the resources either commit together simultaneously or not at all. Transactions provide insurance that a set of changes is complete and the data is always consistent, but they have overhead that hurts performance, which can seem unnecessary when the majority of transactions never roll back. When an update in a transaction does fail, rolling back the transaction can be complex and may itself fail, requiring manual intervention to clean up the resources.

The cloud is rather inhospitable for performing transactions. When necessary, the cloud stops and restarts servers, making them unreliable by traditional IT standards. Cloud workloads are mobile and elastic, and as the platform relocates applications and resources, it stops and restarts them. To compensate for this, tasks need to be interruptible units of work that can start over and retry. Depending on transactions constantly rolling back successfully makes an application less reliable, not more so. To support retry, an application updates each resource separately.

Updating each resource separately fits naturally with performing a complex task as separate simple tasks in separate *Microservices* with separate storage. Yet a complex *Microservice* needs to perform these simple tasks as a unit, all of them or none of them.

Therefore,

Design a *Microservice* that performs complex tasks as a *Service Orchestrator* that coordinates tasks in multiple simpler *Microservices*.

A *Service Orchestrator* is a kind of *Microservice* that performs a complex task as a unit, implementing the complex task by composing it out of simpler tasks. See Figure 4-24.

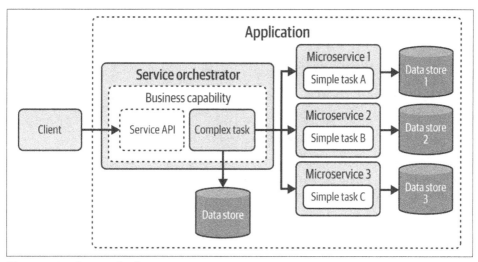

Figure 4-24. Service Orchestrator

A *Service Orchestrator* provides tasks in a *Service API* that are complex, requiring multiple steps to perform. A *Service Orchestrator* may consist of both complex tasks and simple tasks, and a task may combine other complex tasks as well as simple tasks.

A *Service Orchestrator* typically implements business functionality, making it a type of Domain Microservice (130). Because the *Service Orchestrator* does not implement the same business capability as the simpler *Microservices* it orchestrates, it itself is not a **Composite** object (*Design Patterns*, 1994) because it does not have the same *Service API* as the simpler *Microservices*. The *Service API* hides the complex implementation, so a client doesn't know whether the *Microservice* with the business capability is implemented as a *Service Orchestrator* or as a more atomic *Domain Microservice*. A *Microservice* that is first implemented as an atomic *Domain Microservice* could become more complex and evolve into a *Service Orchestrator* with the same *Service API* and its clients would remain unchanged. A *Service Orchestrator* may require its own storage, such as for data it collects from and passes to its simpler tasks, so that an orchestration that is interrupted—such as when the cloud platform relocates it to a different server—can restart where it left off.

By performing a complex task as a unit of work, a *Service Orchestrator* ensures that either all of the steps are performed or none of them are. To accomplish this on the cloud without transactions, a *Service Orchestrator* can be implemented with any of three design strategies:

Orchestration microservice
> The *Service Orchestrator* implements each step in a complex task by invoking another *Microservice* task.

Consolidated microservice
> Combine several *Microservices* into a *Service Orchestrator* that can perform all of the steps itself.

Business process
> Implement the *Service Orchestrator* as a business process that implements each step by invoking a task in another finer-grained *Microservice*.

Let's examine each of these strategies in more detail.

A *Service Orchestrator* implemented as an orchestration *Microservice* simply calls other *Microservices*. For this to work, the complex task and all of its subtasks must be either read-only or idempotent. Read-only means that the task does not change the state of any of the systems it interacts with, nor does it otherwise create any side effects. An idempotent task produces an effect the first time it is run but when repeated produces no additional effects. Because the tasks are read-only or idempotent, if the entire orchestration *Microservice* fails or restarts, it can simply start over and try again. The orchestration *Microservice's* client gets an error instead of a valid result, so it retries the complex task. If a subtask fails or is interrupted, the orchestration *Microservice* retries it. In this way, the entire read-only complex task—including its subtasks—can be retried until it succeeds.

As shown in Figure 4-25, the orchestration *Microservice* implements the steps in its complex task to invoke tasks in other *Microservices*. Each of those *Microservices* uses its own database or other *Backend Services* to implement its task.

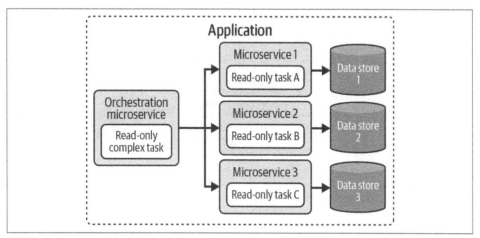

Figure 4-25. Orchestration microservice

The key is that the tasks are all read-only—the state of the databases after the tasks is the same as before the tasks. If one of the subtasks updated its database, but then the complex task failed to complete, it could restart, but then it would perform the successful subtask again and update its database twice, corrupting the data. A read-only task can be run repeatedly if needed without corrupting the data.

For example, an ecommerce task to prepare a product shipment needs to retrieve the customer's shipping address, the product's dimensions and weight, and the warehouse's inventory. All of these tasks are read-only, so preparing a shipment can be implemented as an orchestration *Microservice*.

An orchestration *Microservice* is a perfectly valid strategy but has the limitation that it works only with read-only data or idempotent tasks.

A *Service Orchestrator* implemented as a consolidated *Microservice* implements the complex task and all of its subtasks as one *Microservice* with one persistent *Backend Service*, such as a database. This requires either designing a single *Microservice* from the beginning or refactoring existing code to merge several *Microservices* into a single *Microservice*. When merging *Microservices*, the refactoring merges their data stores as well.

As shown in Figure 4-26, the consolidated *Microservice* implements multiple tasks, and they all share the same database. The *Service API* exposes the complex task and can also expose any of the subtasks clients need to invoke individually.

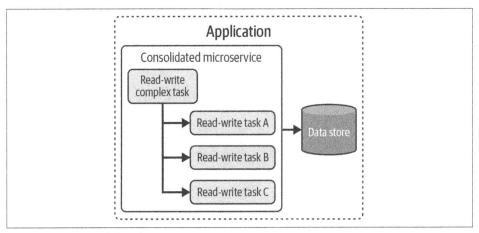

Figure 4-26. Consolidated microservice

The key is that all tasks update data in a single database via a single session that doesn't commit until the end of the complex task. The complex task not only invokes the subtasks but also combines all of their database updates into a single commit in their shared database. This way, if the *Microservice* fails or restarts during its complex task, including any of its subtasks, the database never commits and its session rolls back. The *Microservice* can then restart and retry as if this were the first attempt.

For example, a banking task that transfers funds from one account to another must make sure that the updates occur in both accounts. To implement this service orchestration as a consolidated *Microservice*, the complex transfer task and its simpler deposit and withdrawal tasks must all be implemented in a single *Microservice*, and the data for all of the bank accounts must all be stored in the same database.

A consolidated *Microservice* is a perfectly valid strategy, but it has the limitation that it must be designed from the beginning as a single *Microservice*, or that multiple existing *Microservices* can be merged without breaking their clients. The need for this refactoring is caused by defining too many *Microservices*, each with a single business capability that is too narrowly focused, such that multiple *Microservices* must collaborate to perform a complex task. Instead, design the *Microservice* around a single business capability broad enough to perform complex tasks in the domain.

A *Service Orchestrator* implemented as a business process implements its complex task to run in a business process management (BPM) engine. The business process performs each step in the complex task by invoking a *Microservice* task.

As shown in Figure 4-27, the business process consists of multiple steps, each of which invokes a task in another *Microservice*, where each *Microservice* uses its own database or other *Backend Services* to implement its task. The subtasks aren't required to be read-only or idempotent; each one can read and change the data in its database. The BPM engine can expose the business process as a *Service API*, or a *Microservice* can front the business process to expose it as a *Service API*, kind of an Adapter Microservice (135).

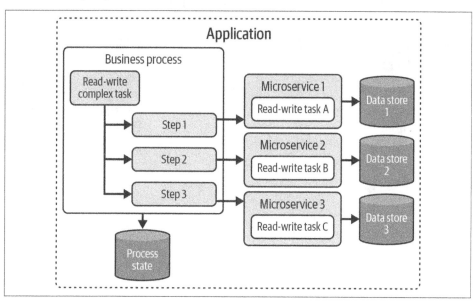

Figure 4-27. Business process

The key is that the business process can perform each step as its own de facto transaction. It invokes each subtask individually; each *Microservice* with a subtask thinks the business process is just any client invoking the task. The business process can keep track of which steps have completed successfully and can retry ones that fail. If the business process fails or restarts, it doesn't repeat the steps that have already completed; it starts again where it was before. The business process might even restart on a different computer and perform the rest of its steps there. A business process can even reverse steps that have already completed by performing *compensating transactions*—tasks that do the opposite of another task, usually implemented in the same *Microservice* as a pair in which the compensating task performs the reverse of the task. The business process works much like an orchestration *Microservice*. It ensures that each step is performed successfully only once, so the steps can be read-write.

For example, the ecommerce application probably has separate *Microservices* for capabilities like customer management, product management, warehouse inventory, shipping logistics, and payment processing. A complex task such as checkout (purchasing the items in a shopping cart) requires coordinating across simpler tasks in multiple *Microservices*. Combining all of those specialized *Microservices* into one generalized consolidated *Microservice* would be a poor Microservices Architecture. Instead, the *Service Orchestrator* will need to implement the checkout task as a business process.

A business process is a perfectly valid strategy, but it requires a BPM engine. The *Microservice* is implemented in the BPM engine or to delegate to the BPM engine.

When choosing among these three strategies (Orchestration Microservice, Consolidation, and Business Process), you need to consider which is most appropriate for your situation, looking at the pros and cons of each. The issue is that that once you make this choice you will often need to follow it for other similar situations in your design. Thus, you will make a choice at least for a subsystem of several *Microservices*, if not for an entire system. An architect should consider each for the system as a whole and choose the most appropriate. For instance, you may choose to select an orchestration *Microservice* as your first choice and then later in a refactoring, change the architecture to use a BPM engine.

Designing a *Microservice* as a *Service Orchestrator* enables it to perform complex tasks by combining other complex and simple tasks. Three design strategies handle read-only tasks, multiple tasks in a single *Microservice*, and multiple *Microservices* with read-write tasks.

A *Service Orchestrator's* design is more complex than traditional IT code that simply performs multiple tasks. The later coding strategy either depends on transaction management, which the cloud does not provide, or worse yet just assumes that multiple updates will always succeed. Code from a traditional IT application migrated to the cloud may run successfully, but without a transaction manager, it will not handle failures correctly.

Compared to simple *Microservices*, *Service Orchestrators* can be more complex to design. Not only do they implement complex tasks, but those tasks need to be designed with a lot more care to ensure that they complete as a unit.

The design for a *Service Orchestrator* must be aware of the *Self-Managed Data Stores* involved in performing the task. As long as only a single data store is involved, or the data stores are used read-only, the orchestrator's design can be simplified. A complex task that uses multiple read-write data stores needs to be implemented as a business process.

To perform short-running tasks, relational databases rely heavily on locking data with read, write, and update locks. Locking in relational databases can cause performance bottlenecks and deadlocks as one session locks data that other sessions also require. Many Cloud Databases (311) strive to avoid these performance problems by incorporating designs that avoid and minimize locking.

A business process *Service Orchestrator* can be hosted in a BPM engine, or can remotely invoke a process hosted in a BPM engine. When invoking the BPM engine remotely, the *Service Orchestrator* is an Adapter Microservice (135) that reuses the business functionality residing in the BPM engine.

A *Service Orchestrator* orchestrates multiple tasks following a predefined plan. Alternatively, multiple tasks can be choreographed dynamically in an Event-Driven Architecture (Chapter 6).

Since each *Service Orchestrator* runs in its own process, Polyglot Development (146) enables developers to implement each *Service Orchestrator* class in a different language or technology.

Examples

As examples of the *Service Orchestrator* pattern, let's examine how an ecommerce website could implement displaying a product's availability using a *Service Orchestrator* with the Orchestration Microservice strategy and managing a purchase using a *Service Orchestrator* with the business process strategy. In between, we'll look at a business process orchestrator implemented using an enterprise integration router.

Ecommerce: Displaying availability

When displaying information about a product for sale, a shopping website might display not only details about the product but also whether the product is currently in stock. In a Microservices Architecture, there are may be one *Microservice* for managing the catalog of products that the website sells and another *Microservice* for managing the inventory currently stored in the warehouse and which of those items have already been sold to other customers. The website needs a single shopping *Microservice* that can provide all the details needed to display a product, including whether the warehouse has any available. The ecommerce application can be architected like the solution shown in Figure 4-28.

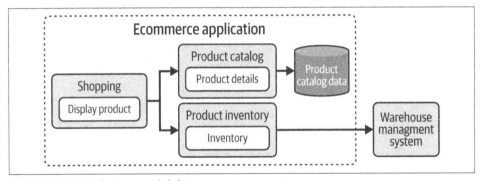

Figure 4-28. Displaying availability

The architecture contains the following *Microservices*:

Shopping
> A *Service Orchestrator* whose display product task is composed of two simpler tasks, product details and inventory

Product Catalog
> A *Domain Microservice* that implements the product details task

Product Inventory
> An *Adapter Microservice* that implements the inventory task by delegating to the Warehouse Management system of record

Neither simpler *Microservice* implements all of the functionality that the ecommerce application requires to display the product completely. The Shopping Microservice doesn't implement all of that functionality either, but it acts like it does, delegating to the simpler *Microservices* and combining their functionality into the complete set that the ecommerce application requires.

The Shopping *Microservice* is a *Service Orchestrator*. Because the product details and *inventory* tasks are read-only, as is the display product task that delegates to them, the Shopping *Microservice* can be implemented using the Orchestration Microservice strategy. Simple code calls one task, then the other, then combines their data for display.

This basic MVP of a Shopping *Microservice* could be expanded to provide additional information, such as pricing in multiple currencies, dynamically fluctuating prices, delivery time estimates, and product ratings. The *Service Orchestrator* probably would not implement any of this functionality, instead delegating to other *Microservices* that specialize in these functions.

Enterprise integration router

When integrating multiple applications, the routing in the middle may function as a service orchestration. When the application interfaces are more or less service oriented and a router combines them with its own interface that is more-or-less service oriented, that's a *Service Orchestrator*.

For example, a **Composed Message Processor** (*Enterprise Integration Patterns*, 2003) uses a **Splitter** (*Enterprise Integration Patterns*, 2003) to split a composite message into a series of individual messages, routes each individual message to its destination, and then uses an **Aggregator** (*Enterprise Integration Patterns*, 2003) to combine the results from the destinations into a single result for the original message. This process is a kind of orchestration, but it may or may not be service orchestration. With enterprise messaging, the messages can be very data-oriented (see **Document Message** (*Enterprise Integration Patterns*, 2003)), simply passing data between applications, which is not a good example of service orchestration. When the destinations' interfaces are *Service APIs* or kind of like *Service APIs*, the message is a request (see **Command Message** (*Enterprise Integration Patterns*, 2003)) that specifies what the destination should do but not how to do it, which typically means that the original composite message is also a request. Likewise, the result message for a request is typically a response. A request split into smaller requests and responses merged into an overall response fits the **Request-Reply** (*Enterprise Integration Patterns*, 2003) pattern, which makes the router a *Service Orchestrator*.

Figure 4-29 shows the solution for a **Composed Message Processor** that acts as a *Service Orchestrator*.

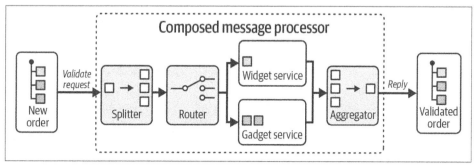

Figure 4-29. Composed Message Processor

The router has a *Service API* with a validate task whose request takes a New Order as a parameter and whose reply returns a Validated Order. That is the *Service Orchestrator's* API. The router orchestrates two services, Widget Service and Gadget Service, which also have *Service APIs*. The router combines their specialized capabilities into a general capability, which is service orchestration.

Another enterprise integration routing pattern, **Process Manager** (*Enterprise Integration Patterns*, 2003), is an even more sophisticated message router that performs a predefined set of steps that can vary based on intermediate results. If it uses service interfaces, this is a *Service Orchestrator*, specifically the business process strategy. The business process strategy is often implemented in a business process engine, as shown in the next example.

Ecommerce: Managing a purchase

When processing a purchase, a shopping website needs to make sure to perform two main tasks: ship the product to the customer and gather payment from the customer. Both tasks are part of a single logical business transaction—either both succeed or neither should be performed. If one fails, it needs to be retried until it succeeds. If one succeeds but the other cannot be completed successfully, the first one needs to be undone, often by executing a compensating transaction that performs the opposite steps. The compensating transaction must complete successfully.

A good approach to perform multiple tasks as a single transaction is to implement the transaction as a business process, which will make the *Service Orchestrator* one implemented using the business process strategy. Figure 4-30 shows a Microservices Architecture with a business process (using the notation for UML activity diagrams) for performing the checkout task in a Purchasing service.

The checkout task performs four activities: receive order, fill order, send invoice, and close order. The Purchasing service implements the fill order activity by delegating to another *Microservice*, Order Fulfillment and its ship product task. Likewise, it implements its send invoice activity by delegating to Payment Processing's charge credit card task.

This design makes Purchasing a *Service Orchestrator*, a *Microservice* that composes its functionality from the simpler Order Fulfillment and Payment Processing *Microservices*. Purchasing is implemented as a business process so that it can run in a BPM engine, which can run fill order and send invoice concurrently and ensure that both complete successfully before running close order. If the BPM engine cannot complete one of the concurrent activities successfully and the other concurrent activity has already completed successfully, the BPM engine will automatically run a compensating transaction to reverse the successful one, often by performing the successful activity in reverse. The Purchasing service is much easier to implement because it can delegate all of this process management to the BPM engine, which is specialized to perform business processes reliably for any application.

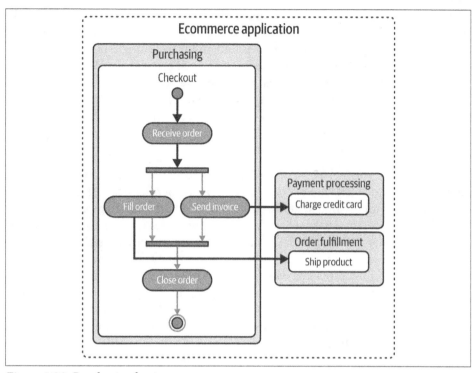

Figure 4-30. Purchasing business process

A *Service Orchestrator* can delegate to other *Service Orchestrators*. For example, checkout delegates to ship product and charge credit card. While charge credit card may be an atomic task—either it succeeds or it fails—the ship product task may be multistep and so Order Fulfillment may also be implemented as a *Service Orchestrator*. In this case, the Purchasing service, a *Service Orchestrator*, delegates to Order Fulfillment, which is implemented as another *Service Orchestrator*.

Conclusion: Wrapping up Microservices Architecture

This chapter discussed how best to build applications that work the way the cloud does: small components that can be replicated easily and distributed across infrastructure. A Microservices Architecture combines Cloud-Native Architecture (58) with a Distributed Architecture (38), forming an architecture that makes an application work the way the cloud does. The architecture structures an application to model a domain as a set of Microservices (119), components that collaborate through well-defined Service API (70) interfaces, where each implements a single complete business capability, manages its own data, is deployed independently, runs independently, and can be developed by a small development team working independently from others.

The main type of *Microservice* is a Domain Microservice (130), what tutorials usually mean when they say "microservice." A *Domain Microservice*, like a domain object in object-oriented programming, models and simulates a single business capability in an enterprise's business domain. Each *Domain Microservice* is designed to work the way the domain does, to model and automate the business's rules and logic. This kind of *Microservice* offers the most design flexibility: the business analysts and programmers have complete control to subdivide the domain into what they consider individual capabilities, scope them, assign them meaningful functionality, and invent an interface for clients to access that functionality.

Another type of *Microservice* is an Adapter Microservice (135), a type that is less commonly documented but very necessary for a Microservices Architecture that needs to work with existing systems. An *Adapter Microservice* wraps an existing system of record or other external SaaS service and includes it as another *Microservice* in the architecture. Whereas a development team has extensive flexibility to design a *Domain Microservice* as a complete business capability, an *Adapter Microservice's* scope of functionality is dictated by that of the existing system it wraps. To the extent the existing system's functionality isn't a very good business capability or its interface isn't very service oriented, the *Adapter Microservice* won't be either. The *Microservice* can try to transform the existing system's capability, functions, and data structures into a well-designed *Microservice*, but the *Microservice* may be little more than a thin veneer around an artifact from a bygone era that nevertheless is still running in the enterprise, providing important business functionality. That functionality should be incorporated into the Microservices Architecture as is, and an *Adapter Microservice* provides the means to do so.

A Service Orchestrator (160) is a composite type of *Microservice* that composes its functionality from other *Microservices*, mostly *Domain Microservices*, as well as *Adapter Microservices* and even other service orchestrators. Each *Microservice* has a different interface that abstracts the functionality it provides. By combining the functionality of other *Microservices*, a *Service Orchestrator* makes bigger parts from smaller ones. A *Service Orchestrator* is in a position to manage transactions, bringing transactionality to Microservices Architecture and Cloud-Native Architecture that otherwise doesn't support transactions. Service orchestrators lend themselves to implementing business processes and are often implemented as business processes in business process management (BPM) engines.

A special kind of *Microservice* is the Dispatcher (140). It forms the interface between a client outside the Microservices Architecture and the ever-changing multitude of *Microservices* inside the architecture. Whereas other types of *Microservices* are composable and appear throughout the architecture, *Dispatchers* are positioned only on the edge of the architecture with the external clients. *Microservices* delegate to other *Microservices*, but not to *Dispatchers*, and *Dispatchers* do not delegate to other *Dispatchers*, only to *Microservices*. Yet like other *Microservices*, each *Dispatcher* can be developed independently, deployed independently, and replicated and distributed across multiple computers. It fails independently and can even scale independently, although *Dispatchers* rarely need to. Whereas *Microservices* provide business capabilities, a *Dispatcher* provides whatever functionality its client requires, modeling the client's capabilities more than the domain's and implementing its functionality using whatever *Microservices* it needs in the architecture. Like other *Microservices*, each *Dispatcher* can be developed by a separate team, one that usually also develops the client that uses the *Dispatcher*.

A Microservices Architecture supports Polyglot Development (146), where each development team gets to choose the language for implementing their *Microservice*. Monolithic applications are usually monolingual, meaning that all of the code has to be written in one language because it all runs in the monolith's runtime. Because each *Microservice* runs in its own process with its own Application Package (62) runtime, separate *Microservices* can have different runtimes and can therefore be written in different languages. Typical cloud-friendly languages for implementing *Microservices* include Node.js, Java, Go (aka Golang), and Python. *Dispatchers* are often implemented in Node.js, and *Domain Microservices* are often implemented in Java. *Adapter Microservices* may be implemented in Java to use the Java Connector Architecture (JCA) but can also be implemented using enterprise service bus (ESB) technologies for adapting service interfaces onto legacy systems of record. Service orchestrators can be implemented in programming code but can sometimes be implemented better using a business process management (BPM) engine. If one language or technology is the best fit for all of the *Microservices* in an architecture, use it; but the architecture also supports implementing each *Microservice* in whatever language or technology works best for its requirements, regardless of what is used to implement other *Microservices*.

Each *Microservice* should persist its data in its own Self-Managed Data Store (154). Replicas of a *Microservice* all share the same data store. Microservices support Polyglot Persistence (375), where separate *Microservices* can choose different types of data stores that best fit each *Microservice's* requirements. Only a *Microservice* can access the data in its data store. The rest of the application can only access a *Microservice's* data by invoking that *Microservice's* interface. The *Microservice* has complete control to decide the format of its data and to evolve that format as necessary, and to manage the data's consistency according to the rules of the *Microservice's* capability.

Microservices can run in a traditional IT environment or in a cloud environment. While the cloud is not required, cloud services such as lifecycle management, load balancing, and autoscaling make *Microservices* much easier to deploy and manage.

Next, we'll explore how to design *Microservices*, especially *Domain Microservices*. It's easy to say that a business domain should be separated into individual business capabilities and that each *Microservice* should model a single business capability, but it is much more difficult to analyze a business domain and figure out what those individual business capabilities are so that they can be modeled. Microservice Design (Chapter 5) 5 shows how to use the event storming technique and domain-driven design concepts to model a domain and discover its individual *Microservices*.

After that, we'll look at Event-Driven Architecture (Chapter 6), an alternative to centrally controlled service orchestration that uses events to choreograph *Microservices* in dynamically discovered interactions. After that, Cloud-Native Storage (Chapter 7) explores how to persist and manage data in a distributed and unreliable cloud environment, and Cloud Application Clients (Chapter 8) describes a range of options for making the UIs that people will use to interact with cloud applications.

CHAPTER 5

Microservice Design

When embarking on developing an application using a Microservices Architecture (Chapter 4), it is important to understand how to best design the Microservices (119) that your application needs. Building a *Distributed Architecture*, such as a Microservices Architecture, has many challenges, and can be difficult to get right, specifically when dealing with possible failure points and distributed transactions.

When developing systems, it has been proven that designing, modeling, and building systems around the domain is a recipe for success. This is true regardless of the architectural style you are using. Understanding the requirements for a system and modeling the domain usually starts with a requirements-gathering phase to gain a better understanding of the domain and the problem we are solving. Requirements-gathering can elicit software requirements from various activities, such as discussing user scenarios, creating user stories, looking at sequences of events for the system, discussing various rules of the system, and examining how to validate the requirements. After the requirements have been gathered, discussed, and validated with the stakeholders, there is usually some form of a modeling phase. In the past, this modeling phase usually included taking your requirements and mapping your domain through some form of a business process modeling technique (i.e., Business Process Modeling Notation (BPMN), Unified Modeling Language (UML) diagrams, flow charts, and data flow diagrams). As useful as these modeling techniques with their diagrams can be, their technical nature means many domain experts are usually not that engaged during the modeling part of the analysis and design phase.

Introduction to Microservice Design

Agile teams promote more lightweight interactive processes that include feedback loops and participation from all stakeholders, including domain experts and end-users throughout the entire development process. Agile approaches encourage domain experts to work closely with the development teams. Most Agile teams deliver working systems, which includes getting valuable feedback and adapting as they learn. This kind of iterative process is at the core of "Agile" development processes. However, even this approach can have problems. The developer acts as a translator, translating the domain expert's mental model into code. But, as in any translation, there can be problems.

Another approach focuses on having the domain experts, the development team, other stakeholders, and (most importantly) the source code share the same model, thus they don't need translation from the domain expert's requirements to the code. Recently, lightweight techniques have become popular such as Event Storming (189), which promotes a more collaborative approach to understanding and modeling the domain. *Event Storming* often uses a subset of concepts from Domain-Driven Design (*https://oreil.ly/7jOfv*) to create an understandable model of the system that can then be mapped to a *Microservices* implementation. The results of these models are useful for creating systems with better availability, scalability, reliability, and modifiability. To be successful with the *Microservices* architectural style, you need to understand the good design principles (*Guiding *IDEALS**) for microservices design.

Guiding IDEALS for Designing Microservices

One might ask, what are good design principles for *Microservices*? Are there principles similar to the **SOLID** principles for designing object-oriented systems?[1] There are some fundamental **IDEALS** that have been outlined for designing modern service-based systems, which are six principles that are key for developing and implementing successful *Microservices*.[2] **IDEALS** is a mnemonic acronym meaning: **Interface segregation, Deployability, Event-driven, Availability over consistency, Loose Coupling**, and **Single responsibility**. Let's examine how these principles relate to *Microservices*.

---

1 In 2000, Robert C. Martin published an article entitled "Design Principles and Design Patterns" (*https://oreil.ly/2O6yC*), which was later compiled into the acronym **SOLID** by Michael Feathers. These design principles for object-oriented programming encourage the creation of software that is easier to maintain, more understandable, and more flexible. The **SOLID** principles are **Single responsibility, Open/closed, Liskov substitution, Interface segregation**, and **Dependency inversion**.

2 These **IDEALS** evolved through a collaboration between Paulo Merson and Joseph Yoder at the end of 2018 and early 2019. Paulo had some original *IDEAS* that we evolved for a talk at the SATURN Software Engineering conference. After some early feedback and discussions, these principles evolved to become what we are calling *Guiding **IDEALS** for Designing Microservices*.

- First there is **Interface segregation**, which tells us that different types of clients (such as mobile apps, web apps, and CLI programs) should be able to interact with services through the contract that best suits their needs. This is similar to **Interface segregation** you see in **SOLID**, except now we are extending it to the interface of our services. Some well-known patterns can help with this. For example, you can use some form of a Dispatcher (140) such as a *BFF* (*Backend for Frontend* is a variation of the **API Gateway** pattern). *BFFs* allow you to develop a specific **API Gateway** for each type of client (or frontend). Each *API Gateway* does routing, transformations, filtering, and the like. The main concept here is to develop different API calls for the different types of clients that need to call your *Microservice*. You can also create different APIs for your service.

- Next we have **Deployability**, which acknowledges that in the *Microservice* era, which can be called the DevOps era, there are critical design decisions and technology choices developers need to make regarding packaging, deploying, and running *Microservices*. Good design and implementation alone don't warrant success. Good **Deployability** practices are essential for the success of any system, and even more so with *Microservices*, as they greatly increase the number of deployment units. Several strategies can be employed to help with successful deployments such as Continuous Delivery, DevOps, Containerization, Serverless architecture, Monitoring, and Logging. There are variations of deployment strategies such as blue-green deployment, canary deployment, and rolling deployment that are very useful for deploying more reliably and safely into production environments.

- Another design principle for *Microservices* is **Event-driven**, which suggests that whenever and wherever possible, we should model our services to be activated by an asynchronous message or event, rather than a synchronous call. Synchronous request-response calls are still needed and used, but today's scalability and performance requirements pose a challenge that can be solved by processing events asynchronously. *Event-Driven Architecture* (EDA) is an architectural style that has been around for a long time. The core of EDA is where components communicate primarily through asynchronous messages or events. It is based upon a publisher/subscriber model (usually referred to as pub/sub) where services or components are decoupled from direct calls. Rather, they publish an event on an event bus, and those interested services or components subscribe to the events of interest.

- The next principle for *Microservices* is **Availability over consistency**, which reminds us that, in general, end users value the availability of the system over strong data consistency, and they are generally OK with this as long as they have eventual consistency. The problem is related to the CAP[3] theorem, specifically when dealing with distributed systems. The CAP theorem outlines that you can guarantee only consistency or availability but *not* both at the same time. So for a better user experience, nowadays it is usually better to favor **Availability over consistency** whenever possible.

- **Loose coupling** has always been an important design concern, and in the case of *Microservices*, has become even more critical, specifically concerning afferent (incoming) and efferent (outgoing) coupling. If you implement *Microservices* with a lot of dependencies, you are in a sense building a distributed monolith, or what we call a macro- or microlith. These systems are far worse than any problems a monolith may have specifically as you still have all of the coupling problems and now they are distributed. These systems can be very difficult when dealing with debugging and distributed transactions!

- The last principle is **Single responsibility**, which focuses on modeling the right-size *Microservices* that are not too large or too slim. Therefore, they will contain the right amount of cohesive functionality. This principle is usually the easiest to understand but one of the hardest to get right. To achieve the right-size service that is designed around a **Single responsibility**, it is important to Model Around the Domain (183). Any good domain modeling techniques can help you build well-designed, right-sized *Microservices* that meet the **Single responsibility** principle.

These design principles are useful when developing modern service-based distributed systems (which today we call *Microservices*). Domain modeling techniques such as those presented in the patterns in this chapter help you achieve these design principles.

Domain Modeling Techniques for Designing Microservices

This chapter presents seven patterns that describe techniques to model and design *Microservices* around the domain (see Figure 5-1). It starts by discussing how to Model Around the Domain (183) by applying *Event Storming* techniques along with a subset of domain modeling concepts to help design the *right size Microservices* (see the section "What's the Right Size for a Microservice?" on page 180).

---

3 More about the CAP theorem is available at Wikipedia (*https://oreil.ly/vxhwg*).

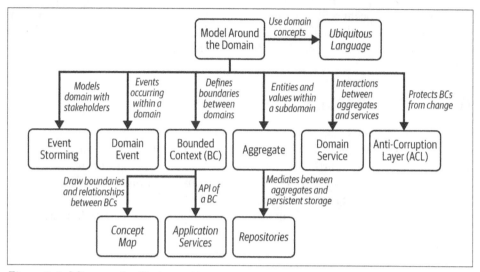

Figure 5-1. Microservice Design patterns

An *Event Storming* session brings stakeholders together to get a better understanding of the domain. The concepts within a domain are defined according to the language of the domain, called the *Ubiquitous Language*. *Event Storming* sessions begin by describing the various Domain Events (193) that happen to the system usually based upon user scenarios. Once you have an understanding of the events within the domain, you can then begin describing the boundaries (Bounded Contexts (201)) of the system. You will then define the types of things with their values (Aggregates (211)) for the domain and their respective *Repositories* to persist them through a persistence layer.

The storming session will also describe various behaviors of the system. Some of these behaviors belong to entities and will be associated with the entities. There will be other behaviors that do not belong to a specific entity but need to interact with multiple entities or *Aggregates* within the same *Bounded Context*. Domain Services (222) are used when the behavior is associated with multiple *Aggregates* independent of a specific entity. Protecting the system from change and allowing various parts of the system (*Bounded Contexts*) to evolve independently is supported by providing an Anti-Corruption Layer (229) which isolates individual parts of the system from one other.

The patterns in this chapter are independent of *Microservice* design and are useful for any type of architecture. However, these patterns are especially useful when applying the Microservices Architecture (Chapter 4) style. Successful design starts by knowing how to design the right size *Microservice* (see the section "What's the Right Size for a Microservice?" on page 180).

Out patterns will begin with our foundational pattern, Model Around the Domain (183). This chapter will conclude with a section that tells you how to take your design that was *Modeled Around the Domain* and implement it using the *Microservices* architectural style.

What's the Right Size for a Microservice?

Microservices Architecture (Chapter 4) has become well entrenched and accepted as an architectural style. Microservices became popular as an architectural style after James Lewis and Martin Fowler published their seminal paper on the subject, "Microservices" (*https://oreil.ly/Dnwyn*), in 2014. Since that time, we've learned some important lessons about building Microservices (119), and one of those lessons has to do with making sure that you think about and design the scope of each *Microservice* in the proper way.

When you think of the term "microservices," the first thing that catches your eye is the prefix "micro." According to most college Classical Greek textbooks, μικρός would have meant only "little" or "small" to Plato or Aristotle. However, in everyday English usage, "micro" tends to denote something astonishingly small—after all, a "micrometer" is a millionth of a meter, and you use a "microscope" to see things that are otherwise invisible to the naked eye because of their extremely small size.

It's in that difference of perception that the trouble lies. A *Microservice* should be "small" in comparison to the monoliths that came before it. However, it shouldn't be *too* small—trying to make your *Microservices* too small is one of the most common mistakes teams fall into when attempting to implement a Microservices Architecture. For example, you could create a *Microservice* for every function. This would create very chatty services that would need to cross many transactional boundaries in order to fulfill a request.

It's this thought that "microservices must be tiny" that leads to our first problem. One of the other common complaints we hear about *Microservices* is that it's too difficult to use them for complex domains such as banking because the REST or messaging interfaces they require don't provide a way to do two-phase commits across multiple *Microservices*. Whenever we hear that complaint, it sets off warning bells in our heads—that complaint is often a symptom that the team is thinking of their *Microservices* as very tiny things.

On the other hand, if *Microservices* are too large, you also have many potential problems. When you develop a Microservices Architecture that looks like the previous architecture, you have essentially gone all the way back to the problem that *Microservices* were intended to solve! You've not only re-created the monolith, but you've made it worse by creating a distributed monolith (or what we sometimes like to call *macroliths*).

Because of this, the term *Microservice* has led many to ponder the question, How big or how small should a *Microservice* be? Many say it should be small enough to be developed in one week by a team that can be fed by two pizzas. This can be a difficult guideline to follow, some of us can eat a lot of pizza. If you google this question, you find many possible answers. Instead, let's formulate an upper and lower bound for consideration.

Lower Bound

A *Microservice* should consist of no less than an *Aggregate* (or at least an independent entity) and the associated Application and Domain Services that operate on the entities of that *Aggregate*.

Aggregates (211) are groups of related entities whose lifecycles are tied together, allowing them to be treated as a single cohesive unit. The canonical example of an *Aggregate* is the Order/LineItem relationship, which we will explore at length.

As we have referred to earlier, a service is a "reification" of a function. We have also pointed out that Domain Services (222) refers to a domain concept that does not naturally correspond to any particular entity or Value Object. The Banking account "Transfer" that we called out in our earlier example is a perfect example of that idea.

The most important design point here is that when thinking about how small to make your *Microservices*, you have to think very, very carefully about transaction boundaries. First of all, you have to think about the lifecycle of the entities involved in your *Microservice*—the create/read/update/delete cycle that we always think about in terms of persistence. But then you have to extend your thinking to all of the updates that can happen to groups of these entities—these are the kinds of things that *Domain Services* will identify. However, it's not just simple one-to-one transactions like transfers that you need to think about. You need to think more widely in the domain about other operations on groups of entities—particularly around things like batch updates and complex queries.

At this point, some purists may be shouting, "But wait! This would require 10, maybe 20, separate REST interfaces on my microservice!" That may be true. If the particular area of your domain is complex enough to warrant that many operations on a single set of entities, that is the smallest unit that you should be releasing as your *Microservice*. It may feel more like a mini-monolith, but it's still better than trying to solve the problems that trying to split it any smaller would create.

What we have found is that it is always better to initially err on the side of making a *Microservice* too large than making it too small. It is easier to take a larger (coarser-grained) *Macro Service* and split (refactor) it into two services than it is to take two fine-grained *Microservices* and combine them.

If this is the right lower bound for a *Microservices* design, how do you practically go about identifying all of those *Aggregates* and especially the services that go along with them? Luckily, there is a very good answer to that question: start your design process by performing Event Storming (189).

Upper Bound

A *Microservice* shall be no larger than the bounded context of a group of related (cohesive) *Aggregates* as you model around the domain.

When you Model Around a Domain (183), a central pattern that delimits the boundaries around the domain model of a subdomain is Bounded Context (201). This is where you can partition your system into different boundaries and discuss the interrelationships between these boundaries. Bounded Contexts define the boundaries within a subdomain and can also be seen as the boundaries of *Microservices*. Within each *Bounded Context*, we have *Aggregates*, which are the related types of things within the domain (Entities), and their values. The *Bounded Contexts* also include the behaviors within that boundary. Therefore, a *Microservice* can have a single *Aggregate*, or two, or more as long as they are cohesive.

One more possible litmus test to apply on the upper bound is to look at the business capabilities. If your *Microservice* were to fail, and it would cause more than one business capability to fail, either your *Microservice* is too coarse grained and you should refactor it or you have a different problem in that you have too many business processes depending on this one particular *Microservice* (e.g., you put it on the critical path of several different flows). Once again, this is where *Event Storming* can help you model around these business capabilities specifically when you find the boundaries through context mapping.

Finding the Right Level of Abstraction

One of the biggest problems that we see in the field with teams building *Microservices* designs is that they don't often start with a technique like *Event Storming* while applying principles of domain modeling. Instead, they start somewhere else, like with the design of their existing system, and try to derive their *Microservices* from there. Or else they start with an architecture (often specified in terms of tools and frameworks) and try to just let the *Microservices* evolve "organically."

In both cases, what you end up with are not what we would call *Microservices*— they tend to be focused on technology and not at all related to terms that the business would recognize. A symptom of inadequate design is that there are few or no Domain Microservices (130) in the solution, because you didn't start with the business vocabulary. Starting with the business vocabulary, the *Ubiquitous Language*, is a critical first step, and that's why we suggest that all teams building *Microservices* apply domain modeling as part of their design process.

A detailed discussion of this topic can be found on the blog entry "What's the Right Size for a Microservice" by Kyle Brown (*https://oreil.ly/CA9Gk*).

Model Around the Domain

You are embarking on developing an application using the Microservices Architectural (Chapter 4) style and deploying it on the cloud. Part of this development starts with stakeholders describing the requirements for building the application. You understand the benefits of using *Microservices* for new applications and refactoring applications to *Microservices*, but you are unsure how to best start.

How can you encourage stakeholders to explain enough of the domain requirements in a way that reveals the relevant capabilities for the application you are building?

Gaining a shared understanding of the requirements for the domain and building the right thing is challenging regardless of the architectural style used. The temptation is to start as quickly as possible and let the system evolve as you learn more about the domain. However, having a clear understanding of the domain and the problem being solved is useful for developing the right solution, particularly if that solution includes *Microservices*.

Many team members understand how to develop a monolithic application. Knowing how to design the *right size Microservice* can be challenging. How big or how small should a good *Microservice* be? How should various parts of functionality be developed and deployed? How should all of those different components relate to one another and communicate with one another?

It can be difficult to know what should be included in a *Microservice* and what should not be part of a *Microservice*. Where should the boundaries be between *Microservices*? What if our services need to share data? Should we have multiple databases, and if so, how do we keep multiple databases consistent?

Although there are many benefits to *Microservices*, building a Distributed Architecture (38) can be very challenging. They can be difficult to test. There can be complexity because of many services. How can we minimize dependencies between *Microservices*? *Microservices* inherit all of the problems or challenges inherent in Distributed Architecture (38).

Therefore,

Model Around the Domain to capture the application's requirements by bringing stakeholders together to describe the subject area in terms of the domain that you are implementing.

Domain modeling techniques help team members acquire an understanding of the system to be built, specifically the requirements from the perspective of the domain experts. You bring developers and key domain experts to describe and model the requirements or subject area of interest. This includes identifying key concepts, looking at the types of things that happen within the domain, identifying the types of things and values needed for the system, and describing the relationships between elements of the domain. The main goal is to get an understanding of the details of the domain and the requirements for the system.

Domain modeling sessions help those involved with the system to acquire an understanding of it and create a description of the domain to translate the requirements for building the system. Domain modeling helps to clarify requirements and usually includes a domain model representation of the problem space. Most domain modeling techniques include a visual representation of the domain model. These sessions are usually informal and use lightweight techniques using whiteboards and sticky notes, either physical or virtual (see Figure 5-2). They avoid discussing technical issues and keep the focus and the discussion around understanding the terminology for the domain.

Figure 5-2. Domain modeling session[4]

A domain model is a representation of real-world ideas that usually include the flow of a system to be built. Domain models include entities or "things" within the system and explore how they are related. Domain models can be represented graphically,

---

4 Photo of Graziela Simone Tonin and Joe Yoder discussing some Domain Modeling principles near Cologne Germany in 2024.

and various diagrams and tools can be used to model domains. A domain model is a conceptual model of the domain that incorporates both behavior and data. It describes both the entities (the types of things included in the domain) and the types of values these entities include. Domain models also include the rules and events for things that happen within the domain.

A domain model also includes the vocabulary and key concepts of the problem domain, and it identifies relationships and the rules among the entities of that domain. Domain modeling helps stakeholders gain a better understanding of the domain and discover the domain in-depth. Additionally, domain modeling can help create a common language that includes business knowledge about the domain. The idea that software systems should be modeled closely to the domain has been around for a long time.

Building a *Distributed Architecture*, such as a Microservices Architecture (Chapter 4), has many challenges and can be difficult to get right, specifically when dealing with possible failure points and distributed transactions. Many have suggested that using a subset of *Domain-Driven Design* (2003) (DDD) modeling techniques can help define the functional scope of *Microservices*. But the techniques needed to apply this idea "in practice" are not clear to everyone. Domain modeling is *not only* an approach to *Microservice* design but is also a proven general technique useful for any design, whether *Microservices* or not.

Domain modeling helps you identify the right business capabilities that map to good *Microservices* and aids in designing the right-sized *Microservices* modeled around the domain. We will focus on that subset of DDD concepts that are most useful for designing *microservices* (or components in a Modular Monolith (29)), such as *Domain (and subdomain), Domain Models, Aggregate, Entity, Value Object, Bounded Context, Anti-Corruption Layer, Ubiquitous Language, Application Service, Domain Event*, and *Domain Service*.

The primary concept discussed as part of DDD is *domain and subdomain*. A definition of a DDD domain outlined by Eric Evans is: "A sphere of knowledge, influence, or activity. The subject area to which the user applies a program is the *domain* of the software." Some examples of domains are banking, insurance, medical, and airline booking services. The main principle of DDD is driving the design around the domain you are working on.

A domain is the area in which you solve a problem with software in an organization—for example, finance, insurance, banking, manufacturing, etc. This includes the concepts and business rules needed to achieve the business goals of the organization. Domain refers to the specific subject that the project is being developed for. The goal is to limit the complexity of a solution by tailoring it as closely as possible to the domain with the help of experts from that domain. When modeling systems, we have to choose the most appropriate domain boundaries with which to align our software and organizational boundaries. When *Modeling around the Domain*, it is important to think about the core domains within the systems you are developing. For example, if we are dealing with the banking domain, you can say that the main domain is everything related to money, finances, and customer relationships. Of course, there are many subdomains for banking, such as personal banking, investment banking, and credit cards.

Most domains are composed of subdomains. What's the difference between a domain and a subdomain? A domain can contain subdomains, which can contain subdomains. Every subdomain is, in a sense, a domain, and most domains are a subdomain. The only time a domain is not a subdomain is when the model does not contain a higher-level parent domain. So for the personal banking subdomain, you can have a subdomain of accounts that could also have a couple of subdomains, such as cash accounts and credit accounts.

The goal is to develop a shared mental model that various stakeholders use to communicate about the system around the domain. This shared mental model is a common understanding of the concepts used by all the teams in an organization. The challenge in *Modeling around the Domain* is to describe the domains with subdomains, and within each subdomain to describe the things (entities and values) along with the behavior (*Domain Events* and domain services). For each subdomain, you have boundaries (called *Bounded Contexts*) and a common business language (*Ubiquitous Language*)[5] for that subdomain.

Ubiquitous Language

In the early days of modeling, there was an emphasis on developing an enterprise model that could be shared across the entire organization. Idealistically this sounded good, but in practice, it led to many problems, specifically as different parts of the enterprise had different views and needs for their various systems and subsystems. Trying to manage and maintain an enterprise model created a maintenance nightmare and often required different systems within your organization to deal with various attributes and behavior they did *not* need. DDD has a concept that helps with this called *Ubiquitous Language*.

Ubiquitous Language is a concept that emphasizes building a common, rigorous language between developers and domain experts about your domain and subdomains. This language should be based on the *Domain Model* using terminology from the domain experts. Eric Evans (*https://oreil.ly/lH-4g*) says, "Domain experts should object to terms or structures that are awkward or inadequate to convey domain understanding; developers should watch for ambiguity or inconsistency that will trip

---

5 *Ubiquitous Language* is an implicit pattern originally described in *Domain-Driven Design* (*https://oreil.ly/5Je0A*) (Addison-Wesley Professional).

up design." *Ubiquitous Language* is a common vocabulary that the entire team shares and uses together as they communicate about the system. The code should also express the *Ubiquitous Language*. For example, entities, values, and events should use the same terms that are part of this *Ubiquitous Language*.

A *Ubiquitous Language* is *not* a *Universal Language*. The same term may mean different things in different subdomains. A domain entity may show up in different subdomains with different attributes and behaviors. For example, think of the concept of an account entity within a banking system. The concept of an account will be seen in many subdomains, such as the CreditCard and SavingsAccount subdomains. The concept of Account for the CreditCard subdomain will have different attributes than the concept of Account for the SavingsAccount subdomain. A credit card account might need attributes such as credit limit, charges, and the like—whereas a savings account will need values such as balance and interest. They may have some common attributes, such as the owner of the account, but they will each have their respective view for their subdomains. So when applying the concept of *Ubiquitous Language*, rather than trying to create an enterprise model representing everything about accounts for all subdomains, we have a language and view of accounts for each domain or subdomain; the CreditCard domain will have its common language for a credit card account, while the Saving Account domain will have its common language for a Savings account. Therefore, we don't have to maintain an enterprise view of *Account*. *CreditCard* and *SavingsAccount* will each have their unique view of *Account*. Therefore, the two subdomains can vary independently as needed without affecting other systems or subdomains.

As the saying goes, "Context is king." The meaning of a concept depends upon the context (the domain) in which it is being used. Another example could be something like a *Customer* (or user) of an online ordering system. For placing the order, we need just enough general information about the *Customer* to place the order. However, when processing payment, we probably need different information about the Customer. Order placement and Payment processing are two different subdomains. Depending upon the context, we allow the different subdomains to have their view of the *Customer* it needs without corrupting it with views from other domains. In other words, different from a Universal or Unified language, *Ubiquitous Language* evolves as it makes sense within a subdomain, without any concern about concepts that are part of other subdomains.

Regardless of the architectural style, modeling around the domain has proved to be very useful to get a better understanding of the domain and the problem you are solving. It also assists with understanding the requirements and finding what types of things with values and events will be happening within the system. *Modeling Around the Domain* helps to create a RESTful service design for *Microservices*. Not all of these will become part of your *Microservices* design—some might be hidden in your service implementation—but you can start to understand the types of things that you're dealing with.

An ongoing argument exists about which comes first: the design of your API or the design of the objects or components that implement your API. Many early distributed-computing proponents advocated designing the *objects* first and then making your API the same as your *Object API*. This approach led to problems in the granularity of the API, which often resulted in APIs that represented technical interfaces instead of interfaces designed around the domain. When you start with the API, you can focus on solving the domain problem and avoid getting lost in the technical details of a particular implementation. This is similar to design by contract in that you focus on the contract forming the agreed-upon API.

The main challenge to modeling is to get the right stakeholders together to get a shared understanding of the domain. It takes time and commitment from people who usually have very busy schedules. The temptation for many agile organizations is to start quickly and let the details of the domain evolve as you go. However, this can come at a cost, especially when the system evolves around the boundaries between subdomains. If boundaries are not properly defined, then the system can become muddy (22), making it hard to evolve and maintain. Fortunately, there are lightweight techniques that can assist with this and are worth the time and effort.

When you design *Microservices* for an application, you first need to get stakeholders together to understand the domain. This can be done through Event Storming (189). *Event Storming* is a popular nontechnical domain modeling technique to help stakeholders gain a better understanding of the requirements by describing them in the language of the business. This technique uses concepts from domain modeling and helps establish the Bounded Contexts (201) (boundaries) for your teams' *Domains and Subdomains*. *Event Storming* helps create an understandable model of the system that can then be mapped to a *Microservices* implementation. The results of these models are useful for creating systems with better availability, scalability, reliability, and modifiability.

When modeling, you define the boundaries of your domain and subdomains, specifically the strategic boundaries called *Bounded Context*. An Anti-Corruption Layer (229) can help *Bounded Contexts* to evolve independently from one another regardless of the interactions between them.

Within each Bounded Context, you will identify the types of things needed within each *BC* (the entities and values), which are grouped together in Aggregates (211). Domain modeling also describes the behavior of the system, called Domain Services (222), which can be triggered by a Domain Event (193). You will also define the API for the *Bounded Context*, which is called *Application Services*. The concepts within a Bounded Context are described using a *Ubiquitous Language*.

The end design goal for these *Microservices* will be to build a Microservices Architecture (Chapter 4) based on an Event-Driven Architecture (Chapter 6).

Event Storming

You are Modeling around the Domain (183) and have started by gathering stakeholders to describe the requirements for designing a system to get a better understanding of the domain and the problem you are solving.

How do you encourage the stakeholders to understand and describe the elements and events around the domain and subdomain?

Domain modeling techniques help team members acquire an understanding of a given project or program and create a description of the domain to translate the requirements of that project into software components. Domain modeling helps to clarify requirements and usually includes a domain model representation of the problem space. Most domain modeling techniques include a visual representation of the domain model. It is often difficult to know how to start the modeling of the domain, especially with many stakeholders with different backgrounds.

Many teams want to start developing the system as fast as possible. This is at the core of agile practices. Designing, modeling and building systems around the domain is a recipe for success. Most agile teams deliver working systems, which includes getting valuable feedback, and adapting as they learn. This kind of iterative process is at the core of "agile" development processes. However, even this approach can have problems. The developer acts as a translator, translating the domain expert's mental model into code. But, as in any translation, there can be problems.

One of the complaints that many people have had about many domain modeling techniques is that they seem to be concerned only with the static functionality of the system. Concepts from modeling can be helpful for getting a better understanding of the vocabulary (the *Ubiquitous Language*) of a business domain. However, many practitioners struggle to determine how to translate the pieces of the *Ubiquitous Language* expressed as *Entities*, *Aggregates*, and *Services* into a complete and functioning system.

A dynamic view of a system allows stakeholders to understand how data is created, how it flows through the system, and how the system should react in response to changes introduced from the outside world. Getting this dynamic view can be challenging and requires many stakeholders to come together to communicate and validate this view.

Therefore,

Perform an *Event Storming* session to elucidate the set of *Domain Events* that flow through a system

This process reveals the boundaries of the system and describes the types of things and actions within a subdomain. *Event Storming* (*https://oreil.ly/bBcc1*) is a brainstorming or design thinking technique developed by Alberto Brandolini in 2012 to quickly find out what is happening in the domain for a system to be developed. Compared to other methods, it is extremely lightweight and intentionally requires no support from a computer.[6] *Event Storming* is not data modeling or object modeling. Rather, it focuses on the events or behavior of the system that can be quickly implemented and validated. The basic idea is to bring together software developers and domain experts to learn from one another. Originally this was done in person at the same physical location.

Event Storming creates a shared common understanding of the domain model. The stakeholders involved include domain experts, technical people, product managers, and product owners. It is intentionally a lightweight, *nontechnical*, workshop-based method that helps participants quickly describe the domain and events of the desired system. It is usually done with sticky notes on a wide wall, although remote *Event Storming* has become popular and can be done with various online tools. Although the results will influence your architecture and technical decision, these sessions *avoid* discussing architectural and implementation issues.

When doing an in-person *Event Storming* session, it is important to have a lot of sticky notes, pens, and markers. Participants are primarily standing and working together placing sticky notes on a wall or board. Therefore, it is good to have a lot of space. The workshop will consist of several steps, so it is a good practice to time-box each step.

Event Storming has various steps to assist with the brainstorming session for eliciting events, *Aggregates*, and views of the system. The following outlines the main steps in *Event Storming*:[7]

1. Identify sequences of *Domain Events*.
2. Add commands that caused the *Domain Events*.

   2a. Add the actor that executes the command.

---

6 While *Event Storming* does not require any computer support, it is perfectly acceptable, but perhaps not optimal, to conduct remote *Event Storming* sessions using computerized sticky note boards such as Mural.

7 A more detailed description of a variation of these steps can be found on "Event Storming by IBM" (*https://oreil.ly/BHFkj*). You can also find an example Microservices implementation that includes an example of *Event Storming* for Container Shipment in the IBM article "Container Shipment Example" (*https://oreil.ly/9BOnS*).

---

3. Add corresponding *Aggregates* (this will reveal the entities and values).

4. Identify *Bounded Contexts* around pivotal events.

The team needs to decide on a legend for the colors of the sticky notes used during the *Event Storming* session. For example, you might consider something similar to that outlined in Figure 5-3 (Domain Events are orange, Command is blue, and Aggregate is yellow).[8] At the minimum, you need something for *Domain Events*, commands, actors, and *Aggregates*. You might also have color stickies for policies, views, errors, questions, external systems, and others. See Chapter 7 in Vaughn Vernon's book *Domain-Driven Design Distilled* (2016) for examples of color options.

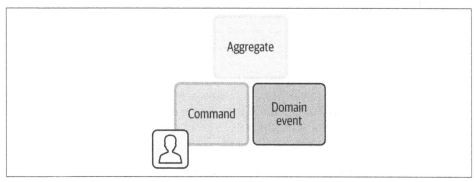

Figure 5-3. Event Storming layout

You begin with identifying the sequences of *Domain Events*. *Event Storming* begins with a team writing down all of the "facts" about their system that they can think of on sticky notes. A fact should be expressed in the past tense, such as, "Deposit has been credited." These facts are the events that can happen to the system. The team then arranges all of the facts they discovered in linear (time-sequence) order horizontally on a wall (usually from left to right). These facts are the *Domain Events* that can happen in the system. They show how one occurrence will be followed in time by another and another and another. Where simultaneous events occur, they can be placed in different horizontal swim lanes separated vertically as seen in Figure 5-4, which outlines candidate system boundaries. These lines for swim lanes and boundaries are usually shown in blue as you create them on a whiteboard with blue painter's tape.

---

8 If you are reading the print book, you will see sticky notes in different shades of gray. For the full color figures, please see the digital version of the text on the O'Reilly online learning platform.

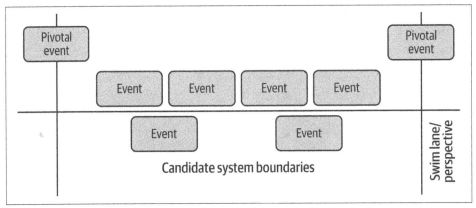

Figure 5-4. Bounded Context around pivotal events

After the team agrees on the sequence(s) of events in time, they can then "decorate" the events by adding: "commands" that create an event, actors that cause commands to be issued, policies that automatically turn one event into another, and data that each event either requires or generates (*Aggregates*). As a result, a dynamic system design begins to emerge from the sequence of time-based events.

Finally, the events can be grouped by data elements and related commands within a scenario to represent a *Bounded Context*. In this way, the *Event Storming* approach has thus helped find and validate the related set of *Entities* with values called *Aggregates*. You also describe the commands and actors within a *Bounded Context*.

Each *Bounded Context* that you identify is a candidate *Microservice*. It is important to start with "Step 1" by identifying the sequence of *Domain Events*, and "Step 2," which identifies the actors and commands for the events. Steps 3–4 can be done in any order by members of the team. For example, after they have identified the *Domain Events* with their respective commands and actors triggering the events, teams can start outlining the boundaries of the events (*Bounded Contexts*) before they describe the *Aggregates*.

Event Storming brings together various stakeholders, including domain experts and other participants with different expertise, to share their domain knowledge by expressing it on colorful sticky notes on a wide wall. *Event Storming* is effective primarily because it is a fast, lightweight, interactive, nontechnical workshop. It is also very straightforward and easy to do. Rather than using complex UML or other modeling techniques, *Event Storming* breaks the process down into simple terms that both technical and nontechnical stakeholders can understand. *Event Storming* is very engaging and effective, its greatest value perhaps being the conversations around the domain and business processes for the system being developed.

The main challenge of *Event Storming* is the difficulty of finding the time to engage the necessary stakeholders. Trying to get the right set of stakeholders together can be difficult. *Event Storming* sessions require a skilled facilitator to guide the discussions and to manage the time in order to keep the participants focused and moving forward. The sessions can provide incomplete information because the model may primarily reflect the views and understanding of the participants with the strongest voices. The sessions may overlook or be missing perspectives from important stakeholders who do not attend. Finally, *Event Storming* can be challenging in that it does not specify to teams all of the necessary parts of an implementation. Fortunately, there are some well-known practices discussed in this chapter that will describe how to meet these challenges.

While performing Event Storming (189), you can use the following concepts to further model your domain:

- Identify Domain Events (193) in terms of the *Ubiquitous Language* for the business logic across Bounded Contexts.

- Identify the Bounded Context (201) around pivotal events that reveal the boundaries of the subdomains for the system.

- Identify *Aggregates* (211) (entities and values) and their respective *Repositories* defined in terms of the *Ubiquitous Language*.

- Identify Domain Services (222) using terms of the *Ubiquitous Language* for the business logic within a Bounded Context.

- When looking at interactions between *Bounded Contexts*, consider an Anti-Corruption Layer (229) to protect from change.

Once you have applied *Event Storming* to identify the *Domain Events*, you will find you are well on your way to beginning to implement an Event-Driven Architecture (Chapter 6). During the modeling session, boundaries (*Bounded Contexts*) will be outlined that will map to the boundaries of a Microservices Architecture (Chapter 4).

Domain Event

You are Modeling around the Domain (183) a system and started by getting stakeholders together to perform an Event Storming (189) session to better understand the domain. The primary goal of this session is to get an understanding of the requirements and what happens in the domain of the system being built.

How do you model those aspects of a design that correspond to things that happen during the various scenarios encountered by the system?

There are many types of things that can happen to a system over time. Sometimes it is some simple change to some data. When this happens, we associate the behavior to make that data change with the entities responsible for that data. The process of making that change may, in turn, also invoke some other domain-specific operation.

However, there are many cases where you have some actions or changes within a *Bounded Context* that are not the responsibility of any specific *Entities*. For example, there are times when some state changes will need to trigger some action to be taken. These actions might need to trigger something to invoke a behavior, possibly in another *Bounded Context*. In other words, something could happen to an *Aggregate* that will trigger an event that might need to change another *Aggregate* either in its *BC* or cause something to happen to another subdomain (a different *BC*).

However, one of the biggest potential issues is one of extension. When all you have is the *Service API* of a module or *Microservice*, the only way to find anything out about the state of the information hidden by that module is to call its API. That API is static; if you want to identify that something has changed over time, your only option is to repeatedly call a part of that API until you get a different response. But the thing is that systems tend to evolve and gain new features associated with whenever changes occur.

As a very simple example, the best time to offer you a paid upgrade to a hotel stay is once you've arrived at the hotel but before you've checked in. Let's say the hotel has upgrades that are unsold—if you've arrived but not checked in, you're at the best possible time to pay for that slightly larger room or bigger bed. You're already thinking about getting to your room, and the promise of a better stay is very enticing—more so than it would have been when you booked your room and were being budget conscious. But to offer you this upgrade, the hotel application (or staff!) has to act fast to offer you that upgrade during that optimal time window.

This is all to say that the time element is important to system design—especially when you want to think about how to extend your system's basic functionality to cover cases (like just-in-time hotel upgrades!) that your original design may not have anticipated. Having a system extension point that allows you to take advantage of changes in time is a critical way of making the system open for extension while remaining closed for modification.

Therefore,

Whenever something changes, create a *Domain Event* noting that something has occurred or changed so that appropriate action be taken.

A *Domain Event* is a representation of something that has happened in the domain and that you want other parts of the domain to know about. A *Domain Event* can also be seen as a statement of a fact that something of interest has happened in the *Ubiquitous Language* of the domain. These facts or events about the system are always expressed in "past tense," such as "Deposit has been credited." *Domain Events* are sometimes called *business events* and express things that occurred to the domain at a specific point in time.

These events signify that something of interest has happened within a domain and can trigger a change or some action in another part of the domain. There are commands that trigger these events and actors that execute the commands. These events can occur in a subdomain of the larger domain and can trigger some action in a different subdomain.

Let's examine the domain of a pizza delivery place called *Joe's Pizza* to illustrate *Domain Events*. *Joe's Pizza* allows customers to order pizzas either online or by phone. When a customer wants to place an order, they will trigger an `Order Requested` event. Once this happens, the system will need to get the pizza types the customer desires, their payment information, and the customer's delivery address. Once the `Pizza Type Entered`, `Payment Info Entered`, and `Customer Address Entered` events have been completed, we can place an order by triggering an `Ordered Placed` event (see Figure 5-5).

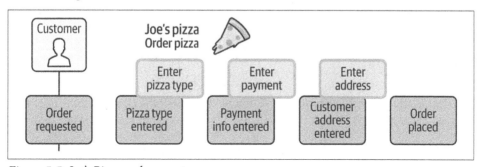

Figure 5-5. Joe's Pizza order events

Domain Events typically represent state change. For example, in our online ordering system, we will have events such as `Order Placed`, `Payment Accepted`, and `Order Shipped`. When these events happen, they usually trigger some actions or behaviors to be invoked. Sometimes an event will trigger a simple action within the same part of the system. For example, in a `ShoppingCart`, you can think of changing the quantity of some item you are ordering. This would simply trigger a call to update the number of items for that order. On the other hand, some events might trigger a more complex action, such as when an "order is placed," you want to trigger an action to `Ship the`

Order. And, once an order has been shipped, it will trigger events that result in actions, such as email the customer.

Domain Events can either be part of the domain or be triggered by something outside of the domain. The most obvious case, of course, is when a human interacts with a system through its user interface to trigger an event (like item added to cart). However, there are many other ways in which external actions or systems can trigger *Domain Events* as well. The Internet of Things is a great set of examples for this— many homes (and most cell phones!) have lots of different types of sensors that can be used to trigger events. For instance, almost every cell phone has a light sensor that's used to determine how to set the brightness of the screen. It turns out that applications can use that same sensor as a movement sensor to guess if a person is moving inside or outside, or if they are moving between rooms with different light levels. RFID (Radio Frequency Identifier) sensors are also built into most phones and can sense when a person moves past a particular radio transmitter (a "beacon"). All of these contribute to geolocation events that can help an application, for instance, locate someone on a map inside a building where GPS signals don't reach.

Finally, external systems may trigger events—you may receive an email, or a text, or some other communication over any of a variety of protocols, old and new. You need to represent those changes inside your system as well, so this is an important way to isolate your system from knowledge of these protocols (perhaps with an Anti-Corruption Layer (229)) while still taking advantage of the notification that the communication has taken place.

Implementation

Implementation of *Domain Events* will vary depending upon the event. You will see in the next section how to partition subdomains into *Bounded Contexts* that ultimately map to the boundaries of *Microservices*. In our pizza example, sometimes there will be events that trigger simple actions, such as the one for requesting the order. When an order is requested, some commands might lead to simply creating the *Aggregates* to represent the customer and the type of pizza they want. On the other hand, some events might trigger an action that needs to interact with another subdomain, such as the example of when the order for the pizza has been placed. *Domain Events* are usually implemented and deployed as part of the *Microservice Bounded Context* for where the event belongs.

When an event triggers something that needs to interact with a different subdomain, it will publish the event as part of a publishing subdomain, and there will be subscribing subdomains interested in the event. Figure 5-6 shows an example of a publishing subdomain (*Bounded Context*) that sends an event to a *messaging mechanism* that will have a subscribing subdomain (*Bounded Context*) handle the event. In other words, these events will represent that something has happened in the publishing domain that the subscribing domain is interested in, which might invoke some action by the subscribing domain.

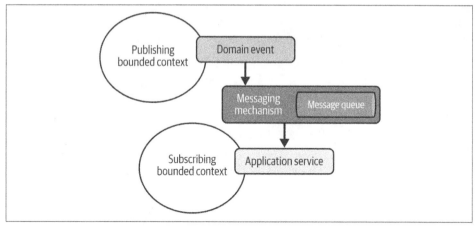

Figure 5-6. Domain Events interacting between subdomains

Domain Events will be implemented using the technologies and message mechanisms that your architecture is built upon. *Domain Events* are usually implemented and deployed as part of the *Microservice* they belong to—the *Bounded Context* in which the *Domain Event* has the most relevance.

Using *Domain Events* to communicate changes across Bounded Contexts (201) can bring several advantages—such as decoupling, scalability, and consistency. *Domain Events* reduce the dependencies and coupling between different bounded contexts, allowing them to evolve independently and avoid tight integration. *Domain Events* help describe and support the **Event-driven** and **Availability over consistency** design principles from **IDEALS**.

A *Domain Event* can be seen as a statement of fact—it represents a set of things tied together by an occurrence of a fact at a particular point in time. You can't "undo" a fact, but you can replace a fact with a new piece of information that comes at a later point in time. Another way of saying this is that facts accrue over time. The issue here is that while events tell you what happened, they don't necessarily tell you the state of something at a particular time unless you can look at the entire history of events affecting that object over the entire span of time. One ramification of this is that if something needs to be reversed, you need to generate a new *Domain Event* that represents the replacement information. That implies that a certain level of auditing of the stream of events should be expected—your system needs to deal not only with the possibility of events arriving out of order and also with them not arriving at all.

Domain Events, not surprisingly, arise out of the Event Storming (189) process. That entire process begins with making a timeline of events that occur within the business domain and then finding the parties involved and identifying data, processing, and interfaces that receive, generate, and react to those events. *Domain Events* are expressed in terms of the *Ubiquitous Language* of the domain.

Domain Events can be used to represent actions between Aggregates (211) within the same *Bounded Context* but also represent interactions across *Bounded Contexts*. So in our online ordering system, when a `Cart` is checked out, a `Cart Checked Out Domain Event` can trigger an action that will create an `Order` in the system and begin the fulfillment process for the `Order`. A *Domain Event* can trigger an action that invokes Domain Services (222).

In Event-Driven Architecture (Chapter 6) we discuss how *Domain Events* are implemented by building Reactive Components (260) that each have a specific Event API (274) and that communicate over an Event Backbone (279).

Examples

The following online ordering, shipping, and airline examples highlight the use of *Domain Events* for describing when something happens within their respective domains.

Online ordering

Let's start with a simple example of online ordering. (Note: we have dramatically simplified this example in a number of ways. We have experience building online shopping systems and know the thousands of complications involved in building a real system—this example is meant to show only the principles and the process.) Let's say you've invented a new widget, and you need an online ordering system to let customers purchase your wonderful new inventions. You've developed a wide selection of widgets for different uses, enough that customers will need to tell you what kind of widget they need in order to find just the right widget for their purposes.

The first step in the design process for building a cloud-native system like this would be to gather the experts and carry out an *Event Storming* exercise. We've covered the process for *Event Storming*, but the first step is to gather all the experts in a room and have them individually write out all the possible facts about the process, and then as a group put them into a single timeline (see Figure 5-7). In this particular case, we'll start with the simplest set of interactions at the start of the process—the process of a `Customer` interacting with your website to select widgets to purchase and then checking out to create an order. You'll note that we indicate that this is all done by the `Customer` by adding a "Persona" sticky for the `Customer`.

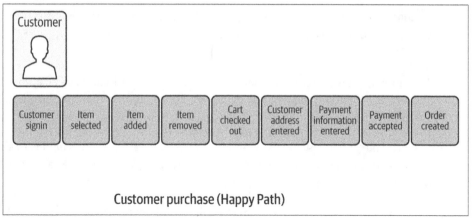

Figure 5-7. Simplest event timeline

There are several important things to call out from this example, as simple as it is. Note that the events have been placed into a single timeline. Sometimes that's difficult to do, especially when actions can be repeated. We see that there is only a single instance of "Item added" and "Item removed" on the timeline, even though those actions may occur in a number of orders and be repeated a number of times. That's fine—in later stages of the process, you can split out different possibilities into different scenarios if it helps you reveal more things about the domain.

The most important thing, though, is that you notice that all of these events are phrased similarly, even though they refer to different aspects of the system. We've mixed up events about the Customer with events about Search and events about Items and Orders. That's fine! They are all *Domain Events*. What this is suggesting to us is that these different *Domain Events* may be related to different parts of the domain. We will see later that this often implies that some of these events are related to different *Aggregates*, which are initially hinted at in the name of the event. We'll find out more about how the *Event Storming* process helps to call these out when we continue this example in Bounded Context (201).

Shipping

We've called out how *Domain Events* come into being as part of the *Event Storming* process, but it's worthwhile to discuss how the simple "sticky-note"-based representation of them is only a subset of the richness that a *Domain Event* can represent. For instance, if you're the owner of a shipping company, you can see why that particular fact would be of interest.

```
The container ship, Anne of Cleves, left the port of Los Angeles,
U.S.A., bound for the port of Hangchow, China, at 7:10 a.m. Pacific
Time, January 3, 2018.
```

After all, your ships have a schedule they need to adhere to, and you have customers who are expecting their shipments to be delivered. Here's another that may be a little less obvious.

```
The container ship, Anne of Cleves, crossed out of U.S. territorial
waters into international waters at 74.23.125N, -23.44.281W at 12:45
p.m., January 4, 2018.
```

Why would the ship owner care about that? Well, the ship owner may not care about that on their own, but they may be required by law to notify customs officials when one of their ships crosses in or out of territorial waters.

Now what is the similarity between these two different statements of fact? Well, there are a few obvious things. For one, they are all statements referring to something that happened at a particular point in time. What's more, both statements contain information about the particular object(s) involved in what happened—in this case, the ship and perhaps the port. They also carry additional descriptive information about the occurrence, such as the type of occurrence, e.g., leaving port or crossing an international boundary. When doing *Event Storming*, it's often useful to list out some of this detailed data about the *Domain Event* as part of the process as you work through real-life scenarios—because it can then lead to a better understanding of the data that makes up the event and the data used by the commands, policies, and other parts of the *Event Storming* process.

Airline

Finally, we can see how *Domain Events* can help solve additional issues about reducing the coupling between different components in your system. For instance, on most airlines, you can register for notification of changes to a flight's departure or arrival time. The *Domain Event* is the fact that the status of the flight changed. What you register for is a notification of these status changes, which can be sent by text, voice, or email. This notification is distributed to any number of recipients, each responding in its own way. That could, for instance, be used by passengers on a flight or by people meeting passengers at the airport.

The important thing to note is that this solution reduces potential coupling between applications. You see, the airline could keep track of the full travel itinerary of each passenger on the flight—not only connecting flights on the same airline but also flights on other airlines, reservations for rental cars and hotels, and any other travel arrangements. For privacy reasons, the passenger may not be comfortable revealing all of this information to the airline. Also, the airline doesn't want to be responsible for storing all of this information and for processing updates to frequently changing travel plans. And even if the airline had the most up-to-date itinerary, it doesn't want to be responsible for having to change the reservations with all of these other travel service providers.

The preceding solution, in which the airline simply gives out a notification of travel changes that allows different people, applications, and organizations to formulate their own solutions, is the best approach. It keeps us from tightly coupling all of these various systems. We'll revisit this idea later when we look at the advantages of an Event-Driven Architecture (Chapter 6)

Bounded Context

You are Modeling around the Domain (183) through an Event Storming (189) session to get a better understanding of the domain and the problem you are solving. This session has revealed many events with the commands and actors that trigger those events. The session might have also outlined the types of things (Aggregates (211) with *Entities* and *Values*) needed for the systems.

How do you clearly define the logical boundaries (edges) of a domain and subdomain(s) where particular terms and rules apply?

The problem with a single domain model (e.g., a single vocabulary and set of entities with values) that covers an entire domain is that it will often be too big to be manageable. Human beings have limits to how much information they can easily keep in their heads at one time. For instance, George Miller's "The Magical Number Seven Plus or Minus Two" (*https://oreil.ly/l07tr*) describes the limitations of our short-term memory.

When more than one team shares a single common model, and common code base, the members of the teams will inevitably run into one another when making changes that are internally consistent with one team's view of the model but can be inconsistent with another team's view. This leads to one of the problems often seen with muddy, monolithic applications—it becomes difficult to test components that simultaneously represent different viewpoints.

Getting the right stakeholders together to understand the system enough to partition a domain into its parts and define the logical boundaries can be a difficult and tedious task. Understanding which concepts are part of a subdomain and which concepts are not can be challenging, especially when there might be some concepts that appear to belong to multiple subdomains or bridge more than one domain. A large domain that has many subdomains will often evolve over time, which might lead to adding, removing, and reconfiguring subdomains as the business changes or you learn more about the domain.

Another motivation is the **Single responsibility** principle from **IDEALS**. One of the hardest parts of domain modeling is determining where one domain (or subdomain) ends and another begins. Many concepts don't have extremely well-defined start and end points but instead blur into each other. For instance, consider education—once we had extremely well-defined start and end points in time that clearly delineated primary education from secondary education and postsecondary education. However, the rise of online learning has begun to confuse those lines. Concepts like apprenticeship and certification blur the lines between work and education. What this means for design is that we need to be very clear in defining our terms limited to the specific purpose we are addressing at the moment. If we're building an online course registration system for courses on domain modeling, we don't need to address all the possible reasons why a person could be registering for a course or where they are in their educational journey; we just need to keep to the particular problem at hand.

Therefore,

Group related aspects of a subdomain into a *Bounded Context* where particular concepts (*Domain Events, Aggregates* and behavior) act as a cohesive whole addressing a particular purpose.

As previously discussed, large domains are usually broken down into smaller domains, which are called subdomains. Domain models describe the logical implementation (or the solution space). When modeling a domain, larger domain models need to be partitioned into smaller pieces or domain models, and we need to put boundaries around them. A *Bounded Context* (*BC*) delimits the scope or boundaries of a domain model. A *BC* is simply the boundary within a domain where elements of that domain apply.

A *BC* defines the boundaries of the applicability of a subdomain. It is an area where certain terms and rules within a subdomain make sense, while terms from other subdomains don't. The scope of a *BC* can be the entire model of a subdomain (highly recommended), or sometimes it can be domain models of 2 or more subdomains (this often happens with dealing when legacy systems or more complex subdomains).

A *BC* is a logical boundary of a domain where particular terms and rules apply consistently. A *BC* represents a boundary around a set of functional features (user stories or use cases) within a domain. For example, it could be everything that is related to customer management in an online ordering system, such as *create customer*, *update customer*, and *update customer address*. A *BC* is simply the boundary within a domain where a particular domain model applies. A *BC* delimits the scope of a domain model.

Let's extend the *Joe's Pizza* example to illustrate how you can go from *Event Storming*, where you gathered *Domain Events*, and to finding the boundaries (*BCs*) of the system and how they relate to subdomains. After further analysis through our *Event Storming* session, we have learned that we can break *Joe's Pizza* domain into three subdomains: Order Pizza, Prepare Pizza, and Deliver Pizza (see Figure 5-8).

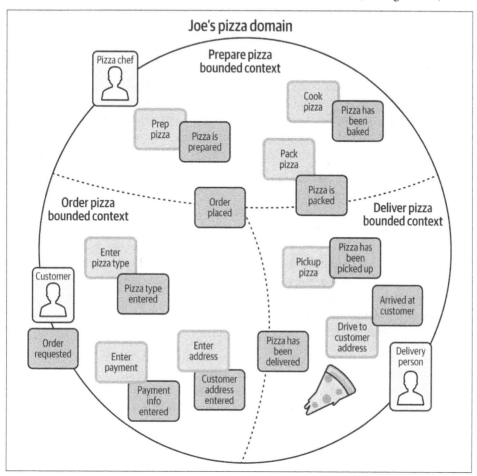

Figure 5-8. Joe's Pizza Bounded Context example

Joe's Pizza allows customers to place orders, which will prompt them to enter the type of pizza requested, the customer's address, and their payment information. In this example, there is an outside *Domain Event* called Order Requested that triggered actions (commands) within the Order Pizza subdomain—Enter Pizza Type, Enter Customer Address, and Enter Payment Info. Once these commands are completed, they trigger the *Domain Events* for the Pizza Type Entered, Customer Address Entered, and Payment Information Entered. Once all of these commands have finished, they will trigger a *Domain Event* that says that the order has been placed. Notice that the Prepare Pizza subdomain is interested in this event, and once it sees that an order has been placed, the pizza can be prepared, cooked, and packed for delivery. The Prepare Pizza subdomain has a different actor, which is the Pizza Chef. The chef will prep the pizza, cook the pizza, and package the pizza. Once the Pizza Is Packed event has occurred, the pizza is ready to be picked up and delivered to the customer by the delivery person.

A *BC* sets the limits around what a specific team works on and helps them to define their domain-specific vocabulary within that particular context. Take the example of a customer in retail. In one context, a customer is a person who buys products from a store. In another context, a customer is a person to whom a retailer markets its products. The customer, in reality, is the same person but will need different perspectives in different *BCs*, each of which acts on the customer entity based on their own rules.

Usually, a *BC* will be the boundary of a subdomain. However, there are times when you might have more than one *BC* in a subdomain. To illustrate this, let's consider the banking domain. We can break that domain down into subdomains, such as credit cards, loans, and accounts (see Figure 5-9). Sometimes a *BC* will be the complete subdomain, such as the Loans subdomain mapping to a single *BC*. On the other hand, there are times when a subdomain will be partitioned into multiple *BCs*, such as the credit card in our example. In this subdomain, we have a Credit Card *BC* that encapsulates information about the credit card, such as the number, code, limit, etc. Then there is the Purchases *BC* that will keep track of the information about purchases for a credit card.

When you define a *BC*, you define who uses it, how they use it, where it applies within a larger application context, and what it consists of in terms of things like Swagger documentation and code repositories. Each *BC* will have its unique *Ubiquitous Language* for that subdomain. For example, the concept and view of an Account for CreditCard will be quite different from the concept of an *Account* in the *Loans BC*, which will also be different than the concept of an Account in the CheckingAccount *BC*.

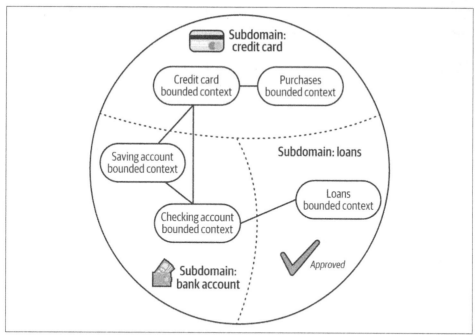

Figure 5-9. Banking Domain with subdomains Bounded Contexts

Application Services

Clients of a *BC* should not have direct access to domain model elements (such as its *Aggregates*). The interaction should be through what is called *Application Services.*[9] An *Application Service* exposes the functionality to the application clients. *Application Services* offers operations that correspond to use cases for the domain. *Application Services* coordinates calls to domain elements and may access different *Aggregates* within the *BC*. *Application Services* does not contain domain-specific business logic. Rather, *Application Services* coordinates outside calls to the *Aggregates* and business logic included within the *BC*. *Application Services* can deal with transactions, access control, logging, and calls to other applications or *BCs*.

So to summarize, a *BC* can be seen as a cohesive grouping of one or more *Aggregates*, with any related behavior related to them, and the interface (*Application Services*) to these *Aggregates* and related behavior. A *BC* explicitly defines the boundaries of your model. This concept is critical in large software projects. A *BC* can be used to define the boundaries of your Microservices (119). When defining *BCs*, it is important to remember that they are autonomous, and a developer should be able to know

---

9 *Application Services* is an implicit pattern originally described in *Domain-Driven Design* (2003) (*https://oreil.ly/7jOfv*) as a type of *Service*.

whether a concept is included in, or out of, a *BC*. *Context Mapping* is a technique useful for finding these boundaries:[10]

Context Map

Once you have identified subdomains, *Aggregates*, events, and boundaries, you can start drawing the relationships between the *BC*—this map of the relationship is called a *Context Map*. A *Context Map* is responsible for defining a boundary between *BC*. These maps should be simple enough to be understood by the domain expert and the technical team. A *Context Map* gives a comprehensive view of the system and can be used to capture the technical and organizational relationships between the *BCs* (see Figure 5-10 for an example in the pizza domain).

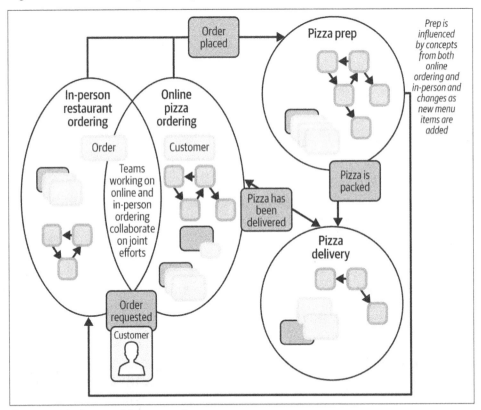

Figure 5-10. Context Map example

---

10 *Context Maps* described by Millet and Tune (*https://oreil.ly/Ga0uE*) are used as a means to capture the technical and organizational relationships between various *Bounded Contexts*.

When building the *Context Map*, it is important to avoid technical details. The following outlines some steps that can be taken to build a *Context Map*:

1. Start with an *Event Storming* session to Identify *Domain Events* and the *Aggregates* (entities/values).
2. Group the *Aggregates* and *Domain Events* into *BC* and start drawing relationships between them.
3. Label the relationships based on the *Domain Events* and how they trigger communication between and within *BC*.
4. Iterate through and discuss, evolving your *Context Map* as you learn.
5. Identify the team responsible for the *BC*.

While doing these steps, it is important to invite domain experts, technical people, and other related stakeholders.

Implementation

In a *BC*, you partition your system into different boundaries and discuss the inter-relationships between these boundaries. To protect the internals of a *BC*, such as *Aggregates* and *Domain Services*, we limit access to *BCs* to be available only through the API of a *BC*.

The basic rule of thumb when going from design to a *Microservice* implementation is to implement a *Microservice* for every *BC* you have modeled. So *BC* are the starting point to define the outlines of your *Microservices*. A *BC* will include *Aggregates* (groups of entities with values) and various behaviors that are either described as part of an entity or *Domain Services* for behavior that does not belong to a specific entity. Finally, a *BC* can include some implementation for the *Domain Events*, which represent that something of interest has happened within a *BC*. These events can trigger actions within the *BC* or might trigger an action in an interested *BC*. You access anything within a *BC* through the interface to your *Microservice*, which is called an *Application Service*.

One of the main advantages of *BCs* is *separation of concerns*. As stakeholders get together and better understand the domain, the system can be better designed and organized to best meet the needs of the organization. By breaking a system into smaller and more understandable pieces, you get the benefit of a smaller, more stable interface that allows the system to more easily evolve to changing requirements. This is an example of applying the **Single responsibility** principle from **IDEALS**. Also, *Application Services* provide a means of **Interface segregation**.

One of the main challenges in finding *BCs* is that it requires coordination between more teams and stakeholders. Coordinating and understanding various domains, sharing models, and understanding the business language is expensive and takes time. How to organize teams according to the *BCs* can be difficult, and understanding the best way for *BCs* to interact can be very challenging. This can in a sense lead to the Inverse of Conway's Law, in that you must design the organization to reflect the design of your software.

An Event-Storming (189) session helps you define the *BC* that map to the logical boundaries of a Microservices Architecture (Chapter 4). This session also helps identify the types of things (Aggregates (211)) that belong to the *BC*. Some behavior belongs to the Entities within a *BC*. There will also be behavior that does not belong to a specific entity in the *BC*. Domain Services (222) and Domain Events (193) can be used for this type of behavior within your *BCs*—and they are often implemented with an Event-Driven Architecture (Chapter 6). *Application Services* are the API into *BCs*, and **Repositories** are used for persisting the *Aggregates* within a *BC*.

A *BC* can also form the boundary of modules in a Modular Monolith (29). When *BCs* are implemented as a Distributed Architecture (38), they become an example of the Microservices Architecture style.

An Anti-Corruption Layer (229) allows *BCs* to evolve independently, thus keeping your *BCs* from becoming entangled and devolving into a Big Ball of Mud (22).

Example

Let's return to our online ordering example. After finding the initial set of domain events, the next step is to look for "pivotal" events. In our particular case, we're just looking at a segment of the entire timeline (we'll see more later), but the first thing that everyone in the group notices is that the person interacting with the system, the persona (in this case, the Customer), changes at a specific point in the process. Initially, everything is done by the customer who is browsing, selecting, and checking out. You can see this in Figure 5-11.

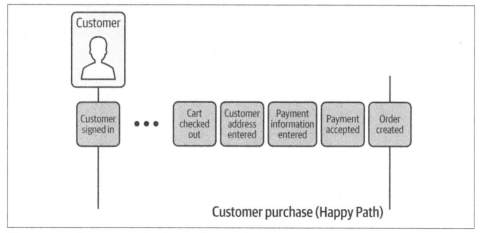

Figure 5-11. Events on a timeline with pivotal events

Once the checkout process is completed, though, the warehouse staff needs to get involved to fulfill the order. Likewise, the shipper will need to get involved to physically deliver the order to the customer. That makes the start of the process (customer sign-in) and the end of this part of the process (customer checkout) uniquely important. That transition suggests that part of the process represents at least one *BC*—in this case, part of what bounds the *BC* is a time boundary that is suggested by the handoff from the customer to your business. That's represented by the lines going vertically through those events. But there are other boundaries that form the remaining outlines of the *BC* that we still need to find.

One important potential boundary that we've implicitly defined so far here is the boundary of who is operating on the events—the *Persona*. If we extend the timeline to the right after Order Created, you'll find that there are different Personas (in this case, Shipping and Warehouse) that get involved in the process. You can see this in Figure 5-12.

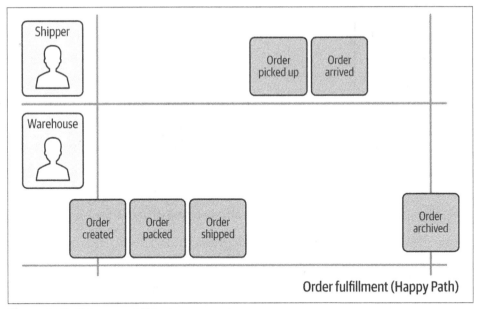

Figure 5-12. Shipper and Warehouse events

That shows us two possible "bounds" for a *BC*. One is time-based and based on pivotal events that signal important process changes. For instance, this entire part of the process begins when the Order is created upon Checkout. That's an important shift in the process. However, the other possibility is that you have a boundary entirely based on who (which Persona) is operating on the events. In this case, you'll see the Shipper is the one responsible for picking up the order and informing everyone that the order has been picked up or that it has arrived. The Warehouse is interested in that but doesn't actually change the status of the order themselves until a far point in the future when the order is archived.

Let's extend our online ordering system example by going back and again looking at user scenarios for when a customer places an order. After a customer logs in to the system, they can browse through the online catalog of products and start adding products to their shopping cart. After they have added one or more items to their shopping cart, they can then checkout and place an order. Checkout is where the customer will enter in their payment and shipping information for the order and then place the order. Once the order has been placed, an event will be triggered for shipping the order.

Returning to our ongoing *Event Storming* example about online ordering, in the phase that follows identifying *BCs*, you start looking more deeply at the common terms referenced in the events or that are suggested by the events. If the events represent facts that have already occurred, then what you are looking for are the things that are referenced in those facts. In our case, we notice quickly that there's a difference between interaction with the catalog (browsing and searching) and interaction with the cart (adding and removing items). Likewise, there are some pieces of information that seem more tied to the customer (like their address and their payment information) than to the order itself—after all, we want repeat customers! Finally, there's a phase change when checkout is complete—the Cart is no longer a Cart; now it's an Order that needs to be fulfilled by the warehouse staff. In *Event Storming*, you can represent this just by sorting the events (still in timeline order) into different swim lanes, as shown by the horizontal lines. You then identify the potential *Aggregates* (Catalog, Customer, Cart, and Order) on which the events in those swim lanes operate. We show those with *Aggregate* stickies (see Figure 5-13).

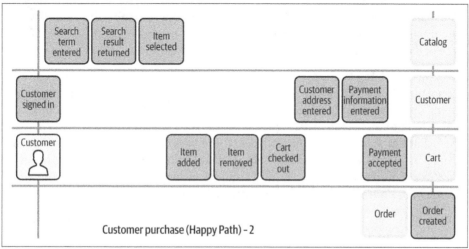

Figure 5-13. Shipper and Warehouse events

What this is leading to is that based on user scenarios for our online ordering system, we have now identified a few core subdomains. There is one for search and another for when a customer adds and removes items to their shopping cart and then checks out. These subdomains include product catalog, cart, and order subdomains. There is also one subdomain for entering customer details around shipping and payment. There are others that we could potentially find in later phases of the process, but we'll leave those for later patterns.

Aggregate

You are performing an Event Storming (189) session to Model Around the Domain (183) so you can design a system to be deployed on traditional IT or the cloud. When modeling, stakeholders come together to better understand and describe the details of the domain and subdomains for the system.

How do you tie together the groups of tightly related concepts and the values that belong within them in a subdomain?

Agile teams like to start quickly by working on their user stories to begin coding functionality into the system. As part of this, they create objects or data structures corresponding to what they currently understand about the system. The problem arises when you need to start understanding how different viewpoints of the same concept apply. You often end up with either multiple classes with slightly different names and responsibilities or (even worse) huge classes with very different responsibilities and vast amounts of shared data.

A domain model is a representation of real-world ideas for your system that will describe the different types of things and values in the system and how they are related. It can be difficult to divide up and correctly describe the concepts in a subdomain. You have to think carefully about the ownership and lifetime of each piece of data and under what context different viewpoints apply.

The concept related to the types of things needed for a system has been around for a long time. They are often called *entities*. Entities are domain concepts within a system that have meaning (and therefore will have a unique id). For example, you might think of an online ordering system, and you have the domain concept of an *Order*. Entities almost always have values. Some values are simple values like strings or integers. Extending on the *Order* example, a simple value for *Order* might be the *orderDate*. Entities can also have more complex values, such as the *Price*, which can include both a numeric value and currency, such as five dollars.

From Entity-Relationship modeling, you know that sometimes entities might be well-defined and have a specific well-known identifier, but they might not live independently. For example, an order will have the line items of products that are part of the order. Describing and grouping these entities can be challenging.

Therefore,

Identify and describe the *Aggregates* needed for your subdomains.

An *Aggregate* is a cluster of domain objects (entities and values) that can be treated as a single, cohesive, conceptual unit. They are a group of related entities and their values. The main purpose of *Aggregates* is to group the related entities and values so they can be treated as a single domain concept.

Every domain, including its subdomains, will need to model the types of things (entities) that you will need to keep track of, and the values and behavior associated with these things. Entities are the things that the system or the domain is about. For example, an online ordering system could have entities such as Customer, Order, and Payment. An entity always has a distinct identity (or ID) that runs through time and different representations. When you think of an entity, imagine something that needs to be tracked over time and whose attributes are likely to change over time. For example, when I place an order, we will need to process the payment and ultimately ship the order. The status of the order will change over time.

Entities are *not* just data; they also have behavior. So rather than entities being simple data objects with no behavior, entities are what we often call *rich domain objects* with behavior related to the entity. Therefore an entity interface favors behaviors, not simply getter and setter functions. Entities should be the first place where we think of putting the domain logic, specifically the logic associated with that entity. Entity is a business concept that exposes behavior.

Of course, entities have values. For example, an order might have a simple attribute such as the order date. These attributes can be represented as simple types such as a string or integer. However, some values for entities can be complex, such as a compound value like Address, Amount, Distance, Price, and Geolocation. These other types of values are referred to in DDD terms as ValueObjects or VOs. The identity of VOs is defined entirely by their state, and they are usually immutable. When thinking of VOs, remember that they are values that don't have and ID or lifecycle. However, they often do have behavior. One way to look at these values is to consider them as smart variables, primarily because they are values with behavior. For example, you could have a *Weight* VO that has a function that converts the value from pounds to grams. Two VOs with the same values for all their attributes are considered equal. *ValueObjects* have no meaning without the entities they are associated with.

Let's look again at *Joe's Pizza* for when someone orders a pizza. Whenever there is an Order Requested event, the system needs to capture information about the Order. When examining the Order Placed *Domain Event*, we noted that we will need an *Order Aggregate* to capture details of an order, such as the size of the pizza, toppings, etc. (see Figure 5-14). It should be noted that this is a simplified subset of the domain for ordering pizzas to illustrate the concept of *Aggregates*.

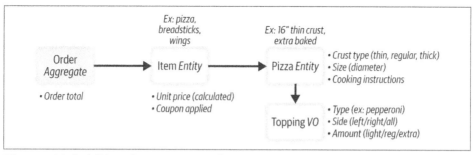

Figure 5-14. Joe's Pizza Aggregate example

In this example, the `Order` *Aggregate* has an `Order` entity associated with one or more `Item` entities. An `Item` is associated with a `Pizza` entity that has the type of crust and the size of the pizza and is associated with one or more toppings that are represented as a VO (type of topping, like pepperoni), what side of the pizza the topping goes on, and the amount (such as extra pepperoni). You might argue or ask, "Shouldn't you have a *Pizza Aggregate*, or better yet a `Product` *Aggregate*?" We could have designed it this way, but we chose not to in this example both to make it easier to understand and also to make a point that you don't always need multiple *Aggregates* in a subdomain. Simpler is often better.

It's important to discuss why `Pizza` is an entity and `Topping` is not. Simply put, one is entirely a subpart of the other. You could return a pizza to have it remade, but you can't have just a single topping removed or added without ruining the entire pizza.

Likewise, you might also ask why `LineItem` and `Pizza` aren't modeled as a single entity since there is a one-to-one relationship between them. You could model these as one entity, but it's better if these two concepts evolve independently. Separating these two concepts into two entities follows the **Single responsibility** principle by allowing rules and information about the pizza to evolve independently from the rules and information needed for calculating the item's price. Therefore, we decided to not have a single entity for both of these concepts. The reason is that if we had to have a single entity for both, we would have to pollute the interface and logic of *Item* with the interface of *Pizza*.

So in summary, within a domain or subdomain, you will have *Aggregates*, which are groups of the types of things (entities) with their values and any behaviors associated with the entities. Entities have ID and can have values that change over time. Some values for entities are more complex (or compound) values with behavior, which are called ValueObjects. VOs usually don't have ID or lifecycle. External objects or services access the *Aggregate* only through the Aggregate Root or API into the *Aggregate*. It is important to define the *Aggregates* (entities and values) in terms of the *Ubiquitous Language* of the domain model.

It is more important to focus on the concept of the API for the *Aggregate* rather than focusing exclusively on the entity that forms the *Aggregate Root*. In other words, there needs to be an API to the *Aggregate*, which may or may not be the API of a single entity. The important concept is that you have a single interface (API) to the *Aggregate* as a whole. Another thing to keep in mind is that *Aggregates* usually either succeed or fail as a whole. They often form the boundaries of transactionality and have a *Repository* associated with them to encapsulate database access.

There are some important considerations when dealing with *Aggregates*. *Aggregates* are the basic element of transfer of data storage for your domain—you request to load or save whole *Aggregates*. Transactions should not cross aggregate boundaries. An *Aggregate* defines a (transactional) consistency boundary that remains transactionally consistent throughout its lifetime. It is often loaded and saved in its entirety from the database. If an *Aggregate* is deleted, all of its entities and VOs are deleted. A database transaction should touch only one *Aggregate*.

Repositories

Repositories were originally described as a pattern by Evans as part of DDD. They have gained traction once again with the rise of domain modeling techniques—specifically in the context of *Microservices*. A *Repository* mediates between the entities and the persistent storage for their values. *Repositories* make it so that your application can work with a simple abstraction of the data associated with your *Aggregates* without having to know the details about underlining persistent mechanisms, such as dealing with database connections, transactions, and the like. The benefit is that the *Aggregates* are now more loosely coupled with whatever persistence mechanism you are using, thus keeping these concerns out of the domain objects. *Repositories* provide a means for the *Aggregates* as a kind of in-memory abstraction of the entities values.

A *Repository* is an in-memory abstraction of all elements of the *Aggregates* entities and values. Therefore, the scope of a *Repository* is an *Aggregate*. A *Repository* is not a Data Access Object (DAO). Rather, *Repositories* provide an interface around their *Aggregates* with methods to add and remove objects and query objects based on some criteria. A *Repository* allows you to populate data in memory that comes from the database in the form of the domain entities. Once the entities are in memory, they can be changed and then persisted back to the database through transactions.

Implementation

Let's examine the concept of Customers and Orders for an ordering system to discuss some implementation alternatives. Any ordering system will have Customers, which will have Addresses associated with them. Address can be modeled in your ordering system as a ValueObject, and you would never have an address without it being associated with a Customer. A Customer will have a lifecycle, and all Customers for an ordering system will have Addresses. Figure 5-15 is an example of the Customer *Aggregate*.

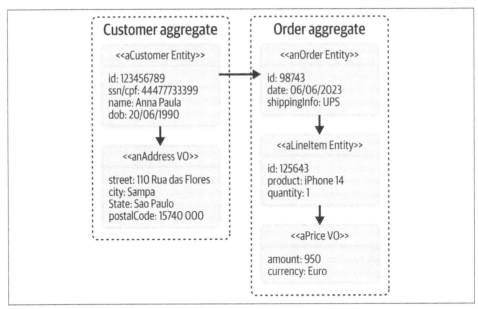

Figure 5-15. Customer and Order Aggregate example

From this example, you can see that an *Aggregate* can have one or more entities with possible VO (you must always have at least one entity). The typical aggregate has one entity and a few VOs, but *Aggregates* with 2–3 entities are also common, as long as they are cohesive. You can have an *Aggregate* with only one entity and no VOs. Each *Aggregate* will have a single API to access anything within the *Aggregate*, which sometimes maps to a single root entity called the *Aggregate Root* in domain modeling terms. The *Aggregate Root* is the main entity within the aggregate, that the *Aggregate* is primarily about. For example, the *Customer Aggregate* would include the Customer and Address entities. Since it doesn't make sense to have an *Address* without a *Customer*, the *Aggregate Root* would be the *Customer* entity. The entities and *ValueObjects* can be implemented in the way we would generally implement them given the language we are using. For example, in Java, we would create a Java class for each entity and VO.

Aggregates will be implemented as part of the *Microservice* they belong to; the *Bounded Context* that contains their *Aggregates*. A couple of design principles to consider when implementing *Aggregates* related to **SOLID** are the **Single responsibility** principle and the **Interface segregation** principle. We want to incorporate and modularize our *Aggregates* so they can evolve independently and be protected from change. There are various ways to achieve these principles, and one way is to create a service for each *Aggregate*. This will encapsulate the domain objects and the *Service API* will be the interface to any entities inside the service.

So a *BC* will be implemented as a *Microservice* that can be packaged as a *Microservice* with a single service when it has one *Aggregate*; or it could contain 2, 3, or more services when there are multiple *Aggregates*, as long as they are *cohesive*. Packaging these cohesive *Aggregates* together into a single *Microservice* creates a transaction boundary for these related aggregates.

The main advantage of *Aggregates* is that they group logically related things (entities and their respective *Values*) as a single cohesive business concept. This provides for encapsulation and also ensures that the related concepts are treated as a single unit, thus supporting the **Single Responsibility** principle from **IDEALS**. This also supports the **Interface segregation** principle. Both of these help when designing *Aggregates* with the end goal being a *Microservice* or a component of a *Modular Monolith*.

That brings up another valuable advantage of *Aggregate*. One of the truisms of Distributed System design is Fowler's First Law of Distributed Object Design (*https://oreil.ly/OkZN5*), which is "Don't distribute your objects!" By that Fowler meant to keep your distributed interfaces, that is to say, your distribution cross-section, small. The more information you transmit, the longer each distributed call takes, which leads to more opportunities you get out of sync with the current database state and a greater chance of polluting one abstraction (or Bounded Context (201)) with another. Aggregates (211) reduce that overall interface size by hiding the entities and value objects inside of them.

On the other hand, it can be hard to find these groups of related things to make up these *Aggregates*—specifically when you are trying to not overdesign. There can be a temptation to try to model your entire enterprise, something that has often been attempted but rarely succeeds.

Event Storming sessions help find the *Aggregates*, which are the related types of things with their values. *Aggregates* with their entities and VOs always belong to a specific *Bounded Context*. Any behavior that belongs to an entity is put into that entity. Domain Services (222) and Domain Events (193) are used for behavior that does not belong to a specific entity or value object. All concepts for *Aggregates* should be defined in terms of the *Ubiquitous Language* for the domain.

Repositories provided an abstraction for handling the interactions between *Aggregates* with their entities and values to the persistent storage. **Repositories**, when implemented within a *Microservice*, is an example of applying the concept of a

Self-Managed Data Store (154).[11] The values for *Aggregates* when implemented using a Microservices Architecture (Chapter 4) as part of a Cloud Application (Chapter 1) will use persistent storage to save their values by applying Cloud-Native Storage (Chapter 7) patterns.

Examples

You can find a simple example of the entity/Aggregate relationship in a retail store. If you go to the soda aisle in a grocery store, you can buy a 12-pack carton of soda. Each can in the carton has a bar code to identify it individually, but you can't buy a single can from the carton. The cans are entities that are referred to as dependent entities. The root entity is the carton. The carton is the Aggregate because it defines the dependent entities' lifecycle (at least as far as the retail store is concerned).

Online ordering system carts

Returning to our ongoing *Event Storming* example about online ordering, in the phase that follows identifying *Bounded Contexts*, you start looking more deeply at the common terms referenced in the events, or that are suggested by the events. If the events represent facts that have already occurred, then what you are looking for are the things that are referenced in those facts.

In our simple example, the customer can add or delete items from the cart. Once they are ready to place the order, the customer can proceed to checkout, enter or perhaps check their payment and shipping information, and place the order.

In our case, we notice quickly that there's a difference between interaction with the catalog (browsing and searching) and interaction with the cart (adding and removing items). Likewise, there are some pieces of information that seem more tied to the customer (like their address and their payment information) than to the order itself— after all, we want repeat customers! Finally, there's a phase change when checkout is complete—the Cart is no longer a Cart; now it's an Order that needs to be fulfilled by the warehouse staff. In *Event Storming*, you can represent this just by sorting into events (still in timeline order) and into different swim lanes (shown by the horizontal lines) and then by identifying the potential *Aggregates* (Catalog, Customer, Cart, and Order) that these swim lanes represent events operating on. We show those with *Aggregate* stickies (see Figure 5-16).

---

11 **Repositories** is an implicit pattern that was originally described in *Domain-Driven Design* (2003).

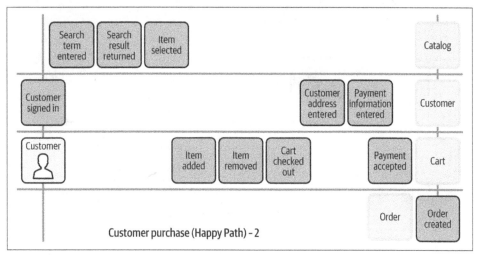

Figure 5-16. Customer purchase Happy Path

These horizontal lines represent another important "boundary line" that helps define a *Bounded Context*. This is the boundary between entities and *Aggregates*. A good rule of thumb is that you shouldn't have single events operate on more than one entity—if you find yourself doing this, that's a signal that you probably are mashing multiple events together, or perhaps that you've missed an *Aggregate* that ties several entities together into a cohesive whole.

Finally, in the last step of the current part of the process, you add the additional "decorations" to the timeline. This includes noting potential data elements that the *Aggregates* contain or refer to on the stickies, as well as adding blue stickies for all the commands (e.g., things the user needs to invoke) that result in these events being recorded. Whenever there's a system-triggered step, you capture that as a pink "policy" sticky, as we see in this case when an Order is created from what used to be a Cart upon checkout (see Figure 5-17).

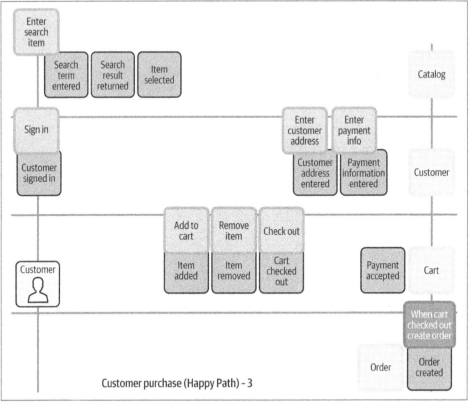

Figure 5-17. Decorated Purchase Happy Path

The command stickies (Enter search item, Sign in, Enter customer address, Enter payment info, Add to cart, Remove item, and Check out) will help you identify the operations on the *Aggregates* that you have found. Along the way you not only find additional attributes for the existing *Aggregate* stickies, but you often find entirely new ones when you have commands that don't seem to operate on any of the ones you've already identified.

Now, at this point, you have a couple of different directions you can take with the expansion of your example. You can either look wider at the other parts of the timeline, or you can go deeper on the entities and potential *Aggregates* you've already found. Let's start with the latter case.

So far, we've seen that the shopping cart will have a list of the items that the customer has added for a potential order. Each item in the shopping cart will need to include the desired quantity for each item as well as the unit price and the total price for the requested quantity of each item. That leads us to the next stage of the domain modeling process, which moves beyond working on the stickies alone and begins to consider details that are closer to implementation.

We've noted that the shopping cart contains products that the customer is thinking about ordering. A bit of thought leads us to conclude there ought to be another entity associated with the *Cart* entity, which is the Item entity. The *Item* can then have attributes for the *productID*, *quantity*, and *unit price*.

That means that in this example, our `Cart` *Bounded Context* has an *Aggregate* with two entities, a `Cart` that is associated with the *Item* (this is a one-to-many relationship—it can have many products the customer would like to order). Because these two entities are closely related, we created an *Aggregate* called the `Cart` *Aggregate* for these two related entities.

This *Bounded Context* is fairly straightforward and includes only one *Aggregate*, which we call the `Cart` *Aggregate*. This *Aggregate* has two entities, `Cart` and `Item`. There is a one-to-many relationship between the `Cart` entity and the `Item` entity. Notice that we will never have `Items` without a `Cart`, therefore the `Cart` is the Aggregate Root in this example.

A bit more consideration makes us think about the relationship between the `Customer` entity and the `Cart` entity. This is a looser relationship. Once a customer enters their address, you may want to save that address for a long time, for instance, in preparation for the next order they place. The customer also doesn't disappear when the `Cart` is checked out—they could then begin to fill a whole new shopping cart if the urge strikes them. That means that while there may be a relationship between the two entities, it's not the same as between `Cart` and *Item*. In that case, the `Customer` may not be a part of the `Cart` *Bounded Context*—it may be an entity that has an independent set of activities associated with it and an entirely independent lifetime. We show this in Figure 5-18.

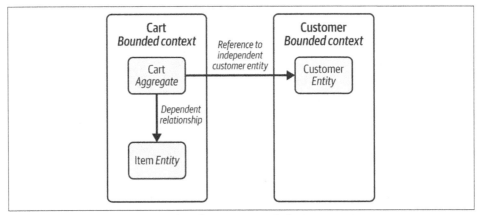

Figure 5-18. Cart Aggregate within the Cart Bounded Context

You would need to maintain a loose reference from one to the other in order to find, for instance, where to ship the order to, but they are not part of the same overall context and thus not part of the same *Aggregate*.

Domain Service

You are Modeling around the Domain (183) a system you are developing and start by getting stakeholders together to perform an Event Storming (189) session to better understand the domain. During this session, various rules and operations are outlined and described for the subdomains of the system being built.

How do you model those operations within a subdomain that do not belong to a specific entity or *Aggregate*?

When developing systems, understanding the rules about a domain and knowing where behavior should be is always challenging. Some behavior belongs to the entities, such as updating a `Customer`'s address. Any behavior specific to an entity or its related entities within the same *Aggregate* is put into those entities. However, there are cases where you have some business rules or behavior in the domain that are not the responsibility of a specific entity or ValueObject.

Consider the simple case of modeling a transfer between `Accounts`. The transfer is not one of the CRUD operations of an account. Rather, it is a concept that affects multiple entities, especially if the transfer is between different account types (such as `Loans` and `Checking`) residing in different *Bounded Contexts*. So how do you represent these functional concepts that do not map to a specific *Aggregate*, especially when they might be behavior related to two or more entities within the same *Bounded Context*?

Previous design methods often tried to force many operations into an entity-based model, usually with adverse consequences. Trying to shoehorn an operation like Account transfer into one or the other of the Accounts would be a violation of the **Single responsibility** principle.

There is also the case where there may be *no* entities that fit a particular concept in a domain. This is particularly true when you have interfaces to things that reside outside your system. For instance, in our online ordering scenario, the shipper lies outside the system—we need to interface with an external API provided by UPS or FedEx to create a shipping label or check on the status of a shipment, but the only connection we have to that system is a single identifier: a tracking number. It would be absurd to force-fit that interface functionality into any of the other entities in our system.

Therefore,

Model operations that do not belong to a specific *Entity* and need to interact with multiple entities within the same *Bounded Context* as a standalone interface declared as a *Domain Service*.

A *Domain Service* performs operations within a *Bounded Context* that do not belong to any specific domain objects. For example, a banking application might have a *Domain Service* that handles the transfer of funds between accounts. *Domain Services* are stateless and are used to perform domain operations and business rules across multiple entities.

Domain Services have three important characteristics: first, the operation relates to a concept that is not part of an entity or ValueObject. Second, the interface is defined in terms of elements of the domain model, and third, the operation is stateless. It is important to define the interface of the service in terms of the *Ubiquitous Language* of the domain model. *Domain Services* are frequently used to orchestrate multiple entities or domain objects.

Let's see how we can extend our model for *Joe's Pizza* to include *Domain Services*. When ordering a pizza, the customer will select the types of pizzas they desire with their toppings. Customers who shop regularly can get a discounted price, and the cost of delivery is dependent upon where the customer lives. Whenever an item is added to the order, the system needs to calculate the current price of the order depending on the items in the order and some customer information. Therefore, the price calculation is dependent upon the Order aggregate with its LineItems of pizzas ordered and the Customer aggregate (see Figure 5-19).

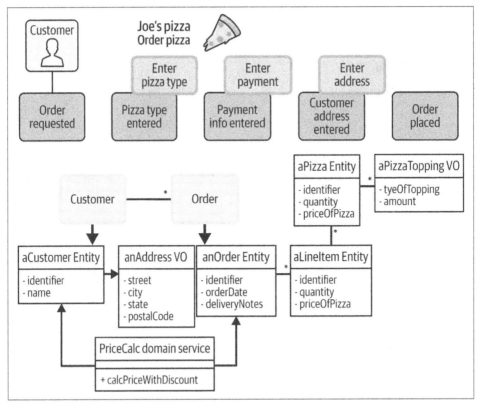

Figure 5-19. Joe's Pizza Domain Service example

One way to model this is to include the business logic to calculate the price in the *Order* aggregate. However, this would couple the *Order* aggregate with the *Customer* aggregate, violating the **Single responsibility** principle. This business logic should be separate and designed to interact with these entities to perform its operation. Thus we create a *Domain Service* for calculating the price, which in this example can be seen as sort of a *Strategy*.

The operations in a *Domain Services* may only read (e.g., calculate a value with input from different entities) or may change the state of one or more entities. These operations are part of the business domain—they are not technical issues of implementation. Things like "Login," "Authentication," and "Logging" aren't appropriate services of this type. However, a concept like "Funds Transfer" in banking, "Adjudication" in insurance, or "Calculating the Price of an Order" in ecommerce might be. *Domain Services* are *not* CRUD operations; those would be put into a **Repository** or perhaps into the interface of an *Aggregate*. They should also not have dependencies on infrastructure elements.

You never directly access a *Domain Service* from outside a *Bounded Context*. Rather, a *Domain Service* can be called by an *Application Service* or other *Domain Services* or entities within the same *Bounded Context*. *Domain Services* are different from *Infrastructure Services* and *Application Services* because they include domain logic and operate on domain entities. *Domain Services* should always be described using the *Ubiquitous Language*. *Domain Services* contain domain logic, whereas *Application Services* orchestrate between domain elements within a *Bounded Context* and do not implement any domain logic.

Implementation

The implementation of a *Domain Service* will be dependent upon the language and technologies you are using for building the system. Let's look at how we might implement something for a banking account subdomain (*BC*) with three *Aggregates*: *SavingsAccount*, *CheckingAccount*, and *AccountHolder*. The *BC* also includes a *TransferFunds Domain Service* that interacts with the *SavingsAccount* and the *Checking Account Aggregates* to transfer money between the two accounts for the *AccountHolder* (see Figure 5-20).

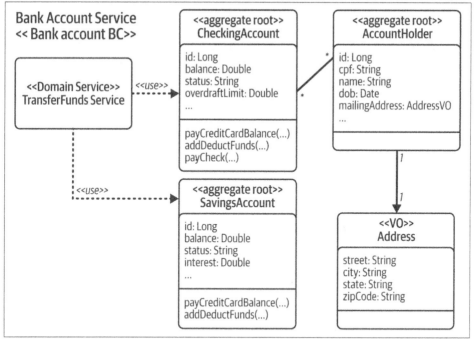

Figure 5-20. Bank account Domain Service example

In this example, the logic for transferring money does not belong to either the *SavingsAccount* entity or the *CheckingAccount* entity. Rather this is business logic that is separate from and needs to interact with these entities to perform its operation.

The *Domain Services* are implemented with the programming language you are using to build your systems. For example, in Java, we would create a Java class for the *Domain Services*. *Domain Services* will be implemented and deployed as part of the *Microservice* they belong to—the *Bounded Context* that contains their *Domain Services*.

Domain Services provide an abstraction for domain logic that does not naturally belong to a specific entity. This abstraction can keep core domain entities clean. This can reduce the coupling between entities within aggregates, allowing them to evolve independently. *Domain Services* help support the **Single responsibility** principle from **IDEALS** by not overloading responsibilities within an entity. It also helps with **Loose coupling** by not entangling related concepts of aggregates with one another.

It can be challenging to understand the domain and know how to organize and partition domain concepts. Various stakeholders—including domain experts—collaborate closely to understand and model the domain. It can be difficult to decide which rules and behaviors belong to an entity and which are independent of a specific entity. This can be especially true when there is poor communication between stakeholders. Insufficient communication between developers, business analysts, and domain experts can result in misaligned expectations and a system that does not meet user requirements.

Some domain logic naturally belongs to a specific entity. When this happens, you implement the domain logic within that entity. Some domain logic does not belong to a single entity; rather, it can include operations across multiple entities. *Domain Services* is a domain concept within a Bounded Context (201) to encapsulate the domain logic between Aggregates (211) and are described in accordance with the *Ubiquitous Language* for its subdomain. *Domain Services* can be invoked by the *Application Service* of its *BC* when an external system needs to call the domain logic of that service. Also, *Domain Services* can be invoked from some action that is triggered by a Domain Event (193).

This last point is worth expanding a bit. For instance, in our online ordering example, an Order is not created until the Cart is completely checked out. Whose responsibility is it to create the Order? It's not the responsibility of anything inside the Cart *Bounded Context*. Placing it there would expose far too many details of how the Order is implemented outside that *Bounded Context*. Instead, that should be the job of a *Domain Service* inside of the Order *Bounded Context*—the process would be initiated by receiving a *Domain Event* that signals that the `Cart` has been checked out. That is why the Event API (274) is so important. It serves as a contract between the *Bounded Contexts* that communicate in this way—the `Order` *Bounded Context* knows it needs to listen on a specific channel for a specific event in order to begin its job.

Example

One of the things we've intentionally kept vague in our online ordering system example is how payment is accepted for the widgets purchased in our online widget store. Even in the earliest *Event Storming* timelines for this example, we had "payment accepted" as an event in the timeline prior to the *Order* being created from the `Cart`. We show that in the segment of the event timeline in Figure 5-21.

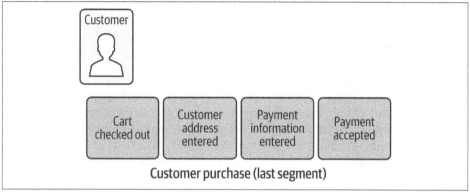

Figure 5-21. Zoom of purchase timeline

We also grouped "payment accepted" as part of the `Cart` *Bounded Context* in the earlier groupings of *Domain Events*. However, we've not paid any attention to that part of the process. We've looked at ways that prices and order totals could be calculated from line items in our other example for *Joe's Pizza*, so we could extrapolate that to our widget example. We've even seen how payment (credit card) information could be gathered from the customer, but an important question comes to mind—what do we do with that payment information?

The long and short of it is we need to use external (third-party) services to complete the crucial step of charging the credit card that the user provided for the total amount (including any applicable taxes and shipping fees) of the `Order`. For that, we need to reach out to these external services. But the question is, where does that behavior go? If you look at the grouping of the *Domain Events*, *Aggregates*, and actions from our *Event Storming* session in Figure 5-22, you'll see that it's not obvious where this behavior should sit.

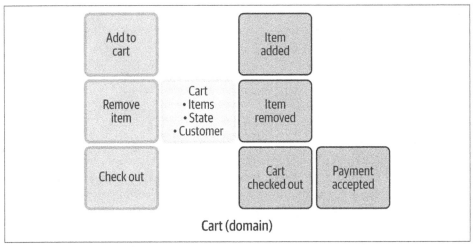

Figure 5-22. Cart Bounded Context

We could potentially try to attach the logic for doing this to the Cart *Aggregate*, but the thing is, it doesn't really fit there. Nor does it fit with the **Repository** that would be needed to find all the Carts and keep them up-to-date as users browse the catalog and add and remove items. Any behavior that is specific to an entity is put into that entity. This doesn't fit those cases. What you quickly conclude is that you need a different location for this domain logic—and that is exactly what the purpose of a *Domain Service* is.

Whenever you have business rules or behavior in the domain that is not the responsibility of a specific entity or ValueObject, you can add an operation to the model as a standalone interface declared as a *Domain Service*. So we can create a Payment Processing *Domain Service* that can be called from the checkout process. You can see this in Figure 5-23.

This is a fairly complicated process, with a lot of moving parts. Once checkout is initiated (let's say from a Checkout Application Service), the Checkout *Application Service* then has to coordinate several pieces. First, it has to find the Cart that is being checked out (from the Cart **Repository**). Then it has to ask that Cart for the total price. Next, it needs to obtain the previously saved payment (credit card) information from the Customer *Bounded Context*. Only now can it ask the Payment Processing *Domain Service* to accept the payment for this amount and use this credit card information.

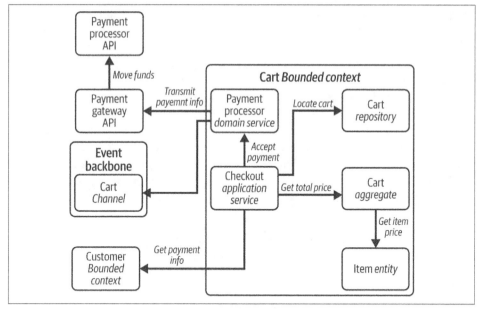

Figure 5-23. Checkout process

That Domain Service can then reach out to the Payment Gateway external API (Payment Gateways are third parties such as Stripe or Square) and securely transmit the payment information to the gateway. The Payment Gateway then handles sending the request on to the Payment Processor (such as PayPal) that will authorize the transaction with the bank or card network. If the payment is authorized, the transaction can complete, and the "Payment Accepted" event can be sent out on the Cart channel of the *Event Backbone*.

Anti-Corruption Layer

You are Modeling around the Domain (183) to design and implement an application to be deployed on traditional IT or on the cloud. There are multiple systems or subdomains (Bounded Contexts (201)) that need to interact with one another.

How can we design the system so that the *Bounded Contexts* (*BCs*) can interact without being tightly coupled together?

Sometimes you need multiple bounded contexts to interact with one another. For example, in a banking domain, you could have a CheckingAccount *BC* that needs to interact with a CreditCard *BC* when making a credit card payment from a checking account. Their domain models are different, and *adapting* the *BC* of CheckingAccounts to the bounded context of Credit Card's interfaces can lead to "corruption" of the *BC* CheckingAccounts model.

There are times when one *Bounded Context* needs to interact with another *Bounded Context*. However, their domain models are different, and "adapting" the two *BC* interfaces can lead to the *BCs* being tightly coupled and dependent on each other. In particular, you need to keep the amount of information exposed by the *Service API* of each *Bounded Context* low—you don't want to expose all the details of how your system operates: if too many external systems know about it, it will become fragile. For instance, you wouldn't want to expose all the details of calculating shipping charges by a third-party shipper in an online ordering scenario to every part of the system if you wanted to be able to explore potentially cheaper, more exotic options like drone delivery. Why would you always generate a tracking number and attach it to all your steps if a drone does the delivery? Instead, it's best to keep each *Bounded Context* tightly in its own lane, which is a way of upholding the **Single responsibility** principle.

There are also times when your system needs to accept a variety of requests from external systems or components. You need to integrate existing inflexible systems with your components. These systems often send requests and data in different formats. You'd like to define a common format for identical requests from external systems, but it is not possible to make them conform to a single interface specification. How can you architect your system to accommodate these variations? How can you support variations in requests and data formats without muddying up your implementation? In a sense, this is a form of **Interface segregation**. You want to keep external things internal and internal things internal.

You would like to keep the interfaces to the functionality provided by components of your system simple and straightforward. However, you need to interact with other systems that may be poorly architected and don't conform to your architecture. When these external systems are muddy, you need to find ways to integrate these systems without compromising your existing interfaces.

There are times when you have limited ability to change existing, possibly muddy, components that are outside your control. You need to integrate your software with these external components. These components are not easily modified and may be poorly designed. How can you preserve the design integrity of your system's core components while integrating with existing components?

As new functionality is added or existing functionality is modified, programmers routinely add code to integrate with external components and systems. Can they do so with minimal impact on existing core components?

Therefore,

Create an *Anti-Corruption Layer* (*ACL*) that handles interactions and adheres to the interfaces of the bounded contexts that need to interact with one another.

The *Anti-Corruption Layer* acts as an isolation layer that offers an interface for the two *Bounded Contexts* (*BCs*) to interact. This isolation layer adapts and translates to the interfaces of the *BCs*. It contains translation logic only, not business logic. It is in a sense the *glue-code* between the two *BCs* that keeps the two *BCs* clean from their respective APIs.

Ideas related to *ACL* have been around for a long time and help two separate systems to evolve independently without becoming tightly coupled, which could lead to a system becoming a *Big Ball of Mud*. An *ACL* helps ensure that the semantics in one *BC* do not "corrupt" the other *BC*'s semantics. *ACLs* provide a specialized interface to your "protected" components, which can perform data verification and possible filtering or data cleansing before delegating the call to the preserved "clean" interface of the component you don't want to be compromised. An *ACL* promotes **Loose coupling** across *BCs*.

This pattern is similar to **Adapters** or **Facades** and sometimes will be a two-way adapter. One way to accomplish this is to implement an **Adapter** or **Bridge** that takes (possibly muddy) requests and translates them into calls that preserve the "clean" interface. This cleansing and transformation can also be implemented using a **Proxy** or **Facade**.

This is especially an issue when you have to couple your internal components to some external systems interacting with your components. This could *muddy* up the code and make it more difficult to support new variations. By separating these concerns about the API and the cleansing and filtering functionality into separate, client-specific components (the adapters or proxies), you allow the common internal component to remain clean and focused on its main responsibility. This also helps solidify the boundaries between different parts of the system, ensuring clear roles and distinct responsibilities. These boundary areas are also where trust regions can be defined and enforced. Both input and outputs to and from the protected component can be filtered and transformed to provide the desired results (see Figure 5-24).

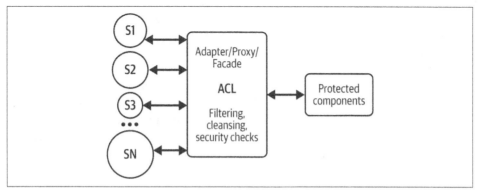

Figure 5-24. Anti-Corruption Layer protecting components

There are many patterns from *Design Patterns* (1994), such as **Adapter**, **Bridge**, **Decorator**, **Facade**, **Proxy**, and **Strategy**, that can be applied when implementing an *Anti-Corruption Layer*. An *Adapter* can be used to translate one interface of a *BC* into a compatible interface for another *BC*. A *Mediator* can be used to implement an *Adapter* that has to communicate and adapt to multiple *BCs*. The mediator provides the glue-code to keep the *BCs* clean. You might also include filtering and security checks. **Interceptors** (*Pattern-Oriented Software Architecture, Volume 1*, 1996), which are dynamically invoked, can be used to filter and do preprocessing before invoking core components.

A handy way of combining several of these ideas from *Design Patterns* is with **Remote Facade** (*Patterns of Enterprise Application Architecture*, 2002). This pattern acts like a **Facade**, which in turn acts like an **Adapter** between internal APIs and external (distributed) APIs. A **Remote Facade** could be built either as a wholly internal *ACL* within the *Bounded Context* (in which case, it also represents the *Application Services* of the *Bounded Context*, particularly in a Microservices Architecture (Chapter 4), or as an external *ACL* that handles external API's in a Modular Monolith (29).

An *ACL* makes it so that services and clients are more loosely coupled. It insulates the clients from knowing how the application is implemented. An *ACL* also simplifies the client by removing dependencies between services. This preserves the integrity of the clean component and its desired interface. *ACLs* provide a place to link in alternatives including untrusted code, thus allowing for validation and verification along with filtering and cleansing without adding complexity to existing components. They separate transformation/validation from code that implements component functionality. Additionally, they make it so that you can add one or more customized interfaces to support muddy code without breaking/changing existing code. *ACLs* are a way of supporting the **Loose coupling** principle from **IDEALS**.

ACLs also have some challenges. One is related to increased complexity—there is another evolving interconnected part that must be understood and maintained. This could cause an increased maintenance and governance burden. *ACLs* have the overhead of the extra network hop via the API, which can decrease performance with translation layers between components. When new behaviors need to be added to a service, you have to evolve the *ACL* for communication with other services. The extra adaptation layer to interact with components increases complexity, and is another spot where mud can start to grow—however, this complexity or glue-code is contained within the *ACL*, and good design principles can help with this.

An *Anti-Corruption Layer* keeps Bounded Contexts (201) from becoming entangled and tightly coupled with one another. They allow interacting *Bounded Contexts* to evolve independently. This is especially useful when you are interacting with *Bounded*

Contexts created by someone else or a third party that you have an incomplete understanding of and little control over. An *ACL* can be implemented with Dispatchers (140) or Adapter Microservices (135).

As referenced earlier, *Anti-Corruption Layers* are often seen in Modular Monoliths (29) and Distributed Architectures (38) as a means to keep components or subsystems clean.

Example

As an example, let's revisit our online ordering system. After an order is created by the system, we will need to fulfill and package the order and then ship the order. One possible solution is to include the fulfillment and shipping within the same *Bounded Context*. The problem with this is that the concept of order fulfillment can evolve independently from how we ship the orders—for instance, we may want to make it possible to change the shipping company in the future or do our own shipping.

We don't want to muddy the concept of orders with the concept of shipping. So rather than put shipping within our *BC*, we separate it into its own subdomain with a different *BC*. Thus, these concepts can evolve independently. However, these two *BCs* will need to interact. For example, when you place an order, you will need to make sure that the order is shipped. To prevent these *BCs* from overlapping or being muddied, we can create an *ACL* between the two. *ACLs* are commonly used to protect our system from changes from external (sometimes third-party) systems that we have no control over. *ACLs* also allow different subdomains (*BCs*) to evolve independently.

Conclusion: Wrapping Up Microservice Design

So far in this book, we've discussed a number of architectural guidelines for building cloud-native, service-based distributed systems, of which *Microservices* are one such architecture. The *Guiding **IDEALS** for Designing Microservices* are one proven set of design principles that motivated the patterns in this chapter.

Our design approach focuses on avoiding translation errors from the domain expert's requirements to the code. The foundational idea presented in this chapter is that Modeling Around the Domain (183) is critical to avoiding these translation errors when designing applications, regardless of architectural style.

Modeling Around the Domain presents a subset of domain modeling concepts that are extremely useful when building applications using the *Microservices* architectural style. To be successful, you must first understand the core domains and subdomains reflecting what the business or software system is primarily about. The goal is *not* to try to create a universal (or enterprise) language. Rather, modeling should be phrased in terms of the *Ubiquitous Language* that makes sense within a subdomain.

That modeling process begins with an Event Storming (189) session. That session describes a linear sequence of Domain Events that represent facts about the system that have occurred. These events can trigger a change or some action in another part of the domain.

Emerging from that process, you delimit the boundaries around the domain model of a subdomain with a Bounded Context (201), or *BC*. The boundary of a *BC* maps well to the boundary of a *Microservice*. We limit access to the internals of a *BC* through *Application Services*—which are the APIs of a *Bounded Context*.

Within a *Bounded Context*, there will be Aggregates (211)—which are the clusters of related domain objects (entities) that are likely to change over time. *Aggregates* include the related entities and their values, together with possible *Value Objects* within a subdomain. **Repositories** provide an abstraction for handling the interactions between *Aggregates* and persistent storage—hiding implementation details of the persistence mechanism.

There is often logic that does not belong to a specific entity. Domain Services (222) handle domain logic that falls between or outside *Aggregates*.

Finally, an *Anti-Corruption Layer* (229) (*ACL*) protects the semantics of a *Bounded Context* from being corrupted by the semantics of another *BC*.

Figure 5-25 shows an example of these concepts working together. In this diagram, we illustrate several key concepts, including how a single *Bounded Context* can have one or more *Aggregates*, each comprised of related entities, and that the persistence of the entities within a *Bounded Context* is handled by a **Repository**. Likewise, external access to the behavior of an Aggregate is provided through *Application Services*, which may be mediated through an *ACL*. This *ACL* can be implemented either as a separate service or may be part of the *Application Service* on either side.

Behavior in between *Aggregates* is handled by *Domain Services*. Finally, *Domain Events* can be created and placed on an *Event Backbone* whenever anything changes within the bounds of a *Bounded Context*. That allows for a style of communication between *Bounded Contexts* that greatly limits coupling between the modules or *Microservices* that make up the implementation of our *Bounded Contexts*.

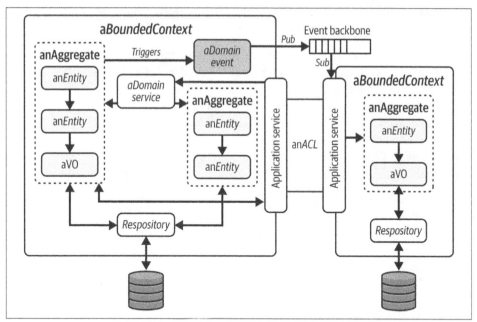

Figure 5-25. Domain modeling concepts

Going from Domain Model to Microservices

Once you have an understanding of the requirements and have completed enough modeling, you might ask, "How do I go from my domain models to a *Microservices* implementation?" Domain modeling techniques are a way to model a domain so that the *Microservices* architectural style can be applied to the implementation of a system.

To see how to go from our modeling sessions to implementation, let's look again at what we mean by *Microservices*. In "Microservices" (*https://oreil.ly/Dnwyn*), James Lewis and Martin Fowler described *Microservices* in the following statement: "The *microservice architectural style* is an approach to developing a single application as a suite of small services, each running in its own process and communicating with lightweight mechanisms, often an HTTP resource API. These services are built around *business capabilities* and *independently deployable* by fully automated deployment machinery."

There are a few distinguishing factors we can pull out of this definition. It is a way of developing or building a system with a suite of small independent services. An important factor is the ability to be independently deployed, and the deployment unit (the *Microservice*) should contain only one service or a few related cohesive services. Critically, this definition also points out that *Microservices* should be modeled and built around business capabilities. This last point is closely related to domain modeling techniques since they focus on identifying the business capabilities within a domain.

So when we get ready to implement our *Microservices*, a *Bounded Context* must be one of the first concepts to consider. A *BC* should be used as a starting point to define the boundaries of your *Microservices*. A *BC* will include *Aggregates* (entities with values) and various behaviors that are either described as part of an entity or as *Domain Services* for behavior that does not belong to a specific entity. Finally, a *BC* should include *Domain Events*, which represent that something of interest has happened within a *BC*. Access to anything within a *Bounded Context* is limited through the interface to your *Microservice*, which is called an *Application Service*.

The basic rule of thumb when going from design to a *Microservice* implementation is to implement a *Microservice* for every *Bounded Context* you have modeled. Then for each *Microservice* that maps to a *BC*, create a service for each *Aggregate* within that *BC*. This encapsulates the *Aggregates* and you provide an interface (API) into the *Aggregate* through the *Service API*. Finally, implement any *Domain Services* and *Domain Events* as part of the *Microservice* that you have modeled within the *BC*. For any *Aggregates* that need to be persisted, you will include a **Repository** for reading and persisting these values.

There are a lot of possible scenarios that influence how your *Microservices* should be implemented. These scenarios will either contain all of the business logic within a *Bounded Context* or there will need to be interactions between bounded contexts.

Business Logic contained within a single Bounded Context

The simplest scenario is when the business logic is contained entirely within the same bounded context and does not need to interact with other *BCs*. When you have this scenario, you implement the *BC* as a *Microservice* and then implement a service for each *Aggregate* within the *BC*. These *Aggregates* contain cohesive entities with their values and behaviors. Communication through the *Aggregate* is only done through the *Aggregate* API, which is sometimes called the *Aggregate Root*. We then deploy all the *Aggregate* services within a *BC* as a single *Microservice*.

A *Microservice* can contain a single service or a few services, as long as they are cohesive. By implementing each *Aggregate* as a service within the *Microservice*, we isolate and protect the *Aggregates* from change, reducing coupling between *Aggregates*.

This follows the **Single responsibility** principle. We expose the interface to the deployed *Microservice* through an application service and use domain events to flag when something happens within the microservice. *Domain Services* include logic that does not belong to a specific entity. The *Aggregates* of entities and VOs, domain events, and domain services are usually considered the domain layer of the *BC*. This domain layer can interact with an infrastructure layer, such as making a call to a **Repository**.

Interactions between different Bounded Contexts

For more complicated scenarios, when there are interactions between different bounded contexts, we will still create a service for each *Aggregate* within the *BC* and deploy them all together as a single *Microservice*. We will also need to deal with interactions between bounded contexts. Sometimes these interactions are done through direct synchronous (HTTP) calls to another *Microservice* for the *BC* we need to interact with. If needed, you can put an *Anti-Corruption Layer* between *Microservices* (for example, an **API Gateway**) to help minimize this coupling.

Other times, we will have asynchronous calls that we implement with events for communicating between *BCs*. Events are communicated asynchronously, which provides the benefit that the system as a whole is still available even if the subscribers are not available. For example, the `Catalog` *Microservice* could continue to work even if the *RecommendationEngine Microservice* is not available—it would just display items in a default order rather than in a recommended order that maximizes potential purchase.

Domain Modeling Concepts Leads to a Layered Design

In *Patterns, Principles, and Practices of Domain-Driven Design* (2015), Millett and Tune point out that modeling with domain concepts can lead to a layered design (see Figure 5-26).

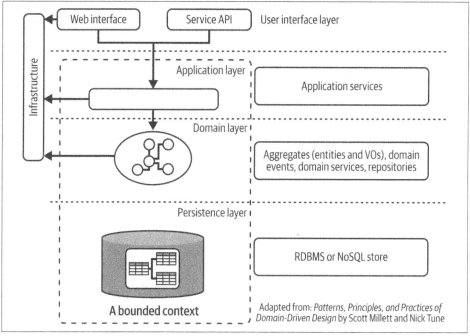

Figure 5-26. Domain modeling can lead to a layered architecture

Within each *Bounded Context*, you will have an application layer (which is the *Application Services*). This is the top-level interface to your *Microservice* and is on top of the domain layer that includes the *Aggregates* of entities and VOs, *Domain Events*, and *Domain Services*.

This layer usually interacts with an infrastructure layer where we can make calls to a **Repository** that will store your *Aggregates* through a persistence layer, such as to an SQL or a NoSQL database. Access to each *Bounded Context* is only through the *Application Services*. So the next layer on top of this is either some API service or GUI service, which sometimes go through a *Dispatcher* such as an **API Gateway** or a **BFF** which is an example of an *Anti-Corruption Layer*.

Now that we have explained the critical concepts involved in *Modeling Around the Domain*, you are ready to implement these concepts in a Microservices Architecture (Chapter 4) compliant with the **IDEALS**. This will set you up for building an Event-Driven Architecture (Chapter 6) for your *Microservices*, which will then rely on Cloud-Native Storage (Chapter 7) for persistence, as you will see in the next two chapters.

CHAPTER 6

Event-Driven Architecture

A recurring theme for evolving an application architecture is to encapsulate components and decouple them. One motivation for identifying modules in a Modular Monolith (29) is to reduce the coupling between cohesive units of code in the same application. Likewise, a Distributed Architecture (38) decouples modules further into services so that they can run on separate computers. Microservices Architecture (Chapter 4) decouples services even more into Microservices (119) so that they can be developed and deployed independently.

Loose coupling facilitates disassembling an application into independent components by minimizing the dependencies of each component on the implementations of other components that it uses. A Service API (70) decouples a service consumer from a service provider, so much so that when one service provider is replaced by another with the same service interface and similar functionality, the overall application still functions correctly. The service interface hides changes in the service provider's implementation from the service consumers. This loose coupling enables the application to evolve incrementally, upgrading individual component implementations one at a time with enhanced versions while preserving the correct behavior of the overall application at each step.

Yet with a service interface, there's another type of coupling that still remains: the components are coupled by the timing and synchronization of the calls they make between one another. When the consumer is ready to invoke the service functionality, the provider must be ready to perform the functionality. The consumer must be able to locate the provider to invoke it, such as via a load balancer. The consumer waits while the provider performs the functionality. If the provider fails, the consumer must handle the error or else it will fail as well.

Introduction to Event-Driven Architecture

This chapter explains how to design applications that avoid coupling not only of their components and the implementation of functionality but also of the location of the service provider and the timing of when the functionality will be provided. Event-Driven Architecture (EDA) accomplishes this by decoupling components so that they interact through *Event Notification* (see Event Notifier (269)) rather than service invocation. Transforming a service invocation into an *Event Notification* produces even greater decoupling between the components.

These patterns assume a basic understanding of how *Event Notification* differs from service invocation, so we'll review that first. We'll review the types of components involved in *Event Notification*, how they help decouple components even more than a Service API (70) can, and how the cloud can make these components easier to host.

With this background on what an Event-Driven Architecture is, we'll then present the patterns that show how to design an Event-Driven Architecture, starting with the root pattern for this chapter, Event Choreography (246).

A Motivating Example

Consider the following problem. Let's say you are building a system to handle onboarding for new employees at a company. When a new person is hired, many components need to be updated to perform tasks such as assigning an email address, starting salary payments, sending a welcome package, etc. Especially if new HR policies are being added frequently, there may be no single centralized business process for onboarding that understands everything that has to be done when a new employee is hired, particularly if there are geographical or divisional differences for onboarding.

It seems like the onboarding process should be able to simply update HR policies about the new employee, and that they should be able to react as needed in turn. We've encountered this idea before, in the Event Storming (189) pattern in Microservice Design (Chapter 5)—this is the idea of an Event (255). An *Event* is an announcement of an interesting occurrence of a phenomenon, typically a state change in an Aggregate (211). That idea can extend the idea of loose coupling to loosening the bounds of who calls a component and how they call it. This leads to what is known as an Event-Driven Architecture.

From Service Orchestration to Event-Driven Architecture

Event-Driven Architecture facilitates composing complex functionality from simple components. An approach from Microservices Architecture (Chapter 4) for composing functionality is to employ a Service Orchestrator (160). *Service Orchestration* couples components tightly and provides greater control for performing preplanned procedures. Event-Driven Architecture couples components loosely and facilitates emergent behavior dependent on context.

A *Service Orchestrator* is tightly coupled with each of the services it orchestrates. When a change occurs in a *Service Orchestrator*, it reacts by invoking a service synchronously, causing the service to react to the change. That couples the orchestrator to the service, because the orchestrator has to know about the service to invoke its behavior, which means that the orchestrator cannot work without the service. It also assumes the orchestrator knows how the service will handle the change and that the service will always handle every change the same way. It also assumes that there's only one service; for more than one, the orchestrator will have to know about all services, know which task to invoke in each, and know which changes each service knows how to handle. The orchestrator will then be coupled to all of those services, such that it cannot run unless they are all available.

To facilitate loose coupling among components, rather than using service invocation, an Event-Driven Architecture incorporates a new style of interaction—*Event Notification*.

Pseudosynchronous and Asynchronous Service Invocation

As explained, to decouple components beyond their *Service API*, the next step is to increase decoupling of the timing and synchronization of the service invocation calls between a service requestor and a service provider. This sounds like a job for asynchronous messaging. When the requestor and provider use messaging (the **Request-Reply** pattern (*Enterprise Integration Patterns*, 2003)), they don't need to know each others' location; the sender can put the message on the queue when it's ready, and the receiver can read the message from the queue when it's ready.

However, a service invocation via asynchronous messaging may not be asynchronous. If the requestor puts the request message on the queue and then blocks waiting for the response, the service invocation is not asynchronous. The blocking requestor makes the service invocation pseudosynchronous, meaning that it's making an asynchronous call synchronously. Pseudosynchronous service invocation consumes threads, complicates crash recovery, and still has to correlate responses with requests, all while turning a single transaction into multiple transactions.

For a service invocation to be fully asynchronous, the requestor needs to listen for responses in a separate thread. The requestor sends the request in one thread and receives the response in a separate thread that listens to the response queue. The requestor uses separate transactions for the request and response, just like asynchronous messaging does. The requestor must correlate each response with its request. Asynchronous service invocation scales better because it doesn't block threads, and any replica of a stateless requestor can handle any response and recover from crashes.

While asynchronous service invocation is an improvement over pseudosynchronous, it still has complexity. Once the request is sent, its logical transaction needs to complete—the provider needs to receive the request, perform the service, and send the response, which the requestor needs to receive and process. For this whole process to be reliable, the messaging system needs to make the network more reliable by providing guaranteed, exactly-once delivery of the request and the response. If either message is lost, the requestor doesn't know whether the provider performed the request and what was the outcome. The requestor can retry, but that may cause the provider to perform the service more than once.

The cloud's unreliable infrastructure makes asynchronous service invocation even more difficult to perform reliably. Message Queuing (MQ)–style messaging systems are able to provide guaranteed, exactly-once delivery of a message because the message is in only one queue manager at any given time. To transfer exactly one copy of a message from one queue manager to another, MQ-style messaging systems implement distributed transactions. As explained in Service Orchestrator (160), distributed transactions do not work well in the cloud. When the single copy of a message is at rest in a queue manager and the queue manager's infrastructure stops working, the message becomes unavailable until the queue manager recovers, and is lost unless the queue is persistent. Event-style messaging systems like Apache Kafka run more reliably on the cloud by embracing replication, similar to a Replicated Database (316) for *Event* streaming. Replication avoids distributed transactions and single points of failure, and replicated messaging systems provide at-most-once delivery and at-least-once delivery, but replication makes exactly-once delivery very difficult to achieve. For a more in-depth discussion of the different types of messaging technologies and messaging styles, including the pros and cons of each, the interested reader should refer to *Enterprise Integration Patterns* (2003).

For all of these reasons, there are limits to how reliably service invocations can be performed asynchronously, and therefore how much more service invocation can decouple requestors and providers beyond the service interface. One of the benefits of Event-Driven Architecture is to provide components that need to communicate an alternative to service invocation. Event-Driven Architecture can decouple components even more than asynchronous service invocation can, by changing the messaging semantics from bidirectional service invocation to unidirectional *Event Notification*.

Event-Driven Architecture provides not just one component like an orchestrator but a set of collaborating components:

Event
  Encapsulates information that describes a change

Event emitter

Detects changes, encapsulates them as *Events*, and sends those out as notifications

Event listener

Receives *Event Notifications* and decides if and how to react

Event channel

Connects *Event* emitters to the *Event* listers that are interested in the emitters' *Events*

These components collaborate to implement *Event Notification* in an Event-Driven Architecture.

Decoupling Listeners from Emitters

Event-Driven Architecture decouples event listeners from event emitters so that both can evolve independently. Multiple event listeners may receive events from multiple event emitters. An event emitter does not know which event listeners receive its events. An event listener may receive events from multiple event emitters and does not know which event emitter sent an event.

The distinguishing characteristics of Event-Driven Architecture are:

One-way transmission

The events are transmitted one way—not bidirectionally—from the event emitter to the event listener. No reply to the event is needed or expected.

Change notification

Event interactions are notifications describing something that has happened. They carry no intent that any particular processing is expected because of the event. Event-Driven Architecture enables two event listeners to react to the same event quite differently.

With these characteristics, Event-Driven Architecture enables a family of interacting components to evolve easily with minimal impact on the overall architecture:

Add an event listener

A completely new component can be added into the family with a new event-handling interface; by expressing an interest in appropriate events, processing in the new component will be initiated at appropriate times using appropriate event data as input, even though no other application or component in the preexisting family explicitly invokes it.

Add an event emitter

New event-producing components and even other applications may be added into the family. Their emitted events will trigger additional appropriate processing by event processors (even though the new event producer is not aware of what this processing is).

Refine an event channel

Intelligence may be added to improve the quality of event-based matching and interactions—for example, duplicate event detection and removal may increase the efficiency of component interactions within the component family by eliminating redundant processing.

This is how Event-Driven Architecture decouples event listeners from event emitters so that the architecture can evolve.

Event-Driven Architecture and Cloud-Native Architecture

An Event-Driven Architecture does not have to run on a cloud platform, but its components work better when they follow a Cloud-Native Architecture (58). Emitters and listeners are often *Microservices*, which are cloud native. Modeling Around the Domain (183) is critical because this helps you both find your *Microservices* and discover the events and relationships between the *Microservices*. Even eventing components that are not *Microservices* will run better if they're Stateless Applications (80). To make them easier to deploy in multiple environments with limited dependencies on the environment, encapsulate their program as an Application Package (62) with an External Configuration (97). Stateless packages are easier to make into Replicable Applications (88). And eventing components that are cloud native can access specialized, reusable functionality as separate Backend Services (106).

Although not required, a cloud environment makes lots of small eventing components much easier to manage. All of the emitters and listeners can more easily share a pool of capacity, and the environment can more easily provision capacity for each individual component as needed. Capacity can also be made available more easily for a new version of a component to replace an old one without causing an outage. The environment can provide messaging services for implementing event buses. Eventing components can get their *Backend Services* from the cloud platform's service catalog.

Developing Event-Driven Architecture

This chapter defines a collection of seven patterns that together explain how to design applications with an Event-Driven Architecture. Figure 6-1 shows the patterns and their relationships.

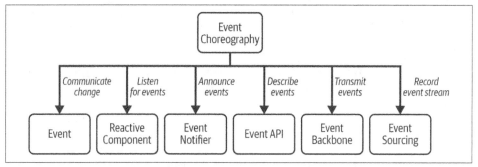

Figure 6-1. Event-Driven Architecture patterns

An Event-Driven Architecture enables application components to coordinate and compose complex functionality via Event Choreography (246).

Event Choreography provides two principle benefits that leverage the decoupling provided by the **Observer** pattern and further increase the decoupling:

Separation of API
    Event notification uses a generic API.

Separation of time and space
    Event notification can queue until the receiver is ready to process the event and works equally well between and within processes.

The participants in *Event Choreography* are as follows:

Event (255)
    Events contain information describing changes. Each one provides notification when a change occurs. Components coordinate by exchanging events.

Reactive Component (260)
    This component listens for events, determines which ones it considers interesting, and reacts to the interesting ones.

Event Notifier (269)
    This component provides notifications of changes by emitting events.

A single component can be both an *Event Notifier* and a *Reactive Component*. It can receive an event and react in part by emitting other events.

Event Notifiers connect to *Reactive Components* via a shared set of channels that transmit events:

Event API (274)
    Defines and describes a set of event types: the format of the events, their meaning, and the circumstances that will create new events. This defined API enables

the event notifiers and *Reactive Components* connected by each channel to agree on how they will communicate.

Event Backbone (279)

Implements a set of channels, one per event type in the *Event API*. Each channel connects the *Event Notifiers* that emit that event type to the *Reactive Components* that listen for that type of event, and transmits the events from the *Event Notifiers* to the *Reactive Components*.

The current state of each *Reactive Component* changes constantly as it receives new events. The record of events for a *Reactive Component* enables Event Sourcing (289) to show the component's current state and the history that led there.

This introduction has covered several topics that are helpful to be familiar with to understand the patterns in this chapter. We've talked about making the loose coupling between service components even looser with *Event Notification*, an example of all the systems that need to be updated when onboarding a new employee, how *Event Notification* differs from *Service Orchestration*, difficulties making service invocation asynchronous, and the component types for *Event Notification* and how Event-Driven Architecture decouples them.

Event-Driven Architecture does not require a cloud platform, but the cloud makes eventing components easier to manage. In this chapter, we will show how *Microservices* can be built using event-driven components. We'll start with the root pattern for this chapter, Event Choreography (246).

Event Choreography

You are developing an application as a distributed set of components in a Distributed Architecture (38), such as a Microservices Architecture (Chapter 4) with Microservices (119). Or you might be refactoring an existing application, possibly a Modular Monolith (29), into distributed components.

When a change occurs in one component, how can a variable number of other components react accordingly?

The real world changes constantly, and changes happen on irregular schedules. Dealing with constantly changing conditions in the real world is difficult. Changes happen often, at inopportune times, and in unexpected ways. Applications need to be updated to reflect those changes. A single change in the real world may affect multiple components or applications. What's more, you don't want to have to wait until everyone who might be interested in a change reacts before you move on with your processing.

When something changes, we want to allow that change to affect many other components without tightly coupling them to the original component. A good design principle is to have loose coupling between components. That was one of the **IDE-ALS** that we discussed earlier in Microservice Design (Chapter 5). Whenever you are developing an application that touches on multiple aspects of your business, you want to communicate information between those components yet avoid tying everything together like spaghetti.

Let's return to an example from Domain Event (193) to see what effects an airline flight running late can have. For example, if you have a connecting flight, you may miss it and need to be rebooked on a later flight, possibly arriving at your destination the next day. If you have a rental car reservation or a hotel reservation and you will not get to that city until the next day, you will not need the reservation for tonight. These are just the consequences and adjustments per passenger. Multiply them times the 100 or so passengers on the flight and you see the issues that can arise and why there are often lines at customer service counters whenever a flight is canceled.

There are also consequences for the airlines. The plane will be delayed for its next flight. Another aircraft may need to be assigned for the next flight and the original aircraft reassigned. The flight crew may miss their next flights. The flights must be delayed or replacement crews assigned. All these consequences occur because one flight is late. Once the airline knows its flight is late, what can it do to mitigate these consequences?

One possibility is that the airline could know the full travel itinerary of each passenger on the flight—not only connecting flights on the same airline but also flights on other airlines, reservations for rental cars and hotels, etc. It could then be responsible for updating all of the applications for each affected passenger. However, the passenger may not be comfortable revealing all of this information to the airline. Likewise, the airline doesn't want to be responsible for storing all of this information and for processing updates to frequently changing travel plans. And even if the airline had the most up-to-date itinerary, it wouldn't want to be responsible for having to change the reservations with all of these other travel service providers.

What this means is that responding to events is important not just within a single application but to interapplication communication as well. When working with things that happen in the real world, you usually don't just have a single application modeling an entire process; you usually have a web of applications, each modeling and managing part of a process. That means that there are many different ways in which applications will want to respond to updates and notifications from a variety of sources.

There are at least a couple of ways in which you could build applications to react to external stimuli:

- Putting APIs into your application is one possible way around this, but that requires something external to your application or component to call the API at the appropriate time. That is the idea behind *Service Orchestration* (see Service Orchestrator (160)), and we've already seen both its advantages and limitations.

- Batch processes are another possible way of forcing updates. You could schedule regular timed updates when components or applications swap information on what has changed in each of them during the interval since the last update. The first problem is that this is not in real time, or even near-real time. Many components can wait an hour or two between updates, but in situations where human lives (or millions of dollars) are at risk, relying on a slow, timed updating process is not enough. Communication between applications often needs to happen at unexpected and impossible-to-predetermine intervals.

- Another possible solution is to use database triggers so that whenever a change occurs in a database, it triggers a change in another table or another database. Database triggers work in real time, but that only updates the information in your database. It does not invoke processing within the application, which both leads to the kind of data coupling we want to avoid with *Microservices* and to the logic of the application being built within the database.

Since none of these solutions fully solve our problem, we need something else that can be made part of the application design itself, like an API, but that can work asynchronously like a database trigger. It also needs to be invoked whenever the change occurs, as opposed to on some predetermined schedule.

Therefore,

Coordinate multiple components through *Event Choreography* so that when one changes, the others can react at their own pace and in their own way.

Event Choreography is the idea that each component can react independently to events they receive and that no central orchestrator is required. Each component (*Microservice*) is truly independent of all the others, even down to not requiring an explicit API to trigger actions that are implemented by the *Microservice*. *Event Choreography* is based on several older, well-established concepts that come together into a consistent architecture. To understand how that happens, we need to start with some simple building blocks.

The first building block is that you can send an abstract notification to any of a number of receivers that register interest in a notification. This comes from the **Observer** pattern (*Design Patterns*, 1994). In this pattern, whenever a change occurs in the sender (called the "Subject"), a notification is sent in **Observer** to all the receivers (called "Observers"). The API of this interaction is generic—different subject/observer pairs didn't have different methods in their API, so all updates from all potential Subjects were processed by the same method on the Observer—the important thing is the parameters sent along with the notification, which indicate who the update came from and what the update was for.

That is the origin of our first principle benefit: Separation of API. This is shown in Figure 6-2 (adapted from *Design Patterns* (1995)).

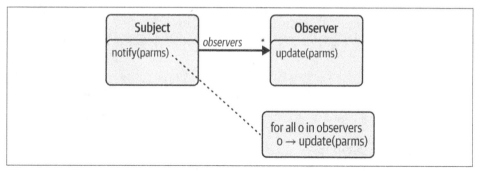

Figure 6-2. Observer pattern

What is critical about this is not only that you don't need a special API on the receiving end but that the relationship is indirect in other ways as well. Observers are optional—a Subject can send out a notification even if there are no Observers to listen for it. Also, Observers can choose to either react to or ignore any notifications they receive.

The next important set of building blocks can be constructed by introducing patterns from *Enterprise Integration Patterns* (2003) (*EIP*). This book looks at the same problem and forces discussed previously and concludes that what is needed is a mechanism (**Messaging** (*Enterprise Integration Patterns*, 2003)) that is not only asynchronous, which the **Observer** pattern did not require, but also multiprocess. This is shown in Figure 6-3 (adapted from EIP).

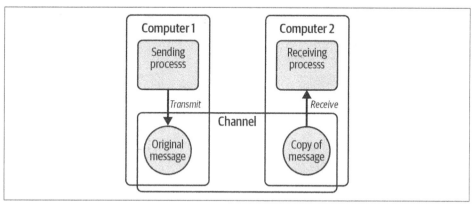

Figure 6-3. Messaging pattern

As we introduced above, the second principle benefit is separation of time and space. Figure 6-3 summarizes this benefit. The first idea is that you need a process between the sender and receiver that handles the implementation of the **Observer** pattern in that it takes abstract messages (data) from any process through a fixed API and then transmits it to any other process that chooses to receive that data, regardless of that process's location. Subjects and observers are connected by a **Message Bus** (*Enterprise Integration Patterns*, 2003), which is made up of many **Message Channels** (*Enterprise Integration Patterns*, 2003) that carry messages. It has its own network protocols to manage that data communication. This provides separation of space since any component inside or outside any process can talk to any other process.

A benefit is that this communication happens asynchronously—that is, once the data is handed over to the channel, the sending process does not need to wait for a reply from any (or all) of the receiving processes. What's more, the messages may be delivered immediately or after an indeterminate amount of time (perhaps if there is a problem in the channel or the receiving process)—the sending process should not care about how quickly the messages are delivered or if they are delivered at all.

The architecture for *Event Choreography* (derived from the one in *EIP*) is illustrated in Figure 6-4. It should be noted that this diagram has replaced computers with applications from the *EIP* drawing. Applications can either run on separate computers or in virtual machines running on the same computer. Additionally, each application can be deployed in the cloud and scaled up by having multiple instances of an application deployed in the cloud.

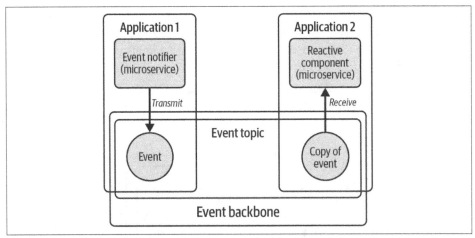

Figure 6-4. Event Choreography pattern

Choreographed components announce changes as Events (255). *Events* are implementations of *Domain Events* and which are transmitted as **Event Messages** (*Enterprise Integration Patterns*, 2003). Events are carried on an Event Backbone (279) through topics. An *Event Backbone* is a special type of **Message Bus** that is optimized to carry *Events* over **Publish-Subscribe Channels** (*Enterprise Integration Patterns*, 2003) and also supports patterns such as Event Sourcing (289).

There are two types of choreographed components: *Event Notifiers* and *Reactive Components*:

- An Event Notifier (269) is a component that is able to announce its changes as events.
- A Reactive Component (260) is a component that is interested in knowing about changes and is able to listen for changes as events.

The set of the descriptions of all the *Events* that are sent out by *Event Notifiers* and the topics on which they are carried makes up your Event API (274).

The *Reactive Components* interested in a set of related *Events* register interest on a topic to connect to the *Event Notifiers* in which the changes represented by those *Events* can occur. *Event Notifiers* connect to the topic to publish events. Different types of changes are transmitted on different topics. The *Event Notifiers* for a type of change and the *Reactive Components* listening for that type of change all connect to the same topic.

An Event-Driven Architecture that enables application components to coordinate and compose complex functionality via *Event Choreography* has a number of advantages from the overall system point of view:

Publishers and subscribers are independent and hence loosely coupled
There's more flexibility to add functionality by simply adding subscribers or events. That creates a very important extension point that is much easier than when you are using *Service Orchestration* as your only mechanism for extension. If you only have a Service API (70) and you want a new action to occur when something changes, you are forced to go into the implementation of a service and add that new feature—adding a new *Reactive Component* to listen to an existing event and perform a new action is much easier.

Scalability and throughput
So far, we've been mostly discussing the design benefits of an Event-Driven Architecture. However, there are multiple performance and scaling benefits as well. Most notably, *Event Notifiers* are not blocked when they publish an event. Since they do not have to wait on one (or many) responses, no threads are blocked and the system can continue processing new actions or events. Likewise, since events can be consumed by multiple subscribers in parallel, if multiple actions need to occur when a single event is detected, you don't need to do them

all serially inside a single component—just build multiple different *Reactive Components* (or multiple listeners within a single *Reactive Component*), each of which performs a different action when it receives the same event simultaneously.

Availability

When you are building an event-driven system, temporary failures in one service that sends out *Events* are less likely to affect others. The reason is that interaction is intermediated through the *Event Backbone*. However, this advantage is offset by the potential disadvantage of reliability, as we discuss in the paragraphs that follow.

Listed here are some of the major challenges of *Event Choreography*:

Message Reliability

This is perhaps the biggest single drawback to an Event-driven approach. An event system does not guarantee delivery. It is, instead, best effort. There are several ways in which an *Event* can be undelivered:

- The event can fail to be delivered and be lost by the *Event Backbone* to any *Reactive Component* because of a failure in the *Event Backbone*. This is rare but still possible when using common *Event Backbone* technologies like Apache Kafka.

- There may be no *Reactive Component* listening on a topic. This is a more common occurrence and can happen due to startup failures of the *Reactive Component* or a temporary failure of the component during the time an *Event* has been published. Most *Event-Backbone* systems have a mechanism to allow a *Reactive Component* to "catch up" on missed *Events* when they restart, but even this has limitations.

- The *Reactive Component* may encounter a failure during processing of an *Event*. Since *Events* are asynchronous and nontransactional, there is often no built-in mechanism for recovery. Once an *Event* is consumed, if something goes wrong, it's up to the *Reactive Component* to do its own recovery by restarting earlier in the event stream.

Event Choreography

Increases the complexity of the control flow for the application, which can make testing and debugging more difficult. There are various interacting moving pieces that might require synchronization points for coordinating activities. Orchestration is particularly useful for managing complex workflows, where several moving pieces need to be coordinated.

Error Handling

In general, error handling in a system based on events is more complicated than in a corresponding system based entirely on synchronous calls through a *Service*

API. The root of this problem is that since event notifications are one-way, there's no easy approach for letting upstream components know that downstream components have encountered problems without creating correction or rollback events, which adds another level of complexity.

Event Choreography is different from *Service Orchestration* in that choreography deals with the possibility that interactions can be unpredictable. Reactive Components (260) may be added at any time or removed at any time. Event Notifiers (269) may decide to add new events or stop sending out events. If interactions are predictable, they can (and should) be orchestrated. It's the constantly changing, unpredictable types of interactions that are best suited for *Event Choreography*.

What this means is that the two principle benefits of *Event Choreography*—the separation of API and the separation of time and space—dramatically reduce the coupling between components that participate in *Event Choreography* as compared to components that take part in *Service Orchestration*. What this amounts to is there are multiple differences between *Service Orchestration* and *Event Choreography*:

- Orchestration can run steps in order or concurrently. Choreography can only run steps concurrently.

- Orchestration knows when a step is completed and what the result or error was. Choreography doesn't know if the step was ever performed; maybe it still will be.

- Orchestration ensures a step is performed once and can be reversed with a compensating transaction. An event may cause zero-to-many steps to run. This may have the effect of running the same step multiple times, making it difficult to reverse a step or even unclear which steps were performed that need to be reversed.

- Orchestration can achieve 100% completeness and ensure consistency. Events can get lost, duplicated, and/or lead to side effects other than the main intended reaction. While events may naturally lead to 99% completeness, for 100%, the application must periodically run auditing to find incomplete or duplicate work and remediate it.

Both orchestration and choreography are useful in system design. However, whenever the emphasis is on reducing coupling—as is often the case in component design—*Event Choreography* should be preferred whenever strict order and transactionality are not required.

Example

Let's say a company wants to provide a travel safety service for its employees. There are many different possible things that it may want to warn its traveling employees about; weather events, public transit disruptions due to strikes, etc. (see Figure 6-5).

The application can receive notifications from various sources, including weather, government travel advisories, and the news. The application can then notify the employees in the affected region through their preferred means of communication if the message matches their notification preference.

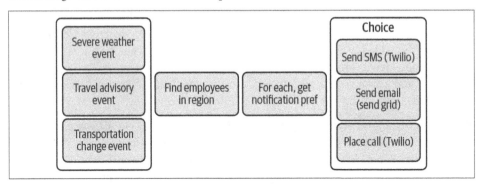

Figure 6-5. Requirements for employee safety notifications

Let's look more closely and find out why *Event Choreography* is such a good solution for this particular problem. We can break the problem down into four stages; first, there are the data sources that might indicate a potential travel problem that we listed in Figure 6-5. Second, there's a stage where you have to identify employees that are within an affected area. Then you want to look at the preferences of each individual employee and send them a notification through their preferred channel (email, text, etc.)

The first set of components (the potential issue sources) are fantastic examples of *Event Notifiers* because they don't care about who, if anyone, gets the notifications they send out! They simply are endless loops gathering and parsing data from sources like The Weather Channel API or RSS news feeds or by scraping government websites and then sending those along as *Events* on the *Event Backbone* as potentially interesting travel disruptions.

Then there is the second stage. Here you can also be driven from events, but the events that drive this stage are travel events—if you require that your employees use a specific travel agency, that agency (or the airlines or train companies they work with) may be able to send out notifications when a flight or train arrives or departs. This is essentially the same as the airline example we looked at the beginning of the chapter. The difference here is that this requires a *Reactive Component* to listen on two different topics, the travel event topic and the travel disruption topic. Whenever it receives a travel event, it updates an internal database of employee locations to show that they have arrived (or departed) from a particular area. When it receives a travel disruption event, it calculates which employees in its internal database are within the potentially affected area. It then looks up their communication preference and sends out another event for each employee, a disruption notification event, to another topic that different *Reactive Components* listen on to send out notifications on the preferred channel.

You see this entire set of interacting components in Figure 6-6.

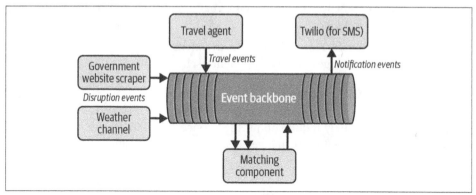

Figure 6-6. Design for employee safety notifications

In short, *Event Choreography* is great for this example since it allows lots of variation. New *Event Notifiers* can be added for new data sources without having to change any existing components. Likewise, new *Reactive Components* on the end can support new notification styles just as easily. And if the company wants to change travel agents, that's also something that is isolated to a single component—again, easy to update or modify.

Event

You are using Event Choreography (246) to coordinate multiple components so that when a change occurs in a component, other components interested in that change can react accordingly yet not be tightly coupled through APIs.

How do you represent a change in one component to be communicated to other components?

There is a tension in the design of any set of communicating components. Components, like the objects they are often built from in object-oriented programming, should avoid revealing too much about their internal implementation details. This is the basic idea of encapsulation, or information hiding, and is an important consideration in component design. At the same time, you also don't want to have to constantly rework every component whenever a new business process step is added—this is essentially the open-closed principle (OCP), first coined by Bertrand Meyer (*Object-Oriented Software Construction*, 1988), that components should be "open for extension, but closed for modification" (*https://oreil.ly/DQePY*). But implementing that principle in practice can be challenging:

- You don't want to overwhelm the system with information, nor do you want to unnecessarily expose internal details of your component to the outside world and thus couple components together too tightly.

- You also don't want to miss important changes that should be communicated with other components.

- You want to provide a mechanism for an extension for your components that does not require changes to the component itself.

It would be great if a component could announce the fact that your state has changed to the world without having to reveal exactly *how* that state changed. That way interested parties could politely inquire about the Service API (70) of your component to find out more details about what changed and not break encapsulation.

Therefore,

Capture the minimal description of each change as an *Event* and communicate that to the other components.

Once emitted, an *Event* is transmitted on an Event Backbone (279) as an **Event Message** (*Enterprise Integration Patterns*, 2003). The critical thing about an *Event* is not the fact that it is a message—in this book, we are actually less interested in the details of the messaging system itself, as that was more than adequately covered in *EIP*. What is most interesting for our purposes is how the message is represented and why the message is being communicated.

In Figure 6-7, we show a very simple example of an *Event*, a "Temperature Change" *Event*, being carried from an *Event Notifier* (presumably a temperature sensor) to one or more *Reactive Components* over an *Event Backbone*, which shows how the *Event* pattern fits together with the others in this chapter.

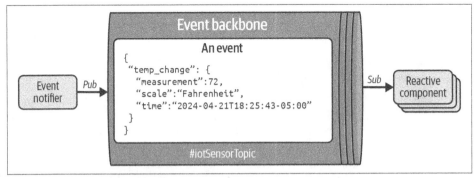

Figure 6-7. Event in transit

To see how this all works, let's go back to the idea of the **Observer** pattern (*Design Patterns*, 1994). In that pattern, the information being conveyed from the Subject to the Observer is described as being a description of a state change. That is fundamental. Earlier in Microservice Design (Chapter 5), we saw how the Event Storming (189) process allows us to find within a Bounded Context (201) the set of commands, Aggregates (211), and policies that form the basic design outline of a *Microservice*. But we also found that the most elementary step in the process was discovering the Domain Events (193) that represent the set of changes of state in the system as a whole.

The set of *Domain Events* discovered in this step is the best place to identify your potential *Events* and the set that you should begin with. But there are other things that can result in an *Event* being triggered as well once you get down into the detailed implementation of a system:

- A database update
- A state change in a process/workflow
- A reported (or even anticipated) problem or other "unusual situation" detected by the system

The simple rule of thumb is that if you think it's possible that another component might be interested in a state change either in your current design or in a future version of your design, you should probably create and send out an *Event* to represent that state change. But at the same time, you want to be parsimonious about how much data you transmit in the schema of the *Event*. You want enough information to do the following:

- Identify the type and cause of the event
- Identify the component (*Microservice*) that was the source of the event

If the data involved is very small, you may pass that along if it is relevant to the notification of what changed. For instance, in an IOT scenario, if you detect a temperature change, passing the new temperature along as part of the *Event* is probably fine. However, if you've updated an entire document or inserted a database row, simply passing along the primary key or equivalent identifier is enough (that is the heart of the **Claim Check** pattern (*Enterprise Integration Patterns*, 2003). In any case, you don't want to break encapsulation and force unnecessary internal knowledge of the *Event Notifier* implementation on your *Reactive Components* if that will more tightly couple your components.

Many of the advantages described in *Event Choreography* also apply to *Events*. One of the main advantages is that with *Events* you can "fire and forget," thus, you don't need to wait for downstream processes. This makes it easier to scale parts of the system independently of other parts. Additionally, you get the advantages of low coupling. It is straightforward to add new behavior by simply adding new services that subscribe to an event. It should also be noted that although the services are loosely coupled through the API of the services, they are still coupled by the events and the topic they are subscribing to. This becomes the contract, so thinking about this carefully and designing these with the principles outlined in Microservice Design (Chapter 5) can help with this.

One of the biggest challenges is to figure out which *Events* are important and what is needed for them. It's important to note that when you are forming your *Events*, you should think carefully about making the data structures consistent across the entire set of *Events* in your system. It would be unhelpful, for instance, to have two representations of the same *Event* that just happen to be emitted from two different components. That is the purpose of a **Canonical Data Model** (*Enterprise Integration Patterns*, 2003) and forms the basis of the Event API (274).

There are two types of choreographed components that interact with *Events*—Event Notifiers (269), which produce *Events*, and Reactive Components (260), which consume *Events*. In many cases, a single component or *Microservice* will take on both roles.

All *Events* travel over the Event Backbone (279) over specific topics unique to a particular set of *Events*. Topics are often separated either by event type (schema) or by the general type of *Bounded Context* that creates those *Events*, which is often implemented as a single *Event Notifier*.

Examples

The following derived events in shipping and clickstream processing are examples that illustrate the *Event* pattern.

Derived events in shipping

One of the more interesting possibilities in the *Event* model is the possibility of forming events from other events. This is the domain of complex event processing (CEP), where multiple events are processed in order to get a result. The point is to look for patterns in the stream of events and take action accordingly. That is why this is sometimes called Event Stream Processing, but it means the same thing.

Earlier, in our description of *Domain Events*, we talked about an example from shipping. When you think about the experience of being loaded on a ship from the container's perspective, you realize that there's a set of closely related events that take place in a time sequence. A container arrives at a port either by truck or by rail and is checked in and placed in a holding area. At some later point in time, the container is moved from the holding area to the place where it will be picked up by a crane and loaded onto a container ship.

That particular string of *Events*—#containerArrived, #containerHeld, #container Prepositioned, #containerLoaded, and (if it's a reefer, e.g., a Refrigerated Container) #containerConnected—are all related by both subject and time. We often find in a *Microservices* approach that a single *Microservice* handles all of these events for that type of situation when they are connected by the same *BoundedContext*.

One of the problems that occurs in shipping is that refrigerated containers have a failure rate—especially in rough seas and on long voyages in extreme temperatures. That can result in wasted goods, due to unit failure and incorrect temperatures. What is needed is a way to predict when a unit is about to fail before it fails and the goods inside become unusable. That would give the crew time to perhaps fix the unit or move the goods inside into another unit.

This is where techniques like machine learning (ML) can come into play. Let's assume that there are a number of different events that are coming in a stream—that the unit is sending out #containerPowerManagement events (how much power per hour is being consumed) and that there are also #containerTemperature events indicating whether the unit is running too hot or too cold. That would allow an ML model built into an *Event Notifier* to perhaps predict (based on known failure data) when a unit is likely to fail in the near future. That model could be built from historical tracking data on existing units. That would allow a system to send out a #predictedContainer Failure event that can be listened for by another *Reactive Component*.

That *Reactive Component* would allow alerts to be sent to responsible parties to "react" in a more timely manner and take actions like running scheduled maintenance, adjusting the unit, or moving the contents if necessary, resulting in an overall reduction in labor costs and increased customer satisfaction.

Clickstream events

Another good example of *Events* of many different types all within the same design can be found when you think about the problem of monitoring (and perhaps monetizing) the interactions that your users have with a website. These are called clickstream events and represent the different links or buttons that a user presses in the specific order in which they interact with them. This can be immensely useful not only in simple tasks like prioritization (putting commonly accessed articles or widgets first) but in more complex situations as well. Let's consider the following typical but not enormously complicated case (see Figure 6-8).

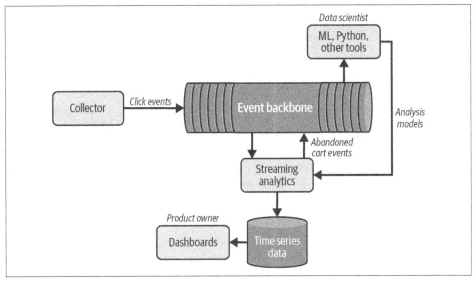

Figure 6-8. Clickstream analytics

You start with a Collector that gathers click information from places like HTTP server logs and then uses that information to pass clickstream events to the *Event Backbone*. At the raw clickstream level, there's not a lot of interest. But when you do some simple analytics like grouping users by demographics (by combining user login events with the events that follow in the clickstream), you can start to gather some useful information, like what kinds of users are clicking on what page. You can do this with simple streaming analytics tools, which can just pull events from the *Event Backbone* and then add metadata before placing it in a time series database. This allows the product owner to later analyze the behavior of the different groups of users. But what is really interesting is the possibility of using existing events to generate entirely new derived events (often called *synthetic* events). For instance, when a user fills a cart with catalog items and then doesn't press the "Check Out" button within a specified period of time, that's called an *abandoned cart*.

Data scientists can use tools to process the extracted clickstream data and look for user struggles and optimization opportunities. For instance, a data scientist could use this data to build more sophisticated models that can determine when a user is about to abandon a cart. They can then publish an *Event* to take action, for instance, offering the user a discount on their cart for a limited time.

Reactive Component

You are using Event Choreography (246) to coordinate multiple components so that when a change occurs in a component, other components interested in that change can react accordingly yet not be tightly coupled through APIs. The choreography communicates information about each change as an Event (255).

How can you construct an application that can react to events?

When building an application that will take advantage of *Event Choreography*, there are a number of issues that need to be addressed within the components:

- You want to allow your components to work together without tightly coupling them to one another.

- You want your components to be able to take advantage of cloud scaling (as in a Replicable Application (88)) as needed without undo restrictions.

- You want to allow each component to be selective in terms of which events to which it reacts.

- You want to allow components to be added or removed easily so that different parts of your application can respond to the same event in different ways

In *Service Orchestration* (see Service Orchestrator (160)), tasks occur in a very orderly, linear fashion, but the sequence and number of things that happen are fixed. But the real world changes constantly. Let's go back to the example of a system that does all the things that need to happen when a person is hired that we looked at in *Event Choreography*. There are some things that everyone will need when they start a new job—an email address, maybe access to some internal systems, perhaps a welcome packet. But as you start to consider all of the variations that can happen when a person comes into a new job, you realize that this is a complex set of possibilities.

If the person who is hired is going to be working in a physical office, they may not need a laptop if there are systems already available. But if they're a remote worker, a laptop is essential. On the other hand, you will need an office or desk assignment if you're working in a physical office. But in an emergency, like a global pandemic, suddenly everyone needs a laptop.

Now, each of these possibilities can be represented by if-then statements within a single business process. That might look like "If the worker is remote, send a laptop; otherwise assign a desk." But as the number of variations increases, this code gets significantly more complicated, and the possibility of mistakes in the complicated branching logic increases. But what if you could instead have each different option be represented by a different component, each of which was reacting to the same new hire event differently?

Therefore,

Build an application from one or more *Reactive Components* that listen for and react to specific sets of events when they occur.

A Reactive Component (260) listens for particular events that are generated from either external or internal stimuli and then determines how to react accordingly (which may well be to do nothing). *Reactive Components* can be built with Reactive Programming techniques, although they are not required to build a *Reactive Component*.

Each *Reactive Component* type decides which topic it listens to (see Figure 6-9). A single *Reactive Component* may listen to one or perhaps more topics and react differently to the *Events* it receives on each topic. Another important distinction is that *Reactive Components* can not only make decisions based on the type of the event but can also choose to react (or not) based on the content of the data that the *Event* carries along.

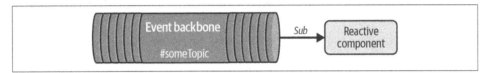

Figure 6-9. Reactive Component

That choice is critical. When a Reactive Component is listening to a topic, it has to receive all the *Events* on a channel's API, but it doesn't have to react to all the events in the channel. It can choose to ignore some of them and throw them away after receiving them. If we break the steps that a *Reactive Component* follows, it comes down to parsing all the events that arrive on the channel (unless your *Event Backbone* allows filtering prior to it being received by the component), deciding what to do with the parsed message, and then reacting to only the subset of messages that the component deems important.

This is quite different from the synchronous nature of a Service API (70). In a *Service API*, the system has already managed the parsing and deciding for you; the only decision in the implementation of a *Service API* is how to react to the call—not whether it should react at all.

In the Event Storming (189) process, we found that each Bounded Context (201) was connected to a specific set of events. As part of the implementation of a *Bounded Context*, a *Reactive Component* will respond to a specific set of events. However, the code that is invoked when asynchronously reacting to an event is not necessarily the same code that will be called synchronously from a *Service API*. In fact, the synchronous elements of the *Service API* come from a different part of the *Event Storming* process, as the *Service API* derives from the Commands (the blue stickies in *Event Storming*) as opposed to the Policies (the pink stickies in *Event Storming*) that correspond to the processing that occurs when an Event is received by a *Reactive Component*.

In many cases, *Reactive Components* are *Microservices*. When this happens, the Event API (274) may or may not overlap with the *Service API*—it's not necessary to have a Service API task for every *Event* on an *Event API*, or vice versa. The two are independent. They may partially overlap, but that is not required. In fact, they are often complementary rather than overlapping. We will explore this in depth in a subsequent examples.

Events are carried over an Event Backbone (279). The *Event Backbone* is responsible for making sure all applications and components that register interest on any particular event channel are notified when an *Event* occurs. Each *Reactive Component* will need to register interest on one or more *Event* topics within the *Event Backbone*.

This design makes *Reactive Components* independent of Event Notifiers (269) in a way that the components that invoke a *Service API* are not. The two are more loosely coupled than the two parts of a synchronous *Service API* since the *Event Notifier* doesn't really care who (if anyone) receives the *Events* that it sends out on the *Event Backbone*. This gives you more flexibility to add functionality by simply adding new *Reactive Components* to the system to react in a different way to the very same *Events*.

However, there are some real challenges to this model, too. The biggest one is the question of testability. It's easy, in principle, to test a *Reactive Component* in isolation—just send the *Event* that it is listening for down the proper channel and observe the results. You can, of course, simulate this entire process with *Mocks* as well. However, the issue comes in when you consider the sequencing of multiple potential reactions to a single *Event*. There is no fixed order of execution of multiple *Reactive Components* listening on the same topic. They could respond in any possible order. If two things need to occur in a particular order, you need to instead rely on *Service Orchestration* to fix the sequence.

What's more, there are potential drawbacks in maintainability when building systems out of *Reactive Components* as well. In general, since there is no fixed order of execution, and since the components are independent, the event-driven programming model is more complex. If you really do need to wait until more than one event happens before an action is triggered, you will need to add persistence and some sort of synchronization mechanism. That is one of the possible uses for Event Sourcing (289), as we will see in that pattern.

Possibly the biggest potential drawback, however, and one that often leads to choosing to use the more predictable *Service Orchestration* instead of *Event Choreography* is the need to ensure that things happen only once. It is important to note that *Reactive Components* are a type of **Event-Driven Consumer** (*Enterprise Integration Patterns*, 2003) and not a **Competing Consumer** (*Enterprise Integration Patterns*,

2003). The difference is subtle but vitally important. What this means is that every *Reactive Component* receives its own copy of the *Event*—and if there are multiple replicated copies of a component because your application is a Replicable Application (88), then each one will get its own copy. Therefore, it is imperative that if you build your application in this way, the *Reactive Component* must be an **Idempotent Receiver** (*Enterprise Integration Patterns*, 2003). An **Idempotent Receiver** means that if a message is received once, or even a hundred times, the effect is the same. This has ramifications for how you build your **Repositories** in that you would need to, for instance, check to see if a row in a Relational Database (334) is already inserted before inserting a new one, or checking to see if a document in a Document Database (339) exists before adding a new one.

Finally, there's one more trade-off that may lead you to mix the *Service Orchestration* and *Event Choreography* models. With *Service Orchestration* (business processes), it's sometimes difficult to know how/when it should end. There could always be more steps. So, for example, even after an order is placed, it must be packaged, and shipping must carry it from origin to destination. Even once it is received, it may be returned. A successful payment may later be rescinded for fraud. The end of an airline flight or hotel stay or the return of a rental car is not necessarily the end of a trip.

This leads you to use *Service Orchestration* to group steps that should either all be completed or none of them—steps that represent a long-running transaction. Let the business process end when its work is complete. In the end, the last step can send events to start other work in other business processes with *Event Choreography*.

Whereas a *Reactive Component* listens for changes as events, an *Event Notifier* (269) announces changes as events. When the internal state of an *Event Notifier* changes, that fact itself is sent out immediately as an event over an event topic.

A *Reactive Component* is often a Microservice (119) with additional functionality to listen for changes as events. The same *Microservice* can be both an *Event Notifier* and a *Reactive Component*. The *Reactive Components* interested in a change use an event topic to connect to the *Event Notifier* where the change can occur.

In addition to these patterns, there are two other patterns that also derive from the *Reactive Component*.

Event Sourcing (289) is a technique by which a component, or an entire application, can rely on the memory of the events within the *Event Backbone* to reconstruct the state of the component at any time. This can improve the resilience of the component.

Command Query Responsibility Segregation (383) is another technique for Microservice Design (Chapter 5) that incorporates the asynchronicity of the *Reactive Component* to maintain independent databases for querying and updating. This is especially useful when you are bringing existing legacy systems into an Event-Driven Architecture made up of *Reactive Components*.

Examples

The following online ordering and airline system examples show the use of the *Reactive Component* pattern.

Online ordering example

To show how a Service API (70) relates to an Event API (274) and how all of that comes together in a single *Reactive Component*, we return to our online ordering example from Microservice Design (Chapter 5). Let's begin by looking at the results of Event Storming (189) for part of that example (Figure 6-10).

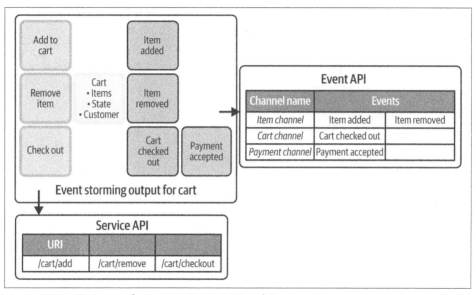

Figure 6-10. Cart contributions to Event API and Service API

In this picture, you see that in the *Event Storming* process, we identified a number of Domain Events (193) that were related to the Cart entity. Likewise, there were several Commands that also operated on the component (Bounded Context (201)) surrounding that entity. As we see, the Commands become part of the *Service API* for that component. The Events (255) generated by the component become part of the *Event API*, with a channel's API being made up of related events carried on a single channel. Those channels can all now be listened to by *Reactive Components* that care about those *Events*. We see something similar (but with more detail) in the next part of the example, where we expand the *Event API* further with additional APIs for individual channels derived from the results of *Event Storming* the Order *Bounded Context*. We show this in Figure 6-11.

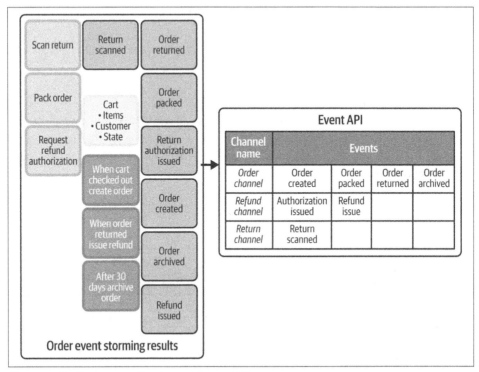

Figure 6-11. Order contributions to Event API

In that example, you see how several additional channels' APIs around Orders, Returns, and Refunds are added to the *Event API*. But how does this all come together in a single component, be that a *Microservice* or a component of a *Modular Monolith*? And how does a *Reactive Component* tie into the *Event API*? You can see how these patterns come together from the *Event Storming* design process in the details of the Order Component implementation in Figure 6-12.

As you can see (as indicated by Arrow 1 in the diagram), Commands become the *Service API* of the component. The Policies that refer to *Events* determine which channel's API the component (acting as a *Reactive Component*) must react to, as indicated by Arrow 2 in the diagram. In our case, one specific *Event* generated by the Cart component (the "Checked Out" event) is exactly what the Order component needs to listen for on the Cart channel in order to know to create a new Order entity. That *Event* would have been triggered by the user interface invoking the checkout function (through a URL) on the Cart component upon checkout.

Finally, the *Events* generated by the component become part of the *Event API* as the Component needs to act as an *Event Notifier* and send those Events out down the corresponding channels whenever the relevant events occur, as indicated by Arrow 3. There may be an opportunity for these different APIs to come together to share code inside the underlying (hidden) component implementation, but that is a detailed design decision and not a requirement.

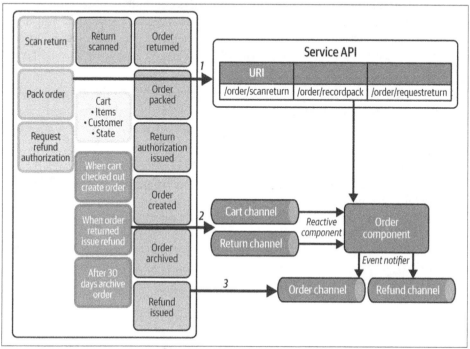

Figure 6-12. Patterns in Order Component

Airline example

For an additional example, let's go back to our airline application described earlier. On most airlines, you can register to receive notification of changes to a flight's departure or arrival time. The notifications can be sent by text, voice, or email. This service can be used by passengers on a flight and by people meeting passengers for a flight. Remember, each *Event* is just a reification of a fact, such as "Flight 999 is delayed by 1 hour" or "Flight 222 is canceled," specific to the business domain. What if we could implement those notifications as an *Event*?

We want to let each *Reactive Component* determine on their own what to do about each event. That could include either making a decision to change their own internal data representation, performing some processing to handle the occurrence of the event, or simply ignoring the event.

Some specific examples of how airline flight notification can help a passenger manage the consequences of a delayed flight are as follows:

- An itinerary component in the airline's computer represents a passenger's flight. It receives notification of the flight delay, determines whether the passenger will miss a connection, and schedules new flights accordingly.

- The reservation record in a rental car company's computer registers for notifications for the renter's incoming flight. When it receives notification of a delay, according to company business rules, it releases the renter's car to other customers and reserves a different car that will be available at the flight's new arrival time.

- The hotel's system has a similar reservation process. When the airline itinerary announces the incoming flight has changed to the next day, the hotel cancels the traveler's reservation for that night and makes the room available for other customers.

- The passenger's calendar program (Google Mail, Outlook, etc.) could register dependency with the airline itinerary and/or travel agency itinerary. When the itinerary changes, the calendar (perhaps with human assistance) can look for conflicts, start rescheduling meetings, and notify meeting participants.

You can see how all of these different *Reactive Components* work together in Figure 6-13.

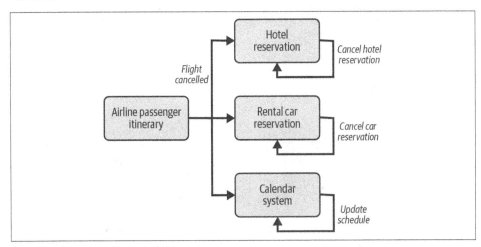

Figure 6-13. Flight Canceled Event

In this way, *Event Notification* (see Event Notifier (269)) can be used to provide complex coordination across multiple complex components, even if each component is developed by a different team or vendor. Each component is responsible for handling notifications when they occur and providing notifications when needed. No component has more information than it needs. It only has to know what resources it depends on (such as a rental car company or hotel needing to know a customer's incoming flight).

Event Notifier

You are using Event Choreography (246) to coordinate multiple components so that when a change occurs in a component, other components interested in that change can react accordingly yet not be tightly coupled through APIs. The choreography communicates information about each change as an *Event* (255).

How and when should a component announce changes to other components?

We've discussed several times in this chapter how *Events* are intended to provide the second principle benefit of *Event Choreography*, the separation of time and space, between components. At the root of that separation is the fact that not every change is necessarily important to every other component. There needs to be selectivity in what changes are communicated and when.

You want to avoid coupling components too tightly, following the principle of **Loose Coupling** from **IDEALS** as described in Microservices Design (Chapter 5). You would like to allow extensions to your system without revealing details of how your components are implemented.

Additionally, you would like to allow components to organize the events that they notify other components about so that *not* every component has to listen for every event. You don't want to overwhelm the system with so many notifications that the system grinds to a halt.

Another thing to avoid is coupling components through their data models. One of the big reasons why a shared database is usually a bad idea between components is that allowing components access to the entire data model of another component means that they can react to what might be minor or temporary changes in an inappropriate way.

For instance, in our shipping example, it would be a bad idea if the order processing team started picking down, packing, and then unpacking and reshelving items every time a potential customer added or removed an item from their shopping cart! There are reasons why these kinds of data and process boundaries are important to preserve the boundaries between each Bounded Context (201).

Therefore,

Design each component as an *Event Notifier* that is able to announce its most important changes as *Events*.

Event Choreography can't exist without *Events* being published. When we looked at the Event Storming (189) process, we saw that one of the key parts of that process was identifying the Domain Events (193) that make up the timeline of what happens within a system. Later on, we found how those can be separated by boundaries delineated by pivotal events (the events in between two pivotal events representing a business process) and by persona. Those boundaries form the edges of a Bounded Context (201) (which group the Aggregates (211) and Commands that are associated with those *Events*) that forms the outlines of a Microservice Design.

Perhaps the most pressing question when deciding how to implement an *Event Notifier* is which events to publish, which gets to the question of where to draw the line between *Service Orchestration* (see Service Orchestrator (160)) and Event Choreography (246). Synchronous request-response calls are still needed and used. Sometimes when something happens, you may need to process it synchronously. For simple sequential tasks that you need to guarantee the results and control the flow, it is good to use synchronous calls. When the tasks are complex, requiring multiple steps to perform, you can process them synchronously as described in *Service Orchestrator*.

However, for complex tasks that are independent and when speed and responsiveness is crucial, it is good to use asynchronous design. In the previous chapter, we described guiding **IDEALS** for designing Microservices (119) that included the event-driven principle, which states that today's scalability and performance requirements pose a challenge that can be solved by processing events asynchronously (a good time to consider *Event Choreography*).

When implementing any event system, we need a way for components to signal when something of interest has happened to them so that any interested components can be notified and take appropriate action (see Figure 6-14). We do this by making the component an *Event Notifier*. At the minimum, the component will implement some notification mechanism that announces when something of interest has happened to it. A component can be an entity, an *Aggregate,* or a *Domain Event* component that belongs to a *Bounded Context*. When an *Event* of interest happens, the component (*Event Notifier*) will publish to a topic that is part of an Event Backbone (279). Notice that an *Event Notifier* does not need to know any details about which component might receive and process the event.

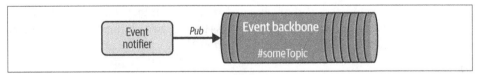

Figure 6-14. Event Notifier

The simplest option is to create an event for every change that happens within a component. One problem with that option is that you may flood your event system with many more events than it can handle, or create thousands of events that, in essence, no one will ever care about. However, events are cheap; you can argue that each individual event is quite small, and most systems run on human timescales—until your system reaches very high levels of performance and scaling. This is a good place to start.

While sending every potential change as an event can be a starting point, it should not be the ending point. What should instead motivate you is to look back to your original intent for the component, particularly if you elucidated that intent by following the *Event Storming* approach. If an event was important enough that a person remembered to capture it on a sticky note as a *Domain Event*, then it is probably at the right level of granularity to preserve as an *Event* to be sent through an *Event Backbone*. Where this may diverge from the original set of *Domain Events* that you see in *Event Storming* is tied to another part of the Microservice Design process.

Remember that *Aggregates* are made up of logical groupings of one or more entities. Often you change the state of an *Aggregate* by adding, removing, or changing one of its components. For instance, if you are representing an internal combustion engine as an *Aggregate*—with the components being all of the various pistons, rods, crankshafts, valves, and other parts that make it up—you have an interesting choice to make if you have another part of your system (like a dash or infotainment component) that wants to know if the engine started when the button was pressed to start it. We show that level of communication in Figure 6-15.

Figure 6-15. Engine component communication

You can issue *Events* from every involved component when the engine as a whole receives its initial "start" command. That may be useful in debugging the engine when something goes wrong; however, the dashboard system only cares about one event, which is #engineStarted, or perhaps #engineStartupFailed. What this means is that your *Event Notifier* will want to send that event on the relevant topic (like #engineStatusTopic) that other components can listen to on an *Event Backbone*. Whether or not the other lower-level events are sent on other topics (like #cylinder StatusTopic) is a component-level design decision that each team can make on their own. Therefore, when starting, you first want to focus on those top-level events that are likely to be used between components.

Related to that decision is another decision on how much data to send along with each event. In general, keep events quite small. Large data changes should not be sent as part of the event. Instead, the **Claim Check** pattern (*Enterprise Integration Patterns*, 2003) should be your guide. If a data element is more than a few lines of text or JSON, consider merely sending along a key that another component can use with the external Service API (70) of your component to discover the relevant details of your component's internal state. That is a better way of ensuring encapsulation and reducing coupling between your components.

In addition to all of the main advantages that you get from any Event-Driven Architecture, you also have the main advantage of an *Event Notifier*, which is that since publishers and subscribers are independent and hence loosely coupled, you can evolve notifier components independently of the *Reactive Components* (260). You can also add some new behavior or a new feature by simply adding a new *Reactive Component* to listen to an existing *Event* and perform a new action.

When building any Event-Driven Architecture, it can be challenging to identify the important *Events* of interest and associate them with the components to trigger the *Events*. Another challenge when designing an *Event Notifier* is control flow, especially if fire-and-forget doesn't work so well. These systems can become more complex when we need to handle control flow, especially if the notifying component will need information from any components reacting to its *Events*. This is especially true when something goes wrong and we have to deal with error handling, which is more complicated than in a corresponding system based entirely on synchronous calls.

As we covered in Microservice Design (Chapter 5), domain objects are gathered into Aggregates (211). One or more *Aggregates* are usually grouped within a Bounded Context (201) that represents the boundary of a Microservice (119)—which may have one or more Service API (70). That leads us to some general recommendations around the use of both *Service Orchestration* (see Service Orchestrator (160)) and Event Choreography (246):

- Within a *Bounded Context*, you'll almost always use a *Service Orchestrator*, and make internal *Events* optional if they seem useful for debugging or extension purposes.
- Between *Bounded Contexts*, you'll mostly use *Event Choreography*. One *Bounded Context* sends an *Event* hoping others will react as necessary; hopefully, another *Aggregate* receives the *Event* and reacts. The exception to this rule is that whenever a response is needed immediately, you should use a *Service API* and invoke

the service using REST or another synchronous protocol. However, there are fewer cases where that is required than you might think.

An *Event Notifier* is part of a *Microservice* with additional functionality to announce its changes as *Events*. The same *Microservice* can include an *Event Notifier* and be a *Reactive Component*. Whereas an *Event Notifier* announces changes as *Events*, a *Reactive Component* listens for changes as *Events*.

The description of the set of *Events* that each *Event Notifier* will send on various event topics makes up the Event API (274) of the system as a whole.

Example

Back in Microservice Design (Chapter 5), in Domain Event (193) pattern, we introduced some simple *Domain Events* that might be generated by an *Event Notifier* tied to a container ship. As you can imagine, these are mostly *Events* that are about the status of the ship as a whole—things like `#DepartedPort` and `#ArrivedAtPort`. It's not too difficult to imagine that there would be other general-purpose events relating to the ship as a whole, like `#LoadingCompleted`. But the unique thing about a container ship is that it is carrying hundreds or thousands of containers—each of which can be also instrumented with sensors and could individually generate events. This is a perfect example of the marriage of Event-Driven Architecture and the Internet of Things (IoT).

This is especially true of containers that aren't just moving dry goods such as TVs or car parts but are special climate-controlled containers that are designed to carry fresh or frozen foods. These are refrigerated containers (commonly called "reefers"), and they are an even better source for imagining multiple types of *Events* that the crew of the ship and the shipping company would be interested in knowing about. Representing each `RefrigeratedContainer` by an *Event Notifier* that emits these events would be an excellent design choice. This could be implemented by a microcontroller connected to the refrigerated container's refrigeration unit, which then connects to the shipwide network.

Sending out events that can be monitored by multiple different *Reactive Components* is important to reduce wasted fresh and frozen goods due to unit failure or incorrect temperatures. So not only could internal temperature measurements be emitted as an event, such as (`#TemperatureMeasured - 4C`), but it would also be useful to take and emit measurements related to power management, such as `#UnitLostPower` or `#UnitPowerConnected`. Detecting whether a unit is running too hot or too cold, or whether a failure condition like a power loss has occurred, is important to alert responsible parties to "react" in a timely manner. This would also allow the shipping company to observe the stream of temperature and power management events and take preemptive actions, such as scheduling maintenance, asking the crew to adjust the unit, or moving the contents if necessary if the unit seems likely to fail.

Event API

You are using Event Choreography (246) to coordinate multiple components so that when a change occurs in a component, other components interested in that change can react accordingly yet not be tightly coupled through APIs. When a change occurs in an Event Notifier (269), it sends an Event (255) to notify interested Reactive Components (260) so that they can react accordingly.

How can the *Reactive Components* in an Event-Driven Architecture know what events to expect?

A Service API (70) defines the interface between a client and a service. A client and service must both implement their respective sides of the same interface so that they'll work together. The interface is fixed and incorporated into the implementations.

While a service requestor and provider are bound directly, the relationship between an *Event Notifier* and a *Reactive Component* is indirect via a shared topic. When an *Event Notifier* and a *Reactive Component* communicate, the communication is indirect via an *Event*. An *Event* is not fixed like a *Service API*; it is transitory. A topic doesn't specify an API. An *Event Notifier* and a *Reactive Component* need to agree on how they are going to communicate, and that agreement will be a lot more indirect than a *Service API*.

A *Reactive Component* needs to know what events to expect. It isn't interested in all of the events in an Event-Driven Architecture; it's interested in ones for a certain purpose. Publish-subscribe messaging uses a topic to publish messages for the same purpose, whereas messages for other purposes are published to other topics. A *Reactive Component* needs to know the set of topics in an Event-Driven Architecture and to subscribe to the appropriate topic. Likewise, an *Event Notifier* also needs to know the set of topics and to publish event notifications to the appropriate topic.

A *Reactive Component* needs to know how to interpret the events it receives. After it subscribes to a topic, it receives **Event Messages** (*Enterprise Integration Patterns*, 2003) from that topic. To make use of an **Event Message**, the *Reactive Component* needs to know the message's format so that it can parse the message. It expects all **Event Messages** on a topic to have that same format so that it can parse them the same way. This means that all of the *Event Notifiers* that publish on that topic need to format the **Event Messages** the same way, which is the way the *Reactive Components* expect to parse the messages.

To communicate properly, the *Reactive Components* and the *Event Notifiers* need to agree on the topics to use and the **Event Message** formats to use.

Therefore,

Define an *Event API* for an Event-Driven Architecture that describes the events the *Event Notifiers* publish and the topics they publish the events on.

An Event API is a contract in an Event-Driven Architecture between the *Event Notifiers* that publish events and the *Reactive Components* that receive the events. It describes the topics events can be published on and the format of the events on each topic. When an *Event Notifier* has an *Event Notification* to announce, it announces the *Event* on the topic for that purpose, publishing an **Event Message** with the format specified for that topic. When a *Reactive Component* needs to receive event notifications for a particular purpose, it subscribes to the topic for that purpose. When it receives an *Event Notification* on that topic, it knows the **Event Message** will have the format specified for that topic.

Figure 6-16 shows an *Event API* for a set of event notifiers that emit events and a set of *Reactive Components* that listen for events. The API describes the list of topics in the Event-Driven Architecture. For each topic, the API describes the format of each of the **Event Messages** on that topic.

An Event API defines what to do for both the *Event Notifiers* and the *Reactive Components*. If an *Event Notifier* and a *Reactive Component* both follow an *Event API*, the *Reactive Component* will always be listening for announcements of a type of change on the same topic that the *Event Notifier* announces the changes on because they both use the topic that the *Event API* specifies for that type of change. If they both follow the same *Event API*, the *Reactive Component* can parse the **Event Message** that the *Event Notifier* publishes because they both use the event format specified for their shared topic in the API. If two development teams implement the *Event Notifier* and the *Reactive Component* and miscommunication occurs, the teams can determine which one is at fault—the problem is in the component that doesn't comply with the *Event API* properly.

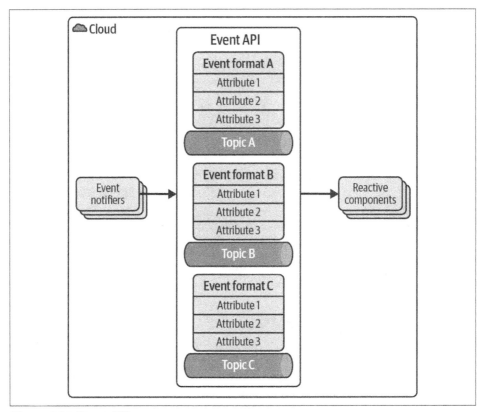

Figure 6-16. Event API

An *Event API* defines a set of topics for an Event-Driven Architecture. For each topic, the API defines the topic's purpose and the format of the **Event Messages** on that topic. The *Event Notifiers* and the *Reactive Components* communicate by using the same topic for the same purpose and by exchanging **Event Messages** formatted for that topic.

Whereas a code compiler can enforce a *Service API*, an *Event* API is not a code construct a compiler can enforce. It is created by tooling, similar to the tooling used to generate RESTful APIs for service components.

An Event Backbone (279) that connects Event Notifiers (269) and Reactive Components (260) implements an event API. The set of topics in an *Event Backbone* defines the scope of the *Event API*.

Examples

AsyncAPI is a specification for describing the API between components communicating asynchronously. Event Storming (189) defines Microservices (119) by discovering them through the events they exchange.

AsyncAPI

An Event-Driven Architecture can specify the topics and event formats in an Event API using AsyncAPI. AsyncAPI (*https://oreil.ly/KRKKa*) provides a standardized approach for describing a set of channels and messages for messaging communication. It specifies asynchronous communication similarly to how OpenAPI (*https://oreil.ly/fCB_r*) specifies synchronous communication, such as REST services. The specification includes open source tools that generate API documentation and validate the code for messaging components, as well as GitHub actions that can be incorporated into a CI/CD pipeline.

An AsyncAPI spec defines a set of channels, operations, and messages. For each channel, it defines the channel's purpose, its URI, a set of operations that the components can request and perform, and message formats that the requestors build and the performers parse. An Event-Driven Architecture can use an AsyncAPI to specify the topics and event formats in an Event API.

Event Storming and the Event API

An Event Storming (189) workshop discovers the set of events in a domain and the Bounded Contexts (201) that exchange them. These events are common to the entire system from end to end. However, there are some bounding assumptions that are implicit in the way you begin the system design process with *Event Storming* (see Figure 6-17).

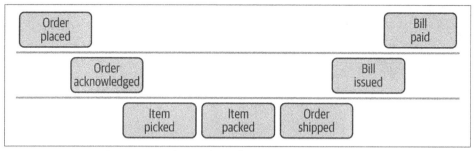

Figure 6-17. Event Storming early timeline phase

The full list of events found in the workshop and communicated on a common *Event Backbone* make up the *Event API*. However, if you remember the rest of the process, it's only in the later phases of the process that you break up the system into components and specify which components generate and receive which events. That set of events (those generated and those received or subscribed to) form the slice of the *Event API* for the component (see Figure 6-18).

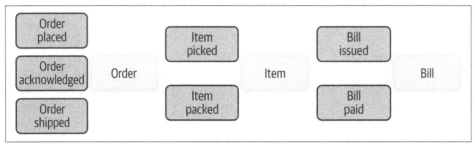

Figure 6-18. Event Storming later timeline phase

This second phase of the process brings in another crucial piece of information: the names of the data elements the *Events* are related to. This is often used to name not only the component that derives from this combination of events, data, and processing but also, crucially, the corresponding topics that the set of related **Event Messages** flow on.

The API for a single channel is effectively the subset of the *Event API* for a single topic and all of the **Event Messages** that are published on that topic. Listing all of the channels' APIs out in a common place, as documentation, provides the benefit that developers of new components can easily decide which channels to subscribe to in order to receive the events they are interested in, but it also reduces duplication—in designing a component, you may find that the component can also generate an already-identified event. Even if an event is new, it may be related to other events and carried on the same channel (particularly in the case of "synthetic" or "derived" events). This is often seen most clearly if the *Event API* is presented in a tabular form (see Table 6-1).

Table 6-1. Event API Example

Channel	Event 1	Event 2	Event 3
Order processing	Order placed	Order acknowledged	Order shipped
Item processing	Item picked	Item packed	
Invoice processing	Invoice issued	Invoice paid	

Each channels' APIs is represented by one line in the *Event API* that refers to that particular topic. This table in and of itself is useful, but let's take the idea one step further. Let's also suppose that you can take the information from the later *Event Storming* phase and decide which information needs to be passed along with each event. In this way, you start thinking about each event in terms of the description of the payload of the **Event Message** that you send. You could represent each event payload description as a JSON document (see Table 6-2).

Table 6-2. Event API JSON Example

Channel	Event 1	EV1 JSON	Event 2	EV2 JSON	Event 3	EV3 JSON
Order processing	Order placed	JSON for order placed	Order acknowledged	JSON for order acknowledged	Order shipped	JSON for order shipped
Item processing	Item picked	JSON for item picked	Item packed	JSON for item packed		
Invoice processing	Invoice issued	JSON for invoice issued	Invoice paid	JSON for invoice paid		

This may seem like a lot of work, but you've gained some additional benefits here— now everyone is aware of not only what possible *Events* can be sent on each channel but also what the detailed data structure of that *Event* would be. Given the wonderful, extensible nature of JSON, you can also maintain version compatibility by always adding additional fields, rather than taking earlier fields away or renaming them. The tabular format we just described is the central idea in AsyncAPI.

Event Backbone

You are using Event Choreography (246) to coordinate multiple components so that when a change occurs in a component, other components interested in that change can react accordingly yet not be tightly coupled through APIs. The changes are represented as Events (255) that are communicated from Event Notifiers (269) and are reacted to by Reactive Components (260).

How can *Reactive Components* receive the events they are interested in without being coupled directly to the *Event Notifiers* that generate the events?

The first principle benefit of *Event Choreography*, the separation of API, has been a feature of all *Event* systems dating back to the earliest implementations of the **Observer** (*Design Patterns*, 1994) pattern in Smalltalk. That is a different way for components to interact than by a Service API (70) in that changes are communicated through a single, common API as data, rather than as separate invocations or REST endpoints.

The second principle benefit of *Event Choreography*, the separation of time and space, specifies that the event system should work asynchronously so that the process or thread generating the event does not need to wait until all receivers receive the event, and the event system should work over the network so that the process or thread receiving the events can be part of a Distributed Architecture (38).

The issue is that each of these elements has often "locked in" developers to particular solutions. For instance, to produce events in an implementation of the **Observer** pattern, the event provider (the Subject) would have to know about each of the event receivers (Observers) in order to deliver events to them.

Finally, you do not want to limit producers or consumers of events to one particular physical location from which to send or receive events. Encoding the location of event infrastructure into the consumer's code limits its ability to scale and to deal with failure situations. A *Reactive Component* should not need to be aware of where the events it subscribes to were originally generated or by which component. An *Event Notifier* should not need to be aware of who receives its events or how many receivers subscribe to its events.

Therefore,

Connect *Reactive Components* to *Event Notifiers* indirectly via an *Event Backbone* that defines a separate topic for each type of event.

An *event topic* is a way to create a publish/subscribe connection for transmitting events. *Event Notifiers* connect as publishers, and reactive components connect as subscribers. This is an example of a **Publish-Subscribe Channel** (*Enterprise Integration Patterns*, 2003). When an *Event Notifier* publishes an event to an event topic, the topic transmits the event to all of the *Reactive Components* that are subscribed, and each of them gets its own copy of the event.

The basic structure of systems that follow this overall architecture is shown in Figure 6-19.

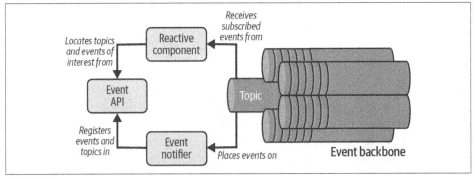

Figure 6-19. Event Backbone

Each event topic is not part of the *Event Notifiers* or the *Reactive Components*; it sits between them. It uses the network to connect but provides publish/subscribe functionality beyond a network's capabilities. All of the topics can reuse the same publish/subscribe functionality if it's implemented in a central place. That is why you need a single component that ties all of the different event topics together. This is the purpose of the *Event Backbone*.

There are some architectural constraints that this *Event Backbone* must allow for:

- It should allow for multiple independent channels or topics that encourages the separation of different event types—receivers should be able to choose to subscribe to those topics or channels that they are interested in and no more
- The *Reactive Components* should not depend on the physical location of the *Event Backbone*. This can be achieved through the use of distributed messaging protocols.

All of the *Event Notifiers* and *Reactive Components* connect to the backbone to communicate via its topics. The backbone spans locations, enabling components in different locations to connect, even if their locations change.

An *Event Backbone* separates the *Event Notifiers* from the *Reactive Components* in both time and space, which is the second principle benefit of *Event Choreography*. They connect to the same topic but run in different processes. An *Event Notifier* can send an event notification when it is ready, and a *Reactive Component* can read that notification later when it is ready.

An *Event Backbone* creates a centralized component that every part of the Event-Driven Architecture relies on. Although the technology can be distributed with replication, the backbone is a logical single point of failure. This is in contrast to a completely distributed technology like REST, where there is no central service that everything must connect to. It is also in contrast to the Microservices (119) approach of Self-Managed Data Store (154), where even if a single *Microservice* can't connect to its database, other *Microservices* (perhaps working with other database services or even just other database instances) may continue to function. While different *Event Backbone* technologies use many different approaches to improve their availability (for example, Apache Kafka replicates topics across multiple brokers in a cluster), this still remains a potential problem.

Another challenge is that once an application is written for a particular backbone technology, such as Kafka or RabbitMQ, it ends up becoming tied to the particular API for that solution or vendor. Vendor lock-in can make it difficult to change to another solution in the future. This is sometimes an opportunity to use an approach like an Anti-Corruption Layer (229), but in many cases that may be more trouble than it is worth. We have found in practice that these types of infrastructure decisions change slowly and rarely. It's best to instead carefully consider the options before picking a technology.

The minimal functionality for an *Event Backbone* is to connect *Event Notifiers* to *Reactive Components* and transmit *Events* between them. Most backbone implementations incorporate publish-subscribe topics rather than point-to-point queues, which facilitates delivering a single notification to multiple *Reactive Components*. Many *Event Backbones* also keep a log of the events they transmit, which can be used to facilitate Event Sourcing (289) so that the sourcing doesn't have to record the event history separately.

An *Event Backbone* is a type of **Message Bus** (*Enterprise Integration Patterns*, 2003), but one that is specialized to carry only **Event Messages** (*Enterprise Integration Patterns*, 2003) and not other types of messages.

Examples

An *Event Backbone* can be implemented using either of two types of messaging systems: event-style messaging systems and MQ-style messaging systems. Both implement the topic functionality needed to build an *Event Backbone*, but they do so with rather different architectures. Event-style messaging systems maximize availability while sacrificing consistency, whereas MQ-style messaging systems do the opposite, maximizing consistency while sacrificing availability when necessary.

Event-style messaging system

Apache Kafka (*https://oreil.ly/oo9BT*) is the most common event-style messaging system, along with products built on Kafka like Confluent (*https://oreil.ly/ApvW_*), IBM Event Streams (*https://oreil.ly/EBqhv*), and Azure Event Hubs (*https://oreil.ly/dVHh0*). Other examples of eventing systems include Amazon EventBridge (*https://oreil.ly/aUIqu*) and Azure Event Grid (*https://oreil.ly/t8pn1*).

An event-style messaging system hosts multiple topics, enabling event notifiers to provide event notifications by publishing events to topics and enabling Reactive Components (260) to receive notifications by reading events from topics. Event-style messaging systems run more reliably on the cloud by embracing replication, similar to a Replicated Database (316) for event streaming.

Figure 6-20 shows an event-style messaging system running in three brokers with one topic split across three partitions. Each partition has two replicas, hosted in two different brokers. All of the events shown here are published on the same topic. Each event is published to one of the topic's partitions. When a *Reactive Component* receives a particular event, it reads the message from the partition that stores that **Event Message**.

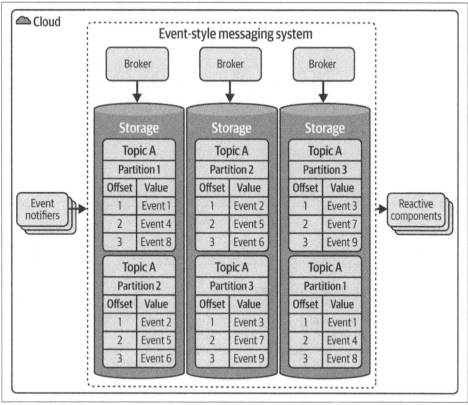

Figure 6-20. Event-style messaging system

Event-style messaging systems are designed to be always available. The replication between partition replicas is eventually consistent, which complicates exactly-once delivery during failure scenarios. If one broker becomes unavailable, the partition replicas in the other brokers keep all messages available, and the messaging clients can still publish and consume events using the functioning brokers.

MQ-style messaging system

IBM MQ (*https://oreil.ly/fQzDQ*) (formerly known as MQ Series) was the first MQ-style messaging system. Others include RabbitMQ (*https://oreil.ly/8PJU2*), Apache ActiveMQ (*https://oreil.ly/L88HP*), Amazon Simple Queue Service (*https://oreil.ly/Rt_FV*) (SQS), and Azure Service Bus (*https://oreil.ly/OExrB*). Many MQ systems are compliant with Java Message Service (*https://oreil.ly/ZrUM2*) (JMS), providing the specification's Queue and Topic features.

Like an event-style messaging system, an MQ-style messaging system also hosts topics and enables *Event Notification* between *Event Notifiers* and *Reactive Components*.

Unlike event-style messaging systems, each queue manager in an MQ-style messaging system is unique, holding its own set of messages and transmitting them from one queue manager to the next.

Figure 6-21 shows an MQ-style messaging system with three queue managers connected to transmit messages. They have one topic defined. Messaging clients connect not to the cluster in general but to a specific queue manager. While the clients can connect to any queue manager, for simplicity, this diagram shows all of the event notifiers connected to the left queue manager and all of the *Reactive Components* connected to the right queue manager. Transmission runs over time and transmits from *Event Notifiers* to *Reactive Components*, so time runs left to right.

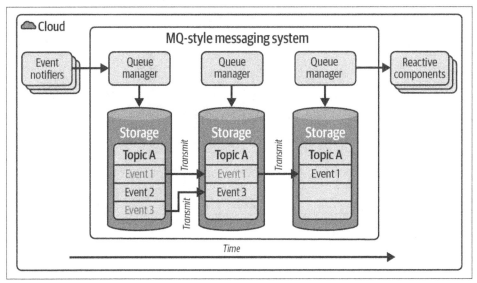

Figure 6-21. MQ-style messaging system

The *Event Notifiers* have added three events to the left queue manager. To transmit them to the *Reactive Components*, the left queue manager has transmitted events 1 and 3 to the middle queue manager, but hasn't transmitted event 2 yet. Perhaps the transmission for event 2 failed. The queue managers will retry transmitting event 2 until it succeeds. The middle queue manager has transmitted event 1 again to the right queue manager, where it is now available to be delivered to the reactive components that are attached to that queue manager and subscribed to the topic.

MQ-style messaging systems maximize consistency at the expense of availability. Each message is stored in only one queue manager at a time. The transmission of messages is always consistent, making exactly-once delivery more reliable. If one queue manager stops running, any transient messages it stores are lost; the messages it stores persistently become unavailable but are recovered when the queue manager recovers or is replaced by a standby duplicate queue manager. Meanwhile, its clients cannot send or receive events unless they reconnect to an available queue manager. If a queue manager becomes disconnected from the others, typically by a network outage, it keeps its messages queued and will resume transmitting them when it reconnects to the other queue managers.

Enterprise backbones

When we described the Microservice Design (Chapter 5) process, we emphasized that *Microservices* (119) are derived from *Bounded Contexts* (201) within a domain. Most domains are composed of subdomains, and you will sometimes discover multiple *Bounded Contexts* within a single domain. This becomes clear during the Event Storming (189) process, where we pointed out that there are often significant events that signal a "change of context" between one or more *Bounded Contexts*.

If we extend this idea a little further, we find that in very large systems or in very large enterprises there is not just a single domain of discourse but potentially several interacting domains.

As an example, let's consider a company that sells software as a service (SaaS), mostly through a self-service website. The sales process is its own rich domain. You need to support your sales teams as they contact leads, turn leads into customers through contracts, and then handle the process of contract renewals and changes.

The process of billing customers for the software they've purchased is its own equally complex domain. There, you have to decipher how individual client IDs roll up to accounts and how accounts are billed to the customers. This can sometimes be a surprisingly complicated process where multinational companies are involved!

Even the bills themselves are complicated, as contracts can specify many different types of discounts, offers, and pricing structures. At some point, you might want to consider paying your sales staff on a commission system. Doing so will require that your sales process be connected to your HR processes—which is again its own domain.

We've not really addressed this level of complexity in this book. We've talked extensively about breaking down complex issues into appropriately sized pieces (*Microservices*) but not about how you manage this level of interdomain connection. Luckily, the *Event Backbone* and *Event API* patterns, with a few simple extensions, can provide part of a very elegant solution for this kind of architectural organization.

If we consider each domain to be comprised of several interoperating *Microservices*, the asynchronous, event-based communication between those services will take place over an *Event Backbone*. What's more, it's probably true that there isn't just one application comprised of *Microservices* in each domain—if the organization is sufficiently large, there may be several applications (potentially dozens or hundreds) in each domain. That warrants each domain having its own *Event Backbone* to facilitate that communication, especially if organizations are free to make their own technology choices. Figure 6-22 shows what this could looks like within an enterprise environment.

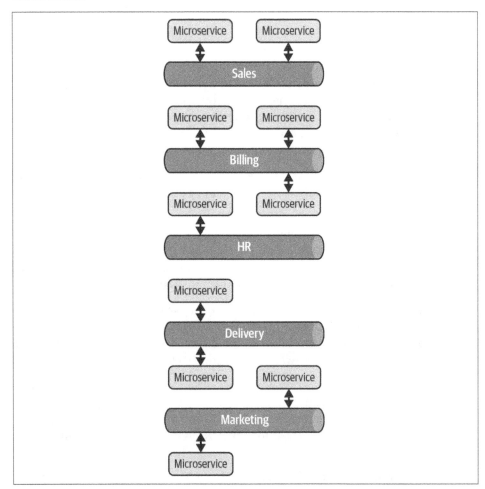

Figure 6-22. Multiple backbones

The Billing backbone may be implemented in an environment such as SAP Event Management (*https://oreil.ly/q3zGY*) because most of the applications in the billing organization are built on SAP. However, in Marketing, a more special-purpose event environment tied more closely to digital marketing, like Twilio's Segment (*https://oreil.ly/90zL-*), might be appropriate. The Delivery team may choose to build their own backbone with Apache Kafka (*https://oreil.ly/oo9BT*).

Where things get interesting is when the different organizations and systems need to communicate. Again, we want this to happen in a reactive, event-driven way. At the same time, it's not appropriate for every low-level sales event (e.g., someone clicked "SCHEDULE A DEMO") to be sent to the *Event Backbone* for Billing or HR. Instead, we need a special *Event API* that is a subset of the *Events* that are published to each *Event Backbone* to be shared across the different backbones.

So while clicking "SCHEDULE A DEMO" may be interesting only to the Sales department, clicking "BEGIN A TRIAL" may be interesting to both Marketing and delivery. Clicking "BUY" would be interesting to both billing and Delivery, since Delivery may need to provision a production instance of the software if it's not naturally multitenant. We show this kind of *Event API* crossing domains in Figure 6-23.

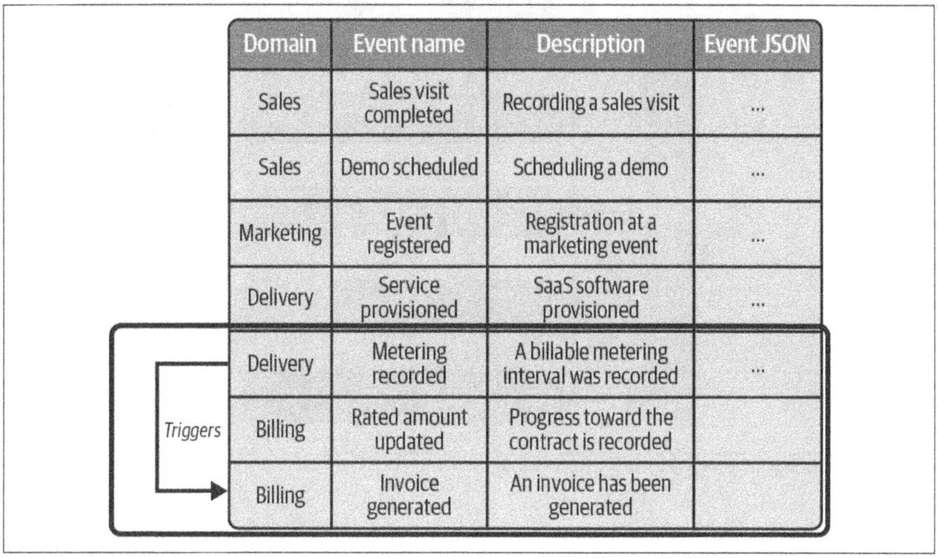

Domain	Event name	Description	Event JSON
Sales	Sales visit completed	Recording a sales visit	...
Sales	Demo scheduled	Scheduling a demo	...
Marketing	Event registered	Registration at a marketing event	...
Delivery	Service provisioned	SaaS software provisioned	...
Delivery	Metering recorded	A billable metering interval was recorded	...
Billing	Rated amount updated	Progress toward the contract is recorded	
Billing	Invoice generated	An invoice has been generated	

Figure 6-23. Multidomain Event API

In this example, we see two events that cross domains. When a metering event is recorded in the Delivery domain (for instance, someone called an API for a SaaS service), that *Event* is interesting to the Billing domain, which must update the current account for the customer by the amount per API call specified in their contract (a process called *Rating*). You can imagine the process of beginning a trial, or converting a trial to a contract, would be even more complex, with many shared events between domains. It's important to note that not every *Event* in an *Event API* will cross domains. Limiting the set of *Events* that are of interest to other domains is part of the challenge of designing systems of this level of complexity.

What this means is that there needs to be a way to connect many or all of the different departments' *Event Backbones* with a backbone of backbones or an Enterprise Backbone (see Figure 6-24).

In this architecture, the Enterprise Backbone receives selected events from the other backbones and then retransmits them to any interested parties, including other backbones. This kind of inter-backbone connectivity is often carried out through a "bridge." A bridge may be a standalone piece of software or merely a feature of the backbones themselves. Each bridge acts as a *Reactive Component* in that it receives events from one backbone that it sends on to a second backbone by acting as an *Event Notifier* to the second backbone.

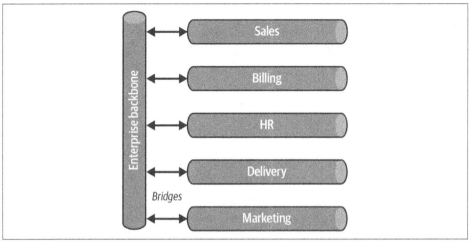

Figure 6-24. Backbone of backbones

That **Messaging Bridge** (*Enterprise Integration Patterns*, 2003) may be a standalone piece of software or merely a feature of the backbones themselves—for example, AMQ Streams to Kafka (*https://oreil.ly/ZAT14*) or Segment to Kafka (*https://oreil.ly/kN1sw*).

Jim Episale gives an example of how this kind of Enterprise Backbone was built in the IBM CIO office, along with the benefits of this type of architecture in James Episale's blog post "Building a Cross-Pipeline Data Registry for Multi-Application Ecosystems." (*https://oreil.ly/2xEQS*)

Each team that is responsible for a domain—for example, Billing—should be responsible not only for the *Microservices* in that domain (as we have discussed earlier) but also for the backbone for that domain. That then means they are also responsible for the *Event APIs* for their domain as well (intradomain). If each individual domain team is then responsible for their own backbone, then who is responsible for the Enterprise Backbone and the shared *Event API* that goes across domains (interdomains)? That needs to be the responsibility of a shared services team, perhaps composed of representatives of the individual domain teams. That same shared services team can form the core of a governance team for the overall architecture as a whole—this shared services team will be responsible for publishing the shared *Event APIs* and can be responsible for bridging between backbones.

Event Sourcing

You are using Event Choreography (246) to coordinate multiple components so that when a change occurs in a component, other components interested in that change can react accordingly yet not be tightly coupled through APIs. The choreography communicates information about each change as an Event (255), which the Reactive Components (260) use to update their state.

As an application's state changes constantly and unpredictably due to evolving conditions, how can you audit the history that created the current state?

Let's say you're building an application to represent a complex, evolving process. One of the hardest parts of applications like this is figuring out how to represent the state of the current process but also explaining how the process got into the state it's currently in. In other words, the history of the process is an important part of the process itself.

This is true in a number of fields. For example, in accounting, there's an entire field called *forensic accounting* that uses investigative techniques to uncover financial fraud by examining the history of transactions to trace funds or identify where assets have been directed. When you're trying to trace something such as a theft of cryptocurrency, the ability of the blockchain to serve as a history of all the transactions that happened and how they relate to one another is an important enabler. In medicine, knowing the history of a patient in terms of what treatments they have been given, what tests have been performed, and what the results were are likewise immensely valuable in understanding a patient's current state. In shipping or transportation, knowing where something has been is important in determining questions like what taxes or duties need to be paid or what delays or adverse conditions it might have experienced, or in making predictions about things like arrival times.

It seems like trying to store all of these things separately might be too complicated. You could have a single state variable of the latest test result (say, their body temperature) for a patient, for instance, but that doesn't give the same information as if you had all of their temperature records. If a single state variable is not a reasonable solution, then what is? You could try having multiple state variables that each represent each of the different cases, but that quickly becomes too complex to manage. Imagine trying to line up all of the different records for a patient's temperature with when they were given medication if those are stored in separate arrays or lists. If we can't line up the times in which they happen, it would be difficult to figure out whether a test result is an indication of a medication working or whether the abnormal result is a side effect of the medication.

The worst part comes when something in a complex system has to be undone or reset. This happens all the time. To reverse a financial fraud (say, a stolen credit card), you need to remove or undo invalid credit card transactions. To cancel a financial transaction that is in flight, you need to rewind all of the different parts of the transaction to the state they were in before it began. *Undo* is an interesting verb. It means we want to turn back time to before something happened and change the past. What if we could do exactly that? What if we could rewrite history?

Therefore,

Log the history of events that each *Reactive Component* receives so that *Event Sourcing* can understand the component's current state and reconstruct its state if necessary.

To do this, you need to first record the history of a *Reactive Component* as an ordered set of the events that were received. You next need to allow queries (navigate) over this history to understand how the component got into its current state. Then you should allow the system to simulate a change in its state by changing its "current position" in the event stream and selectively replaying events. Finally, allow the system to repair its final state by either replaying the events on the real component or compensating for the difference between the simulation and the original state.

The first part of the solution is a history of the events that have occurred on a particular event topic. Every critical change to the *Reactive Component* has to be able to be represented by or "created from" an event in this history. It's important that these events be stored in the order in which they arrived. Ships, trains, and airplanes don't arrive at their destinations before they depart their origins, and likewise, the order of orders placed and payment received for an online store is also critically important. If one of the desired properties of our solution is to "turn back time" to an earlier state, we need to understand how the system was put into that state—that's recorded not just in the events themselves but importantly in the order in which they arrive on the topic (see Figure 6-25).

Figure 6-25. Event sourcing

So let's take a very simplified and low-stakes example. Let's say that we're teaching a course on event-driven development. During the course, we give out homework, which is turned in and graded—and then give quizzes, which are also turned in and graded. A simple history early in the course for one student (corresponding to a single event topic) can be seen in Table 6-3.

Table 6-3. Event history example

Assignment	Grade
Homework 1	98
Homework 2	100
Quiz 1	84
Homework 3	92

The next part is the ability to navigate (forward and backward) through that history—both for simple queries answering the question "how" the process got to this particular state but also to use this history to make decisions about which events are good and which might be problematic. Thus, searching through the history is important. But it's not only search but also simulation of internal states at a particular point in time that becomes critical.

Returning to our motivating example, let's say that we have to report midterm grades halfway through the course. This could just be a simple weighted average where a quiz is worth twice as much as a homework assignment, and then you use a simple 90-80-70-60 scale for letter grades A (superior) through D (failing). Our student has the following history at the time that midterm grades are calculated (see Table 6-4).

Table 6-4. Event history midterm grades

Assignment	Grade
Homework 1	98
Homework 2	100
Quiz 1	84
Homework 3	92
Quiz 2	41
Reported Grade	C

At this point, we report the midterm grade of C (passing but unexceptional) to the registrar and it goes out, possibly influencing the student's chances at a scholarship. But then the student runs into class and shows us their second quiz—two pages had stuck together and one page had not been graded at all! The grade should not have been a 41 but a 91!

When we change history and update the 41 to a 91, the weighted average immediately changes to 91 for all assignments—a solid A grade for one of our brightest students. What we need to do, though, is not just determine that the new average should be

91—which is simulating what really would have happened without the mistake—but instead change the actual reported grade; in essence, we want to go back to the point in time before the second quiz and replay events forward with the new set of events (see Table 6-5).

Table 6-5. Event history changed example

Assignment	Grade
Homework 1	98
Homework 2	100
Quiz 1	84
Homework 3	92
Quiz 2	91
Reported Grade	A

When you put all three of these pieces together, you get the ability to take the following steps:

1. Pick a point in time (which may be the beginning of time) and reset the state of the component to the state it had at that point in time. If the point of time is the beginning of time, that means resetting everything to where the component initialized to.

2. Search the event history to find the set of events forward from that point

3. Select only those events that you judged as good (perhaps leaving out things like fraudulent or incorrect events or replacing them with other events, as in our example).

4. Replay those good events by having the *Reactive Component* respond to them in the same way that it had originally responded to them in the first place.

One of the ramifications of this tiny example is that we have found that to be able to undo or re-create a state, you need the ability to identify a starting point in the event stream and reset the component's state to the state at that point in time. In our simple example, we could rewind to the beginning of the semester and play everything forward. If your critical state is a simple number like our weighted average or a current account balance in a financial system, it's easy because you can always rewind to the beginning and start at zero. However, storing that state (such as a current account balance) at another point in time allows you to go back to that earlier point and then restore the state of the account to where it was at a known point in the past. In that case, storing the critical state of a component as a snapshot or checkpoint can simplify the calculations going forward (see Figure 6-26).

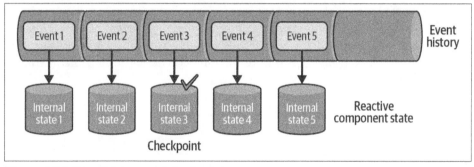

Figure 6-26. Event history and checkpoint

Here, having a checkpoint between events 3 and 4 is important because it means that if we need to rewind event 4 or 5, we need only go back to that last checkpointed state, not necessarily all the way back to the beginning, and then play forward only from the last checkpoint.

When implementing *Event Sourcing*, you need to decide on how and where to store your event history. In simple cases, you may be able to take advantage of the capabilities of the *Event Backbone* and use the *Event Backbone* as the event history (*Option 1* in Figure 6-27). However, most systems that serve as an *Event Backbone* limit how long they store messages. In the case of Kafka, for instance, the default retention period is one week (although that is configurable). That is enough for many case, but not all.

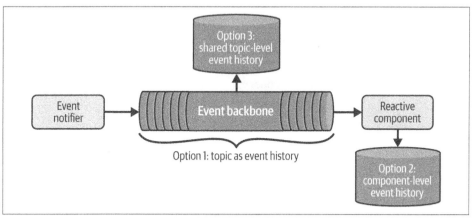

Figure 6-27. Alternatives for Event Sourcing

If you need a history that is longer than that, you may want to consider using an external database, like a time-series database, to store your event history (*Option 2* and *Option 3* in Figure 6-27). *Option 2* will store the component level history as it receives events, while *Option 3* will store the topic-level event history that arrives to the *Event Backbone*.

One of the main advantages of *Event Sourcing* is that because you have the events and the order they were processed, you can replay the events if needed. This could also result in replaying the events with new features. For instance, imagine a financial system where one of the actions is the calculation of a daily interest payment on a short-term loan. Now, further imagine that for some period of time—due to an incorrect interest rate being entered—we have been calculating that daily interest wrong for a few weeks. The problem is that this means that the balance every day (on which the new balance is calculated) is also wrong. We need to at a minimum know the history of the debits and credits to the system to replay the interest calculations correctly in order to find what the daily interest should have been over that time, and then we need to create a new credit or debit at the end to make up for the incorrect calculations.

A potential downside of keeping the state of an application as a series of events in an event stream is that reconstructing the current state of the application always involves a query to the history, which can take a varying amount of time depending upon how long the event stream is (how many events it consists of) and the performance of your query. When formulating your queries, even in the simplest case, you need to come up with a mechanism for knowing how far back in time you want to query the event stream. Essentially, you always need to have a way of identifying a bounding event that marks the beginning of a query.

Another challenge to *Event Sourcing* arises when you are dealing with external systems that were not designed with this approach. Additionally, you need to manage how you store the events, as noted earlier, which may add extra cost to your solution. Also, if reversal of events is required and is not straightforward, you might need to build into events how to reverse themselves.

Obviously, you can't have an event history without Events (255), so *Events* are fundamental to the pattern. Likewise, as we've mentioned, the history of events received is specific to a particular event channel, so knowing the Event API (274) of your events is critical. Likewise, the event history is either part of the *Event Backbone* or should be pulled off the Event Backbone (279) and stored separately by a Reactive Component (260), depending upon your particular needs.

Examples

The following financial services and ride-hailing examples illustrate the use of *Event Sourcing*.

Financial services

One of the most common domains in which we have seen the pieces of the *Event Sourcing* pattern come together is in the financial services domain. Let's consider a common structure that emerges in that domain constantly. We are all used to seeing financial statements—such as a bank account statement—represented as rows of text arranged as columns for descriptions of the transaction, with numbers in one or the other column representing whether the transaction is a credit or a debit, possibly accompanied by a running total or balance (see Table 6-6).

Table 6-6. Event-Sourcing transactions

Date	Description	Credit	Debit	Balance
010224	Starboots Coffee		5.24	104.10
010224	Public Grocery		27.19	76.91
010324	EBX, Inc (Paycheck)	1017.99		1094.90

This kind of representation is called a "Ledger" and has been common in accounting since it was adopted by Italian merchants in the fourteenth century. For our purposes, what is critical is that each entry in the ledger is important—be it a credit or a debit—but also that the order of the entries is important. When financial transactions are represented in this way, it provides a history of the account. That would make it possible, for instance, for the account owner to locate and dispute a transaction if there was financial fraud (like someone stealing a debit card and buying lots of extra-fancy coffees).

If we view each credit or debit as a separate *Event* and then view the sequence of events as a time series, we've fulfilled the first criteria for *Event Sourcing*. The reason we don't think of this as being an example of *Event Sourcing* is that we're so used to this kind of representation of financial transactions that we almost can't imagine them being represented in any other way (as we said, this has been around since the 14th century).

The next criterion is to look at what you can do with the time series of Events. We've already seen that the history allows you to traverse it forward and validate that every transaction is valid. This is especially helpful in today's world of opt-out subscriptions, where a seemingly innocent online purchase can lock you into a recurring (and often unwanted) monthly fee. This is the domain of a number of different software solutions today that (when given access to your accounts) will search for these types of transactions and tell you how much you could save in a month if you dropped all of your subscriptions. That fulfills the second criterion, search and simulation. A calculation of what your monthly checking account balance looks like without your bacon of the month club subscription is a simple case of simulation.

But the final criteria (repair) is the one that often leaves developers scratching their heads. This gets to the difference between simple and complex cases. In the simple, one-account case, having a reverse operation for the two operations (debit and credit, which are themselves their reverse operations) is a decent solution. In fact, you can even see that in your own bank and credit card accounts if you dispute a charge. You may see entries in your bank account ledger similar to those shown in Table 6-7.

Table 6-7. Event-Sourcing disputed charge

Date	Description	Credit	Debit	Balance
010224	Starboots Coffee		5.24	104.10
010224	Public Grocery		27.19	76.91
010324	EBX, Inc (Paycheck)	1017.99		1094.90
010424	BigBank - Provisional Credit -012424 Starboots	5.24		1100.14

Where things really get interesting, and where replay and replacement becomes helpful, is when you don't just have a single account but multiple, linked accounts with complex transactions moving between them. Consider the following scenario. Let's say you have a retirement account (like a 401K) that contains lots of different exchange traded funds (ETFs), mutual funds, and individual stocks and bonds.

From the perspective of the account holder, even a complicated thing like an account rebalance should look to them like one single transaction—they just set up what they want their new portfolio to look like in terms of what ETFs, funds, stocks, and bonds they want to own in what percentages, and tell the system to make it so. Internally, that's a pretty complicated, but usually trouble-free, process. ETFs, stocks, and bonds are traded to other parties at the current market price, the proceeds move into one or more "sweep" cash accounts, and then the resulting cash is used to buy the desired set of equities and other products to make up the final percentage. If everything goes well, this is like a well-oiled machine, with the amounts in all those different subaccounts for each financial product being predictable from the moment the rebalance is requested, and the account holder being no better or worse off than when they started.

However, things can go wrong, sometimes badly, and sometimes it's the broker's fault. Systems can freeze, trades can be halted or reversed by the other party, and, ultimately, it's the broker that holds the account that has the fiduciary responsibility to make things whole for the account holder if they are the ones who screw up. That's where replay really comes into the forefront. Even if something goes horribly wrong and one or more trades can't complete, or worse, complete at a loss caused by the broker's actions, the broker can use the event stream to then rewind and playback a simulation of what should have happened, then make things whole for the customer by doing their own internal compensation for any losses that were the broker's fault.

Ride-hailing

A simple example of *Event Sourcing* can be drawn from ride-hailing services. Let's say we have a driver that's participating in a car-hailing service (like Uber). All day long the driver will receive notifications of hails, decide whether to respond to those hails, pick passengers up, take passengers to locations, drop them off, and then repeat the process. The problem with a point-in-time representation is that it is hard to keep a single state variable up-to-date, especially when there is the possibility of network lag or having the driver's app drop off the network when cellular coverage is bad. What's more, it's also hard to figure out the logic of how to "undo" things when conditions change.

For example, let's imagine that a driver receives a request to pick up a passenger. We could say that the current state of the car is that it's on a trip. But what if the passenger cancels the request before they are picked up? Or what if the passenger arrives at a destination only to let the driver know they wanted to use an ATM and then be carried to another location, which was their real destination? The conditions evolve quickly and are hard to represent in a static form.

Trying to represent this complex set of conditions as a single state variable would be difficult. You could implement it as a state machine, but there's always the chance that your state machine may not represent all of the possible edge cases of what can happen in reality—like passengers canceling both before the ride begins and after it begins or the driver deciding they want to cancel the ride for some reason (like fearing for their safety).

Instead, if we keep a history of events, in whatever order they were received, you can find the current state of the car by simply examining the last event on the event stream. But representing your application state this way brings other advantages too:

- You can easily derive other information that is useful to the application by querying the event stream over time. For instance, calculating the average trip time for a trip simply amounts to scanning the event stream from a given point (like the initial sign-in of the day) and then summing the timestamp differences between trip starts and trip completes, then dividing by the number of start/complete pairs found during that day.

- Undoing amounts to adding new events to the event stream that reverse previous actions. Likewise, if you need to restore the state of an application to that of a previous point in time, you can simply replay the event stream from an earlier save point to that point.

- It is possible to go back in time and reconstruct the state of the application at any point in time. For instance, if there is a dispute between a passenger and a driver over who canceled a ride or whether a car arrived at the right pickup point at a specific time, you can rewind the event stream to find what the state was at that particular time.

This kind of backward-looking through time over an event stream is illustrated in Figure 6-28.

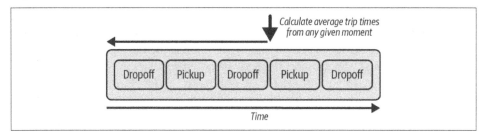

Figure 6-28. Ride hailing Event-Sourcing example

In this car-hailing example, the last trip end event can be a bounding event that serves as a good point to take a checkpoint. You can reconstruct the status of a ride at any point between the time it starts and the time it finishes, but rides themselves are bounded. You would not need to look for any events prior to the previous trip end event in constructing the current status of a ride.

Conclusion: Wrapping Up Event-Driven Architecture

This chapter discussed how to design components to coordinate without ever knowing about one another. Event-Driven Architecture builds on Microservices Architecture (Chapter 4), developing a different approach for how *Microservices* or entire applications can collaborate.

Event-Driven Architecture designs components to collaborate through Event Choreography (246). These choreographed components can be as simple as a Microservice (119) to as complex as a Modular Monolith (29). Choreography enables components to collaborate without a central plan, to handle unexpected changes, and to evolve independently with changing requirements.

A Service Orchestrator (160) follows a predefined plan and coordinates executing each step in order by tightly coupling the orchestrator with its services and invoking them synchronously or pseudosynchronously. This contrasts to *Event Choreography* where you coordinate multiple components so that when a component of interest changes, it triggers an Event (255) allowing any components interested to react to that change. While both approaches compose greater functionality from simpler services, they accomplish the composition very differently. *Event Choreography* is coupled only to its topic, announces a change that propagates asynchronously, and then lets the simpler services individually decide whether they consider the *Event* important and how to process it.

Orchestration ensures that the overall function is performed correctly and completely, whereas choreography enables components that were never designed to work together to collaborate to fulfill a collective purpose, doing so with greater scalability and resilience. We can debate which approach is better, and of course, each has advantages in the right circumstances. Rather than choosing a one-size-fits-all solution, an application can have the best of both worlds by incorporating both Microservices Architecture and Event-Driven Architecture taking advantage of each when it fits the functional requirements best.

Microservice Design (Chapter 5) helps you discover the boundaries of your *Microservices* and reveals when and where your *Microservices* can benefit from Event-Driven Architecture. The events discovered in Event Storming (189) and used to scope *Microservices* are recast as event notifications that choreograph the Aggregates (211). Event-Driven Architecture recognizes that event design and incorporates it back into the running application.

Event-Driven Architecture enables choreography by organizing *Microservices* and other components not only as Service API (70) consumers and providers but as Event Notifiers (269) and Reactive Components (260). Notifications are communicated as *Events* that are sent on topics on one or more Event Backbones (279). An Event API (274) describes the topics and the **Event Message** (*Enterprise Integration Patterns*, 2003) formats to teams who will produce or consume *Events*. *Event Notifiers* are designed to send *Events* to topics shared with *Reactive Components* they collaborate with. These *Events* have well known formats understood by both sides of the collaboration. New *Event Notifiers* and *Reactive Components* can easily be added to the collaboration, and unneeded ones can easily be removed, all without causing changes to the existing components. The components need never know that they're collaborating with one another.

This chapter also shows how Event Sourcing (289) records a log of changes to *Reactive Components* that explains their current state. The log is the history capturing a paper trail of the *Events* that impacted the components, one that can be queried to explain how the components' current state came to be. The application can replay portions of the history to re-create a component's previous states, effectively looking at the component back in time, and can replay events selectively to create new states for the component. Furthermore, if the current state of the component is found lacking, the application can replace the current component with the result of a simulation, effectively undoing *Events* that corrupted the current component by skipping them the second time around. All of this *Event Sourcing*—history, querying, simulation, and replacement—is made possible by an Event-Driven Architecture that updates *Reactive Components'* state via *Events*.

Next, we'll explore how stateless components store their state externally. Cloud facilitates a wealth of Cloud-Native Storage (Chapter 7) options and databases that work the way the cloud does. A range of database options enables persisting data the way the application wants rather than the way the database wants. Database services make it easy for development teams to create and manage their own databases without needing a separate database administrator (DBA) and enable each *Microservice* to have its own Self-Managed Data Store (154) hosted in a manageable set of database servers.

CHAPTER 7

Cloud-Native Storage

For cloud-native applications to work better in the cloud, they need to persist their data in storage that works better in the cloud.

A Cloud-Native Application (Chapter 3) can pose a difficult problem: you would like for one to be a Stateless Application (80), and yet most applications have state. If the application's state isn't in the application, where does the state go? Microservices Architecture (Chapter 4) seems to compound this problem because each Microservice (119) has its own Self-Managed Data Store (154). So the question is not just what one application does with its one set of data but what all of its *Microservices* do with all of their separate sets of data.

The cloud has brought developers and architects a wealth of new options for data storage. Long gone are the days when the only data storage option was an enterprise relational database for all applications, regardless of whether the type of data that was being stored was suited for a table-based representation. However, with new choices come new potential problems. In particular, the nonfunctional requirements that an enterprise relational database addresses now become more important, as the number of ways in which these requirements can be addressed increases.

Introduction to Cloud-Native Storage

This chapter explains how to store data in ways that work better on the cloud and that enable applications to use the data more easily. While the cloud includes storage infrastructure, databases hosted in the cloud work more the way Cloud-Native Applications work. The patterns in this chapter show how databases on the cloud provide more sophisticated data management than storage infrastructure does by managing the storage for the application, thereby simplifying applications while providing them with additional capabilities.

To introduce these patterns, we'll first review the problems with making storage infrastructure work the way Cloud-Native Applications work.

With this background, we'll then present patterns for how *Cloud Applications* can best use storage, starting with the root pattern for this chapter, Cloud Database (311).

Storing Data for Cloud-Native Applications

A cloud platform provides storage infrastructure—typically three types: block, file, and object. An application can use raw storage directly. However, storage often doesn't provide the nonfunctional requirements that applications require, such as resiliency, backup, performance, and security. The limited capabilities of storage forces the application to do a lot of the work of managing the data.

Cloud-Native Applications work better on the cloud. To do so, their data storage also needs to work better on the cloud. Making storage work the way Cloud-Native Applications work introduces some key questions:

- How should you represent your data if each *Microservice* or module should manage its own data? What ramifications does that have for how many databases you have in an application and the types of data they should manage?

- How does the database contribute to and help meet the quality-of-service (QoS) requirements of your application, such as availability, redundancy, and data consistency? How can your database keep up with the scaling requirements of your application if you have a Replicable Application (88)?

- How should you host and manage all of these different databases?

The patterns in this chapter address these questions.

Architecting Applications with Cloud-Native Storage

This chapter defines a collection of thirteen patterns that explain how to design applications that use cloud-native storage to persist data. Figure 7-1 shows the patterns and their relationships.

An application or *Microservice* persists its data in one or more Cloud Databases (311), rather than using raw storage such as file storage or disk storage. (Object storage is a special-case alternative to a Cloud Database.)

Most databases run in the cloud as a Replicated Database (316), making the data reliably available on the cloud's unreliable infrastructure and scaling the way the application scales. Whereas databases can be designed for replication, storage either doesn't replicate or the replication has limitations. Database replication is far more flexible and configurable.

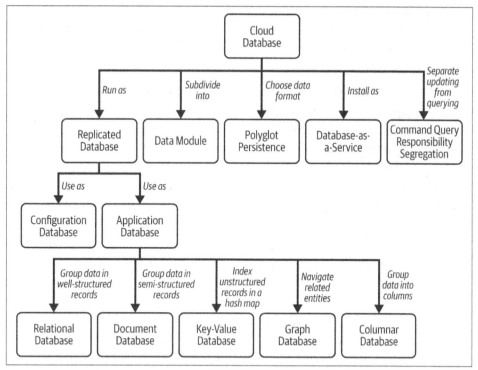

Figure 7-1. Cloud-Native Storage patterns

Some cloud databases are Configuration Databases (324), used to persist and share the settings for cloud services and platforms. While useful for implementing cloud capabilities, they generally are not used directly by cloud-native applications.

Cloud-native applications do have state that they need to store. For the application to remain stateless, it persists its data in an Application Database (329). There are several different types of application databases, optimized for different strategies for storing and accessing the data:

Relational Database (334)

> Stores well-structured records in tables, normalized to optimize for dynamic querying

Document Database (339)

> Stores semi-structured data in unnormalized records with direct access via keys

Key-Value Database (345)

> Stores unstructured records indexed in a hash map for direct access using their keys

Graph Database (352)
> Stores semi-structured entities optimized for navigating the relationships connecting entities

Columnar Database (357)
> Stores structured records in tables optimized for analytics

Rather than use a single database for the entire application, a cloud-native application typically separates data into Data Modules (367), such as each *Microservice* storing and managing its own data separately. The application should store each data module in a separate database.

Data Modules facilitate Polyglot Persistence (375), where the database for each module can be a different type best suited to how the application formats and uses that set of data.

Having selected a database to use, rather than the developers or operations installing it manually, a Database-as-a-Service (379) hosts databases that it installs and manages. One service instance can host multiple databases for multiple *Data Modules* that are all stored in the same database type.

A database can optimize the performance of either updating data or querying data, which becomes a problem for data that is constantly being queried while it is also being updated. Command Query Responsibility Segregation (383) (*CQRS*) is a database strategy that optimizes the throughput of both querying and updating the data simultaneously.

This introduction has covered several topics that are helpful to be familiar with to understand the patterns in this chapter. We've talked about how stateless applications have an even greater need to persist data, and *Microservices* require an even greater number of separate data stores. Meanwhile, raw cloud storage doesn't work the way cloud-native applications do, but the cloud platforms host databases that do work like cloud-native applications.

Before we begin, it is useful to review some topics from the section "Database Topology and Database Selection" on page 304 that become critical when understanding the decisions behind some of these patterns. With this background in mind, we will then move on to discuss patterns for architecting and designing the storage for cloud-native applications. That discussion starts with the root pattern for this chapter, Cloud Database (311).

Database Topology and Database Selection

To understand how to best address the concepts of resiliency and horizontal scalability, it's worth surveying some topologies for database management systems and how they address these issues. This evolution toward better solutions for these two areas is important in understanding the issues involved in choosing a database management system (DBMS) for a cloud-native system.

The first topology to examine is the single-server, single-storage approach. This is illustrated in Figure 7-2. For most of us, a system like this is our first introduction to a DBMS. It may have been a single-server instance of MySQL or Postgres or (for those of us older than that) a single-server system like Microsoft Access. Note that in this and all the following diagrams, a rectangular box represents a server process, with the text showing whether clients can read or write to that process (or both) with a database icon representing storage.

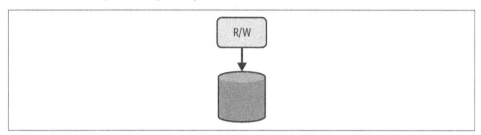

Figure 7-2. Single-server topology

The advantage of this approach is that it is simple. It gives you the ability to use a DBMS without spending a lot of time on installation, configuration, or setup. It is also relatively cheap in that it requires only one server, VM, or container and attached storage.

The disadvantage is that it provides neither scalability nor redundancy. The single database server process creates a single point of failure—as does the single location for storing the data. If a physical disk fails, even in the cloud, the data may become unavailable or corrupted. Nevertheless, this is a great way to get started with understanding the programming model of a DBMS system, and the simplicity makes it easy to build simple systems, perhaps MVPs, that can later scale if needed. That is why this is the simplest choice not only for traditional Relational Databases (329), including PostgreSQL, but also for the most elementary installations of Redis (single node) and CouchDB (single node). You do not gain scalability or redundancy but only a slight modicum of resiliency through containerizing these databases—if you connect from a container to persistent storage, the quick restart time of a container will mean that if the container dies, it will be quickly restarted.

Seeking to address the resiliency problems of a single-server model, the next model to evolve was the leader-follower model. In a leader-follower model, reads and writes are all directed to the leader. However, there is an unseen (to the user) second database server, connected to a separate storage, that receives a copy of all the updates to the leader as they are made (usually through a mechanism like log shipping (*https://oreil.ly/Npj20*)). That means that the follower storage holds a copy of the data (minus perhaps the last transaction in progress) and that the follower database server process is ready to accept reads and writes but is not yet doing so. In the event of a leader failure, the follower takes over and begins processing reads and writes to the database (this process is called *fail-over*, and when the leader process becomes functional again, a similar process called *fail-back* must occur). This is shown in Figure 7-3.

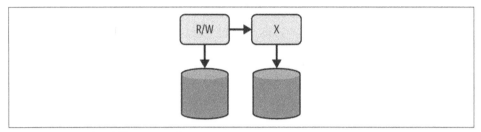

Figure 7-3. Leader-follower topology

Now you have a measure of redundancy in that the leader-follower model can survive the failure of a single process or the failure of its attached storage. However, this doesn't address the question of scalability—you're still limited to the number of transactions in a unit of time that the single server can support.

That leads us to the next variation on the leader-follower model. You can easily add some horizontal scalability if you allow reads on one or more follower processes—so long as writes are forbidden, you have no possibility of a conflict requiring resolution. That leads you to the model shown in Figure 7-4.

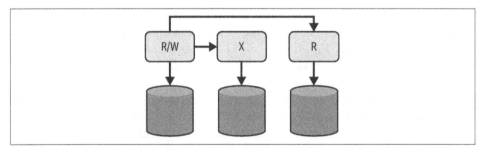

Figure 7-4. Leader-follower with read replicas topology

These additional follower processes are called read replicas. While this adds some scaling, it works best when the read/write ratio is heavily skewed toward reads. This occurs, for example, in the retail industry, where people view items more often than they choose to add them to their cart. It also occurs in many types of web applications where the output is primarily informational—if a website is semi-static this is quite useful. However, if you need to scale this to cloud sizes, even this approach will fail to scale as you will quickly reach the limitations of the single-writer process.

What's more, there is an insidious problem lurking below the surface that can also create issues, even if you do not reach that level of scaling; it takes a finite amount of time to transmit the changes from the leader to all the followers. If this happens synchronously (e.g., all followers must be updated before the transaction completes and control returns to the writer process) the total time for any transaction will increase as you add additional follower processes, eventually reaching a point where it becomes noticeable or restrictive. If, on the other hand, you update the followers asynchronously, you introduce a different problem—the problem of consistency, where two copies of the data can get out of sync for a period of time. We will address the issue of consistency later in this section.

Even though this approach has issues as described, it is quite common in the industry as it does address many real-world problems. For instance, it is used in Redis Sentinel, in MongoDB with replica rets, and in SQL databases, such as MySQL (when configured with InnoDB clusters and mirrored), and even in Enterprise databases like DB2 HADR.

In fact, enterprise databases were the first to introduce the next variation on the theme, which looks at the problem we have considered by relaxing the other constraint—gaining linear scaling while leaving the problem of data redundancy to a different solution (see Figure 7-5).

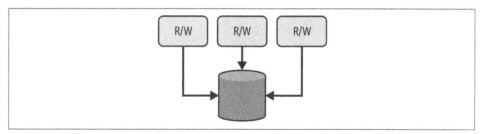

Figure 7-5. Shared-storage topology

In this model, you have a shared, networked filesystem that is available to all the processes running in all of the distributed computers that are part of the solution. This has several advantages:

- You can add nearly as many read/write processes as you want, and the solution will scale linearly so long as you can manage load balancing across all the processors (load balancing is not shown in the diagram but is assumed either through an external load balancer or a client-based load balancing scheme).

- Failure of any read/write process does not affect any of the remaining processes. Read/write processes can be added or removed at will, which allows scaling up and down.

- Managing the concurrency of reads and writes to the database across all these processes reduces the problem of managing shared file access in a multiprocess operating system, something that operating systems have been able to do since the 1960s.

The downside of this is that it requires a shared, networked filesystem. And these have their own issues. First, they are often difficult to set up and sometimes expensive to manage, even in cloud systems, which limits their use. Second, they have their own problems similar to the problems we've seen with databases themselves. To perform adequately, the clients will often take advantage of approaches like caching, buffering, and prefetching. This creates additional complexity and may reduce the overall performance of the system, particularly in complex read/write scenarios involving conflicts to the same file or parts of a file (the most common assumption in shared file systems is that most files are read-only, which is not the case in this scenario). What's more, it moves the failure point away from the database server processes to the process (and associated hardware) hosting the shared file system. That can, in some cases, create a single point of failure but more often simply requires expensive, special-purpose storage hardware with multiple redundancies.

Nonetheless, this is the approach taken by Oracle RAC and IBM DB2 pureScale in providing scaling for enterprise databases. The complexity and cost of this solution and its reliance on distributed file systems are what led to the evolution of the final solution we will examine, as shown in Figure 7-6.

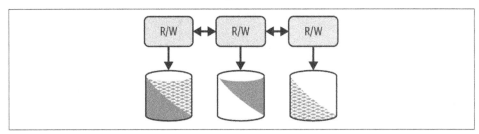

Figure 7-6. Partitioning with replication topology

This solution is called *partitioning with replication*, and it combines the replication of data we've seen in the preceding solutions. It avoids the issues with distributed file systems by not requiring them; it instead uses a local file system for each process. What is unique is that all the data is not stored in each local file system. Instead, only a part of the data is stored on each file system, and only a part of the data is accessible to each read/write database process. This requires splitting up the data by some feature of the data, which is called *partitioning*. Each partition of the data is then stored multiple times across different servers (a minimum of two servers per partition is required for redundancy in case of database server failure, but there is no theoretical maximum).

Almost all *Replicated Databases* are designed as distributed consensus systems. These are systems that enable multiple nodes in a distributed system to come to a consensus on a shared value or state. They provide a way for nodes to coordinate their activities and reach an agreement on a common set of data or configurations. The most common approach for achieving consensus is called the Raft protocol. The Raft protocol works by selecting a single node in the system to act as the leader and by having the other nodes in the system follow the leader and replicate its actions. The leader is responsible for receiving and processing requests from clients and for replicating those requests to the other nodes in the system.

The Raft protocol ensures that all of the nodes in the system agree on the order in which requests are processed and the state of the system by requiring that all nodes communicate with one another and reach a consensus on the order of requests. If a node becomes unavailable or fails, the Raft protocol allows the other nodes in the system to detect the failure and to elect a new leader so that the system can continue to operate without interruption. This ensures that even if a leader node fails, the database as a whole can continue to service requests.

This seems to have all the advantages you need; it can scale infinitely (you just need to add more partitions of your data), survives the failure of one or more database servers easily, and does not require a distributed file system and all its associated complexity. However, there is something important that is sacrificed to gain these advantages. The reality of the matter is that once you add both clustering and partitioning to your database design, you are now at the mercy of Brewer's CAP theorem ("Towards Robust Distributed SystemsDistributed System" (*https://oreil.ly/z7PlD*)). CAP stands for Consistency, Availability, and Partition Tolerance. The theorem states that you can have, at most, two in any design. For each database, it is important to know which two the designers have chosen.

The most common case is the that "C" of CAP, Consistency, is the one sacrificed. To maintain consistency across multiple copies in a cluster, you either need to lock all the copies of a partition for the duration of an update or allow only one process to update any partition (which brings us back to leader-follower with read replicas). Instead, most databases that take this approach adopt the model called eventual consistency. In Eventual consistency, it's accepted that some reads to partition copies will be "out of date" for a short period of time, but that over time updates will propagate across the network to all the copies of a partition.

This solution is used by many NoSQL databases, so many that by default when people think of NoSQL, they immediately assume eventual consistency, even when that is not true of that particular database. It is used by Redis Cluster, Scylla Rings, and Couchbase Cluster but also by some NewSQL databases like Cockroach DB.

For most applications, this is not a bad assumption. Especially when data is being used for analytics purposes, or when the timing of updates is not ultimately that important in the grand scheme of things (is it that much of a problem if a post in your social media feed is delayed by even a second or two, much less a few milliseconds?), the combination of scaling, lack of special infrastructure or network storage support, and redundancy in this solution makes it the obvious choice. However, not all applications fit this model. Banking applications are one example where consistency is very important.

To summarize which two of the three are chosen from Brewer's Theorem for the most common cases:

CA databases

As exemplified by traditional relational databases (e.g., most Relational Databases (334)), these databases prioritize consistency over availability. To achieve ACID semantics, synchronous replication is most commonly used, where a write is not considered complete until it has been replicated to all nodes.

AP databases

Many NoSQL databases focus on being partition-tolerant and ensure that the system remains operational even during network events where the database nodes become separated (or "partitioned") and cannot communicate and remain consistent. They may use strategies like eventual consistency, where consistency is achieved over time, or provide tunable consistency levels to balance between consistency and availability. All nodes remain available when a partition occurs, but some might return an older version of the data. CouchDB, Cassandra, and ScyllaDB are examples of AP databases.

CP databases

Some databases aim to provide both consistency and partition tolerance by sacrificing availability under some scenarios. These systems often use synchronized clocks and distributed transactions to achieve strong consistency. MongoDB and Redis are good examples of this kind of database.

However, you can't just select a database entirely on this assumption. Most databases have a range of options that will balance which (if any) of the elements of the CAP Theorem are sacrificed under particular conditions. You may have noticed, for instance, that we have described that Redis has several different options that correspond to different distribution models. This allows you to decide which option suits your needs under any particular circumstance—balancing complexity against the elements of redundancy and scalability. Most other databases also allow multiple options to choose from. What you should do instead is select the database type first based on your data structure needs, then select the best database architecture to suit your redundancy and scalability needs.

Cloud Database

You're developing an application with a Cloud-Native Architecture (58) that has domain data and needs to persist it. Perhaps you're developing a Self-Managed Data Store (154) for a Microservice (119).

How should a cloud-native application store data persistently in a cloud environment?

As discussed in Stateless Application (80), applications manage two types of state: session state and domain state. A database of record is storage for the most reliable copy of the domain state.

Where should an application store its domain state? An application needs to persist its domain state so that the data can be recovered after a crash and shared among replicas of the application, users of the application, and other applications. Raw storage—such as block, file, and object storage—seems like a tempting place, and that is ultimately the infrastructure where data is persisted. But storage presents two challenges for applications that need to persist and access their domain state:

Concurrency

> Storage can easily manage data when there's only one application client thread at a time reading or writing. But when one thread tries to read data while another is updating it, applications can retrieve inconsistent data from storage. If two threads try to write data at the same time, it's possible to overwrite or corrupt the data in storage. Even if a *Microservice* is the only application accessing the data in its Self-Managed Data Store (154), concurrency still occurs between the *Microservice's* replicas (see Replicable Application (88)) that share the data store.

Querying

> Storage works well when an application knows what data is stored and what data it wants and can specify where in the storage to find that data. But if an application needs to perform a search, all it can do is read all of the storage and filter for the data it wants, which is terribly inefficient, especially as data sets grow in size.

Databases, such as the Relational Databases (334) in traditional IT, help applications manage storage. However traditional enterprise databases may not fit the cloud well in three respects:

Schema

> Traditional databases force data into a common schema, thereby telling the application how to structure its own data. Applications have to accommodate the database, with many applications having to implement complex object-relational mapping just to make their **Domain Model** (*Patterns of Enterprise Application Architecture*, 2002) (see Domain Microservice (130)) fit the database schema. An

application with data that doesn't follow a strict structure will have difficulty mapping it to a fixed schema database.

Storage minimization
An enterprise database strives to write as much data as possible into as little storage as possible. Such databases typically update records in place, which uses storage more efficiently but requires aggressive use of locking, hurting the performance of concurrent threads and lowering the database's overall throughput and scalability.

Single process
Enterprise databases often run as a single active process that scales vertically but not horizontally and so is a single point of failure.

Cloud-native changes the architecture of an application so that it works better in the cloud. Likewise, databases need a new architecture so that they work better in the cloud.

Therefore,

Persist the data for a *Cloud Application* in a *Cloud Database*, one that scales horizontally as *Cloud Applications* do and offers the application flexibility in how it stores and accesses the data.

A *Cloud Database* works well hosted in the cloud and stores the state for a stateless Cloud-Native Application (Chapter 3), as shown in Figure 7-7.

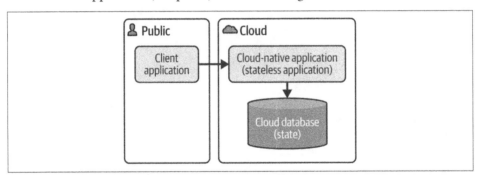

Figure 7-7. Cloud Database

A *Cloud Database* is much like a traditional IT database in that it is responsible for storing and managing data, handling much of these responsibilities so that the application doesn't have to. A *Cloud Database* differs from its traditional IT counterpart in that it is able to run reliably on a cloud's unreliable hardware, can easily accommodate a range of topologies, and stores data in the way that applications model domains.

Databases organize data into records that can be stored anywhere on the disk, simplifying an application to work with records as units of data and not needing to know where and how the records are stored. Databases must be designed to do the following well:

Concurrency

A database isolates threads to keep the data consistent. A database will not allow two applications to write to the same record at the same time, and when one application thread is writing a record, a database will not allow any other thread to read that data. A database caches data so that multiple read threads for the same data access only the disk once and organizes the records on the disk to avoid thrashing. Without a database, all of the applications are responsible for coordinating all of their threads to avoid conflicts.

Querying

A database separates the identity of a record from where it is stored on disk, understands the records' structure to know which ones have the data an application is searching for, can index the structure to find records more easily, and can navigate between related records. Without a database, this functionality becomes each application's responsibility.

Whereas enterprise databases are designed to accommodate data, *Cloud Databases* are designed to accommodate *Cloud Applications* in the following ways:

Schema

Whereas an enterprise database has a one-size-fits-all approach that tells the application how the data will be stored, an application tells a *Cloud Database* how to store the data. Many *Cloud Databases* are schemaless, able to store an application's state the way it's stored in the domain model. This makes the state easier and faster to store and retrieve, and facilitates managing not only well-structured data but also data that is semi-structured and unstructured, as well as data representing networks of connected records.

Data access

Whereas an enterprise database will excel at storing maximum data in minimum disk space, as disk has become cheaper, *Cloud Databases* have focused on enabling data access to meet the flexibility and availability of cloud environments, simplifying data access for applications and maximizing concurrency and throughput.

Multiple, horizontally scalable processes

Whereas an enterprise database often runs in a single active process, a *Cloud Database* runs in multiple replica processes that can scale horizontally to work the way the cloud works. It also replicates the data to keep it available even when a database process becomes unavailable. A database may have difficulty updating multiple distributed copies of a record concurrently. *Replicated Databases* tend to rely on eventual consistency, where each copy of a record receives an update over time.

A *Cloud Database* manages storage better than an application accessing storage directly, works more like how the application works, and works more the way the cloud works.

Cloud Databases work the way the cloud does and the way applications do and reduce the effort applications need to manage data persistence.

Because most *Cloud Databases* work differently than the *Relational Databases* most traditional IT developers are accustomed to, the developers need to learn new databases and new approaches to persisting and accessing data. Eventual consistency can be a challenge since application design tends to assume a single version of the truth.

There are many *Cloud Databases* to choose from. The best database for a *Cloud Application's* requirements depends on three criteria:

Replication
A Replicated Database (316) runs multiple server processes for accessing the same data. With these processes, the database comprises horizontally scalable redundant units, much like a Replicable Application (88).

Redundant data storage
A database running process replicas often also replicates its data, storing copies of a record in multiple processes, both to reduce single points of failure and to improve read throughput. The section "Database Topology and Database Selection" on page 304 has a detailed discussion of how this is accomplished across various database implementations.

Data structure
An Application Database (329) enables applications to persist data and access it in a way that is appropriate to a particular application's data structures and algorithms.

In addition to application databases, cloud platforms also host Configuration Databases (324), which cloud platforms and services use to manage highly concurrent shared configurations.

Just as an application monolith can be refactored into Microservices (119), a large set of data (such as an existing enterprise database of record) should be refactored into separate modules. A Data Module (367) stores each independent set of data in a separate logical database. Multiple databases can be hosted in the same database server or in separate database servers. Database-as-a-Service (379) (DBaaS) makes it easy to create and manage multiple database server instances to manage multiple *Data Modules*. A single DBaaS server can store multiple *Data Modules* that are designed for the same type of *Cloud Database*.

Multiple *Data Modules* enables the opportunity for Polyglot Persistence (375), which allows for resolving these three criteria differently for different sets of data. Since each application module or *Microservice* maps to its own *Data Module*, which is stored in a separate logical database, each database can easily be of a different type, making the overall application's persistence polyglot.

Often a key set of data needs to be queried extensively while it is also being updated frequently, which makes the database a significant performance bottleneck, even a *Cloud Database*. The Command Query Responsibility Segregation (383) (*CQRS*) pattern helps resolve this problem.

Examples

With a range of database services to choose from with different capabilities, *Cloud Applications* do not all need to use a single enterprise database.

Several NoSQL databases work like cloud services whether deployed on traditional IT or on a cloud platform, including Apache CouchDB (*https://oreil.ly/DeWo2*), MongoDB (*https://oreil.ly/xVCf1*), Apache Cassandra (*https://oreil.ly/gF41J*), Redis (*https://oreil.ly/xk6wh*), and Neo4j Graph Database (*https://oreil.ly/vVtIT*).

Most cloud platforms include several *Cloud Database* services:

Amazon Web Services (AWS)
> Hosts several DBaaS services, including Amazon Aurora (*https://oreil.ly/69rlX*), Amazon DynamoDB (*https://oreil.ly/6-Bxi*), Amazon ElastiCache (*https://oreil.ly/Ttgk-*), Amazon DocumentDB (*https://oreil.ly/P269V*), and Amazon Neptune (*https://oreil.ly/3-0k-*)

Microsoft Azure
> Hosts databases such as Azure SQL Database (*https://oreil.ly/iVnJf*), Azure Database for PostgreSQL (*https://oreil.ly/cuPYR*), Azure Cosmos DB (*https://oreil.ly/NDTys*), and Azure Cache for Redis (*https://oreil.ly/5gr-X*)

Google Cloud databases
> Include Cloud SQL (*https://oreil.ly/B2ajL*), AlloyDB for PostgreSQL (*https://oreil.ly/rh907*), Bigtable (*https://oreil.ly/CMpzC*), Firestore (*https://oreil.ly/Mn7kw*), Memorystore (*https://oreil.ly/v7hVO*), and MongoDB Atlas (*https://oreil.ly/OCGKJ*)

IBM Cloud

Hosts a number of DBaaS services, such as IBM Db2 on Cloud (*https://oreil.ly/ LKjup*), IBM Cloud Databases for EnterpriseDB (*https://oreil.ly/a5RLp*), IBM Cloud Databases for PostgreSQL (*https://oreil.ly/jmety*), IBM Cloudant (*https:// oreil.ly/xWSrU*), IBM Cloud Databases for MongoDB (*https://oreil.ly/1m1ok*), and IBM Cloud Databases for Redis (*https://oreil.ly/1ldjO*)

These *Cloud Databases* implement a number of the different patterns, which we will see later in this chapter.

Replicated Database

(aka Distributed Data Store)

You are building an application following a Cloud-Native Architecture (58) and are in the process of choosing a Cloud Database (311). For your application to be highly available, its database also needs to be highly available.

How can a *Cloud Database* provide the same quality of service as a cloud-native application, with the same availability, scalability, and performance as the application?

For a Cloud-Native Application (Chapter 3) to work well in the cloud, all of the Backend Services (106) it depends on also need to work well in the cloud. An application is only as reliable as its *Backend Services*. The single most important *Backend Service* for many applications is its database, which is key to implementing most of an application's functionality. For an application to be highly available, its database must also be highly available.

A common approach to make a database highly available on traditional IT is for it to run in two processes, one active and one standby. The clients use the first process to access data. If the first process fails, the database makes the second process active, and the clients switch over to use it to access data.

This active-standby approach has limitations. If the processes share storage and that fails, both processes become useless. Therefore, each process needs its own storage, which means that every time the first process updates its data, the second process needs to copy the update and do so with zero latency between the processes to avoid any data loss in an outage. A detail that simplifies keeping both copies synchronized is that changes occur only in the active copy, so copying data is performed in a single direction, from active to standby.

Even with redundant storage, other problems remain. Switching the clients from the first process to the second process takes time, during which the clients experience an outage. If the second process also fails before the first process recovers, the clients experience a prolonged outage until one of the processes can recover. By cloud standards of always-on availability, active-standby is a less-than-perfect solution.

The unreliable nature of cloud infrastructure is especially problematic for the active-standby approach. Failover from active to standby because of infrastructure failure is no longer an unusual occurrence caused by a major outage; it can occur frequently on the cloud simply as part of frequent routine maintenance. Database clients can experience frequent outages because of frequent failover. Active-standby has no way to avoid this problem other than wishing the active process could run as reliably on cloud infrastructure as it does on traditional IT, which it cannot.

A cloud-native application is able to scale elastically, which helps it maintain steady performance, using more capacity when client load increases and releasing capacity when the client load decreases. The active-standby approach has just one active process, which has limits on how much client load it can handle from its applications. An active process can grow bigger when the load increases, but only until its server runs out of capacity. And it usually cannot grow smaller when load decreases. Even if the active process can grow large enough, network I/O may become a bottleneck, throttling numerous database clients accessing data through a single process.

For a database to scale, not only does the server process need to scale, but the storage needs to scale as well. Just as a process cannot grow once it has used all of the capacity of its server, the database's data cannot grow once it has used all of the capacity of its storage. Even if the storage capacity is huge, the active process has limits as to how much storage it can manage effectively. A single process accessing huge amounts of data will eventually be throttled by storage I/O.

For a database to be as scalable and reliable as its cloud-native application, it needs an architecture that scales better than active-standby.

Therefore,

Select a *Replicated Database*, one that runs multiple active server processes for accessing the same data, that stores multiple copies of the same data, and that applies updates to the data consistently across the copies.

A *Replicated Database* runs not as a single server process but as a cluster of nodes, each of which is a database server process with its own storage, as shown in Figure 7-8. The database coordinates these nodes so that they work like one large database server process. Clients access the database as though it runs in a single process (as was shown in Figure 7-7).

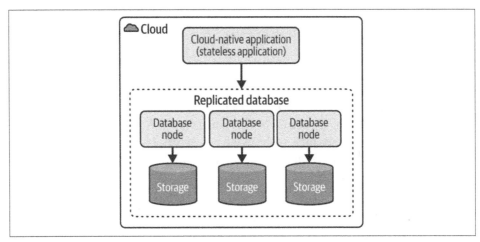

Figure 7-8. Replicated Database

The nodes in a *Replicated Database's* cluster can all run on a single computer but can also be distributed across multiple computers. Each node has its own storage, either local to the computer hosting the node or accessible from the node's computer. The database stores its data redundantly by replicating copies across the nodes, making the data highly available using commodity storage, thereby eliminating the need for specialized high-availability storage such as a RAID array.

A *Replicated Database* works much like a Replicable Application (88), if the application were stateful and each replica also had storage. A *Replicated Database* scales by adding nodes. While some of the nodes can run in standby mode, the database has multiple active nodes capable of serving client requests, thereby distributing client requests across multiple nodes.

The *Replicated Database's* architecture makes the database more reliable and increases the data availability, improves the scalability of client I/O, and enables the storage to grow to store more data while also improving storage I/O performance. The database runs reliably on unreliable cloud infrastructure because when a node and its storage become unavailable, clients are still able to access the node's data using other nodes and their storage. A more reliable database improves the availability of its data. When too many clients become a bottleneck for accessing data, the database scales to run more nodes on more computers with more network connections and bandwidth. When storage I/O becomes a bottleneck, by scaling to run more nodes with more storage, the database scales to lower each node's storage I/O demands.

Replicating across multiple nodes with redundant copies of the data works really well for read-only data, but becomes a challenge for updating data. Whenever a client creates or updates data, the database synchronizes its replicas. Because each data record is stored redundantly in multiple nodes, when a client updates a data record, synchronization duplicates that update on each copy of the record. While the database is updating multiple copies, those copies can become temporarily inconsistent for clients reading that record.

While a single database server can keep its data always consistent, a data record in a *Replicated Database* can become inconsistent temporarily while the database synchronizes an update. A single database server keeps its data *immediately consistent* by locking one or more records while it updates them. For a *Replicated Database* to lock a set of records, it needs to establish a distributed lock across all of the nodes that store copies of the records.

While some *Replicated Database* implementations do support distributed locking, its complexity lowers the database's reliability and performance. To avoid that complexity, the preferred configuration achieves *eventual consistency*, often by employing multiversion concurrency control (MVCC) (*Transactional Information Systems*, 2001) so that each replica can update at its own pace and clients can read the records while they are being updated. Eventual consistency enables a distributed database to maintain availability with good performance. This advantage becomes most evident when a node is unavailable and cannot be updated. Rather than blocking the whole database and all of its clients while it waits for all nodes to be available, the database keeps operating without the missing node by using the other nodes and their redundant copies of the data. When the unavailable node rejoins the cluster, the database restores the node by performing the data updates that it missed, thereby reestablishing its consistency with the rest of the cluster.

During eventual consistency, while the database is updating each copy of a data record individually, different clients reading the record may see different versions of the data. During synchronization, clients reading the same logical record from different nodes will each see a consistent version of the data, but they may be different versions of the data. Effectively, some clients see the newly updated data, while others still see the old data before it has been updated. Eventually, often in a matter of milliseconds when the cluster is stable, the database will update all of the copies and all clients will see the updated data. Another source of inconsistency can occur in a *Replicated Database* when two clients update different copies of the same record. When two clients make two different changes to two different copies of the same data, the result is a conflict that the database will log as an error to be resolved manually.

To simplify synchronizing updates across replicas and avoid deadlock and write conflicts, many *Replicated Databases* store their data differently than a traditional *Relational Database* does. A *Relational Database* often normalizes the data for a single entity across multiple tables, optimizing storage efficiency and enforcing consistency within shared data. Conversely, many replicated databases avoid normalizing the data by storing each logical entity as a single record. A replicated database can synchronize updates to a single record more easily, improving performance and reliability and shortening the time that the replicas are inconsistent, thereby avoiding conflicts. Data in a single record is not only easier for the database to manage, but it also simplifies client access to the data and improves throughput to the client.

A *Replicated Database* has higher availability because its servers and its data are replicated, yet the relationship between the replicas affects how well the replication works. There are two main replication models, which differ in the relationships between the replicas: leader-follower (formerly known as master-slave, aka primary-secondary) and quorum-based consensus. The leader-follower model is simpler because one node is in charge but becomes a problem when the leader becomes unavailable. Without a node that's in charge, the followers don't know what to do, and the cluster stops working until it can either reestablish communication with the leader or identify a new leader. With the quorum-based model, all of the cluster members are equal, so as long as two out of three of the members are working, they can agree on what to do and the cluster keeps working. The leader can become a bottleneck and a single point of failure. A quorum-based cluster can avoid single points of failure by distributing members across anything that can fail, such as multiple computers in multiple data centers in multiple regions.

Replication as a pattern is a basic requirement for a cloud-scale database. However, there are multiple different topologies that can support data replication. These include both solutions that use a leader-follower approach and those that use a clustering approach. The section "Database Topology and Database Selection" on page 304 explains the different potential topologies, but the key is that whichever solution you choose must have a topology that supports both the replication of the data and the process for accessing the data. In the end, this decision is internal to the database and hidden from the application, and therefore not a decision for you to make.

A *Replicated Database* scales the way a Cloud-Native Application scales, making the database as scalable and reliable as the application. It makes the data highly available on unreliable cloud infrastructure and maintains performance even as the size of the data set and client load increase.

To maintain reliability and performance, a *Replicated Database* avoids distributed locks and instead employs eventual consistency, which increases availability but means clients may temporarily see old data in some replicas that has already been updated in other replicas. To make synchronization more reliable, *Replicated Databases* often store all of the data for an entity in a single unnormalized record. However, that single record is often also easier for an application to use. Some replicated databases use different replication strategies than others, which can affect how well the database works in a distributed outage.

The architecture for a *Replicated Database* is similar to that of a Replicable Application (88). Just as the application can scale by running in more replicas, which also makes the application more reliable, a *Replicated Database* runs more nodes to increase its scale and reliability.

To maintain immediate consistency, a *Replicated Database* would need to establish a distributed lock so that it can update all of the copies of a record in a distributed transaction. Service Orchestrator (160) explains the complexity of distributed transactions, especially in a cloud's unreliable infrastructure, and why they should be avoided.

Replicated Databases are used for two purposes, Configuration Databases (324) and Application Databases (329). Different types of *Application Databases* store data records in different formats to facilitate different usages. Polyglot Persistence (375) enables different Data Modules (367) to be stored in different types of databases.

The database provided by a Database-as-a-Service (379) is often a *Replicated Database*, making it a perfect Backend Service (106) to provide persistence or caching for a Cloud-Native Application.

Examples

Most NoSQL databases are replicated. Let's consider three of the most popular ones: MongoDB, Redis, and CouchDB. Each runs in a cluster of multiple nodes that can be distributed across multiple computers, and each database's cluster can remain functional even when some nodes fail, enabling these databases to run reliably on unreliable cloud infrastructure. However, each one has a different cluster architecture that makes some more resilient than others.

MongoDB

A MongoDB (*https://oreil.ly/Nua37*) cluster, as shown in Figure 7-9, consists of a set of data baring nodes with exactly one primary node and multiple secondary nodes. On a cloud platform, each node can run on a different computer, thereby distributing the set across computers and making the database run more reliably on unreliable infrastructure.

The cluster synchronizes the data throughout the nodes in the set. The primary node replicates data updates to the secondary nodes asynchronously, keeping their data in sync. Because the data in the secondary nodes is synchronized with that in the primary node, when a node fails, data is not lost.

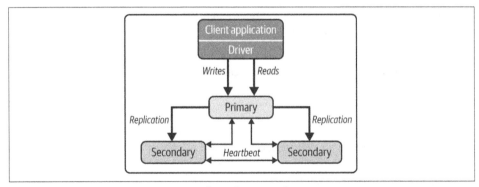

Figure 7-9. MongoDB primary/secondary cluster architecture

The cluster ensures the set always contains exactly one primary node, even when the primary node fails. The secondary nodes maintain heartbeats with the primary node and with one another. When the primary stops communicating with the other members of the set, the secondary nodes elect one of the secondaries and make it the new primary. If the original primary becomes available again, one of the new primaries is demoted to become a secondary so that only one primary node remains.

The primary node receives all write operations from the database clients so that it can maintain data consistency. By default, clients read from the primary, but clients can specify a read preference to send read operations to secondaries. However, because of asynchronous replication, reads from secondaries may return data that does not reflect the state of the data on the primary.

Because all client write operations and most client read operations in a MongoDB database go through the primary node, it can become a throughput bottleneck and single point of failure (temporarily). A MongoDB database is more resilient than a database that runs in a single server but can be less resilient than other *Replicated Databases*.

Redis Cluster

A Redis cluster (*https://oreil.ly/ZCANz*) is a variation of a Redis database that runs in a cluster of multiple equivalent nodes, as shown in Figure 7-10. Each node can run on a different computer in the cloud, distributing the nodes to avoid a single point of failure and making the database run reliably on unreliable infrastructure.

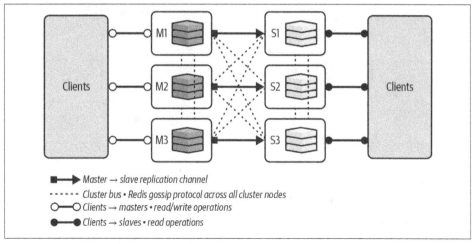

Figure 7-10. Redis grid cluster architecture

A Redis database cluster is a mesh where every node is connected to every other node in the cluster via the cluster bus. Asynchronous replication propagates updates to replicas. While the nodes are equivalent, they can run in two different modes. A primary node can service read and write operations, whereas a secondary or replica node can only service read requests. Clients can connect to any node; the cluster routes write requests to primary nodes and read requests to any primary or replica node.

A Redis cluster can remain operational when partitioned, such as when some of its nodes fail or the network fails. However, at most one partition remains operational. The operational partition must contain the majority of the primary nodes that are reachable and must also contain at least one reachable replica for every primary node that is no longer reachable. Any other partitioned nodes are unreachable. If the reachable nodes are insufficient, the entire cluster fails until it recovers.

Apache CouchDB

An Apache CouchDB (*https://oreil.ly/V4fr8*) database runs in a cluster of equivalent nodes, as shown in Figure 7-11. Each node can run on a different computer in the cloud, distributing the nodes to avoid a single point of failure and making the database run reliably on unreliable infrastructure.

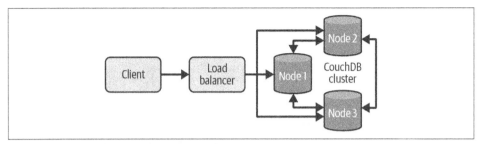

Figure 7-11. CouchDB peers cluster architecture

Clients access the database through a load balancer that distributes requests across the nodes. Any node can perform both read and write operations.

All of the nodes in the cluster synchronize via the network. When data is written to one node, the cluster propagates the update to the other nodes asynchronously.

When the cluster becomes partitioned, each partition operates independently, serving the clients that can reach it. When partitioning is resolved and all of the nodes in the cluster are reachable, they all propagate their updates to resynchronize. When the resynchronization detects conflicts where the same document was updated differently in partitioned replicas, it logs the conflict for manual remediation.

Configuration Database

(aka Distributed Coordination Service)

You are implementing a cloud service – not a Cloud Application (6) but a service that an application can use as a Backend Service (106). It will run distributed across multiple computers in the cloud.

How can a cloud service store its service state such that all of the nodes in the service can share and access the state?

A cloud service runs in multiple redundant nodes across multiple computers. Much like a Replicable Application (88), distribution across multiple nodes improves a cloud service's resiliency, availability, scalability, and performance. Multiple nodes make a cloud service more resilient on unreliable cloud infrastructure: when one node fails or becomes inaccessible on the network, the cloud service is able to keep running properly on the remaining nodes.

Replicating nodes is simpler for an application than for a cloud service because a cloud-native application is stateless, whereas most cloud services are stateful. An application with a Cloud-Native Architecture (58) is not only a *Replicable Application* but is also a Stateless Application (80) that stores its state externally. The state in a *Stateless Application* goes in the *Backend Services*, which therefore are stateful. For example, databases store data, secrets managers store credentials, monitoring services log events, and API gateways track requests. When a cloud service runs distributed across multiple nodes, it needs to share its state across those nodes.

Most cloud services are also configurable. When an administrator changes the configuration in one node, the other nodes must also update with those configuration changes.

The cloud service needs to store its state independently of any one node and continue to be able to share its state across the operational nodes. A cloud service needs data storage that does the following:

- Ensures that all of the nodes in the service can access and update the shared state at all times

- Ensures that the entire service and each of its operational nodes retain access to the shared state when nodes fail

- Ensures that each of the nodes in the entire service is notified when configuration data changes

A cloud service could use raw storage, such as block or file storage, to store its state. But as Cloud Database (311) explains, raw storage makes data difficult to replicate and to read as individual records.

Data stored in multiple copies on multiple computers to survive when a node fails —that sounds like a job for a Replicated Database (316). However, most replicated databases employ eventual consistency, which can be a huge problem for the nodes in a cloud service. For the service to work correctly, all of its nodes need to work the same at all times, which means they all need to see the latest data at the same time and cannot wait for it to eventually show up.

A cloud service needs to store its state in something that has all of the advantages of a replicated database but none of the disadvantages.

Therefore,

Store the session state for a cloud service in a *Configuration Database*, a *Replicated Database* that is reliably consistent and notifies all of the nodes whenever the data changes.

A *Configuration Database* is a *Replicated Database*, so it consists of multiple nodes, each a server process coupled with its own storage. Unlike a *Replicated Database*, a *Configuration Database* is reliably consistent, providing all clients the same single version of the truth at all times. See Figure 7-12.

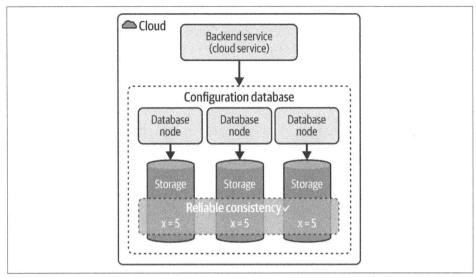

Figure 7-12. Configuration Database

A *Configuration Database's* reliably consistent state means that once a record is updated in any node, all of the nodes have the update, so a read from any node always gets that latest data. Clients see the same data at the same time, and writes are immediately visible to all clients. A *Configuration Database* typically employs the leader-follower replication model, where a single leader node coordinates updates and maintains the latest set of data.

A *Configuration Database* achieves reliably consistent data by doing what a *Replicated Database* normally avoids: it performs each update as a long-running distributed transaction. A write to the database is not complete until a majority of the nodes have recorded it. The *Configuration Database* still provides very good performance, handling thousands of reads and writes per second. It also enables clients to register for notification when the data changes, so a client using a record knows its data has changed.

A *Replicated Database* that keeps its data reliably consistent sounds too good to be true, so of course there are limitations. To maintain reliable consistency and never return an incorrect result, it favors consistency over availability. When a *Configuration Database* becomes partitioned, the partitions become either read-only or unavailable. A *Configuration Database* is able to keep its data reliably consistent by restricting the format of the data and the amount of data it can manage. The database can scale across many nodes, but it is optimized for small amounts of data.

To make its data easy to manage and quick to access, a configuration database typically is a Key-Value Store (345) that stores its data as key-value pairs organized in a hierarchy. The database does not support querying other than lookup by key.

Clients access and modify data using simple get and set operations that specify the key. The database does not try to parse the values, storing each one as a binary or character large object (BLOB or CLOB). Clients register for notification by specifying the keys of the records they depend on.

A *Configuration Database* is reliably consistent with high throughput, but that works for only relatively small amounts of data, and it has to be formatted as key-value pairs. A configuration database is specialized to store the configuration for cloud services. Reusable services often have to deal with issues of availability, performance, and security stemming from multitenancy that most standard applications do not need to be concerned with. As such, they need lower-level access to how their topology is managed, controlled, and serviced than most applications do.

There are some challenges with *Configuration Databases*. With very complex systems, it can be difficult to anticipate the impact of small configuration changes. For example, a change as small as an incorrect digit in a port number for a database connection could render an entire system inoperative. Therefore, you need to make sure that the data is up-to-date, accurate, and complete. If configuration changes affect multiple systems, it can be challenging to trace the full impact of the change across all the systems.

Applications typically need a more general-purpose database—an Application Database (329), particularly one that favors **Availability over consistency** when partitioned and that supports storing large amounts of data in a variety of formats. Many *Application Databases* in turn use a *Configuration Database* as part of their implementation so that a database cluster can configure all of its replicated nodes consistently as they each persist large amounts of data.

Each cloud service stores its own configuration data separately, making that data a Data Module (367).

Different cloud services do not all have to store their configuration data in the same type of *Configuration Database*. Instead, cloud services can use Polyglot Persistence (375), where each cloud service can store its configuration data in a different type of *Configuration Database*.

Like any cloud database, a *Configuration Database* can be hosted by a cloud platform as a Database-as-a-Service (379).

Examples

Three common *Configuration Databases* are etcd, ZooKeeper, and Consul. Many *Application Databases* incorporate these *Configuration Databases* into their own implementations.

Etcd

Etcd (*https://oreil.ly/TGxou*), Cloud Native Computing Foundation (a CNCF project), is a distributed, consistent *Key-Value Database* for shared configuration that keeps working through node failures and network partitioning. Etcd gained fame as the *Configuration Database* used to implement the Kubernetes container orchestrator, storing the desired state and current state for all of a Kubernetes cluster's nodes and containers and enabling all of the nodes to maintain a consistent view of the state of the cluster at all times.

Etcd employs the leader-follower replication model using the Raft consensus algorithm to distribute states across a cluster of computers. A client can connect to any etcd node to perform an update, but when the node is a follower, it forwards the update request to the leader, which logs the update and tells the followers to do so. When a quorum of the followers confirms the update, the leader confirms it to the client, and it becomes the new value for all nodes. When the leader becomes unavailable, the followers elect a follower and promote it to the leader.

For more details about the Raft consensus algorithm, see the section "Database Topology and Database Selection" on page 304.

Apache ZooKeeper

Apache ZooKeeper (*https://oreil.ly/riJy2*) enables highly reliable distributed coordination through a centralized repository of configuration information. ZooKeeper was created by Yahoo as part of Hadoop (*https://oreil.ly/FY7n1*), who donated it to the Apache Software Foundation. It became famous when Netflix incorporated it into Netflix OSS, their Open Source Software foundation for Microservices (119).

Like etcd, ZooKeeper employs the leader-follower replication model. Writes to a follower are forwarded to the leader, which acknowledges the write when the followers have updated.

HashiCorp Consul

Consul by HashiCorp (*https://oreil.ly/wllwa*) has many features, including a distributed coordination service implemented as a distributed *Key-Value Database* for storing configuration data and other metadata. It also provides service mesh features like service discovery with health checks and encrypted communication between services.

Like etcd and ZooKeeper, Consul employs the leader-follower replication model implemented using the Raft consensus algorithm.

Distributed Databases

Many database services use *Configuration Databases* to centrally store configuration information:

Apache HBase (https://oreil.ly/kbaL9)
> Also part of Hadoop from Yahoo, is a distributed Columnar Database (357) that is built on top of Apache Hadoop and uses ZooKeeper for distributed coordination

Apache Cassandra (https://oreil.ly/GrcCR)
> Donated by Facebook, is a distributed NoSQL *Columnar Database* that uses a peer-to-peer architecture and ZooKeeper for distributed coordination

CockroachDB (https://oreil.ly/fpYvE)
> A distributed SQL database (a Relational Database (334)) that uses a hybrid logical clock and vector clock algorithm based on Raft and etcd for distributed coordination and consensus

On the other hand, many *Cloud Databases* do not incorporate etcd or ZooKeeper but instead implement their own synchronization mechanisms. These include Apache CouchDB (*https://oreil.ly/V4fr8*) and Redis Cluster (*https://oreil.ly/d8Kc7*).

Application Database

You are writing a Cloud Application (6) or Microservice (119) structured with a Cloud-Native Architecture (58), so it is a Stateless Application (80). Yet a *Stateless Application* has state and needs to persist it.

How should a Cloud-Native Application store the data it uses so that it can run as a *Stateless Application*?

As Cloud Database (311) explains, a *Cloud Application* should store its data not in raw storage but in a database. The question then is what capabilities a database should have to work well for *Cloud Applications*.

Cloud Applications strive not merely for high availability but for continuous availability. Yet most applications are highly dependent on their database, so an application is only as available as its database. A cloud database needs to also be continuously available. A Replicated Database (316) can have very high availability, but when the cluster becomes partitioned, consistency and availability become a trade-off.

Cloud Applications strive for scalability, which means they not only need to serve more users but also need to store more data for those users. As more users perform more tasks, they use more data, so the applications need to access more data more quickly to serve all of those users. The easier it is for an application to access its data, the less code application developers have to write, and the application will get better performance accessing data.

A *Cloud Application* needs a database that is highly available, even if that means its data becomes inconsistent temporarily. It needs to be able to scale in multiple respects: store large amounts of data, enable the application to access the data easily, and support large numbers of users concurrently accessing data.

Therefore,

Store the domain data for a Cloud-Native Application or a *Microservice* in an *Application Database*, one that like the application is highly available, can store large amounts of data, scales to support numerous concurrent users, and simplifies data access for the application.

An application database tends to be a *Replicated Database*, although some types distribute across multiple nodes better than others. Some are reliably consistent, but the ones that distribute well tend to use eventual consistency. No one diagram can capture this range of capabilities, but the important feature to focus on is availability.

As shown in Figure 7-13, as a *Replicated Database*, an *Application Database* runs across multiple nodes. When one of the database's nodes becomes unavailable due to failure or network partitioning, the database uses the remaining functional nodes to keep working, keeping the database available so that the application maintains access to its data.

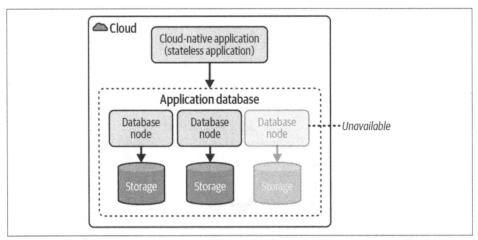

Figure 7-13. Application Database

When one node becomes unavailable, the data remains available in other nodes. A database typically replicates a minimum of three copies of each data record in three different nodes but may replicate many more copies to survive losing a large number of nodes. For ultimate availability, a database can not only run a large number of nodes but also replicate all of the data across all of the nodes, so then a single surviving node can still keep the database available.

There are lots of ways to replicate across multiple nodes. For an exploration, see the section "Database Topology and Database Selection" on page 304.

There are many types of cloud application databases, which fit into three broad categories:

SQL databases

These traditional *Relational Databases* employ relational algebra to organize data into tables, rows, and columns that clients can search and filter using structured query language (SQL). SQL databases are well-suited for applications that require complex queries, transactions, and referential integrity and are often used in enterprise environments.

NoSQL databases

These are non-*Relational Databases* that do not use SQL as their primary query language. They are designed to handle large amounts of unstructured and semi-structured data, and are often used in environments where scalability and high availability are important. NoSQL databases are often used in web-scale applications, such as social networking sites, online retailers, and other applications that require fast read and write performance. *NoSQL Distilled (https://oreil.ly/M1XZ2)* describes many different aspects of NoSQL databases.

NewSQL databases

These are a new generation of *Relational Databases* that are built to provide the scalability and high availability of NoSQL databases, while still maintaining the transactional consistency and SQL support of traditional SQL databases. They are often used in environments where both scalability and strong consistency are important, such as in financial and ecommerce applications. NoSQL databases are typically less efficient at SQL-like queries because of differences in approaches to query optimization. For an application that depends on SQL-centric complex query capability, a solution such as a NewSQL database or a distributed in-memory SQL database may be more efficient.

All of these categories are *Application Databases*, but they differ in how they store data and make it accessible to applications, making some easier for some types of applications to use and others better suited for other uses. They optimize their querying and update capabilities for a particular mechanism of data storage and retrieval optimized for different application requirements:

- Some applications need a database to be highly optimized for efficient reads, while others need it to be equally efficient at reading and writing.

- Some applications need to simply store data as is and retrieve it in its original format, whereas others need the database to understand the data format to facilitate searching and navigating it.

- Some applications need a database to enforce data format, whereas others want a database that can handle variable formatting.

No *Application Database* is a one-size-fits-all solution, so there are many different ones to choose from.

Application Databases are databases, so they facilitate storing and managing large amounts of domain data and enabling applications to easily access and manipulate individual data records. A range of *Application Databases* differ in the trade-offs they make between consistency, availability, and scalability. And perhaps most importantly, they differ in the way they store and organize data and the types of data they are designed to handle.

Because of the range of database categories, it is important to choose the right database structure and retrieval mechanism for the job the application needs to perform. Performance, scalability, and other application requirements will determine the particular type of database to choose. An application's component design should be the driving factor in selecting a database, not the other way around. That is true in both the structure of the data the application is storing and in the way in which the application needs to query or search data.

Compared to an *Application Database*, a Configuration Database (324) is much more specialized. It manages a much smaller amount of data and only supports looking up data record by their keys with no querying. It scales across numerous nodes while keeping its data reliably consistent, but it does so by favoring consistency over availability, whereas applications strive for availability.

There are several types of *Application Databases*. Each type works best for certain requirements:

Relational Database (334)
> Works well for relational data, an acknowledgment to the fact that relational representations are still sometimes the right way to store and manage certain types of application data. SQL and NewSQL databases are optimized for scalability and free-form querying.

Document Database (339)
>Works most like a relational table row that the database can easily replicate across multiple nodes. The records are schemaless JSON data, much like the parameters in web services. The documents can be searched but not easily reformatted to entirely new configurations as in the *Relational Database* approach.

Key-Value Database (345)
>Works like a hash map, enabling an application to access unstructured data directly with $O(1)$ performance for many use cases.

Graph Database (352)
>Excels at storing entity-relationship-attribute (ERA) data structured as entities with relationships and attributes, and at easily traversing those relationships from one entity to another. This works well for the data in social media networks, travel networks (highways or flights), and the mathematical operations for constructing and formatting large-scale neural networks.

Columnar Database (357)
>Works well for data analytics, storing well-structured data and enabling rapid access to all records with a specified value.

A single large application may make use of multiple Data Modules (367) that are independent of one another. Different modules may require support for different data types and access styles, so Polyglot Persistence (375) enables an application to store each module in a different type of database. Each database should ideally be hosted by the cloud platform as a Database-as-a-Service (379).

Examples

The IT industry offers many different database products and open source projects that are suitable for applications to use to store their domain data. Examples of each *Application Database* category include the following:

SQL databases
>SQL *Relational Databases* include Oracle database (*https://oreil.ly/Ov31z*), IBM Db2 (*https://oreil.ly/Lqs7Y*), Microsoft SQL Server (*https://oreil.ly/8WILY*), PostgreSQL (*https://oreil.ly/uqhNB*), and MySQL (*https://oreil.ly/SRv7W*). Public cloud platforms host SQL database services based on those products.

NoSQL databases
>Examples of NoSQL databases include MongoDB (*https://oreil.ly/PRLaZ*), Apache CouchDB (*https://oreil.ly/fqe5c*), Redis (*https://oreil.ly/YKAUz*), and Memcached (*https://oreil.ly/nd3yZ*). Cloud services include ones that host those products as well as IBM Cloudant (*https://oreil.ly/wyn1u*), Google Cloud Datastore (*https://oreil.ly/O-Dp0*), and Amazon DynamoDB (*https://oreil.ly/0r1vg*).

NewSQL databases

> NewSQL databases include CockroachDB (*https://oreil.ly/NRVsG*), MariaDB Xpand (*https://oreil.ly/Ye_p-*) (originally known as Clustrix), and SingleStore (*https://oreil.ly/jBxsU*) (originally known as MemSQL). Public cloud NewSQL databases include Google Cloud Spanner (*https://oreil.ly/yTe3Y*) and Amazon Aurora (*https://oreil.ly/-RJPh*).

As shown earlier, major public cloud platforms host many of these types of databases as services and host their own cloud-only databases as well.

Relational Database

You are writing a Cloud Application (6) or Microservice (119) structured with a Cloud-Native Architecture (58) and are selecting an Application Database (329) for your application to use to persist its domain data.

How can an application store well-structured data that it needs to query dynamically?

Cloud vendors often support newer databases generally categorized as NoSQL databases. Developers often assume that a cloud database is always a NoSQL database, but not all applications and not all data lend themselves well to NoSQL databases.

Most existing data in an enterprise's traditional IT systems is typically stored in tables in a *relational database* management system (RDBMS). When the data is already structured to be stored in well-defined tables, converting it to a NoSQL format often provides little benefit.

An enterprise's existing traditional IT applications are typically written to use an RDBMS. The applications expect to have data that are well-structured records, or access those records by performing CRUD operations (create, read, update, and delete), to update those records using ACID (atomic, consistent, isolated, and durable) transactions, to query the records using SQL (structured query language), and to take advantage of database views to structure the same data as different record formats for different uses. As long as the application works well as is, a NoSQL database provides little advantage and in fact will require significant modifications to keep the application working.

Even when developing new *Cloud Applications* that need to store new data in a cloud database, a NoSQL database may not be the best choice. An application's data may naturally be well-structured, such as the records gathered from users filling in forms. The application's domain logic may do little more than CRUD and query the data. An application like this needs a database that is optimized for performing these functions on well-structured data, which is probably not a NoSQL database.

If a new or existing application would work well on traditional IT using an RDBMS, a NoSQL database in the cloud will actually make it work worse.

An advantage of many NoSQL databases on the cloud is that they provide better availability than a traditional IT RDBMS does. Many NoSQL databases run distributed across multiple nodes so that if one node fails, the others keep the data available. Ideally, applications should get the availability of data stored in a NoSQL database without having to convert RDBMS data to NoSQL.

Therefore,

Store well-structured data that applications will query frequently in a *Relational Database*—hosted in the cloud.

A *Relational Database* is an *Application Database* that stores its data formatted as a schema of tables, rows, and columns. It enables an application to search its data using SQL queries and can use database views to present the same data in different formats. A *Relational Database* implements ACID transactions, so it favors consistency over availability. Yet a *Relational Database* can run in multiple active processes to maximize availability and scalability, making at least some of its data available at any given time. As shown in Figure 7-14, a *Relational Database* stores each table row once, a single consistent source of truth for that row's data.

A *Relational Database* is usually a Replicated Database (316), but some *Relational Databases* replicate better than others. Older SQL databases run active-standby, with a single active node that stores all of the data and handles all client requests, and a standby node that stores a copy of the data. Newer SQL databases run in multiple active nodes.

The trick for a *Relational Database* running in multiple active nodes is to implement ACID transactions that preserve the data's consistency and referential integrity. The database achieves this by storing each table row in only one node and storing related table rows in the same node. One copy of each table row acts as a single source of truth for the record, and storing related table rows in the same node enables the node to maintain referential integrity within the data. Storing a table row in a single node makes the node a single point of failure for all of its table rows. The database can compensate for this shortcoming by maintaining a standby copy of each active node.

A *Relational Database* server can host multiple schemas (i.e., a set of tables) in the same node but can also host each database in a different node.

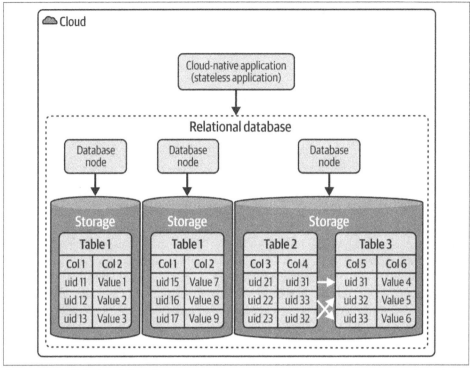

Figure 7-14. Relational Database

Some *Relational Database* servers not only distribute different databases to different nodes but also distribute a schema's tables across nodes, and can even split a single table and distribute it across nodes (this is called *partitioning* and is described in detail in the section "Database Topology and Database Selection" on page 304). Figure 7-14 shows a single table, Table 1, split across two nodes, Database Node A and Database Node B. It stores each of the table's rows in a single node, but some of the rows are stored in one node, while other rows in the same table are stored in another node. The database uses distributed queries to search a table split across nodes, running the query in both nodes and merging the results. The diagram also shows a set of records normalized across two tables, with the rows in Table 3 referring to rows in Table 4. Because of this relationship, the database stores both tables in the same node, Database Node C, and that node is responsible for maintaining the referential integrity within the data.

Using these techniques, a *Relational Database* can achieve massive scalability and wide distribution while preserving ACID transactions and efficient querying.

A *Relational Database* can be a good choice for a cloud-native application or *Microservice* that needs access to existing relational data or has well-structured data it needs to be able to query easily. The *Relational Database* enables moving existing relational data to the cloud without needing to significantly alter the data or the applications that use it. It also offers great flexibility for searching the data and presenting different views of the same data for different uses. Many *Relational Databases* are more highly available and scalable than their traditional IT counterparts while still preserving ACID transactions.

While a *Relational Database* can be highly available as a whole, the availability of any one record can be more limited. Each record is stored in a single node, so when that node becomes unavailable, that record becomes unavailable unless and until the database replaces it with a standby node.

A cloud-native application or *Microservice* is often implemented with an object-oriented language such as Java, especially code developed using techniques like domain-driven design. Storing data in a *Relational Database* necessitates object-relational mapping (ORM), which can be difficult to develop and maintain and can perform poorly at runtime.

Many cloud-native applications and *Microservices* work better with a Document Database (339) in which semi-structured data is stored the way the application represents it. While *Document Databases* are often highly scalable and available, the data can become inconsistent temporarily and inefficient to query, shortcomings a *Relational Database* does not share.

Sometimes the data in a *Relational Database* is just binary or character large objects (BLOBs or CLOBs). A Key-Value Database (345) can store unstructured data more efficiently and optimize access.

Relational Databases are terribly inefficient at following relationships between data because doing so requires performing querying and joins across tables. A Graph Database (352) maintains referential integrity between entities and simplifies navigating relationships efficiently.

A *Relational Database* is for storing and accessing rows of data. When an analytics program is interested in all of the unique values in a column and not in the rest of the data in the row, use a Columnar Database (357).

An application using a *Relational Database* should use it to store a single Data Module (367) and use Polyglot Persistence (375) to store modules of table data in *Relational Databases* and modules of other data formats in other types of databases.

A *Relational Database* should be hosted by the cloud platform as a Database-as-a-Service (379). Most public cloud platforms host multiple table DBaaSs.

Examples

There are literally dozens of examples of *Relational Databases*. The oldest and most familiar ones are enterprise SQL databases. An application does not require a traditional enterprise database to use SQL. At least two other types of databases also implement SQL: Small SQL and NewSQL.

Enterprise SQL

Databases for hosting an enterprise database of record include Oracle database (*https://oreil.ly/PqO2u*), IBM Db2 (*https://oreil.ly/ZjVGz*), and Microsoft SQL Server (*https://oreil.ly/9w4ag*). These have usually been hosted on traditional IT, and many public cloud platforms host at least some of these databases as a service (Database-as-a-Service (379) or DBaaS).

Small SQL

Small SQL databases such as MySQL (*https://oreil.ly/C-4iN*) and PostgreSQL (*https://oreil.ly/7o8Jm*) have these advantages:

- These databases are very well supported, both by the open source community and by many vendors. It is relatively easy to find documentation and tutorials for them and to find developers skilled in them.
- These databases are small and lightweight enough to containerize easily and deploy and update through the same GitOps mechanisms used to deploy application code.
- These databases are supported in DBaaS services on the public cloud platforms.

A major shortcoming of Small SQL databases is that, as the name implies, they often do not support the same level of scale (particularly with regard to sharding) that enterprise databases can provide.

NewSQL

Scalability is where NewSQL databases shine. They combine the best attributes of Small SQL databases and the scalability of NoSQL databases. These include CockroachDB (*https://oreil.ly/SPwNP*), Apache Trafodion, (*https://oreil.ly/hx9Jr*), MariaDB Xpand (*https://oreil.ly/eL902*) (originally known as Clustrix), and SingleStore (*https://oreil.ly/j_eXV*) (originally known as MemSQL). Public cloud NewSQL databases include Google Cloud Spanner (*https://oreil.ly/y933e*) and Amazon Aurora (*https://oreil.ly/RYNyE*).

NewSQL databases can be a good choice for any application that needs ACID transactions, an SQL engine that fully supports the relational model, and extensive scaling and sharding capabilities. Yet that choice comes at a cost—these databases are often more complex to set up and manage than the older Small SQL solutions. It is also harder to find people with skills in these databases. Regardless, when selecting a *Relational Database*, these should be considered as options.

Document Database

You are writing a Cloud Application (6) or Microservice (119) structured with a Cloud-Native Architecture (58) and are selecting an Application Database (329) for your application to use to persist its domain data.

How can an application most efficiently store and retrieve data when the future structure of the data is not well known?

When developing a new application, often the requirements for the domain data it will need to persist are rather unknown. As the application evolves, the data format can change. The application could start out using a Relational Database (334) with a schema for well-structured data. By the time the data requirements are well understood and the data format can be designed accordingly, it may be too late and the application is locked into the existing schema.

One of the advantages of cloud is that it supports agile development. An application can start as a minimum viable product (MVP) and then incrementally improve as new features are discovered. For an application to evolve easily, its database must be able to evolve easily as well. A *Relational Database* with a strict schema is difficult to evolve. If early deployments of the application have created data, migrating the data to new versions of the schema becomes cumbersome.

Another aspect of agile development is that an application must be able to access data easily. *Relational Databases* require applications to implement object-relational mapping (ORM) code to transform the relational data into the application's domain object model and back again. When developers spend time writing code to make the application work with the database, they aren't developing user functionality. The application needs a database that works the way the application does, storing data in the same format the data uses with minimal mapping. The database should make it easy for an application to access a set of data that it needs as a single record that can easily be read or written as a single task.

While a *Relational Database* is designed to store well-structured data, much of the world's data is not well-structured data. Real-world data tends to be semi-structured, with enough structure to figure out what its fields are but with variability in the structure from one record to the next. Even storing something as common as a customer's mailing address or phone number becomes complicated for an enterprise with an international customer base. Trying to store data with such variable formatting in a fixed schema is difficult.

A *Cloud Application* needs to scale the way the cloud does, and so does its database. A *Cloud Application* needs a Replicated Database (316) with the same availability, scalability, and performance that the application has. A *Replicated Database* runs in multiple nodes that can be distributed across multiple computers and make use of multiple sets of storage, enabling the database to grow and run reliably even on unreliable cloud infrastructure.

Therefore,

Store the application data in a *Document Database*, a database that structures its data the way the application does.

A *Document Database* is a kind of NoSQL database and is schemaless, so it can store data without a predefined schema, simply by storing data the way the application delivers it. A *Relational Database* and a *Document Database* both store domain entities, but rather than storing each entity as a table row normalized across several tables scattered across the disk drive, it stores each entity a single document that it can access in one easy step from one area of the disk drive without joins. A *Document Database* typically represents its data externally as JSON data. It is typically a *Replicated Database* that runs in multiple nodes and replicates each document across those nodes.

Figure 7-15 shows a *Document Database* running in three database nodes that stores two documents and has replicated both of them to all of its nodes. The database can route each client request to any of its nodes. Since every node stores a replica of all of the data, any node that receives the client request can serve its data. If each node replicates only some of the data and a client requests data in another node, the node that receives the request can redirect it to a node that stores a replica of the data.

A *Document Database* enables the data to evolve as the application evolves, facilitating agile development. A *Document Database* does not have a fixed schema for its data. Most *Document Databases* represent their data externally as JSON data, which doesn't mean that's how the database stores it necessarily but explains how the database's client APIs format data to be read and written. JSON records are nested with individual key-value fields at each level, so the database understands the structure of the data. Yet JSON can structure any data this way, and then so too can a *Document Database*. By simply persisting the JSON data as is, the database doesn't require any prior knowledge of the data's structure and doesn't force the data to fit into any predefined structure.

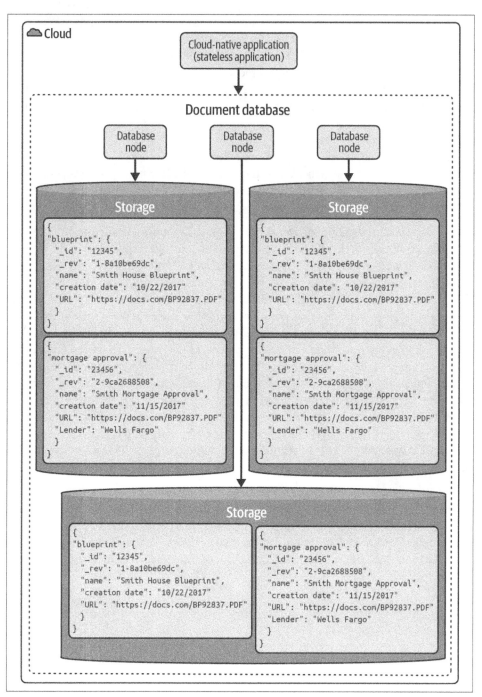

Figure 7-15. Document Database

Many *Cloud Applications* and web applications already structure data as JSON, so doing it for the database is natural and no extra effort. Even if your application is not written in JavaScript and thus already uses JSON, there are available libraries to serialize and deserialize JSON into object structures in Python, Java, Golang, and most other languages. A JSON-structured *Document Database* makes it easy to store the data the way the application is already using it and to read the data back in that format, which makes the database easy for the application to use and makes tasks efficient because so little data transformation is needed. No ORM is needed since the database and the application use the same structure to store the data. Because the database understands the structure of the documents, it can facilitate more efficient querying by indexing the shared attributes across many different item types.

A *Document Database* makes persisting data much easier so that developers can focus their efforts on implementing user requirements. *Document Databases* model their data the same way their applications do and do not normalize their data beyond the normalization that the application does as part of modeling the domain. When the application has data about a customer, product, or account and persists it to the database, the database stores all of that data as a single record—a document. The database can easily replicate that document to other nodes as an atomic unit. Every document has a unique ID and a revision ID, making it easy for the database to keep track of replicas in different nodes, as well as determine which replica has the latest revision and which ones need to be synchronized. Two-way replication—where some changes occur in one node and some in another and need to be synchronized in both directions—is relatively easy to perform. Meanwhile, the application has complete flexibility to normalize the data the way the domain does naturally. If multiple members of a household share the same house, the application can store that house once and share it among records for multiple residents. This same structure is persisted in the database and can be navigated by the same relationships.

A *Document Database* also has shortcomings. Because a *Document Database* offers so much flexibility in how it stores data, the database has little ability to enforce data consistency or referential integrity, pushing those responsibilities back into the application. Very large documents can limit performance, compelling the application to decompose (i.e., normalize) a large document into smaller ones that it can query and access individually.

A *Document Database* works the way a *Cloud Application* does, storing semi-structured data in the same format the application uses, storing each data entity as a document, and enabling individual documents to vary in format. A *Document Database* makes agile development easier because it requires limited code in the application for persistence and can evolve with the application. As *Replicated Databases*,

Document Databases can be highly replicated for maximum availability on unreliable infrastructure.

Document Databases make data easy to store and retrieve but do not enforce data consistency or referential integrity. Querying the data may not perform well.

For well-structured data, consider a Relational Database (334) for a database that enforces data consistency, maintains referential integrity, and optimizes query performance.

For unstructured data that cannot be queried, consider a Key-Value Database (345) for a database that provides direct access to binary or character large object (BLOB or CLOB) entities via keys.

For data where the applications navigate the relationship between the entities more than they use the data in the entities, consider a Graph Database (352), which manages each entity like a document but is optimized for lookup via references.

An application using a *Document Database* should use it to store a single Data Module (367) and use Polyglot Persistence (375) to store modules of document data in document databases and modules of other data formats in other types of databases.

A *Document Database* should be hosted by the cloud platform as a Database-as-a-Service (379). Most public cloud platforms host multiple document DBaaSs.

Examples

Document Databases are NoSQL databases, but not all NoSQL databases are *Document Databases*. (Others are *Key-Value Databases* or *Graph Databases*.) There are a number of common *Document Database* products and public cloud platform services. A common example of an application using a *Document Database* is an ecommerce application storing a catalog of products.

Document database products and projects

These products and open source projects implement *Document Database*:

MongoDB (https://oreil.ly/sdtPR)
    A very commonly used *Document Database* that is distinguished by its flexible schemas, powerful built-in query capability, and scalability and availability

Apache CouchDB (https://oreil.ly/NcR7U)
    Incorporates synchronization techniques from Lotus Notes that features built-in conflict resolution and supports incremental replication

Couchbase (https://oreil.ly/dvgm5)
    A document-oriented database that emerged from the team that built Memcached

Many cloud platforms also host these databases as DBaaS services.

Cloud platform document databases

These cloud platform services provide a *Document Database* (as a DBaaS):

IBM Cloudant (https://oreil.ly/MEXT6)
  Built on Apache CouchDB

Amazon DynamoDB (https://oreil.ly/tNJRS)
  Supports the document model in addition to the key-value model

Amazon DocumentDB (https://oreil.ly/hMgTk)
  Compatible with MongoDB

Azure Cosmos DB (https://oreil.ly/PsyLq)
  Can be used as a *Document Database* or a *Relational Database*

Google Cloud Firestore (https://oreil.ly/_G7fb)
  A document-oriented database that supports the Google Firebase application development platform

In most cases, the particular product you choose matters less than how well suited your particular usecase is for a *Document Database*.

Document Database ecommerce example

When making a decision as to which NoSQL database to choose for any particular *Microservice*, perhaps the default, first type to consider should be a *Document Database*. As stated earlier, *Document Databases* have the flexibility to represent anything that can be serialized as a JSON document—which includes most object structures in most languages. Thus, for simple object structures where the individual objects are going to be searched by any one of several fields of the objects, it's a good solution to start with.

An example of this that we have seen in the ecommerce field is a product catalog. In the online ordering example for Bounded Contexts (201), we discussed how most users will begin their interaction with the catalog by performing a search. However, we left the details of that search to be defined later!

Searching a product catalog can be a difficult process, because representing a product can be complex. Different types of products have different attributes, so there is no single product type with a fixed schema. It is difficult to model products in a *Relational Database* because different types with different attributes need different schemas, such as different database tables. The data for all of the products in each table has to fit that schema, even if some products are missing some attributes or have extras. Then all of the different tables need to be searched differently.

A *Document Database* can keep all products in a single group, where the data for each product lists whatever attributes it needs. Products can be searched by any attributes that seem relevant, enabling customizable searching. If a product doesn't have a particular attribute that's part of the search, the search can assume a default value or ignore that product as not a match. If all products had the same attributes, a *Relational Database* might be the best solution. But when they do not, a *Document Database* may well be a better solution.

Let's consider a couple of simple examples of different product types. The first is something simple, like laundry detergent. The product description, size of the container, and manufacturer are most of what someone might search. That's a simple product representation. However, searching for soft goods like clothing involves several different aspects that weren't part of the laundry detergent example—gender, sizes or measurements, colors, and materials all would be added to the fields already described for simple products. You may want to display many more pictures of a piece of clothing than you would for a container of laundry detergent as well.

At one online merchant we worked with, the most complex search of all was for car tires. Specifying a tire involves not only complex sizing and description codes but also lots of additional attributes about the tire itself—for instance, the weather it's for and the details of the warranty on the tires. Complicating this was the fact that very often people would search not by any attribute of the tire but by the vehicle models that the tire is designed to fit!

All of these add up to different object representations, perhaps even an inheritance hierarchy rooted at simple catalog items, and then with subclasses or other separate representations for specialized types like clothing or car tires. Any or all of these attributes will need to be searched, and what's more, as the catalog expands and new items are added to the products the vendor carries, they want to want to be able to do that quickly, without having to change any of the existing catalog contents. This is why a *Document Database* is perfect for this particular problem. You may not only have different representations of the different products but also build and optimize (index) different searches for all these different cases and add to it on the fly.

Key-Value Database

You are writing a Cloud Application (6) or Microservice (119) structured with a Cloud-Native Architecture (58), and are selecting an Application Database (329) for your application to use to persist its domain data.

How can an application most efficiently store and retrieve independent data entities that are always looked up by the same key?

Sometimes an application wants to store an isolated data record using a unique ID that the application can use later to retrieve the record as is. The application doesn't need to query the database to look for the record; the unique ID specifies the exact record the application needs.

This scenario is common for session management and for caching data. A session stores data for a web application on the server to track the history and context of the web user. A database cache stores data retrieved from a database so that the application can avoid repeatedly retrieving the data from the database.

When an application stores and retrieves data by specifying a unique ID, a database can easily index those data records. The database uses the unique ID as a key and stores the record indexed by that key. The next time the application specifies the same unique ID, the database uses that as a key to retrieve the record. The database can store the record as an atomic value and doesn't need to understand the content or structure of the value it is storing. As far as the database is concerned, the record's data type might as well be a binary or character large object (BLOB or CLOB).

Other databases like Relational Databases (334) and Document Databases (339) add a lot of overhead that isn't needed in this scenario. The records in those databases don't necessarily have unique IDs, or those UIDs aren't necessarily apparent to the application. The application expects to search for multiple records matching its criteria and does not assume the match will always be exactly one record. The database understands the structure of each record and the fields it contains, storing the field values separately and indexing certain ones to enable applications to query for those values. The database also understands the relationships between separate records, managing them as a collection and enabling an application to retrieve multiple related records more easily. This overhead is helpful for applications that use the data more generally but isn't needed when the application knows the exact ID of the record it needs.

Applications need a more efficient, specialized database without this general-purpose overhead.

Therefore,

When an application always performs lookup on the same key, store its data in a *Key-Value Database* optimized to work like a hash map.

A *Key-Value Database* is a kind of NoSQL database and is schemaless, so it can store data without a predefined schema, simply by storing data the way the application delivers it. *Key-Value Databases* are often the most scalable type of database with the best performance. A key-value database is optimized to store unrelated, unstructured data records indexed by their unique IDs. It uses each record's UID as a key and stores its unstructured data as a value. It is typically a Replicated Database (316) that runs in multiple nodes, storing its data in one or more partitions (i.e., tables) that it replicates across multiple nodes.

Figure 7-16 shows a *Key-Value Database* running in three database nodes that stores records in three partitions with two replicas of each partition. The database can route each client request to any of its nodes. If a node receives a request for a partition it does not store, it reroutes the request to another node that does store the partition.

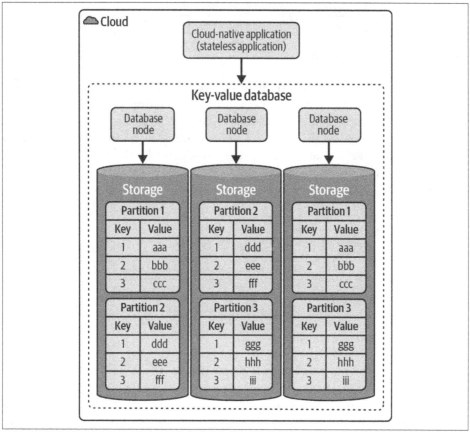

Figure 7-16. Key-Value Database

A *Key-Value Database* works like a hash map in a programming language like Java. A hash map rapidly calculates the hash of the data in a key and uses that hash as an index into an array structure. The hash map uses the hash index to insert a value directly into the array and to directly access the value in the array to read it back out. A key-value database replicates that approach as a database that can store billions of individual values over multiple servers. Figure 7-17 shows the basic idea.

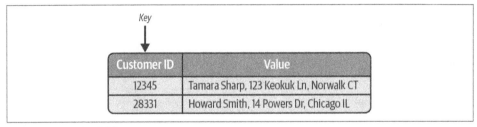

Figure 7-17. Key-Value concept

This simplicity is extremely useful for situations like the caching scenario described earlier, and *Key-Value Databases* are designed to take advantage of this simplicity. For simple key lookup operations, most *Key-Value Databases* offer O(1) performance. This is even true when the data is stored across multiple nodes in a cluster because it is easy to partition key-value data and prepend the partition ID to the key, forming a compound key, as is shown in Figure 7-18.

Partition ID	Customer ID	Value
1	12345	Tamara Sharp, 123 Keokuk Ln, Norwalk CT
1	28331	Howard Smith, 14 Powers Dr, Chicago IL
2	27715	Rose Cheng, 9889 Highmark St, Santa Clara CA

Figure 7-18. Compound Key-Value

The basic API for a *Key-Value Database* is very simple. The API is fundamentally two operations: get(key) and set(key, value). Each key's value is a primitive, such as a string (i.e., character array) or integer. For the SET operation, the database stores each value exactly as is. For the GET operation, the database returns the value as is, deferring to the application to interpret the value's format. When setting a value with a key that is already in the database, the SET operation doesn't update an existing record; it replaces any existing record.

Many *Key-Value Database* implementations store each value as more of a document that has structure. The *Key-Value Database* may support value types such as string and binary, which are just CLOB and BLOB; other primitive types such as number, Boolean, and null; collection types like list, set, and map; and JSON, which is a string or CLOB that the database parses as a document. Databases that recognize these value types typically enable them to be indexed and enable applications to query on the values, which gives the database some *Document Database* functionality.

Key-Value Databases excel at looking up data records by their keys. They are schemaless and handle unstructured data, storing it as is and returning it as is. This simple approach means they are usually the most scalable and best-performing type of database.

Most *Key-Value Databases* make querying by value either impossible or quite slow. Every value within a partition needs a unique key; if two values in the same partition inadvertently use the same key, the last one replaces the one that was already in the database.

If an application caches data using a Document Database (339), the performance may be significantly worse than it would be with a *Key-Value Database*. That is because *Document Databases* optimize for more complex cases such as searching by the contents of the documents stored.

Sometimes an application stores its data in a Relational Database (334) when it should instead use a *Key-Value Database*. For example, a Java enterprise application may persist its domain objects in a *Relational Database*, presumably storing the objects as relational data. Surprisingly, the persistence code in many of these applications serializes the objects and stores the data as BLOBs. This occurs as the result of a team throwing up their hands at the complexity of trying to map their domain objects into relational tables and columns. BLOBs in a *Relational Database* have many disadvantages: the database cannot query the data because it has no columns, and the database manages such huge blocks of data inefficiently. Worse, if improvements to the code change the object's structure, the existing data may no longer be readable because the persistence code cannot deserialize it. This is a scenario where a *Key-Value Database* would work much better.

There are multiple types of databases—the trick is to use the best tool for the job. A *Key-Value Database* is not always the best option. Rather than serializing Java objects, the persistence code may be able to use a database more efficiently by serializing the objects as JSON data rather than binary data and storing the JSON documents in a document database. When an application wants to search for data, a *Key-Value Database* is typically suboptimal if not useless, so the application should store its data in a *Relational Database* or *Document Database*.

An application using a *Key-Value Database* should use it to store a single Data Module (367) and use Polyglot Persistence (375) to store modules of key-value data in *Key-Value Databases* and modules of other data formats in other types of databases.

A *Key-Value Database* should be hosted by the cloud platform as a Database-as-a-Service (379). Most public cloud platforms host multiple key-value DBaaSs.

Examples

Here are some common *Key-Value Database* products and public cloud platform services, as well as a domain-specific example for caching session data.

Key-Value Database products, projects, and services

These products and open source projects implement *Key-Value Databases*:

Memcached (https://oreil.ly/SRkeT)
> A free, open source, in-memory *Key-Value Database* that is specifically targeted at caching. It is very performant and is often used for storing session state and web page caches.

Redis (https://oreil.ly/rMpK3)
> A source-available, in-memory *Key-Value Database* but one that is more generally usable for a variety of use cases. It has a more extensive API than the simple get-and-put semantics of Memcached, which makes it more useful as a general-purpose NoSQL database. As a result, it has become one of the most commonly used NoSQL databases. Valkey (*https://oreil.ly/C7wAV*) is a fully open source fork of Redis that was started in 2024 when the Redis license changed from open source.

Riak KV (https://oreil.ly/C6UW8)
> A *Key-Value Database* built on a general-purpose, open source distributed systems framework, Riak Core. Riak is a formerly commercial product that went entirely open source in 2017. Other extensions of the Riak Core include Riak CS (Cloud Storage) and Riak TS (Time Series), demonstrating that it is possible to build multiple types of application databases on the same underlying distributed systems model.

Ehcache (https://oreil.ly/wchQq)
> An open source Java distributed cache project that is based on *Key-Value Database* functionality.

These cloud platform services provide *Key-Value Databases* (DBaaSs):

Amazon DynamoDB (https://oreil.ly/C3rux)
> Supports both the key-value model and the document model

Google Cloud Bigtable (https://oreil.ly/u5nlt)
> A *Key-Value Database* that is also a wide-column database (i.e., a Columnar Database (357)), meaning that it supports very wide tables with tens of thousands of columns

Azure Cosmos DB (https://oreil.ly/Csjbs)
> Provides *Key-Value Database* functionality.

While all *Key-Value Database* products function in the same way, they are optimized for different usecases. So you need to carefully consider your usecase when selecting a product.

Session Data and Key-Value Databases

As briefly described, a simple example of the use of *Key-Value Databases* that is very common is managing HTTP session data. We will use Java as an example; however, most web frameworks in other languages operate similarly. Jakarta Enterprise Edition (*https://oreil.ly/QX26_*) defines the HttpSession object as part of its servlet framework for building Web Form Applications (414).

This interface serves as a key-value lookup mechanism for managing the user's state data (which can be literally anything but often represents selections the user has made on previous pages in a navigation). There are two approaches for storing HttpSession objects: in the JVMs and in a database.

The default implementation of most application servers stores the HttpSession objects in an in-memory cache inside each web container's JVM. Each user is identified by a unique value, the JSESSIONID, that is encoded either directly in the URL of the request or (more commonly) in a cookie that is stored on the user's browser. In this cache, the key is the JSESSIONID, and the value is the user's session data.

This solution, while very simple, has a lot of downsides. The first is that if the JVM crashes, all of the customer records stored in that in-memory cache are lost. The second is that a complex routing solution (i.e., sticky sessions) is needed to ensure that user requests are always routed to the JVM that holds the entries for that particular user. This solution must be implemented in front of the JVMs being used as application servers, often in a frontend proxy like NGINX. All of this adds up to complexity that developers do not want.

That is why many teams have turned to using *Key-Value Databases* like Redis or Memcached to instead store HttpSession data. The match between session data and a key-value store is so straightforward that it's hard to imagine teams choosing nearly any other solution once they begin using them together. One common combination for users of the Tomcat server is to use Redis along with the open source Redisson (*https://oreil.ly/cYjxm*) library for using Redis as the backing store for HttpSessions. Likewise, Spring Boot (*https://oreil.ly/SJ4s2*) users will use Spring Session to connect to Redis as a backing store. Commercial application servers like IBM's WebSphere Liberty (*https://oreil.ly/pXQ_5*) support the same type of functionality as well.

Graph Database

You are writing a Cloud Application (6) or Microservice (119) structured with a Cloud-Native Architecture (58) and are selecting an Application Database (329) for your application to use to persist its domain data.

How can an application most efficiently store and retrieve interrelated data entities by navigating their relationships?

When we think of the structure of data, there are some obvious ways of representing data that seem "natural." Perhaps the most straightforward is with key-value data, where an application performs a lookup on a single field value to find another field value, or in document data, where an application stores data that reflects the way that people still tend to think in terms of separate pieces of paper, such as forms.

But there's a more challenging complex data type that we have to think about—and that is the data model, consisting not only of a simple data structure, like the attributes for a person, but also the very complex ways in which that person relates to other people and other entities like employers, property, and community organizations. A single person can belong to multiple different types of relationships:

- A `Person` relates to the other `Persons` in their family and has relationships with those family members.

- A `Person` relates to the people they work with and may have friendships and relationships outside of a company hierarchy—in other words, all of an employee's friends and coworkers may not report to the same boss.

- A `Person` has friends that they may know through multiple different venues, such as social clubs, their neighborhood, school, etc.

What this amounts to is that while it may be possible to represent a `Person` as a simple data structure, mapping out their social networks gets complicated. The data model starts adding more and more attributes to try to represent all of the relationships to other people. The problem is that all of these relationships are similar in some ways but different in others. A cousin can also be a friend, or a coworker could be someone you went to school with. Managing when a `Person` is removed from one subnetwork or added to another becomes complex. What is needed is a simple way to represent these different networks such that an application can easily navigate a particular network when it is focused on one particular type of relationship but that easily enables it to also explore how these relationships intersect.

Therefore,

Model and navigate relationships among entities with a *Graph Database*, which represents relationships as a mathematical graph with nodes (entities) and edges (relationships between nodes).

A *Graph Database* is a kind of NoSQL database and is schemaless, so it can store data without a predefined schema, simply by storing data the way the application delivers it. *Graph Databases* excel at modeling domain entities connected to one another by numerous relationships. This capability simplifies implementing application functionality to determine the other entities that one entity is related to and then follow the relationships of interest to explore those related entities. Each entity is like a document in a Document Database (339), often represented externally as a JSON document, but a *Graph Database* gives much better support for modeling the entities' relationships and navigating to other entities via their relationships. A *Graph Database* makes navigation much more efficient than querying. It is typically a Replicated Database (316) that runs in multiple nodes and replicates each entity across multiple nodes.

Figure 7-19 shows a *Graph Database* running in three database nodes that store six different entities—three people, two books, and a paper—and the relationships between the entities. What this doesn't show is that the database typically replicates each entity and distributes the replicas across its nodes. The database can route each client request to any of its nodes. If a node receives a request for an entity it does not store, it reroutes the request to another node that does store the entity.

Graph data fits the structure of an entity-relationship-attribute (ERA) model. An entity is an object in a domain. Its attributes are properties about the entity, similar to the columns in a table or the fields in a document. Its relationships point to other relevant entities.

A *Graph Database* solves several types of problems more easily than comparable database types. For example, consider if an application needs to do any of the following:

Navigate deep hierarchies
    An application may have the functionality to look for relationships in a very large family tree. For example, the University of Oxford has assembled the largest ever human family tree (*https://oreil.ly/4201T*), one that contains 27 million individuals, both living and dead, in order to perform genetic research. Navigating this structure to track small genetic changes across tens of thousands of individuals spanning dozens of generations requires search optimizations that are simply not feasible in other database types like *Document* or *Key-Value Databases*.

Find hidden connections between distant items
    This is where *Graph Databases* become helpful for optimization problems. For example, a transport network might have a bottleneck like a train derailment

due to a washed-out bridge. To find another way around, a graph of data may show that two distant cities are connected directly through a different type of transport link (like a ship route) that ordinarily may not be an option, but may end up saving time in this situation. A similar example is graph theory's traveling salesman problem (TSP), which searches for the shortest overall route through several geographically disbursed points.

Investigate interrelationships between items

This is the largest set of potential cases where *Graph Databases* shine. For example, navigating the complex web of websites a person visits is absolutely critical to making recommendations from retail websites based on shared interests, common attributes, and similarities.

Graph Databases make these types of problems easier, simpler, and faster to solve.

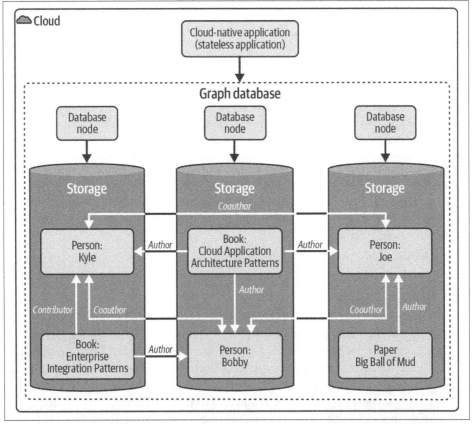

Figure 7-19. Graph Database

While *Graph Databases* do have advantages, they also have somewhat significant drawbacks. The first is difficulty finding developers with the skills to use these databases. *Graph Databases* are not as widely used as Relational Databases (334), or even Document Databases (339) or Key-Value Databases (345), so developers have less experience using them. What's more, there is not a single dominant *Graph Database*, nor is there a commercial product or an open source project. That means that the user community of each database product is somewhat small and may make it difficult to find skills or obtain answers when problems occur.

Another issue with *Graph Databases* is that there is not yet an accepted standard for graph queries such as SQL for *Relational Databases*. As a result, several query languages are available. For example, both Neptune and Cosmos support both Gremlin and SPARQL, while Neo4J supports the Cypher query language. This lack of standardization for the client API creates challenges when moving applications from one database to another, as well as for developers learning to write code that uses *Graph Databases*.

There are also issues with the nature of graph data, which impact *Graph Databases* managing that data. For example, bulk updates are generally complex in a *Graph Database*, since each entity must be updated separately, and updating an entity also involves updating all the relationships to that entity. So, for example, if a company was splitting up, to split a company directory built in a graph database, the process would have to address each employee individually and re-create the new relationships separately. That can be slow and computationally expensive.

Graph Databases naturally store data consisting of interrelated entities and simplify an application's ability to navigate those relationships.

However, *Graph Database* products are not widely used, so finding experienced developers is difficult. The querying API is not standardized, leading to vendor lock-in for applications using a particular database. Also, graph data is complex. Graph databases help handle the complexity, but management can still be difficult.

There are multiple types of databases; the trick is to use the best tool for the job. A *Graph Database* is not always the best option. Entity data with few relationships can probably be managed more easily in a Relational Database (334) or Document Database (339), especially for applications to search the data. If the entities are unrelated, they can be stored in a Key-Value Database (345).

An application using a *Graph Database* should use it to store a single Data Module (367) and use Polyglot Persistence (375) to store modules of graph data in *Graph Databases* and modules of other data formats in other types of databases.

A *Graph Database* should be hosted by the cloud platform as a Database-as-a-Service (379). Some public cloud platforms host graph DBaaSs.

Examples

Here are some common *Graph Database* products and public cloud platform services, as well as a domain-specific example implementing a recommendation engine.

Graph Database projects, products, and services

There are several *Graph Databases* in common use on the cloud:

JanusGraph (https://oreil.ly/gvh7o)
> A Linux Foundation project, this is a scalable graph database optimized for storing and querying graphs.

Neo4j Graph Database (https://oreil.ly/MqvY3)
> A scalable, open source graph database that is available as the Neo4j Aura cloud service.

Apache TinkerPop (https://oreil.ly/nU3EO)
> A framework for graph databases that incorporates the Gremlin query language.

Azure Cosmos DB (https://oreil.ly/7cZ3R)
> On Microsoft Azure, this is a multimodal database that includes graph database functionality that supports the Apache Gremlin API by incorporating most Apache TinkerPop functionality.

Amazon Neptune (https://oreil.ly/MaThy)
> On Amazon Web Services (AWS), this is a fully managed *Graph Database* service.

There are not as many choices on each platform for *Graph Databases* as there are for other *Application Databases*. This means that your application might need internal code to address features that are not available on the platform databases.

Ecommerce Product Recommendations and Graph Databases

Users of ecommerce sites are probably familiar with the section below the particular item you are browsing titled "similar items" or "purchased together with." This is the result of a product recommender system, and once you start looking for them, you will find them everywhere. Amazon and other shopping websites typically recommend other products that fit well with this product. A recommender system is famously part of Netflix, which held annual contests to improve its recommendation algorithms. It is the basis of systems like Spotify, which is essentially only a big recommendation engine.

But what is a recommendation engine? At its heart, it's an exercise in data science and linear algebra. It usually comes down to constructing vectors for which you can calculate cosine similarity showing how close two or more items are to each other in that vector space. But how do you even construct those vectors? Where do the numbers in this data science exercise come from? That's where a *Graph Database* comes in and excels.

In a common implementation, whenever a user interacts with a system—purchasing a product, filling a cart, or even browsing a page—the system records that interaction as nodes and edges in a *Graph Database*. So if a user buys two products, edges are created between the user node and the product nodes. That could allow your analytics system to traverse those edges later and find that the user had purchased the two products, and use that information to recommend the second product to someone who is browsing the first.

More accurately, the recommendation system would construct vectors from the records of the interactions of hundreds or thousands of users, each adding their own information to strengthen specific connections between the nodes (incrementing use counts), and then use the magic of linear algebra to find those products for which the connections are the strongest.

When you throw in individual user interactions and their own preferences, this can give you highly accurate and personalized recommendations.

Columnar Database

You are writing a Cloud Application (6) or Microservice (119) structured with a Cloud-Native Architecture (58) and are selecting an Application Database (329) for your application to use to persist its domain data.

How can an application most efficiently store data for performing analytics, such as in a data warehouse?

Often an application needs to store data that it uses to calculate statistics or perform *Aggregate* queries. This is especially common in Microservices Architecture (Chapter 4) when one *Microservice* pulls together data from several *Microservices* to perform queries or *Aggregate* data.

An interactive user application requires online transaction processing (OLTP), and Relational Databases (334) perform OLTP well. A user fills out a form, and the database writes the fields from the form to a database table. As multiple users also fill out that form, each user's answers are written to a row in the table using a transaction for each user. The answers are all the same format because they all come from the same form, so the database table's strongly typed schema handles it well. When a user wants to see the form with the data they previously filled out, that database read is a transaction. The application can use a couple of transactions to show the user their data, let the user edit the data, and commit the changes. Similarly, for data that is not as well structured, a Document Database (339) can perform transactions on individual documents.

In these OLTP scenarios, a read or write transaction involves an entire table row, using all of the data in that record. The application can query to find the rows that it needs, then reads or updates all of the data in those rows. *Relational Databases* do this well because they are optimized to manage data as complete table rows. OLTP requires both inserting data into the database as well as reading it back out again. *Relational Databases* tend to be equally good at both, providing reasonable performance.

Data analytics requires online analytical processing (OLAP). When a *Relational Database* tries to perform OLAP, it becomes a performance bottleneck, limiting how much data can be processed quickly and not scaling well even with additional hardware. Data analytics requires sorting through large amounts of data and finding interesting data quickly. A *Relational Database* tends to approach the problem by reading all of the data from disk and iterating through it linearly, which doesn't scale well. Analytics often is not interested in much of the data in a record, focusing more on knowing which records or how many total match a search. Analytics needs a database that can query data as efficiently as possible, even if that hurts the performance of inserting and updating data. While an OLTP database can efficiently insert and update individual records, this is uncommon in OLAP databases. An analytics database often loads data in bulk, writing the data in large batches, not one record at a time as with OLTP. Analytics data is typically loaded once and then read repeatedly, as the data is analyzed and reanalyzed for different purposes.

Analytics data often isn't as well-structured as OLTP data. The data to be analyzed can be gathered from multiple places that collect varying details about each record. Force-fitting the semi-structured data into a strongly typed schema will at best make the database table sparsely populated and at worst force the application to throw away data fields that don't fit into the schema.

OLAP needs a database optimized for reading and sorting through large amounts of data, even if that means its performance suffers when writing individual records, and that can still organize semi-structured data for efficient querying.

Therefore,

Store the data for an application that performs analytics in a *Columnar Database*, a database optimized to find records quickly, even in semi-structured data.

A *Columnar Database* is often described as NoSQL but more precisely is schemaless or wide-column but still based on tables. *Columnar Databases* support very rapid SQL-style querying of large amounts of semi-structured data, rows of data that the database organizes into columns. It is typically a Replicated Database (316) that runs in multiple nodes, storing its data in one or more keyspaces that it replicates across multiple nodes.

Figure 7-20 shows a *Columnar Database* running in three database nodes that store records in three keyspaces with two replicas of each keyspace. The database can route each client request to any of its nodes. If a node receives a request for a keyspace it does not store, it reroutes the request to another node that does store the keyspace.

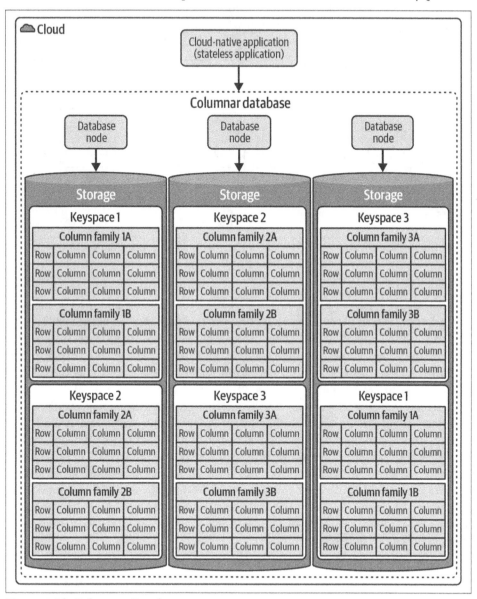

Figure 7-20. Columnar Database

True to its name, a *Columnar Database* stores data not in rows but in columns. For example, consider a table that stores the first names, last names, and zip codes for a set of customers. A standard *Relational Database* would store each row separately as a record written to disk, the data for one row all together on disk, followed by another. Instead, a *Columnar Database* stores each column separately as a record written to disk, the data for one column with the values for all rows all together on disk, followed by another. Figure 7-21 shows the difference.

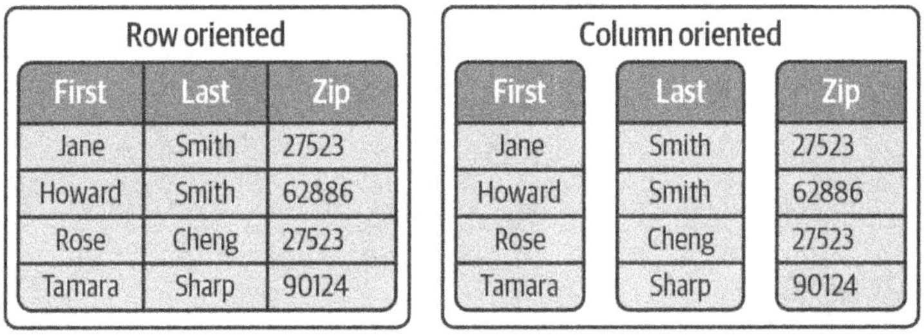

Row oriented			Column oriented		
First	Last	Zip	First	Last	Zip
Jane	Smith	27523	Jane	Smith	27523
Howard	Smith	62886	Howard	Smith	62886
Rose	Cheng	27523	Rose	Cheng	27523
Tamara	Sharp	90124	Tamara	Sharp	90124

Figure 7-21. Column orientation

This differentiation may seem trivial, but when querying large data sets to look for certain column values, this arrangement of the data makes the database much more efficient.

A major disadvantage of a *Columnar Database* is that updates and inserts may take much longer than in other types of application databases. An application still inserts data records by row, but the database does not insert a single row. Instead, the database must break the row into columns and insert its values into each of the columns, writing the new column data to the same area of the disk as the existing column data to keep it all contiguous. OLTP applications perform a lot of inserts of individual records and therefore will work better with a *Relational Database* or a *Document Database*. Once an OLAP application inserts or updates data, it then reads it many times, making read efficiency a higher impact than write efficiency. When an OLAP application does insert records, it tends to load the records in bulk, so the database can perform the insert overhead once for all of the records. When data is needed for both OLTP for user interactions and OLAP for analytics, an application can store it twice in two different databases, where the application continuously updates the OLTP database but queues the updates for the OLAP database to perform them in bulk as a batch job.

Understanding how a *Columnar Database* is able to query data so much more efficiently than a *Relational Databases* requires understanding how the *Columnar Database* is implemented and how it organizes its data. A *Columnar Database* groups entities that will be searched together, splits up rows to store the data by column, skips empty column values, and compresses data for reading from disk faster.

A common *Columnar Database* implementation groups its data into keyspaces containing column families. A column family stores records that externally seem like rows of data with a UID for the record and a tag on each column value that specifies the column. The column tags enable records in the same column family to specify different columns. This makes each column family act somewhat like a *Relational Database* table and each keyspace act like a schema (i.e., a collection of tables).

Figure 7-22 shows a keyspace with column families for two different entity types. The database performs each search in a column family, essentially by retrieving a column in that column family, so the application should put data that should be searched together in the same column family. Each record in a column family needs a UID, so if two records somehow have the same UID, they need to be put into two different column families.

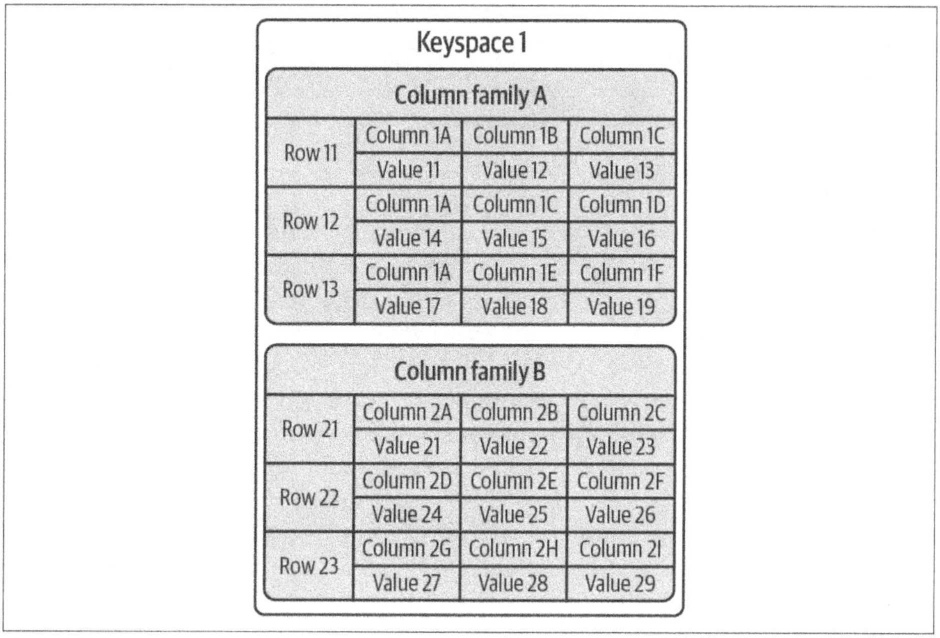

Figure 7-22. Columnar Database keyspaces

Although all of an application's data can be stored in a single column family, a good approach typically is to store each type of entity in its own column family, such as customers in one column family and products in another, which enables the entity types to be searched separately.

While an application still externally inserts data records by row, the database internally stores the data by columns, as shown in Figure 7-23. The database can more efficiently read a set of column values from one contiguous section of disk and reads only the data for that column, making the amount of disk to be read minimal and the amount of RAM needed to load the data smaller. Then the database can search that smaller amount of RAM more efficiently to develop statistics about the data. Many OLAP use cases are multidimensional, with each dimension being a column. Arranging the data by columns enables the database to read only the data in the dimensions' columns and then quickly find their intersection.

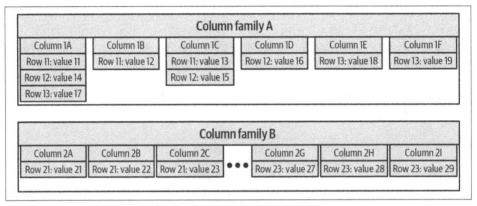

Figure 7-23. Columnar Database columns

For an example of how storing data by column makes querying more efficient, consider looking up how many customers live in a particular zip code. A *Relational Database* would need to iterate through all of the customer records, filtering for the ones with the particular zip code, and then would return all of the data for all of those records just to compute a count of the number of records. Even by optimizing the database with indexing and performing the count in the database instead of the application, a *Relational Database* cannot perform this search as efficiently as a *Columnar Database*. A *Columnar Database* instead would store a column of zip codes and could quickly find how many of those match the particular zip code. It might even optimize the column to list each unique zip code once and, for each unique zip code, list the rows with that zip code, which makes searching for a particular zip code as instantaneous as finding that one value from that one column.

A *Columnar Database* can compress data, which enables it to perform queries even faster. Compressing the data stores it using less disk space, which makes it faster to read and allows more data to be loaded into the same amount of RAM. To accomplish this compression, rather than storing all rows in a column, the database stores only the rows that have values for that column, as shown in Figure 7-23. The shorter the column, the more compact its data is, with no loss of data. For example, the zip code column does not store data for all customers it only stores data for customers with zip codes, making it more compact. If a customer does not include a zip code, its data is stored in other columns but not in the zip code column. Columns are also more efficient to store because all of the values in a column have the same type so the database can store them with no wasted disk space. As mentioned earlier, the database can compress the column further by listing each unique column value only once and then listing the IDs for the customers with that value, which for a lengthy column value saves more disk space as well as makes a query for that value more direct.

While the structure of data in a *Columnar Database* is more flexible and can seem semi-structured compared to the well-structured data in a *Relational Database, Columnar Database* data still needs structure. A *Columnar Database* can work efficiently as a wide-column database, storing records where most of the columns are blank. In a *Relational Database*, all of the missing values would produce very sparsely populated tables, as shown in Figure 7-24.

Column family A as a table						
	Column 1A	Column 1B	Column 1C	Column 1D	Column 1E	Column 1F
Row 11	Value 11	Value 12	Value 13			
Row 12	Value 14		Value 15	Value 16		
Row 13	Value 17				Value 18	Value 19

Column family B as a table									
	Column 2A	Column 2B	Column 2C	Column 2D	Column 2E	Column 2F	Column 2G	Column 2H	Column 2I
Row 21	Value 21	Value 22	Value 23						
Row 22				Value 24	Value 25	Value 26			
Row 23							Value 27	Value 28	Value 29

Figure 7-24. Columnar Database column families as tables

Since a *Columnar Database* stores only the columns that have values, it stores the data with high density. Yet while columns can vary between records, the data needs enough structure that it can be searched effectively, which means the records require the important columns that the application will search. The *Columnar Database* doesn't force two records with the same data type to store both in the same column, but if they have different column names, they will be very difficult to search. When data has very little structure, where every record has different columns, the database will store that data in a huge range of columns with very few rows per column, which will be very difficult to search. For example, Column Family B in Figure 7-24 will be very difficult to search effectively since none of the rows have the same column, so any column value matches at most one row.

Although a *Columnar Database* is often characterized as a NoSQL database, that perspective is misleading. A *Columnar Database* can appear somewhat schemaless because it can act as a wide-column database where each record populates only some columns. Yet it still has a schema, albeit not a predefined fixed schema but one the database determines dynamically to include numerous columns as needed.

Whereas NoSQL *Document Databases* and *Key-Value Databases* work well with semi-structured and unstructured data, a *Columnar Database* needs data to have enough structure that it can be queried effectively. Many *Columnar Databases* store their data in *Relational Databases*, which are definitely not NoSQL. And unlike a NoSQL database, many *Columnar Databases* can still be queried with SQL and can be ACID compliant—even though their inserts are slow, they are consistent. In this situation, you can think of a *Columnar Database* as an SQL database with a dynamic wide-column schema.

A *Columnar Database* manages data for OLAP, optimizing data storage for query efficiency at the expense of performance for inserting and updating data. It organizes data records into columns to make it more efficient to query. It can handle semi-structured data, although the data has to be structured well enough for efficient querying.

Analytics focuses on finding a small amount of interesting data within a large amount of data. *Columnar Databases* make it possible to do this much more efficiently.

However there are some challenges, such as limited suitability for transactional workloads, higher overhead for writing data, and complexity in handling joins. Also, they can be resource intensive for small queries with increased complexity for certain operations. Finally, there can be a learning curve along with scalability and concurrency challenges.

For OLTP, use a Relational Database (334) or Document Database (339).

Each keyspace in a *Columnar Database* is a Data Module (367). Use Polyglot Persistence (375) to store *Data Modules* for OLAP in a columnar database and *Data Modules* for OLTP in relational and document databases.

A *Columnar Database* should be hosted by the cloud platform as a Database-as-a-Service (379). Most public cloud platforms host at least one columnar DBaaS.

Examples

Here are some common examples of *Columnar Database* products and public cloud platform services, as well as a domain-specific example implementing marketing using an airline application.

Columnar Database products, projects, and services

These products and open source projects implement *Columnar Databases*:

Apache HBase (https://oreil.ly/STfSV)
> An open source, column-oriented, distributed, versioned, non-relational NoSQL database modeled after Google's Bigtable. Contributed by Yahoo as part of Hadoop, HBase stores its data in the Apache Hadoop Distributed File System (HDFS) or Amazon's Simple Storage Service (S3) and is designed to support real-time read and write access to large data sets.

Apache Cassandra (https://oreil.ly/PeBk1)
> A distributed NoSQL database contributed by Facebook that uses a column-oriented storage model and is designed to handle large amounts of unstructured or semi-structured data.

ScyllaDB (https://oreil.ly/6Nxpu)
> An open source wide-column database designed to be API compatible with Apache Cassandra while offering significantly higher throughput and lower latency.

IBM Db2 Warehouse (https://oreil.ly/sbp0m)
> A column-organized data warehouse with in-memory processing designed for complex analytics and extreme concurrency.

These cloud platform services provide *Columnar Databases* (DBaaSs):

IBM Db2 Warehouse on Cloud (https://oreil.ly/pUKH7)
> Supports columnar storage and is hosted on IBM Cloud using IBM Cloud Object Storage and on AWS using Amazon Elastic Block Store (EBS) with Amazon Elastic File System (EFS).

Google Cloud Bigtable (https://oreil.ly/_74Gp)
> A hosted distributed NoSQL HBase–compatible database that runs on top of Google File System (GFS), is designed to support real-time read and write access to large data sets, and is integrated with the Google Cloud Data Platform. Google describes it as "a sparse, distributed, persistent multidimensional sorted map."

Amazon Redshift (https://oreil.ly/S053Q)
> A hosted petabyte-scale massively parallel processing (MPP) cloud data warehouse service with columnar storage designed to handle large-scale, high-performance data storage and analysis needs for applications on AWS.

Amazon Keyspaces (https://oreil.ly/rTd9H)
> A hosted, scalable, and highly available database service that supports the Cassandra Query Language (CQL) API.

Azure HDInsight HBase (https://oreil.ly/t5a_N)
> Apache HBase hosted in a managed cluster using Azure Storage.

When choosing a *Columnar Database*, an important factor is compatibility with other parts of your analytics toolkit. You want to ensure, for instance, that your reporting tools are compatible with your *Columnar Database* when making your product selection.

Airline marketing example and Columnar Databases

Marketers often want to target a promotional offer to existing customers who are likely to be interested. To do so, they search through a sea of historical data about lots of customers' purchases to look for activities similar to the new offer, reasoning that customers who have made purchases like this in the past may be interested in doing so again. This searching through historical data and looking for interesting patterns is data analytics, and *Columnar Databases* are especially good at performing OLAP. Other types of databases are tuned for OLTP, which provide poor performance for analytics, but *Columnar Databases* are optimized for analytics to provide much better performance.

For example, let's consider an airline that is running a route to San Francisco from Chicago. To drum up more business for this route, a marketer with the airline may wish to find customers who might be interested in this route and offer them a special promotion. To find these customers, the marketer runs a query on the airline's historical data along the lines of "Find all frequent fliers who purchased flights leaving Chicago where the yearly spend was over $100,000 in the last year." This is a very complex query: it needs to filter for customers who are frequent fliers, have departed from Chicago, have spent a lot on flights, and have done so in a limited time frame. A *Relational Database* might contain the data for all customer flights flown in the past several years, and running SQL across that much data would require a lot of I/O that reads a huge amount of disk. The data needs to be filtered in multiple independent ways—frequent fliers, Chicago departures, high spenders, recent activity—and each filtering process will consume considerable memory and CPU. Ultimately, the filtering will throw away data that never needed to be read in the first place. When the querying finally produces a list, the marketer may find it contains too many names or too few, necessitating adjusting the query and running it all over again!

A *Columnar Database* is optimized to run multidimensional queries across huge sets of data and read only the data that is needed. If the data for all flights flown in the past few years is stored in a columnar database, the database will perform this marketing search much better. It will have a much easier time producing a list of customer IDs for frequent fliers, for fliers with Chicago departures, and for fliers who are high spenders based only on their activity for the past year, than producing the intersection for all three. Using a columnar database, the marketer will get their results much faster, placing much less load on the infrastructure because it reads much less data from the disk—only the customer IDs from the desired columns.

They can look at the number of customer IDs and judge whether that's a meaningful number without reading all of the customer records. They can more quickly adjust their query to find a meaningful list, even if that means running queries multiple times to find one that works best.

With that list of customers who are likely to be interested, the marketer can then recommend to those fliers that a vacation in San Francisco would be a great idea!

Data Module

You're developing an application with a Cloud-Native Architecture (58) that has domain data and needs to persist it. Perhaps you're developing a Self-Managed Data Store (154) for a Microservice (119).

How can I align my data model with my application model so that both are easier to maintain and can evolve quickly?

An enterprise application often stores all of its data in a single large *Relational Database*. Furthermore, in many enterprises, the majority of the enterprise applications share one huge set of data stored in one or a few enterprise databases of record. Even when an application has some data that none of the others will use, it stores that data in the same enterprise databases of record because that's where all of the applications store all of their data.

An enterprise database of record is difficult to maintain. No one application is responsible for any set of data; it is shared by many applications, and they are all responsible for it. Some of it may not even be used anymore—the applications that once used it have changed, yet it still remains in storage. If one application corrupts the data, all of the other applications that use the data are adversely affected, all assuming the data is valid and having no way to determine which application introduced the problem. Once data is stored in a certain schema, that schema cannot be changed because multiple applications share the data, and they would all need to be updated to the new schema at the same time that the database is updated. Thus, an enterprise database of record becomes an ever-growing warehouse of data, much of which is never used, stored in a schema that may no longer be ideal and that the enterprise has no ability to improve.

Data is often convenient to store in an enterprise database so that any data can be referenced and connected to any other data. Referencing data in separate databases is difficult, but doing so in the same database is easy, and the database can maintain referential integrity. Yet the more connected data is, the more difficult it is to change. Schema is already difficult to change in a shared database. Connections between sets of data create dependencies such that changes to some of the data, even without changing the schema, impact other data such that it may also need to be updated.

Large sets of interconnected data make the data more difficult to maintain and much slower to evolve.

Therefore,

Divide the application's total set of data into *Data Modules*, sets of data with no or limited dependencies with one another, and store each in its own database or schema.

Data Modules divide a large set of data into smaller sets of data. The data inside a module is closely related, whereas the data in one module is more loosely related to the data in another module. While one database can store multiple modules, to maintain their independence, each module should be stored in its own database (aka schema or set of tables). Each database can be hosted in its own database server, but it can be more efficient to consolidate multiple databases into one database server.

Figure 7-25 shows the set of data for an application divided into four modules. Each module includes multiple data types that together implement an encapsulated unit of data. The data in one module can reference the data in another module, but most of the references are within a module with relatively few references between modules.

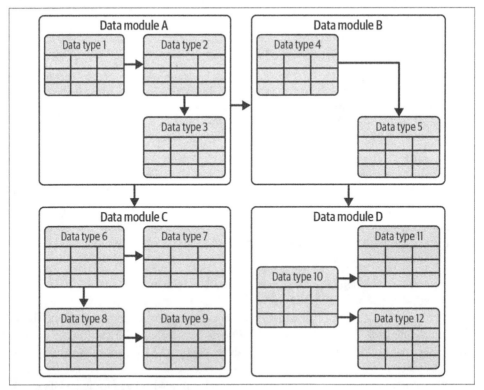

Figure 7-25. Data Module

Data Module is the data version of the Modular Monolith (29) and Distributed Architecture (38) patterns for applications. Just as an application is more difficult to maintain as a Big Ball of Mud (22), dividing data into modules and storing them in separate databases makes the data easier to maintain.

Applications and modules should connect only to the databases with the *Data Modules* that the code uses. Each application in an enterprise should not connect to all of the *Data Module* databases in the enterprise; they should only connect to the ones whose data it uses. This approach leads to fewer applications connecting to a given module's database, making that data easier to maintain and evolve. For applications with a *Modular Monolith* architecture or *Distributed Architecture*, each module should only connect to the databases of the data it uses.

The modularity of the data should reflect the modularity of the application so that each application module typically uses a single data module. This alignment between application modules and *Data Modules* becomes especially apparent in an application with a *Microservices* architecture. Each *Microservice* manages its own data, which is a data module, and stores it in its own Self-Managed Data Store (154), which is the database that hosts the *Data Module*. Each *Microservice* has its own database, as shown in Figure 7-26.

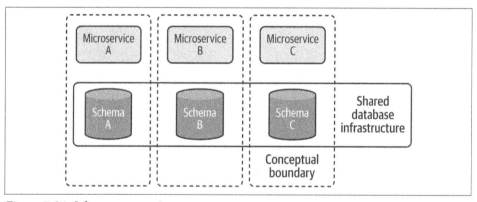

Figure 7-26. Schema per service

Figure 7-26 also shows that the databases for multiple *Microservices* can all be hosted in a single database server. A single server enables multiple *Data Module* databases to share the server's infrastructure resources, administration effort, and licensing costs. Each *Microservice* owns its data and stores it in a separate *Data Module* it controls, yet shares the overhead of the database server. Each *Microservice* owning its *Data Module* helps developers avoid coupling their microservices and the database (either intentionally or unintentionally). To enforce this, configure each *Microservice* so that it can connect only to its database, and vice versa.

A data model with a good design groups data into well-organized modules. At one extreme, every data type could be stored separately in its own module. At the other extreme, all data types could be stored in a single module. Here are some guidelines for figuring out a good set of modules:

- If one logical data type is normalized across multiple tables, those tables should all be hosted in the same module.
- If two data types need to be updated in a single transaction, they should be hosted in the same module.
- If two data types have the same lifecycle, such that when the record is created or deleted, records for the other data types should be created or deleted as well, put them in the same module.
- If two data types have very different lifecycles, such that one is still viable after another is deleted, host them in separate modules.
- If one data type is shared by two other data types, host them in separate modules.

For an enterprise with an enterprise database of record, refactoring the application into modules may be much easier than refactoring the database. The application has limited scope, whereas a database that is used by multiple applications cannot be changed without also changing all of the applications. These constraints often result in a set of *Microservices* that all share the single enterprise database just like the other enterprise applications do. Ideally, the *Microservices* should each have their own database, and they may be able to do that for new *Data Modules*, but when the existing data is all one big module, multiple *Microservices* will have to share it as is.

Data that will be modified together should be stored in the same data module so that it can be modified in the same transaction, but that creates a quandary when two different sets of data need to be modified together. Two different *Microservices* should store their data in separate *Data Modules* in separate databases, but then two sets cannot be modified in a single transaction. This situation may require connecting together the two *Microservices* through Service Orchestrator (160) or Event Choreography (246). Then when one *Microservice* updates its data, it invokes or notifies the other *Microservice* so that it can update its data as well.

Data Modules enable making data as modular as the application. Data that is updated together should go in the same module; data that is merely used together can go in separate modules. Each module should be hosted in a separate database, and multiple databases can be hosted in the same database server. Application modules should connect only to the data modules with the data they use.

An enterprise database of record can be much more difficult to refactor than an application. A database may be shared by multiple applications, which would require updating all of those applications when the database is updated. And data all stored in one database may be highly intertwined and difficult to separate.

Store each *Data Module* in its own separate database, which is an Application Database (329).

Since each application database is separate, data in two *Data Modules* do not have to be stored in the same type of application database. For each *Data Module*, use Polyglot Persistence (375) to choose the type of application database that works best for the data in that module.

Multiple *Data Module* databases can be stored in the same database server. On a cloud platform, that database server can be hosted as an SaaS service, an instance of a Database-as-a-Service (379).

Examples

Let's explore what different types of databases and database products call the construct for dividing the server into databases for separate *Data Modules*. Then we'll look at a simple example of an ecommerce application that uses multiple *Data Modules*. Finally, we'll consider a quick example of refactoring a monolith with one large database into Microservices (119) that each have their own database, all hosted in a single database server.

Database server terminology for hosting multiple databases

Most database servers have a construct for dividing the server into databases for separate *Data Modules*, but different types of databases and database products have different names for that construct. Many NoSQL databases advertise themselves as being "schemaless." but the general concept of a boundary of separation that a *Relational Database* schema provides is also provided in those databases. However, exactly what it is called differs from database to database and (unfortunately) is often tied up in the details of the clustering and management structure of each database. Nonetheless, we can point to a single concept in most Application Databases (329) that represents a distinct set of data and a description of the structure of that data that acts as a single Self-Managed Data Store (154) that the operations of a single *Domain Microservice* can operate on.

Here are a couple of different types of databases and the feature in each that represents a *Data Module*:

PostgreSQL schema (https://oreil.ly/didyW)

In PostgreSQL, a schema is a collection of tables that represents a single logical database. PostgreSQL also has a concept it calls a database, which is a collection of schemas tied together by a common set of users. Of these two concepts, schema aligns most closely with *Data Module*.

MongoDB collection (https://oreil.ly/ylxGo)

In MongoDB, a collection is a set of documents. That collection represents both a scope for searching documents and also the mechanism for finding the structure of the documents. Thus each *Data Module* stored in MongoDB should be stored in its own collection. MongoDB does not require that all the documents in a collection fit the same schema, but when a collection has schema validation enabled, MongoDB validates the format of data during updates and inserts it into that collection.

Apache Cassandra keyspace (https://oreil.ly/PeBk1)

In Cassandra, a keyspace is a collection of tables and types tied to a replication strategy. Store each Cassandra *Data Module* in a separate keyspace.

Neo4j Graph Database (https://oreil.ly/xx2ag)

In Neo4j Graph Database, the best equivalent to a *Data Module* is the database, which is a single connected graph made of nodes, their properties, and the relationships that tie them together. A single Neo4J installation can host multiple databases (at least in the Enterprise Edition of Neo4J).

Redis shard key (https://oreil.ly/5BkQ0)

Redis is the most difficult choice in which to implement this concept. In Redis, there is no single built-in concept within the database API that directly corresponds to a *Data Module*. Redis partitions by sharding the key, so to store data in *Data Module*, construct keys that include a unique identifier for each module.

Likewise, other database products and services have their constructs for organizing *Data Module* as sets of data.

Ecommerce application

An ecommerce application keeps track of customers who order products. Figure 7-27 shows a potential modularized *Data Module* for the application.

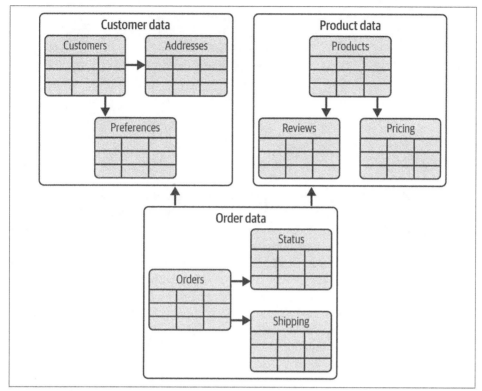

Figure 7-27. Ecommerce Data Modules

This *Data Module* separates the data into modules for customers, products, and orders. While customer seems like a single type of data, each customer also has closely related data, like their mailing addresses as well as the customer's preferences. Likewise, the data for a product also includes pricing data that tends to change independently of the product, and each product can have multiple customer reviews. Order brings these two units together, relating a customer to the products they ordered. A separate order data type enables one customer to have multiple orders and for multiple customers to order the same product. Even Order contains more than one type of data. Orders must track the status of the order as it shifts through its lifecycle and the details of the shipping process that also has its own lifecycle.

Refactoring a Big Ball of Mud and its database into Microservices with Data Modules

Let's say that you are currently using a single, large *Relational Database*. In that case, problems arise when you have two different *Microservices* that use the same information—the same tables within the same schema. The problem is that when everything references everything else, it is difficult to figure out how to split them apart. You see what we mean in Figure 7-28.

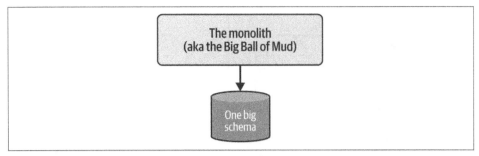

Figure 7-28. Monolithic Application working off One Big Schema

As you transition to *Microservices*, you must realize that there are many fewer problems caused by sharing hardware at the server level—in fact, when doing the initial refactoring to *Microservices*, there are a lot of advantages to keeping the new, more cleanly separated schemas in the same enterprise servers because companies usually already have teams and procedures in place for database backup and restore, and for database server updates—which the teams can take advantage of. In a sense, what the enterprise is providing through providing the hardware and software and management of an enterprise database is a limited version of a Database-as-a-Service (379). This especially fits well with an approach that begins with more cleanly separating parts of your monolith by functional area—starting out with a *Modular Monolith*, as shown in Figure 7-29.

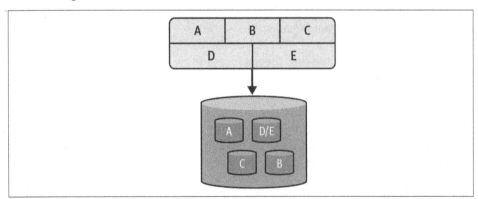

Figure 7-29. Schema per module

In this example (meant to show a refactoring work-in-progress). you can see how the database has been broken up by separating out tables corresponding to three new schemas (A, B, and C) that correspond to specific modules in the refactored application. Once they have been separated like this, they can be cleanly broken out into distinct *Microservices*. However, D and E are still being refactored—they still share a single schema with interconnected tables.

You can easily see how this is a step toward the desired end state of a set of microservices that each manage their own data.

Polyglot Persistence

You're designing an Application Database (329) for an application to store its Data Modules (367). There are many types of *Application Databases* to choose from.

How can an application store its *Data Modules* in the type of database that works best for the application's data structure and how it accesses the data?

When all of the applications in an enterprise share the same enterprise database of record, choosing what database to use is simple: always use the enterprise database of record; it's the only choice. Furthermore, selecting the database technology for hosting the database is simple because it is always a *Relational Database*. The only real decision is whether to use Oracle, Db2, or SQL Server, and usually the enterprise has already standardized on one of those long ago. So for any application with some data to store, the decision is simple: store the data in the enterprise database of record which is a *Relational Database* hosted in the database product the enterprise has always used.

Cloud and distributed architectures have motivated innovation in database technologies, resulting in numerous database products and open source projects to choose from, implementing several types of *Application Databases*. While an application has many databases to choose from, it's not clear which one it should choose. Relational Databases (334) have many advantages and disadvantages compared to Document Databases (339), while Key-Value Databases (345) excel at some tasks but not others, and so on for the other database types. An application can treat all of its data like table data, but that may not work very well for some of the data.

Even with multiple database types and database products to choose from, an enterprise may feel compelled to standardize on one product. One product shares licensing costs across more data and makes staffing projects easier when all of the developers have skills in the same database. Yet uniformity for licensing and developer skills may stifle the opportunity for each application to use the best database for its requirements.

An application works better if it is modularized into a Modular Monolith (29) or Distributed Architecture (38) such as Microservices (119). Likewise, the application will have more flexibility if it modularizes its data model into *Data Modules*. If the application has modularized its data, to standardize on one database, it needs to store all of its *Data Modules* in the same database, such as storing them all in a *Relational Database* or all of them in a document database. For an application with diverse sets of data, any database choice will work well for some data, but another database choice would work better for other data.

What is needed is a database that is optimized for each module in the data model. Yet no one database is going to work best for every module.

Therefore,

Use *Polyglot Persistence* to store each data module in the type of database that works best for that module.

Polyglot Persistence stores each *Data Module* not just in a separate database but also in a different type of database. Some modules may happen to use the same type of database, not because they all need to be stored in the same type but because that type is the best choice for each of them. If two application modules both use table data, they should store both of their *Data Modules* in *Relational Databases*. But if one of them uses semi-structured data, it should store its *Data Module* in a *Document Database* even though the other module uses a *Relational Database*. *Polyglot Persistence* gives this flexibility.

Figure 7-30 shows an application split into three modules that split its data into three *Data Modules*. While all three *Data Modules* could be stored in the same type of database, the application modules have different types of data that can be managed better by different database types, and *Polyglot Persistence* enables the design to store each *Data Module* in a different database type. The first module has well-structured data, so its *Data Module* works best in a *Relational Database*. The semi-structured data in the second application module means its module of data stores most easily in a *Document Database*. The third application module uses a *Key-Value Database* because its data is unstructured. With *Polyglot Persistence*, the design stores each *Data Module* in the database type that works best for that data.

Polyglot Persistence is the data version of Polyglot Development (146). Just as two different *Microservices* can be implemented in the same language but do not have to be, two *Data Modules* can be stored in the same database type but do not have to be. Polyglot creates the opportunity not only to implement two *Microservices* in two different languages but also to store two *Data Modules* in two different types of databases. Since two *Data Modules* should be stored in two separate databases anyway, when needed, those two databases can be of two different types.

Polyglot Persistence supports storing *Data Modules* in separate database servers but does not require it. When a designer chooses to store two *Data Modules* in the same database type, they can be hosted in two different databases within the same database server. To host two data modules in two different database types, the two databases must be hosted in two different database servers.

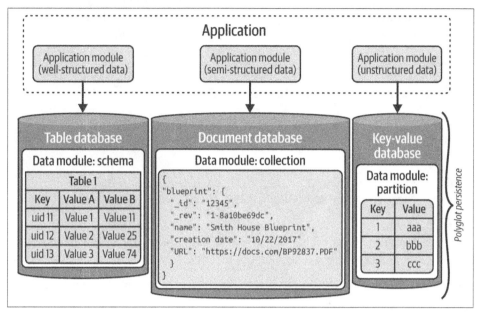

Figure 7-30. Polyglot Persistence

While providing multiple database types gives applications flexibility in persisting data, supporting them may introduce complexity. Each new type means hosting new database servers, and servers of different types mean that a team will need database administrators and application developers with skills to handle multiple types.

Polyglot Persistence enables storing each *Data Module* in a different database type but does not require it. It enables development teams to choose the best database type for each *Data Module*. *Data Modules* that store their data in the same database type can be hosted in the same database server.

Multiple database types mean hosting and administering multiple database servers of different types, skills, and costs that can increase application complexity.

Each database type is easier to host and administer if it is a Database-as-a-Service (379).

Example

Let's revisit our earlier example drawn from a simple ecommerce application consisting of a few easily understood Domain Microservices (130) and consider the different types of *Data Modules* and thus *Application Databases* that would be found in this application:

Catalog
> Enables the user to browse information on different products, see descriptions, view images of the item, and find out the price of the item.

Shopping Cart
> Enables the user to select items from the catalog and then store them for later purchase.

Product Recommendations
> Helps the user have a better shopping experience.

Order
> Once you have passed through the purchasing process, including arranging for payment and shipping, the order must be fulfilled

Each of these different *Microservices* requires different types of data, each of which may fit a different set of storage requirements, and thus a different type of Application Database (329), for example:

- The Catalog is a perfect example of document data. Each catalog entry is a mix of different fields with different types of data in each, and what's more, the set of information may differ from product to product. (For example, there are more things to describe in a complex item like a car than in a screwdriver.) A Document Database (339) enables flexible data formats, efficient searching, and support for returning multiple data types to the frontend as individual JSON documents.

- The Purchase button will need to take the shopper through multiple screens (get shipping address, get credit card information, confirm the purchase, etc.), which requires them to move back and forth between the screens. This session data can easily be cached in a Key-Value Database (345).

- Product Recommendations require fast navigation through lots of different types of data, stored multidimensionally: what the user has purchased before, what other users similar to them have purchased, their demographic data, etc. A Graph Database (352) is exactly the right solution for navigating this data.

- The Shopping Cart allows for multiple possible solutions, such as a *Document Database* or a *Key-Value Database*. Either way, the Shopping Cart data is its own Data Module (367) that separates the data for the Shopping Cart *Microservice* from the *Data Modules* for the catalog *Microservice* or purchase *Microservice*.

- Once an Order has been created from a Shopping Cart, the order fulfillment, packing, and shipping process often involves lots of small changes to distinct parts of the original order (for instance, items may be shipped separately or in small groups and also returned separately). That kind of searching and updating of small pieces of information is perfect for a Relational Database (334).

As previously described, *Polyglot Persistence* is a necessary tool to solve the problem of optimizing each *Microservice* to address its own unique set of problems in the domain. For more information on each of the different specific use cases for this example, see the corresponding examples in each of the individual patterns.

Database-as-a-Service

You're designing an Application Database (329) to store the data for your Cloud Application (6).

How does an application have access to an *Application Database*?

An enterprise database of record is not optimized for applications to persist data; it is optimized for database administration. When an enterprise wants a new database, or even a new table in an existing database, the developers submit a request to the database administrator (DBA) team. The DBAs specialize in database management—such as creating backups, restoring backups, normalizing and optimizing schema, and software licensing—which relieves development teams of these responsibilities.

In their request to the DBAs, the developers must justify the need for yet another database or tables and specify details like the schema, how much data will be stored, and how it will be queried, details developers often do not know early in a project. The DBAs limit the number of databases because a few big databases are easier to manage than many smaller ones. Keeping track of which applications need access to which databases is easier when all applications have access to all databases. Assigning a database a large but limited amount of storage up front makes storage easier to manage.

Database administrators and enterprise databases become an impediment to agile development, especially of Microservices (119). Each *Microservice* should have its own Self-Managed Data Store (154) to store its data as a Data Module (367) in its own database. The team that develops the *Microservice* should also be responsible for its database, creating a database when needed and controlling how it stores the *Microservice*'s data.

Creating a database isn't simple and could require a whole new set of skills for the development team. The team needs to provision a set of bare metal servers or virtual servers (aka virtual machines (VMs)), as well as a set of block storage. The team then needs to download the database software, install it on those servers, and configure it with software licenses and to perform backups. All of this requires database administration skills a developer may not normally have, and these skills differ for each database product.

Since a *Microservice* is a Replicable Application (88), it can scale linearly, which means its database needs to be a Replicated Database (316) so that it can scale linearly as well. A replicated database is more difficult to install, if for no other reason than because it requires provisioning multiple servers and installing the database software on each of them.

Since the developers are using a cloud platform, rather than the development team having to install and administer its own database, a service the cloud could provide is to already have databases installed for development teams to use.

Therefore,

Create your *Application Database* by using a *Database-as-a-Service*, a cloud service that handles much of the work of installing and managing a database.

A *Database-as-a-Service* (DBaaS) is a software-as-a-service (SaaS) in the cloud. Whether the service is built into the cloud platform, loaded onto the cloud platform, or accessed remotely as a web service hosted by a vendor in their data center, the application accesses a database in the service as a Backend Service (106). The service manages a set of database servers and installs databases by hosting them in those servers. The service simplifies creating databases in those servers, handles the licensing, and simplifies management tasks like scheduling backups. Developers can easily create a database and set it up with schemas and other database configurations to store the application's data.

Figure 7-31 shows three *Cloud Applications* that each has its own cloud database. All three cloud databases are hosted by the same DBaaS. Each DBaaS is for a particular database product, so this single DBaaS assumes that all three databases are instances of the same product, such as all PostgreSQL or all MongoDB. Applications that need two different database products, like a PostgreSQL database and a MongoDB database, will need a DBaaS for each.

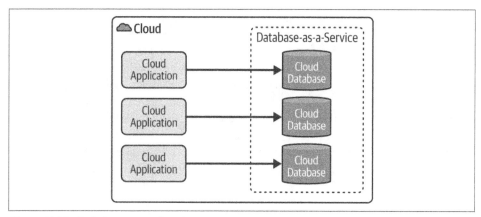

Figure 7-31. Database-as-a-Service

While developers have a range of application database products to choose from, they are limited to the DBaaS services available on their platform. The easiest ones to use are ones built into the cloud platform as SaaS services. A second option is databases that can be downloaded from a marketplace, such as the Kubernetes operators in OperatorHub (*https://oreil.ly/tPMRR*) and Red Hat Marketplace (*https://oreil.ly/x1hS-*). Much like the cloud platform, the operator both installs the database service and manages it. A third option is database services hosted by the vendors in their own data centers and made available remotely as web services. If a development team wishes to use a database that is not made available via one of these three methods, the development team is back to having to manually download, install, and manage the database.

A problem with development teams creating and using their own databases is that application developers may not have the skills to administer databases. Database administrators (DBAs) have more practice performing database tuning, Relational Database (334) works better with optimized table normalization and indexing. A Document Database (339) works better when the granularity of the documents is scoped to simplify data management. A Replicated Database (316) works better when configured with customized partitioning and sharding policies.

To help development teams administer their databases, a common solution is to form a dedicated team of experienced DBAs that the development teams share to tune their databases. DBaaS will free the DBAs from creating and managing databases so that the administrators can focus on configuring and optimizing the databases. The DBA team can also look for opportunities to optimize the usage of the database servers by hosting multiple databases in a shared set of DBaaS service instances. A skilled DBA team is most important for administering production databases. For other stages of the software development lifecycle (SDLC), such as dev and test, DBaaS databases with default settings may be adequate, requiring minimal administration or tuning.

Finally, a last element to consider in using *Database-as-a-Service* are the security requirements of the data. In some cases, enterprises may prefer to keep data local rather than store it in the cloud, negating the ability of teams to use *Database-as-a-Service*. This may be due to regulatory requirements or merely to policy preference on the part of the company building the application. Regulatory issues are increasingly less of an issue since cloud providers have worked diligently to provide security features that are certified by regulatory agencies. However, there still may be cases such as those involving proprietary data (particularly when the cloud provider competes with the company using the provider's services), in which avoiding the use a *Database-as-a-Service* may be a logical choice when made out of an abundance of caution.

A *Database-as-a-Service* greatly simplifies creating and managing databases in the cloud. The service has already installed the database servers, handles licensing, and manages backups. Developers use the service to create a database and configure it to store the application's data, which is much simpler than installing the database manually.

Developers are limited to the DBaaS services the platform makes available. For any other options, the developers must manually install the database. Even with a DBaaS to create and manage databases, development teams may not have the skills to optimize databases and so can benefit from a dedicated DBA team to administer the application's databases, particularly its production databases. Additionally, there can be vendor lock-in by a DBaaS provider, which may not allow your organization direct control over the servers executing the database. Often the cloud service DBaaS provider is in charge of monitoring the database platform and supporting infrastructure, which might lead to security or confidentiality concerns along with compliance or regulatory challenges.

All of the types of *Application Databases* and *Configuration Databases* that we cover in this chapter can be hosted as a *Database-as-a-Service*. Rather than list them all individually here, we provide multiple examples of different DBaaSs of each type in the respective patterns.

Examples

There are literally dozens of examples (perhaps hundreds) of this kind of service on cloud platforms. Among some of the most popular are:

Amazon Relational Database Service (RDS) (https://oreil.ly/-C7KE)
    A popular DBaaS offering in AWS that enables users to launch and manage a variety of *Relational Database* engines, including MySQL, PostgreSQL, Oracle,

and others. Amazon RDS provides automated backups and point-in-time recovery and is designed to be easy to use. It supports read replicas for these databases, which improves the scaling characteristics and addresses many cases requiring horizontal scaling.

Amazon DynamoDB (https://oreil.ly/l2_Qr)
An offering in AWS that enables users to create and manage a highly scalable, fast, and flexible NoSQL database that supports both document and key-value data models, and is designed to be highly available and durable.

Azure Cosmos DB (https://oreil.ly/eO9UW)
A DBaaS offering in Azure that enables users to create and manage a globally distributed, multimodel database. Cosmos DB supports multiple data models, including document, key-value, graph, and columnar, and is designed to be highly available, scalable, and low-latency.

Google Cloud Bigtable (https://oreil.ly/Y95LG)
A hosted distributed NoSQL database that supports real-time read and write access to large datasets.

IBM Cloudant (https://oreil.ly/v5Hg2)
A document database that is available as an SaaS service on IBM Cloud and as a third-party web service.

The choice of which DBaaS offering to use will depend on the specific requirements of the application, the availability of the services on the application's cloud of choice, and the trade-offs between cost, performance, and features that are acceptable for the use case.

Command Query Responsibility Segregation (CQRS)

You are designing a Cloud Database (311) to store the complex data structures for multiple Cloud Applications (6). The application must manage complex *Aggregate* object data that must be consistent during concurrent updates by multiple clients. The applications will independently modify these complex data structures while they also read the data.

How do you optimize throughput for query and updates by multiple clients that have numerous cross-cutting views of the data?

At its simplest, the way an application uses the data in a database can be pretty straightforward: the application CRUDs the data, which is to say that it creates, reads, updates, and deletes the data records in the database. The application writes the data with a particular format and reads it back in the same format. Some of the time it writes data and at other times it reads data, but it usually doesn't read while it's writing or try to update data while it's reading that data. Each data item is a fairly flat record of primitives that maps easily to a row in a Relational Database (334) or rows in normalized tables.

Yet many real-world applications are more complex. Data structures are nested, parts are shared by multiple records, and relationships exist between seemingly independent entities. For example, the product catalog for an ecommerce application has many data elements for each product, some of which are relevant to multiple products, and products are often related. Applications employ complex domain logic to validate data changes, keep it consistent, and maintain referential integrity. That verification works for one client updating the data, but when multiple concurrent client threads update the data at the same time, the domain logic only verifies the changes in each thread and cannot detect conflicts between threads. The domain logic needs to be applied sequentially, making it a bottleneck that handles only one update thread at a time and does not support replication (see Replicable Application (88)).

Another complexity is optimizing data access. To help maximize data throughput, database administrators often optimize a database mostly for reading or mostly for writing. This approach is difficult to apply to a database with data that is frequently updated and read, especially data that is read while it is being updated. For example, the product inventory in an ecommerce application is updated whenever items are added to the warehouse and whenever a new order is placed. Meanwhile, the inventory is simultaneously read as users browse products and update their shopping carts. Database tuning that makes the data easier to update makes it more difficult to read, and data must be locked during updates specifically to prevent other threads from reading it. Writing data updates tends to take priority, creating a bottleneck for reading data, one that replication doesn't improve and actually makes worse by adding client threads accessing the database.

Yet another complexity is that not all applications look at the same data the same way. The application for a buyer may need to view inventory data by geography, whereas the application for restocking inventory needs it organized by quantity. The application for shipping current orders is interested only in products that are currently for sale, whereas an application for browsing order history needs data for old products that were available in the past. Querying can find these different sets of data, but a query can run more efficiently if the data is organized for that query. Yet for data that will be used in many different ways, there is no one right way to organize it. Any approach for organizing the data will help in using it in some ways but hurt in others ways.

What is needed is a database and an approach for organizing data that handles complex data structures, maintains validity throughout concurrent updates, and serves different views of the same data efficiently while the data is also being updated.

Therefore,

Store the data in a *Command Query Responsibility Segregation* solution that duplicates the data in two databases, one that clients use to update the data and another for clients to read the same data.

Command Query Responsibility Segregation (*CQRS*) stores a set of data not in one single database but as two copies in a pair of databases: one for reading and another for updating. The solution keeps the two copies synchronized—whenever the data is updated in the write database, it is likewise updated in the read database. Clients using the data do not access either database directly. Instead, the solution presents clients with two separate APIs: one for making modifications to the data and another for retrieving data. Clients need to choose which API to use; a client that wants to read and write uses both APIs but uses them separately. The APIs segregate the querying activity from the updating activity, directing each to the read and write databases, respectively.

Figure 7-32 shows the *Command Query Responsibility Segregation* solution as two segregated parts, a write solution and a read solution, connected by an Event Backbone (279). The solution implements two databases, one in each part, each of which stores a copy of the same data. There are many approaches for implementing the *CQRS* solution; this shows one very comprehensive design with all of the solution's features clearly designated.

The write solution manages the write database and the API that updating clients use to modify data in the write database. The write database is the database of record for the entire solution because it always contains the latest consistent copy of the data. Clients cannot access the write database directly. Rather, clients that want to update the data do so using the modify API. The write solution implements the API to encapsulate each update as a **Command** (*Design Patterns*, 1994). The command facade can pass the update commands directly to the write model, or it can optionally queue the update commands on a **Command Bus** (*Enterprise Integration Patterns*, 2003). In cases with relatively few simultaneous updates, the write model and its updates to the database of record can process commands as fast as the command facade creates them, so the command bus isn't needed. In cases where the write solution has many clients simultaneously using the command facade to create update commands, queueing may be needed to help the write model manage concurrency by serializing the update commands on a queue and enabling the write model to throttle its consumption of update commands from the queue.

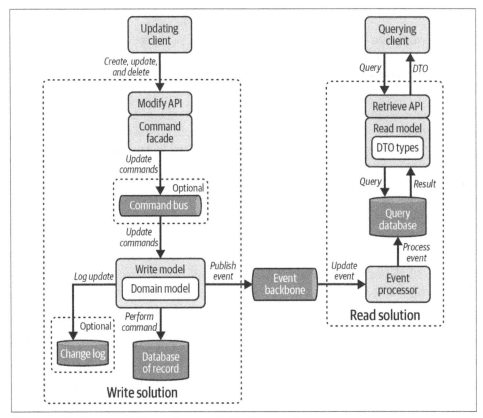

Figure 7-32. Command Query Responsibility Segregation

A write model updates the database much as any application would, using a domain model to enforce data validity. The write model performs the update commands serially, performing each command to update the data in the database of record. At the same time, the write model also creates an update event for the command and queues it on the event backbone. The write solution can optionally include a log of the changes made to the database of record. If it does, whenever the write model performs a command and publishes an update event notification, it also records the update history by logging the update to the change log.

As the write model reads and performs commands, to enforce data validity, it needs to perform the commands sequentially and perform each command on the latest set of data from the previous commands. To do so, the write model can be implemented as a **Singleton** that reads commands one at a time, completing one before starting the next. This design enforces serialization but makes the write model a performance and availability bottleneck. To avoid the bottleneck, the write model should be replicable (see Replicable Application (88)), which then means it must also be stateless (see Stateless Application (80)). To perform each command statelessly, a write model replica must use a single database transaction to lock and read the data from the database of record, use the domain model to update the data with the new data from the command while maintaining validity, and write the valid data back to the database. This is how the write model is able to serialize updates that the clients make concurrently and preserve the validity of the data—even complex *Aggregate* objects—after each update.

The read solution manages the read database and the API that querying clients use to query the data in the read database. The read database mirrors the write database, maintaining a replica of its data. Clients cannot access the read database directly. Rather, clients that want to query the data do so using the retrieve API. The read solution implements the API as a read model that queries the data from the query database, a read-only replica of the data in the database of record; encapsulates the results as **Data Transfer Objects** (*Patterns of Enterprise Application Architecture*, 2002) (DTOs); and returns the DTOs to the client. Meanwhile, the read solution keeps the data in the query database synchronized with the data in the database of record. An event processor reads the update notification events from the event backbone (that were published by the write model) and reacts to each event by updating the data in the query database. Only the event processor can update the query database; the read model and its clients treat the query database as read-only.

CQRS is a complex solution to a complex problem that accomplishes a number of key goals:

Serialize concurrent updates
> By serializing the database updates as a queue of commands, the write model performs multiple updates sequentially, even when they're initiated concurrently by independent clients. Sequential updates are not a bottleneck because they are queued, so clients can queue updates as rapidly as they like. By performing updates one at a time, the write model uses the domain model to validate each update and resolve conflicts.

Manage complex data structures
> The write model uses the domain model to organize a consistent set of complex data and map it to the database efficiently.

Separate client workloads
> Clients updating the data and clients querying the data no longer conflict because they use separate databases. Locking to update the database of record does not block clients from retrieving data from the query database. Read clients can query concurrently because the database is read-only. Reading is only blocked by the event processor synchronizing the data from the database of record.

Load distribution
> The client load of updating and querying data is distributed across two databases.

Schema optimization

>The database of record can have a schema, storage strategy, and tuning optimized for inserting and modifying data. The query database can have a different schema and storage strategy and be tuned differently to optimize it for querying data as defined by the retrieve API. While both databases can be Relational Databases (334) or Document Databases (339), the two databases can easily be two different types of Application Databases (329), such as a Key-Value Database (345) to store primary copies of the data quickly and a Columnar Database (357) for optimized querying. Try accomplishing that with any single database.

Update history

>The write solution can maintain a change log. Logged changes can be used to repeat missing updates and to perform Event Sourcing (289) to selectively update the query database.

CQRS is an alternative to the strategy of each Microservice (119) storing a separate Data Module (367) in a Self-Managed Data Store (154). When a *Microservice* manages its own data in its own database, it can avoid the complexities that *CQRS* handles. *CQRS* is most useful with monolithic databases of data that has not been modularized. Until those databases and their applications can be modernized, *Cloud Applications* have to coexist with them, and *CQRS* is an approach for coexistence.

If a *Microservice* has a complex data model and its clients concurrently update the data while reading it, the *Microservice* may benefit from implementing its *Self-Manged Data Store* using the *CQRS* design. A *Microservice* with a complex data model needs a domain model to keep the data valid. Meanwhile, multiple concurrent threads in multiple *Microservice* replicas can cause conflicts between the concurrent updates. Multiple *Microservice* threads attempting to read the data can conflict with other threads that are updating the data. Just like *CQRS* can help multiple applications coordinate, it can also help multiple threads in the same *Microservice* coordinate.

CQRS is not limited to two databases. If multiple querying clients want very different views of the data, design a retrieve API for each along with a separate query database optimized for that API. All of the query databases can synchronize with the database of record by all subscribing to the event backbone for the update event notifications. Likewise, a query database can replicate data from multiple databases of record that each have their own modify APIs, as long as each write solution manages a separate set of data. All of those write solutions publish their updates as event notifications on the event backbone, which the query database merges into one combined set of read-only data.

Querying clients must be designed to expect eventual consistency. *CQRS* introduces latency between the database of record and the query database that leads to eventual consistency between the updating clients and the querying clients.

Designing the modify and retrieve APIs can be daunting for developers accustomed to direct database access, turning that access into contracts akin to Service APIs (70). The APIs make accessing the database into tasks that can be performed on behalf of the client. Implementing the modify API requires mastering the command pattern and message queuing.

Command Query Responsibility Segregation separates clients that update data from those that query it, combining two synchronized databases that act as one. This separates handling of concurrent updates to complex data structures from concurrent querying of the data as it's being updated, performing both tasks more efficiently. It is able to perform both inserts and queries efficiently since the read solution and write solution can use different database architectures.

CQRS is a complex solution to a complex problem. The synchronization must work well or the read clients will query incorrect data. The read-and-write solutions are more complicated than direct database access. One challenge of *CQRS* is that it is arguably more complicated. Complexity has been moved from the database into the application. For those used to dealing with *Relational Databases*, the transfer of complexity can be difficult to adapt to. You also have to deal with eventual consistency. *CQRS* makes the asynchronous aspects explicit, but it can take some getting used to especially because it is unfamiliar to most developers. They may have to learn additional database technologies.

Event Backbone (279) is a key component of a *CQRS* solution, connecting the write and read solutions and implementing the basis for synchronizing the databases.

CQRS is an amazingly powerful idea. *CQRS* was introduced to most people in *CQRS* (*https://oreil.ly/yGdxQ*) by Martin Fowler. It has been elaborated further in many places, such as **Command-Query Responsibility Segregation (CQRS)** (*https:// oreil.ly/EM0R_*), which also elaborates on the transformation from a simple application using a database to a full-blown *CQRS* solution.

Examples

The following examples illustrate some implementation considerations for *CQRS* and an example of refactoring to get the benefits of *CQRS*.

Implementation variations

Command Query Responsibility Segregation (CQRS) is a technique inspired by Bertrand Meyer's "command query separation." The basic idea behind *CQRS* is to separate commands from queries. Commands are operations that change data (and don't return any data). Queries are operations that read data but don't change anything. In distributed systems, changing data efficiently and consistently is challenging. Commands require a more complex design than queries. Also, it's common for query operations to be called far more often than command operations. There are design alternatives for separating queries from commands when implementing *CQRS*. You need to decide whether to implement it either with One Service or Two Services. Query operations read from a dedicated data store, which is a replica of the primary data store that is updated by command operations. The query data store can be optimized for queries.

One service. In a single service, you separate query from command operations, but they're still part of the same service. Query processor and command processor share some of the service logic. You include an optimized query data store for quick queries (read-only) of the data (see Figure 7-33).

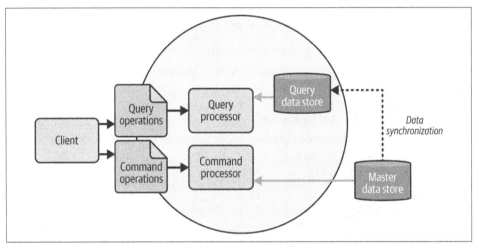

Figure 7-33. CQRS one service implementation

Data from the "primary data store" is replicated to the "query data store," which can be either internal or external to the service. For example, you might optimize your queries by creating an in-memory database. Because the data is replicated, it is important to note that sometimes you might be querying *stale* data.

Two services. You can also implement *CQRS* with two services (Figure 7-34), each with its own contract and design. This approach gives you more flexibility for independently scaling the query and command operations.

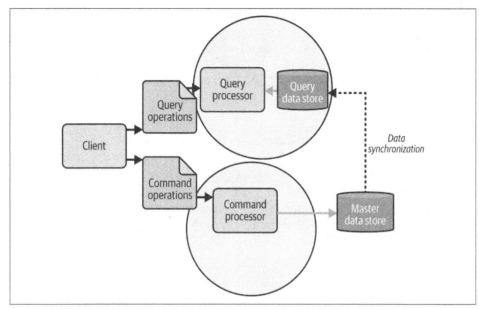

Figure 7-34. CQRS two-service implementation

For example, you can deploy the query service to 20 instances and the command service to 3 instances. You could then have the query service get data from Elastic Search while the command service uses MySql.

Refactoring example

Let's give an example of when *CQRS* becomes important. Let's say we have a team that is not operating in a complete greenfield—there are existing sources of functionality or data that must be reused to complete the application on time and within budget. In particular, you cannot transition all at once to a *Cloud Database* because critical data is stored in a large, existing monolithic database. In that case, how do you deal with the fact that you can't usually transition all at once between existing monolithic data stores and the database-per-microservice approach?

The problem is that reading from data is different from writing data. A service implementation usually has a specific "projection" of a set of relational data that represents a specific view of the data. That view can usually be cached using any of the data caching patterns described in this pattern language. The issue is that writing to the database often involves writing to multiple tables with complex business rules dictating how the information being written needs to be validated and updated. It's that latter code, often encoded in legacy applications, that is difficult to change.

One of the key aspects of *CQRS* is that when it is used for modernization purposes, it requires a data replication approach to keep the Read Model and the Write Model in synchronization. In some cases, this can be done with specific data synchronization tools for the databases being used for the Read Model and Write Model (for instance, Oracle GoldenGate (*https://oreil.ly/2420N*) or IBM DataGate (*https://oreil.ly/Z_a13*)), but these technologies often have significant limitations on which databases can be used for the data source and the data target.

However, by combining existing patterns, we can accomplish this more generally. We create a new Read Model that is a projection of a data set in an existing application by creating a brand new Domain Microservice (130). We have also created a new Write Model that is an Adapter Microservice (135) that translates from the new API to the existing API of the old application. This will require us to set up some type of data replication between the two so the projection of the existing data will keep up with changes to the Write Model. See Figure 7-35.

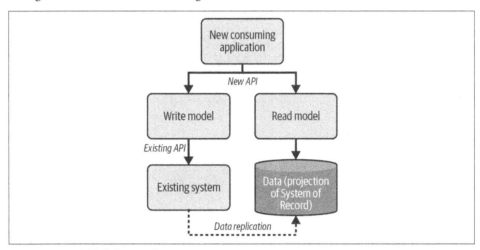

Figure 7-35. CQRS data replication

The most common way of setting up this data replication in this case would be by introducing an Event Backbone (279) between the existing application and the Microservice (119) that is serving as the Read Model (Figure 7-36). In this way, the new Read Model can subscribe to changes made to the existing system and update its data accordingly.

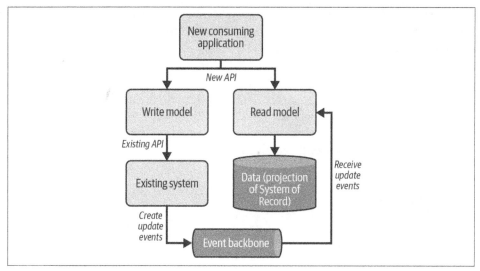

Figure 7-36. CQRS with Event Backbone

The update events can be created directly in the existing application if you have the ability to modify the existing application. That is by far the most general-purpose solution for this problem. But if you do not, you can still use a technology like Change Data Capture to record changes to the application's underlying database. Many existing Change Data Capture tools, such as IBM Infosphere Change Data Capture (*https://oreil.ly/iJAFY*) and Oracle GoldenGate support connecting to a Kafka Event Backbone directly, as do open source platforms like Debezium (*https://oreil.ly/QWSuz*).

What's more, you can even take this further. By introducing Event Sourcing (289), you don't even necessarily need a database for your Read Model that represents the point-in-time. Instead, we can simply re-create the current state by reading the event sequence either stored directly on the Event Backbone (279) or in a longer-term archival event database.

Conclusion: Wrapping Up Cloud-Native Storage

This chapter has addressed several questions about how to store data effectively in the cloud so that you can build efficient, reliable, scalable Cloud-Native Applications (Chapter 3). This data storage strategy enables the application to run as a Stateless Application (80). Each Microservice (119) that has state should store its data in its own Self-Managed Data Store (154), multiplying the challenge of storing data effectively.

The chapter showed the advantages of applications storing their data in a cloud database that can be distributed and replicated. It showed how some databases are designed for implementing cloud services whereas others are meant for use by *Cloud Applications*, and how different kinds of databases for applications offer options for the types of data to be stored, how the database stores it, and how it enables access. The chapter showed how to organize data across multiple databases, how different databases within the same application can have different structures, and how cloud platforms can make databases available as managed services. Finally, it showed a common solution for managing data that must scale for concurrent writing as well as concurrent reading.

Cloud Databases and Replication

While it may be tempting to store data in the cloud infrastructure's block storage or file storage, a *Cloud Application* or *Microservice* should store its data in a Cloud Database (311). Better than storage, a cloud database manages concurrency between multiple application threads, enables querying, stores the data more like the way the application stores it, and makes the data easy for the application to access it.

More than just a database hosted in the cloud, most cloud databases are Replicated Databases (316), running in multiple node processes that can scale horizontally the way a Replicable Application (88) does. A replicated database works the way the cloud does, making its data more highly available in unreliable cloud infrastructure and distributing client load for better throughput. Older *Relational Databases* with a single active process are not replicated, even when running in the cloud, and still depend on vertical scaling. Other databases that are replicated have different architectures for coordinating their nodes: primary/secondary, mesh, and peer. The section "Database Topology and Database Selection" on page 304 explores these database management topologies in greater detail.

Cloud Database Categories

This chapter showed patterns for the two broad categories of cloud databases, both replicated:

Configuration Database (324)
A Configuration Database implements cloud services as well as container orchestrators. Whereas most replicated databases are eventually consistent, propagating and updating across nodes over time, a Configuration Database is reliably consistent because each update is made to all of its nodes at the same time. This way, all of the replicas of a service always have the same configuration. Distributed computing is hostile to reliable consistency, so to make it work, Configuration Databases place restrictions on the format of data and how much of it the database can store, and their performance can suffer. These restrictions mean

that a Configuration Database does not have the flexibility of a general-purpose database.

Application Database (329)

An Application Database is a general-purpose database for an application or *Microservice* to store the domain data that constitutes its state. Designed for applications, these databases are highly available, can store large amounts of data, and can scale to support numerous clients. Different types of application databases store data more like the way the applications do. On the cloud, a database node can become unavailable because of the less-than-100% reliability of cloud infrastructure's computing and networking. Even when a node becomes unavailable, the rest of the database keeps working and the replicated data remains available. Types of databases include SQL, multiple types of NoSQL, and NewSQL.

In a cloud environment, availability and consistency are a trade-off, and the architectures of the two database categories solve this trade-off differently. When the cloud infrastructure and database nodes are working well, both database categories are available and consistent. But in failure scenarios, something has to give. Configuration databases are reliably consistent, meaning that they favor consistency over availability. Application databases are the opposite: they favor availability and sacrifice consistency and as a result provide eventual consistency. *Cloud Applications* favor availability, which is one reason why application databases are more suitable.

Application Database Types

The patterns in this chapter explained the five broad types of application databases:

Relational Database (334)

The easiest way to store data from a *Relational Database* in traditional IT is in a *Relational Database* in the cloud. It doesn't have all of the new features of a NoSQL database, but it does work the way older applications expect, with features like SQL querying, ACID transactions, and database views. It can be the best way to store well-structured data that will be queried dynamically. Newer SQL databases are replicated across nodes and distribute their data, but because of the immediate consistency of their ACID transactions, they cannot replicate their data, which limits the availability of the data during failures.

Document Database (339)

A *Document Database* is one designed to store data the way the application does, making it easy for the application to access and easy for the database to replicate across nodes. They provide great distribution of client load and great availability, at the expense of eventual consistency. Some of the best-known NoSQL databases, such as MongoDB and Apache CouchDB, are document databases.

Key-Value Database (345)

A *Key-Value Database* works like a hash map, providing the simplest way to store and retrieve data, which provides some of the best performance and scaling of any NoSQL database. At its simplest, a *Key-Value Database* stores a record of data as a binary block, storing the data exactly as the application delivers it and delivering it back to the application in exactly the same structure. The limitation is that the data in a *Key-Value Database* cannot be queried; it can be accessed directly only via its key. Some *Key-Value Databases* can parse each value to support querying, which means they also work like document databases.

Graph Database (352)

A *Graph Database* works like a *Document Database* where the documents are highly interconnected, enabling easy navigation among the entities by following their relationships. Graph data efficiently models networks such as cities and geographies, social networks, transportation routes, and other interrelationships.

Columnar Database (357)

A *Columnar Database* acts as a data warehouse for performing analytics. Whereas other databases are optimized for online transaction processing (OLTP), where data is frequently inserted as well as read, a *Columnar Database* is optimized for online analytical processing (OLAP), where data is queried far more than it is updated. A columnar database is especially efficient at finding all of the rows that have a particular value. They are good at storing data that is schemaless, wide-column, or sparse, though that can make the data difficult to query effectively.

The different kinds of databases excel at storing different data with different levels of consistency:

- Well-structured data fits well in a *Relational Database* with immediate consistency.

- Semi-structured data fits well in a *Document Database* or *Graph Database* with eventual consistency, or in a *Columnar Database* with immediate consistency.

- Unstructured data fits well in a *Key-Value Database* with eventual consistency.

Application databases with immediate consistency have lower availability, while those with eventual consistency can often achieve higher availability.

Many database products offer features of more than one kind of database and can excel at storing data with multiple levels of consistency.

Organizing and Accessing Data

Rather than store a large set of data in a large database, the more data can be divided into smaller independent Data Modules (367), the more manageable each set of data will be. *Microservices* not only modularize domain functionality into individual units of functionality; they also modularize data, and each manages its data in its own *Self-Managed Data Store*. The data for any one *Microservice* (not shared by others) is a *Data Module*. Each *Data Module* should be stored in its own database. Multiple databases of the same type can be hosted in separate database servers or grouped in the same database server.

With each *Data Module* hosted in its own database, the *Data Modules* do not all have to be stored in the same kind of database. With Polyglot Persistence (375), if the data in one module works best in one type of database or specific product and another module works best in another type or product, then store each module in a different type of database, the one that suits it best. An application team or enterprise may prefer to limit the range of database choices that will be supported, but within that range, store each *Data Module* in the choice that suits it best.

Managed Databases

With so many different database types and products to choose from, it can become a full-time job just learning how to install and manage all of these databases. A database administrator (DBA) team may have the time to do this but not the range of skills, and an application development team will probably have neither the time nor the skills. With a cloud platform, they don't have to. Many clouds provide at least one Database-as-a-Service (379) (DBaaS), which provides a database as a managed service. A DBaaS has installed a database, providing it as a service instance that hosts database servers. Development teams can simply use the service instance to create databases. The service instance then manages the databases, performing tasks such as creating backups. When a platform provides a range of DBaaS services, a development team can choose from among them and easily experiment with different databases to find the one that works best for their application.

Multiuse Data Solution

A database with commonly used data can easily become a performance bottleneck. Multiple threads concurrently writing to a database can bog down its performance, as can too many threads concurrently reading from the database. Threads trying to read data as it is being updated suffer especially poor performance. Command Query Responsibility Segregation (*CQRS*) (383) can help remedy this situation by duplicating the data in two or more databases whose access is controlled by two APIs, one for modifying the data and another for reading it. By duplicating the data in separate write and read databases, the *CQRS* solution can optimize each. It is responsible for keeping the data synchronized across the databases, treating the write database as the database of record, and ensuring that each update to the DoR is replicated in the read-only database.

Next we'll explore how humans and other application clients access cloud applications. Cloud Application Clients (Chapter 8) provides several types of user interfaces (UIs) and other types of clients that enable users outside the cloud to access applications hosted inside the cloud. The clients support different types of devices and different preferences for access and can even facilitate one application accessing another. They ensure that all users receive consistent functionality regardless of how they access the application.

These Cloud-Native Storage patterns, together with the *Microservices* patterns you've already seen and the Cloud Application Clients patterns, complete the core of a simple application. You will see these patterns used again as we look into the problems of modernization and refactoring existing applications into a Cloud-Native Architecture.

CHAPTER 8

Cloud Application Clients

A cloud application must provide consistent functionality to users accessing the application from a variety of devices.

Today's frontend client world is challenging. Your user community will often be spread across multiple devices from multiple vendors, operating across several different potential technology platforms such as smartphones, tablets, or laptops. When you want to provide the best user experience on each device and need the interface to be best-in-class on each platform, it is difficult to build a single application in one form factor that serves the diverse user community at all points in the interaction lifecycle.

Perhaps the best example of this that we have encountered took place at a major airline. In this airline, there are three major vehicles for customer interaction: the airline's mobile application, the airline's website, and the check-in kiosks available at the airport. What we saw is that the same users would sometimes use all three points of interaction; they would buy tickets on the website and check in on the mobile application but print bag tags from the kiosk! Of course, there was significant functional overlap between all three points of interaction; you could, for example, print a boarding pass at home or at the airport or display a mobile boarding pass in the mobile application.

Introduction to Cloud Application Clients

This chapter explains how to design applications that can be accessed by users via not just one type of device but by a variety of devices. One application that can be accessed via different devices enables each user to access the application via their preferred user interface (UI).

To introduce these patterns, we'll review some basics about developing user interfaces. We'll review the motivation for multimodal interfaces. Next, we'll confirm the need for the UI to be separated from the domain. We'll review the **Ports and Adapters** architecture, which highlights some principles for making an application able to support a variety of user interfaces. Finally, we'll review principles that make application user interfaces work well.

With this background about user interfaces, we'll then present patterns for how they fit in a cloud application architecture, starting with the root pattern for this chapter, Client Application (406).

Multimodal User Interfaces

Different users want to access the application using different types of devices. To support this, an application architecture must be *multimodal*, enabling an application to provide users with multiple modes of interacting with the application. This is most common when you consider that even a single user may access an application in multiple forms on several different devices.

The application can't support just one client technology for one device type. Multimodal architecture means developers must leverage different technologies to reach different user communities. An application can still provide traditional web applications, but developers must also be prepared to build more sophisticated frontends such as mobile applications and single-page applications (SPAs).

Separate UI and Domain

To avoid descending into a hell of duplicate code for all of these device types, developers should design application clients to interface with a more general-purpose backend server representing the resources within a business domain, such as Domain Microservices (130).

One of the fundamental principles that sits behind all of the advice in these patterns is that there should be a distinct and firm boundary between UI code and domain business logic. While this advice is so old that giving it again here may seem almost quaint, the problem is that in practice, many teams fail to follow this principle. Perhaps one of the best examples of this architectural principle is the **Ports and Adapters** architecture, sometimes called the Hexagonal architecture.

Ports and Adapters (Hexagonal) Architecture

Previously, we have presented diagrams that looks like Figure 8-1, where we are illustrating the parts of a cloud application. By now you should be familiar with this three-tier representation of the architecture and understand what we mean by *client*, *application*, and *backend service*.

Figure 8-1. Three-tier architecture

Let's now take a bit of a deeper dive into an application of this type. Let's say that you're building an airline reservation application for a brand-new domestic airline (another example we revisit several times in this book). When you first start out thinking about this application, you may anticipate that it will only be used by users from within a web browser. So it begins with an application implemented with JavaScript, HTML, and CSS and running in a browser, accessing database services provided by the application running in the cloud.

However, over time your airline becomes more successful, and you find that you need to support not only a browser-based client but an iOS-based mobile client as well. What's more, your airline is getting ready to add its first international flight, to a country that requires that all passengers first upload a digital copy of their passport page prior to boarding the flight. That means that you not only have two different client types but also two different cloud Backend Services (106) (object storage and a database-as-a-service), as shown in Figure 8-2.

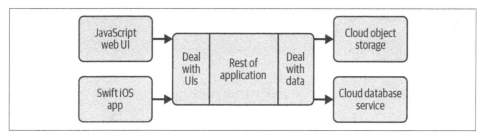

Figure 8-2. Modular application tier

This is where things begin to get really interesting. At first, you may have been fine if your application had been architected to be a single Big Ball of Mud (22) without much division between the parts that handled UI issues and the parts of your application that handled database issues. However, as the number of client types increases, you find that it becomes more important that you make distinctions in your code between those parts of the application that handle UI and those that handle databases. This is when you start to refactor your application into more of a Modular Monolith (29).

What's more, it's not just that you want to separate out the UX code from the database code and from the domain logic, but you also want to make sure that you handle those parts that are unique to either the iOS mobile client or the JavaScript browser client separately from one another. The same is true of separating out the parts that deal with each backend server. The API for object storage is different from a database API such as the API for PostgreSQL, and it doesn't make sense to call them from the same code.

Luckily, there is a well-known design pattern that addresses exactly this kind of problem—the **Ports and Adapters** (*https://oreil.ly/U2icd*) pattern by Alistair Cockburn, originally called the Hexagonal Architecture pattern. Figure 8-3 shows our example architecture from Figure 8-2 expanded with an adapter for each client type and an adapter for each storage type. These adapters can be thought of as ports into and out of your application, with ports on the driving side for clients that drive your application and ports on the driven side for services that get driven by your application.

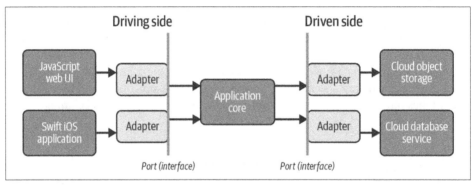

Figure 8-3. Ports and Adapters

The simple idea behind this pattern is that your application core (your domain model code) should not have to know anything about the specifics of how data is stored or managed. Likewise, even though the code needed to fill up and handle navigation between screens is different between different UI types, the way in which they interact with the core domain model code should remain the same. The constant interfaces (on the "driving," or UI side, and the "driven," or data side) are called *Ports*. Ports can have multiple implementations that either call into the domain code (on the driving side) or are called from the domain code (on the driven side). These implementations are called *Adapters*.

Although it was called the Hexagonal architecture, there is nothing special about the number six (e.g., a hexagon)—it was just convenient for the first description of the pattern. This visual effect allows people drawing these types of architectures to insert ports and adapters as needed. Figure 8-4 shows the same application architecture shown in Figure 8-3 as a Hexagonal architecture where it is rotated 45 degrees and put on top of a hexagon.

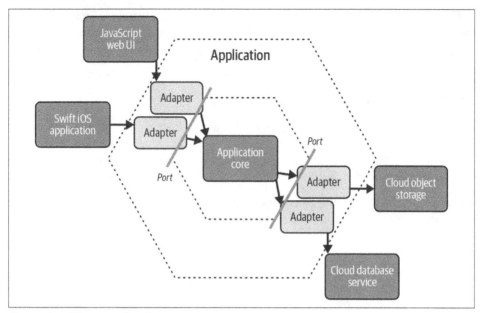

Figure 8-4. Hexagonal architecture

There are different types of driving and driven interfaces that can still fit with the **Ports and Adapters** approach. We've called out two types of interfaces—user interfaces and databases. Notifications (or what we would call *outgoing events*) are another driven interface that the application core would interact with. Likewise, you can think of incoming events as being another driving interface. The overall effect is that you can have as many of these different incoming and outgoing types as you need.

In our case, what we want to point out is that several times in our individual patterns, we will call them out as acting like **Ports and Adapters** in a Hexagonal architecture. For instance, back when we covered the Dispatcher (140) pattern, you can see how they were acting as ports for Domain Microservices (130). Adapter Microservices (135) are also a variation on **Ports and Adapters** in that they act as adapters for existing systems and provide them with a port type that matches your domain API. When we discussed **Repositories** in Aggregates (211) as a technique for keeping database code away from your domain code in the process of Microservice Design (Chapter 5), they were also functioning as adapters for databases implementing a port type. Similarly, in the Event-Driven Architecture (Chapter 6) chapter on building event-driven systems, Reactive Components (260) were likewise acting as adapters to port types defined in an Event API (274).

If we only concern ourselves with the user interface portion of this approach, we realize that what this approach was presaging was the separation of the code of a *Domain Microservice* from the UX code that calls a *Domain Microservice*. The entire Microservices Architecture (Chapter 4) is an architectural and organizational mechanism for enforcing this type of separation. This is just another way to decrease coupling between components.

Principles for Application User Interfaces

This concept of an application core surrounded by different types of adapters for different purposes illustrates a key concept that the patterns in this section implement. The different UI style is meant to be separated from the business logic it relies upon. In a sense, they are all "adapters" in a *Ports and Adapters* architecture.

There are a handful of basic principles about client architecture that underlie the patterns we will introduce in this chapter. These principles are as follows:

- Separate presentation logic from business logic.
- Provide the users a consistent view of the application regardless of how they interact with it. Ideally, this consistent view should be supported by the application's domain services (requiring you to explicitly model the user, which is natural in many domains).
- Meet the application's users where they are, in a form that is best suited to the particular type of interaction. This requires realizing that users are not homogeneous, nor do they always interact with an organization in the same way all the time. This means the application logic must be accessible in a variety of form factors and through multiple channels.
- Enable development teams to work on complete end-to-end business processes; the same team should be responsible for both the frontend and backend parts of this user interaction (e.g., the user experience in all its forms and the domain services that implement the business process).

These principles help design an application that can be accessed with a variety of user interfaces.

Architecting Applications with Multimodal Clients

The patterns in this chapter all stem in one form or another from these basic principles:

Client Application (406)
  This is the root pattern of this section and it describes the overall structure of applications that must work across multiple types of user interaction. In particular, you need a way of explicitly capturing and representing each particular style of user interaction.

Browser Application (410)

This is the parent of a number of different subtypes of applications that run within a browser and require only commonly available open technologies in order to present a user interface.

Web Form Applications (414)

These are one of the oldest types of *Browser Application* and still should be the default option for small, simple applications. This approach combines server-side rendering (using a template language) with simple forms-based navigation. It is well suited for interacting with users who are on less-than-ideal hardware platforms and places few requirements on the user's side beyond opening a URL in a browser application.

Single-Page Applications (421)

These are a common approach to building complex client-side web applications that fully leverage the power of modern browsers. These applications take advantage of the power of browser-based JavaScript, CSS, and HTML to build highly interactive user experiences.

Micro Frontends (426)

These are a way to avoid recommitting the mistakes of monoliths within a client-side application built using the Single-Page Application architectural approach.

Mobile Application (430)

This describes the most customizable solution for consumer-facing client applications. While *Web Applications* are still enormously common and are often the best solution for internal corporate applications, many consumers now expect the bulk of their interactions with many companies to take place through a dedicated *Mobile Application*.

Command-Line Interface (437)

This is a way of interacting with the user at an operating system command line. This is important because many simple types of actions the user may want to take in order to automate interaction with the system are more easily done at an OS command line than through other mechanisms.

Public API (443)

This is the mechanism for making your *Application Services* available to the world of developers outside of your own team. They are important wherever you have interactions with third parties, such as suppliers, business partners or governmental entities, or if you want to build an ecosystem of independent developers around your services.

An Interaction Model (448)

This represents an interaction with a user in a particular technology stack or channel. It allows for the separation of user interface and business logic while encouraging commonality across interactions of different types.

There are multiple different types of technology, dependent patterns that are kinds of or subtypes of *Client Applications*. The relationships between these patterns are shown in Figure 8-5.

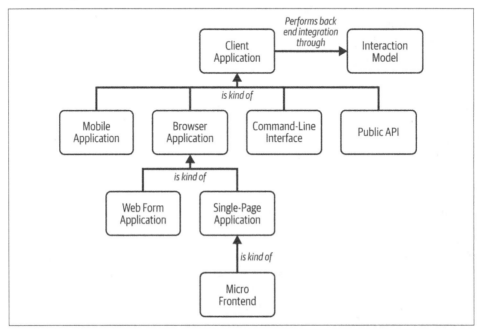

Figure 8-5. Client Application patterns

We will begin the discussion of these patterns with the root pattern of the section that encompasses all the others, Client Application (406).

Client Application

You've developed a Cloud Application (6), perhaps with a Cloud-Native Architecture (58), perhaps using Microservices (119). Users need to be able to use this cloud application.

How can an end user take advantage of the services provided by an application running in the cloud?

A user accesses any application via its user interface. This is simple when the application runs on a personal desktop computer. It is a monolith, where the entire application runs on the computer, including the user interface. The user has access to the user interface because it is running on the user's desktop computer.

An application running in the cloud is not running on the user's desktop computer. Whether the application is a monolith or a set of *Microservices*, it is running in the cloud and the user is outside the cloud. Perhaps the user could run the application on their computer, but then it wouldn't be running in the cloud. Hosting the application in the cloud creates a challenge for the user to access the application from their desktop computer.

The user may not even be using a traditional desktop computer application. Instead, the computer may be running a web browser. The user may not even be using a desktop or laptop computer but instead may be using a smartphone or tablet. Nevertheless, the problem is the same: the application isn't running on the user's computer, browser, phone, or tablet; it's running in the cloud. Yet the user needs to be able to access the application from their device.

Therefore,

Develop a *Client Application* that implements a user interface for users to access the cloud application. Each user runs the *Client Application* on their computer or device and connects to the cloud application via a network such as the internet.

This problem was solved long ago by the client/server application architecture. Client/server architecture splits the monolithic application into two parts, a client portion that runs on the user's local computer and a server part that runs on a remote computer. The client portion is typically a user interface, while the server part is the application's headless domain functionality. Since the server application never knows when a client may need to connect, it is always running and available, often by hosting it in an application server.

In cloud computing, the server computer is the cloud, or more precisely compute infrastructure in the cloud. The server application is no longer hosted in an application server—it is a cloud application hosted in the cloud, often a cloud-native application with a Microservices Architecture (Chapter 4).

Whether the server application is hosted in an application server or on a cloud platform, the user interface runs on the client as a separate application. Each user runs the client application on their computer or device. The *Client Application* connects to the *Cloud Application* via a network such as the internet and interfaces with the server application as a service provider. The *Cloud Application* runs in the cloud, whereas the *Client Application* runs outside the cloud, as Figure 8-6 shows.

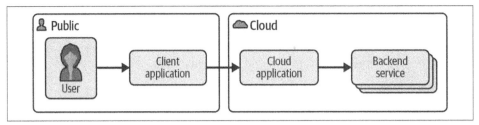

Figure 8-6. Client Application

Because the *Cloud Application* is hosted in the cloud, it has access to Backend Services (106) that are also hosted in the cloud. The *Client Application* may be capable of running in the cloud or anywhere outside the cloud, but to be useful as a user interface, it runs on the user's device, such as their desktop computer. The user has local access to the *Client Application*, which provides the user remote access to the *Cloud Application*.

A single *Cloud Application* can have multiple *Client Applications* specialized for different user roles and different client computer architectures. A *Cloud Application* may provide different *Client Applications* for the same type of computer or device but for different types of users, such as employees versus customers, usually to provide different subsets of functionality available in the *Cloud Application*. It may also provide different *Client Applications* for the same user functionality on different types of computers or devices, such as for a laptop versus a smartphone. The *Client Application* can tailor the user experience for the computer or device it's designed to run on, to compensate for constraints such as screen size or network bandwidth, and to take advantage of capabilities such as GPS location and authentication mechanisms like fingerprint readers and facial recognition.

A *Client Application* enables a user to access a *Cloud Application* by running a user interface on the user's device that remotely accesses the functionality in the application running in the cloud. Each user gets their own copy of the user interface running on their own device. Different types of user interfaces can support different types of users and different types of devices.

Each *Client Application* is something additional for the development team to implement and manage separately from the rest of the application that runs in the cloud. An enterprise with a wide range of users that have a wide range of devices will have to implement many similar but separate *Client Applications*.

The *Client Application* should interface with the *Cloud Application* via a Service API (70), typically implemented by a Dispatcher (140). The API remains stable even as the *Cloud Application* changes so that the *Client Application* can remain stable, enabling developers to independently evolve the *Client Application* and *Cloud Application*. The *Client Application* and *Dispatcher* must work together, united by the API, and so the same development team should implement the client, API, and *Dispatcher* together.

There are different kinds of *Client Applications* that support a multimodal architecture—different kinds of clients accessing the same functionality in a *Cloud Application*:

Browser Application (410)
> This runs in an HTML web browser running on the user's client computer or device.

Mobile Application (430)
> This runs on a client smartphone or tablet.

Command Line Interface (437)
> This runs in an OS shell on the client computer or device, providing commands for invoking individual functions in the server.

There are many other specialized types of interfaces that exist for additional types of platforms, such as airport kiosks and bank automatic teller machines (ATMs). Other application client types we will not cover include telephone voice menus, chatbots, and more. However, these three form the basic set that other types can often be derived from.

Examples

Any application running in the cloud that has users has *Client Applications*:

Websites
> Any interactive website for ecommerce, banking, travel, driving directions, email, etc., connects to a backend that these days is probably running in the cloud. Likewise, many of an enterprise's internal applications used by its employees now often run in a web browser to access an enterprise-specific backend that may be hosted in the cloud. The web interface is typically designed to run in any web browser on any device.

Mobile Applications
> An app running on a smartphone or tablet may seem standalone, but most don't work in airplane mode because they require a network connection—internet access via cellular or WiFi. Like a website, these mobile apps delegate to a server application to perform the heavy lifting, access vast amounts of data, and apply domain logic, and those server applications often run in the cloud.

CLIs

Developers commonly use CLIs to administer infrastructure and services. Administering equipment in a data center used to require walking into the data center, but now most equipment has a *Service API* and a lightweight web server that enables any authorized user with network access to remotely administer the equipment. Many cloud platforms extend this model to all of the cloud services so that entire environments can be created and managed via the CLI.

As mentioned, airport kiosks are clients, and the services they access are often hosted in the cloud. ATMs were developed long before the cloud or even the popularity of the internet, but newer ones can access banking systems hosted in cloud environments.

About the only *Cloud Applications* that don't require *Client Applications* are those that process data and perform analytics or machine learning. Yet even those have *Client Applications* that enable data scientists to set up the processing tasks and view the results.

Browser Application

You are building a Cloud Application (6)—such as a Cloud-Native Application (Chapter 3)—that is hosted in the cloud. Users need a Client Application (406) to be able to interact with this cloud application.

What is the easiest, most universal *Client Application* for any user that does not assume a specific hardware or software configuration?

Every application is based on a set of assumptions about the hardware and software platform it is built to run on. However, this creates an issue: if there are too many assumptions—that is if the required hardware and software is too specialized—then the application may not find wide use. The class of applications that make relatively few assumptions about the hardware and software they run on serve an important purpose. They fill in a gap in the computing landscape that is sometimes difficult to fill:

- Users may prefer not to have to download and install a *Client Application* if they are not committed to using it on a constant basis.

- Different users have different computers and devices running different operating systems, making it difficult to develop a single *Client Application* that will run on all of them. Often a web page is the only available lowest common denominator that can be used by many different types of devices.

- HTML web browsers with basic capabilities like JavaScript are ubiquitous and available on every computing platform

Therefore,

Develop a *Client Application* as a *Browser Application* that will run in any HTML web browser.

A *Browser Application* at its heart is a bit of a misnomer because the simplest form of the application does not run in the browser at all. Instead, it is a dynamic website that is merely accessed through the user's browser over the internet (see Figure 8-7).

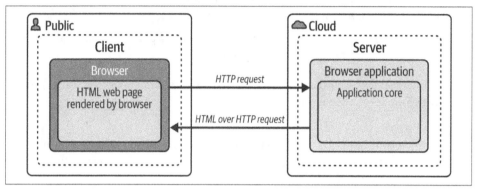

Figure 8-7. Browser Application

The principle behind any sort of *Browser Application* is simple—there is a program running on a remote server that listens for HTTP requests at a particular URL. It then responds to those requests by generating the appropriate HTML to form a web page that represents the response to the HTTP GET, POST, or other HTTP verb. Within that general statement, however, are many different variations. The program could be embedded within another program like a web server (e.g., CGI), or it could be standalone (as with Node). It could respond back with only HTML, or it could respond with other content types as well—such as images, but more importantly CSS and JavaScript. What's more, the server can also respond with content types that represent only information, like JSON (which becomes important when you consider AJAX).

The benefits of developing an application as a web page (something that can show up in a browser) are many:

- Any computer or device that has an HTML web browser (that is, nearly all of them) can run a *Browser Application* since all that is required is conformance to HTTP and HTML.

- A *Browser Application* doesn't have to be installed; it entirely runs within the browser accessing the website.

- *Browser Applications* tend to be lightweight, require limited memory on the client, and work well with low-bandwidth network connections.

However, as common as they are, *Browser Applications* have their drawbacks:

- *Browser Applications* cannot take advantage of the unique features of a device (such as the camera, GPS, or magnetic compass on a smart phone) as easily as a *Mobile Application* can. In some cases, this is worth the trouble of building a *Mobile Application* simply for access to the device features.

- A *Browser Application* is not easily expanded by third parties in the same way that a *Public API* or *Command Line Interface* allows.

The advancement of web technologies has led to several forms of *Browser Applications*, which we cover in later patterns:

Web Form Application (414)
: A simple application built from HTML pages rendered server-side with no JavaScript where transitions between pages are triggered by following links or by submitting HTML forms

Single-Page Application (421)
: An application built from many different pieces of HTML assembled and rendered on the fly within the same webpage, constructed client-side using JavaScript and CSS

Micro Frontend (426)
: Mini-applications that can be composed into a *Single-Page Application* via a framework

All of these have evolved from the many content types that a *Browser Application* can return in response to an HTTP request.

Examples

When the web was first imagined by Tim Berners-Lee (*Weaving the Web*, 1999), all that was envisioned was the idea of a Web Server serving up static HTML web pages and images. The web did not stay static for long, as the following examples show.

CGI

Soon after HTML 1.0 was released, another proposed standard called CGI (Common Gateway Interface) came into being to make websites dynamic through various means, such as programmatic generation. The first versions of this would call programs externally to generate specific pages within a URL tree—some pages would be served by the web server, while others would be delegated (through a special directory called *cgi-bin*) to dynamic pages generated by these external programs (see Figure 8-8).

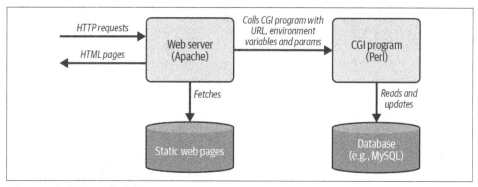

Figure 8-8. Web with CGI

Template Applications and PHP

The next evolution of browser applications was to combine the program generating the HTML and dynamic content within a single template mechanism by which programmatic statements are embedded inside an HTML page. A canonical example of this approach is PHP (a recursive acronym for PHP, the Hypertext Processor). PHP runs inside virtually any web server software and will work with most databases. PHP programs are written inside of HTML pages where PHP statements are interpreted inside special tags that are differentiated from HTML tags, usually with the syntax. Any PHP code inside the tag is dynamically interpreted and evaluated to render HTML that is then inserted into the appropriate place in the HTML page as it is returned to the page requestor by the web server. This type of architecture is shown in Figure 8-9.

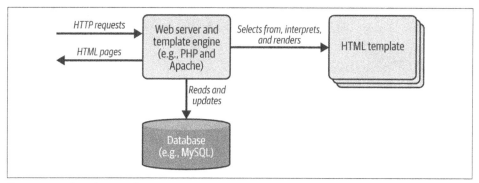

Figure 8-9. Simple templating system

ASP.NET, Servlet, and JSP

Developers soon realized that making the HTML template the target for requests made it very difficult to choose what page to render when an HTTP request is received. That led to a separation of the request processor from the template engine. This approach was commonly used in ASP.NET and Java Enterprise Edition, where the request processor such as a Java Servlet was separated from the template, which was a Java Server Page or JSP. This is shown in Figure 8-10.

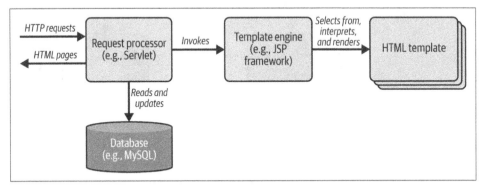

Figure 8-10. Separate template system and request processor

JavaScript and AJAX

The next major development in web application development was the introduction of JavaScript into the browser between 1995 and 1997. Initially, JavaScript was only used for small, standalone applications, much like other competing technologies like Flash. However, this changed in 2006 with the introduction of a new feature in Internet Explorer that allowed calls to a backend system from within a JavaScript application. This approach (still called AJAX, or Asynchronous JavaScript and XML, even though XML is now rarely used) was the cornerstone of a new approach to web applications. We cover much more of that in the Single-Page Application (421) pattern.

Web Form Application

You are building a Browser Application (410) that needs to reach the largest possible user community. You likewise need to get something out quickly to your users.

How do you build a user interface to provide basic functionality to the largest possible set of users using the largest possible set of devices and hardware?

Some applications are meant for greatness. Most, however, are not. One of the downsides of taking all of your architectural and business lessons from unicorns and hyperscalers is that it is easy to believe that all applications will become virally successful, require unheard-of scalability, and attract millions of adoring fans that hang on every font and icon change with bated breath. The truth is, that while there are applications that fit that category, the reality is that much more than 90% of all applications written will be written for an unchanging audience, whose size is well-known ahead of time and whose usage patterns are both consistent and sporadic. For instance, how many times have you had to update your home address at your auto insurance company? The total number of times that particular part of their website will be used in a year can be calculated very precisely from the size of their covered population and a coefficient derived from some population movement statistics obtained from the Census Bureau.

Even setting aside the fact that most enterprise applications are much more like our hypothetical address-change app than a widely-used website like X or Facebook, there are other fundamental issues that often make it less advisable to try to keep up with the cutting edge of user interface technology. Probably the most important, and least considered, is developer skill—if you adopt a new frontend JavaScript framework, then you are implicitly saying that it is worthwhile to spend the time for your developers to learn this framework—something that will make you even more likely to want to use it to its fullest extent once that learning time is committed. What this leads to is an example of the sunk cost fallacy—if your developers spent time learning something, you want to get the benefit out of that time, which will often result in applying technologies to problems for which they are, at best, overkill.

On the other hand, what if there were a set of technologies that were already well understood, widely available in commercial and open source implementations, completely compatible with cloud-native principles and, what's more, could give you the fastest path to value for many types of user interfaces? That would seem to be a godsend to teams who struggle to learn all of the other parts of cloud adoption. And what if those same technologies allow you to reach the widest possible user community at the same time? In fact, that technology exists.

Therefore,

Build a *Web Form Application* that serves up HTML pages from a server-side application and that takes input through HTML forms.

This approach works best for relatively small and simple applications, particularly those that do not require intense graphical interaction or those that are used sporadically or rarely. *Web Form Applications* rely on the structure of HTTP for the basic interaction with the user. Remember that there are only a handful of HTTP verbs. Following are two most commonly used ones (and the ones most applicable to our purposes):

GET

GET is a request from a browser to retrieve a web page from a server and can be sent by typing a URL address in or from a link.

POST

POST is sent from a browser to the server in response to the submission of a web form.

If we consider only those two verbs, that determines the flow of how pages are shown and how the user interacts with them. The flow for this kind of application is shown in Figure 8-11.

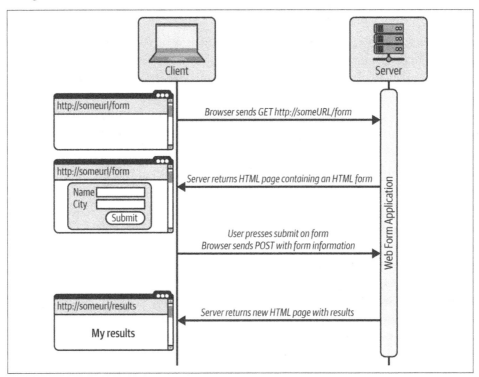

Figure 8-11. Web Form flow

The important thing about this (very simplistic and highly simplified) summary of HTTP 1.0 and 1.1 is that this approach is independent of the many different mechanisms for implementing this. Note that this description doesn't specify whether you are using a single server process to handle everything on the backend or multiple processes (such as a web server and application server combination). It doesn't specify if you use a templating mechanism or not. The fact is that *any* of these are valid technical choices for different reasons.

Many of you reading this may already be saying, "That's what our old monolith was! That's what we're trying to move *away* from!" You will note that we are merely describing the approach that this type of application takes in constructing user interfaces but do not say anything about how large or small each application would be. The rejection of *Web Form Applications* entirely as a solution is an unfortunate application of the principle of tarring two very different things with the same brush.

Just because many teams built *Web Form Applications* as *Big Balls of Mud* does not mean that all *Web Form Applications* must necessarily be implemented as *Big Balls of Mud*. First, there are many lightweight technologies today that allow you to build *Web Form Applications* that are small and very lightweight. Node is perhaps the most obvious one, but there are corresponding lightweight web form applications for other languages like Python Flask. Even in the Java world, which often was derided the most for large, unwieldy applications that require enormous Web Application Servers to run, there are technologies like Spring Boot and Quarkus that allow you to build small, cloud-native applications in Java that follow the *Web Form Application* pattern.

Servlet and JSP with Microservices and Interaction Models

We mentioned in the introduction to this chapter that one of the key principles in building user interfaces should be the separation of domain logic from presentation logic. One of the problems with many implementation architectures is that there is no good way to enforce that separation. In fact, early template architectures like PHP almost required that the two be mixed together, and to avoid doing so in later template architectures like Servlet/JSP or ASP takes great discipline in building application **Facade** (*Design Patterns*, 1994) objects that would act as adapters to the core of the application. This is something many teams never took up, instead coding business logic directly from the servlets or other request processors or (even worse) the JSP or ASPs themselves.

Instead, a better way to do this is to formally separate the two by introducing separate Interaction Models (448) and Domain Microservices (130). This version of the *Web Form Application* architecture is shown in Figure 8-12.

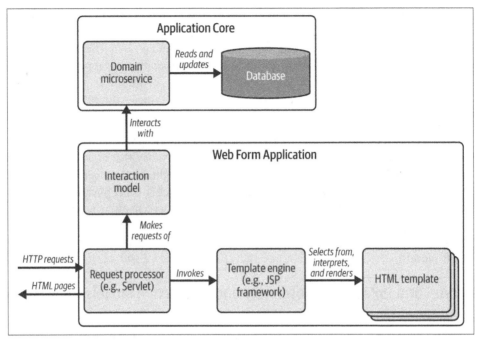

Figure 8-12. Interaction with Domain Microservice

By splitting away the Domain Microservice, we have created what Alistair Cockburn refers to as the Application Core in the **Ports and Adapters** architecture.

In this way, the three parts of a **Model View Controller** (*Patterns of Enterprise Application Architecture*, 2002) or **Model View Presenter** (*https://oreil.ly/TjDRX*) pattern are introduced. We can call the common parts of these the "Model View X" approach, or "MVx". The Request Processor handles the issues of control flow (X), the *Interaction Model* (and *Domain Microservices*) handles domain logic (M), and the template engine handles building the HTML page (V). Building applications in this way can be a very fast path to a minimum viable product, as fast or even faster than building a Single-Page Application (421) depending upon the complexity of the screen flow. What's more, building this kind of application is something that many developers already have skills in; Java programmers often learn Servlets and JSPs before learning frameworks for building REST services, and PHP skills are common in the industry as well. The tools, frameworks, and runtimes for building this kind of application are very mature and stable, available as open source, and run both on premises and in every available container technology and cloud provider—meaning that developers will not be running on the bleeding edge of a new technology or locked into a particular vendor.

Here are some of the most important advantages of a *Web Form Application*:

- It is relatively simple to build. There are relatively few things to learn, and you can start building applications with common tools (like Node.js, ASP.net or JSP) very quickly.

- Since the only requirement placed on the user is that they have a browser capable of rendering HTML (or HTML and CSS) it is possible to provide a user interface that can be rendered on many different types and ages of devices. This is especially important when considering the percentage of a user population that is not on the latest hardware or operating system versions.

- The technologies needed to build these applications are well established and available in open source versions, and skills are easy to find.

- Since a *Web Form Application* follows the strict rules of HTTP 1.0/1.1 and HTML/CSS, the browser's back button and browser history will always work. This is something that users often expect to work and are surprised when applications running as a *Single-Page Application* violate that implicit assumption. A *Web Form Application* will follow that implicit assumption about how browsers "should" work, causing fewer instances of lost work through inadvertent use of the back button.

However, there are plenty of drawbacks of *Web Form Applications* as well, which is why many other choices now exist for *Client Applications*:

- *Web Form Applications* are not nearly as responsive to user input as *Single-Page Applications* can be. The page-at-a-time mechanics of *Web Form Applications* make them slower to react to input, especially over slow networks. HTTP/2 was specifically designed to improve the speed of browser-based applications processing multiple requests at once (e.g., *Single-Page Applications*), and *Web Form Applications* cannot take advantage of all of those speed improvements.

- Complex user interactions are difficult if not impossible to represent in a *Web Form Application*. You can always use JavaScript to make your user interactions more sophisticated, but once you start using JavaScript in your pages, you are already well on your way to a *Single-Page Application* and should probably think carefully about implementing that pattern instead.

That last set of disadvantages gets to the best way to use *Web Form Applications*. They are best suited for very simple, form-driven interactions that can (often) be characterized by CRUD (Create, Read, Update, Delete) functions. Essentially, if you are building a simple frontend on a database, a *Web Form Application* may suffice. If you're doing anything that requires more sophisticated interaction with the application than updating or fetching tabular data, you probably want to look at other *Client Application* choices.

Likewise, a key principle to follow in sizing a *Web Form Application* is that each individual application should perform only *one* business function. If this sounds like the same principle that applies to *Microservices*, that's because it is. Not only will that make the business logic more cohesive, but it will keep the presentation logic simpler and more readable as well. If you keep the user interface of each application small (fewer than ~10 pages per application) and directly reflective of a single business process flow in the domain, many of the issues that led to the problems we saw with large, monolithic Web Applications can be avoided. This is true regardless of what technology combination you use—you can choose to construct your application with template technologies like JSP, PHP or ASP or directly code your HTML into your Node.js applications in JavaScript. The decision is yours, although most teams will have an easier time when using a templating technology.

Whenever a business process (and screen flow) crosses from one domain entity or Aggregate (211) to another, you should also cross over to another application to handle that flow. Thus, your web application boundaries should roughly correspond to the boundaries of a *Microservice*. Going beyond that can lead to grouping unrelated logic and leads to building a monolith. There also may be a temptation to build multiple Web Applications that all communicate through a shared database, which again should be avoided.

If you find yourself moving in that direction, or if you have a user interface that is complex and not easy to express as simple forms and results pages, you probably need a more capable client-side application based in JavaScript with backend logic provided by Domain Microservices (130). In that case, a Single-Page Application (421) is the best option. Of course, the ultimate in user interface customization is possible if you build a Native Mobile Application (430), so you also need to consider your options in that regard.

This pattern is related to **Template View** (*Patterns of Enterprise Application Architecture*, 2002) pattern and in fact may be considered a blending of **Template View** and **Application Controller** (*Patterns of Enterprise Application Architecture*, 2002). However, building a *Web Form Application* is only one user interface choice of many that developers now face, so many of the reasons for separating the two are no longer necessarily applicable given this plethora of choices. The *Web Form Application* pattern is one of many such choices that "won out" in the end, even to find itself replaced by other technology options.

Examples

There are many examples of *Web Form Applications* that were originally built to highlight or explain particular languages, tools, or programming models. They all began, however, with the original Java Pet Store (*https://oreil.ly/TiNFp*).

This application was introduced as the original reference application for the Java Platform, Enterprise Edition (JEE) around 2001. That application was based on Servlets and JSP and followed an MVC-style architecture as introduced in *Core J2EE Patterns* (2003). Describing what it calls the Web Tier of the application (which was a three-tier application, having a client tier consisting of a browser, a web tier, and an Enterprise JavaBeans tier that represents the domain model and database interaction), the Java BluePrints site (*https://oreil.ly/y1aIt*) stated, "The Web tier is responsible for performing all Web-related processing, such as serving HTML, instantiating Web page templates, and formatting JSP pages for display by browsers." The last available version of the Java Pet Store 1.0 can be downloaded on the Oracle website (*https://oreil.ly/dWCZS*).

Single-Page Application

You are developing a new Browser Application (410) that has complex navigation, or you are refactoring a section of a Web Form Application (414) to make it more interactive.

How do you design the frontend of your application to provide the best mix of client responsiveness and server optimization?

When the user's experience is of critical importance to your application, you find the following criteria to be true when designing your frontend:

- You want your application to be responsive, fast, and to feel as much as possible like a native application.

- You want to provide the user with a very responsive application that they can interact with easily despite network lags. You do not want to make your application become completely unusable when internet connectivity is spotty or slow. This means moving as much processing as possible to the frontend browser.

- You want the user to be able to interact with the application naturally, without arbitrary restrictions in user interface design. This means that you want to allow the use of controls that provide immediate user feedback without requiring long wait times while you contact a backend system.

- You want to enable your designers to provide the cleanest, most attractive user interface possible and to be able to make design modifications without requiring them to work through your development team. This means the HTML pages should be served up naturally through a Web Server and should be developed and managed using a Content Management and Authoring system. You don't want extra steps where a development team would pick up and modify a page after it was built by the design team.

The traditional Web Form Application (414) (even using page template technologies like ASP.NET or JSP) does not meet these conditions. The page-at-a-time back and forth trips to the server make the applications slow and at the same time usually require changes to both the frontend and backend code at the same time since the backend code is often mixed with the frontend HTML.

However, that is not the only possible solution—all modern browsers now have the ability to let JavaScript dynamically modify HTML, and what's more that same JavaScript can make its own requests of the server.

Therefore,

Design your *Browser Application* as a *Single-Page Application*, such that all interaction takes place within a single logical page within the browser.

At its heart, the major element of a *Single-Page Application (SPA)* that makes it different from a *Web Form Application* is that there is a JavaScript program running within the web browser as part of what the browser loads as a single page. That application will be responsible for the following:

- Handling user interaction. The JavaScript will provide event handlers that are invoked when the user interacts with any screen controls within the HTML page, such as buttons, scroll bars, or text boxes.

- Communicating with the backend server responsible for providing information to the JavaScript in response to user requests. That service is pictured here as a Dispatcher (140) and a set of Domain Microservices (130), although any other type of Cloud Application (6) that understands HTTP will also serve, such as a Modular Monolith (29).

- Producing or modifying the DOM (Document Object Model) of the HTML page that the browser displays from a template HTML page (something like in the ASP or JSP model for a *Web Form Application*) that is augmented with information that the JavaScript code obtains from the backend server.

The *SPA* approach is a variation on the traditional MVx patterns (MVx meaning **Model View Controller, Model View Presenter,** and all of the variants of those patterns) used in the dynamic web approach used by all *Browser Applications* in that views are not complete web pages. They are simply portions of the DOM that make up the viewable areas of the screen. The initial HTML load is simply a shell that is broken up into child containers (or regions). Developers often use an MVx framework, such as React, Angular, or Vue, to handle the difficult parts of the application management, such as routing to the right view, combining data from AJAX calls with template HTML fragments, and managing the lifecycle of each view. The components of the *SPA* program and the backend server are shown in Figure 8-13.

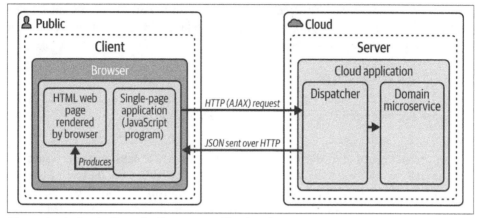

Figure 8-13. Single-Page Application and backend

The *SPA* approach lets you store page state within the client and connect to the backend through REST services. This approach is called "single page" because all of the HTML, CSS, and JavaScript code necessary for a complex set of business functions, which may represent multiple logical screens or pages, is retrieved as a single page request.

The *SPA* approach allows for very responsive, fast applications that render quickly. JavaScript code that executes within a web page can control the look and feel of the application by generating and manipulating the client-side DOM in any way it chooses, and it also can request information from the server at any point based on user interactions—resulting in more responsive user interfaces. The overall flow of information in the AJAX approach that is fundamental to *SPA* is shown in Figure 8-14.

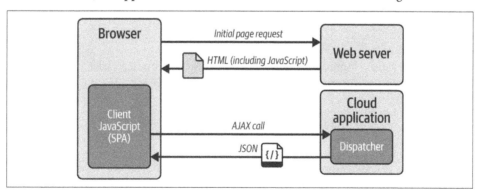

Figure 8-14. AJAX interactions

SPAs are often written to take advantage of Responsive Design principles (*Modern Web Development with IBM*, 2014) to optimize user experience for screen layout and size. CSS media queries are often used to include specific blocks that apply for only specific screen types. This technique allows a different set of CSS rules to be specified for tablets, mobile phones, or laptops, resulting in screens that are laid out and configured specifically for those devices.

There are a number of distinct advantages to the *SPA* approach:

Speed
An advantage of the *SPA* approach is that the AJAX calls that are issued by the *SPA* to the server have generally smaller payloads, and thus are faster to execute, than corresponding calls that would transmit a completely rendered HTML page. Since an *SPA* doesn't have the same round-trip issues that a *Web Form Application* has, they are often faster in responding to user requests.

Improved experience
An *SPA* will generally give you a more responsive user experience than a *Web Form Application*, partially due to the improved rendering and processing speed we discussed, but also because it allows for more fine-grained control of the user experience. Each action by the user, be that typing a character, pressing a button, or simply scrolling the application, can result in a small update to the DOM being rendered by the browser, making the application seem very responsive as a result.

Decoupling
The *SPA* approach effectively decouples presentation logic (particularly rendering and entry validation logic) from server-side domain logic. This makes it possible in many cases to make UI changes without having to update a corresponding server component.

State stored locally
Since the state is stored locally as part of the application, it's easier to manage the state from a development perspective than the entirely remote state management in a *Web Form Application*.

There are also a set of disadvantages to the approach that teams need to consider:

Complexity
Any time you split the application logic across two computers (and often two or more computer languages), you are increasing complexity. The navigation logic of an *SPA* will be more complex in that respect than a *Web Form Application* would be.

Initial load speed

The downside of the *SPA* is that the initial download of the application is significantly slower when you use client-side rendering since all of the potential parts of the *SPA* are loaded at once. You load a significant amount of HTML, CSS, and especially JavaScript before you can use the application, particularly if you use a library like React or Vue. You may remember that one of the advantages of *Browser Applications* is that they are relatively lightweight—once you start adding sets of large libraries to your *SPA*, you may find that this is no longer true.

Lack of browser history and the back button

An additional downside of the *SPA* approach is that it works counterintuitively to the way that web browsers are "supposed to work" in that each page is available for navigation one at a time with the forward and back buttons. Since the entire application is within the context of a single page, hitting the back button wipes the entire application, and whatever changes were in progress and not updated to the backend are lost. As a result, many *SPAs* disable the back button entirely. Some browser APIs mitigate this, but that requires additional development to make this work.

Security issues

Since *SPAs* by nature use AJAX to communicate between the server that hosts the HTML and JavaScript, the client and the server that the AJAX calls are made to, the potential for cross-site scripting attacks exists.

In a complex business application, you may implement several *SPA* instances. Each one represents a single logical set of screen interactions that perform a business function. This approach maps extremely well into the Microservices (119) approach, as you can match an *SPA* to the capabilities of one or more Domain Microservices (130). However, you may need to perform some translation or conversion of the results of a *Domain Microservice* in order to match the unique user interface requirements of your *SPA*. That will naturally lead to the need for a Dispatcher (140).

Unfortunately, *SPAs* can sometimes grow to the same size and complexity as the monoliths they are expected to replace. To avoid that, build complex applications as a set of Micro Frontends (426) that are composable.

Examples

Just as with *Web Form Applications*, there have been hundreds of examples of *Single-Page Applications* have been developed to explain different libraries, tool suites, and frameworks for JavaScript. For example, the jQuery (*https://oreil.ly/c0r6d*) and jQuery UI (*https://oreil.ly/YrXp9*) projects host dozens of sample applications highlighting how to use those venerable frameworks for user interface interaction, AJAX, and DOM manipulation.

The original Java Pet Store demonstrated the *Web Form Application* approach with Servlets and JSPs using traditional Web 1.0 techniques. When the Web 2.0 techniques embodied by the *Single-Page Application* came into use, Sun (now Oracle) produced a new version of the application. It takes advantage of those techniques to show, among other features, the infinite scrolling techniques popularized by applications like Facebook and Twitter. You can find the Java Pet Store 2.0 (*https://oreil.ly/JUv0G*) on the Oracle website.

Micro Frontend

(aka Microapps)

You are developing a new Single-Page Application (421) or you are refactoring a section of an existing *Single-Page Application* to make it more modern. You realize that the temptation exists to place unrelated functionality for several business processes together in the same *Single-Page Application*, even though that "feels" contrary to the Microservices (119) approach. You are already applying a Microservices Architecture (Chapter 4) to divide your domain into separate services.

How do you avoid creating a monolithic *Single-Page Application* by placing too much functionality in a common frontend?

Just as the desire to separate concerns and avoid placing business logic that doesn't need to go together into a monolith led to the *Microservices* approach, the same type of concerns apply to frontend UI presentation and logic written in HTML, CSS, and JavaScript as well. In particular, you'll want to address the following concerns:

- You want to enable teams to be able to independently develop and release end-user functionality without having to retest or redeploy the entire UI.

- You want to enable cross-functional teams that own a feature from frontend to backend.

- You want to enable teams to have the freedom to choose from multiple frameworks (such as Angular or React) when appropriate.

While the *Single-Page Application* approach is fantastic in that it allows teams to entirely replace the UI layout and controls within a particular screen region at any time, when a team building a large application tries to apply that approach to many different areas of the business, the result can often be delays and unexpected conflicts as different aspects of the business may need slightly different UI representations. For example, the optimal screen layout in an airline website for choosing a flight may not be the optimal layout for viewing your frequent flyer status. What's more, you want to allow for different customizations in different parts of your application. The payment flow of your airline website may be different, for instance, if the customer is paying with airline points (and started in the loyalty section of the application) than if they are paying by credit card.

Therefore,

Split your *Single-Page Application* into several *Micro Frontends* that align to specific business features.

"Micro Frontends" (*https://oreil.ly/So0DO*) by Cam Jackson introduced this concept. A *Micro Frontend* is a *Single-Page Application* that consists of HTML, CSS, and JavaScript. Each *Micro Frontend* has its own main container region and is loaded in a single HTML upload. The *Micro Frontend* is contained within a parent application that performs activities such as routing to the correct *Micro Frontend* and bringing it into the foreground page. This allows the team responsible for that business feature to implement the full flow of the frontend for the feature.

An example of this kind of architecture, drawn from our shopping cart example from Microservice Design (Chapter 5) is shown in Figure 8-15.

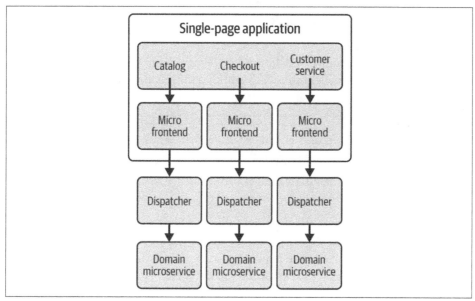

Figure 8-15. General Micro Frontend architecture

Like both *Microservices* and other *Single-Page Applications*, a *Micro Frontend* should be an independent, self-contained application that has no dependencies on other *Micro Frontends* or shared libraries. For example, a change to a JavaScript library or CSS in one *Micro Frontend* should have little or no impact on any other *Micro Frontend*.

This level of isolation allows several *Micro Frontends* to be placed on a single web page that can operate independently of one another, be deployed independently, and even use different frameworks. For example, two different *Micro Frontends* on the same page could use Angular and React, respectively. To make this function, you will often have to use a *Micro Frontend* framework like single-spa (*https://oreil.ly/CrHLJ*), which is a router that enables the different frameworks to communicate.

Micro Frontends, being *Single-Page Applications*, share all of the advantages of *SPAs* over *Web Form Applications*. But the unique split of a *Micro Frontend* brings its own advantages as well:

Smaller deployable units
Each *Micro Frontend* is a small subset of the entire set of functionality of the website as a whole. That means that each unit is faster to develop and test and will individually load faster than a monolithic *SPA* that contains all of the functionality for the entire application.

Independent deployment
Breaking up a monolithic *SPA* into *Micro Frontends* enables you to also break up a larger team into smaller units, each working independently on a different *Micro Frontend*.

Independently updated
Since each deployable unit is smaller, it enables teams to perform updates and make changes independently from the other *Micro Frontends*.

Likewise, in addition to the disadvantages of *Single-Page Applications*, there are added drawbacks:

Added complexity
Breaking up a *Single-Page Application* into a set of *Micro Frontends* adds to the overall complexity of the solution since you now need added coordination between the *Micro Frontends* at the parent *SPA* level.

UX inconsistency
While teams have the flexibility to choose any MVx framework they choose, and also to specify their own look and feel choices through CSS, this freedom can lead to inconsistency in the UI as you move from view to view. Instead, it is often better for teams in an enterprise to consistently use a single MVx framework, or at most a very small set of them, and share some common CSS files to specify a consistent look and feel for the entire web application. Note that having a separate team define that common set of styles and CSS files is an anti-pattern. This is actually a better application of a loose "guild" approach to ensure that

your UX designers and HTML developers are working together toward common goals.

Micro Frontends should be aligned to the backend *Microservices*, especially those *Microservices* that implement the Dispatcher (140) pattern. The best way to do this is not to separate these teams but to keep development of an end-to-end feature together as a single unified team. This implies that each *Micro Frontend* would correspond to a different *Dispatcher*. This also allows the same team to own features and functionality from frontend to backend and work independently.

In a sense, this pattern bears a similar relation to *Single-Page Application* that Modular Monolith (29) does to Big Ball of Mud (22). This is a recurring theme that we've also seen before with Data Module (367). *Micro Frontends* make the *Single-Page Application* more modular.

Examples

There are many examples of *Micro Frontends*, particularly (as we touched on) on the tool websites that are often used for building *Micro Frontends*, such as the single-spa (*https://oreil.ly/AjuY5*) site. In our experience, we have seen it applied successfully in many different domains, particularly in one that we mentioned earlier, which is in the airline industry.

An example of an architecture (and team organization) that follows this pattern is shown in Figure 8-16.

In this example, a team building a customer website for an airline is divided into three stream teams, each one responsible for one major epic that represents a major chunk of functionality in the application. That means each team is responsible for both the backend *Microservices* and the *Micro Frontends* representing those epics. Each stream team implements both the frontend and backend development of their epics, although teams may connect at the *Microservices* level, such as the booking team needing to be able to find flight availability if a flight is canceled and must be rebooked.

By implementing the *Micro Frontend* pattern, you can develop and deploy small features with more agility than in a monolithic *Single-Page Application*. This enables cross-functional teams, ownership of frameworks, and end-to-end ownership of features and reduces complexity.

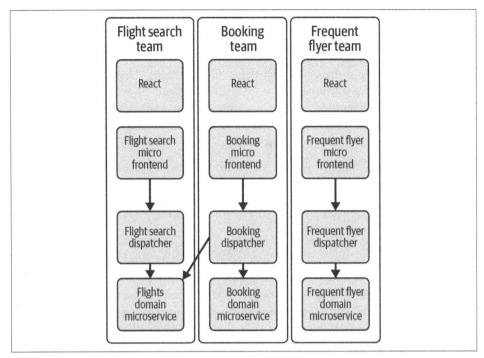

Figure 8-16. Micro Frontend division

Mobile Application

You've developed a Cloud Application (6), such as a Cloud-Native Application (Chapter 3), that is hosted in the cloud. Users need a Client Application (406) to be able to interact with this *Cloud Application*. Many of your customers are going to use a mobile device as their preferred means of accessing your application.

How do you provide the most optimized user experience on a mobile device and take advantage of the features that make mobile computing unique?

A Browser Application (410) that runs well on a desktop or laptop computer might seem sufficient for a mobile device too. After all, mobile devices also have browsers, and this way the application can be reused on multiple devices. Yet an application that works well dynamically updating in a laptop browser that has a mouse, keyboard, and a large screen may be difficult to use on a mobile device.

There are several aspects of building mobile applications that are fundamentally different from building web applications (either Web Form Applications (414) or Single-Page Applications (421)):

Smaller, more varied screens

Mobile device screens are smaller and vary widely in size—as with phones and tablets—and often a large part of the screen is obscured by a virtual keyboard. The amount of content and detail that fits well on a laptop screen is often too much for a mobile screen. The amount and layout of the content need to adjust to the size of the screen and whether a widget such as a keyboard or an enumerated list of choices is being displayed.

Human-machine interaction

Browsers can support interaction conventions that mobile screens typically do not, such as pop-up menus and multiple tabs or windows.

Input

A touchscreen with a virtual keyboard works differently than a physical keyboard and mouse. Scrolling and selecting may be more difficult, and typing long strings of words can be tedious. Touchscreens often provide unique features like haptic feedback that are not part of the web computing experience.

Sensors and integrated features

Mobile devices have many attached sensors and include capabilities that users become accustomed to using in a variety of ways. These can include cameras for scanning QR codes and taking pictures of checks, GPS for precise locations, integrated calendars, and notification systems.

Platform evolution

The two major mobile ecosystems change rapidly. Applications that emulate a mobile device's look and feel often seem outdated when the native user interface libraries of the mobile OS change.

Unreliable networks

Mobile networks can be slow and spotty. *Single-Page Applications* use AJAX, which is specifically designed to be very chatty and assumes a fast, reliable network. A mobile client's connection to the server needs to be less chatty and transfer less data to consume less bandwidth.

Local caching

A mobile client can cache state locally so that it connects to the serverless often and may even be able to run disconnected, including in airplane mode.

Mobile home screen

A mobile device features a home screen that displays a catalog of programs it can run. The user of a browser-based application must remember to bookmark the webpage of the application. Failure to do so may make the browser-based application more difficult to find next time.

While *Single-Page Applications* provide a user interface that can be adapted to different screen sizes and orientations—albeit often with a lot of scrolling— no browser-based application can take advantage of all the features and capabilities of a mobile device. What's more, even though advances have been made in the speed and performance of JavaScript in many browsers, the performance of applications in mobile browsers is still noticeably worse than in laptop browsers.

Therefore,

Develop a *Mobile Application*, an app that runs natively on the user's mobile device and enables users to interact with the cloud application.

A *Mobile Application* enables users to interact with the application running directly on their mobile device without requiring a web browser. You develop *Mobile Applications* using the tools and capabilities provided by the native platform development tool suite. This means that you will need to develop a different *Mobile Application* for each major mobile platform, such as iOS and Android. Developing directly to the platform enables the app to take advantage of the hardware capabilities of that mobile platform by invoking the facilities built into the mobile OS APIs.

The users download a *Mobile Application* from a secured, managed app store, which enables the provider of the OS to vet the applications that are available for their platform to make sure they are not malicious or do not violate the TOS of the platform. A *Mobile Application* acts as a client of a *Cloud Application* and invokes the capabilities of the *Cloud Application* in the same way as the other types of *Client Application*. We show the basic structure of a *Mobile Application* in Figure 8-17.

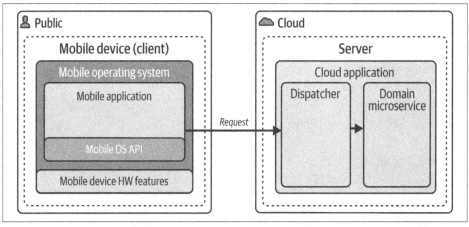

Figure 8-17. Mobile Application

A *Mobile Application* does not have many of the problems that an *SPA* does when running on a mobile device. What's more, there are several advantages to writing a *Mobile Application* instead of an *SPA*. A *Mobile Application* enables the developer to take maximum advantage of the platform's capabilities. Users can easily locate and download the application through the platform's application store and add it to the device's home screen for easy access. For most capabilities in a *Mobile Application*, this will be the path of least resistance and will enable the easiest use of new device capabilities as they evolve (see Figure 8-18).

A *Mobile Application* is not a world entirely on its own. It should fit within the architectural guidelines and strategies we have outlined in the rest of this book. In particular, it should communicate with backend domain services implemented using standard component strategies, such as Microservice (119) or Modular Monolith (29). Specifically, there is often a need for a Dispatcher (140) in front of those *Microservices* or other components to mediate between the requirements of the mobile user experience and the backend server. Another key strategy is to realize that wherever possible you should share other code between multiple incarnations of your *Mobile Application*. This is true not only for code to invoke services on the backend server but for UX logic as well—since the different platforms recommend different default toolsets and even languages for building applications, teams must often make the decision to use frameworks and platforms that allow for development of applications on multiple mobile platforms.

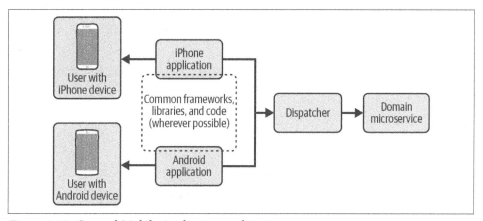

Figure 8-18. General Mobile Application architecture

Similarly, a design choice that many teams building *Mobile Applications* often struggle with is how much of their entire application space to implement in the *Mobile Application*. In a multimodal architecture, you often have more user functions in the web application than may be available in the *Mobile Application*. In particular, there is the question of how to enable access to seldom-used functions from within a *Mobile Application*.

Sometimes, teams have used native functions such as web views to access existing web content from within the *Mobile Application*, but that often leaves users confused as the interface of the web application is not consistent with the native *Mobile Application*. Instead, what has emerged as a solution to this problem is the use of frameworks such as React Native and Ionic that enable teams to embed application code written as Single-Page Applications (421) inside of existing iOS or Android applications. The advantage of this approach is that React Native is compatible with existing web applications written using React, while likewise Ionic works with web applications written in React, Angular, and Vue. Figure 8-19 shows an example of this kind of overall architectural approach.

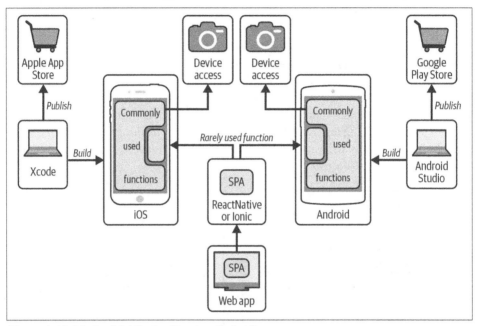

Figure 8-19. Native Mobile Application (hybrid)

While *Mobile Application* applies mainly to native applications on mobile devices (as the name implies), it can also more broadly apply to any computer with a windowing system. Web-based applications like team communications, email, and music and video streaming can be accessed not only through web browser interfaces but also through native applications. These native applications run not only on iOS and Android devices but also on Windows and macOS computers, typically a different distribution of the same application for each platform. Thus *Mobile Application* is a subtype of native application, which applies to any client application implemented to use its platform's windowing system. While native applications for desktop and laptop computers are somewhat common for commercial applications, this approach is rarely used for enterprise applications.

Since the introduction of the iPhone in 2007, there has been an entire generation of users and developers for which interaction with a *Mobile Application* is the default expectation. That has been fostered by the multiple advantages that *Mobile Applications* bring to the table:

User interface specialization
This is perhaps the biggest advantage of a *Mobile Application* versus a *Browser Application*. When an application is deployed as a *Mobile Application*, it is fully integrated with the user experience of the mobile device. That includes placement on the home screen, integration with the device features, and optimization of the screen size.

Discoverability through the app store
For the "mobile generation" and many other user communities, the first place to look for a solution to a problem would be to look in their respective app stores for an application to solve a problem or interact with a company. The benefits of discoverability should not be discounted as a marketing strategy. Many times placement within an app store is just as important as placement within a search engine.

User lock-in
When a user uses a *Mobile Application*, they tend not to want to leave the confines of the application to move to another application. This is the genesis of "all-in-one" applications that are common in certain parts of the world like WeChat, which added features like mobile payment into a chat application so that users would not have to leave the application. This is becoming increasingly common in other parts of the world as corporations like Meta seek to build their platforms in similar ways by expanding horizontally into adjacent areas. While an advantage to the developer, this is perhaps a dark pattern that may not be in the best interests of the users.

There are, however, many disadvantages to writing a *Mobile Application* that teams must also think about:

Development effort
Mobile Applications are often much more complex (and therefore expensive) to write than corresponding *Browser Applications*, especially for relatively simple user interfaces. What's more, where there are fairly significant differences in UX capabilities between different devices running in the same platform (such as tablets versus phones), you may need additional effort to write user interfaces optimized for those different devices.

Duplication of effort

> When you write a *Mobile Application* in addition to a *Browser Application*, you are absolutely duplicating effort and now have at least twice as much code to maintain.

Specialized skills

> One of the biggest drawbacks of writing *Mobile Applications* is that they often require specialized skills and libraries. There are multiple tool suites you can use to reduce this specialization, such as React Native, but you still need to have mobile development skills to deploy and debug the applications.

Mobile development ecosystem (app stores) restrictions

> Perhaps the biggest drawback for many developers is that you need to live within the restrictions, and especially the cost structures, of the two mobile development ecosystems. Deploying an application into the Android or Apple App Stores requires developer registration, and application certification, and puts restrictions on the kind of content that can be placed within the application (such as the mandate for in-app purchases through the app store).

Just as with Single-Page Applications (421), Microservices (119) are a good match to *Mobile Applications* since the business-oriented capabilities of a Domain Microservice (130) map cleanly to the complex screen flow and interaction capabilities of a *Mobile Application*. *Mobile Applications* are often paired with Dispatchers (140) that can filter and translate results to data formats that are specific to the mobile platform.

Examples

There are literally hundreds of sample *Mobile Applications* that show the advantages of working within the capabilities of the standard platforms. Apple's Sample Application Library (*https://oreil.ly/P96js*) and Google's Android Sample Library (*https://oreil.ly/eF21P*) both provide many examples. Google also provides an application called Now in Android (*https://oreil.ly/x6ObB*) that is designed to highlight capabilities and best practices and is built in Kotlin and Jetpack Compose.

A simple, straightforward example of building *Mobile Applications* for multiple platforms with a toolkit that maximizes common code can be found on the Ionic website (*https://oreil.ly/iTpcJ*), where they describe how a team built an application for the 2021 Enterprise Application Summit (EAS) using Ionic. This application was designed to handle all of the standard features of conference software, such as allowing attendees to browse talks, build a schedule, and provide reminders for talks that the users are interested in. Since the application was built using Ionic, not only was the content shared across Android and iPhone, but the content and logic were also shared with the website since most of it was implemented as a *Single-Page Application*.

Command-Line Interface

You've developed a Cloud Application (6) such as a Cloud-Native Application (Chapter 3) that is hosted in the cloud. Users need a Client Application (406) to be able to interact with this cloud application. The users want to interact with the application in a repeated or automated way—e.g., they may want to repeat an operation on a schedule or repeat an operation many times, such as over a set of variables or parameters.

How can an end user automate activities like bulk loads, bulk changes, or scheduled execution of activities while using the services provided by an application running in the cloud?

When most of us think about the user interface of a system, the most common interpretation of the term *user interface* brings to mind a graphical user interface of some sort. Since the advent of the WIMP (Windows, Icons, Mice, Pointers) paradigm in the 1980s and early 1990s, it's hard to conceive of any other way to interact with a computing system. In fact, two entire generations of developers have grown up such that this may be the only way in which they have ever interacted with computers.

However, there are times when a WIMP approach, be it on the web, or in a mobile or desktop application, has its limitations. The simplest case of this is when a procedure needs to be automated. Let's says that you have a simple web page that shows you how many people are registered for an event, such as a Meetup or a book club. If no one registers for a particular event, you will still be charged for the event venue, even if no one shows up. It would be great if you could look at the event signup just prior to the cutoff time, see if anyone is registered and if not, cancel the event.

If you have only a Mobile Application (430) or Browser Application (410), then unless the developer adds this functionality to the application, you are out of luck. You might be lucky and the developer may have provided you with an API to the application, but that is not guaranteed since web-facing APIs present their own challenges to the application developer, nor is it necessarily something that would make it easy for you to write your simple check and cancel the action.

What we need is something that facilitates these simple types of automation tasks yet at the same time doesn't require the complexity of programming to an API.

Therefore,

Build a *Command-Line Interface* (CLI) that enables the cloud application's APIs to be invoked from the command line of a shell in an operating system.

Your *Command-Line Interface* takes advantage of the services of a *Cloud Application* by enabling users to execute APIs at the operating system command line. A

Command-Line Interface will usually be built up out of individual CLI commands that each correspond to the major functions of your application.

The architecture for a *Command-Line Interface* has two parts, as shown in Figure 8-20: a CLI client that implements the commands and the Cloud Application that those commands invoke. The user must install the CLI client in their client machine's operating system.

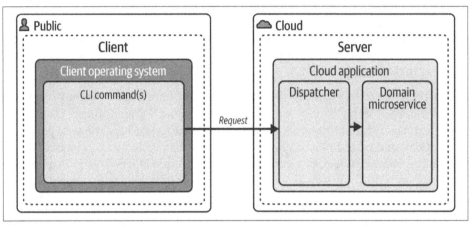

Figure 8-20. Command-Line Interface (CLI)

This example shows how to implement the Cloud Application (6) with a Dispatcher (140) and one or more Domain Microservices (130), but this client pattern applies equally well to other cloud architecture patterns, like a Modular Monolith (29).

A *Command-Line Interface* for a *Cloud Application* enables users to invoke functionality in several ways: from scripts, from unit testing tools, or through an automated platform such as a Robotic Process Automation tool. A key element of a good *Command Line Interface* is composition. This is a great way to facilitate the **Pipes and Filters** architecture. The **Pipes and Filters** (*Enterprise Integration Patterns*, 2003) architecture is a classic way to implement an extensible architecture. In that approach, as exemplified by Unix pipes and filters at the command line, the output of one *Command Line Interface* command can be piped into the input of another command, enabling the composition of multiple tools.

In any case, each CLI command (composable or not) serves as a point of connection between the backend business logic (the *Dispatcher*) and the scripting code that calls it. It also can serve as a point of contact to other code, such as schedulers (to run tasks at a particular time) or to testing code that can automate development tasks like regression testing (see Figure 8-21).

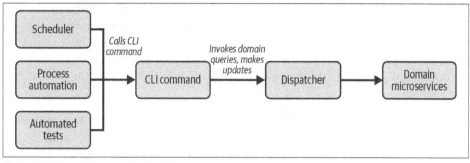

Figure 8-21. CLI command architecture

The simplest implementation of a CLI (perhaps a degenerate case) is using cURL (or another equivalent tool) in place of a custom CLI client to invoke the REST endpoints in the server-side application's API. However, that's not a great solution to the problem in that the parameters required to run cURL in this way would be quite complex—cURL just moves the parameters of the HTTP request into the command line, so while you make it possible to script or automate different combinations, it does not make it easy to do so. Instead, one of the biggest design points of a *Command-Line Interface* is that the commands should format the input and output to be easily human-readable and human-writable. However, if the commands become too fancy with formatting, that may interfere with the ability to pipe the output of one command into the input of another without requiring additional complex command-line switches to move between modes.

Going back to our simple hypothetical Meetup example, we can easily imagine that there could be two commands, one equivalent to "Get Event Registration Details" and another one equivalent to "Cancel Event." They could be tied together with a simple shell script in Linux, which could then be scheduled to run every night as a Cron job. However, this is not the only program that could be easily written using a *CLI*. With a little bit of an extension of the *CLI* (to include creating events), an application could look for open dates and times for events at the venue, and then to schedule events at those times. The ability to compose commands together creates many possibilities.

However, there are requirements on the *CLI* to make this kind of scripting feasible. The **Pipes and Filters** pattern discusses that a common data format needs to be in place among the different commands in the CLI to facilitate piping the output of one command into the input of another. There also need to be facilities for managing the identity of the user of the *CLI* integrated as part of the command set in order to authorize access to the backend tasks that the *CLI* will need to call.

If you are building user interactions for a complex business process, one factor worth considering is the order of development of the different patterns in this section. We have found that in many cases the appropriate order of development should be

API, CLI, and then GUI. The reason is that the most important thing to do is to develop the services in the backend server that make up your business logic (e.g., the API). However, once that is done, the most difficult issue is often how to facilitate end-to-end testing of that API. Writing a web-based or mobile user interface and then testing that user interface with a GUI automation tool like Selenium is possible but often challenging.

Instead, if you begin by building a simple *CLI* that embeds the most important commands, you can use that with simple scripting tools (such as Shell) to try out different combinations of the APIs. This will often expose integration issues that would otherwise be difficult to identify and fix when also facing the added complexity of UI testing. Once the basic flows have been built and tested, you can move on to building the user interface, but this always enables the scripting alternative for more complex interaction combinations.

Since the *Command Line Interface* is such an old approach for user interaction, many teams don't even think of it as a possibility for modern solutions. But it comes with a number of advantages:

Simplicity
> The primary advantage of building a *CLI* is that they are easy to build. The simplest CLIs require nothing more than the stdin and stdout libraries that all languages support.

Resource consumption
> *CLI* applications often consume fewer compute and network resources when compared to graphical applications.

Ease of testing
> A *CLI* is remarkably easy to test. Again, since the input and output are entirely in terms of text, it's simple to formulate test cases and feed them to the program and to evaluate the responses.

Composition
> A simple *CLI* is composable at the operating system level. So long as it is well-behaved and treats input and output as text, standard operating system features that have been available since the early Unix versions (such as piping outputs into inputs and invoking commands through scripting) allow you to take advantage of a wealth of abilities built into the operating system itself. This includes scheduling through commands like Cron in Unix/Linux and the Windows task scheduler.

However, there are many drawbacks to using a *Command-Line Interface* that must be addressed:

Installation
> The main disadvantage is that the *CLI* must be installed on the user's device. Luckily, for simple *CLIs*, this is a well-understood and easily solved problem. In Linux, there are multiple package installers (such as apt in Debian derivatives or yum in Centos and RHEL) that allow you to define and build packages that can be easily installed by users. In the Mac world, homebrew formulas are similar descriptions (which are actually small ruby programs) that define how a new tool can be installed.

User-friendliness
> A *CLI* is not intuitive to use. When compared to a web or graphical interface, it is often difficult to understand how to use a *CLI*, and it usually requires referring to documentation to even get started.

Discoverability
> Most users don't work day to day at the command line, even on computers and devices that have *CLIs*. Thus, your application may not be easily discoverable once installed if a user has to use it. Once again documentation (both on your computer and on the web, where it is search-indexed) becomes critical for usability.

As noted, the simplest implementation of a *CLI* has a command for each task defined by an API. But your *CLI* can also provide more complex commands, each implemented using multiple API tasks. This effectively makes each complex command a Service Orchestrator (160), which means the different API tasks are performing separate transactions, so you need to consider cases of rollback and failure.

The API can build in dynamic hook points (*https://oreil.ly/q0cVO*) for overriding behavior. This is especially useful with **Pipes and Filters**, providing places (hook points) to override behavior at various points in the process. An added benefit of a *CLI* is that it makes it easier to quickly test things manually while also facilitating automated testing.

CLI commands can also serve as simple event triggers in an Event-Driven Architecture (Chapter 6). You might even consider an Event-Driven Architecture to be an alternative to a *CLI*, but the problem with this view is that while an EDA easily solves the problem of hooking into different stages of the business process easily, you are still completely locked into the event system as the only means of expansion or automation, which may or may not be what you want.

CLIs may use Interaction Models (448) within their design to more cleanly separate connection with the backend logic (*Dispatcher*) from the mechanics of processing command-line input and output.

Finally, one thing to consider in your design of your *CLI* is exactly how far you want to take the *CLI*. One of the assumptions that goes into this pattern is that each command is (more or less) standalone and that sequencing and especially control structures (loops, conditionals, etc.) are provided by a scripting tool that invokes each command (such as Unix Shell or PowerShell). If you choose to make your language more complete, including these kinds of control structures, you are probably better served in writing a Domain Specific Language (DSL) (*Domain-Driven-Design*, 2003).

Examples

We show three different examples of *CLIs*, starting with the first generally recognized *CLI* and then looking at more modern examples of how *CLIs* can be useful even in the era of the web.

Multics and the origin of command lines

The first steps toward a command line (and perhaps the first CLI to see the light of day) were part of the Experimental Time-Sharing System (ETSS) (*https://oreil.ly/zskiH*) demonstrated at MIT by Fernando Corbato in 1961. It was based on an earlier paper by Christopher Strachey (*https://oreil.ly/1YXTd*) in which he envisioned a way to have one user debugging a program while another user was running another program. ETSS featured just over a dozen or so commands related to loading, running, and debugging programs. It replaced a more cumbersome interface involving punched cards to represent the program and switches and buttons to indicate what should be done with the programs. What is generally recognized as the first fully formed CLI (which was not named such until after the development of Graphical User Interfaces—they were often just called "consoles" as they emerged simultaneously with the development of video-based system terminals) was developed in 1964 as part of the pioneering Multics time-sharing operating system by the combined efforts of MIT, Bell Laboratories, and General Electric. Multics was the major inspiration for Unix by Bell Laboratories, whose features have inspired every command line interface developed since.

cURL

Perhaps the best example of the utility of a *CLI*, even for a task that on the surface seems completely wrong for it, is in Daniel Stenberg's now-ubiquitous utility cURL. cURL is a utility for getting and sending data, including files, via URLs. Essentially, you can think of it as a command-line version of the address bar in a graphical web browser. cURL has been used for testing websites, testing REST APIs, retrieving data, uploading data, transferring files, and perhaps a thousand other uses. It is now built into the operating system in macOS and Windows and was even part of the software of NASA's Ingenuity Mars Helicopter (*https://oreil.ly/E4vgk*).

Hyperscaler CLIs

In the next section we relate the story of how AWS embraced the concept of the *Public API* from the introduction of their first cloud Backend Service (106). Likewise, another common feature that cloud services from AWS and all the other hyperscalers have provided is a *CLI* that enables users to create and manage instances of those services from any remote system. The AWS CLI is one example of this, and *CLIs* exist for Azure (*https://oreil.ly/OdcxU*), IBM Cloud (*https://oreil.ly/PZhDE*), and Google Cloud (*https://oreil.ly/LhxkN*). In theory, an advantage of having multiple interface types like this (web interface, CLI, and Public API (443)) is that they should be completely identical and any new feature should be introduced into all three simultaneously, but in practice, there are often delays, differences, or gaps in coverage among the choices, leading to frustration for automation developers.

Public API

You've developed a Cloud Application (6) such as a Cloud-Native Application (Chapter 3) that is hosted in the cloud. Third-party applications developed and used outside of your enterprise need to interface with your application and invoke its functionality.

How do you best enable third-party applications to interact programmatically with a *Cloud Application*?

A problem we have often encountered in enterprises that need to work with third parties (business partners, governmental entities, etc.) is that they don't pay enough attention to the communication between what's inside their own walls and the entities. There are two extremes in which we have seen companies fail in their public API approach:

- The farthest end of the spectrum is assuming that you can simply publish your internal Microservices (119) as APIs to the world. The result is that as these *Microservices* change, the changes are inflicted on third parties outside of the company that depend on those APIs. This often results in teams having to support multiple versions of API (we have seen up to six supported at once!) because the third parties cannot change their code as fast as the internal development teams can.

- The other end of the spectrum is that the APIs never change, resulting in lots of work and lost opportunities inside the company itself. For example, many retailing companies still practice FTP file exchange with their suppliers for catalog entries, making it difficult to update catalog entries in real time and forcing teams to write batch jobs to do daily or even weekly bulk updates. This becomes untenable when manufacturers become better at tailoring products for small market segments—especially when the number of products increases dramatically.

Neither end will work—both ends put an undue burden on one or the other partner, often both. What is needed is something that moderates the changes and isolates internal changes to some degree from the external API.

Therefore,

Build a separate service that implements an externally facing *Public API* that third-party applications can use to access the *Cloud Application's* functionality.

There are two cases in which to consider a *Public API*:

- Often, you have the need to support applications that are completely outside your enterprise. These are applications implemented by third parties (such as business partners, governmental entities, etc.).

- Even within an enterprise, you may have applications that are part of the enterprise but are implemented and maintained completely separately from the team that builds the backend logic.

The APIs for the first group will usually have public internet-facing URLs or some other way to access them from anywhere, such as a VPN. That is the primary use case for the *Public API*. APIs for the second group have private/internal URLs that are not generally publicly or externally accessible. Those are generally not initially published as *Public APIs* but may become *Public APIs* if the functionality ever needs to be exposed to business partners or third parties.

Public APIs are sometimes subdivided yet again into partner (closed) APIs and public (open) APIs. The difference between these two is that partner APIs are usually controlled through some contractual agreement and thus are more restricted in how fast they can change in comparison to a *Public API*. In either case, you need to think about both subtypes as being products—they have consumers outside of your development organization, and you have to think about the impact of any changes on that external user community.

That is why the Dispatcher (140) approach of creating unique *Public APIs* is so powerful. It enables you to isolate changes that affect your external user community (the *Public API*) from changes to your internal services (see Figure 8-22).

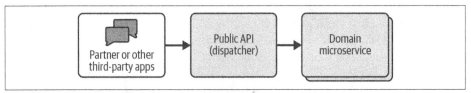

Figure 8-22. Public API

A *Public API* should preferably be stateless, as it should require any state to be the responsibility of the client program that invokes the *Public API*.

The service that you implement as a *Public API* essentially operates as a **Facade** (*Design Patterns*, 1994) to internal services. This service acts as a specialized *Dispatcher*. It differs from the *Dispatcher* pattern in at least two ways:

- In many cases, your own client applications need finer-grained access than those provided by *Public APIs*. There are often features you don't want to expose to applications outside of your control. As a result, *Public APIs* usually provide only a courser-grained level of access that limits the functionality third parties can provide over your systems. As an example, administrative interfaces are usually not provided as part of a *Public API*. Likewise, fine-grained data access may be disallowed in a *Public API*, but summary access may be allowed to preserve privacy. This is, for example, the way the U.S. Census Data APIs (*https://oreil.ly/pgDtI*) operate—they enable access to summary data but not data on individuals.

- A *Dispatcher's* API should evolve over time—at the same rate as the *Client Applications* that use them. This is possible because you can adapt and maintain both the *Dispatcher* and the *Client Applications* accordingly. However, a *Public API* needs to be much more stable because changes can very easily break existing third-party applications and also annoy third-party developers, potentially causing them to stop using your products.

Here are the primary advantages of creating a *Public API* for your applications:

New business opportunities
> A *Public API* may allow for the creation of new applications that you can't anticipate, which provides for new markets and new avenues for monetization of your data and function.

Creating an ecosystem
> The primary advantage of a *Public API* is that it creates an ecosystem of other developers. By opening up your program to be called externally over the internet, you are allowing the creativity of the rest of the programming community to expand your vision in ways you could not imagine. That can, however, be both a blessing and a curse, as you may find that use cases you had not intended for your application to cover may become predominant, stretching your resources in unintended ways.

Creating a *Public API* is not something that should be done lightly. There are several issues and potential disadvantages that teams need to carefully consider:

Versioning

Whenever you publish an API (internally or externally), you face a problem of how to control the API's evolution over time. One side effect of this is the need to publish the version of the API and to werfor the detection of that version by external clients so that they can determine if they are compatible with that version of the API. You can do this by naming the APIs (including the version number in the URL, for instance) or by including the version number in metadata such as HTTP headers. That's just the tip of the iceberg, however. You also need to consider how many versions of the API you will maintain on your server at once—if a change is a breaking change, one is probably too few. Determining the upper limit depends on your tolerance for maintaining multiple versions of the API.

Security

When you make an API available on the public internet, you open yourself up to potential security issues. You have to determine ways of preventing things like injection attacks (where hackers try to send information to your APIs to gain access to your underlying data), man-in-the-middle attacks (where hackers impersonate your APIs to steal user data), and even Distributed Denial of Service (DDoS) attacks where hackers will attempt to overwhelm your compute and network capacity. Having a robust security posture (often through what is called a Zero Trust security approach) is a requirement for publishing a *Public API*.

A *Public API* is one type of Service API (70). One major difference here is that it is a specialization of this pattern for a very specific purpose. All web services, especially *Microservices*, must have a *Service API*. In that pattern, we spoke about how one of the benefits is that it slows down the rate of change for clients by enforcing a separation between API and implementation. However, the need for that separation and the need to keep the rate of change of client and service implementation separate is exacerbated by the fact that in a *Public API*, there is an expectation of stability— external organizations are less tolerant of rapid change than internal teams are. That is why protocols like FTP have remained so popular for B2B information exchange even after multiple generations of innovations (such as SOAP and XML, REST and JSON) have emerged to replace file transfers as better carriers of information.

Something else that is important to understand is that a *Public API* is *not* the same thing as an **API Gateway**. The **API Gateway** (*Microservices Patterns*, 2018) pattern solves a slightly different problem caused by the creation of *Public APIs*. *Public APIs* should be discoverable, documented, and versioned—and access to them should be limited to those clients that are properly authenticated and have the right level of authorization. What has happened is that many **API Gateway** products also provide a form of the Adapter Microservice (135) pattern as part of their implementation—thus people have often built the implementations of their *Public APIs* directly into the **API Gateway**. This is limiting in several ways; first of all, it locks you into that particular **API Gateway** vendor implementation, and second, these products are often limited in how sophisticated the adaptation can be—resulting in *Public APIs* that are often barely disguised versions of internal *Microservices* implementations. This is dangerous in that it exposes too much of your private implementation to the outside world, and it also limits your ability to change your underlying implementation. Taking the architectural approach that a *Public API* should be its own, carefully designed entity avoids this problem.

However, having said this, the **API Gateway** is an often useful addition to the *Public API* pattern because you can use these products to secure, manage, and track your *Public API* usage as well as provide a place to publish their documentation. Figure 8-23 expands on the design in Figure 8-22 to show an example of an architecture that combines both.

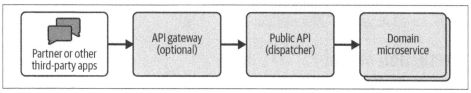

Figure 8-23. Public API with gateway

Examples

An important part of technology lore that emphasizes the importance of the *Public API* is the "Bezos Mandate" that Jeff Bezos (CEO of Amazon) supposedly sent out to all Amazon developers around 2002, as related in 2011 in "Stevey's Google Platforms Rant" (*https://oreil.ly/7saql*). As the story goes, Jeff Bezos sent out an internal email that had the following points:

1. All teams will henceforth expose their data and functionality through service interfaces.

2. Teams must communicate with each other through these interfaces.

3. There will be no other form of interprocess communication allowed: no direct linking, no direct reads of another team's data store, no shared-memory model, no back-doors whatsoever. The only communication allowed is via service interface calls over the network.

4. It doesn't matter what technology they use. HTTP, Corba, Pubsub, custom protocols—doesn't matter. Bezos doesn't care.

5. All service interfaces, without exception, must be designed from the ground up to be externalizable. That is to say, the team must plan and design to be able to expose the interface to developers in the outside world. No exceptions.

6. Anyone who doesn't do this will be fired.

This story has never been denied by Jeff Bezos or anyone else in leadership at Amazon—it should be noted that the original email would have predated the founding of AWS by four years. A culture of promoting APIs at Amazon was critical to the development of the first AWS services.

The very first cloud service ever offered on AWS was the AWS Simple Queue Service (SQS), which was initially released in beta form in 2004. SQS was a commoditization as a service of a networked queuing mechanism that had previously been provided only as end-user installed software from companies like IBM or TIBCO. The announcement of the first publicly available version of SQS in 2006 ("Amazon Simple Queue Service Released" (*https://oreil.ly/D_hUf*)) featured its "straightforward APIs to let you create queues, send messages, receive messages, delete messages, list your queue collection, and to delete entire queues."

Interaction Model

(aka Application Model, Application Controller)

You are building multiple Client Applications (406) for different use cases (for instance, an end-user client application and an admin interface). You want all of the *Client Applications* to work consistently, but you find it's very easy to embed your business rules directly into the code that handles your user experience (UX) actions. That makes maintaining the application difficult, especially as libraries and frameworks evolve.

How do you avoid mixing business and presentation logic inside your *Client Application*?

Mixed business logic and presentation logic is the bane of many corporate developers' existence. Unfortunately, it is a common problem. This is one reason why Refactoring the Monolith (484) by Strangling the Monolith (Chapter 10) has become so popular—often little attention was paid to the separation of presentation and business logic, resulting in business logic that is spread throughout different layers of a system, and that is inconsistent in its handling of user input and requests, sometimes leading to security issues.

What's more, user interface frameworks and libraries change, evolve, and fall in and out of fashion over time. For example, in JavaScript, just since the introduction of the AJAX approach (see Single-Page Application (421)), we have seen frontend applications be rewritten multiple times because it became difficult to find people skilled in a particular framework, because the community supporting the open source project behind the library started to shrivel or because the development team wanted to take advantage of new features that were only available in another framework. So in one application alone, we've seen it move from Dojo, to AngularJS, to Vue, to React over a period of several years. Rewriting your entire frontend to deal with these changing frameworks is something that teams would like to avoid.

Therefore,

Encapsulate the *Client Applications'* interactions with the *Cloud Application*, and manage the state of the user interaction as an *Interaction Model*.

The primary reason for the *Interaction Model* is to isolate domain logic from presentation logic. If you think about the reason we have a *Dispatcher*, this is the inverse of that—it isolates the presentation logic away from having to know too much about the backend but also serves as a bulkhead to keep the user interface from "polluting" the backend. That means that it separates any channel-specific libraries—such as those for *Mobile Applications* on iOS or browser-based applications in React—from the rest of the application as well. Thus, the *Interaction Model* will interface with both of these libraries and the backend Microservices (119) model (either through a Dispatcher (140) or directly). You can see this in Figure 8-24.

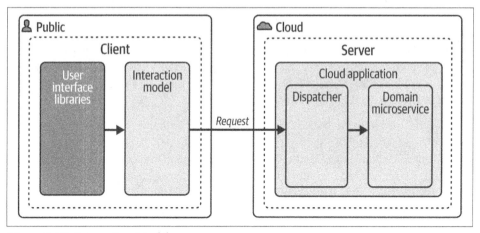

Figure 8-24. Interaction Model

If you are careful in the design of the interface of your *Interaction Model*, you can also make it easier to deal with changing winds of frontend libraries. If your *Interaction Model* has an interface that specifies the abstract interactions of your user interface but does not take (for example) specific JavaScript library objects as parameters, your code is better able to handle changes when your team decides on a new user interface library.

Interaction Model is a concept that VisualWorks Smalltalk (*https://oreil.ly/KyJXC*) called Application Model. VisualWorks updated the model-view-controller (MVC) framework to split the model into two parts: the domain model and the application model (see Figure 4-2). An application consists of one **Domain Model** (*Patterns of Enterprise Application Architecture*, 2002) and multiple application models, one for each GUI. A GUI's application model made the domain model work the way the GUI expected it to, focusing only on the domain functionality the GUI needed, presented via an API the GUI preferred, and structuring the domain data the way the GUI preferred. While the concept is sound, the name "application model" was always a bit of a misnomer, because it wasn't modeling the application, it was modeling a specific user interaction with the domain model. Therefore, this pattern calls it an *Interaction Model*.

An *Interaction Model* interfaces with the domain model via a Service API (70). A Cloud-Native Application (Chapter 3) provides clients access to its domain model via *Service APIs*, which the *Interaction Model* uses to serve its GUI. A Microservices Architecture (Chapter 4) structures its domain model as a set of Domain Microservices (130), which the *Interaction Model* accesses via Dispatchers (140).

Interaction Models are related to specific business processes. The same boundaries that apply to domain models (for example, those found in the Event Storming (189) process) also apply to the *Interaction Model*, since the *Interaction Model* captures the interactions with the users that lead to the actions and events in the event model. Likewise, *Interaction Models* are often also specific to a particular user persona as a single business process usually has transition points where the focus shifts between different personas; each individual section between the intersection of business process and persona would be its own *Interaction Model*.

Perhaps the single most important aspect of an *Interaction Model* is that it is the locus of management for state of the current user interaction. Users interact with a user interface framework through different mechanisms like button click events, text submission in a text window, or voice input, among myriad other possibilities. These interaction events have to be translated into meaningful actions in the business domain. Doing so requires a "memory" of what the context of the button click, chat request, or voice input represents in terms of the state of the current business process that the UX is processing for that user.

An important question to address is how many *Interaction Models* you have in your system. This is a similar and related question to how many *Dispatchers* you have in a system using *Microservices*. There are no absolute hard and fast rules, but we can generally say the following is true:

- You will have different *Interaction Models* for each of your major business processes because that tends to be the differentiation between different major ports of the user experiences. For example, in our ongoing online shopping example, you could imagine that the purchasing business process (with customers using it) has a very different user interface flow than the order fulfillment process (which is used by the internal shipping team).

- You will often (but not always) have different *Interaction Models* for each channel in a multimodal architecture. So in the simplest case, you'd have different *Interaction Models* for a web channel as part of your Browser Application (410) and the mobile channel for your Mobile Application (430). However, those two may be able to share some code and, in the best case, could potentially be the same implementation, depending on how unique the user experience in the two channels would be.

Finally, relating back to the discussion in the section "Ports and Adapters (Hexagonal) Architecture" on page 400, *Interaction Models* can be classified as Adapters in a *Ports and Adapters Architecture*. However, there are other types of adapters in this model that are not *Interaction Models*—you don't want to take the analogy too far. An *Interaction Model* may be distinguished by the fact that ultimately there is a human on one end of the interaction and not a system or other piece of software. This is not a hard-and-fast rule, as there will always be ways to simulate human interaction or automate a system that is designed to interact with a human (such as user interface testing software like Selenium). However at least part of the software design process should be devoted to making sure that the interaction can be carried out with a human in mind. Thus, it is intimately and inextricably tied into issues of UX and UI design. An upfront Design Thinking approach (*Design Thinking*, 2011) should always be employed in the development of an *Interaction Model* to ensure these issues are considered.

Interaction Models may not be something that all developers naturally build into their *Client Applications*, but they bring a wealth of advantages to *Client Applications* including the following:

Testability

One key advantage of introducing an *Interaction Model* is that it improves the overall testability of your system by introducing a point at which the two halves (the client side and the server side) can be separated so that each half can be tested individually using techniques like Mocks. Your *Interaction Model* should have a limited set of external dependencies, usually represented by one or two components (like *Domain Microservices*) or in more complex cases, by a *Dispatcher* that acts a facade for several *Domain Microservices*. That limited API makes it easy to replace those with a Mock so that your UI testing can occur without invoking a backend server. Likewise, you can often using web mocking frameworks to automate unit testing of interactions with the backend code without having to rely on a complex UI test.

Separation of Model from View

Separating the abstract interaction with the backend from the detailed implementation of the frontend also makes it possible for you to isolate that backend code from minor changes to the frontend. Even if you are practicing Responsive Design principles, it is often true that you need slightly different web page designs and detailed interaction design between mobile (or tablet) and desktop versions of an application. Keeping those details separate from the backend interaction is easier to maintain if you have one implementation of that logic instead of two or more, leading you to want to share code between different *Interaction Model* implementations.

Independence from frontend libraries

Frontend client libraries change with the seasons. In one example we are familiar with inside IBM, the JavaScript client component libraries have changed three times over the lifetime of the application—which is actually fairly typical in the industry. Migrations from (for instance) Vue to React or from jQuery to Angular are a common occurrence. An *Interaction Model* isolates your backend code from that very changeable frontend code.

But no solution is perfect, and there are some trade-offs as well:

Extra maintenance

Adding an additional layer means that you have additional code to maintain. It also means that you have to think about how to avoid polluting the *Interaction Model* with details of your frontend client libraries while still representing the client interactions appropriately.

Additional code size

Writing an *Interaction Model* results in more code—which when in JavaScript as part of client application means that the code must be downloaded each time into the browser. That means a longer load time.

There are other ramifications as well. In a multimodal architecture (where you are building several different *Client Applications* for different purposes or communities), there are concepts that span multiple different technology platforms. The concept of a user is something that exists regardless of whether the user is interacting with a system through a web application or through a *Mobile Application*. Allowing the user to carry their identity through the different channels is important to the user in order to follow the principle of least astonishment but also is vitally important in debugging problems where users may find different results for the same interaction on different platforms. This also leads to the need for consistent logging. To implement this, you sometimes have to implement duplicate logging logic for each channel type. This ensures that these complex multimodal systems can be debugged.

The *Interaction Model* serves as the only point of interaction between any user interface frameworks and the backend server. This makes it possible for the *Interaction Model* to also serve as the point of contact to other common libraries that may also change, such as logging libraries. If you have common code (or at least dependency injection aspects) to deal with tracing and observability, it is possible to trace requests through all layers of the system regardless of the particular UI being used. This interaction, including sharing common code like a User object between multiple *Interaction Models*, is shown in Figure 8-25.

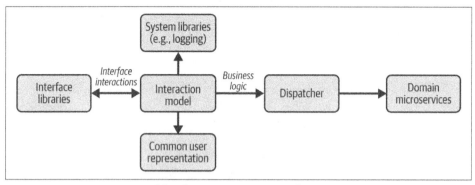

Figure 8-25. Interaction Model Relation to common code

In this case, the minimum code sharing you can have across multiple *Interaction Models* in a system is to reuse common objects like a user or a logging library. In some cases, if the language you are working in allows it, you may also want to have the different *Interaction Models* descend from a common superclass to allow you to push up some of these common functions like logging, user management, or even connection to backend *Dispatchers* into the superclass. This is difficult if, for instance, you implement your *Mobile Application* in Swift and your *Single-Page Applications* in JavaScript, but if you are choosing to use the same language (for instance, JavaScript with a framework like React) for multiple different types of *Client Application*, you may be able to reduce overall code bulk in this way.

The *Interaction Model* is a broadened view of the **Application Controller** (*Patterns of Enterprise Application Architecture*, 2002) pattern. That pattern was also concerned with the separation of UI from business logic, and sequencing or selecting UI operations, but is more tightly tied to page-based web interface technology, which is only one example of the *Interaction Model*—see Browser Application (410) and its newer descendants, Single-Page Application (421) and Micro Frontend (426). However, the idea of business logic separation and explicit modeling of user interaction expands to many other areas as well—most notably as Mobile Applications (430) and Command-Line Interfaces (437) but also to other technologies, such as chatbots.

Conclusion: Wrapping Up Cloud Application Clients

In this chapter, we've looked at an important but often overlooked set of decisions that make up a critical part of a cloud application: examining your choices for the application's user interfaces. We emphasize user interfaces, plural because too often teams make only one choice in how to implement the user interface. Today, multimodal interfaces have become the norm and should be considered when building user interfaces for Client Applications (406). This multimodal interface decision allows for the development of user interfaces for optimal use of the user's device that remotely accesses the functionality in the application running in the cloud—allowing you to provide different types of user interfaces to support different types of users and different types of devices.

This is achieved by surrounding an application core by various adapters that serve different purposes. The UI styles we introduced help separate the business logic they rely upon through the adapters in a **Ports and Adapters** architecture. A *Client Application* should interface with the Cloud Application (6) via a Service API (70), typically implemented by a Dispatcher (140). Thus the API can remain stable while the *Cloud Application* evolves so that developers can evolve the *Client Application* and *Cloud Application* independently of each other.

There are different kinds of *Client Applications* that support user experience of their cloud applications—these can come in many forms, from the most common approach, a Browser Application (410), to Mobile Applications (430) and other forms that teams should also carefully consider, like a Public API (443) or a Command-Line Interface (437). These are usually built using some form of a **Ports and Adapter** architecture, which often uses *Dispatchers* that provide a unified API for clients to interact with the internal business logic. In this case, to complete an end-to-end architecture across the chapters up to this point, we also see how **Repositories** map to specific Backend Services (106) and Cloud Databases (311), allowing requests to pass all the way from user interface to database or other service (see Figure 8-26).

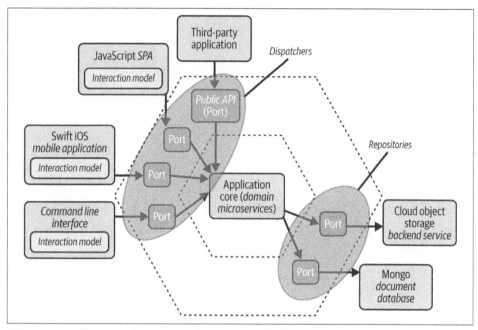

Figure 8-26. Client Applications within Ports and Adapters

The history of the *Browser Application* provides several implementation options that teams, again, may not consider by default but should consider carefully. A Web Form Application (414) is something that can be quickly built for simple cases—and even in more complex cases may be the best option for implementation. The Single-Page Application (421) based on JavaScript running in the browser is the most common choice, but even that has issues, some of which are resolved by building Micro Frontends (426). When building these *Client Applications*, Interaction Models (448) can help abstract away user interface library details and allow for better testing and separation of concerns.

What we've covered up to now are all of the necessary pieces to build new cloud applications. However, not every application starts fresh. You may have existing applications that are not in the cloud. The next chapters will cover how to make existing applications available on and better suited for the cloud.

CHAPTER 9

Application Migration and Modernization

While an application can be designed new for the cloud, a *Cloud Application* often begins as one that runs in traditional IT and then is moved to the cloud.

So far in this book, we have assumed that when designing and architecting an application for the cloud, you are creating a new greenfield application from scratch. While greenfield development can be ideal, the reality is that many Cloud Applications (6) start their lifecycle as traditional IT applications that are later moved to the cloud. These existing applications were designed for traditional IT and not for the cloud. As explained in Cloud Applications (Chapter 1), legacy applications often embed characteristics that work fine on traditional IT but are poorly suited for cloud computing.

This chapter explores how to move an existing application to the cloud and make it run better on the cloud. For these legacy applications to work well in the cloud, developers need to not only move the application to the cloud but often also modify the application to incorporate more of the best practices in this book.

Introduction to Application Migration and Modernization

The development effort to move an application to the cloud is often described as *migration and modernization*. *Migration* moves the application to the cloud, while *modernization* modifies the existing application to make it work better in the cloud.

Before we dive into patterns for moving applications to the cloud, we'll review some background information that is helpful for understanding them. While some of this background comes from industry practices, much of it draws from principles presented earlier in this book. Presenting a recap of these principles here serves as a refresher—as well as an opportunity to show how they fit together to facilitate migrating and modernizing applications.

To develop this context, we'll review several concepts. First, we'll return to the NIST's definition of cloud computing, specifically expanding on the three service models and the capabilities they provide for hosting applications. Second, we'll explore inhibitors to modernizing legacy applications, particularly the relationship between existing user requirements and technical debt. Third, we'll review the fundamentals of structuring and hosting an application—platform, architecture, and packaging—as well as how client/server and Cloud-Native Architectures (58) contribute to modernizing an application for the cloud. Fourth, we'll review industry-standard cloud migration strategies, which include modernization.

Finally, we'll introduce the four patterns for migration and modernization: Lift and Shift (470), Virtualize the Application (475), Containerize the Application (478), and Refactor the Monolith (484). We'll also introduce two best practices for how to do it: Start Small (492) and Pave the Road (496). We'll summarize how these fit together while also incorporating these foundational principles from earlier in the book.

Cloud Computing Service Models

The primary difference between a traditional IT application and a *Cloud Application* is how it is hosted. The introduction to Cloud-Native Application (Chapter 3) discussed the National Institute of Standards and Technology (NIST) definition of cloud computing, including the NIST's three service models of cloud computing. A cloud platform organizes cloud services into these three service models:

Infrastructure-as-a-service (IaaS)
　　Physical and virtual servers with compute, storage, and networking capacity

Platform-as-a-service (PaaS)
　　Orchestrated application runtime environments

Software-as-a-service (SaaS)
　　Complete application software

Figure 9-1 illustrates the models, showing which services are managed by the cloud platform and which the user must manage.

All of the service models—as well as traditional IT—are composed of nine services (i.e., capabilities) for hosting applications. With each successive service model, the cloud platform manages more of these capabilities:

Virtualized infrastructure - IaaS
　　The cloud platform manages compute servers, storage, and networking, as well as their virtualization

Managed runtime environment - PaaS
> The cloud platform extends IaaS to also manage the runtime, middleware, and operating system for the user-provided application and data

Managed application services - SaaS
> The cloud platform manages all of the services, including providing the application and its data as software for applications or users to consume as a service

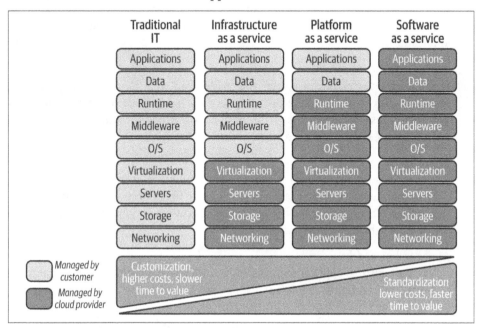

Figure 9-1. Cloud computing service models[1]

With each level, the standardization increases, thereby lowering time-to-value and making solutions faster to develop. With increased standardization comes less opportunity to customize the environment, so the application must conform to the environment.

Modernization and Technical Debt

Whenever you are developing an application that runs in the cloud, you need to know whether you are migrating an existing traditional IT application to the cloud or developing a new greenfield application specifically for the cloud. Much like with traditional IT applications, the decision of whether to create a new application from scratch or update an existing application depends first on whether there's an

---

1 Function-as-a-service (FaaS) has become a popular cloud model which is beyond the scope of this book.

existing application that matches the current user requirements and, if so, how much technical debt (*https://oreil.ly/3u9vS*) is embedded within that existing application. These scenarios determine whether to modernize an existing application or create a new one:

Novel user requirements
> If the user requirements are sufficiently novel—perhaps to enable an enterprise to support a new line of business or a new and highly innovative approach to serve an existing customer base—then a good choice is to start developing a new application.

Established user requirements
> If the user requirements are ones that have been well-known to the enterprise for some time, the enterprise probably already has at least one application that performs those requirements. If an application exists for most of the current requirements, the decision hinges on technical debt:

> *Minor technical debt*
>> If an existing application is fairly easy to maintain, it may be relatively easy to migrate to cloud and is a good candidate for migration. Of course, it only makes sense to migrate the existing application as long as the application matches the current requirements.

> *Major technical debt*
>> If the existing application is already difficult to maintain, it may be quite difficult to migrate. If it is not a very close match to the current user requirements and would need a lot of changes just to fulfill the requirements, it may not only be difficult to maintain but also not worth maintaining. In this case, you should consider either starting a new application from scratch or planning on a modernization effort that sooner or later requires rewriting so much of the code that it may feel like a new application.

Even if an application has a lot of technical debt, there are techniques to move it to the cloud with relatively few changes, which may be worthwhile as long as it fulfills the current requirements well. However, moving an application to the cloud as is does not fix its technical debt, so the debt will move to the cloud as part of the application. For the application to truly take advantage of the strengths of the cloud, the technical debt will have to be repaired, and that may still require significant rewriting of the application.

Application Fundamentals

What are the options for migrating an application to the cloud and modernizing an application for the cloud? To answer that, first let's consider the aspects of what we call an *application*—cloud or otherwise.

An application can vary in three aspects:

Platform
> The location for hosting the application can be *traditional IT* or *cloud*.

Architecture
> The application can be structured as a *Big Ball of Mud*, a *Modular Monolith*, or a *Distributed Architecture*.

Packaging
> Each process can run in a *bare metal server*, a *virtual server*, or a *container*.

Each of these aspects varies independently, so any combination is possible. A *Big Ball of Mud* can be virtualized or containerized and hosted on traditional IT or on the cloud, as can a *Modular Monolith*. Many cloud platforms provide bare metal servers as a service, just like traditional IT infrastructure, and so bare metal can be used to host an application with any architecture on traditional IT or on the cloud. Virtual servers and containers can be hosted on traditional IT or the cloud. Rather than explore all 18 possible combinations, we will explore each aspect individually, knowing that they can be combined as needed.

An application embodies a combination of those three aspects. For any combination, two more optional aspects can be added:

Client/server
> Separate the user interface from the rest of the application so that it can be hosted in the user's web browser or mobile device while the rest of the application is hosted on a remote server or in the cloud.

Cloud native
> For an application to run well in the cloud, it must be architected for the cloud, which also structures the application to run better on traditional IT as well.

Let's explore all of these aspects of structuring and hosting an application in more detail.

Platform

There are two fundamental choices for how to host an application:

Traditional IT
> This is the newish term for what we previously called an application installed on a computer. Each enterprise had its own equipment it managed, which was the hardware that applications were deployed onto. The application developers knew exactly what infrastructure the application would be deployed on, and if the enterprise changed the infrastructure significantly, the application would have to be modified accordingly.

Cloud

> This is computer equipment that is virtualized to abstract the infrastructure that the operations team manages and separate it from the applications that the development team creates. Cloud computing facilitates a vendor/customer relationship between the provider of the cloud infrastructure and customers who provision capacity for their applications.

Cloud Applications (Chapter 1) explained common characteristics of traditional IT applications that hinder them from working well on the cloud. This chapter explains how to move an existing application from traditional IT to the cloud.

Architecture

In Application Architecture (Chapter 2), we reviewed three fundamental application architectures:

Big Ball of Mud (22)

> A monolithic application with no discernible structure, where any code has access to all other code and variables

Modular Monolith (29)

> A monolithic application composed of loosely coupled, well-encapsulated code modules

Distributed Architecture (38)

> An application composed of code modules that can run on separate computers

The first two architectures are monoliths where the application runs as a single workload in a single executable process. In an application with a *Distributed Architecture*, each module runs as a separate workload in a separate process.

These architectures are independent of the platform. Any of these architectures can be hosted on traditional IT infrastructure or cloud infrastructure. Whichever platform hosts the application, its architecture doesn't change.

Application migration and modernization

An application can be migrated to change its platform and modernized to change its architecture.

Figure 9-2 shows how migration relocates the application from one platform to another without changing its architecture, whereas modernization transforms the application from one architecture to another without changing its platform.

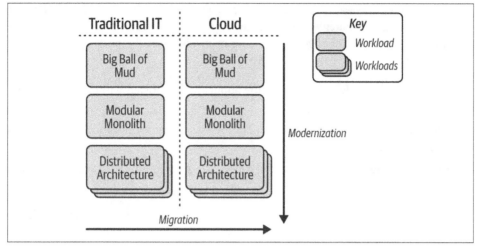

Figure 9-2. Application migration and modernization

Either or both approaches can be taken. A traditional IT application can be migrated to cloud, maintaining the same architecture. An application on traditional IT or cloud can be modernized to a more sophisticated architecture. An effort to update an existing application will often both migrate it to a new cloud platform and modernize its architecture.

Packaging

Another way to modernize an application, in addition to evolving its architecture—is to package the application, which encapsulates it better to simplify its deployment. Each of an application's components that will run as its own process can be packaged for deployment in one of three ways:

Bare metal server
> Don't package the component; just install it and its runtime directly onto a computer's operating system.

Virtual server
> Install the component with its runtime and operating system into a virtual server image that can run in a hypervisor.

Container
> Install the component with its runtime and operating system libraries into a container image (ideally one that is Open Container Initiative (OCI)–compliant) that can run in a container engine.

An application's packaging does not change its architecture. The way the architecture is packaged determines how its runtime will be hosted.

With these three ways an application can be packaged for deployment, this chapter describes migration strategies that take an application currently running on a bare metal server and either changes the hosting or modernizes the packaging. There are three options:

1. *Lift and Shift* simply changes how the application is hosted without modernizing the packaging.

2. *Virtualizing an Application* modernizes the packaging so that the application can run in a hypervisor.

3. *Containerizing an Application* modernizes the packaging so that the application can run in a container engine.

Virtualizing an Application and *Containerizing an Application* are alternatives. Either can be combined with *Lift and Shift* to both modernize an application's packaging and migrate it to the cloud.

The packaging options are shown in Figure 9-3.

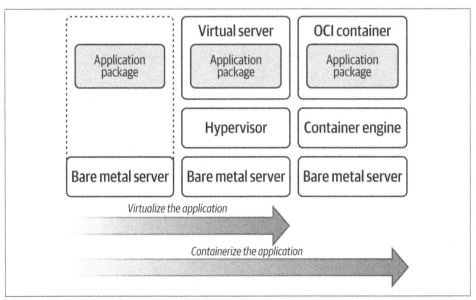

Figure 9-3. Application packaging modernization

Modernizing an application's deployment packaging evolves it to make it more sophisticated. Figure 9-4 shows the three deployment packaging options and how each is more sophisticated than the last.

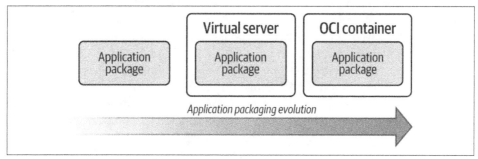

Figure 9-4. Application packaging evolution

Developers may evolve an individual application through these stages over its life-time. In Application Architecture (Chapter 2), we saw that an application's architecture can evolve—much like how bicycles have evolved to become more sophisticated. Similarly, an application's packaging can also evolve, from a bare metal application to a virtualized application to a containerized application. The application or distributed module is still the same, but each stage improves how it is deployed and run. The intermediate stage is optional.

Client/server

If an application is hosted centrally where it can be managed and shared, its user interface needs to be hosted on the user's computer. The Introduction showed how application architecture evolved from a monolithic application that ran on a single computer to one with a client/server architecture where the client application runs on the user's computer and the server application runs remotely on a centralized, shared computer. Cloud architecture is a specialization of client/server architecture where the server is the cloud. In Cloud Application Clients (Chapter 8), we saw that an application hosted in the cloud needs this client/server split.

Modernizing an application's architecture for the cloud requires dividing the application into two client/server parts:

Client Application (406)
    The user interface that runs on a user's computer

Cloud Application (6)
    The shared, multiuser functionality that runs in the cloud

This architecture enables users to access a *Cloud Application* remotely via a network connection (such as the internet), which in turn enables a range of user interface types (e.g., web browser, smartphone app, etc.) to access the *Cloud Application*. A simple app on a smartphone can have the power of a supercomputer via its connection to its *Cloud Application*.

Cloud native

The Introduction went on to show how application architecture evolved from client/server, where the server might be the cloud, to a Cloud-Native Architecture (58) that structures the application to run well on the cloud. Cloud-Native Application (Chapter 3) elaborated on this goal, explaining the advantages of an application with a Cloud-Native Architecture, with other patterns showing details of how to establish this architecture within an application. *Cloud-Native Architecture* can be optionally added onto any of the structure architectures: A *Big Ball of Mud* can be made cloud native (although it won't be easy!). A *Distributed Architecture* is usually easier to evolve further into a *Cloud-Native Architecture*.

Modernizing an application's architecture for the cloud requires transforming it to a *Cloud-Native Architecture*, one designed to use the cloud to run as well as possible. This evolution divides the two-part client/server application into three parts:

Client Application
> The part that runs on a user's device (same as with client/server architecture)

Cloud Application
> The part that runs in the cloud that is developed custom for a particular user functionality

Backend Service (106)
> The platform services that are developed by third-party vendors to be reused by multiple applications

This architecture enables developers to focus on developing the functionality specific to their enterprise's domain that makes their application unique while reusing platform services to perform common tasks.

A *Distributed Architecture* combined with a *Cloud-Native Architecture* forms a Microservices Architecture (Chapter 4), where each cloud-native *Distributed Architecture* module is a Microservice (119).

Cloud Migration Strategies

Developers often refer to the Rs of cloud migration, which are strategies for how to perform migration and modernization well. Gartner (*https://oreil.ly/OWOfn*) published in 2010 what became known as the 5 Rs of cloud migration: *rehost, refactor, revise, rebuild,* and *replace.* In 2016, Stephen Orban revised these into "6 Strategies for Migrating Applications to the Cloud" (*https://oreil.ly/mo4vN*). The 6 Rs of cloud migration are:

Rehosting (rehost)
> Also known as lift-and-shift, this strategy moves an application from traditional IT to the cloud with as little change as possible—making it the quickest and

easiest way to move to the cloud. It doesn't improve the application, but hosting it in the cloud can be more efficient and less expensive than maintaining private data center capacity. An application may be easier to rearchitect for the cloud after it's already been moved to the cloud.

Replatforming (revise)

Also known as lift-tinker-and-shift, it moves an application to the cloud as is but rehosts parts of the application in the cloud platform's managed services when possible. For example, a component hosted on prem on a bare metal server or in a VMware VM might be migrated to the cloud's virtual server platform, such as AWS's EC2. Relational data hosted in an Oracle database on prem might be rehosted in a relational database service on the cloud, such as Azure Database for PostgreSQL. The application maintains its current code and architecture but takes advantage of the cloud platform's operations and software licensing.

Repurchasing (replace)

This strategy replaces an application with commercial software hosted in the cloud. For example, rather than continue to maintain a custom on-prem application for customer relationship management (CRM), enterprise resource planning (ERP), or human resources (HR), replace it with an application hosted in the cloud, such as Salesforce, NetSuite, or Workday.

Refactoring / Re-architecting (refactor, which can evolve into rebuild)

This strategy modifies an existing application for cloud, typically to make it more cloud native. This is the most effective strategy for an existing application to take advantage of the cloud but also the most difficult. An application can be so difficult to refactor—perhaps because it is customized for specific hardware or simply because it contains so much technical debt—that the effort effectively becomes replacing the application. If replacement looks necessary, it is easier to rebuild it from scratch rather than trying to refactor it.

Retire

An application may be running but without anyone using it. If so, rather than move it to the cloud, simply shut it down—no one will miss it.

Retain

If an application is too difficult to move to the cloud, but is still useful and still works, simply continue to run it where it is. An application may be too locked into its on-prem environment to move to the cloud, a multitenant public cloud may be considered too much of a security risk, or hosting an application in a data center in another country may not be allowed. Or the application may be too riddled with technical debt to refactor. In any of these situations, leave it alone.

Any of these strategies is a viable decision for how to move an application to the cloud (or, in the case of retiring or retaining, deciding not to move it). Of these, three focus on migrating and modernizing an application on the cloud: rehost, replatform, and refactor.

Migrating and Modernizing Applications in the Cloud

The considerations for developing an application that runs in the cloud are as follows:

- How to host the application in the cloud.
- Whether to modernize an existing application or start a new one.

You need to assess whether you have an existing application for the current requirements, what technical debt is embedded within it, and whether it will be less effort to migrate that existing application to the cloud than to develop a replacement application from scratch. Once you have that in mind, you are ready to choose from a set of patterns for migrating and modernizing an application:

Existing application

If you have an existing application that runs on traditional IT that you'd like to migrate to the cloud, you have a couple of options:

- Lift and Shift (470): Rehost an application by migrating it without modernizing it, and perhaps replatform it as well to host some components in the cloud's managed services. A traditional IT application with any architecture and packaging can be moved as is to the cloud. It's a good way to start a cloud journey, but it often leads to modernizing the application as well.

- Virtualize the Application (475): Replatform an application's program and its components in a hypervisor. An application with any architecture that is deployed onto bare metal servers can be modernized by packaging it to run in a set of virtual servers, aka virtual machines. In the cloud, this approach uses the IaaS service model. The *Lift and Shift* strategy is often combined with this one to move an application from bare metal servers on traditional IT to a similar set of virtual servers on the cloud.

- Containerize the Application (478): Replatform a program and its components in a container engine. An application with any architecture that is deployed onto bare metal servers or in virtual servers can be modernized by packaging it to run in a set of OCI-compliant containers. This enables the application to be hosted in a container orchestrator on traditional IT or the cloud. In the cloud, this approach uses the PaaS service model.

- Refactor the Monolith (484): Refactor an application with a monolithic architecture, on traditional IT or the cloud, into a more modular architecture. A *Big Ball of Mud* can be refactored into modules to become a *Modular Monolith*. The modules in a *Modular Monolith* can be refactored to each run separately in a *Distributed Architecture*. Strangle the Monolith (Chapter 10) is a strategy for refactoring the application incrementally.

New Cloud Application (6)

The ultimate in refactoring an application is to rebuild the application entirely. Whether starting from scratch or rebuilding an existing application, you must design it from the beginning to run well in the cloud. Rebuild is the correct strategy for an existing application with so much technical debt that it should be replaced with a new one. While the new application can be designed for any platform, architecture, and packaging, a *Distributed Architecture* will have the most flexibility, and modules packaged as containers for a container orchestrator on the cloud will be the easiest to deploy and give the cloud the greatest ability to manage them. This may end up being the most challenging of all since in the end you will be writing a new application.

These options are listed in order from the least to most cloud-friendly, from the least amount of changes to an existing application to the most changes to writing a new application from scratch. You can write a new application with the most basic platform (traditional IT), the most basic architecture (*Big Ball of Mud*), and the most basic packaging (bare metal, which is no packaging). But when starting from scratch with no technical debt, developers these days should typically choose to start with the most sophisticated approaches: a *Distributed Architecture* of containerized modules to be deployed on the cloud. A refactored *Cloud Application* and a new *Cloud Application* produce equivalent results. By embodying distributed containerized modules, both are well suited for the cloud. Where they differ is not in the resulting application but in how they began. Either an existing application was converted to embrace the cloud or a new application was built from the beginning to work well on the cloud.

The list is effectively ordered from the least cloud-native outcome to the most cloud-native outcome. Because the cloud is distributed, any application deployed to the cloud should ideally have a *Distributed Architecture*, either because it was written that way from scratch or because an existing application was refactored to make it modular and distributed. Until that is possible, the next best option is to containerize the existing monolithic application so that it can be hosted in a container orchestrator in the cloud. If that is not possible, at a minimum, host the application in virtual servers in the cloud; the application is not much different, but at least it can more easily be hosted on a cloud platform.

To perform these strategies, follow these best practices:

Start Small (492)[2]
>   Perform the work incrementally—not all at once, but in manageable chunks.

Pave the Road (496)[3]
>   Don't make each team and developer invent their own practices; rather, build a foundation of tools, environments, and policies for the developers to follow.

With these practices, migration and modernization will go much more smoothly.

This introduction has covered several topics that are helpful to be familiar with to understand the patterns in this chapter. We've talked about the cloud computing service models, modernizing applications in the face of technical debt, the fundamentals of architecting and hosting applications, and standard cloud migration strategies, and we've introduced the patterns.

With this background in mind, let's explore patterns for how to migrate and modernize an existing application: Lift and Shift (470), Virtualize the Application (475), Containerize the Application (478), and Refactor the Monolith (484). Then we'll look at how to perform these tasks: Start Small (492) and Pave the Road (496).

Lift and Shift

(aka Rehost)

You have an existing application, typically hosted in bare metal servers, that you want to migrate onto the cloud. To minimize time and effort, you want to change the application as little as possible. Although that will not give your application many of the advantages of the cloud, you still want the advantages of hosting the application in cloud infrastructure because it provides more flexibility and efficiency than traditional IT infrastructure. The cloud infrastructure is presumably a vendor's public data center but could also be your enterprise's private data center.

What is the simplest possible way to move an existing application to the cloud?

The existing application may or may not be well-architected for the cloud, but you don't have the luxury of rewriting the existing application right now. Making significant changes to an existing application to make it run better in traditional IT takes time, effort, and skill, complexities that are magnified when modernizing a traditional IT application for the cloud. Maybe later you'll modernize it to make it more cloud

---

2 Note that the Start Small and Pave the Road patterns evolved from the Strangler Patterns (*https://oreil.ly/ApoZy*) presented at Pattern Languages of Programs 2020 (*https://oreil.ly/2RSFH*) by Joseph Yoder and Paulo Merson and a variation of these patterns were described in the "Leading a Software Architecture Revolution" paper (*https://oreil.ly/Bs_9W*) presented at Pattern Languages of Programs 2022 (*https://oreil.ly/pTd8s*) by Marden Neubert and Joseph Yoder.

3 *Ibid.*

native, but for now, you just need to get it out of your enterprise's data center and into a public cloud–or at least off of traditional IT and into a private cloud. There are other issues you may also have to consider:

- Writing an application following a Cloud-Native Architecture (58) requires skills that your team may not possess. They may not be familiar with how to refactor into Microservices (119), or they may not have experience with the new tools, frameworks, and languages that a *Cloud-Native Architecture* would require.

- You may not be able to afford the development effort to rewrite or refactor an application into a *Cloud-Native Architecture*. You may have financial constraints on how much you can spend on rewriting or refactoring your application.

- You may have constraints on how rapidly a solution to move to the cloud must be. You may, for instance, be shutting down an on-premises data center, requiring applications to move to a new location, which increasingly means moving them into the cloud. Often these moves need to happen quickly, meaning that you don't have the luxury of exploring other options.

What you need is an environment in the cloud that closely matches the traditional IT environment the application runs in.

Therefore,

Lift and Shift an existing application to the cloud by creating a set of compute servers in the cloud that match the traditional IT computers the application has been installed on and reinstalling the application into those cloud servers.

This is the first of the 6 Rs of cloud migration: Rehosting. Relocate (rehost) the application as is from a set of traditional IT computers to a similar set of cloud servers. The relocated application will still run the same way it always has, but it will run in the cloud. Figure 9-5 is an example of how to *Lift and Shift* a monolithic application to the cloud without making any changes to the application. Note that could be a very entangled system or modularized. It could have pieces of the application that could be *Lifted and Shifted* to different cloud servers, especially if there were remote calls in the original system.

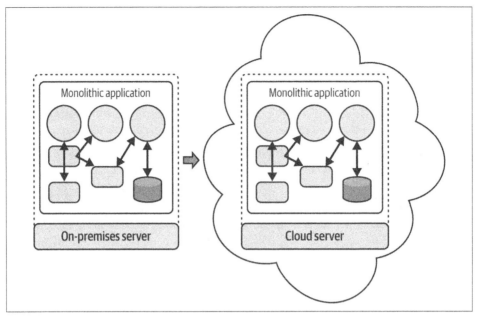

Figure 9-5. Lift and Shift

A *Lift and Shift* migration is the most straightforward and least intrusive path for cloud adoption. It migrates the application but doesn't modernize it. It moves the application to the cloud while keeping code changes to a minimum. Whereas most approaches to application migration and modernization rearchitect your application to work in the cloud, the *Lift and Shift* approach preserves the application's architecture and instead changes the cloud to match your existing traditional IT environment.

There are four basic steps that you need to take to make a *Lift and Shift* possible:

1. *Duplicate compute environment*

    You need to ensure that you can create a compute environment in your cloud provider that duplicates as closely as possible the compute environment the application was built for. You need to ensure that the cloud vendor supports the operating system product and version that the application was built for, or that the application dependencies on the version are so minimal that no code changes are necessary to run on a new version.

2. *Duplicate network environment*

    You need to ensure that you can duplicate the application's networking dependencies in the cloud. This requirement depends on the application. While some traditional IT applications may be flexible enough that the network dependencies between components can be adjusted in configuration files, many require customizing the network configuration. Cloud servers are typically hosted in a Virtual Private Cloud (VPC), which creates a private network. For applications that require network customization, the VPC's private network can be configured with any application dependencies, such as specific network addresses. Many public clouds facilitate this by enabling you to Bring Your Own IP (BYOIP) addresses to the cloud, relocating IP address ranges from traditional IT on prem to the cloud. A VPC's private network can also manage application isolation using virtual firewalls, routers, and gateways.

3. Connect to on-prem resources

An application may need to continue to connect to existing on-prem resources that cannot be relocated to the cloud, such as systems of record and databases of record, as well as the enterprise's existing corporate security components, such as single sign-on (SSO) and authorization products, monitoring, and backup utilities. The enterprise's security requirements may require all requests to the application to come in through an enterprise intranet rather than directly from clients on the global internet. Many public clouds facilitate connecting to remote data centers using features such as dedicated network connections over private telephony networks (often called direct connect or direct link) as well as virtual private networks (VPNs) over the internet.

4. Resolve data dependencies

You need to ensure that the application can access the data it needs, either in a Cloud Database (311) or through an external connection through the enterprise intranet to existing databases of record. Moving the data to a *Cloud Database* provides much better performance and is easier to set up than a secure remote connection to the enterprise intranet, but shared databases are difficult to move, and data residency requirements may mean that the database isn't allowed to be moved.

This is a seemingly daunting list, but this is the minimum set of steps that have to be carried out to move an existing application onto the cloud. The good news is that there are many tools provided by cloud providers and other vendors that can help you perform this kind of migration. For example, the AWS Application Migration Service (*https://oreil.ly/FRMYt*) assists in workload migration. Azure Migrate (*https://oreil.ly/cOhQ4*) likewise guides users through discovery, assessment, and migration to their cloud.

Lift and Shift is a lightweight migration strategy and has the potential advantage of being able to complete the migration in a short amount of time. It can also be less complex for migrating features and various permissions. This technique also minimized risk for disruption during migration.

Lift and Shift has the drawback of not getting the full advantage early on of a full-featured *Cloud-Native Architecture*. This might lead to missed opportunities and poor cost optimizations. Third-party applications can also be challenging to migrate using *Lift and Shift* if you cannot exactly duplicate the on-premises environment that the vendor application requires.

Finally in a *Lift and Shift*, you often don't gain any operating expense benefits. Essentially, in a *Lift and Shift*, you are only moving the application without changing the processes and tools you use to manage, operate, or deploy the application. You trade operating expense (aka OpEx; the monthly bills from a hyperscaler) for capital expense (aka CapEx; purchasing, operating, maintaining, and depreciating your own data center equipment). If you do not take advantage of the operating features of a cloud-native platform (such as DevOps tools, Containers, etc.), your agility gains will likewise be minimal as development and operating tasks will likely take the same amount of time as in the on-premises environment.

The term *Lift and Shift* often refers to a combination of strategies:

- Move the application from traditional IT to the cloud.
- For an application hosted on a bare metal server, Virtualize the Application (475) to host it in a virtual server that can be configured the way the traditional IT computer is configured. You can even Containerize the Application (478) so that its parts can be hosted in a container orchestrator. If the application is hosted in parts on multiple bare metal servers, virtualize or containerize each part.
- Migrate the application's dependencies to the cloud by hosting them in the cloud platform's Backend Services (106). This involves migrating to Application Databases (329), which can be hosted as Database-as-a-Service (379).

Often the application being moved using *Lift and Shift* is a monolith. Refactor the Monolith (484) to modernize it into a Modular Monolith (29) or even an application with a Distributed Architecture (38). This process can be performed incrementally by Strangling the Monolith (514).

Examples

Capital One has spoken at several conferences about its cloud modernization journey. They have described (*https://oreil.ly/gKJGf*) how rehosting (e.g., *Lift and Shift*) has been one of many strategies they followed across their portfolio.

Accenture has an interesting case study (*https://oreil.ly/3I6Ts*) of how they helped Corteva (formerly part of Dupont) to migrate their LIMS (Laboratory Information Management Systems) onto Azure through a *Lift and Shift*.

Virtualize the Application

You have an existing application that you want to migrate onto the cloud, perhaps using Lift and Shift (470). You want to avoid changing the way the application is written but are willing to change how the application is packaged for deployment so that it will run better in the cloud.

What is the simplest possible way to package an application so that it can easily be deployed to traditional IT or to the cloud?

Lift and Shift deploys an application to the cloud as closely as possible to the way it was deployed to traditional IT. An application is typically deployed on traditional IT by installing it in the operating system running on a bare metal server.

Bare metal servers are also an option on many cloud platforms. They are good for specialized uses like high-performance computing (HPC) and workloads that need an extremely customized environment, such as a specialized CPU or GPU. But for general workloads, bare metal servers are unnecessarily inflexible and difficult for the platform to manage. Most applications do not require bare metal's efficiency. Rather, they would benefit more from the flexibility that the cloud enables for many workloads to share a set of hardware. Some of the problems of bare metal servers are as follows:

- Bare metal servers require relatively more operational resources than other computing options, such as virtualization or containerization. To run an application on a bare metal server, operations personnel must first install the operating system (OS) on the server, install any middleware or other dependencies needed to run the application, and then install the application into the OS. This process can be at least partially automated using automation technologies like Ansible (*https://oreil.ly/kja4G*), but that automation must still be written or at least located and tested.

- Bare metal servers do not benefit from the ability of Cloud Applications (6) to transparently take advantage of any available server on the cloud. If a bare metal server fails, another server must be provisioned and the OS, application, and all its dependencies reinstalled.

An application installed on the operating system running on a bare metal server is therefore tightly bound to that server. Ideally, operations should install the application into the operating system once and then be able to move that package from one server to another without having to start from the ground up each time.

Therefore,

Virtualize the Application by packaging the application as a virtual server so that it can be hosted in a hypervisor. The hypervisor can be hosted in the cloud, thereby hosting the application in the cloud.

When you *Virtualize the Application*, the application does not change; what changes is how it's installed. Rather than install the application on a bare metal server, install it in a virtual server, which can run in a hypervisor in the cloud (see Figure 9-6). All cloud providers support at least one hypervisor type as part of their infrastructure-as-a-service (IaaS) offerings.

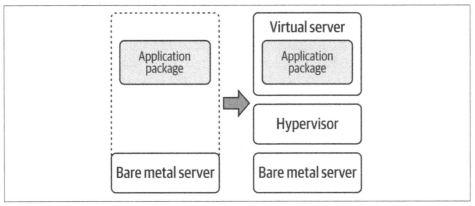

Figure 9-6. Virtualize the Application

A virtual server packages an application installed in an OS so that the package can run in a hypervisor. If an application is packaged as an Application Package (62), it is especially easy to deploy, including installing into a virtual server's OS. Wherever the hypervisor can be hosted, the virtual server can be hosted, and so the application can be hosted there as well. Virtualizing the application avoids having to install the application into the OS more than once. The application is installed in the OS once and is packaged as a virtual server, and that virtual server can be run repeatedly in multiple hypervisors hosted in multiple environments without having to reinstall the application in each one.

Cloud works more effectively by running workloads in the infrastructure-as-a-service (IaaS) service model, where all of the hardware components are virtualized. Virtualization enables the cloud to manage workloads more efficiently, such as enabling a single set of hardware to host multiple workloads that share the hardware, easily relocating a workload from one set of hardware to another. Virtualization also enables the cloud to allocate each workload exactly as much capacity as it needs, and perhaps even to grow and shrink that capacity elastically to adjust to changes in client load.

To host an application in a virtualized environment, developers need to package the application so that it can be deployed to a virtualized environment. Packaging applications as virtual servers makes them all look alike to the hypervisor, enabling a hypervisor to run a server without regard to the application's specifics.

Most applications can run successfully in virtual servers because virtual servers work very much like their physical counterparts, bare metal servers. An application usually requires an OS, so the bare metal server must host the necessary OS, which may need to be customized for the application. Likewise, each virtual server hosts its own OS, which the hypervisor calls the server's guest OS and which can also be customized for the application. The application can be installed on the guest OS the same way it's installed on the OS on a traditional IT's bare metal server. Each virtual server can host a different guest OS, enabling applications that require different OSs to run in the same hypervisor on the same bare metal server.

The biggest advantage of *Virtualize the Application* is that once an application is virtualized, it is no longer tied to a specific physical machine (like a bare metal server). It can move to any hypervisor within the cloud environment, which makes it easier and faster to recover from failures (in fact, this is automatic as images will restart on another hypervisor or machine whenever an image crashes). What's more, patching of the OS or application becomes a more repeatable process, as the work is done in a development environment where the new version of the OS and application are tested outside of production long before the new image is released into production.

Perhaps the biggest drawback of *Virtualize the Application* is that when you virtualize an application, you are doing so for a specific hypervisor. If you want to use the Amazon Elastic Compute Cloud (EC2) service, you need to package your application as an Amazon Machine Image (AMI). If you are using VMware as your hypervisor, either on premises or in the cloud, you must package your application as a VMware Virtual Machine Disk (VMDK) file. There are tools like HashiCorp Packer (*https:// oreil.ly/UasiD*) that aid you with building images for multiple different formats, but you must build these into your deployment process.

Because of this need to build images for a specific hypervisor, images often end up becoming "sticky" to a particular hypervisor as teams are less incentivized to move the application to another hypervisor, even if there are technical or cost advantages, because of the work required to repackage and redeploy the application. What's more, even in the cloud, there are operational differences (in tools and procedures) between managing images on each of the different cloud providers, which again, leads to "stickiness" to hypervisors and cloud providers.

To move an application to the cloud, *Lift and Shift* and *Virtualize the Application* are often combined: each application hosted on a bare metal server in traditional IT is converted into a virtual server hosted in a hypervisor in the cloud. Most applications can be virtualized, and this approach enables IaaS to host and manage the application rather than traditional IT.

Most applications that can be virtualized can further be containerized, and Containerize the Application (478) enables the cloud to host the application even more efficiently than virtualization.

If the application to be virtualized is a monolith—Big Ball of Mud (22) or a Modular Monolith (29)—developers can Refactor the Monolith (484) into a Distributed Architecture (38).

A virtualized application can be redesigned further to make it embody more of a Cloud-Native Architecture (Chapter 3), which makes it even easier to run on the cloud.

Examples

Application virtualization has been well-established for so many decades that there are literally hundreds of case studies on the advantages of virtualization over running on bare metal servers. Among those are the following:

- Amazon has published a case study of how Swire Coca-Cola (*https://oreil.ly/3ag8X*) used both *Lift and Shift* and *Virtualize the Application* to move from their on-premises data centers into the AWS cloud.
- VMware, together with Forrester, has done a Total Economic Impact study of adopting VMware on AWS at a public university (*https://oreil.ly/4hgX3*).

What makes these studies interesting is that they show the advantages of *Virtualizing the Application* into a cloud environment.

Containerize the Application

You have an existing application that you want to migrate onto the cloud, or you have already used Lift and Shift (470) to move it onto the cloud. You want to avoid changing the application but are willing to change how the application is packaged for deployment so that it will run better in the cloud.

How can an application be packaged to facilitate greater deployment density and platform portability?

With greater deployment density, more applications can run on the same amount of capacity, thereby using the hardware more efficiently. Platform portability enables packaging an application once that can then be deployed on any cloud, public or private. The developers can change their minds about which cloud platform to use and redeploy to a new platform without having to repackage the application.

One way to package an application is to Virtualize the Application (475), which packages an application as a virtual server image. Virtual servers are highly customizable, which facilitates being able to host just about any traditional IT application, but are also very heavyweight. You can be more efficient with cloud resources when you host an application in a container rather than a virtual server because containers are lighter weight than virtual servers. When a packaged application is lighter weight, it starts up faster and can scale more easily within the same memory and CPU footprint.

However, most IT shops are very comfortable with virtual server technology because it has been available on premises with traditional IT for decades and skills exist to support well-known technologies (such as VMware ESXi). That makes virtualization an easy place for teams to start since they believe they can build on existing skills, even though the particular hypervisors and tools for virtualization on the cloud are often different.

But there are other aspects of virtual servers that also make using them sometimes challenging:

Patching
Virtual servers are originally created from images that begin from a known level of software (operating system, middleware, and application). The problem is that virtual servers often run for a very long time, incentivizing operations teams to apply patches to the running software rather than build a new server image and entirely replace the existing virtual server. That causes drift, which means that it becomes more difficult to debug problems in virtual servers when they occur. This is why patching is an anti-pattern, as explained in The Twelve-Factor App: V. Build, release, run (*https://oreil.ly/cd6Sg*), which was introduced in the Cloud-Native Application (Chapter 3).

Proprietary
Virtual server technology has not been standardized to the level of other packaging technologies. There is often significant work involved in porting a virtual server image to another hypervisor or virtual image format.

Overhead
Virtual server technology often has a higher operating cost than other technologies (such as containers) because of the lower density and greater effort required to create, manage, and patch existing virtual servers. Even though startup costs may be relatively low, the ongoing operating cost can be significant.

So, much like *Lift and Shift*, *Virtualize the Application* often starts off very well as a first step—it's a great way to Start Small (492). However, as you get to the point of scaling to greater numbers of applications and begin thinking about standardizing techniques and approaches that work across your enterprise, you find that the lower initial effort leads to higher effort over the longer term.

Therefore,

Containerize the Application by packaging the application as a container so that it can be hosted in a container engine. The container engine can be hosted in a container orchestrator that is hosted in the cloud, thereby hosting the application in the cloud.

When you *Containerize the Application*, the application does not change; what changes is how it's installed. Rather than install the application on a bare metal server or even in a virtual server install it in a container, which can run in a container engine (see Figure 9-7). A container engine can run on a bare metal server or in a virtual server, and is even more useful when running on a node in a container orchestrator such as Kubernetes.

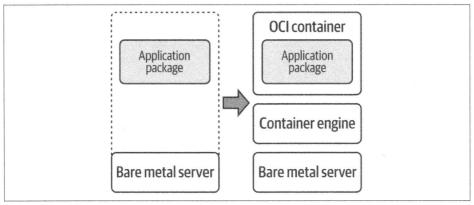

Figure 9-7. Containerize the Application

Containerization is the next evolution of application packaging beyond virtual servers. A container packages an application with the OS libraries it requires so that the package can run in a container runtime as part of a container engine. If an application is packaged as an Application Package (62), it is especially easy to deploy, including installing into a container. Whereas a virtual server includes a full guest OS, a container includes only the additional OS libraries that the application requires. Rather than each container including duplicate OS kernels, which is the biggest part of the OS, multiple containers running in a single container engine share a single OS kernel. This makes a container much more compact than a virtual server. Compared to virtual servers, containers can be run in greater density on the same hardware, can start more quickly, and can reliably be shut down cleanly, making them ideal for cloud-native applications. There are other advantages to containerization as well:

- Since a container shares the underlying OS kernel with the container platform, you can fit more containers into the same memory space than you can virtual servers. Container images also take up less disk space than virtual servers due to the way in which the container file system is built.

- Containers start up significantly faster than virtual servers because of the shared OS kernel and the fact that containers are running in a common shared process space—there is simply less inside each container that needs to be started up.

- The way in which containers are built means that it is harder (by no means impossible, but much harder) to change a running container from the original configuration (image) with which it was built. This sounds like a negative but is instead a major positive to container technology. That means that containers do not drift from their original configuration from when they were packaged, making them easier to operate since all containers created from the same container image are absolutely identical. If a container fails, the new container that starts up will be identical to the original in every way. This embodies The Twelve-Factor App: V. Build, release, run (*https://oreil.ly/Z1CqQ*).

- Containers are more portable than virtual servers. The container approach standardized early around image configurations (dockerfiles) and container runtime engines built on a small set of open source projects. As additional projects expanded on container technology, the creators of those projects were careful to maintain compatibility with the earlier projects. Starting in 2015, the Open Container Initiative (*https://oreil.ly/Qudy0*) (OCI) then proposed specifications within which all vendors should maintain compatibility. As a result, if you build a container, it can usually be moved across clouds and on-premises environments (such as Kubernetes environments) more easily than a virtual server.

Cloud works more effectively by running workloads in the platform-as-a-service (PaaS) service model, where the platform manages the application runtime and OS, such that the developer has to supply only the application. A container orchestrator (such as Kubernetes (*https://oreil.ly/bE4Nk*)) accomplishes this, managing container engines running on OS kernels. The developer is responsible only for the container that includes the application.

The key question for adoption of *Containerize the Application* is, can the application (that is, each of its processes) run in a container? There are a few considerations when deciding whether an application can be containerized:

Operating system
    A container, such as a Docker container, can run either Linux or Windows. The application needs to be able to run in a current version of one of those OSs for

containerization to work. This limits your options if your application only runs on an OS that is not supported by a base container image, but luckily these two options cover most applications.

Middleware

Does the application run in or depend on middleware, such as an application server or database? If your application runs in a simple programming language runtime that runs in a container OS (such as an Application Package (62)), the application can be made into a container pretty easily. If the application requires that it run in a more extensive application server or other middleware, that server must be able to run in a container OS. Again, luckily this covers most modern versions of middleware but may force you to migrate your application to a supported version if only the latest versions are supported on a container.

Base image

You can create a container image from scratch for an application, but vendors already provide base images for standard runtimes and application servers. So if your application runs in a fairly standard runtime or application server, you should build your image by starting with a vendor's base image. If your vendor does not provide a standard base image, you must build your own image and install the middleware or application into the OS by writing your own installation scripts and automation. This in particular means you may be at the mercy of the vendor if the installation scripts are not amenable to automation (as is true in many Windows installation scripts) or if it places requirements on the installation (like connection to the internet) that may not be easy to meet in all circumstances.

In the end, if your application is written in a common programming language, runs on the latest versions of Linux or Windows, or uses standard commercial or open source middleware, you are likely to be able to run it within a container fairly easily. However, if your application or middleware places unusual restrictions on the runtime environment, you may find it difficult to containerize and instead will be better off *Virtualizing the Application*.

Containers are lightweight, can be more portable than virtual servers, and are faster to manage and deploy than virtual servers. All of these factors can save time and money with application deployment. Due to the standardization of container images and runtimes, developers can package applications once and run them anywhere. Containerization can make managing applications easier as they are isolated and operated independently. Containers can assist developers in creating and deploying apps faster, and thus containers help in supporting decomposition of a monolith into Microservices (119).

However, containerization as a process is not without its challenges:

- Existing development and deployment automation is often built to support virtual server deployments. It takes time and effort to convert older automation to containerization.

- Existing middleware or third-party applications may also be built or optimized only for virtual server environments. You may have to convert the middleware to a version or product that supports containerization, which may involve rewriting or updating your application.

- Lack of skills in container environments may be a barrier to converting development and deployment processes and automation to support containers. You may need to train your staff in this technology, which comes at a cost.

Containers can be difficult to build, especially manually. You are much better off if you spend effort developing automation to build and deploy your containers in a standardized way within your DevOps pipelines instead of letting each team solve this problem on their own. This is a great way to Pave the Road (496) and let the first teams adopting containers build reusable assets that later teams can adopt.

Container orchestration can be especially difficult to get right. Many teams try to adopt container orchestration without having the skills in place to manage the container orchestration environment—it's much better to have a common team with those skills that can manage many different applications within shared orchestration environments to leverage these rare skills. Adopting a common DevOps process to make deploying applications as containers easier is also important, particularly a build pipeline that compiles an application into deployment artifacts and packages them in a container.

A containerized workload may not be the final destination in a cloud modernization journey. Containerization may be all that's needed in some cases, particularly if the monolith is relatively small or if the team is able to deliver features at the rate and pace you need. However, for larger monoliths where the complexity of the monolith and/or testing time makes it impossible to deliver features at the pace the business needs, you will want to Refactor the Monolith (484) to redesign it using *Microservices*. Use Strangle the Monolith (514) to refactor it incrementally.

Another step in a cloud modernization journey is to redesign an application to make it embody more of a Cloud-Native Architecture (Chapter 3). For example, if it runs as a single process, its availability will improve as a horizontally scalable workload if you can make into a Replicable Application (88).

Examples

Containerization has been a well-accepted part of the computing landscape since Docker was introduced in 2013, and as a result, there are many case studies available that describe its successful adoption:

- The IBM CIO Office has been on a multiyear application modernization journey (*https://oreil.ly/W1-Y8*) that has resulted in thousands of applications being moved from virtual servers to containers in Kubernetes. This move to containers has resulted in a cost reduction of 90% in operations costs and a 55% reduction in total operational actions performed, as detailed in a case study (*https://oreil.ly/RzZ0P*).

- Tinder has documented how they moved their applications to containers and Kubernetes (*https://oreil.ly/Qp_IO*) and the advantages they gained from the move.

- The Warehouse Group has also documented the advantages (*https://oreil.ly/63M-2*) they found in their move to containers with Docker.

Finally, the Cloud Native Computing Foundation (*https://oreil.ly/OJlor*) (CNCF) has a comprehensive list of case studies that describe the advantages of many of the different projects within the CNCF, all of which depend on beginning with containerization.

Refactor the Monolith

You have an existing application that works but has grown haphazardly. It's a Big Ball of Mud (22), and you'd like to modernize it into a Modular Monolith (29). Or you'd like to modernize it from a monolith into a Distributed Architecture (38). It should look like it was designed from the beginning as a new Cloud Application (6).

How can I make an existing application easier for multiple teams to maintain and able to run effectively in a multicomputer environment?

Some application architectures are more sophisticated than others. Depending upon the choices made in that architecture, an application's architecture can either support small development teams working independently or impede them. It can enable the application to run more efficiently in an environment composed of multiple computers or prevent it.

But not every application needs to run as a *Distributed Architecture*, or even follow a Cloud-Native Architecture (Chapter 3). There are a set of decisions that lead you to decide that your application cannot be supported in the long term in its current form:

- If your application changes often, and it is difficult to update the application because of its design, that may indicate that its current architecture is unsupportable and should be changed. This is common with *Big Balls of Mud*.

- If you have tried and failed to Virtualize the Application (475) or Containerize the Application (478) because the application has too many dependencies on its current hardware and software environment, you should consider changing the architecture of the application.

- If your application is very inefficient at using computing resources, its architecture and packaging may be causing inefficiency. For example, if it is a Replicable Application (88) but one in which the unit of replication is very large, it may consume a lot of memory and/or disk compared to the CPU resources used. Enabling more efficient replication may require a better architecture for better packaging.

In the first case, small development teams working independently are more efficient than one large development team. To enable them to work independently, the application must be modular, with limited dependencies between components. That enables each team to work on a different module with limited dependencies between teams. A team can make changes to their module with less concern that it will adversely affect other modules.

In the second case, if an application is developed from the beginning to be modular and distributed, it's easy to maintain and deploy that way. However, some applications, intentionally or otherwise, end up with an architecture that is more like a *Big Ball of Mud*. The application performs user requirements correctly but was not designed to be easy to maintain or flexible to deploy.

Finally, any environment composed of multiple processes is more scalable and resilient than a single process, and an application can be as well but only if it is designed to run distributed across multiple processes. A monolith can only run as one process, but a distributed application can run each module in different processes and in a different computer. A distributed application has the flexibility to run all of the modules on the same computer, each on a different computer, or any combination in between.

Once an application is working, there's hesitancy to change it. An improved application is only an improvement if it still works. The trick is to take a working application that wasn't designed for modularity and distribution and adapt it for your purpose without breaking it.

Therefore,

Refactor the Monolith to convert it from an unstructured blob into a set of modules that can run distributed across multiple computers.

This process starts by finding the parts of a monolith that are entangled and refactoring them where possible to be modular (see Figure 9-8).

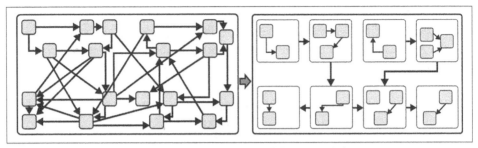

Figure 9-8. Refactoring a Big Ball of Mud to a Modular Monolith

Refactoring takes code that already works and changes it into code that still works but has a better structure that is easier to maintain. In *Refactoring* (2018), Martin Fowler describes refactoring as a way to improve the design of existing code "to make it easier to understand and cheaper to modify without changing its observable behavior." Refactoring will always involve some level of rewriting. However, how much you need to rewrite depends on both the approach to refactoring you take and the overall design of your application.

The first decision is: do you keep any of the existing parts of the system at all? Sometimes the monolith needs to be reconceptualized and reimplemented from scratch. If the application was written using a language, framework, or toolkit that is no longer supported, or that the current team has few skills in using, rewriting completely may be the only possible decision. However, the cost and duration of a complete rewrite often make it infeasible. If rewriting it is not feasible, the best approach is to refactor the existing code to improve its structure without changing its behavior.

The next decision deals with whether to keep the monolith whole or split it into pieces that can run on separate computers (e.g., as a *Distributed Architecture*). Sometimes keeping the monolith whole and refactoring it to make it more modular is the right approach. A well-partitioned application deployed as a single process (a *Modular Monolith*) can be a viable solution.

A key decision point in making this determination is whether the different parts of your application have different requirements for scaling. If all the parts of your application have similar scaling requirements, you may want to keep them together, at least at first. On the other hand, if they do have different scaling requirements, that is a factor leading to splitting the application into different distributed components using the Strangle the Monolith (Chapter 10) approach.

Refactoring a large application is not something that is done in a single step. It involves lots of learning about how the cloud works and a deep understanding of how your application functions. Teams often Lift and Shift (470) to the cloud as a first step to gain experience with working on the cloud. As part of that *Lift and Shift*, they also may decide to adopt Cloud Databases (311) or other Backend Services (106). While not a prerequisite to *Refactoring the Monolith*, addressing this may give the team confidence to proceed with a more involved refactoring effort.

Refactoring a monolith so that it is more modular can make it so that the application is easier to maintain, test, and deploy. However, a key aspect of any type of refactoring is that it is a behavior-preserving transformation. You need to ensure that the behavior of the existing application does not change during the refactoring. That means you need to have adequate test coverage of the application and also have an automated testing strategy that allows you to run the tests quickly both before and after any refactoring step. We refer readers to Michael Feathers' book *Working Effectively with Legacy Code* (2004), which discusses the strategies needed to add test coverage to existing code that does not have unit tests in order to address this issue. An improvement in the last several years since that book was written is that automated test generation tools like Tackle (*https://oreil.ly/OEnNu*) have come along to help in the generation of unit tests to speed up this process. You can use generative AI coding tools such as Microsoft Copilot (*https://oreil.ly/gu_kR*) and IBM watsonx Code Assistant (*https://oreil.ly/V_MkD*) to speed up the process of adding appropriate tests to legacy code where there are none.

Making a monolithic application, even a Modular Monolith (29), into a distributed application is no small task. Finding Hairline Cracks (530) to separate modules and remove duplications can be difficult. What we have found is that the amount of effort required to accomplish this can sometimes prevent people from adopting and using the Distributed Architecture (38) approach. Sometimes it is simply easier to rewrite the application directly as cloud-native Microservices (119) from scratch. That is especially true when the code base of the monolith is not well documented or understood, particularly if none of the original developers are still part of the development team. Contributing to this is that distribution technologies have acquired a well-deserved reputation for adding complexity to application development and testing. Making an application into a *Distributed Architecture* is often a useful goal, but it is not easy.

In this vein, converting a large application entirely into cloud-native *Microservices* can take considerable time and effort, especially if the application is already being used in production and needs to be maintained while the conversion is being performed. To make this conversion process manageable, perform the process incrementally by *Strangling the Monolith* (see Strangling Monoliths (Chapter 10)). Part of this strangulation process is making packaging decisions about the new (and existing) parts of the application. You may also Virtualize the Application (475) or Containerize the Application (478), or virtualize or containerize each of the distributed components.

Converting the application into a distributed set of *Microservices* makes it easier to take advantage of the platform-as-a-service (PaaS) capabilities of cloud. Modernizing a traditional IT monolith into a set of cloud *Microservices* is a significant transformation. The ultimate goal is an application with Cloud-Native Architecture (58) that is furthermore a Microservices Architecture (Chapter 4).

Examples

After mentioning a couple of case studies of refactoring a monolith, we will consider in depth an example of refactoring an airline's customer-facing application.

Published case studies

Following are two published case studies of refactoring a monolith:

- Allen Fang published a case study of how Shopback refactored a monolithic application (*https://oreil.ly/LiygT*) that used a lot of the patterns we have already covered in this book, such as *Command Query Responsibility Segregation* (*CQRS*) (383) and Anti-Corruption Layer (229).
- The VMware Tanzu team documents how they refactored the sample monolithic SpringTrader application (*https://oreil.ly/uRYzq*) into *Microservices* for deployment onto Cloud Foundry.

The downside of these examples is that they don't address the problem of coexistence between the refactored and existing applications. The following example discusses this.

Airline example

Several times in this book, we have shown examples drawn from a "hypothetical" airline that has used the patterns to build a cloud-native application. In fact, this has been a real transformation use case that one of the authors led. We can now dive deeper into how a team at this airline used *Refactor the Monolith* along with other patterns in this chapter (and a few from Strangling Monoliths (Chapter 10)) to pull off a major architectural feat of taking a large existing application and making it cloud native.

The team began with a traditional, on-premises Java application that implemented their website as a Web Form Application (414). The customer profile information and in-progress reservation data were stored locally in an Oracle relational database, while the transactional work of booking the reservation once selections were made and reserving seats was done by a backend mainframe application (which is still common across the travel and transportation industry). This is shown in Figure 9-9.

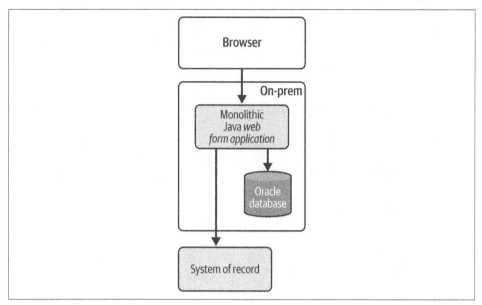

Figure 9-9. Original airline monolith

The team knew they wanted to work toward a more cloud-native application, but there were many skeptics, both inside and outside the organization as to whether or not the reimplementation would work. However, the team had an ace up their sleeve, as it were. There was a high-priority executive request for a new feature to their website that had been delayed for several months because it was so difficult to make changes to the existing monolith. That feature, automatic rebooking upon flight cancellation or delay, had the right combination of executive support and enough need for development speed that their management was willing to try something new.

The team used this opportunity to not only *Start Small* with this one single feature but also to try out several new elements. First, the team built a Single-Page Application (421) inside their more traditional website that would manage rebooking; additionally, it served as an introduction to new design elements and approaches. Second, they used a cloud-native approach using *Microservices* on the cloud to build the new business logic. The resulting design was implemented over four months from the inception of the project. This included training time, setup time, and the time needed to spin up the new squads. The design—which was based on Domain Microservices (153) and used a new Cloud Database (311) and Dispatchers (140) between the *Microservices* and the *SPA*—is shown in Figure 9-10.

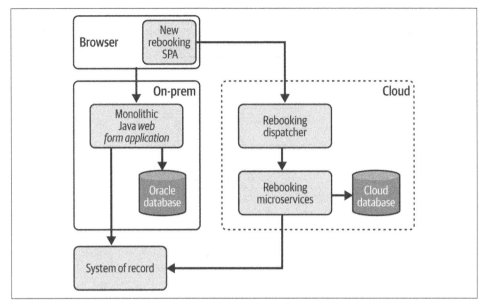

Figure 9-10. Start Small example with rebooking

So far, we haven't shown any refactoring, so why is this an example of *Refactor the Monolith*? Everything up to this point has all been a means of Paving the Road (496) to allow the team (and their management) to become comfortable with the technology and to establish the principles and tools that would be needed for the next phase, such as common DevOps pipelines and approaches. The real work happened in the next phase, when the team took a few pieces of the existing code from within the website and refactored it into new *Microservices* so that not only rebooking but all booking could occur via the new Cloud-Native Application (Chapter 3). This also required the team to modify their *SPA*-based approach to one that used Micro Frontends (426) to represent multiple parts of the user experience within the new parts of the website (see Figure 9-11).

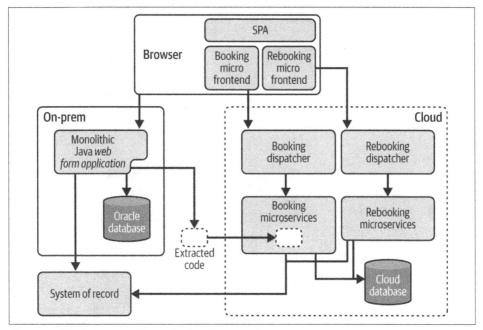

Figure 9-11. Refactoring Pave the Road example

This process happened over a period of more than a year as the team slowly chipped away at the existing system and built new *Microservices* for each of the major pieces of functionality. Finally, all that was left were the pieces of the original website that were rarely used or that did not directly affect the revenue of the airline to a substantial degree. The team then decided to containerize the remaining monolith (see Containerize the Application (478)) and move the remaining bits of the application, still packaged as a single monolith but now substantially smaller, onto the cloud, changing it only to the extent needed to move it to a Cloud Database (311) instead of the original Oracle database. We see the final form of the system in Figure 9-12.

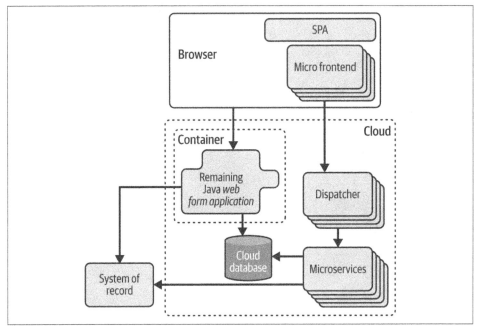

Figure 9-12. Refactored Airline Monolith example

This clever technique, which is a variant of Lift and Shift (470) called **Lift and Shift at the End** (*Cloud Native Transformation*, 2019), was the capstone to their effort in *Refactoring the Monolith*.

Start Small

(aka Gradually Evolve the System, Baby Steps)

You either have an existing application running on your environment that has been providing value to your organization for years or you need to develop a new application. The decision has been made to begin moving toward a Cloud-Native Architecture (58), but there are many different teams with different technologies and skill levels in your organization. You are new to developing Cloud Applications (6) and want any new or existing applications to take advantage of cloud technology, possibly using the Microservices Architecture (Chapter 4) style.

How can we start adopting cloud services and moving existing applications to the cloud or writing new applications for the cloud, possibly using *Microservices*?

The organization wants to minimize or amortize costs to evolve to the cloud architectural style and would like to do this fully as soon as possible.

Teams and people want to start right away and successfully take advantage of the cloud. This may include implementing Microservices (119). However, the organization is not ready for a major move to this new architectural style in terms of infrastructure and operational practices. The operations team worries about the prospect of multiple environments proliferating.

Possibly only a few of the developers have the technical skills and the drive to evolve the current system to the new architectural style. How can we motivate developers to overcome the hurdles in creating their first *Cloud Applications*, and show the way to the others?

Therefore,

Take baby steps when starting. *Start Small*, either by writing some new functionality as an application that is deployed to the cloud or by refactoring or rehosting a small existing application and running it on the cloud.

The main idea is to start small and take a lot of baby steps toward your goal. This can be done by implementing something simple and deploying it on the cloud. If you have an existing system, you can consider pulling a few existing items out of your current system (usually a monolith) and deploying these items (components or services) on the cloud. The latter can be a good way to warm up, especially if you have some simple and fairly decoupled capability. Figure 9-13 shows Service A being moved (refactored out of the monolith) and deployed to a cloud server. It also shows a new small simple application being built and deployed on the cloud.

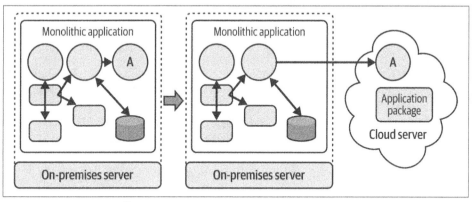

Figure 9-13. Start Small

The main thing here is to start small. There are several good reasons why you may want to do so:

1. A lot of learning has to happen before you can be successful on the cloud, even on a small scale. Every cloud provider has a set of tools, APIs, and account

management rules that have to be mastered. What's more, even deploying the simplest application requires understanding security policies, identity management, and issues like key management. This is a lot of cognitive load to put on a team—starting with a small, easily understood application with relatively few features reduces this overall cognitive load.

2. Corporate processes have to be changed in order to move things to the cloud. Many companies, especially those with complex approval processes, will need to change or adapt their practices for validation, auditing, deployment, and security in order to deploy applications on the cloud. It takes time and energy to change these processes, and doing this while also trying to work out how to deploy a large and complex application can be too challenging for many teams.

3. Teams need time to adjust to their new roles. While the role of a developer may be the least affected by a move to the cloud, operational and security teams have greater changes that they have to adapt to. Even a DBA will often have to adjust to new database tools or limitations or differences they may not face in on-premise databases. Even simple procedures like backup and restore are different between cloud database services and on-premises databases, so mastering the changes takes time as they work through the differences.

Because of this increased cognitive load, we strongly suggest that you begin with the simplest possible application that can be moved to the cloud and still provide measurable business value. This is why the idea of a Lift and Shift (470) is a popular one for the first *Cloud Application*. One way to start small is to focus only on the parts that are new, and a *Lift and Shift* eliminates any new application functionality from the mix. Also, we have seen some new functionality that can easily be written (possibly as *Microservices*) and deploying to the cloud can be a good first step.

Another popular option is to Containerize the Application (478)—although that adds additional complexity to the problem in that not only do you need to master the account management, tracing and monitoring, and potentially deployment tools of your cloud provider, but you also need to learn how to build and deploy container images as well. While this is a good longer-term solution, unless you have already adopted containers and/or Kubernetes on premises, this is a lot to ask of any team. Instead, building a common containerization environment that many teams can use and benefit from is a good way to later Pave the Road (496).

Other solutions such as Refactor the Monolith (484) provide a better path to cloud-native development but require a minimum level of operational readiness. Refactoring to *Microservices* requires having a DevOps deployment environment, with a continuous delivery pipeline to independently build, test, and deploy executable services, and the ability to secure, debug, and monitor a Microservices Architecture (Chapter 4). Operational readiness maturity is required whether we are building greenfield services or decomposing an existing system. While these early baby steps can help teams better understand Microservices Architecture, you cannot forget that this also must include getting the needed infrastructure in place. This evolution to operational readiness impacts the organization that will need to evolve and adapt practices.

The main advantage to *Starting Small* is that the organization does not incur the high cost and risk of a widespread change in technology. Initial projects will face several challenges and technical roadblocks. By *Starting Small*, future *Microservices* won't have to pay the same price because you will be able to apply principles that you learn from these beginning projects. Also, by *Starting Small*, you can potentially get some benefits sooner (new technologies, small changes, etc.).

On the downside, adoption could take longer, and you have to maintain and govern the old systems as well as the newer cloud solutions for a long time. The diverse technology increases the total cost of ownership (TCO). Finally, it takes longer to get the full benefits of the new architecture because there is a slower evolutionary process, specifically because you are taking baby steps rather than "commit and move forward" with most of your teams.

This pattern is closely related to *Pave the Road*, which can add organizational and technological elements that encourage and enable the successful initial steps prescribed by *Start Small*. Adding these elements doesn't happen at once. More likely, the organization will run a pilot project that will drive the adoption of tools, technologies, and practices. By *Starting Small*, you can learn how to *Pave the Road* by building up the infrastructure and getting things running. You will also learn how to start developing and deploying into the cloud. This pattern is similar to **Baby Steps** (*More Fearless Change*, 2015).

Start Small sometimes begins with Refactoring the Monolith (484) by possibly extracting some "larger services," where you extract components from the system into services that you can move and deploy in the cloud. If needed, you create a Monolith to Microservice Proxy (514) to communicate from the monolith to the extracted piece on the cloud. This can be the beginning of Strangling the Monolith (514).

Example

In a migration and modernization effort of a financial system that strangled a fairly large monolith to be replaced with a microservices implementation, the team *Started Small* by moving a fairly decoupled component out of the monolith and implementing it as a microservice. This is shown in Figure 9-14, which illustrates an example in that X in the figure is re-created as microservice X′ deployed on the cloud. This diagram does not reveal the details of the actual system but rather illustrates what was done to get started.

The company also started creating new logic using the Microservices Architecture (Chapter 4) style and deploying these microservices in the cloud (shown by Z in the figure). The diagram shows that a new microservice (Z) may need to make service calls to the monolith. The scenario where component X is being called by other components within the monolith is addressed either by adapting those calls to call X' or by the design solution described by creating a Monolith to Microservice Proxy (514).

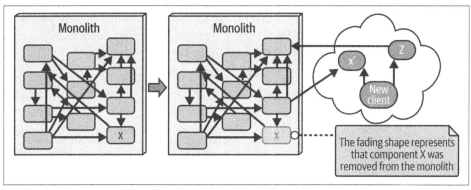

Figure 9-14. Start Small example of moving functionality to microservices

It might be a small, simple step to extract something larger (a *Macro Service*)[4] from the monolith as you learn. You can then further refactor these larger *Macro Services* into smaller Microservices (119). One way to find these larger pieces is to look for Hairline Cracks (530). Other times you might Refactor then Extract (542). Once you have been successful in *Starting Small*, the organization might create a directive to add New Features as Microservices (521), restricting the implementation of new features in the monolith.

Pave the Road

(aka Make Cloud Adoption Easier, Make Cloud Development Easier, Make Microservice Development Easier)

You either have an existing application you need to modernize or need to develop a new application. The decision has been made to move to the cloud and adopt architectural styles such as Microservices (119). Your organization is new to the cloud. You want to grant teams as much autonomy to make their own decisions as

---

4 This is a subpattern described in the Extract Component (535) pattern.

you can, but at the same time you do not want to waste time and effort by having teams make the same mistakes over and over again.

How can we encourage teams to move to the cloud and adopt these new technologies without letting each team go in their own direction and work at cross purposes?

Some developers are excited about building applications using new technologies such as cloud architectures and microservice-related architectures. However, when your organization has little or no experience building cloud-native or *Microservice*-based applications, it means that there will be many opinions as to the best way to begin making that move.

Teams in your organization work side by side with business units to develop solutions and want to focus on the problem domain and create and deploy applications faster. New architectures promise to address some of those aspirations. However, moving to a new architecture also brings anxiety and risks. Some developers have been working with legacy applications for a long time, and the new architecture brings up some concepts that may be foreign to them.

Your deployment process may require the coordination of different development teams and operators. Such a process can hinder the organization's agility. The practices, policies, and technologies for establishing a DevOps environment may not be in place. Developers may not be familiar with containerization, continuous delivery, log consolidation, *Microservices*, and other recommended practices for cloud development. That means that teams would be responsible for developing each of these on their own while at the same time learning a new set of tools and techniques.

Therefore,

Pave the Road by creating platforms, environments, and shared elements that ease the fundamental tasks of creating or migrating applications to the cloud.

There are many ways to *Pave the Road*. The first step is to get the infrastructure up and running. To be successful with the cloud, it is important to have a good DevOps environment. This includes an automated pipeline of building, good tests, deployment, and monitoring as part of the process. This also usually includes creating a containerized environment and deploying an example application in this environment. Figure 9-15 illustrates an example of building a DevOps pipeline and releasing a containerized application in the cloud. Documenting this process and sharing the best practices with examples is a good early practice to help *Pave the Road*.

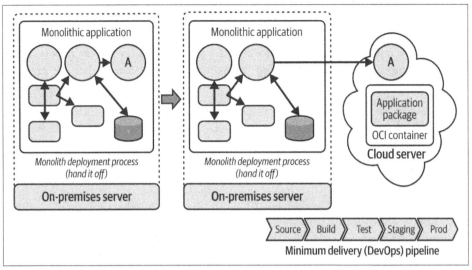

Figure 9-15. Pave the Road example

There are a number of common tasks that in aggregate can be overwhelming when taken on by a single team writing their own application. If a team is not highly motivated and or given the amount of time necessary to learn the best way to perform these tasks, they may choose to go back to their former ways of working and abandon moving their applications to the cloud. Aiding teams in this task by reducing the amount of work and cognitive load that they must be responsible for is critical. Often these tasks are carried out by one or more **Platform Teams** (*Team Topologies*, 2023) that create a common shared platform for application development, deployment, and operations or software architecture.

On the application development side, some of these common tasks include:

- Creating simple examples, templates, and/or scripts to show developers how to write applications for the cloud. If teams will be deploying *Microservices* to the cloud, simple examples and templates for building *Microservices* should be included.

- Establishing standard DevOps practices, such as continuous delivery (*Continuous Delivery*, 2010). This often means building common DevOps pipeline elements, including tool integrations, standard deployment options, etc. This should include defining processes and setting up tools that provide the infrastructure for automating the pipeline for building, testing, and deploying components, including *Microservices*.

However, application development tasks are not the only tasks that take up an application team's time and energy. There are a set of platform-level issues that also contribute to this cognitive load and reduce the amount of time that can be spent on core application development tasks. These include platform technology elements related to the runtime environment, such as containerization, container orchestration, log consolidation, monitoring, and distributed tracing. This also involves establishing practices like External Configuration (97) and infrastructure as code (*Infrastructure as Code*, 2016).

Following are some of the solutions we have seen that aid in these tasks:

Building a common/shared container infrastructure
> In particular, one of the downsides of adopting a container orchestrator (such as Kubernetes) is that many times teams build their own infrastructure—infrastructure that includes high overhead from the necessary control plane of the container orchestrator. **Stream Teams** (*Team Topologies*, 2023) usually do not have the time or the expertise to manage these efficiently.

Establishing centralized account management for public clouds
> This is also an essential element for reducing overall public cloud spend. Note that there is a fine line to tread here—you don't want to take over full control (e.g., the cloud should remain self-service), but you also don't want teams to have to swipe their own credit cards.

Building standardized automation for VM and service provisioning, building common VM images or common setup automation, or creating common container base images
> If you adopt open source tools such as Ansible or Terraform, or even cloud-specific tools like AWS CloudFormation, you can save time and effort on tasks that are often performed manually by development teams. However, this can cause different development teams to build similar, simple automation tasks multiple times. Sharing and standardizing of this automation code can drastically reduce overall effort.

Establishing and maintaining common operational tools for observability, monitoring, and debugging
> Having common tools means that developers can share expertise in these tools, and (importantly) it makes it possible to establish end-to-end observability across all the disparate parts of a large system.

Then there is a set of architectural tasks that can aid multiple teams in large-scale development. These are often taken on to create more consistency in application development and architecture and to facilitate easier movement of team members among teams:

Creating and documenting reference architectures for cloud adoption
> This should include a description of all the implementation details required to allow **Stream Teams** to implement them. This may include descriptions of common patterns, preferred choices for Backend Services (106) to maintain easy

communication across teams and development of documentation guidelines, shared architectural principles, and guidelines for tool selection.

Developing or purchasing tools that generate the core of a system from a higher-level specification or through a wizard UX

This can be done either algorithmically through the generation of templates or through the use of generative AI tools to develop an application core from a specified standard template. You can also build these tools yourself if you want the maximum level of customization. For example, you can build a Domain Specific Language (DSL) (*Domain-Driven Design*, 2003) to generate the beginning of a Cloud Application (6) using *Microservices*, which includes the pipeline for deploying to the cloud. This requires a lot of effort and should be done only once an organization is more mature in cloud development and needs to expand the number of teams working on Cloud Applications rapidly.

From the preceding list, you can see that there are many things to consider when deciding on an appropriate solution. Our advice is to start with the simplest thing possible that minimizes your maintenance effort and evolves as you learn. This usually begins with building pipelines and deploying services (DevOps) and establishing some level of common infrastructure like a container orchestrator.

Finally, it's important that you hire experienced people and provide training and/or mentoring. Nothing *Paves the Road* like someone who has been through the process before showing teams the common pitfalls and helping them navigate past them.

With or without an expert in the ranks, the organization will typically launch a pilot project. The team for this project should have ace developers who are also good at transferring knowledge. They shall *Pave the Road* while building the pilot project and documenting what is needed for other teams to follow their steps. The documentation can take the form of README files, instructions on a wiki, architecture decision records (*https://oreil.ly/jY6JN*), a template for cloud projects, a reference architecture, and more.

One of the main benefits of *Paving the Road* is that it creates an **Easier Path** (*More Fearless Change*, 2015) for developing *Cloud Applications*. New teams or people can roll out their first *Cloud Applications* more quickly by learning from the examples, documents, and templates created by the pioneer teams that *Paved the Road*. On the other hand, it requires a lot of time and effort to build the software, process, template, docs, etc. Some of these can be difficult, such as building out new DSLs. Also, there can be maintenance issues associated with these items. The initial projects that will *Pave the Road* will take longer and require a high upfront investment that will only pay off later.

The main anti-pattern that can emerge from the misapplication of *Pave the Road* is "Build it and they will come." In this, a team proceeds with building infrastructure, automation, or tooling that is not wanted or needed—because they are choosing technologies that the **Stream Teams** do not want or need to use or because they are working either too far in advance or too far behind the Stream Teams. You have to rely on the **Stream Teams** to "forge the trails"—in most cases, you only *Pave the Road* where tracks have already been created by one or more **Stream Teams**.

This pattern goes hand in hand with Start Small (492). An initial small project might be the pilot project that will shed light on the various new technologies and tools that get to be adopted for cloud development. You can then *Pave the Road* by abstracting the common features of the pilot and *Paving the Road* for other later projects. If you are considering a move to *Microservices*, consider the homonymous pattern **Pave the Road** (*https://oreil.ly/25JtE*) for specific details on proven practices on how to pave the road for the Microservices Architectural style.

It is a good idea to build a **Quality Delivery Pipeline** (*https://oreil.ly/3285q*) using deployment strategies such as **Blue-Green Deployment** (*https://oreil.ly/gQ6ui*) and **Canary Deployment** (*https://oreil.ly/VHpF3*) when you are *Paving the Road* for cloud development with *Microservices*.

This pattern is similar to **Paving over the Wagon Trail** (*https://oreil.ly/wCgA_*) from the perspective of creating reusable templates, scripts, or components. However, this pattern also talks about other things that help, such as building the infrastructure, documentation, training, and hiring good people.

Another important consideration is to rethink the way applications deal with persisted data, as they move from a more centralized database approach to the typical data decentralization used in *Distributed Architectures*. For example, there might be the need to use the **Saga** (*Microservices Patterns*, 2018) pattern in place of the original single-connection transaction in the monolith.

Example

The following examples are from real-world systems that two of the authors have worked on. The first is a fast-growing financial system in a Latin American company, and the second is an experience from IBM.

Financial system

This pattern was used during a migration and modernization effort of a financial system that strangled a fairly large monolith to be replaced with a *Microservices* implementation. The company started growing rapidly as new business opportunities emerged. The business was more than doubling every year in terms of revenue and users. There was also a large growth in teams, which grew by an order of magnitude in less than five years. Although the original architecture was suitable for the original needs, there was a point where they needed to make a more radical change to the architecture (called a *Software Architecture Revolution* (*https://oreil.ly/2whaK*)), which led to a committed effort to evolve to using the Microservices Architectural style and deploying parts of the system on the cloud.

At the beginning of this initiative, the organization *Started Small* by having a few teams experiment with building some functionality with *Microservices* ultimately to be deployed in the cloud. Part of this early effort required them to *Pave the Road* by building the infrastructure for a **Quality Delivery Pipeline**, which became the common CI/CD pipeline used by teams. This early work defined processes and set up tools that provided the infrastructure for automating the pipeline for building, testing, and deploying the microservices. They also created simple examples, templates, and/or scripts to show developers how to write the *Microservice* and deploy it to production.

They also *Paved the Road* for microservice projects by addressing several technology elements related to the microservice runtime environment—such as containerization, container orchestration, log consolidation, monitoring, and distributed tracing. It also includes creating and documenting DevOps practices, some of which require infrastructure and tool automation. The result led to a successful migration and modernization of the system as the company continued to grow and evolve. They are now able to release very frequently using the Microservices Architecture (Chapter 4) style deployed in the cloud.

IBM CIO Common CI/CD Pipeline

For several years, there has been an effort at the IBM CIO Office (*https://oreil.ly/of675*) to foster large-scale migration into a container-based hybrid cloud environment by first *Paving the Road* with a common CI/CD pipeline. As noted earlier, building up a **Quality Delivery Pipeline** is a common first step to encourage teams to adopt the cloud by helping them get past some common problems in deploying to a new cloud environment.

In this particular effort, one of the issues they faced in trying to encourage teams to onboard their applications into their container-based hybrid cloud environment was that teams were reluctant to move from their existing CI/CD approaches. In the past, each team had been responsible for building their own CI/CD pipelines on a common Jenkins hosting infrastructure. That led to a great diversity of pipelines, with little commonality across how different applications performed their build and deployment. A ramification of this was that teams were each also responsible for meeting internal security guidelines by running required open source license and usage checks and running required Dynamic Application Security Testing (DAST) and Static Application Security Testing (SAST) tooling on their applications. The problem was that since each team did this on their own, both the frequency of checks and the recordkeeping of the checks for these tools were spotty, causing audit failures.

The team responsible for migrating applications onto the hybrid cloud environment *Paved the Road* by introducing a new, common CI/CD pipeline approach based on Tekton that performed these checks, among other fixed steps like a common build approach, common testing tools, and common deployment step. The common pipeline logged all the test and scan results into a common database, fixing the recordkeeping problem that the teams had earlier encountered. The pipeline is configuration-driven and flexible in that it supports multiple languages, and multiple deployment targets, while still enforcing a set of shared goals for security and architectural commonality. As teams adopted the new pipeline, it reduced their overall development effort, improved security, and at the same time automatically managed deployment into the new shared hybrid cloud environment. As a result, well over 2,000 applications were moved onto the common cloud environment over a period of less than two years with a minimum duplication of effort.

Conclusion: Wrapping Up Application Migration and Modernization

In this chapter, we've examined a set of patterns related to moving an existing application from traditional IT to the cloud and improving it to work like an application that was originally written to run well on the cloud. Up until this chapter, this book has discussed how to make an application work well on the cloud assuming that it's a new application being written for the cloud.

Moving an existing application to the cloud is performed in two broad stages, migration and modernization. Migration moves an application from one platform to another, in this case from traditional IT to the cloud. Modernization changes an application to make it work better, in this case by changing its architecture so that it runs better on the cloud as well as by changing its packaging so that it can more easily be deployed on the cloud and so that the cloud platform can manage the application more easily. This often includes applying the Microservices Architectural (Chapter 4) style.

Performing Migration and Modernization

Moving applications to the cloud requires many decisions that need to be made by architects, lead developers, and managers as organizations get used to the benefits and restrictions that the cloud provides. Examining different architectural approaches needed to build new cloud-native applications or evolving existing applications toward a cloud-native approach is a long and necessary journey. Early on, an organization needs to design its cloud approach focused on business value that is delivered rapidly so that it can take advantage of these small successes. This can build excitement and help teams realize that there is a way forward into the cloud. So when you are new to either developing an application that runs or moving an existing application into the cloud, it is best to follow the practices:

Start Small (492)

> Start Small by having a team implement some new functionality in the cloud—this is a good way to learn about cloud architecture principles and to build up the infrastructure.

Pave the Road (496)

> If the team is facing its first cloud project, you need to make sure you have the infrastructure and the environment (both technical and organizational) to make it easier to implement *Cloud Applications*.

Cloud development is not something that teams master all at once. Teams must be substantially mature in DevOps and Agile practices before they can be successful in applying this architectural style. Designing *Cloud Applications* should always be an iterative process, where you build on small successes and then apply them over and over again until teams are comfortable with one level of technology before moving on.

Lift and Shift (470) and Virtualize the Application (475), the rehost and replatform strategies, are terrific starting points for teams because they build on skills they already have. However, it generally shouldn't be the ending point of a cloud journey. While virtualization has a low barrier of entry, it also has relatively low benefits since it doesn't change the way teams develop or operate their applications. Containerize the Application (478) is a further step in the right direction in that it forces the teams to adopt better (more modern) operational processes and requires that applications be Replicable Applications (88). Finally, when a team is ready to Refactor the Monolith (484), they are ready to take advantage of the principles of Cloud-Native Architecture (58).

Migration and Architecture Modernization Patterns

This chapter presented a migration pattern that can be used to move an application from traditional IT to the cloud:

- Lift and Shift (470) is the move-to-cloud pattern, the rehost strategy. Instead of deploying the application to traditional IT, replace it with a copy deployed to the cloud. The application is deployed to the cloud the same way it is to traditional IT, which means that the cloud must have the same sort of servers (hardware or virtual machines) and operating systems that the application uses with traditional IT.

This *Lift and Shift* relocation provides some of the advantages of a Cloud Application (6). Moving the application to the cloud enables taking advantage of the cloud's shared infrastructure. The cloud's virtualized infrastructure provides scalability and resiliency, which the application may be designed to exploit. If the platform is a public cloud, the application owner can rent capacity rather than own it—converting the cost of application hosting from CapEx (i.e., a capital expense) to OpEx (i.e., an operating expense), enabling the application to utilize pay-as-you-go pricing.

After a lift-and-shift, an application does not run differently or better in the cloud than it did in traditional IT. The cloud provides more shared capacity, which the application may be able to use, but the application still works and runs the same.

This chapter has also presented an architecture modernization pattern, used to improve the application's architecture:

- Refactor the Monolith (484) is the pattern for improving the architecture of an application, the refactoring/rearchitecting strategy. It does not change the user functionality in the application but rather changes the structure of the software that provides the functionality.

There are two main paths for refactoring an application to improve its architecture:

- Refactoring a Big Ball of Mud (22) into a Modular Monolith (29) improves the application by making its architecture more modular. It still runs as a monolith in a single process on a single computer.
- Refactoring a *Big Ball of Mud* or *Modular Monolith* into a Distributed Architecture (38) improves the application by making its architecture modular (if it starts as a *Big Ball of Mud*) and making the modules into services that run in different processes that can run on separate computers. No longer bound to the capacity of a single computer, a distributed application can better utilize the capacity of multiple computers.

Either of these strategies make it easier for separate development teams to maintain the individual modules or distributed components.

Strategies for Migrating and Modernizing Applications

The patterns can be combined to produce common migration and modernization strategies. Figure 9-16 shows several strategies to use when applying the patterns during migration and modernization and how these patterns can be applied:

Lift and Shift (1)
    Migrates the application to the cloud

Refactor the Monolith (4)
> Modernizes the structure of the application's architecture

New Cloud Application (5)
> Can produce an application with any architectural structure

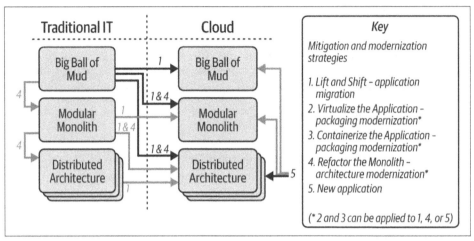

Figure 9-16. Application Migration and Modernization strategies

These strategies can be used individually, incrementally, or in combination. How they're used goes back to our options for migrating and modernizing an application: what platform and structure are we starting with, and what do we want to end up with? Find those two points in the diagram, and the path that connects them shows the strategies to apply.

Following are the most commonly used strategies:

Lift and Shift (1)
> Simply move the application from traditional IT to the cloud, preserving the application's architecture.

Lift and Shift (1) and Refactor the Monolith (4)
> Move the application to the cloud and improve its architecture.

New Cloud Application (5)
> A new application typically has a *Distributed Architecture*, but it could also be structured as a *Big Ball of Mud* or *Modular Monolith*. Creating a new application is an alternative to migrating and modernizing an existing application.

As part of moving the application to the cloud, developers should refactor the architecture to add two more improvements:

Client/server

Refactoring a *Big Ball of Mud, Modular Monolith*, or *Distributed Architecture* into a client/server architecture improves the application to separate the Client Application (406) from the rest with the user functionality that will run on the server. If the application's architecture is still a monolith, refactoring will extract the presentation logic from the domain logic so that they can be deployed separately. If the application has a *Distributed Architecture*, if the same service implements both presentation logic and domain logic, this refactoring will separate them and combine the presentation logic into a single module that can be deployed on a user's computer.

Cloud native

Refactoring a client/server where the server is a *Big Ball of Mud, Modular Monolith*, or *Distributed Architecture* into a *Cloud-Native Architecture* will ensure that the server portion of the application will run better on the cloud. This refactoring will restructure the application to delegate to Backend Services (106) for middleware functionality, the repurchasing/replace strategy for the middleware so that the rest of the application primarily implements domain functionality and can run in a standard language runtime.

A *Distributed Architecture* where each service has a *Cloud-Native Architecture* evolves into a Microservices Architecture (Chapter 4).

Hosting and Deployment Modernization

In addition to migrating an application to the cloud and/or modernizing its architecture, another aspect of modernizing an application is to improve the way it is packaged, which makes it easier to deploy and easier for the cloud to manage. There are two main strategies for modernizing an application's packaging, which can be applied to migration and architecture strategies 1, 4, or 5 described previously:

Virtualize the Application (475) (2)

Packages the application or each of the services in a *Distributed Architecture* as a virtual server that runs in a hypervisor. This is the how-to-leverage-IaaS pattern, enabling the application or service to take advantage of the infrastructure-as-a-service (IaaS) service model. By packaging the component as a virtual server, the cloud platform manages the virtualized compute, storage, and networking so that the application developers don't have to.

Containerize the Application (478) (3)

Packages the application or each of the services in a *Distributed Architecture* as a container that runs in a container engine. This is the how-to-leverage-PaaS pattern, enabling the application or service to take advantage of the platform-as-a-service service model. By packaging the component as a container, the cloud platform manages the runtime, middleware, operating system, and virtualized infrastructure so that the application developers don't have to.

In the cloud platform service models, IaaS enables the cloud platform to provide more standardization than traditional IT does, and PaaS provides more standardization than IaaS. More standardization lowers costs and enables developers to achieve faster time to value. More specifically, the developers achieve this greater standardization by applying these patterns to package the application as a virtual server (that runs in IaaS) or better yet as a container (because it runs in PaaS).

These packaging patterns are orthogonal to the application's platform and architecture. They modernize how the application is deployed and can do so on traditional IT or the cloud. They can be applied whether the architecture is a *Big Ball of Mud*, *Modular Monolith*, or *Distributed Architecture* and can be applied to an architecture that's been further modernized into client/server and cloud native. The combinations are not endless, but numerous combinations are possible.

This chapter presented some migration and modernization techniques to use when an organization moves a traditional IT application to run in the cloud. Another common technique for migration and modernization incrementally develops a new application around the original legacy application (usually a monolith). The next chapter will examine how to Strangle the Monolith (514) by gradually migrating a monolith architecture to a Microservices Architecture (Chapter 4) running in the cloud.

CHAPTER 10

Strangling Monoliths

Microservices (119) have been increasingly adopted by many organizations to better address their software needs. *Microservices* encapsulate different parts of an application as independently deployable units that contain their own application logic, data, and more. After the term "microservices" appeared, previous systems or architectures developed were labeled as "monoliths." Unfortunately, the term *monolith* gained a bad connotation because these systems are often considered to be legacy systems or Big Balls of Mud (22). Developing a system using the monolith architecture style is not necessarily a bad design decision or an anti-pattern. Sometimes it is the right choice. Building any kind of a Distributed Architecture (38) can be very difficult and has many challenges. A well-designed Modular Monolith (29) is often the best choice for organizations, especially when starting a new project.

Typically, a monolithic application is packaged as a single deployment file that runs on an application server. The monolith consists of many components that may contain business logic from various subdomains. These monolith components can include services, modules, libraries, or any type of implementation. They also have dependencies among themselves that typically increase over the years. Monolith components that are visible on the network may use protocols, message formats, and API design standards that are not fully compatible with network calls being used in new client applications. For example, the monolith may provide Enterprise JavaBean (EJB) services, and new applications in Python are not able to directly call these services.

Over time even a great design can be compromised by successive architectural revisions, especially as technical debt (see the section "Modernization and Technical Debt" on page 459) grows. The claim that the architecture that predominates in practice was the *Big Ball of Mud* was first made in 1998; *Big Ball of Mud (BBoM)* architectures are still seen today. They are the culmination of many design decisions that gradually result in a system that can be difficult to change and maintain. However, *BBoMs* usually do not result from well-intentioned design ideas gone wrong. Nor are they simply an accretion of expedient implementation hacks. Rather, they stem from a mix of doing what it takes to meet expedient business requirements along with paying insufficient attention to technical debt growth.

When a monolith becomes muddy, adding new functionality to it becomes difficult, and it can be challenging to take advantage of new protocols and technologies. Additionally, deployment becomes more difficult, especially for large entangled *BBoM* systems; changes require testing the whole system because the changes might have affected other parts of the system. When you are dealing with these issues, your best option can be to replace the existing system with a Microservices Architecture (Chapter 4) by implementing new features as *Microservices* while gradually transforming your monolithic system by "strangling" it—replacing existing parts of the monolith with *Microservices*.

Introduction to Strangling Monoliths

Adopting the Microservices Architectural (Chapter 4) style yields benefits such as shorter development times and increased flexibility for experimenting with new ideas and technologies. However, most organizations have existing systems that were developed before *Microservices* yet still provide value. As organizations evolve, a monolithic system can become harder to maintain and hinder the ability to keep up with new business needs. The poor flexibility of monoliths has driven many organizations to apply the Microservices Architecture (Chapter 4) style, which leads to the questions, 'What do you do with the existing monolith?' or 'How do I transform my monolith to *Microservices*?'

Martin Fowler coined the term *Strangler Application* as a metaphor to describe one way of rewriting a system. The "Strangler Application" is based on an analogy to "strangler vines" that "strangle" a tree that they are wrapped around.[1] In software, this means gradually creating a new system by adding new functionality outside the original system and by replacing/rewriting existing functionality inside the original system with new components outside the original system. You continue this process until the old system has been "strangled"—that is, replaced by a new system. When you are finished, all (or almost all) of the original system is implemented outside of that system and the original is no longer needed or used.

The "Strangler Application" concept is independent of services (or *Microservices*) because you can transform a system to a new architectural style without using services—for example, you could evolve the current application to become a *Modular*

---

1 Fowler later renamed this *Strangler Fig Application* (*https://oreil.ly/D4Qbh*).

Monolith gradually by adding new functionality outside the entangled system and by refactoring functionality within the system to be more modular. Over time, the original system will be replaced (strangled) by this new better-designed modular system. However, for this chapter, the focus on "strangling" is about transforming a monolith architecture to a Microservices Architectural (Chapter 4) style while keeping the monolithic system running.

Simply put, you "strangle" a monolith by replacing/rewriting it bit by bit as a fresh system implemented using *Microservices*. During strangulation, some functionality is provided to clients by the new system and some by the monolith, depending on what has been migrated. Strangulation requires two mutually supporting activities: abandonment and migration.

You "abandon" (rarely or never-used) functions in the monolith by performing all new development in the fresh *Microservice*-based system. In some extraordinary situations, you can replace a monolith by using only abandonment: for example, if usage patterns are changing rapidly, the functionality provided by the monolith might well become obsolete over time, and only the functionality provided by the *Microservice*-based system is required—in this case, at some point the monolith can simply be thrown away.

You "migrate" functionality by reimplementing pieces of it in the *Microservice*-based system. During migration, some functionality originally provided by the monolith will still be provided by that monolith, while functionality already migrated will be provided by the new system. You might need to implement some functionality by a combination of code running as *Microservices* and code running in the monolith; this can happen when some parts of a cluster implementing a coherent chunk of functionality have been migrated while others have not yet.

Strangler Patterns

When deciding to strangle a monolith, one of the first decisions is whether to completely rewrite the monolith at once or move to *Microservices* by Strangling the Monolith (514) over time.[2] Sometimes rewriting the monolith is the right approach. For example, if business needs have substantially changed, then the monolith may need to be reconceptualized and reimplemented from scratch (possibly using *Micro-services*). However, often the cost and duration of a complete rewrite make rewriting a monolith infeasible. If the monolith has become hard to maintain and is hindering new projects, and rewriting it is not a viable path, it is time to start *Strangling the Monolith*.

---

[2] Some of these *Strangler Patterns* (*https://oreil.ly/b3cyn*) were originally presented at Pattern Languages of Programs 2020 (*https://oreil.ly/78fxy*) by Joseph Yoder and Paulo Merson.

Once you have decided to *Strangle the Monolith*, there are many possible variations and proven practices that help you successfully evolve the system. Figure 10-1 is a pattern map of techniques you can apply when moving a monolith application incrementally to a *Microservices* application—this pattern map includes relationships between the patterns. When *Strangling the Monolith*, it is a good idea to Start Small (492) with manageable changes and Pave the Road (496) to enable teams to progress faster and more reliably during the "strangling" process. This is usually done by having a team implement some new functionality with *Microservices* and is a good way to learn about *Microservices* principles. This also allows you to build the infrastructure and the environment (both technical and organizational) to make it easier to implement *Microservices*—this can include setting up DevOps with a delivery pipeline that allows you to build, test, and deploy *Microservices*.

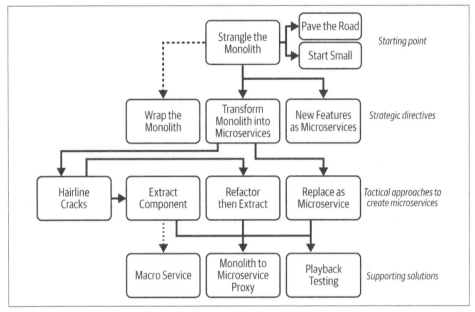

Figure 10-1. Strangling Monoliths patterns

Once teams have successfully set up the environment and have successfully created some *Microservices*, you can make strategic directives early on that help with the strangling process. It is usually a good idea to protect the system from change by **Wrapping the Monolith**.[3] **Wrapping the Monolith** is commonly achieved by creating a **Proxy** (*Design Patterns*, 1994) or **Facade** (*Design Patterns*, 1994) for existing external systems. New requirements will inevitably need to be implemented and released during the strangling process. Once you have validated that *Microservices*

---

3 This is a scaffolding pattern, described in the Strangle the Monolith (514) pattern.

development can be done successfully within the organization, you create a directive that encourages and enforces any new development efforts to be done by adding these New Features as Microservices (521). This strategy helps ensure you do not continue to add the existing monolithic application.

However, there will still be a lot of functionality inside the monolith that needs to be replaced with a *Microservice* implementation. This is achieved by Transforming the Monolith into Microservices (526), which includes finding and prioritizing areas that can be extracted, refactored, or replaced by *Microservices*. During the transformation process, you will be moving and replacing pieces of functionality within the monolith with *Microservices*.

You start the transformation by looking for Hairline Cracks (530) within the monolith—areas where you can easily extract pieces of functionality out of the monolith and replace them with *Microservices*. Sometimes these *Hairline Cracks* reveal code segments that are straightforward and easy to extract as components; if *Hairline Cracks* reveal well-defined APIs, you can the Extract These Components (535) to a *Microservice* implementation.

You extract this functionality out of the monolith by copying code out of the monolith and reimplementing it as *Microservices*. Extraction often starts by extracting larger pieces of functionality as single pieces (**Macro Services**),[4] and after extracting, you refactor these larger pieces to smaller *Microservices*; it helps to first understand the domain and *Microservice* design. This is a recursive process of breaking down the monolith by extracting functionality around domain concepts.

Other times these *Hairline Cracks* will reveal some functionality that, with some changes inside the monolith to the existing code, you will be able to Refactor Then Extract (542) to *Microservices*—in other words, you refactor parts of the monolith first to make these parts easier to extract to *Microservices*. You achieve this by looking for areas inside the monolith that, despite some coupling, can be refactored to a better design, such as modular components with well-defined APIs.

However, most monoliths will have many places where the functionality is tightly coupled, and the only alternative is to lock it down in the monolith and to rewrite and Replace as Microservice (546) that functionality. You achieve this by freezing the code for this functionality in the monolith and reimplementing the functionality with new *Microservices*. You remove the original implementation from the monolith after the implementation has been validated.

There are a couple of supporting patterns to use when replacing functionality within the monolith. Any place within the monolith that needs access to the new services can use a Monolith to Microservice Proxy (552). This **Proxy** provides an access

---

4 This is a supporting pattern described in the Extract Component (535) pattern.

solution from any existing monolith components to either extracted or newly created *Microservices* needed by the monolith. After extracting or reimplementing code from the monolith to *Microservices*, you should validate that the new implementation is running properly by testing the new implementation and comparing it to the original implementation. You achieve this by Playback Testing (556) a set of inputs and actions on the new implementation from the same set of inputs and actions on the original system and comparing results.

To summarize, *Strangling a Monolith* primarily consists of two processes: implementing new features as a *Microservice* outside the monolith and recursively replacing pieces of functionality within the monolith with *Microservices*. Adding new features as a *Microservice* is a good way to start because it not only helps you learn about *Microservices* but also helps ensure that you do not continue to add any new functionality to the monolith that you might have to transform later. Once you start moving to Microservices (119), the challenging part, and what most of this chapter is about, is how to *Transform a Monolith into Microservices* until your monolith application has been "strangled" and replaced with a new *Microservices* application.

Strangle the Monolith

(aka Strangler Application, Evolve System with Microservices)

You have a monolithic application that still provides value to your organization and thus can't be discontinued or shut down. Large parts of the monolith have devolved into a Big Ball of Mud (22), although parts of the system may possibly be considered a Modular Monolith (29). You have decided to replace your monolith system with a Microservice Architecture (Chapter 4).

How can we replace a monolithic architecture with a Microservices Architecture while reducing overall risk?

Microservices can help you better meet the needs of the organization, but moving existing applications to Microservices (119) involves risk. However, reducing the overall risk of your software development is critically important. For instance, software requirements may be changing more rapidly than your organization can accommodate, creating business risk. Adding features and managing existing features within a monolith can be difficult due to significant coupling between components in the monolith, so adding new functionality often creates bugs. Likewise, complex synchronization among the teams working on the monolith makes replacing or adding functionality challenging because the additional communication paths between teams create misunderstandings and delays.

Reconceptualizing and implementing the monolith from scratch with *Microservices* can be the right approach. However, rewriting an entire application can be difficult, expensive, and can introduce an unacceptable amount of risk. Most organizations don't have the appetite for that much risk at once.

Replacing the entire monolith at once can be extremely risky for the following reasons:

- A full all-at-once rewrite and replace would also not show value until the complete rewrite is finished.
- Critical changes may not be made on the original system when time and effort are prioritized on the rewrite.
- Demands on the changes to the original system may make it impossible to staff the teams needed for refactoring or rewriting the monolith.
- Testing an entire replacement at once may be difficult, if not impossible.
- There is a chance that the teams rewriting the system cannot keep up with changes to the original system, making the rewrite fail.
- If your legacy monolith is used by client applications, protecting those existing client applications is important because external clients are often unwilling or unable to make large changes to their software on the same schedules as your internal teams.

Organizations grow and change because business needs change over time. Since the software architecture (according to Conway's Law) parallels the structure of your organization, your software organization also needs to grow and change accordingly. When these changes result in growth, it creates more communication paths and makes change harder. What's more, organizational growth means developers with varying ranges of experience make changes to the system. That results in technical debt that makes it harder to change the monolith.

In most systems, changes require testing the whole system because they might affect other functionality within the monolith. Also, a legacy monolith rarely shows obvious seams for separating it cleanly into *Microservices*. Deployment time also increases with the size of the deployment unit, making deploying the entire monolith difficult and long.

From the preceding discussion, we see that modernizing to *Microservices* has a lot of potential benefits, but rewriting an entire application all at once is risky. So how can we address this?

Therefore,

Gradually replace the existing monolithic application with *Microservices* by iteratively replacing existing functionality in the monolith with *Microservices* and by implementing any new features as *Microservices*.

These *Microservices* are developed and deployed independently of the monolith. Apply the process recursively until the monolith is replaced (strangled) by the new *Microservices* application. This strangling process is illustrated in Figure 10-2.

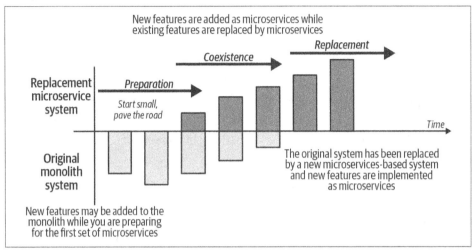

Figure 10-2. Strangling the Monolith process over time

When beginning the strangling process, you need to make sure you have the infrastructure and the environment (both technical and organizational) to make it easier to implement *Microservices*. Therefore, if your team is facing their first *Microservice* project, you Pave the Road (496). *Paving the Road* for *Microservice* projects includes technology elements related to the *Microservice* runtime environment, such as containerization, container orchestration, log consolidation, monitoring, and distributed tracing. It also includes adopting DevOps practices, some of which require infrastructure and tool automation, for example, continuous delivery, External Configuration (97), and (*Infrastructure as Code*, 2016).

Once you have *Paved the Road*, it is time to start writing your first *Microservice*. Starting Small (492)—by having a team implement some new functionality—is a good way to learn about *Microservices* principles and practices. Once one or a few *Microservices* have been successfully created, the team might redirect any new development efforts to add New Features as Microservices (521). *Starting Small* is also a good way to help *Pave the Road*.

During the strangling process, at some point, you begin to Transform the Monolith into Microservices (526). Once you start to replace functionality from the monolith with *Microservices*, you often need to redirect requests to new services from existing clients or monolithic code. There will also be times, especially early on in the process, when the new *Microservices* need access to the monolith. Figure 10-3 is an example of this, showing where new pieces of functionality have been created outside of the monolith as *Microservices* (*X'*, *Y*, and *Z*).

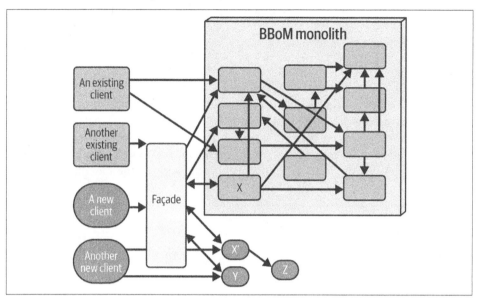

Figure 10-3. Architecture example while Strangling the Monolith

Note that in this example, X' is a *Microservice* replacing the functionality of X, while Y and Z are new *Microservices* providing some new functionality. Any code within the monolith that needs access to X can be directed either to the original implementation or to the newly replaced X' implementation. Any new or existing clients can access the monolith through a **Facade** (*Design Patterns*, 1994), thus not entangling any current or new code with the *BBoM* monolith.

Many teams don't consider *Strangling the Monolith* because they believe it will cost more—specifically because you have to maintain both the original and new systems. However, the alternative—completely rewrite the monolith—is just as costly and time-consuming but riskier. An important reason to consider *Strangling the Monolith* over a cut-over rewrite is reduced risk because the risk of new code introduction is incurred in smaller increments spread over time. Another advantage is cost amortization because many organizations cannot afford an overall rewrite of the monolith in a single undertaking. For these reasons, along with others, many organizations make the decision to undertake this process of evolving their existing monolith to a new *Microservice* implementation of the system.

A common strategy used to select pieces of the monolith to replace with *Microservices* is to focus on high-value items or tasks first. Another technique is to find some low-hanging fruit or places where you can easily pull out pieces of the monolith. This can be thought of as a divide-and-conquer technique where you continue pulling pieces out of the monolith until the system has been replaced. During this iterative process, you often start by *Wrapping the Monolith* to help keep the *Microservices* and the monolith decoupled from one another.

Wrap the Monolith

Extracting logic out of the monolith into *Microservices* may create a situation where the same logic (either in the monolith or implemented as *Microservices*) needs to be accessed by both old and new client components.[5] Existing clients need to access the logic the old way, and new clients access the logic the new way, using current protocols and API standards. A general approach is to create a **Proxy** (*Design Patterns*, 1994) or **Facade** for old external systems or client components (see Figure 10-4). This **Facade** sits between the client components and the logic in the monolith moved to *Microservices*.

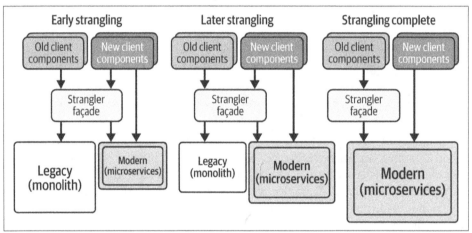

Figure 10-4. Wrapping the Monolith

Initially, this **Facade** doesn't do anything but pass all traffic, unmodified, between old client components and the legacy application (monolith). This approach protects old clients from change. As *Microservices* replace monolith components, this **Facade** converts and transforms protocols from old clients into the protocols, technologies, and contracts used by the new *Microservices* being created. Note that this could be a two-way **Facade** as there could be communication coming back from the monolith to the calling client components.

---

5 **Wrap the Monolith** has not yet been written as a pattern but could be. **Wrap the Monolith** is an optional scaffolding pattern and one of the first decisions that should be made after you have decided to *Strangle the Monolith*.

The ideal goal is to completely *Strangle the Monolith*, eliminating it completely; however, there are cases where the benefit of doing so will not be worth the effort. Sometimes, part of the monolith might not be worth completely rewriting. For example, some core pieces of the monolith may provide value and change infrequently. If you have wrapped these pieces so that they are easy to use, the benefit of extraction is minimal. Likewise, if a core piece of code is entangled and quite difficult to rewrite or extract, it could make sense to leave this code as is. This is especially true if you have addressed the essential problems in the monolith and don't need to go any further.

Strangling the Monolith helps you take advantage of the Microservices Architecture (Chapter 4) while the old architecture continues to provide value to the organization. Having many frequent releases helps you monitor the strangulation progress while adding new functionality, thus making sure the monolith system continues to function properly. When features are moved from the monolith to *Microservices*, parts of the monolith become strangled, and these parts can be retired. This pattern enables any existing client calling code to continue to access the required functionality whether it is part of the monolith or has been moved to *Microservices*.

Even with the previously mentioned benefits, there are also trade-offs when *Strangling the Monolith*. There is an overall challenge of maintaining and governing two types of software architectural styles—the monolith and the microservice—that typically use different implementation technologies, runtime environments, infrastructure elements, and deployment procedures. This technology diversity may increase the total cost of ownership (TCO) for the organization. Additionally, because the strangling process is a gradual evolution, it can take quite a bit of time before you start to get the advantages of the new architectural style.

There is also a challenge related to data. A monolithic application typically uses a centralized database, whereas *Microservices* typically follow the Self-Managed Data Store (154) approach. There are many issues that arise when you are dealing with issues related to distributed databases. Some of these challenges are ensuring data consistency, handling transaction management, syncing data across *Microservices*, retrieving data from multiple data sources, and more. You need to think carefully about these issues during the strangling process and apply both Microservice Design (Chapter 5) principles and Cloud-Native Storage (Chapter 7) practices.

Strangling a Monolith is an iterative process. Therefore, to be successful, it is a good idea to Start Small (492). Also, you want to ensure that changes do not break existing functionality and to limit making changes to any client code that needs access to the new *Microservices* by *Wrapping the Monolith*. You can use a Dispatcher (140) to implement the **Facade**, which applies a technique similar to the **Wiping Your**

Feet at the Door (*https://oreil.ly/RKiRW*) pattern and can be considered a type of Anti-Corruption Layer (229).

After starting and once you have built the infrastructure, you can encourage teams to move toward the new architecture by having them add New Features as Microservices (521). After initial success with building *Microservices*, you are ready to begin the process of Transforming the Monolith into Microservices (526).

Examples

There are many examples of small, medium, and large organizations that have *Strangled the Monolith*.

Uber

In a blog post (*https://oreil.ly/v2stg*), Uber shared their experience through this process during a period of hypergrowth. During this challenging period, they broke down their original monolith system into hundreds of *Microservices* to support their needs for scale and growth, all while continuing to evolve their running system.

Netflix

Netflix went through a strangling process (described in a blog (*https://oreil.ly/OlPsH*)), during which they rebuilt their video processing pipeline using *Microservices*; they thus maintained their rapid pace of innovation and continuous improvement for member streaming and studio operations. It was originally created as a single monolithic system that handled all media assets. Over time, as the system expanded, there was a significant increase in the complexity of the system, leading to coupled functionality, long release cycles, and reduced development velocity. Netflix gradually transitioned (*https://oreil.ly/pAd1r*) from their monolithic system to *Microservices* partitioned based on business capabilities. There of course were challenges during this transition related to data consistency, interservice communication, and the availability of the system—effective monitoring and logging were crucial for dealing with and resolving these issues.

eBay

eBay had an application that had evolved over more than a decade and contained hundreds of features in monolithic modules, and because of the growth of the app, the code became increasingly harder to maintain and thus needed to evolve their monolith to *Microservices* (*https://oreil.ly/_twy6*). They incrementally migrated from their monolithic system to the new Microservices Architecture (Chapter 4) while continuing to build new features and release the app on a regular cadence.

Amazon

Amazon, which has one of the biggest ecommerce systems in the world, similarly embarked on a journey of *Strangling the Monolith* over time to *Microservices*. Initially, Amazon's original architecture was a monolithic system. During the rapid growth of the business, many challenges arose, including addressing the complexity of the original system, responding to change, and dealing with scaling issues. Over time, they transformed their monolithic architecture into hundreds of *Microservices* developed around their business capabilities. This transformation helped with scaling, improved development velocity, and helped teams to work more autonomously.

PagSeguro

In a presentation at Agile Brazil called "Microservices for Agility: The PagSeguro Story" (*https://oreil.ly/5dAEz*), a couple of people shared their *strangling* experience of modernizing a large monolithic system to many hundreds of *Microservices* to meet their growing business needs during a fast-growing time at their organization. This transformation of their system to *Microservices* helped the company continue to grow rapidly and be quick and agile while adapting to evolving business needs. One of the keys to their success was making sure to *Start Small*, *Pave the Road*, and Model Around the Domain (183) during the *strangling* process.

These are just a few of many organizations that have gone through a process of transforming an originally successful monolithic architecture to a Microservices Architecture (Chapter 4) to meet their current and future needs. This was usually done during a fast-growing period at these organizations and the choice to use the Microservices Architectural (Chapter 4) style helped them address their challenges during this growth.

New Features as Microservices

(aka New Functionality as Microservices, Microservices First Strategy[6])

The decision has been made to move toward the Microservices Architecture (Chapter 4) style. You have started the strangling process by Starting Small (492) and Paving the Road (496) to build the infrastructure for implementing *Microservices*.

While *Strangling a Monolith*, how do you avoid adding new functionality to the monolith that will later have to be modernized into *Microservices*?

During the long-running process of strangling a monolith, it's natural that developers, and especially product managers, feel inclined to add pieces of functionality to

---

6 This pattern was originally called **Microservices First Strategy** in the *Strangler Patterns* (*https://oreil.ly/1Phl4*) by Joseph Yoder and Paulo Merson.

the monolith. Some developers may not fully engage in *Microservice* development, perhaps because they didn't get acquainted with the new technologies and tools. These developers are more prone to keep adding code to the monolith.

Adding to the monolith is typically faster and less expensive in the short term than providing the same functionality by implementing it with *Microservices*. Teams may prefer to take the shortest path and finish their tasks sooner by implementing it in the monolith; especially if they do not know and understand the long-term benefits of evolving the architecture to *Microservices*.

On the other hand, if teams are free to keep adding and changing features in the legacy system, the initiative to Strangle the Monolith (514) may never reach its goals. If there are no design standards or policies set forth to require new or modified functionality to be created in the new architectural style, the monolithic system may see continued growth despite efforts to reduce its scope.

Many developers have been working on the monolithic system for a long time and are focused on feature creation and not familiar with the new technologies and tools. Others may realize that the new architecture provides new technologies they could benefit from but are unsure about how to use it, especially because this might involve integration with some parts of the legacy system.

Therefore,

Create a new directive that whenever you add new functionality to the system, these new features are implemented as *Microservices*.

The main objective is to avoid or contain the growth of the monolith and to get teams to start to move to using *Microservices* for any new functionality. This is done by encouraging teams to implement new features with *Microservices*. Figure 10-5 illustrates a *Microservices*-first directive that limits development in the monolith while encouraging any new development to be done through *Microservices*.

One way to make sure that teams start adding *New Features as Microservices* is to create a directive that is part of your governance process that promotes adding new functionality first as *Microservices* while discouraging adding new functionality to the monolith. It is important to explain this decision to stakeholders such as product owners and developers and provide support to help them be successful using *Microservices*. This discussion can be very challenging—you might need to show the risks of continuing with the monolith and the need for transforming it. You may have to use various tactics to convince them to use *Microservices* more often for their implementations, such as providing them with tools that make building and testing *Microservices* easier, emphasizing the organizational advantages of *Microservices* (e.g., it strengthens team autonomy), or pointing out specific flaws and difficulties in maintaining the existing monolith.

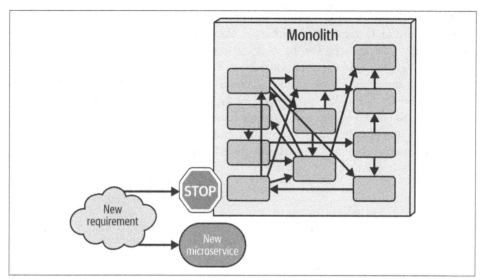

Figure 10-5. Microservices-first directive to promote New Features as Microservices

Sometimes you can do this by communicating with and encouraging teams to add new functionality using *Microservices*. Some team members or developers will be excited to do this, and the system will start to see some of the benefits. Teams can also be encouraged by creating templates or examples, making it easier to add functionality with *Microservices* (e.g., *Paving the Road*). This is an example of a "carrot" approach to encourage the desired behavior. You can also encourage teams to consider using *Microservices* when they are modifying existing features.

However, you may also need to restrict changes (the "stick" approach) when making changes in the monolith. Teams and developers might be tempted to take the more expeditious way to add new features by relying on what they have always done in the past. In these cases, a "stick" may be more appropriate. Organizations might want to add "speed bumps"—for example, using a governance committee to approve changes to the monolith. This committee permits new code to easily be added using *Microservices*, but if you want to change the monolith, you need to convince the committee that the change needs to be implemented this way.

You usually do this by having a mechanism in place for reviewing any changes to the system as a whole. This mechanism includes teams explaining why the change should be made to the monolith rather than implementing the change with *Microservices*. This review mechanism needs to ensure only critical (absolutely necessary) changes are made within the monolith.

When adding new features, the best scenario is when the new feature can be added independently of the monolith. However, there will be cases where adding a new feature might best be achieved by making some changes to parts of the monolith. When this happens, you can look for ways to Extract Components (535) to move the functionality out of the monolith into *Microservices*. Sometimes you may have to first Refactor then Extract (542) some pieces of functionality. Additionally, there may be cases where the functionality is so tightly coupled that your only alternative is to lock the original functionality in the monolith and completely Replace as Microservice (546) that functionality to implement the new desired feature.

An advantage of adding *New Features as Microservices* is that the organization can expedite the move toward the new architecture, thus reaping the benefits of *Microservices* throughout the organization sooner. This helps teams learn more about the Microservices Architecture (Chapter 4) and how to be more productive and successful with this architectural style. There is an additional advantage of not making things worse in the monolith that will have to be reimplemented with *Microservices* later.

However, it can take longer to implement new features because you can no longer simply add features into the monolith by using copy/paste techniques. Also, many teams are comfortable and productive with making changes quickly in the monolith. You will also need to spend time and effort to set up a governance committee that can initially slow down development efforts that need to go through the new approval process. Also, there is a cost for providing the training, tools, people, and support for transitioning your teams to be productive with *Microservices*.

While implementing a new requirement with a new *Microservice* or for some changes to existing functionality, you will sometimes need to Transform the Monolith into Microservices (526) as part of this process. While adding new *Microservices*, you sometimes will need to create a Monolith to Microservice Proxy (552) for any monolith functionality that needs access to the new features implemented as *Microservices*. Additionally, you can use a **Facade** (*Design Patterns*, 1994) to access any functionality inside the monolith that any new *Microservices* need access to—this could be the **Facade** you used to **Wrap the Monolith**.

This pattern is similar to the **Restrict Changes to the Legacy Application** and **Freeze** patterns described in *Leading a Software Architecture Revolution* (*https://oreil.ly/vo1ZH*). **Restrict Changes to the Legacy Application** establishes a directive that requires approval for any changes to the legacy system, while **Freeze** locks changes in the old architecture to achieve faster results.

Example

Cyberark talks about how they began with a *Microservices First* strategy in the development of Conjur (*https://oreil.ly/w68Uq*).

The airline example we described in Refactor the Monolith (484) began with a directive to add *New Features as Microservices* for the new implementation of automatic rebooking of flights on disruption.

A longer example of this pattern is illustrated through a migration and modernization effort of a financial system that strangled a fairly large monolith to be replaced with a *Microservices* implementation. This company created a directive early on that encouraged teams to develop new features by implementing them first with *Microservices*. Although this worked for some teams, many teams were reluctant because they were more comfortable making the changes in the monolith, and often there was a lot of pressure to get the new requirement out quickly. Therefore, this organization created a governance committee to restrict changes to the monolith during the "strangling" process.

This committee included representatives from both the technical and other areas of the organization, including Products, Business, Sales, and Marketing. It was important that this committee be made aware of the risks of continuing to add to the monolith and agree on the importance of moving toward implementing new features with *Microservices* whenever possible. The committee reviewed every proposed change to the monolith, discussed impacts versus opportunities for the whole organization, and decided whether the changes needed to be done in the monolith for business reasons.

Figure 10-6 outlines the process this governance committee used to restrict changes to the monolith while encouraging new changes to be added with *Microservices*. A new feature can always be implemented by using *Microservices* without getting approval from the committee. Any new requirements that needs to be implemented in the monolith must be approved by this committee.

This governance committee reviews why the team thinks the change needs to be made in the monolith and then decides whether to accept the change being made in the monolith or reject the change and demand that the team implement it with *Microservices*. Additionally, the committee can postpone the decision by requesting more details or alternatives from the change proponents.

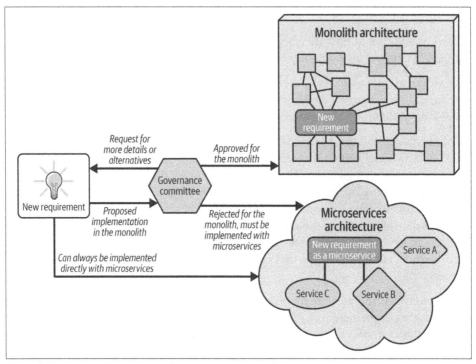

Figure 10-6. Example process of governance committee

Transform Monolith into Microservices

(aka Replace Monolith Functionality with Microservices, Divide and Conquer)

The decision has been made to Strangle the Monolith (514), which included creating a directive to add New Features as Microservices (521). You would like to move some of the functionality out of the monolith into Microservices (119) to improve the maintenance of the monolith and reduce the blast radius of new changes to it.

How do you keep the original monolithic system working while you substitute pieces of functionality with *Microservices* over time?

Once an organization has started to reap some of the benefits of using the Microservices Architecture (Chapter 4), there will be a lot of pressure to take advantage of the new architectural style for pieces of functionality that are contained within the monolith. However, the existing system will still require changes and necessary updates.

There is a temptation to completely rewrite the monolith. However, it is more often the case that the cost and duration of a complete rewrite make it infeasible to take this path. Instead, if the monolith has become hard to maintain and is hindering new projects and desired features, and rewriting it is nearly impossible, you'd like to find a path to move functionality out of the monolith while keeping it working. It is critical that your system continues to work during your transition to *Microservices*.

In particular, existing clients need to keep working. Sometimes you have no control over these, especially if they belong to other teams or are third-party clients. This is challenging when implementing *Microservices* that use new protocols and message formats. Likewise, it can be challenging to rewrite functionality in the monolith into *Microservices*. The following situations can complicate the process of transforming a monolith into *Microservices*:

- The monolith may use old versions of libraries and frameworks. Developers want to upgrade to the latest versions, but the upgrades are not fully backward compatible and require updating a lot of code in the monolith. These upgrades have been postponed time and again over the years, and now the discrepancy between the old version and the latest makes the upgrades costly and risky.

- The monolith may have been written in a programming language that is no longer the best choice for the current context of the organization.

- Teams often want to develop new applications using different programming languages, different frameworks, or simply newer but incompatible versions of languages or frameworks. Consequently, these new applications cannot directly call components in the monolith.

- Teams want the potential benefits of using new protocols and technologies. However, client applications make use of the monolith by calling services that use old protocols and technologies (e.g., SOAP, EJB) or by adding module dependencies to the monolith and directly calling the logic inside it.

Most monoliths are usually large systems that contain business logic from various domains. It can be difficult to understand where and how to break apart a monolith. Teams often don't know where to start with such an effort. It usually requires a lot of time, effort, analysis, and refactoring of the monolith before pieces of the systems can be separated. Also, once you start, when do you stop? How can you know the best approach for replacing functionality in a monolith with *Microservices*?

Therefore,

Iteratively transform your monolith into *Microservices* by identifying the places where you can split the monolith into components that you then extract, refactor, or replace into smaller components that are modeled around the domain.

The main task is to find partitions (clusters of functionality) within the monolith that can be replaced with *Microservices* and then prioritize and replace these pieces over time. You are gradually transforming your monolith application into a *Microservices* application (see Figure 10-7). This transformation process can be thought of as a divide-and-conquer technique where you continue pulling pieces out of the monolith until the system has been transformed and replaced with *Microservices*.

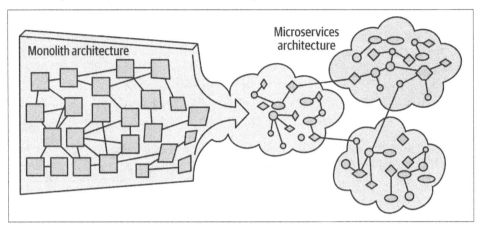

Figure 10-7. Transforming a Monolith into Microservices

This transformation process can take a lot of time to completely replace the mono-lith, especially for an entangled monolith. A good starting point is to find some low-hanging fruit or places where you can easily pull out pieces of the monolith—this helps teams learn about *Microservices* and motivates them by delivering some results. Another strategy you can use is to focus on high-value items or tasks first—those areas that are causing problems and will provide a big win if you can replace them with *Microservices*. These should be prioritized based on what yields the most value to the teams and the organization.

There are various techniques that can assist with finding places (partitions) to pull functionality out of the monolith—these partitions are found and replaced by apply-ing other strangling patterns (see Figure 10-8).

You begin this process by searching the monolith for obvious places that can be exploited to extract functionality to a *Microservice*. These are areas that already have well-defined interfaces—for example, a service inside your monolith. You find these places by examining the monolithic application for Hairline Cracks (530) around pieces of functionality that can easily be extracted. In these situations, you look for specific areas within the code that are loosely decoupled in the monolith.

If you find a place already mostly decoupled from the monolith, you can then Extract the Component (535) from the monolith, replacing it as a *Microservice*. *Extract Component* works well for components or functionality within the monolith that have well-defined interfaces and can easily be extracted and wrapped as *Microservices*. Sometimes *Hairline Cracks* will reveal areas with some coupling that you might need to first Refactor then Extract (542) the components from the monolith into *Microservices*.

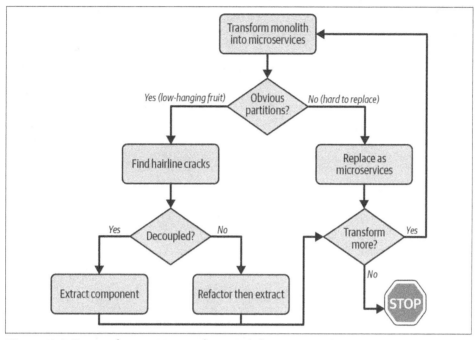

Figure 10-8. Process for partitioning the monolith into Microservices

However, many monoliths, especially entangled ones, will have a lot of places within their code that have less cohesion yet are tightly coupled. This is where you may need to Replace as Microservice (546) that functionality. It can be extremely challenging to find code groupings from these entangled parts of a monolith that can be replaced. When transforming these more entangled areas within the monolith, it is usually a good idea to focus on functionality that is changing a lot and causing a lot of problems.

The main advantage when you *Transform a Monolith into Microservices* is that the monolith application continues working and providing value to the organization during the transformation process. Additionally, it can be easier to maintain, change, and deploy functionality for any parts of the monolith that are transformed.

However, it can be difficult to *Transform a Monolith into Microservices*. It takes a lot of time and effort to find and replace these pieces of functionality that could be used for releasing new features or maintaining the system. Another challenge is that of maintaining two systems during the transformation process—for example, you may have to synch data between the *Microservices* and the monolith and also make updates to the monolith when something changes to a *Microservice*.

For any code that is extracted or replaced from the monolith, you can use a Monolith to Microservice Proxy (552) so that any monolith code that needs access to this new code will continue to work. During this transformation process, it is a good practice to use Playback Testing (556) to validate the migration.

Whenever you are *Transforming a Monolith*, it is a good idea to wrap up pieces within the monolith by applying well-known wrapper design patterns (*Design Patterns*, 1994) such as **Adapters**, **Decorators**, **Facades**, and **Proxies** so that you can protect the new services from being entangled with the monolith.

Examples

All of the examples described in the Strangle the Monolith (514) pattern apply here. Additionally, the examples described in Hairline Cracks (530), Extract Component (535), Refactor then Extract (542), and Replace as Microservice (546) are examples of *Transforming a Monolith into Microservices*.

Hairline Cracks

(aka Fracture Plane, Design Seams (*Working Effectively with Legacy Code*, 2004))

You have decided to Strangle the Monolith (514). You are evaluating an existing monolithic application and have decided to take some or all of the functionality of the application and rearchitect it for Microservices (119).

How do you identify the areas within a monolith application that are candidate boundaries for *Microservices*?

You would like to separate functionality from the monolith to improve the maintenance of the application and reduce the blast radius of new changes to it. It's not easy to understand how a monolithic application can be broken apart into *Microservices* to achieve this desired result. When evolving to Microservices Architecture (Chapter 4), there is often pressure to take advantage of the new architectural style as soon as possible.

It can be time-consuming and difficult to find places where the monolith can be split apart and extracted into *Microservices*. You need to find places inside the monolith that can be replaced with *Microservices*. If your monolith has multiple interfaces, there are usually good odds that one or more of them can be separated from the others.

Therefore,

Look for *Hairline Cracks* inside the monolith—these are the places where the monolith will be easier to break and replace with *Microservices*.

Hairline Cracks reveal places (clusters of functionality) within the monolith that can more easily be separated for extraction from the monolith (see Figure 10-9). You use these *Hairline Cracks* to either extract pieces out of the monolith to *Microservices* or to refactor to a better design before extracting to a *Microservice*. This is analogous to a hairline crack in a piece of metal or a fracture plane in some rocks.

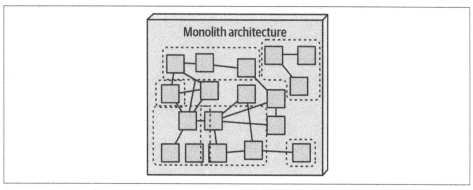

Figure 10-9. Finding Hairline Cracks in a monolith

The challenge is finding these *Hairline Cracks*. Monoliths usually contain components or services that provide seams where you more easily split the monolith apart and extract it to *Microservices*. A good place to start is to look for cohesive pieces of functionality that are loosely coupled inside the monolith—these are usually included as part of a component within the monolith with a well-defined interface. For example, in large monolithic applications, there are at least three very simple cases where you can find obvious cracks that can be exploited regarding services, often exposed by Service APIs (70) (see Figure 10-10).

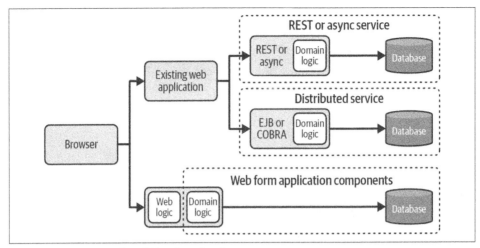

Figure 10-10. Examples of Hairline Cracks

Following are the three cases illustrated in Figure 10-10:

Case 1: Existing REST or Async services

This is by far the easiest case for refactoring. It may be that you have existing services that are already compatible with a Microservices Architecture (Chapter 4), or that could be made compatible. Start by untangling each REST or simple Async service from the rest of the application package, and then deploy each service independently. At this level, duplication of supporting files is fine—this is still mostly a question of packaging. Here you can begin the process of *Extracting Components*, but remember that this is often an iterative process toward refactoring to *Microservices*. Your new *Microservices* will still need to each perform one and only one business function while following accepted cloud DevOps principles.

Case 2: Existing older distributed services like CORBA, SOAP, or EJB

If you have existing services, they were probably built following a functional approach (such as the **Service Facade** (*SOA Design Patterns*, 2008) pattern). In this case, functionally based services design can usually be refactored into an asset-based services design. The reason is that in many cases, the functions in the **Service Facade** were originally written as CRUD operations on a single object. In the case where that is true, the mapping to a RESTful interface is straightforward—just re-implement the EJB session bean interface or SOAP interface as a RESTful interface. You may need to convert object representations to JSON to do this, but that's usually not very difficult. In cases where it's not a simple set of CRUD operations (for instance, account transfer), you can apply a number of different approaches for constructing RESTful services (such as building simple functional services like /accounts/transfer) that implement variants of the **Command** (*Design Patterns*, 1994) pattern.

Case 3: Simple web interfaces

Many programs are really just simple Web Form Applications (414) (for example, Servlet/JSP in Java) acting as frontends to database tables. If this code has a domain layer, that can be extracted and a new *Microservice* built around it. However, they may not have a domain object layer at all, especially if they follow design patterns like the **Active Record** (*Patterns of Enterprise Application Architecture*, 2002) pattern. In this case, creating a domain layer that you can then represent as a RESTful service is a good first step and an example of Refactor then Extract (542). Identifying your domain objects by Modeling Around the Domain (183) will help you identify your missing domain layer. Once you've built the domain layer (and packaged each new service separately), you can either refactor your existing *Web Form Application* to use the new service or you can build a whole new interface following a multichannel architecture approach.

In addition to these cases, there are often components or modules within a monolith that can potentially be extracted to *Microservices*. It is usually a good idea to focus on business capabilities to find these areas. These places often reveal partitions within the code that may be easier to wrap into a component that can then be extracted to a microservice—once decoupled from most of the monolith, they are usually fairly easy to extract out of the monolith to be replaced with *Microservices*.

Perhaps the biggest problem in finding *Hairline Cracks* arises when the business capabilities are not well-defined within the code or well-identified. In that case, the best approach is often to begin with the data and work backward into the code. This is particularly true when there is substantial interprocess communication through the database and when logic is implemented within the database (perhaps as stored procedures). In this case, it can be quite difficult to identify any business concepts at all from the code.

In that case, beginning with the database structures and the stored procedures that operate on them is the first step. That will help show you what domain concepts may exist. Then you can begin working backward to find the pieces of code that invoke the stored procedures and then continue moving backward from there to the data structures in the code that represent domain concepts, even if they are not well-named or well-defined. That can become the seed from which you can go forward and begin *Modeling Around the Domain*. If you repeat that process several times, you may then be able to identify the *Aggregates* within the system and begin tracing out the edges of a Bounded Context (201) in earnest.

Hairline Cracks reveal areas where you can refactor the monolith to a better design as it is being strangled. Breaking a monolith along an easily identified *Hairline Crack* is often a good introduction to the refactoring process and provides a team with the confidence they need to proceed with more complex refactoring.

The main challenges are related to time and complexity because it can be difficult and time-consuming to find these **Design Seams** (*Working Effectively with Legacy Code*, 2004) and refactor them to a better design. What's more, as with any refactoring effort, the benefits are not realized until after the refactoring is completed, so making the effort to pay back the technical debt requires advanced planning and agreement between the product owner and the technical team.

Finding these *Hairline Cracks* is similar to finding **Design Seams**. Finding these **Design Seams** can help you find places where you can Extract Components (535). Sometimes these *Hairline Cracks* reveal places where, although they have some coupling, there is potential to Refactor then Extract (542) the functionality from the monolith to *Microservices*.

When finding *Hairline Cracks*, it is good practice to apply proven Microservice Design (Chapter 5) modeling techniques to determine the best design and domain boundaries to refactor toward. The goal is to build the right-size service that is Modeled around the Domain (183).

Examples

The first example describes a tool for finding *Hairline Cracks* with a reference to a case study of using it. The second example looks for *Hairline Cracks* in an ecommerce app for extracting features to *Microservices*.

Mono2Micro

IBM Mono2Micro (*https://oreil.ly/OwXFY*) is a tool for identifying parts of your Java code that are loosely coupled externally while more tightly coupled internally. The tool will find the appropriate *Hairline Cracks*, partition the code into those sections, and then generate wrapper code to refactor the partitions into *Microservices*. Jay Talekar and Sachin Avasthi from the IBM CIO Office have written a case study (*https://oreil.ly/bMcXs*) of using this tool on a number of applications as part of a larger modernization exercise.

Shopping cart and checkout from ecommerce

Let's consider an ecommerce monolithic system that includes functionality for a shopping cart and for checking out and paying for the order (see Figure 10-11). In this example, after some analysis within the monolith, we decide to refactor the shopping cart and checkout features to a better design to make it easier to maintain and extract this functionality into a *Microservice*.

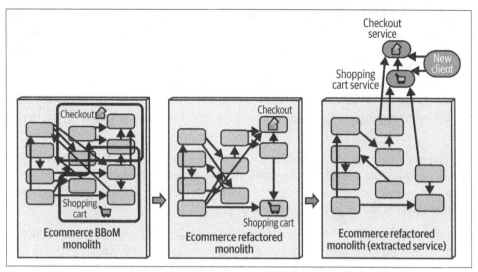

Figure 10-11. Ecommerce Find Hairline Cracks and refactor to Microservice

After this refactoring, the checkout and shopping cart features can be extracted into a separate service. Sometimes *Hairline Cracks* reveal components that can be extracted with little or no refactoring to the monolith. Other times you might need to do quite a bit of refactoring to extract the functionality.

Extract Component

(aka Extract Service, Extract Functionality to Microservice, Extract Component and Add Facade[7])

You have started the strangling process and are looking for ways to Transform the Monolith to Microservices (526). You have identified some Hairline Cracks (530) within the monolith that reveal some potential services or modules (pieces of functionality) that would be beneficial if modernized to Microservices (119).

How do you separate loosely related parts of the code in our monolith into distinct deployable units?

A monolith by definition is a large deployment unit that encompasses functionality pertaining to many different subdomains. Some changes to the system require changes across subsystems, often creating bugs or other issues. Teams often do not have a full understanding of the domains and subdomains.

---

7 A variation of this pattern was originally called **Extract Component and Add Facade** in *Strangler Patterns* (*https://oreil.ly/9ZpqJ*) by Joseph Yoder and Paulo Merson.

Teams will want to pull out pieces that are causing pain and start using new approaches—specifically *Microservices*. Since monoliths are large, different development teams work on different parts of the monolith. However, these teams are usually organized in ways that are detrimental to this desire—such as organizing teams by layer within a layered architecture. This requires teams to coordinate closely and work together to make changes to the system. Any change in one part of a monolithic system often requires changes to another part. which is usually owned by a different team.

Developers usually have the freedom to take shortcuts, which often add dependencies across components within the monolith when implementing new features or fixing bugs. As a result, many monoliths are significantly tangled. Component interdependencies then make it difficult to isolate fine-grained, cohesive components.

Despite this, there are often places inside the monolith that have some functionality grouped around aspects of the domain. The monolith may include components with well-defined interfaces that can be separated from the monolith. Monoliths often also include some components or pieces that contain related pieces of functionality that can be pulled out into their own component(s) or service(s).

Therefore,

Extract functionality identified by a *Hairline Crack* out of the monolith into its own separate distributed component. Apply recursively until the components are appropriately sized for *Microservices*.

To extract functionality, you start by examining those places (functionality or components) within the monolith identified by *Hairline Cracks* that show the most promise for extracting into *Microservices*. You then gradually extract these components from the monolith, working toward implementing them as *Microservices*. Any access from existing clients that need access to extracted functionality can be routed through a **Facade** (*Design Patterns*, 1994). Figure 10-12 illustrates the application of this pattern to component X, which is extracted and becomes microservice X'.

Note that in Figure 10-12, component X is mostly decoupled from the rest of the monolith. Usually, some detangling is needed to extract components from the monolith. If components inside the monolith were clients to X, you can either adapt those clients to have them calling the new *Microservice* X' through the intercepting **Facade**, or, if possible, adapt them to directly call X'. In this example, an existing client and component Y was calling X directly. These calls are now directed through the **Facade**, which will call X' by transforming any protocols and respond accordingly. This example also shows that a new client application may also call *Microservice* X' directly if the extra features of the **Facade** are not required for the interaction.

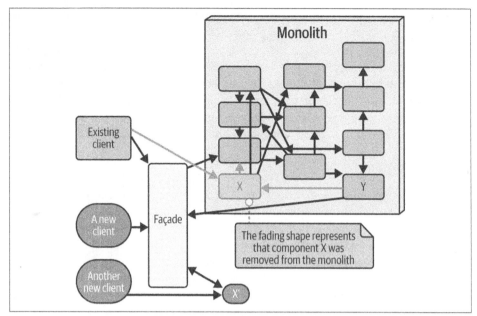

Figure 10-12. Extract Component from monolith and add Façade

There are two approaches you can take when *Extracting Components*: top-down or bottom-up. You can get some **Quick Wins** by applying a bottom-up approach, which examines the low-hanging fruit (obvious places) you found when looking for *Hairline Cracks*, and then extracting that functionality from the monolith to a *Microservice*.[8] For example, as described in *Hairline Cracks*, you may already have some services being implemented in the monolith, such as REST or Async services. There might also be older distributed services such as CORBA, SOAP, or EJB. These services can usually be extracted into a *Microservice* that is deployed independently of the monolith in a straightforward way.

Also, some *Hairline Cracks* might reveal components or modules within the monolith that have well-defined internal interfaces and are loosely coupled with the rest of the monolith. These pieces are also good candidates for extracting out of the monolith and require less effort than more tightly coupled pieces. You get to take advantage of *Microservices* early on by extracting these components.

However, it is usually more often the case that an entangled monolith will contain larger pieces or components that are tightly coupled internally and thus harder to

---

8 **Quick Wins** is a pattern described in *Leading a Software Architecture Revolution* (*https://oreil.ly/FAEQq*) by Marden Neubert and Joseph Yoder. When beginning any migration or modernization endeavors, it is a good idea to start with less risky and less coupled subsystems before you engage in more complex activities so teams can learn about the new architecture and the migration/modernization process.

break into smaller pieces without a lot of refactoring. This is when you can apply a top-down approach by taking larger pieces of functionality and extracting them from the monolith even though they contain some entangled parts. In these cases, pulling out these larger pieces first can help you begin to get the benefits of moving toward *Microservices* and can make refactoring these entangled pieces to smaller *Microservices* easier. Therefore, for a lot of the monolith, you will be extracting larger pieces of functionality into a **Macro Service** and then breaking each of them down into a *Microservice* after this functionality has been successfully extracted.

Macro Service

When *Extracting Components*, you often start by extracting high-level components and then recursively breaking those pieces into smaller and smaller pieces.[9] You continue this process until you have reached the level of *Microservices*, where each piece stands alone and meets the requirements for a *Microservice*. You can think of the monolith as the biggest piece, and then we apply a divide-and-conquer technique to break the monolith down into smaller and smaller pieces. An example is shown in Figure 10-13, where tightly coupled components A and B are extracted as a **Macro Service**.

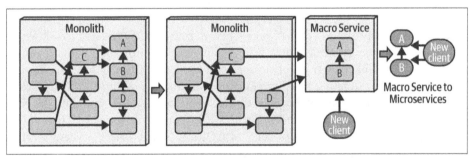

Figure 10-13. Extracting Macro Service to Refactor to Microservices

Any original functionality within the monolith that needs access to the extracted functionality is redirected to call the newly created service that implements the functionality outside the monolith—for example, components C and D are redirected to the newly created **Macro Service** as seen in Figure 10-10.

Extracting a **Macro Service** is the first step toward *Microservices*, but it begins as a larger service because of coupling within the monolith that makes it difficult to extract the smaller pieces. Once this intermediate solution is stable, you can then begin to separate the **Macro Service** into smaller *Microservices*. After the **Macro**

---

9 *Macro Service* is a supporting subpattern that was originally called **Macro then Micro** in *Strangler Patterns* (*https://oreil.ly/FAEQq*) by Joseph Yoder and Paulo Merson.

Service has been extracted, new clients can begin to access and use the functionality of the extracted service. There may be some larger pieces of functionality that you need to first refactor into a component with a well-defined interface that can then more easily be extracted to a service.

When you are extracting a **Macro Service**, you may not be as concerned with all the attributes that make a service qualify as a *Microservice*. For instance, it is common for a **Macro Service** to perform more than one business function yet still be loosely coupled to the rest of the monolithic application. An example of this is when there is complex decision logic that chooses from among various options that are difficult to refactor into separate components, but pulling out all of the decision logic plus the additional domain logic behind the decision logic as a single large component is still a good first step toward refactoring into *Microservices*.

Implementation Issues

Once you have decided on a component to extract, you clone the code that can be extracted as is and release it as a *Microservice*. The next step is to test and validate the extracted pieces. Once you are comfortable with the newly released *Microservice*, you can then route any necessary calls to it. Existing client applications or components that use functionality moved out of the monolith into a *Microservice* can be handled as follows:

- They can be rewritten to call the new *Microservice*. This option takes time to be rewritten and may not be achievable before these components become *Microservices*.

- They can remain unchanged and have their calls go through a routing interceptor (the **Facade** component) to the new *Microservice*. This component performs the protocol bridging and message transformations for the existing client components to interact with the new *Microservice*. This option is your only choice when there are clients that you cannot change (i.e., third-party clients).

In addition to protocol bridging and message transformations, the **Facade** component, which can also act as a reverse proxy, can perform several operations, such as security controls, dynamic message routing, traffic monitoring, circuit breaker, and even caching.

Sometimes you can use refactoring tools such as IBM Mono2Micro (*https://oreil.ly/ wxluv*) to extract the component. This tool can find the appropriate *Hairline Cracks* within a monolith and then partition the code into sections that can generate wrapper code to refactor the partitions, extract them into **Macro Services** or *Microservices*, and provide wrapper code to delegate code from the monolith to the new *Microservice*.

The main advantage is that you get the benefit of using the Microservices Architecture (Chapter 4) for functionality that can be extracted from the monolith. You are also able to change, test, and deploy the extracted piece more quickly without affecting or releasing the monolith. The **Facade** component has the benefit of enabling existing clients or code inside the monolith to seamlessly interact with the newly created *Microservice*.

However, it can be difficult to find decoupled pieces within the monolith, and sometimes you don't see the immediate benefit of extracting these pieces. Also, for larger pieces, the team might not have the time or inclination to refactor them to smaller *Microservices*. Extracted **Macro Services** usually contain tightly coupled pieces, which still makes modification of the code to add new functionality more difficult than it would be if you completed the refactoring to *Microservices*.

Whether you are Starting Small (492) or not, you can *Extract Components* whenever desired functionality in the monolith can benefit from being moved to a *Microservice*. Hairline Cracks (530) reveals potential places in the monolith that can be extracted. It is common to first extract a larger **Macro Service** and then refactor it into smaller *Microservices*.

You might need to first Refactor then Extract (542) the components from the monolith. If the functionality is tightly coupled in the monolith, you may need to Replace as Microservice (546).

For any functionality in the monolith that needs access to the extracted behavior, you can create a Monolith to Microservice Proxy (552), which can also act like a **Facade** for external clients. The new *Microservice* likewise might need to access the **Facade**.

Modeling Around the Domain (183) is an important technique for finding the right-size services (180) as the system evolves. Larger functional pieces being extracted are usually modeled around Bounded Context (201) pieces of the domain.

Examples

The following airline and ecommerce examples describe how to apply the *Extract Component* technique.

Airline example

In an airline refactoring example we worked on, we found that the initial monolithic application was performing three major sets of business functions suitable for refactoring to better separate them:

1. "fly" represents "day of flight" functions like check-in, bag check, and upgrade purchase
2. "try" represents flight search
3. "buy" represents the purchase process

This logical division gave us the ability to start looking for smaller logical units within each group (or "chunk" as we called them).

We were then able to look through the code of each part of the monolith, looking first for **Macro Services** to extract; one such was the ticket purchase process. This process was large and tightly coupled internally—for example, it had many internal logic switches, such as whether the customer was purchasing an upgrade or a new ticket. Nevertheless, it was at the right level to be extracted as a **Macro Service**. This reduced duplication in the overall system because the purchase function had originally been replicated multiple times in the original code. It was a good early step toward refactoring the system into *Microservices*, which continued as a refinement process over several later releases.

Ecommerce

Figure 10-14 extends our example of extracting a **Macro Service** from an ecommerce monolith similar to the example shown in *Hairline Cracks*. Note that Checkout is well-defined functionality within a subdomain of an ecommerce system. In the Checkout subdomain, you can check out and pay for any items you have added to your shopping cart.

Analysis of the *Hairline Cracks* within the monolith revealed that we could extract the Checkout functionality from the monolith without too much effort. We were then able to refactor the extracted functionality into two smaller *Microservices* called Checkout and Shopping Cart. Note that in this example, components Y and Z were updated in the monolith to call the newly created services outside of the monolith.

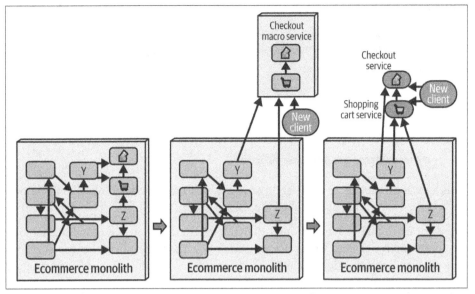

Figure 10-14. Extracting Macro Service ecommerce example

Refactor then Extract

(aka Reorganize Monolith then Extract to Microservices)

You have been Strangling the Monolith (514) with a focus on finding ways to Transform the Monolith into Microservices (526). Some areas have been identified by Hairline Cracks (530) that you have been able to extract into Microservices (119). However, there are other areas inside the monolith with some internal coupling (at least partially) that you would like to get the benefits of being implemented with *Microservices*, especially parts of the monolith that change frequently.

How do we address coupling within the monolith to facilitate extraction into *Microservices*?

Monoliths are often tightly coupled with many dependencies between internal components, making it difficult to easily extract existing code. You need to find ways to reduce that coupling to make it possible to extract that code.

However, the code may be very complex or difficult to understand, leading the team to be cautious in making any changes at all to specific sections. A change in one part of the monolith can break other parts of the system, and those breaks can be difficult to detect, especially if the test coverage of the monolith is inadequate.

Therefore,

Reorganize the monolith by refactoring partially coupled pieces to be more modular with well-defined interfaces, and then *Extract Components* to Microservices.

You start by finding places within the monolith that you can refactor into modules; these modules can later be extracted from the monolith into *Microservices*. Figure 10-15 shows functionality "a" and "b" being refactored to components *A* and *B* within the ecommerce monolith. Such refactored modular pieces can then be extracted into *Microservices*.

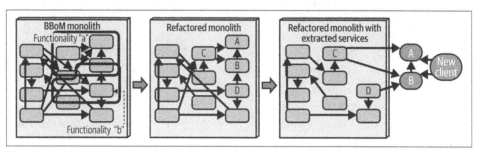

Figure 10-15. Refactor then Extract to Microservices

In this example, both "a" and "b" functionalities are places that could be refactored to separate modules (A and B) within the monolith. You can then *Extract the Components* (modules A and B) and add a **Facade** (*Design Patterns*, 1994) to migrate the functionality of *A* and *B* to *Microservices*. Note that components *C* and *D* now call the newly extracted *Microservices*. Alternatively, we could have left an interface for *A* and *B* in the monolith to **Proxy** (*Design Patterns*, 1994) calls to the extracted *Microservices*.

There are various techniques you can apply to help with this. If there are pieces of functionality that have coupling, analyzing these pieces can identify places where you could make the code more modular, thus making it easier to extract into a *Microservice*. First of all, any *Hairline Cracks* that cannot directly be extracted are potential places that can be refactored inside the monolith to make extracting them easier. Code smell tools and refactoring tools can assist with finding these places and will refactor the code inside the monolith.

While adding new features or fixing existing features, there will be areas within the monolith that need to evolve to address the desired changes. When making these changes within the monolith, there is an opportunity to see if there are pieces that can be refactored and extracted to *Microservices*. This is often an evolutionary process—for instance, you may begin by pulling multiple related calls together into a common point using the **Facade** pattern—perhaps also using language features like Interfaces in Java or Traits in Rust to facilitate this. You can then, over time, evolve that **Facade** into a Service API (70), even while the code remains within the monolith. This gives you time to update the clients that used the original **Facade** into clients that consume the *Service API* instead. Once you have done that, you are more likely to be able to successfully pull out the code behind the *Service API* using Extract Component (535).

When the code is difficult to understand, it can be a good idea to "refactor to understand," which helps you learn more about the domain and the current implementation and often reveals areas that can be extracted. Often, it is useful to split your data before extracting the components—especially if you are using a large shared database and communicating with other components through the database. Database refactoring mechanisms like denormalization can facilitate that, especially if you combine that with refactoring components to communicate through interfaces rather than through the database.

The are two main advantages to this approach. First of all, parts of the monolith are refactored to a better design, making it easier to evolve and maintain. Also, these refactored components can more easily be extracted to *Microservices* when needed.

One disadvantage is that you might have to wait longer until you get the benefits of *Microservices*. In addition to taking longer, it could also increase complexity in the monolith as you create new abstractions. Learning and maintaining these abstractions could be costly in terms of time and expertise.

After refactoring the functionality in the monolith, the next step is to apply the Extract Component (535) pattern. Sometimes you will need to refactor larger pieces or components from the monolith, then extract them as **Macro Services**, finally breaking them down into smaller *Microservices*. After applying *Refactor then Extract*, you can create a Monolith to Microservice Proxy (552) for any functionality in the monolith that needs access to the extracted behavior.

This pattern is related to Refactor the Monolith (484) because you are refactoring parts of the monolith so that you can more easily extract these pieces to *Microservices*. The main difference is that you are not trying to refactor the complete monolith, which might be independent of applying the Microservices Architecture (Chapter 4) style. Rather you are finding pieces of functionality inside the monolith that have the potential to be refactored to assist you in extracting that functionality into a *Microservice*.

Examples

The following are examples of systems that have applied the *Refactor then Extract* pattern.

Financial services system

What we often seem to think about most in Refactor the Monolith (484) is the process of breaking down complex components into ever smaller pieces. However, sometimes the exact opposite approach is required. In one financial services system that one of the authors worked on, the problem was that the developers had tried to anticipate scaling in an altogether inappropriate way; they had essentially violated Fowler's First Law of Distributed Object Design (*https://oreil.ly/JkDVi*)—"Don't distribute your objects!"—and had made *everything* in their system a distributed object, requiring remote calls. They did this by taking an overly layered approach to their system, where not only their top-level domain concepts (like Retirement Plan) were distributed components, but all of their data representations were distributed components as well. The overhead from all of these remote calls was enormous and brought system performance to a standstill.

We recommended a two-step approach. First, refactor the internal (data representation) calls to everyday Java method invocations instead of remote calls. This in itself dramatically improved the overall performance of the system and allowed us to then move on to the next stage—refactoring the domain concepts on the top of the tree into components with RESTful interfaces that each performed one and only one business function. The entire process from beginning to end is shown in Figure 10-16.

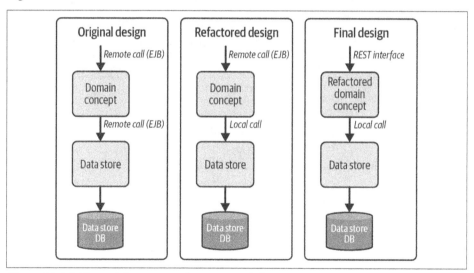

Figure 10-16. Financial services refactoring and then Extract to Microservices

The advantage of this approach is that the team could show substantial results early on in terms of reduced system complexity and improved performance before completing the transition to a *Microservices*-based approach.

Ecommerce system

We previously showed an ecommerce example where we found *Hairline Cracks* in a monolith, refactored the Checkout and Shopping Cart functionality, and then extracted the two functionalities into a single service (see Figure 10-11). We also showed how to take this extracted **Macro Service** and break it down into smaller *Microservices* (see Figure 10-14).

Figure 10-17 is an example of applying both of these techniques together for an ecommerce monolith to extract the Checkout and Shopping Cart functionality. This is an example of Starting Small (492) and taking some *Baby Steps* toward a *Microservice* implementation.

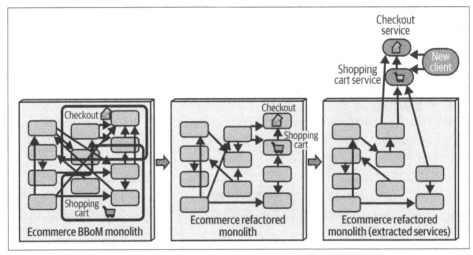

Figure 10-17. Ecommerce refactoring then Extract to Microservices

In this example, both the Checkout and Shopping Cart functionality were identified as *Hairline Cracks* within the monolith as places where the functionality could be refactored to separate modules within the monolith. Once this functionality is refactored to separate modules within the monolith, you can then *Extract the Components* to migrate this functionality into a Checkout **Macro Service** that includes both the Checkout and Shopping Cart functionality. After this has been extracted, then this *Macro Service* can be split into Checkout and Shopping Cart *Microservices*.

Replace as Microservice

(aka Replace as Service, Reimplement as Service, Reimplement as Microservice)

You are Transforming the Monolith into Microservices (526). You have been able to extract into Microservices (119) certain areas identified by Hairline Cracks (530).

However, there are other areas inside the monolith that you would like to get the benefits of being implemented with *Microservices*.

How can we move complex and important pieces of functionality that are tightly coupled in the monolith to *Microservices* with minimal impact?

In a monolith, especially one not well organized into modules, changing a single feature often requires changing several parts of the monolith in a coordinated fashion. For parts of the monolith that change frequently, you'd like to replace those parts with *Microservices*, which makes them easier to change with less impact on other parts of the monolith.

You may want to extract frequently changing parts of the monolith; however, because they are tightly coupled with many dependencies between internal components, they are difficult or nearly impossible to separate from existing code. The existing monolith may be too fragile to add any new code to it, as any change can cause side effects.

Therefore,

Reimplement (rewrite) components or functionality from the monolith as *Microservices*. While doing this, lock down this functionality in the monolith.

When you have functionality within the monolith that cannot easily be extracted and would be useful to implement with *Microservices*, you lock down the original functionality in the monolith and rewrite the component(s) that provides core functionality as a microservice—Figure 10-18 is an example of component X in the monolith being locked down and then rewritten to *Microservice X'*. For many entangled monoliths, this functionality will be spread across different parts of the monolith rather than just one component; we are using a single component to illustrate this pattern.

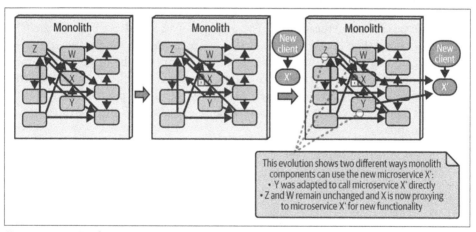

Figure 10-18. Replace as Microservice

In this example, any development or changes to the original component X (or functionality related to X) in the monolith is locked down (frozen). A new version of the functionality for X is then implemented as *Microservice X'*, and it becomes the primary locus for that functionality. After the new *Microservice X'* is tested and validated, new client components can start using the functionality of *Microservice X'*.

Once the new *Microservice* becomes part of the new system and starts to evolve, other components inside the monolith may need access to the new functionality that is in the *Microservice*. In this case, there are two alternatives to access the new *Microservice* from inside the monolith. One way is to rewrite any client components in the monolith to directly call the new *Microservice*; Figure 10-18 shows Y being updated to directly call X'. Another way is to create a **Proxy** (*Design Patterns*, 1994) from the original component X in the monolith to call the newly implemented feature in *Microservice X'*; this alternative is illustrated in Figure 10-18, where Z and W are still calling X and then being delegated to X' for the updated functionality.

The following outlines the steps for the *Replace as Microservice* approach:

1. Code-freeze[10] the functionality you want to replace in the monolith.

2. Create a new *Microservice* implementing the functionality from the monolith that you want to replace.

3. **Canary Release** (*https://oreil.ly/3Iyvb*) the new *Microservice* while carefully testing.

4. Change the interface of the original implementation of the functionality in the monolith to call the newly created *Microservice*.

5. Gradually rewrite the old client components to call the new *Microservice* instead of the old component in the monolith.

6. Eventually remove the original implementation of the functionality if feasible.

There are variations to these steps. For example, you could start by freezing the functionality and then create a new interface or abstraction to the functionality. This interface could be a direct call (implemented as a **Proxy**) to the original implementation of the functionality. Then, you update any monolith client code to call this new interface. After you create the new *Microservice* and you are confident with the new implementation, you can then switch the interface to use the new *Microservice* implementation.

---

10 Code-freeze is an example of **Freeze** described in *Leading a Software Architecture Revolution* (*https://oreil.ly/ 7FZxY*). **Freeze** locks changes in the old architecture to achieve faster results when *Replacing as Microservices* the original implementation.

Addressing Challenging Areas in the Monolith

Entangled monoliths by definition will include many areas inside them that have less cohesion and are tightly coupled. This makes it extremely challenging to find code groupings that can be extracted. You are trying to find areas or partitions within the monolith that can be decomposed and possibly extracted or replaced. Sometimes analysis can reveal *Hairline Cracks* where there are pieces of functionality that can be refactored to a better design, creating components within the monolith that can more easily be extracted. In these situations, you look for specific areas within the code that can be decoupled from the monolith. On the other hand, there will be many areas where this is not possible, and you will need to lock changes to that functionality in the monolith and reimplement them with *Microservices*.

When addressing these entangled areas in the monolith to replace that functionality with *Microservices*, it is usually a good idea to focus on key business capabilities that change a lot, especially if the changes are causing problems. An entangled monolith usually includes functionality that is coupled around these capabilities. The goal is to decouple these capabilities by focusing on the domain. To find these, look for boundaries inside the monolith around related business objectives and responsibilities, even if they include many pieces of functionality. These boundaries reveal areas that can potentially be grouped together and replaced with a *Microservice*. You can find these places inside the monolith in the following ways:

- Look for high-level groupings of related functions that go together (examples include account management, invoicing, quoting, contracting, billing, shipping, etc.).
- Look for smaller repeated use cases within those groupings of functions (examples include tax calculations, shipping provider selection, credit card payment, loyalty point redemption, etc.).
- Identify code-level components within those repeated use cases to build into *Microservices*.

To search for these areas within your code, you can also analyze your commit logs and examine problems from your issue-tracking tools such as Jira. You may also want to use tools that show coupling and other code smells, such as SonarQube. Parts of the system that change frequently and affect other parts of the system should be included as potential sections to be moved to *Microservices*—it is valuable to extract these pieces out of the monolith as soon as possible.

Replacing functionality with *Microservices* provides flexibility and the benefits of being able to use new technologies, frameworks, and platforms. Also, teams can experiment with new ideas with less risk of breaking the monolith. Rewriting these pieces also makes this functionality easier to change in the future because you have decoupled it from the monolith.

On the other hand, the organization loses the benefit of adding features in the monolith for that frozen piece of code. While the code is locked down, you cannot add new features for this part of the system. Also, it can be complex for pieces in the monolith to take advantage of the new features implemented in *Microservices*. Finally, there could be data-syncing issues between the data stored in the monolith and data stored in the new *Microservices*, specifically in the data used in the frozen code.

If any components within the monolith need access to the new features in the newly created *Microservice*, you update them to directly call the *Microservices*, or you can create a Monolith to Microservice Proxy (552) from the original locked component to call the new *Microservices*. You can use a **Facade** (*Design Patterns*, 1994) to access any functionality inside the monolith that the *Microservice* needs access to.

When you *Replace as Microservice*, the new implementation should be validated through Playback Testing (556) by comparing the new *Microservices* implementation to the original implementation from the monolith, especially because you are rewriting and replacing the original implementation.

Branch by Abstraction (*Monolith to Microservices*, 2019) is a special case of *Replace as Microservice*, where specific steps are outlined for replacing the code in the monolith with *Microservices*. In **Branch by Abstraction**, you create an abstraction point for the functionality that will be replaced and have the code inside the monolith call to this new abstraction. *Replace as Microservice* includes this scenario but also includes other variations of replacing the functionality of the monolith with *Microservices*— for example, by simply locking this functionality down and completely rewriting it without creating the new abstraction inside the monolith.

Examples

The following examples illustrate the *Replace as Microservice* approach.

Major hotel chain

In this example, the hotel chain followed the *Replace as Microservice* approach to replace an existing complex subsystem used for viewing and redeeming hotel reward points within a large Web Form Application (414) that was being broken apart into services. The existing code was buggy and complex, so they chose to rewrite the entire rewards section as a distributed service (this was before *Microservices* became known as such). The advantage of this approach in the long-term was that a few years later, the hotel chain decided to replace their home-grown rewards tracking system with a commercial rewards tracking application. They could only do this because they had a single remote API to the previously developed service that minimized the amount of work needed to entirely change out the implementation of the rewards system.

Ecommerce

Figure 10-19 is an example of an ecommerce system where functionality for the "Authorize Payment" inside the monolith is *Replaced as a Microservice*. Authorization is an approval of credit or debit cards that validate that the cardholder has sufficient funds available to pay for the transaction that they are attempting to make. There are third-party systems that provide this functionality, usually for 1.5% to 3.5% of the transaction. For a lot of transactions, this cost can add up to quite a bit of money, which sometimes is a good reason to implement this functionality internally.

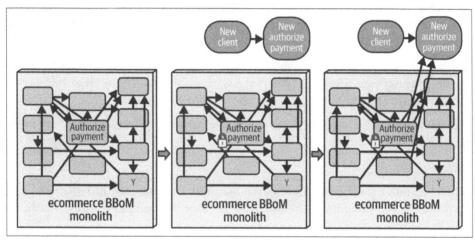

Figure 10-19. Replace as Microservice ecommerce example

Note in Figure 10-16 that the "Authorize Payment" functionality is tightly coupled inside the ecommerce monolith and also makes a call out to a third-party service (not shown) to authorize a credit card payment. Because of this coupling, they decided to lock any changes to this part of the monolith and rewrite this functionality outside the monolith as a new service.

Once this new service was released, they were able to start testing and **Canary Release** this service to new clients. Over time, they were able to rewrite parts of the monolith to directly call this new service; Y is redirected to call the new "Authorized Payment" service. This example also illustrates the use of a *Monolith to Microservice Proxy* that delegates from the locked component in the monolith to call the new *Microservice* implementation.

Monolith to Microservice Proxy

(aka Proxy Monolith Components to Microservices, Proxy Monolith Service to Microservice)

You are in the process of transforming your monolith to Microservices (119), and you need existing monolithic code to call the new functionality made available as *Microservices*.

How can developers change the code in the monolith to access and use the functionality that was replaced with *Microservices*?

During the long-running process to Strangle the Monolith (514), components in the monolith are gradually replaced with *Microservices*. The *Microservices* may use protocols and message formats that are different from what is used in the monolith. However, evolving the monolith to use the same standardized message formats used in *Microservices* can be expensive.

You would like to have the monolith take advantage of the new features provided in the *Microservices*. However, the cost and risk of updating a large number of components in the monolith to call the new *Microservices* is high.

Old client applications require access to components in the monolith that are being extracted as *Microservices*.

Therefore,

When you move functionality out of the monolith components into *Microservices*, keep the old components in the monolith but rewrite them as *proxies* to redirect calls to the new *Microservices*.

The main idea is that the interface of old client components remains unchanged. Monolith components that are replaced by *Microservices* no longer implement the business logic to directly process the calls themselves. These components still expose the same contract, but all they do now is route calls to the new, *Microservice*-based implementation. Now that there's a *Microservice* that does something the monolith does, rather than trying to update all of the client code in the monolith, just replace the monolith code that used to do the functionality with proxy code that calls the *Microservice*. Figure 10-20 illustrates the application of the pattern to components X and Y.

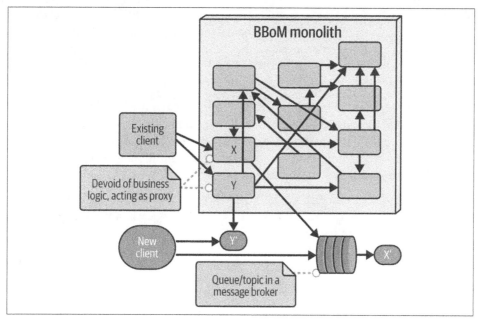

Figure 10-20. Monolith to Microservice Proxy

The components are extracted or rewritten as *Microservices* X' and Y'. The diagram illustrates that these extracted or rewritten services can be synchronous or asynchronous. For example, service Y' can be a synchronous REST service, and service X' can be a consumer of a message queue (e.g., a Kafka topic) and hence be activated by asynchronous messages or events. In this example, Y is proxying directly to Y', while X is proxying by sending a message to a queue that X' subscribes to.

Additionally, it should be noted that in this example, components X and Y are called by existing clients and by components inside the monolith. These clients and the components within the monolith are unaffected by the solution because they still see the same contract exposed by X and Y, even though the actual business logic got delegated to *Microservices* X' and Y'.

Instead of adding a **Facade** (*Design Patterns*, 1994) interceptor component, you have the monolith components acting as **Proxies** (*Design Patterns*, 1994) to the new *Microservices*—in a sense, parts of the monolith are being converted into **Facade**. Because new *Microservices* may have different contracts, monolith components acting as *Proxies* may need to perform the message transformation and protocol bridging.

The main benefit of this pattern over the generic **Facade** solution is related to handling calls from within the monolith. Clients and components within the monolith are unaffected by the solution because they still see the original contract. We don't have that benefit when you simply **Wrap the Monolith** because you still have to redirect calls from inside the monolith in some way.

Unlike *Wrapping the Monolith*, this pattern does not require creating, configuring, and monitoring a **Facade** component to allow existing clients to seamlessly communicate with new *Microservices*. Therefore, this pattern is generally easier to implement and govern than that one. However, similar to the solution with the **Facade**, the performance overhead exists of an extra network hop.

This pattern requires rebuilding and redeploying the monolithic application whenever you Extract Component (535) as a *Microservice*, which is not the case with the **Facade** solution. In that pattern, internal clients would need to be adapted to calling the new *Microservices*, as the **Facade** typically would not intercept the in-process calls within the monolith.

There are possible failure scenarios inherent in distributed systems that must be dealt with when applying this pattern. These failures could compromise meeting the reliability and performance requirements of the system.

This pattern is a variation of the traditional **Proxy** pattern applied to distributed systems. In this case, the proxying components are also known as **Remote Facades** (*Patterns of Enterprise Application Architecture*, 2002) or **Ambassadors** (*https://oreil.ly/ rr1re*).

Examples

The following examples are from real-world systems (a payment system and a major retailer) that two of the authors have worked on.

Payment System

One of the authors was involved in a migration and modernization effort for a payment system that is similar to PayPal and Square together. This system involved a transformation from a large monolith to a *Microservices* implementation over a few years. A critical part of this system was the ability for customers to place their orders and pay for items either with existing money in their account or by using a credit card. This piece of functionality was known as Checkout. The Checkout process needed to evolve, and they made the decision to replace this functionality within the monolith as a *Microservice*. The functionality in Checkout was entangled within the monolith, specifically because there were many calls to the Checkout API inside the monolith. After they implemented and validated the Checkout functionality as a *Microservice*, they were able to route calls to the new Checkout service by creating a

Monolith to Microservices Proxy. A benefit of this *Monolith to Microservices Proxy* was that it gave us the ability to **Canary Release** and validate the Checkout service.

Major retailer

A simple example of this approach was implemented by a major retailer several years ago. In this case, the retailer had a very complex Web Form Application (414) that had a custom-built frontend portion that enabled catalog browsing and cart filling, which then passed on the cart information to a commercial Order Management System (OMS) for recording and fulfilling the order upon checkout.

In this case, the original design had a flaw—the system was implemented as a monolith, with the OMS being directly integrated into the monolith as a library. Thus, everything the user did happened within the same set of threads, controlled by the same shared thread pool, of the application server the *Web Form Application* ran on.

Three hundred and sixty-four days out of each year, this was fine. The problem happened the first Black Friday (the day after the US Thanksgiving holiday, the busiest day for retail in the year) that this system was in place. On that day, the system reached its maximum capacity—the bottleneck turned out to be in the capacity of the database the OMS was running on, which could only write orders to the database at a fixed rate. This backed the system up when the thread pool filled up with orders waiting to be written, which caused the entire system to crash.

So the next year, we implemented the previously discussed approach—we refactored the OMS by *Extract Component* into a **Macro Service** that ran in its own process (and turned the entire system into a Distributed Architecture (38)). We then used a queuing system between the catalog section of the monolith and the OMS, which we hid behind a *Monolith to Microservices Proxy*. Thus, we could let the catalog section run as fast as it could, with the only difference being that orders were placed on the queue instead of being written to the database immediately. The OMS could write to the database at its own rate, and eventually, as orders slowed down, it would catch up and empty the queue. We show the old design and the new refactored design in Figure 10-21.

This change worked well in this example because the problem never repeated itself, especially given the additional capacity to the system as a whole that allows independent scaling of both parts of the system created.

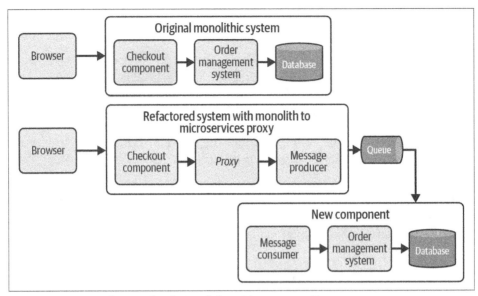

Figure 10-21. Retail example of Monolith to Microservice Proxy

Playback Testing

(aka Parallel Run (*Monolith to Microservices*, 2019), Validate New Implementation)

You are modernizing an existing application that includes replacing components from the monolith with *Microservices*.

How do you ensure that the new Microservices Architecture maintains the same functionality as the old monolithic system, especially when the amount of detailed end-to-end application knowledge of the existing application may be limited?

When you evolve to a new architecture, there is a period of time where new and old systems coexist. It is important to plan for the transition and think about the coexistence period and the special challenges that emerge during that period.

One of the unexpected difficulties of this coexistence period occurs just before the new functionality goes live. A basic principle of refactoring is that before you begin any refactoring effort, you should have a solid set of tests of the existing system that you can also run against the new system. However, when refactoring legacy systems, you can't assume that this solid set of tests covering all potential code paths exists.

Systems that were not built with detailed testing in mind usually don't have adequate test coverage. In many cases, teams must work on building tests to validate new systems without detailed knowledge of the underlying system they are reimplementing. That makes it difficult for teams to determine if a refactored system really will respond in the same way as the existing system. What further complicates this is that even subtle bugs in the existing system may have become enshrined in workflows and UIs—in such a way that they have become hidden or undocumented features rather than bugs.

All this means is that teams would like to have a mechanism for ensuring that the behavior of the new system can reasonably be determined to be "the same" as the old system when a portion of the old system is reimplemented in the new system.

Therefore,

Test the new system by capturing a set of inputs and actions on the original system and running a playback of the same inputs and actions on the new implementation. Then, compare the results of the two systems for any differences.

The main idea is to first capture then *Playback* a set of transactions on both the existing and new systems and then log a report of the comparison of the values discovered throughout the entire playback sequence. Figure 10-22 outlines an example of running the new and the old followed by a comparison of the results.

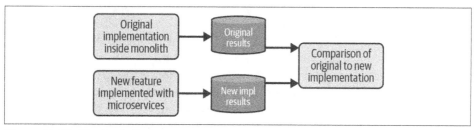

Figure 10-22. Playback Testing

Running and comparing two systems has been around for a long time. In many refactoring and replacement situations, particularly with older systems, not only are the developers that built the system long gone, but the code may not even be able to be fully analyzed for all possible functional outcomes. In many older systems, including commercial off-the-shelf (COTS) systems, the source code may be unavailable or may be written in a language (such as Assembly Language) that is not easily understood.

However, even if the code itself cannot be easily understood or analyzed to build a functional test suite, the data (particularly data in flat files or a database) that the code produces is usually much easier to understand. What's more, the data has the advantage of being persistent—you can often write new programs that run asynchronously that the team can use to read the values of the persistent data and report on it to other programs.

Your situation is complex—simply checking for the final state of the system after running a number of transactions through the playback might not be sufficient. This may be because it is hard to understand the way the current system functions or because you do not have a full test suite for the existing system.

There are various ways to implement this playback. For example, if the functionality that is being changed is creating transactions in a database, and the results of running the system are simply updating and making some changes to a database, you can simply compare the results of running both systems on two identical databases, comparing the results. If your new system has a different database structure, this comparison can be a little more difficult. If this is the case, you may need to write scripts to extract and compare the results of the two systems, which might require some transformation of the data before a comparison is done.

Another approach is to capture live transactions from existing calls over a period of time from the old system as Events (255). You then transform those *Events* as necessary to match the API of the new system and play them back as *Events* on the new system to ensure that the behavior of the old and new systems match. These *Events* should be selected around Domain Events (193) that occur in the original monolith system.

There are three issues in implementing an approach like this. The first is capturing the *Domain Events*. If you are following a *Command Query Responsibility Segregation (CQRS)* (383) approach using Event Sourcing (289), one possibility is to capture a set of existing calls to the write model, especially if the write model is just serving initially as an Adapter Microservice (135) to the existing system. The calls can be wrapped up as *Events* and then added to the Event Backbone (279) in this case. If there are still calls going to the underlying existing system that do not go through the write model, this becomes a little more complicated, as you may need to construct your *Events* from log messages or other data capture mechanisms. A simplified form of this is shown in Figure 10-23.

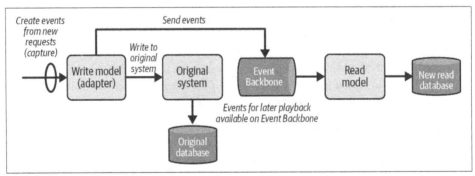

Figure 10-23. CQRS read model and write model for Playback Testing

Once the captured *Events* are added to the *Event Backbone*, the next decision is how long you need to capture the events for playback. Often creating a database for these events may be required if playback will cover a longer period than a few hours. In any case, the *Events* must be transformed to the format consumable by the new (refactored) write model—if you are capturing them from an adapter-based write model, this is already done for you but otherwise will be required if you are capturing them from any other source.

The final stage of this is playing back the captured events on the new (refactored) write model. One key decision is to determine whether the state of the new write model reflects the state of the existing system after each transaction is played back and executed. In the simplest case, you can do this at the end of the playback (perhaps comparing summary and total information, by pulling reports, for instance) but in more complex cases, a step-by-step comparison of all of the entities with their values may be required.

Applying this pattern will help your team gain confidence in the functional test coverage of the new application even when it is impossible to determine all of the functional requirements of the existing application.

It can be difficult and time-consuming to create a test framework for validating and comparing the old system to the new architecture. You also have to maintain both systems during the testing phase.

This pattern is commonly used for validating your new implementation when you are applying the Replace as Microservice pattern (546) and can also be used when applying the Refactor then Extract (542) and Extract Component (535) patterns.

A **Parallel Run** (*Monolith to Microservices*, 2019) as described by Newman is part of *Playback Testing*, although *Playback Testing* includes more details about the setup and the infrastructure needed than is covered in **Parallel Run**.

Examples

This idea of comparing an old implementation with a new implementation has been around for a long time. Many organizations have been applying this technique to validate the new implementation with the original implementation of a system for years. The following examples outline a couple of applications of *Playback Testing*.

Invoicing system

One of us worked on migrating and modernizing an invoicing system where the client used *Playback Testing* to validate the new system. The original invoice system was a monolith that calculated invoices for all the clients at the end of the month. We replaced the system with invoice services that made it easier to create new invoices for clients and calculate the invoices more efficiently and quickly. Calculating invoices correctly was very critical for this organization, and making sure that the new implementation calculated the charges correctly for each client was necessary before releasing and using the new invoice services. Therefore, to ensure the new implementation was correct and good enough to release, they *Playback Tested* the old invoice system before going live—comparing the results to the new invoice services for all clients. Once they were satisfied with the results, they **Canary Released** (*https://oreil.ly/hKMep*) the new invoice services, ultimately retiring the old invoicing system.

US financial institution

A major US financial institution applied an example of *Playback Testing* as part of a much larger modernization and refactoring effort. In this situation, the team was building a new system using *CQRS* with a separate write model and read model. At the same time, the team was transitioning from the existing system to the new system. This example performed the capture through an adapter-based write model and playback comparison through summaries. The overall approach is shown in Figure 10-24.

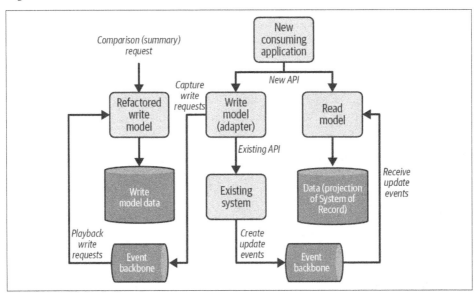

Figure 10-24. Complete Playback Testing prior to shutdown

The team used *Playback Testing* with the goal that the existing system would be completely eliminated and replaced with the new (refactored) write model, as shown in Figure 10-25.

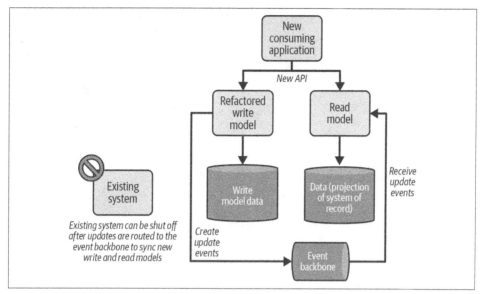

Figure 10-25. Playback Testing after shutdown

It was only when all the reports were run simultaneously between the old and new systems, showing the same results regardless of which system they were run on, that the old system was finally shut down. In fact, after traffic was redirected to the new system, making it the primary system, the old system continued to run for a time. The reason the traffic was being directed to the old system was so that the reports could be compared for a time after the new system became the primary system.

Conclusion: Wrapping Up Strangling Monoliths

In this chapter, we've examined a set of patterns to apply when modernizing a system by migrating a monolith architecture to a Microservices Architecture (Chapter 4). Sometimes a monolithic architecture is the right approach. Moving to Microservices (119) brings several technical and organizational challenges. If an existing monolithic solution works fine and allows the organization to address new requirements, there's no pressing reason to change it. Sometimes refactoring the monolith to make it easier to change is the right choice.

If the monolith is getting harder to change and adapt to new requirements, a decision needs to be made whether to refactor the monolith to make it easier to change, completely rewrite the monolith by applying *Microservices*, or apply these Strangler patterns. If the decision is to evolve the monolithic architecture to a Microservices Architecture, there are strategies that can help you during this effort. Figure 10-26 outlines some possible paths that can be taken during the strangling process.

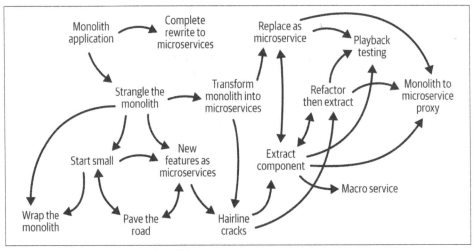

Figure 10-26. Strangling a Monolith sequences

For organizations and teams that are new to *Microservices*, it is good to Start Small (492) by having a team implement some new functionality using *Microservices* and to Pave the Road (496) by building the infrastructure and the environment (both technical and organizational) to make it easier to implement *Microservices*. This can also include developing templates and training to make it easier to implement *Microservices* and help with beginning the transition to the new architecture. You may also want to **Wrap the Monolith** so that when you replace some pieces of the monolith with *Microservices*, you can redirect any existing clients to these new *Microservices*, adapting them as needed.

Once you have created a few *Microservices* and verified that designing and implementing your system with *Microservices* is a good idea, you are ready to apply the "strangling" process. A good way to begin is to encourage and enforce teams to develop New Features as Microservices (521). This creates a directive that requires that all new functionality be added via a *Microservice*, thus not adding to the monolith. This directive can also encourage teams to make any changes to the monolith by first attempting to implement the changes with *Microservices*.

Although implementing *New Features as Microservices* is a good start, a lot of functionality within the monolith will still need to be pulled out to fully take advantage of the Microservices Architecture (Chapter 4) style. Therefore, after getting comfortable with *Microservices*, the next step is to start Transforming the Monolith into Microservices (526). This is an iterative process that finds places in the monolith that can be extracted, refactored, or replaced with *Microservices*.

To find pieces in the monolith that can be transformed, a good starting point is to search for Hairline Cracks (530), which are areas of functionality or components inside the monolith where you can Extract Components (535) to a *Microservice* implementation. Sometimes it will be easier to extract larger pieces of functionality into **Macro Services** and then refactor them to smaller *Microservices* as you learn the domain. *Hairline Cracks* can also reveal places in the monolith that, although they have some coupling, with some changes you can Refactor then Extract (542) them to a *Microservice* implementation. When the functionality is tightly coupled within the monolith, your only option may be to rewrite and Replace as Microservice (546) that functionality.

Transforming the Monolith into Microservices is a recursive process where you apply both bottom-up and top-down approaches to partition and break down the monolith into smaller and smaller pieces. For any extracted or replaced functionality, you can use a Monolith to Microservice Proxies (552) to access the new *Microservices* from the monolith. Playback Testing (556) should be used to validate any extracted or replaced implementations of the original system during the strangling process.

Strangling Scenarios

There are various strategies or scenarios to follow when strangling. The following outlines a few scenarios (stories) that an organization can enact during the strangling process: Add New Feature, Pull Out Painful Pieces, and Can't Use That Protocol.

Add New Feature scenario

When you need to add new functionality to the application, you try to implement it as a *Microservice* wherever possible. This scenario describes a way for adding *New Features as Microservices*, which mandates adding new features by implementing them with *Microservices*. For example, you could implement a small piece of new functionality as a *Microservice*, calling it from the monolith or external clients if needed. Another possible way to add this new feature is to find *Hairline Cracks* within the monolith related to that feature and then *Extract Components* from the monolith to *Microservices*. This extraction is especially beneficial for new functionality that extends or replaces old functionality in the monolith that became hard to change and evolve. Sometimes it is easier to start by extracting a larger **Macro Service**. Then after you have successfully implemented and released the extracted component and after you learn more about the domain and the implementation, you can refactor it into smaller *Microservices*. Whenever you replace functionality in the monolith, you might need to create a *Monolith to Microservice Proxy* for any monolith code that needs access to the new *Microservice*. You should always validate your new *Microservice* implementation with some form of *Playback Testing*.

Pull Out Painful Pieces scenario

You have different components from the monolith you would like to extract to Microservices (119). Some of these are painful areas within the monolith that are causing issues when adding new functionality or changing existing functionality. The desire is to make it easier to make changes or add new functionality without breaking the system. A good way to start *Transforming the Monolith to Microservices* for these painful pieces is by finding *Hairline Cracks* in the monolith related to these pieces, especially looking for components or services with well-defined interfaces. You can then *Extract Components* from the monolith to the a *Microservices* implementation. *Extracting Components* from the monolith enables the team to more easily make changes to this extracted functionality or to add new functionality related to these extracted modules by simply changing the extracted *Microservice* while minimizing potential issues and changes to the monolith. If the original functionality is part of a larger set of components coupled within the monolith, you can extract a **Macro Service** and then refactor it into smaller pieces afterward. Sometimes the functionality you need to move to a *Microservice* is tightly coupled within the monolith. One way to approach this problem is to freeze the functionality within the monolith and completely rewrite it and *Replace as a Microservice* that functionality. Whenever extracting or replacing functionality in the monolith, you often need to create *Monolith to Microservice Proxies*. For any pieces of functionality that you pull out of the monolith, validate the new *Microservice* implementation through *Playback Testing*.

Can't Use That Protocol scenario

The organization has already *Started Small* and *Paved the Road* and has been successfully using *Microservices* for new software solutions for some time. There is a legacy monolithic application that uses an old communication protocol that is no longer supported in new solutions. Part of the functionality in this monolith is now required by new *Microservices* and is entangled within the monolith. To move this functionality and *Transform It from the Monolith to Microservices*, we employ the *Replace as Microservice* to rewrite that functionality as a *Microservice*. When the rewrite is complete, we make the new *Microservice* known to other teams. Sometimes you do this by applying *Refactor then Extract* to the code within the monolith to make it easier to replace as a *Microservice*. Usually, you cannot tease out or rewrite small pieces from the monolith, so you might start with a larger component or service and then refactor it later after you start with a **Macro Service**. A team that has a software solution that is using the original functionality in the monolith and then decides or needs to use the new version in the *Microservice* can work with the team that created the *Microservice* to implement a **Facade** (*Design Patterns*, 1994) that can do the translation and **Proxy** (*Design Patterns*, 1994) calls to the new *Microservice*. Note that it is common to create *Monolith to Microservice Proxies* whenever you create new *Microservices* to replace functionality from the monolith. You should validate your new implementation through some form of *Playback Testing*, which will compare the monolith implementation to the new *Microservices* implementation. Other teams that use that functionality in the monolith gradually follow suit.

These are just a few examples of scenarios the authors have seen that can be applied when *Strangling a Monolith*. There are many other sequences for different organizational and technological contexts, and anyone *Strangling a Monolith* is encouraged to create their own sequence of steps to best meet their strangling needs.

Other Strangling Considerations

The strangling process involves preparing, writing your first *Microservices*, and replacing functionality in the monolith with *Microservices*. When starting, sometimes it is best to protect the system from change by *Wrapping the Monolith*, which is usually done by applying standard wrapper patterns such as **Facade**, **Proxy**, or **Adapter** (*Design Patterns*, 1994). This wrapping supports the strangling process by providing access to the new system (*Microservices*) through the old way (existing client code)—additionally, this allows access to the newly developed *Microservices* from the original system without being coupled to it. This wrapping can also be achieved by using a Public API (443), an Adapter Microservice (135), or a Dispatcher (140). This will encourage and facilitate existing clients to use the *Microservices* that will replace parts of the monolith. By clients, we mean any existing code, components, or systems that are accessing the monolith. Some of this client code could be from a third party that you cannot change.

When *Strangling a Monolith*, you can sometimes completely strangle the monolith (the monolith is gone); though it is often the case that completely *Strangling the Monolith* might not be worth the effort—part of the monolith might be providing value and it costs too much to rewrite. We've seen many strangling examples where most of the monolith has been strangled, as outlined in Figure 10-27, but there are some parts of the monolith remaining that are providing value and won't change.

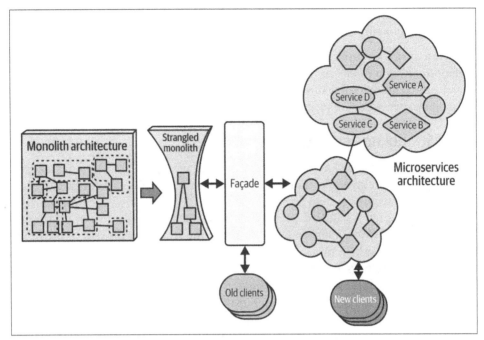

Figure 10-27. Strangled Monolith

Although this chapter addresses some database challenges when applying these patterns, we deferred writing additional patterns on "evolving or decomposing the database" while migrating your monolith. For a description of patterns that cover database decomposition and the trade-offs around data synchronization, transactional consistency, and referential integrity, we refer the reader to Sam Newman's book (*Monolith to Microservices*, 2019).

Conclusion

In this book, we have shown how to architect and design applications that run well on the cloud and how to modernize an existing application as part of migrating it to the cloud. Applying the patterns in this book produces applications that work with the qualities of cloud computing such as universal access, shared resources, distributed computing, virtualized computing, elastic computing, multitenancy, self-service, API driven, and multicloud. Let's review what we've learned, how to apply these patterns, and what comes next.

What We've Learned

Cloud computing works differently than traditional IT. Applications for the cloud need an architecture and design better suited for cloud computing, requiring application developers to adopt a mindset embodying a new set of practices. Our patterns have demonstrated these practices.

Applications that incorporate these patterns compensate for and take advantage of the characteristics that cloud computing embodies. These characteristics include unreliable infrastructure, eventual consistency, generic hardware, application mobility, multitenancy, horizontal scaling, statelessness, immutability, componentization, service catalogs, cloud databases, and self-provisioning. Given these characteristics, there is no one right way to architect Cloud Applications (Chapter 1); rather, there are numerous decisions that can help make an application work better or worse in the cloud.

The patterns help you with the decisions that make your applications work well on the cloud. Some of these decisions include the following:

Monolithic or distributed

To what extent should an application be monolithic or distributed? It can start out as a monolith when that's easier, and then be converted to distributed when that becomes advantageous. How will you know when a *Distributed Architecture* is becoming more advantageous than a monolithic one? When multiple teams need to work on different parts of the application, and when producing maintainable code with limited technical debt becomes more important than hacking together new functionality as quickly as possible. See Application Architecture (Chapter 2).

Cloud native

What qualities should be baked into an application's design to make it run well on cloud computing? An application doesn't need to be stateless or replicable, bundled into an application package, or exposed with a Service API. Indeed, most traditional IT applications don't have these qualities. But the more an application does have these qualities, the better it will run in the cloud. See Cloud-Native Application (Chapter 3).

Microservices

When developing a *Distributed Architecture*, what components should be developed as *Microservices* and why? Components designed as *Microservices* can be developed and deployed, and scale and fail independently, which is usually worth the extra design effort. How do we know how many different *Microservices* an application should be decomposed into and what the scope of each one should be? Model how business functions in the domain interact. Then implement each of those business functions as a *Microservice*. See Microservices Architecture (Chapter 4) and Microservice Design (Chapter 5).

Orchestration or choreography

How can *Microservices* collaborate when the interactions between them are complex, dynamic, and unpredictable? Since each *Microservice* is specialized for a single task, to perform complex tasks, multiple *Microservices* must collaborate. It's difficult enough to model the collaborations when they are simple, stable, and well-known. Rather than orchestrate the interaction, choreograph it. Within a single application, simpler interactions that need to be more reliable can be orchestrated, whereas unpredictable ones can be discovered through choreography. See the Service Orchestrator pattern (160) and Event-Driven Architecture (Chapter 6).

Storing state

Because cloud-native *Microservices* are stateless, where does the state go? Is a relational database always the best way to store an application's data? How can storage work more the way the cloud does? See Cloud-Native Storage (Chapter 7).

Application clients

How do users access applications running in the cloud? How can an application support users on different types of devices, such as computers, phones, and tablets? How can other applications collaborate with your application? See Cloud Application Clients (Chapter 8).

These patterns also prepare you to modernize a traditional IT application so that it will work well in the cloud. These decisions include the following:

Migration and modernization

If an application runs well on traditional IT, why won't it run well in the cloud? What can be done to facilitate making an existing application run better in the cloud? See Application Migration and Modernization (Chapter 9).

Strangling

What if an application running on traditional IT is too big and too important to move to the cloud all at once? How can it be moved incrementally while the users are still using it? See Strangling Monoliths (Chapter 10).

The patterns in this book will help you make these decisions wisely, in a way that is customized to your application's needs as well as to your team's skills and preferences. By doing so, you will develop an application that is ready to work well in the cloud.

Applying What We've Learned

Early on we presented Figure 1-1, which outlined the structure of a prototypical Cloud Application (Chapter 1). Now we can annotate that diagram with how the structure of the application embodies the chapters in this book, which we show in Figure C-1.

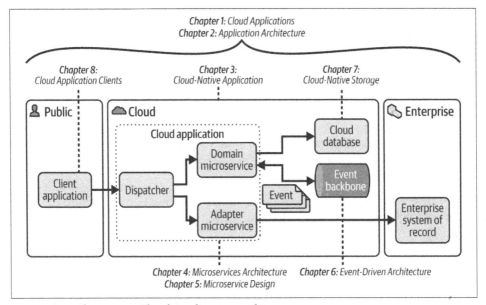

Figure C-1. Chapters in Cloud Application architecture

Each of the chapters in this book work together to inform decisions for building applications that work well on the cloud:

Chapters 1 and 2
  The entire application is a Cloud Application (6), as described in Cloud Applications (Chapter 1). It can be structured as one of several Application Architectures (Chapter 2), where Distributed Architecture (38) is the most flexible one that works more the way the cloud does.

Chapter 3
  The application shown here is a Cloud-Native Application (Chapter 3) with a Cloud-Native Architecture (58).

Chapters 4 and 5
  This application's *Cloud-Native Architecture* is constructed as a Microservices Architecture (Chapter 4), composed of a set of Microservices (119) discovered by Modeling Around the Domain (183) to produce a Microservice Design (Chapter 5).

Chapter 6
  This diagram shows only one application, but if there were multiple, they could connect via an Event Backbone (279) and coordinate through Event Choreography (246) in an Event-Driven Architecture (Chapter 6).

Chapter 7

The Cloud-Native Application and its *Microservices* are stateless, storing their state in one of the options described in Cloud-Native Storage (Chapter 7), typically a Cloud Database (311).

Chapter 8

Users access the application using a Client Application (406), one of the types described in Cloud Application Clients (Chapter 8).

Chapters 9 and 10 (not shown)

While an application can be created new from scratch for the cloud, often an existing application is moved from traditional IT to the cloud using the techniques in Application Migration and Modernization (Chapter 9), starting with Lift and Shift (470). Strangling Monoliths (Chapter 10) describes how to perform this transition iteratively, even on an application that is running in production, starting with Strangle the Monolith (514).

These chapters have laid out a process for producing an application architecture, starting with components of domain logic, how they collaborate, how they persist their data, and how how the outside world can interact with them. While each chapter describes the best practices for one aspect of creating a *Cloud Application*, they all fit together to show how to architect and design a complete *Cloud Application*.

Knowing what decisions to make and when to make them is half the battle, and we hope these patterns will help you make those decisions. You get to decide how to apply these principles based on your application requirements, your enterprise's priorities, and how your development teams prefer to work.

What Comes Next

As first laid out in the Introduction, IT professionals can adopt cloud computing in three main phases:

- Application Architecture and Design
- Application Development and Deployment
- Cloud Operations and Nonfunctional Requirements

Phase 1 is accomplished using the patterns in this book: how to architect and design an application so that it will run well on the cloud.

Phase 2 comes next. To perform application development and deployment, apply three main concepts:

Application deployment

Having implemented an application or *Microservice*, it then must be deployed to the cloud.

Build automation

Having figured out how to deploy the application or *Microservice*, the deployment process should be automated.

Continuous delivery

Deployment, even automated deployment, shouldn't be performed just once; it should be part of an iterative development process.

This still isn't everything you need to be successful with the cloud, but it is a good next few steps in maturing your journey.

Application Deployment

A developer may have written the world's greatest Cloud Application (Chapter 1) or *Microservice*, but it's not doing anyone any good sitting on the developer's hard drive. For users to benefit from this creation, it must be deployed into the cloud, where it'll run and users can access it.

Deployment sounds like one task but involves several steps. To deploy an application to cloud infrastructure, each application component needs to be packaged, either virtualized (see Virtualize the Application (475)) into virtual servers to be deployed in a hypervisor or containered (see Containerize the Application (478)) as containers to be deployed in a container orchestrator such as Kubernetes. The packaged components are managed using registries, which work differently for each package type and platform. The deployment platform must be configured to host the application correctly, which is done differently for each platform. Only then can the application be packaged and deployed onto the configured platform so that it can actually run successfully.

Build Automation

While application deployment can be performed manually, that quickly becomes tedious and error-prone. To make deployment reliably repeatable, it should be automated. This requires understanding not only how to deploy an application but the steps for deploying an application reliably—this process is commonly known as continuous integration and continuous deployment (CI/CD). It also requires understanding common tooling for performing CI/CD, tooling that can be used to make an application deployable with a single command.

Continuous Delivery

Deploying an application should be part of a larger process of continuously improving the application. As long as an application is being used, users will find bugs and request new features. Developers can make these improvements, but an improvement sitting on a developer's hard drive doesn't help the users. For the users to benefit from the improvement, it must be deployed into the running application so they can use it.

If a new application release is deployed only once a year, users need to wait a long time for improvements the developers made months ago. An improvement waiting for the next release is not benefiting the users. Rather, as soon as an improvement is available and approved, it should be deployed into production so that the users can start benefitting from it.

Continuous delivery is a process to improve an application as frequently as is practical. As agile development iteratively improves the application's functionality, continuous delivery integrates, approves, and releases those improvements into production. Users are able to benefit from each improvement as soon as possible, enabling the enterprise to start realizing return on investment (ROI) as soon as possible.

Final Thoughts

The cloud has become the dominant platform for hosting computer applications. Much like the way applications used to be designed for mainframes and then desktop computers, modern applications must now either run well on the cloud or risk becoming irrelevant. Architects and developers who do not know how to design applications that run well on the cloud risk becoming irrelevant.

The intention of this book is to help application developers remain relevant and increase their success using the cloud. Hosting applications on the cloud involves much more than simply redeploying a traditional IT application onto a cloud platform or designing a new application the same old way. Developers need the skills to design new applications that will run well on the cloud, and to modernize existing applications so that they too will run well on the cloud. The patterns in this book go a long way toward helping developers learn these skills so they can be successful with the cloud.

Welcome to the cloud. You may as well get comfortable—we're all going to be here for a while.

Index

and AJAX, 414
AJAX frameworks, 45
Node Package Manager (NPM), 68
in Single-Page Applications, 423
single-page applications implemented in,
152
JDK (Java Development Kit), 68
jQuery and jQuery UI projects, 425
JRE (Java Runtime Environment), 65, 68
JSON
Document Databases representing data as,
340
JSP (Java Server Page), 414, 417

K

Kafka, 242, 281
Key-Value Databases, 328, 333, 337, 345-351
advantages, disadvantages, and alternatives
to, 349
compound key-value, 348
Configuration Databases, 326
optimized to work like hash map, using for
applications using same lookup key, 346
products, projects, and cloud platform services, 350
session data and, 351
storing values as documents having structure, 348
working like hash maps, 347
keyspaces (Columnar Databases), 361
Kubernetes, 481

L

Language Server (VS Code), 46
layered architecture, 20
leader-follower database topology, 305, 320
in Configuration Databases, 326
with Read Replicas, 306
legacy code, adding test coverage to, 487
libraries
programs' dependency on, 63
Lift and Shift, 458, 464, 470-474
advantages of, 473
combination of strategies referred to, 474
combination with Virtualize the Application, 478
deployment of applications to the cloud, 475
drawback and challenges to, 474
examples of, 474

steps to make it possible, 472
tools provided by cloud platforms to help
with, 473
using to gain experience working in the
cloud, 487
using to migrate Distributed Architecture
applications to the cloud, 41
using to migrate existing applications to the
cloud, 468
using with Big Ball of Mud applications, 27
lift-tinker-and-shift, 467
Linux, xvii
Linux Foundation
Cloud Native Computing Foundation
(CNCF), 54
listeners (see event listeners)
load distribution in CQRS, 387
locking
Replicated Databases and, 319
use in traditional enterprise databases, 312
log shipping, 305
logging, consistent, for Interaction Models, 452
loose coupling, 226, 239
of components, provided by events, 269
decoupling components using Event-Driven
Architecture, 241
of Event Notifiers and Reactive Components, 272
for microservices, 178
Anti-Corruption Layers supporting, 232
lower bound for microservices, 181

M

machine learning (ML)
model built into Event Notifiers in shipping
events example, 259
Macro Services, 496, 513
extracted from monolith, issues with, 540
refactoring larger pieces from monolith
then extracting as Macro Services, 544
using with Extract Components, 538
"Make it work, make it right, and make it fast"
(Beck), 26
managed runtime environment, 459
Maven, 68
Mediators, 232
Memcached, 350
Message Bus, 282
messaging, 169

---

platform as a service (see PaaS)

platforms

    application packaging facilitating greater platform portability, 478

    for hosting applications, 461

    issues with, reducing time spent on application development, 498

Playback Testing, 514, 550, 556-561

    CQRS read model and write model for, 558

    ensuring new microservices maintain functionality of old monolith, 556

    example applications of

        invoicing system, 559

        U.S. financial system, 560

    validating new implementation when applying Replace as Microservice, 559

    ways to implement playback, 558

plug-in architecture, 36

Polyglot Development, 9, 67

    in Adapter Microservices, 139

    in Domain Microservices, 134

    in Microservices Architecture, 127

    support by microservices, 119

    using in microservices, 146-153

        example using Node.js, Java, and Go, 148

        examples of, 151-153

    using to store each Data Module in database type best for it, 376

Polyglot Persistence, 10, 151, 375-379

    as data version of microservices, 376

    Data Modules facilitating, 304, 315

    example, ecommerce application, 377

    for microservices, 158

    storing Data Modules in database type best for application's data structure, 375

Ports (Ports and Adapters Architecture), 402

Ports and Adapters Architecture, 400-404

POST method (HTTP), 416

PostgreSQL, 305

private cloud, 53

programming languages

    application architectures independent from, 20

    Application Packages specific to, 64

    deciding which to use in cloud applications, 62

    enterprise governing selection of languages for microservices, 150

    examples of languages with runtime environments and packaging managers, 67-70

    modern, cloud-friendly languages, 64

    not supporting packaging applications and running them in runtime environments, 67

    VS Code support for different languages, 46

programs

    program in Application Package, requirements for, 67

    terminology for components in an architecture, 19

proxies

    monolith components acting as proxies to new microservices, 553

    rewriting old components in monolith as, 552

Proxy pattern, 231, 530

    Monolith to Microservice Proxy, 514

    Monolith to Microservices Proxy, 524, 554

    use in Replace as Microservice, 548

    using in Wrapping the Monolith, 512

pseudosynchronous and asynchronous service invocation, 241-243

Public API, 139, 145, 405, 443-448

    advantages of creating, 445

    versus API Gateway, 446

    cases to understand when considering, 444

    differences from Dispatchers, 445

    examples of, 447

    with gateway, 447

    sometimes divided into partner (closed) and public (open) APIs, 444

    specialization of Service API, 446

public cloud, 53

publish-subscribe messaging, 274

publishers and subscribers, 251

Q

quality delivery pipeline, 501, 502

querying

    databases designed for, 313

    domain state storage and, 311

    no accepted standard for graph queries, 355

    optimizing throughput for query and updates by multiple clients simultaneously, 383

queuing systems, passing messages via, 40

Quick Wins pattern, 537

R

Rabbit MQ, 281
Raft protocol, 309, 328
React Native, 434
Reactive Components, 10, 198, 261-269
    bridges between Event Backbones in enterprise backbone acting as, 288
    building an application from that listens for and reacts to specific events, 261
    challenges to building applications from, 263
    connecting to Event Notifiers via Event Backbone, 280
    Event API defining what to do, 275
    in Event Choreography, 251
    Event Notifiers and, 273
    Event Notifiers connecting to via shared channels, 245
    example, airline application, 267
    example, online ordering service, 265
    example, online ordering system, 265
    failures in Event Choreography, 252
    independence from Event Notifiers, 263
    interacting with Events, 258
    listening and reacting to event topics, 262
    listening to event topics, 254
    logging history of events received for Event Sourcing, 290
    as microservers, being both Event Notifiers and Reactive Components, 264
    mixing Service Orchestration and Event Choreography models, 264
    need to be built as Idempotent Receivers, 264
    in shipping events example, 259
    subscribing to event topics and reacting to events, 274
Read model and Write model, synchronizing for databases, 391
read replicas, leader-follower topology with, 306
recommendation systems (ecommerce), Graph Databases and, 356
Redis, 305, 310, 315, 350
Redis cluster, Replicated Database example, 322
Redis Sentinel, 307
redundancy

redundant data storage in Cloud Databases, 314
Refactor the Monolith pattern, 468, 484-492, 544
    challenges to converting large application entirely into cloud-native microservices, 487
    deciding that application cannot be supported in the long term in current form, 484
    decisions in refactoring, 486
    ensuring behavior of application doesn't change in refactoring, 487
    examples of
        airline application, 488
        published case studies, 488
    making existing application easier to maintain and run in multicomputer environment, 484
    making monoliths into distributed applications, 487
    refactoring Big Ball of Mud application to Modular Monolith, 486
    Start Small beginning with, 495
Refactor Then Extract pattern, 496, 513, 528, 533, 542-546
    addressing coupling in the monolith to facilitate extraction into microservices, 542
    applying Extract Components after refactoring, 544
    difference from Refactor the Monolith, 544
    examples of use
        ecommerce system, 546
        financial services system, 544
    refactoring partially coupled pieces in monolith then extracting components to microservices, 543
    refactoring to understand difficult code, 544
    techniques to help with, 543
    using Playback testing with, 559
    using with extracted components from monolith, 540
refactoring
    in cloud migration of applications, 467
    defined, 486
    having set of tests of existing system to run against new system, 556

SoRs integrated by Adapter Microservices, typically monolithic applications, 138

T

technical debt, 18, 509
    application modernization and, 459
    arising from overlooking architectural concerns, 23
    in Big Ball of Mud pattern, 26
technologies used in cloud computing, xvii
template applications and PHP, 413
template architectures, 417
Template View pattern, 420
three-tier architecture, 400
throughput
    of Event-Driven Architecture, 251
Tinder case study, moving applications to containers and Kubernetes, 484
trade-offs in application architecture, 18
transactions
    capturing then playing back on existing and new systems, 557
    Columnar Databases and, 364
    Configuration Database updates as long-running distributed transactions, 326
    distributed, implemented by MQ-style messaging, 242
    Event Sourcing, 295
    online transaction processing, 357
    performing multiple tasks as single transaction, 170
    scoping Domain Microservices for, 133
    transaction boundary for cohesive Aggregates, 217
    transaction manager, 166
Transforming the Monolith into Microservices, 513, 516, 526-530
    difficulty of, 529
    examples of, 530
    main advantage of, 529
    process for partitioning monolith into microservices, 528
    using Extract Components pattern, 528
    using Monolith to Microservice Proxy for extracted or replaced code, 530
    using Replace as Microservice pattern, 529
    using while adding new features as microservices, 524

wrapping up monolith pieces with wrapper patterns, 530
Twelve-Factor App practices, 55
    dependencies and, 66

U

Uber, use of Strangle the Monolith, 520
Ubiquitous Language pattern, 182, 186-189
    building common language between developers and domain experts, 186
    Domain Services, interfaces defined in, 223
    importance of context, 187
    versus Universal Language, 187
UIs (user interfaces)
    building user interactions with complex business process, 439
    Client Application UI enabling access to Cloud Applications, 408
    interaction Model connecting UI to back-end services, 453
    multimodal UIs, 400
    principles for application user interfaces, 404
    separating UI and domain, 400
    specialization in Mobile Applications, 435
Universal Language versus Ubiquitous Language, 187
Unix pipes and filters at command line, 438
updates
    optimizing throughput for query and updates by multiple clients simultaneously, 383
    serializing concurrent database updates, 387
upper bound of microservices, 182

V

ValueObjects (VOs), 214
values (entity)
    in Bounded Contexts, 188
view (four-layer applications), 120
views, 422
virtual servers, 463
    advantages of containers over, 480
    benefits of, 479
    challenges to, 479
virtualized infrastructure, 458
virtualized, multitenant computing with shared infrastructure, 61

About the Authors

Kyle Brown (*https://www.kyle-brown.com*) is an IBM Fellow and vice president and CTO for the IBM CIO. He has been programming professionally since he was sixteen and has been focusing on design and implementation of large-scale enterprise systems for over thirty years. Kyle speaks at IBM and industry conferences, has written for multiple publications, hosts web chats, and records YouTube videos for IBM. He has also written ten books, including *The Cloud Adoption Playbook* (Wiley).

Bobby Woolf (*https://www.linkedin.com/in/bobbywoolf*) has worked with IBM clients and partners to help them develop enterprise applications deployed on cloud incorporating the latest best practices and technologies. Bobby has published numerous technical articles and presented at conferences, and has been writing patterns since the first Pattern Languages of Programming (PLoP) conference in 1994. He is an Open Group certified Distinguished Technical Specialist and a coauthor of a few books, including *Enterprise Integration Patterns* (Addison-Wesley).

Joseph (Joe) Yoder (*https://joeyoder.com*) is a research collaborator at IME/USP; president and a fellow of the Hillside Group, a group dedicated to improving the quality of software development; and a founder and principal of the Refactory, a company focused on software architecture, design, implementation, consulting, and mentoring on all facets of software development. He is best known as an author of the "Big Ball of Mud" pattern, illuminating fallacies in software architecture. Joe is also a coauthor of *A Scrum Book: The Spirit of the Game* (Pragmatic Bookshelf), which includes 94 patterns and 2 pattern languages about getting the most out of Scrum. Joe received the New Directions award at the Software Engineering Institute's conference on Software Architecture. The ACM recognized Joe as a Distinguished Member in the category of "Outstanding Engineering Contributions to Computing," and the Hillside Group awarded Joe as a Hillside Fellow.

Colophon

The animal on the cover of *Cloud Application Architecture Patterns* is the European bee-eater (*Merops apiaster*). Part of the bee-eater family, they can be found in southern Europe, parts of North Africa, and Western Asia. They inhabit a variety of settings, such as meadows, orchards, and forests, but tend to nest near water.

Like other species in the bee-eater family, the European bee-eater is a mid-sized, brightly colored bird. Their bodies are a mixture of gold, yellow, brown, green, and turquoise. They have rust-colored feathers and a slightly curved, sharp black beak often with a white stripe running down through its eye. While males and females often share the same coloring, females tend to have more green than gold feathers.

The name implies the European bee-eater only feeds on bees, but they also consume insects such as wasps, butterflies, dragonflies, and hornets. To avoid being stung while eating, they capture their prey mid-flight and either rub or hit it against a hard surface until the stinger and venom are removed.

The cover image is based on an antique line engraving from Wood's *Illustrated Natural History*. The series design is by Edie Freedman, Ellie Volckhausen, and Karen Montgomery. The cover fonts are Gilroy Semibold and Guardian Sans. The text font is Adobe Minion Pro; the heading font is Adobe Myriad Condensed; and the code font is Dalton Maag's Ubuntu Mono.

Chapters in Cloud Application Architecture

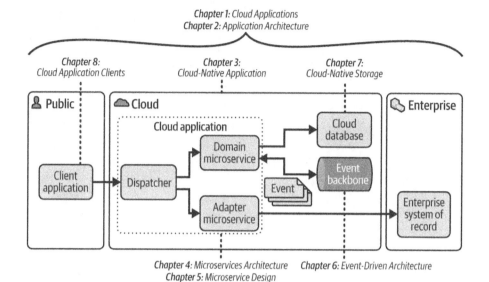

O'REILLY®

Learn from experts.
Become one yourself.

60,000+ titles | Live events with experts | Role-based courses
Interactive learning | Certification preparation

**Try the O'Reilly learning platform
free for 10 days.**

www.ingramcontent.com/pod-product-compliance
Lightning Source LLC
Chambersburg PA
CBHW080129060326
40689CB00018B/3726